## More Praise for *The Law of the Exe*

MW01157002

"For constitutional scholars, the publication of a new book...
In *The Law of the Executive Branch: Presidential Power*, Fisher covers the field, demonstrating his expertise in an incredible number of diverse areas. By providing ready access to primary materials, the book allows readers to reach their own judgments about the appropriate scope of presidential power. Like the framers of the Constitution, Fisher rejects dogma, pragmatically exposing all claims about presidential power to the light of experience in the real world. This book will be an essential, invaluable resource for scholars, students, legislators, judges, and executive branch officials."

Chris Edelson, Assistant Professor, Department of Government,
American University, School of Public Affairs

"Louis Fisher's work has for many years been indispensable to me while I served in Congress. His superb scholarship on the separation of powers and the encroachment of the imperial presidency will be ever more valued when the history of our era is written. With the publication of *The Law of the Executive Branch: Presidential Power*, Dr. Fisher makes an enormous contribution to the study of the presidency. The book is a masterwork of scholarship, a remarkable milestone in a remarkable career. We all owe him an enormous debt of gratitude."

Ron Paul, M.D.
former Member, US House of Representatives

"Lou Fisher is an intellectual giant among constitutional scholars who has consulted with all three branches on separation of powers issues. In *The Law of the Executive Branch*, Fisher draws on nearly a half century of his scholarship based in original documents, precedent, and historical analysis while highlighting the legal controversies surrounding each constitutional provision related to presidential power. This authoritative analysis provides a major intellectual benchmark that will inform and inspire present and future constitutional scholars."

James P. Pfiffner, University Professor of Public Policy,
George Mason University

"Lou Fisher's *The Law of the Executive Branch: Presidential Power* is must reading for anyone who is interested in our constitutional system. Fisher brings a wealth of experience and understanding about the Framers' design and how it has evolved over time. In many important areas that have been debated since the founding—such as the war powers, executive privilege and claims of inherent presidential power—Fisher provides encyclopedic analyses of how the Executive has been changed from a subordinate constitutional branch that carries out policies made by Congress into the most powerful branch of the government."

Robert J. Reinstein
Clifford Scott Green Chair Professor of Law
Temple University, Beasley School of Law

"They could not have picked a more ideal subject-author combination to launch such a project. Professor Fisher enjoys unparalleled status as an acclaimed national expert on questions of separation of powers, in general, and on presidential authority, in particular. Given the author's background, this particular offering in *The Oxford Commentaries on American Law* series fulfills an important and pressing need. No significant topic in the law of the executive branch goes uncommented on in this volume's 400-plus pages of case analysis and commentaries."

David Alistair Yalof, Professor and Department Head,
Department of Political Science, University of Connecticut

# THE LAW OF THE
# EXECUTIVE BRANCH

# The Oxford Commentaries on American Law

*The Editorial Advisory Board*

## The Oxford Commentaries on American Law:

## An Introduction to the Series

Welcome to *The Oxford Commentaries on American Law*. In this series, Oxford University Press promotes the revival of the art of the American legal treatise by publishing careful, scholarly books that refine the laws of the United States, synthesizing them for the bench, for the bar, for the student, and for the citizen–while providing a foundation for future scholarship and refinement.

The treatise, sometimes called the commentary or, in its elementary form, the hornbook, is the most traditional of law books. Written for use by lawyers, judges, teachers, and students, the treatise is a source of law in itself. From the Roman *Institutes* of Gaius and for Justinian, through the great volumes on English law called the Glanville and Bracton, to the *Institutes* of Sir Edward Coke and the *Commentaries* of Sir William Blackstone, and even to their criticisms in the manuals and codes of Jeremy Bentham, treatises were – along with case reports and statutory collections – both a repository and a source of the law.

This was true in the United States throughout the nineteenth and the twentieth centuries, when the treatise was the dominant law book for the mastery of any given field. Great lawyers–the likes of Joseph Story, James Kent, Oliver Wendell Holmes, John Henry Wigmore, William Prosser, and Allan Farnsworth–wrote elegant books that surveyed the law from a unique perspective and that were read and quoted by judges, lawyers, and scholars. These books were studied by generations of students, who consulted them anew throughout their legal careers. They remain essential to understanding American law. Yet in the last decades of the 1900s, as the law book marketplace changed, treatises became less fashionable in the U.S.

Treatises remain significant to the legal systems of Europe, Asia, and South America, as well as in some specific fields of U.S. law. However, the general need for new ideas in U.S. law to incorporate changes and answer new questions has hardly grown less. Thus, the need persists for clarification in the law by careful analysts seeking to define the most useful and balanced approaches to legal rules as applied to specific situations. The purpose of such analysis is to organize, explain, and apply the most significant sources in a field of closely related laws, rather than to account for every single decision or variation in it.

The treatise is therefore a tool to describe rules and principles in the law and to organize them for applications to specific situations, in answer to questions in the law that are likely to arise. These principles and rules are derived sometimes from the statements and texts of legislators and regulators, sometimes from the practices of judges, lawyers, and officials, sometimes from the context of older legal customs, and sometimes from the logic and justice that bind the law, as understood by the author of the treatise. Treatise authors work within a tradition to create a new source of law, like Sir Edward Coke said, bringing new corn from old fields.

It is my great pleasure to work not only with the authors of these books but also with a world-class staff of professionals in the English and North American offices of the Oxford University Press, and with an outstanding editorial board. I am grateful to each of you for your care and persistence in developing this grand initiative.

Stephen M. Sheppard
Series Editor

# Other Works by Louis Fisher

- *Congress: Protecting Individual Rights* (2016)
- *The Democratic Constitution* (with Neal Devins, 2nd ed., 2015)
- *Constitutional Conflicts between Congress and the President* (6th ed., 2014)
- *American Constitutional Law* (with Katy J. Harriger, 10th ed., 2013)
- *On the Supreme Court: Without Illusion and Idolatry* (2013)
- *Presidential War Power* (3d ed. revised, 2013)
- *Defending Congress and the Constitution* (2011)
- *Political Dynamics of Constitutional Law* (with Neal Devins, 5th ed., 2011)
- *On Appreciating Congress: The People's Branch* (2010)
- *The Supreme Court and Congress: Rival Interpretations* (2009)
- *The Constitution and 9/11: Recurring Threats to America's Freedoms* (2008)
- *In the Name of National Security: Unchecked Presidential Power and the* Reynolds *Case* (2006)
- *Military Tribunals and Presidential Power: American Revolution to the War on Terrorism* (2005)
- *The Politics of Executive Privilege* (2004)
- *Nazi Saboteurs on Trial: A Military Tribunal and American Law* (2003)
- *Religious Liberty in America: Political Safeguards* (2002)
- *Congressional Abdication on War and Spending* (2000)
- *The Politics of Shared Power: Congress and the Executive* (4th ed., 1998)
- *Encyclopedia of the American Presidency* (with Leonard W. Levy, 4 vols., 1994)
- *Constitutional Dialogues: Interpretation as Political Process* (1988)
- *The Constitution Between Friends: Congress, the President, and the Law* (1978)
- *Presidential Spending Power* (1975)
- *President and Congress* (1972)

# THE LAW OF THE EXECUTIVE BRANCH

*Presidential Power*

*Louis Fisher*

**The Oxford Commentaries on American Law**

Stephen M. Sheppard
Series Editor

**OXFORD**
UNIVERSITY PRESS

# OXFORD
**UNIVERSITY PRESS**

*Oxford University Press is a department of the University of Oxford. It furthers the University's objective of excellence in research, scholarship, and education by publishing worldwide.*

Oxford    New York
Auckland    Cape Town    Dar es Salaam    Hong Kong    Karachi    Kuala Lumpur    Madrid
Melbourne    Mexico City    Nairobi    New Delhi    Shanghai    Taipei    Toronto

With offices in
Argentina    Austria    Brazil    Chile    Czech Republic    France    Greece    Guatemala    Hungary
Italy    Japan    Poland    Portugal    Singapore    South Korea    Switzerland    Thailand
Turkey    Ukraine    Vietnam

Oxford is a registered trade mark of Oxford University Press in the UK and certain other countries.

Published in the United States of America by
Oxford University Press
198 Madison Avenue, New York, NY 10016

First printing in paperback, 2015.
ISBN 978–0–19–938211–8 (paperback : alk. paper)

The Library of Congress has cataloged the hardback edition as follows:

Library of Congress Cataloging-in-Publication Data
Fisher, Louis.
   The law of the executive branch : presidential power / Louis Fisher.
      pages cm. — (Oxford Commentaries on American Law)
   Includes bibliographical references and index.
   ISBN 978-0-19-985621-3 ((hardback) : alk. paper)
1. Presidents—United States. 2. Executive power—United States. 3. War and emergency powers—United States. I. Title.
   KF5053.F57 2014
   352.23'50973—dc23
                                                                          2013019898

*To the William and Mary Law School*

# Contents

# Preface to the Paperback Edition

IN DEFINING THE SCOPE OF PRESIDENTIAL POWER, THIS TREATISE BEGAN WITH questions that are even more relevant for the paper edition. In determining presidential powers that are legitimate, do we automatically rely on judicial rulings, especially those by the Supreme Court? That has clearly been the pattern, but the treatise then asked: "what if a decision rests on a plain misconception about presidential power, often because the Court fails to properly understand historical precedents? No matter how frequently a decision is cited by courts and scholars, this treatise does not regard a judicial error as a valid source of law. Instead, the treatise has been prepared to encourage courts and scholars to revisit misconceptions and correct them."[1]

Why do we accept judicial rulings grounded in error? Developments after publication of the hardcover edition underscore the need to analyze the capacity of the judiciary to not only make errors about presidential power but leave errors uncorrected. Part of the reluctance to challenge judicial errors is that we are told that when the Supreme Court decides a case it speaks with finality. In 1953, Justice Robert Jackson expressed that view: "We are not final because we are infallible, but we are infallible only because we are final."[2]

A clever sentence with remarkable twists and turns, but Jackson in 1953 fully understood that the Court is neither final nor infallible. Consider the 1940 compulsory flag-salute case. The Court voted 8 to 1 to require children of Jehovah's Witnesses to salute the American flag or face dismissal from public schools.[3] The top-heavy majority might indicate finality, if not infallibility, but three Justices (Hugo Black, William Douglas, and Frank Murphy) read critiques of the decision and soon regretted their willingness to join the majority. Two years later they announced in a decision that the 1940 case had been "wrongly decided."[4] The 8-1 majority now fell to 5-4. Two Justices of the majority of eight retired and were replaced by two new Justices, who proceeded a

---

1. Louis Fisher, The Law of the Executive Branch: Presidential Power xvii (2014).
2. Brown v. Allen, 344 U.S. 443, 540 (1953).
3. Minersville School District v. Gobitis, 310 U.S. 586 (1940).
4. Jones v. Opelika, 316 U.S. 584, 624 (1942).

year later to join the four dissenters to overturn, 6 to 3, the 1940 decision.[5] The person who wrote the 1943 decision was one of the new Justices: Robert Jackson.

The 1940 decision could be described not as a judicial "error" but rather a poorly reasoned decision that found no support from scholars, law reviews, newspapers, and the general public. Under either interpretation, the Court was neither final nor infallible. The history of the Supreme Court to make mistakes was described bluntly by Chief Justice William Rehnquist in 1993: "It is an unalterable fact that our judicial system, like the human beings who administer it, is fallible."[6] His observation is particularly telling because Rehnquist had clerked for Jackson.

Despite the Court's record of issuing decisions that are poorly reasoned and erroneous, scholars and reporters continue to promote judicial supremacy and finality. Tom Goldstein, who frequently argues cases before the Supreme Court, stated in 2013 that when the Court "interprets the Constitution, that is the final word. The President and Congress can't overturn the decision. The only option is to amend the Constitution which is basically impossible."[7] Adam Liptak, writing for the *New York Times* in 2012, noted that "only a constitutional amendment can change things after the justices have acted in a constitutional case."[8] Robert Barnes, in an article for the *Washington Post* in 2014, wrote that *Marbury v. Madison* "established the court as the final word on the Constitution."[9]

In terms of errors that result from the Supreme Court failing to properly understand historical precedents, there should be little doubt about judicial weaknesses in this area. An article by Justice Jackson in 1945 observed that judges "often are not thorough or objective historians."[10] Writing in 1989, Justice Antonin Scalia acknowledged that the judicial system "does not present the ideal environment for entirely accurate historical inquiry."[11] He said that the "inevitable tendency of judges to think that the law is what they would like it to be will, I have no doubt, cause most errors in judicial historiography…"[12] In a book published in 2011, Justice John Paul Stevens described judges as "merely amateur historians" whose interpretations of past events, "like their interpretations of legislative history, are often debatable and sometimes simply wrong."[13]

My legal treatise focused on Supreme Court errors that have magnified presidential authority, limited congressional power, and weakened the system of checks and balances. A prominent example is the "sole organ" doctrine announced by Justice George Sutherland in the 1936 *Curtiss-Wright* case. The issue before the Supreme Court involved only *legislative* power, not presidential power, but Sutherland proceeded to refer to "the very delicate, plenary and exclusive power of the President as the sole organ of the federal government in the field of international

---

5. West Virginia State Board of Education v. Barnette, 319 U.S. 624 (1943).

6. Herrera v. Collins, 506 U.S. 390, 415 (1993).

7. http://www.scotus.blog.com/2013/06/power.

8. Adam Liptak, *In Congress's Paralysis, a Mightier Supreme Court*, N.Y. TIMES, Aug. 21, 2012, at A10.

9. Robert Barnes, *Addressing the Supreme Court with Fun*, WASH. POST, Oct. 25, 2014, at Al.

10. Robert H. Jackson, *Full Faith and Credit—The Lawyer's Clause of the Constitution*. 45 COLUM. L. REV. 1, 6 (1945).

11. Antonin Scalia, *Originalism: The Lesser Evil*, 57 U. CINN. L. REV. 849, 861 (1989).

12. Id. at 864.

13. JUSTICE JOHN PAUL STEVENS, FIVE CHIEFS 225–26 (2011).

relations."[14] Obviously the President does not have "plenary and exclusive" power over international relations. One need only read Articles I and II of the Constitution to see powers vested exclusively in Congress (such as regulating "Commerce with foreign Nations") or shared between the President and the Senate (such as the treaty power).

The "sole organ" doctrine might appear to have some initial credibility because Justice Sutherland relied on a speech that John Marshall gave when he served in the House of Representatives in 1800. A year later he became Chief Justice of the Supreme Court and served in that position until 1835. But when one reads the speech, it is obvious that Marshall did not promote plenary and exclusive power for the President in external affairs. Instead, he merely defended President John Adams for turning over to Great Britain an Englishman charged with murder. Adams did not claim independent presidential power to *make* policy. Instead, he relied on extradition authority granted him in the Jay Treaty to *implement* policy. In doing so, he performed his constitutional duty under Article II to "take Care that the Laws be faithfully executed," with treaties under Article VI considered to be "the supreme Law of the Land." Nothing in Marshall's speech advocated plenary and exclusive authority for the President in external affairs. Those points are fully detailed in the treatise.[15]

The treatise notes that on July 23, 2013, the D.C. Circuit supported the President's implied authority to recognize foreign government's over the implied authority of Congress to legislate on passport policy. This decision in *Zivotofsky v. Secretary of State* relied five times on the erroneous "sole organ" doctrine in *Curtiss-Wright*.[16] The perpetuation of judicial error, heavily relied on by the Justice Department to augment presidential power, prompted me to file an amicus brief with the Supreme Court on July 17, 2014. I explained that the D.C. Circuit was at fault for relying not merely on dicta, but erroneous dicta. Moreover, the dicta had evolved over time to be accepted as the holding. My brief asked the Court to correct "the erroneous dicta that appear in *Curtiss-Wright*, errors that have misguided federal courts, the Justice Department, Congress, some scholarly studies, and the general public."[17] The *National Law Journal* accepted my brief in a column called "Brief of the Week," asking this basic question: "Can the Supreme Court Correct Erroneous Dicta?"[18]

The judicial error in *Curtiss-Wright* lasted for 79 years until the Supreme Court, on June 8, 2015, issued *Zivotofsky v. Kerry*, involving the Jerusalem passport case. As Chief Justice Roberts noted in his dissent, the Solicitor General invoked *Curtiss-Wright* "no fewer than ten times in his brief," including reliance on Justice Sutherland's description of the President as the "sole organ" in foreign affairs. The majority, without explaining how Sutherland misrepresented John Marshall's speech, analyzed *Curtiss-Wright* and the sole-organ doctrine and concluded that it "does not extend so far" as the administration argued in its briefs. Instead, the description of the President's exclusive power over foreign affairs "was not necessary to the holding of *Curtiss-Wright*—which, after all, dealt with congressionally authorized action, not a unilateral

14.  United States v. Curtiss-Wright Corp., 299 U.S. 304, 320 (1936).

15.  FISHER, THE LAW OF THE EXECUTIVE BRANCH, at 3, 4, 265–68, 387, 391–92, 415, 417.

16.  Id. at 297; Zivotofsky v. Secretary of State, 725 F.3d 197 (D.C. Cir. 2013).

17.  *Brief Amicus Curiae of Louis Fisher in Support of Petitioner*, Supreme Court of the United States, Zivotofsky v. Kerry, No. 13-626, July 17, 2014, at 35; available at http://www.loufisher.org/docs/pip/Zivotofsky.pdf.

18.  Jamie Schuman, *Brief of the Week: Can the Supreme Court Correct Erroneous Dicta?*, National Law Journal, Nov. 3, 2014; available at http://www.loufisher.org/docs/pip/fisherbrief.pdf.

Presidential determination." The majority then noted: "whether the realm is foreign or domestic, it is still the Legislative Branch, not the Executive Branch that makes the law."

As a result, it appears that the majority finally rejected the sole-organ doctrine in *Curtiss-Wright*. Yet it did not part company with other erroneous dicta in that decision. According to the majority in *Zivotofsky*, the President "has the sole power to negotiate treaties, see *United States v. Curtiss-Wright Export Corp.*, 299 U.S. 304, 319 (1936)." Justice Sutherland claimed that the President makes treaties with the Senate but "he alone negotiates. Into the field of negotiation the Senate cannot intrude; and Congress itself is powerless to invade it."[19]

There are many ways to discredit Sutherland's understanding of the treaty negotiation process. One is to start with his twelve years as a U.S. Senator, from March 4, 1905 to March 3, 1917. In his book, published in 1919, he recognized that Senators participated in treaty negotiation and that Presidents often acceded to this "practical construction."[20] In describing treaty-making, he said the power of the Senate "is co-ordinate, throughout, with that of the President."[21] The record is clear that Presidents have often invited Senators to participate in treaty negotiation in order to build political support for a treaty. Similar reasoning led Presidents to include members of the House in treaty negotiation when treaties are not self-executing and require authorization and appropriation by Congress.[22]

Despite this ample and clear record of congressional participation in the treaty process, the Office of Legal Counsel in 2009 cited Justice Sutherland's "clear dicta" in *Curtiss-Wright* that "Into the field of negotiation the Senate cannot intrude; and Congress itself is powerless to invade it."[23] Clear, yes, but falsely grounded in terms of historical practice. OLC's memo is just one of many examples of the executive branch relying on erroneous dicta in *Curtiss-Wright* to advance presidential power. It would have been constructive for the Supreme Court in *Zivotofsky* to state that Justice Sutherland was wrong here as well but it chose not to do so. A judicial error in existence for 79 years will continue without correction, misleading authors and their readers.

For example, consider an article by Steve Coll in the April 27, 2015 issue of *The New Yorker*. He wrote critically of Republican members of Congress who "have meddled in unprecedented fashion to undermine President Obama's nuclear diplomacy with Iran, as he seeks—with Britain, France, Germany, Russia, and China—to cap Iran's nuclear program in exchange for relief from economic sanctions." The most "egregious example," he said, came from 47 Senate Republicans who signed "an open letter to Iranian leaders, which contained a dubious analysis of the Constitution and warned the mullahs not to rely on any deal that Congress failed to approve."[24]

In repudiating this congressional interference with presidential leadership, Coll turned to *Curtiss-Wright*, in which he said the Supreme Court issued "a thumping endorsement of a President's prerogative to lead foreign policy." Coll quoted from the decision: "In this vast

19.   United States v. Curtiss-Wright Corp., 299 U.S. at 319.

20.   George Sutherland, Constitutional Power and World Affairs 122–24 (1919).

21.   Id. at 123.

22.   Fisher, The Law of the Executive Branch, at 272–76; Louis Fisher, *Treaty Negotiation: A Presidential Monopoly?*, 38 Pres. Stud. Q. 144 (2008); Louis Fisher, *Congressional Participation in the Treaty Process*, 137 U. Pa. L. Rev. 1511 (1989).

23.   Office of Legal Counsel, *Memorandum Opinion for the Acting Legal Adviser, Department of State*, June 1, 2009, at 9; http://www.justice.gov/olc/2009/section7054.pdf.

24.   Steve Coll, *Dangerous Gamesmanship*, The New Yorker, April 27, 2015, at 19.

external realm, with its important, complicated, delicate and manifold problems," only the President "has the power to speak or listen as a representative of the nation. . . . He alone negotiates" and Congress is "powerless" to interfere.[25]

The letter from the 47 Republican Senators claimed that "while the president negotiates international agreements, Congress plays the significant role of ratifying them." That is not always the case, but the Obama administration erred in insisting that the President has full constitutional authority to enter into agreements with other countries. An effective challenge came from Senator Bob Corker, chairman of the Senate Foreign Relations Committee. His draft legislation, to require the White House to submit the Iran agreement to Congress for a vote, gained bipartisan support of all committee members. In late March 2015, 367 House members, including 129 Democrats, sent a letter to President Obama, expressing their concerns about the agreement with Iran.[26]

Although President Obama initially criticized members of Congress who raised objections to his negotiations with Iran, the breadth of the opposition and its bipartisan quality forced him to yield. He said he would sign a bill giving Congress a voice on the proposed nuclear accord with Iran. The bill required the administration to send the text of the final accord to Congress, along with classified material, giving lawmakers an opportunity to vote on allowing or forbidding the lifting of congressional imposed sanctions.[27] The bill passed the Senate 98 to 1 and the House 400 to 25. Justice Sutherland's theory of the President possessing plenary and exclusive control over external affairs found no support from the elected branches. President Obama signed the bill on May 22, 2015.

Although the Supreme Court in *Zivotofsky* jettisoned the sole-organ doctrine, it came close to creating a substitute by describing the President as the "one voice" in foreign affairs. Between the two elected branches, "only the Executive has the characteristic of unity at all times" with the capacity to speak "for the Nation." Deprived of Sutherland's sole-organ dicta, the executive branch will have ample opportunity to cite these contemporary broad judicial doctrines to advance presidential power.

---

25. Id.

26. Mike Lillis, *Obama risks backlash in pursuit of Iran nuclear deal*, THE HILL, March 25, 2015, at 5.

27. Jonathan Weisman & Peter Baker, *President Yields, Allowing Congress Say on Iran Deal*, N.Y. TIMES, April 15, 2015, at A1; Karen DeYoung & Mike DeBonis, *Deal struck on Iran oversight*, WASH. POST, April 15, 2015, at A1.

# Preface to the Hardcover Edition

THE PRINCIPAL PURPOSE OF THIS TREATISE IS TO EXPLORE THE SOURCES and limits of presidential power. How should we determine which powers are legitimate? Do we treat judicial rulings, including those by the Supreme Court, as legitimate sources of law? We do, but what if a decision rests on a plain misconception about presidential power, often because the Court fails to properly understand historical precedents? No matter how frequently a decision is cited by courts and scholars, this treatise does not regard a judicial error as a valid source of law. Instead, the treatise has been prepared to encourage courts and scholars to revisit misconceptions and correct them.

Judicial and scholarly errors are apt to draw from secondary sources. This treatise relies on original sources and explains why and when the Court and scholarly studies misrepresent a precedent. Links are provided to original sources to permit readers to independently form their own judgment. The treatise has a second purpose. Disputes about legal and constitutional powers of the executive branch are often discussed as wholly detached categories, with one power cleanly separated from another. Issues range from the war power to federal appointments to executive privilege. An objective of the treatise is to keep seemingly distinct and autonomous categories connected to a larger framework of overarching principles and values. To do that, Chapter 1 identifies twelve fundamental concepts to provide general guidance.

A treatise on "the law" of the executive branch, with a special focus on the presidency, is somewhat misleading. Law is generally regarded as fixed, clear, and binding. Much of the law on executive and presidential power is fluid and subject to change. Moreover, few legal and constitutional powers of the President are exercised in an exclusive fashion. Most are shared with other branches, in large part or small, depending on how those branches assert their own powers. Other constraints and encouragements come from scholars, the public, and outside pressures. In the Steel Seizure Case of 1952, Justice Jackson said that presidential powers "are not fixed but fluctuate, depending upon their disjunction or conjunction with those of Congress."[1]

The scope of presidential authority has been the center of constitutional disputes since the Framing, with increased scrutiny and complexity after World War II. The breadth of presidential

---

[1] Youngstown Co. v. Sawyer, 343 U.S. 579, 635 (1952) (Jackson, J., concurring).

appointment and removal powers, the natural competition with Congress and the judiciary, control over military and foreign policy, and the capacity of the President to discharge multiple duties in a legal and constitutional manner have all been the subject of intense controversy. That power reaches to the White House, executive departments and agencies, independent commissions, and the judiciary through the appointment process.

This treatise analyzes the law of the executive branch in the context of constitutional language, the Framers' intent, and more than two centuries of practice. The result is shaped partly by litigation but also by presidential initiatives, congressional responses, and public and international pressures. Each provision in the Constitution is evaluated to determine the contemporary meaning and application of presidential power. Judicial misinterpretations are sometimes in dicta, but they can nevertheless greatly influence the perception and reality of presidential powers. The "sole organ" doctrine of *Curtiss-Wright* (1936) is one example, but there are others. This treatise identifies legal and constitutional errors and explains, when possible, why they occur. Often it is a court taking something out of context or accepting, without independent verification, executive branch assertions.

I participated in a number of issues covered in this treatise. After writing an article on constitutional issues of Presidents who impound funds, published in the October 1969 issue of the *George Washington Law Review*, the Senate Committees on Government Operations and the Judiciary asked me to assist in the drafting and eventual passage of the Impoundment Control Act of 1974. I sat behind Senator Sam Ervin at committee hearings to provide counsel, set next to him at committee markup to offer my thoughts on amendments to the bill, wrote the impoundment section of the conference report, and prepared a floor dialogue between Senator Ervin and Senator Hubert Humphrey to explain the objectives of the legislation. I received a letter and signing pen from President Nixon.

My work was not limited to defending legislative interests. At times I urged protection for the President and the judiciary. In 1985, I appeared before the House Committee on Government Operations, testifying that the Gramm-Rudman-Hollings deficit control bill encroached on presidential power. I regarded the bill as unconstitutional because it gave executive duties to legislative officers (the Comptroller General and the Director of the Congressional Budget Office). In testifying against an item-veto bill, I objected to empowering the President to cancel funds for the judiciary. I said the executive branch, in court more than any other party, should not have control over the judicial budget. I received a letter from the executive director of the Administrative Office of the U.S. Courts, thanking me for defending judicial independence. On four occasions I testified in support of legislation to give federal judges greater authority to review executive branch claims of the state secrets privilege.

In 1987, I served as research director of the House Iran-Contra Committee and wrote the sections of the final report dealing with constitutional and institutional issues. In these and other experiences, I worked on a nonpartisan basis with Democrats and Republicans and had the opportunity to meet with lawmakers, their staff, executive officials, White House and Justice Department experts, and federal judges. Participation in public conferences helped me gain a better understanding of political and legal issues. In 1994, after publishing numerous studies on secret spending, I was asked by the House Permanent Select Committee on Intelligence to testify on the confidential budget of the Intelligence Community. It was my judgment that the Constitution required the aggregate budget to be made public. In 1998, I testified three times in support of the CIA Whistleblower Act and worked with both the House and Senate Intelligence Committees on a bill that became law that year.

Over a period of more than four decades, I testified repeatedly on such issues as the item veto, the pocket veto, legislative vetoes, presidential reorganization authority, presidential removal power, executive privilege, executive lobbying, biennial budgeting, the balanced budget amendment, recess appointments, whistleblower protection, war powers, Congress and the Constitution, restoring the rule of law, and NSA warrantless surveillance. With regard to the claim that the President possesses "inherent" authority to create military tribunals, I filed three amicus briefs in the *Hamdan* litigation stating why the President lacks that authority. I filed amicus briefs on a number of other issues that arose after 9/11. After retiring in August 2010, I testified on the "Fast and Furious" issue of gunrunning, budget reform proposals, and the constitutionality of President Obama's military operations in Libya.

# Acknowledgments

PRESIDENTIAL POWER HAS BEEN A PREOCCUPATION SINCE MY DAYS AS a graduate student in the 1960s, leading to my first book, *President and Congress* (1972).That interest continued during four decades at the Library of Congress from 1970 to 2010, where I served as Senior Specialist in Separation of Powers with Congressional Research Service and as Specialist in Constitutional Law with the Law Library. Over that period of time I published 20 books, almost 500 articles, and hundreds of reports at the Library of Congress. I testified 50 times before congressional committees on a range of constitutional disputes, explained in the preface. Upon my retirement in August 2010, I continue to work with congressional offices and committees. Many of my articles, books, and congressional testimony are available on my personal webpage: http://loufisher.org.

After leaving the Library of Congress it was my good fortune to join the Constitution Project as Scholar in Residence. I had been active with the Project over the preceding decade on a number of research projects, including war powers and the state secrets privilege. Shortly before my retirement, Professor Stephen Sheppard of the Arkansas Law School asked about my interest in writing a treatise on "The Law of the Executive Branch." It was an opportunity to build on what I had done and deepen my understanding. Steve guided me through the steps needed to submit a proposal for this Oxford series. Three outside reviewers offered a number of excellent suggestions to my initial outline. After finishing the manuscript, I received many thoughtful evaluations from six reviewers.

I am very pleased to dedicate this book to the William and Mary Law School. While at the Library of Congress, I taught a number of courses at the law school over a period of two decades and continue to teach there after retirement. With a close friend and member of the faculty, Neal Devins, I have coauthored two books, *Political Dynamics of Constitutional Law*, now in its fifth edition, and *The Democratic Constitution*, about to be issued in a second edition. In the course of preparing this manuscript, I had the luxury of using online sources at the law school, including HeinOnline and JSTOR, and I had access to various presidential, congressional, and judicial documents. Extra time available during retirement allowed me to carefully read and reread thousands of books and articles devoted to constitutional government. These scholarly works helped clarify and sharpen my understanding. I could not possibly identify every author, but my citations will bear witness to how much I benefited from their individual labors and insights.

Many colleagues helped me identify the issues that required analysis. Three read the entire manuscript: Reb Brownell, Mort Rosenberg, and Mitch Sollenberger. Chris Edelson read Chapters 7, 8, 9, and the Conclusions. Henry Cohen read Chapter 9 and the Conclusions. A number of colleagues read particular portions of the manuscript: Dave Adler, Curtis Copeland, Jeff Crouch, Neal Devins, Jenny Elsea, Jasmine Farrier, Mike Glennon, Joel Goldstein, Bob Havel, Henry Hogue, Chris Kelley, Mike Koempel, Harold Krent, Jack Maskell, Walter Oleszek, Dick Pious, Mark Rozell, Mike Shenkman, Bob Spitzer, Charles Tiefer, Bill Weaver, and Don Wolfensberger. They joined with others who commented on my draft table of contents, which changed on a regular basis to accommodate new topics: Moe Davis, George Edwards, Herb Fenster, Sharon Franklin, Katy Harriger, Nancy Kassop, Jim Pfiffner, Harold Relyea, and Jim Thurber. My deep gratitude to all. I greatly appreciate the exceptionally thoughtful and careful copyediting by Michele Bowman.

# Note on Citations

ALL COURT CITATIONS REFER TO PUBLISHED VOLUMES WHENEVER AVAILABLE: *United States Reports* (U.S.) for Supreme Court decisions, *Federal Reporter* (F.2d or F.3d) for appellate decisions, and *Federal Supplement* (F. Supp. or F. Supp. 2d) for district court decisions. There are also citations to *Opinions of the Attorney General* (Op. Att'y Gen.), *Opinions of the Office of Legal Counsel* (Op. O.L.C.) in the Justice Department, and opinions by the Comptroller General (Comp. Gen.) of the Government Accountability Office, formerly the General Accounting Office. When citing a court ruling, I do not use the lengthy name that appears on the first page. I use the shortened version placed at the top of pages. For example, instead of McConnell, United States Senator, et al. v. Federal Election Commission, et al., I use McConnell v. Federal Election Comm'n. Second, I use the name of a case as reported and do not change the name of a position to a particular occupant. If the name of a reported case is Zivotofsky v. Secretary of State, I use that and do not change it to Zivotofsky v. Clinton. Several standard reference works are abbreviated in the footnotes by using the following system:

| | |
|---|---|
| Elliot | The Debates in the Several State Conventions, on the Adoption of the Federal Constitution (5 vols., Jonathan Elliot, ed., Washington, DC, 1836–1845). |
| Farrand | The Records of the Federal Convention of 1787 (4 vols., Max Farrand, ed., New Haven, Conn.: Yale University Press, 1937). |
| The Federalist | The Federalist, Benjamin F. Wright, ed. (New York: Metro Books, 2002). |
| Goldsmith | The Growth of Presidential Power: A Documented History, William M. Goldsmith (3 vols., New York: Chelsea House Publishers, 1974). |
| Landmark Briefs | Landmark Briefs and Arguments of the Supreme Court of the United States: Constitutional Law (Philip B. Kurland and Gerhard Casper, eds., Washington, DC: University Publications of America, 1978–2013). |
| Richardson | A Compilation of the Messages and Papers of the Presidents (20 vols., James D. Richardson, ed., New York: Bureau of National Literature, 1916). |

# ONE

# Fundamental Concepts

THE THEME AND PERSPECTIVE OF THIS TREATISE IS TRADITIONAL BUT ALSO contemporary. The system of separation of powers requires engagement by all three branches in defining the scope and use of executive and presidential power. That engagement depends on knowledge of the past, applied in a usable manner to meet problems of the day. All three branches must be willing to be full partners in exercising checks and balances. That constitutional principle is not served by a retreat by the courts or by Congress when responding to presidential initiatives, either in the name of efficiency, national security, or deference. An ongoing commitment and independent judgment are needed to reach outcomes that serve the general public and protect constitutional values.

## 1. ENUMERATED AND IMPLIED POWERS

Some presidential powers are enumerated in Articles I and II, including the veto power and the power to nominate. Those powers, clear as they may seem, have invited many questions and controversies. Presidents early exercised both the regular veto and the "pocket veto." In recent decades they have opted for a third form: claiming to pocket veto a bill but then returning it to Congress for a possible override. The practice of Congress is to treat such hybrids as a regular veto, not a pocket veto. As detailed in Chapter 5, the scope of the veto power has been fleshed out not by the text of the Constitution or amendments to it but by presidential initiatives, congressional responses, and judicial rulings.

Article II provides that the President "shall nominate" public officers, subject to the advice and consent of the Senate. Does that language empower the President alone to select the person to be nominated, or are individuals outside the executive branch involved in that decision? Chapter 4 explains that a few Presidents regarded nomination as exclusively an executive matter, only to learn it was politically necessary to share that task with others. Senators perform a prominent role in naming federal district judges and even appellate judges and Supreme Court Justices. The veto and nomination powers illustrate the difficulty of understanding the scope of presidential power simply by looking at the text of the Constitution.

In addition to enumerated powers, all three branches possess a number of implied powers: powers that can be reasonably drawn from express powers. In Article II, the President has the express duty to "take Care that the Laws be faithfully executed." If the head of an executive department cannot or will not carry out a statutory responsibility, the President has the implied power to remove the individual. The integrity of the Constitution is safeguarded when all three branches are limited to enumerated and implied powers. As the treatise explains, the Constitution is endangered by asserting other types of powers, such as "inherent."

Are decisions by the Supreme Court reliable guides on the breadth of presidential power? Not always. Article II empowers the President, by and with the advice and consent of the Senate, "to make treaties." Does the President have the exclusive authority to negotiate treaties? Justice Sutherland, in the 1936 *Curtiss-Wright* case, claimed that treaty negotiation is purely a presidential power into which "the Senate cannot intrude; and Congress itself is powerless to invade it."[1] In that understanding he was fundamentally mistaken (Chapter 7, section 3A). His earlier writings as a U.S. Senator acknowledged that Senators participate in the negotiation of treaties.[2] Members of the House of Representatives have also been included in treaty negotiation.

# 2. OVERLAPPING POWERS

Nominations and treaty-making necessarily involve the executive and legislative branches. So does the presidential response to legislative requests for executive branch documents and testimony. President George Washington was the first to recognize some discretion on the part of the executive branch to withhold documents from Congress, although in this particular investigation into heavy military losses under General Arthur St. Clair he fully cooperated. Since that time, there have been many controversies over the President's "executive privilege" and the capacity of Congress to receive documents and testimony it needs to carry out legislative duties. Some of those disputes enter the courts and are resolved there. Most are settled through political accommodations reached between the two elected branches (Chapter 5, section 7).

Overlapping powers are a dominant theme with the war power, balancing the Article I powers of Congress with the Article II powers of the President. The Constitution empowers Congress to "declare war." An early exception was the Quasi-War against France in 1798, which was authorized rather than formally declared. The Framers recognized that the President may use military force to "repel sudden attacks," especially when Congress is not in session and unable to respond immediately. May Presidents initiate war without receiving from Congress either a declaration or an authorization? That was never the understanding until President Harry Truman in 1950 bypassed Congress by going to war against North Korea on the basis of resolutions passed by the UN Security Council. The constitutionality of that precedent is explored in Chapter 8, section 5. Federal courts have been involved in war power disputes from 1800 to the present, although through much of the Vietnam War-era courts at every level avoided war power disputes by invoking a number of threshold principles (Chapter 8, section 7D). Those judicial doctrines, discussed throughout this treatise, include standing, ripeness, mootness, political questions, and "prudential considerations."

---

1. United States v. Curtiss-Wright Corp., 299 U.S. 304, 319 (1936).
2. GEORGE SUTHERLAND, CONSTITUTIONAL POWER AND WORLD AFFAIRS 123 (1919).

# 3. JUDICIAL MISCONCEPTIONS

In addition to express and implied powers, does the President also possess powers said to "inhere" in his office? Justice Sutherland made this claim in *Curtiss-Wright*: "As [John] Marshall said in his great argument of March 7, 1800, in the House of Representatives, 'The President is the sole organ of the nation in its external relations, and its sole representative with foreign nations.'"[3] According to Sutherland, the sole-organ doctrine invests the President with certain exclusive, plenary, and independent powers in foreign affairs. Recent administrations have invoked the sole-organ doctrine to assert broad and unchecked presidential powers. From the context of his speech, it is clear that John Marshall referred strictly to the authority of President John Adams to implement an extradition provision in the Jay Treaty. That is, Adams relied not on inherent power but authority conferred upon him by treaty. He thus exercised his express constitutional duty to take care that the laws (in this case a treaty) be faithfully executed. Details of that story appear in Chapter 7, section 1B.

Justice Sutherland's misrepresentation of the sole-organ speech is not unusual. Justice Robert Jackson observed: "Judges often are not thorough or objective historians."[4] Writing in 1989, Justice Scalia stated that the judicial system "does not present the ideal environment for entirely accurate historical inquiry."[5] Referring to the experience with his own staff, he said courts do not "employ the ideal personnel."[6] Justice John Paul Stevens, in a book published in 2011, wrote: "judges are merely amateur historians" whose interpretations of past events "are often debatable and sometimes simply wrong."[7] Another recent study by Judge J. Harvie Wilkinson III underscores these judicial limitations. He explains that historians spend years studying a period of time "and investigating its nuances," while judges have only months to decide each case "and even that time has to be divided among all the cases on the docket."[8] History professors, he points out, have the benefit of research assistants trained in the tools of historical research. Judges have their law clerks, "and although these newly minted lawyers are intelligent and capable, they are typically unversed in the historian's methods."[9] Granted these limitations, if federal judges decide to characterize a speech by John Marshall, they have an obligation to actually read it and reach an informed understanding. Undergraduate students are required to do that; so should judges.

---

3. United States v. Curtiss-Wright Corp., 299 U.S. 304, 319 (1936), citing ANNALS OF CONG., 6th Cong. 613 (1800).

4. Robert H. Jackson, *Full Faith and Credit—The Lawyer's Clause of the Constitution*, 45 COLUM. L. REV. 1, 6 (1945).

5. Antonin Scalia, *Originalism: The Lesser Evil*, 57 U. CINN. L. REV. 849, 861 (1989).

6. Id.

7. JUSTICE JOHN PAUL STEVENS, FIVE CHIEFS 225–26 (2011).

8. J. HARVIE WILKINSON III, COSMIC CONSTITUTIONAL THEORY: WHY AMERICANS ARE LOSING THEIR INALIENABLE RIGHT TO SELF-GOVERNANCE 50–51 (2012).

9. Id. at 51.

Judicial misconceptions and errors about history are serious because, once uttered, they are likely to be cited on a regular basis as reliable precedents.[10] It should be the duty of courts to revisit their errors and correct them. Many scholars have taken Sutherland to task (Chapter 7, section 1B), but courts continue to cite his language from *Curtiss-Wright* as though it is credible and trustworthy. It is not. Every time his misinterpretation is cited it gains apparent strength and legitimacy, adding support to the concept of independent and exclusive presidential power.

The executive branch invoked inherent presidential power to defend the decision of President Truman in 1952 to seize steel mills to prosecute the war in Korea. The Supreme Court denied that he possessed any emergency, residual, or inherent authority to act as he did.[11] Assertions of inherent presidential authority have reappeared frequently since then, including by President Richard Nixon (impoundment of funds and warrantless domestic surveillance) and by President George W. Bush after the terrorist attacks of 9/11 (creating military commissions). As explained throughout this treatise, the attempts by Truman, Nixon, and Bush to use inherent powers were turned back by Congress and the judiciary. Chapter 3, section 4 focuses on the concept of inherent presidential power. Specific instances of that power being rejected by the other branches appear in Chapter 8, section 6 (Truman's steel seizure), Chapter 6, section 6 (Nixon's impoundments), Chapter 9, section 8B (Nixon's domestic surveillance), and Chapter 9, section 8C (Bush's military tribunals). Chapter 3, section 5 analyzes the "prerogative" power. Some scholars distinguish between "inherent" and "preclusive" presidential powers.[12]

# 4. HISTORICAL FRAMEWORK

Legal analysis, when narrowly applied, can become hypertechnical and divorced from important principles. The framers were not primarily theoreticians. Those who drafted the Constitution and fought for its ratification had served in public life and wanted a government that would function effectively. Committed to self-government and influenced by the Enlightenment, the framers were at the same time distrustful of human nature. They wrestled with and attempted to reconcile these competing values. At the Philadelphia Convention, John Dickinson advised his colleagues: "Experience must be our only guide. Reason may mislead us."[13]

In analyzing particular provisions of the Constitution, it is important to appreciate some of the lessons the framers brought to the Philadelphia Convention. How did they react to the model of British monarchical powers, especially in war powers, foreign policy, and external

---

10. CHARLES A. MILLER, THE SUPREME COURT AND THE USES OF HISTORY (1969). See also Alfred H. Kelly, *Clio and the Court: An Illicit Love Affair*, 1965 SUP. CT. REV. 119, and John G. Wofford, *The Blinding Light: The Use of History in Constitutional Interpretation*, 31 U. CHI. L. REV. 502 (1964).

11. Youngstown Co. v. Sawyer, 343 U.S. 579 (1952).

12. David J. Barron & Martin S. Lederman, *The Commander in Chief at the Lowest Ebb—Framing the Problem, Doctrine, and Original Understanding* (Part 1), 121 HARV. L. REV. 689 (2008), and *The Commander in Chief at the Lowest Ebb—A Constitutional History* (Part 2), 121 HARV. L. REV. 941 (2008).

13. 2 Farrand 278.

affairs? What was their opinion of executive power in the Continental Congress, from 1774 to 1787? What did "separation of powers" mean to them: an abstract theory or something more practical to include the associated (and seemingly conflicting) system of checks and balances? Those questions need to be addressed when analyzing the constitutional text. The framers rejected the British model as placing too much authority in the executive but also understood that executive officers in the Continental Congress were far too weak. Debates from 1776 to 1789 demonstrate an effort to move away from an impractical model of pure separation of powers (as promoted by Montesquieu) to an overlapping of powers and dependence on institutional checks.

## 5. THE BRITISH MODEL

The framers closely studied the British political system that centered war-making and foreign policy in the Executive. They broke decisively with that model and warned against the hazards of executive wars. After careful consideration, they transferred many powers of external affairs to the legislative branch to secure the principle of self-government and popular sovereignty. They understood the need of the President to "repel sudden attacks," but reserved to Congress the decision to take the country from a state of peace to a state of war against another country (Chapters 7 and 8).

Although the English Parliament gained the power of the purse in the 1660s to restrain the king, the power to initiate war remained a monarchical prerogative. In his *Second Treatise of Civil Government* (1690), John Locke identified three functions of government: legislative, executive, and "federative."[14] The last included all powers over external affairs. Those same principles appear in the writings of William Blackstone, the British eighteenth-century jurist. Book 1 of his *Commentaries on the Laws of England* (1765) defined the king's prerogative as "those rights and capacities which the king enjoys alone."[15] Some of those powers are "rooted in and spring from the king's political person," including the right to send and receive ambassadors and the power of "making war or peace."[16] Those formulations are parallel to the contemporary claim of "inherent" presidential power.

The American framers transferred many of Blackstone's executive powers to Congress or divided them between the President and the Senate (as with treaties and the appointment of ambassadors). Unlike England, with its long history of monarchy over which Parliament gradually gained some powers, America as a national government began in 1776 with a legislative branch and no other. In the debates at the Philadelphia convention, state ratifications, and essays in the Federalist Papers, the framers explicitly rejected British monarchy and the political models of Locke and Blackstone.

---

14. John Locke, Second Treatise of Civil Government §§ 145–46 (1690).

15. 1 William Blackstone, Commentaries on the Laws of England 232 (1765).

16. Id. at 232–33.

## 6. ARTICLES OF CONFEDERATION

No separate national executive existed when America broke from England in 1776. All national powers were exercised by one branch of government: the Continental Congress. The ninth article of the first national constitution, the Articles of Confederation, provided: "The United States, in Congress assembled, shall have the sole and exclusive right and power of determining on peace and war."[17] The single exception to that principle lay with the sixth article, which allowed states to engage in war if invaded by enemies or when threatened by Indian tribes.[18] The new national government needed the approval of nine of the thirteen states when it wanted to engage in war, enter into treaties, borrow money, appropriate funds, and make other commitments.[19]

Delegates to the Continental Congress handled not merely legislative chores but also administrative and adjudicative duties. The Articles of Confederation authorized Congress to appoint a committee to sit during a legislative recess and permitted Congress to appoint other committees and civil officers as may be necessary to manage the general affairs of the national government. Committees of that character had been operating for several years before the drafting of the Articles. They were established in 1774 to petition the King, examine matters relating to trade and manufacture, and to prepare addresses to the people of Great Britain and Quebec.[20]

A rapid proliferation of committees made it difficult for members of the Continental Congress to perform their legislative duties. As a compromise between its committee system and the selection of single executives, Congress experimented with multi-member boards of men recruited from outside Congress. These boards were regularly criticized for moving too slowly and lacking accountability. Who among the board members was actually responsible? Pressure mounted for single executives, a step taken in 1781. The new positions were Superintendent of Finance, Secretary at War, and Secretary of Marine. Congress created an office of Attorney General to prosecute all suits on behalf of the United States and to advise Congress on all legal matters submitted to it. These executive positions were not independent of Congress. They were agents of Congress, subject to full legislative control and direction.[21]

## 7. CONSTITUTIONAL CONVENTION
## AND RATIFICATION

The belief that the U.S. Constitution consists of highly theoretical principles hammered out over a few months in Philadelphia received wide currency from William Gladstone. He described the draft constitution as "the most wonderful work ever struck off at a given time by the brain

---

17. MERRILL JENSEN, THE ARTICLES OF CONFEDERATION 266–69 (1963).

18. Id. at 264–65.

19. Id. at 269. The Articles of Confederation are reprinted at 1 U.S.C. L.

20. 1 JOURNALS OF THE CONTINENTAL CONGRESS 26, 53, 62, 101.

21. LOUIS FISHER, PRESIDENT AND CONGRESS 6–14 (1972).

and purpose of man."[22] He put the emphasis more on borrowed theory than first-hand experience drawn from colonial government and more than a decade of the Continental Congress. Political theory played an important role, but it was always circumscribed and tested by experience. The concept of separation of powers developed from a painfully slow evolution of executive departments. In a striking phrase, Francis Wharton said that the Constitution "did not make this distribution of power. It would be more proper to say that this distribution of power made the Constitution of the United States."[23]

Notes taken by James Madison and others at the Philadelphia convention are available in the multi-volume work edited by Max Farrand.[24] Madison, Alexander Hamilton, and John Jay wrote essays in defense of the Constitution, which are known as the Federalist Papers and published in various editions. Valuable commentary, referred to as the Anti-Federalist Papers, reflects the analysis of those who opposed the draft Constitution. Debates in the state ratification debates are in volumes edited by Jonathan Elliot.[25]

# 8. SEPARATION OF POWERS

The years from 1774 to 1787 marked a search for administrative efficiency. Illuminating the practical evolution of separated powers are the experiences of John Jay and Henry Knox as single executives in the Continental Congress. In taking over as Secretary for Foreign Affairs in September 1784, Jay strengthened the powers of that office. He served throughout the remaining years of the Continental Congress and continued in that capacity as Acting Secretary of State under George Washington's first administration, until Thomas Jefferson assumed those duties in March 1790. Knox, elected Secretary at War on March 8, 1785, remained in that post until the final days of 1794. Another remarkable example of administrative continuity is Joseph Nourse, who served as Register of the Treasury from 1779 to 1829.[26]

Madison, Hamilton, and other framers explained why the separation of powers model developed by the French theorist Montesquieu would not be appropriate for America. Powers had to overlap to assure the vital safeguard of checks and balances. In the Federalist Papers, Madison compared the overlapping of powers in the draft Constitution with the abstract

---

22. William Gladstone, *Kin Beyond Sea*, 127 NORTH AM. REV. 185 (Sept.–Oct. 1878).

23. 1 FRANCIS WHARTON, THE REVOLUTIONARY DIPLOMATIC CORRESPONDENCE OF THE UNITED STATES 663 (6 vols., 1889).

24. Appropriate caution has been directed at notes taken at the Philadelphia convention and the state ratifying conventions. No doubt James Madison did not capture everything said at Philadelphia. James H. Hutson, *The Creation of the Constitution: The Integrity of the Documentary Record*, 65 TEXAS L. REV. 1 (1986). Earlier studies also warned about reliance on the "framers' intent." Jacobus tenBroek, *Admissibility and Use by the United States Supreme Court of Extrinsic Aids in Constitutional Construction*, 26 CAL. L. REV. 287 (1938); John G. Wofford, *The Blinding Light: The Uses of History in Constitutional Interpretation*, 31 U. CHI. L. REV. 502 (1964).

25. Hutson, *supra* note 24, at 12–24, calls attention to comparable problems of reliable transcription with the work of Elliot.

26. E. JAMES FERGUSON, THE POWER OF THE PURSE: A HISTORY OF AMERICAN PUBLIC FINANCE, 1776–1790 (1961), HARRY M. WARD, THE DEPARTMENT OF WAR, 1781–1795 (1962), JENNINGS B. SANDERS, THE PRESIDENCY IN THE CONTINENTAL CONGRESS, 1774–89 (1971 ed.), and WILLIAM B. MICHAELSEN, CREATING THE AMERICAN PRESIDENCY, 1775–1789 (1987).

and impracticable partitioning of power advocated by others. His instructive essays include Federalist 47, 50, and 51. Hamilton in Federalist 66 insisted that the true meaning of the separation maxim was "entirely compatible with a partial intermixture." For critics who disliked the treaty process because it mixed the executive with the Senate, he dismissed such complaints in Federalist 75 as "the trite topic of the intermixture of powers."

By the late 1780s, the concept of checks and balances had gained dominance over the pure doctrine of separated powers, which one contemporary pamphleteer called a "hackneyed principle" and a "trite maxim."[27] After ratification, three states (North Carolina, Pennsylvania, and Virginia) urged that a separation of powers clause be added to the Bill of Rights. Virginia recommended that the "legislative, executive, and judiciary powers of Government should be separate and distinct." Pennsylvania and North Carolina offered their own versions of a separation clause. The compromise language presented to Congress reads: "The powers delegated by this constitution are appropriated to the departments to which they are respectively distributed: so that the legislative department shall never exercise the powers vested in the executive or judicial[,] nor the executive exercise the powers vested in the legislative or judicial, not the judicial exercise the powers vested in the legislative or executive departments." The separation clause was one of 17 constitutional amendments sent to the Senate, which struck it from a list of proposed amendments on September 7, 1789. Also voted down was a substitute amendment to make the three departments "separate and distinct" and to assure that the legislative and executive departments should be restrained from oppression by "feeling and participating the public burthens" through regular elections.[28]

It is often argued that the separation doctrine, while not explicitly stated in the Constitution, is nevertheless implied. No doubt it is, but that does not help us understand exactly what is implied and to what degree the three branches must remain separate. We are told that powers are separated to preserve liberties. It is equally true that too much emphasis on separation can destroy liberties. The historical antagonism in France between executive and legislature, characterized by an oscillation between administrative and representative forms of government, is a classic example of the danger of extreme separation. The constitutions of 1791 and 1848 represented the most ambitious attempts in France to establish a pure separation of powers. The first experiment led to the Committee of Public Safety, the Directory, and the reign of Napoleon Bonaparte. The second effort produced Louis Napoleon, reaction, and the Second Empire. "It is hardly surprising," wrote Professor Vile, "that this last flirtation with the pure doctrine ended in the same way as others had ended in France—in absolutism."[29] The American framers wanted to avoid that kind of political fragmentation and paralysis of power. Justice Joseph Story explained that they endorsed a separation of powers but "endeavored to prove that a rigid adherence to it in all cases would be subversive of the efficiency of government, and result in the destruction of the public liberties."[30]

27. M. J. C. Vile, Constitutionalism and the Separation of Powers 153 (1967).

28. 1 Annals of Cong. 453 (June 8, 1789). See Edward Dumbauld, The Bill of Rights and What It Means Today 174–75, 183, 199 (1957); Fisher, supra note 21, at 24–27, 277–78.

29. Vile, supra note 27, at 207.

30. 1 Joseph Story, Commentaries on the Constitution of the United States 396 (1905).

# 9. ARTICLES I AND II

The framers placed presidential powers in Articles I and II. Sections 2, 3, 6, 7, and 9 of Article I contain provisions that relate to the President, including impeachment, the Vice President as President of the Senate, the Senate President pro tempore filling in for the Vice President when the latter has to exercise the office of the President, the Incompatibility and Ineligibility Clauses, the veto power, and suspension of the writ of habeas corpus.

Article II begins: "The executive Power shall be vested in a President of the United States of America." At times this is referred to as the Vesting Clause, analyzed in Chapter 3, section 2. Does the "executive Power" consist solely of the powers specifically enumerated in Article II? That position is not tenable. It was recognized in 1789, the first year of the new national government, that the President has an *implied power* to remove the head of an executive department if that individual interferes with another express power of the President found in Article II: "he shall take Care that the Laws be faithfully executed." The constitutional obligation of the President to carry out the laws necessarily trumps a Cabinet officer's right to hold office. Here a presidential implied power is drawn necessarily from an express power. The President's removal power is analyzed in Chapter 3, section 7.

Does it matter if a constitutional provision is placed in Article I or Article II? Article I, section 9, provides: "The Privilege of the Writ of Habeas Corpus shall not be suspended, unless when in Cases of Rebellion or Invasion the public Safety may require it." Does the location of this language in Article I mean that the power of suspension is reserved to Congress alone and not to the President? Had this language been placed in Article II, would that have shifted the suspension power to the President? In some cases it should not matter where a constitutional provision is placed. Article II, section 2, provides that the President "shall have Power, by and with the Advice and Consent of the Senate, to make Treaties, provided two thirds of the Senators present shall concur." Transferring that language to Article I would not affect the relative powers of the President and the Senate.

Article II, section 1 vests "the executive Power" in the President, whereas Article I, section 1 grants Congress powers "herein granted." Is the difference in wording significant? Does the former give the *whole of the executive power* to the President, and the latter only *part of the legislative power* to Congress, as some proponents of presidential power argue? Chapter 3, section 3, analyzes the herein-granted issue. Other chapters explore the extent to which Congress is confined to powers specifically stated and whether the President somehow has access to powers beyond those expressly provided.

It should be clear that all three branches have access to powers not expressly stated. They are *not* confined to enumerated powers. All exercise a range of implied powers, including the power of Congress to investigate and issue subpoenas, the power of the President to remove certain executive officials, and the power of federal courts to exercise judicial review. Moreover, the powers placed in Congress are quite broad, such as the commerce power and the taxing power. The "sweeping clause" in Article I, section 8, gives Congress the power to pass all legislation "necessary and proper" to carry into execution not only its foregoing legislative powers but "all other Powers vested by this Constitution in the Government of the United States, or in any Department or Officer thereof."

## 10. EVOLVING POWERS

The dominant trend after World War II has been a steady climb in presidential power, accompanied by marked increases in the size and budgetary resources of the White House and the executive branch. Checks and balances against presidential power have become less effective and reliable.[31] Some studies focus not on legislative weaknesses but chronic deficiencies within the presidency.[32] On a regular basis, members of Congress have expressed concern about their dwindling powers and have taken steps intended to strengthen the independence and capacity of their branch. Despite those efforts, Congress has become less protective of its institutional powers.[33] During that same time period, the Supreme Court found it necessary to reevaluate its constitutional authority to police and limit the boundaries of presidential power, including in the sensitive field of national security policy.

For much of U.S. history, presidential power fluctuated depending on who occupied the office, creating a cycle between strong and weak Presidents. Presidents who pressed and expanded their powers were followed by a Congress determined to reassert and recover its prerogatives. That pendulum effect is less present after 1945. From the progressive movement of the early 1900s to contemporary Republicans, political forces have pushed toward greater presidential power, a reduced role for Congress, and less interest in the framers' commitment to checks and balances.[34] Some scholars now advocate a "unitary executive" to further insulate the President from outside constraints (Chapter 3, section 10B).

Contemporary Presidents inherit a large bureaucracy and multiple statutory programs, acting on the basis of powers steadily accumulated by their predecessors. Presidents of either party vow not to leave the office weaker than when they entered. White House aides and department officials do what they can to encourage a broad assertion of executive power with few checks. Many scholars have promoted an idealized model of the presidency, claiming that its occupant is devoted to the "national interest" and surrounded by advisers with unrivaled

---

31. Peter M. Shane, Madison's Nightmare: How Executive Power Threatens Democracy (2009); Gene Healy, The Cult of the Presidency: America's Dangerous Devotion to Executive Power (2008); James P. Pfiffner, Power Play: The Bush Presidency and the Constitution (2008); Frederick A. O. Schwarz, Jr. & Aziz Z. Huq, Unchecked and Unbalanced Presidential Power in a Time of Terror (2007); Charlie Savage, Takeover: The Return of the Imperial Presidency and the Subversion of American Democracy (2007); Matthew Crenson & Benjamin Ginsberg, Presidential Power: Unchecked and Unbalanced (2007); Andrew Rudalevige, The New Imperial Presidency: Renewing Presidential Power after Watergate (2005).

32. Richard M. Pious, Why Presidents Fail: White House Decision Making from Eisenhower to Bush II (2008).

33. Jasmine Farrier, Congressional Ambivalence: The Political Burdens of Constitutional Authority (2010); F. Ugboaja Ohaegbulam, A Culture of Deference: Congress, the President, and the Course of the U.S.-Led Invasion and Occupation of Iraq (2007); George I. Lovell, Legislative Deferrals: Statutory Ambiguity, Judicial Power, and American Democracy (2003); Louis Fisher, Congressional Abdication on War and Spending (2000); Stephen R. Weissman, A Culture of Deference: Congress's Failure of Leadership in Foreign Policy (1995); and Barbara Hinckley, Less Than Meets the Eye: Foreign Policy Making and the Myth of an Assertive Congress (1994).

34. Richard H. Pildes, *Law and the President*, review of The Executive Unbound: After the Madisonian Republic, by Eric A. Posner and Adrian Vermeule, 125 Harv. L. Rev. 1381 (2012).

expertise and reliable political judgment.[35] Countering this trend are the uncertain and less organized efforts of the legislative and judicial branches.

# 11. APPROACHES BY LAWYERS AND PROFESSORS

Lawyers are often surprised by techniques employed by university specialists who analyze executive and presidential power. The two university fields most concerned with those questions are law and political science. Writing in 2005, Robert Delahunty and John Yoo suggested that law professors "have reached a formalist stalemate over the powers of the Presidency and that this stalemate has diverted attention away from interesting avenues of scholarly research."[36] As explained in the next section, lawyers rely on both formalism and functionalism when they study presidential power. Formalism is a broad concept, but often it means studying constitutional texts in a narrow context. Delahunty and Yoo say that political scientists focus on "the individual characteristics of the Chief Executive as a political leader," possibly referring to the works of James MacGregor Burns, Richard Neustadt, Clinton Rossiter, and Arthur M. Schlesinger, Jr.[37]

Delahunty and Yoo conclude that "the two disciplines have been talking past each other—law examines the formal constitutional powers, while political scientists have focused on the unique political character of individual Presidents."[38] Of course the two disciplines are not cleanly divided. There is substantial overlap between them, and many scholars have both a law degree and a doctorate in political science. Still, political science is more distant from public law than it was in the past. From the 1880s to the 1950s, public law was an integral part of political science. Scholars in that discipline did not hesitate to study formal constitutional powers.

A prominent example is the work of Edward Corwin.[39] Actually, his doctorate was in history. During his period, historians were quite comfortable in analyzing constitutional issues and writing broadly about public law. Contemporary historians have largely vacated that field. That is unfortunate. Analysis of public law, including executive and presidential power, is not and should not be the sole preserve of one discipline, be it law, political science, or history. Balkanization of disciplines creates artificial barriers that prevent an accurate understanding of public law aspects of the presidency and the executive branch.

35. Louis Fisher, *Teaching the Presidency: Idealizing a Constitutional Office*, 45 PS: Political Science & Politics 17 (2012); David Gray Adler, *Textbooks and the President's Constitutional Powers*, 35 Pres. Stud. Q. 376 (2005); Louis Fisher, *Scholarly Support for Presidential Wars*, 35 Pres. Stud. Q. 590 (2005); and Thomas E. Cronin, *The Textbook Presidency and Political Science*, 116 Cong. Rec. 34914–28 (1970).

36. Robert J. Delahunty & John C. Yoo, *Thinking About Presidents*, 90 Corn. L. Rev. 1153, 1161 (2005).

37. James MacGregor Burns, Presidential Government: The crucible of Leadership (1965); Clinton Rossiter, The American Presidency (1956); and Richard E. Neustadt, Presidential Power: The Politics of Leadership (1960). Schlesinger's works include The Age of Jackson (1945) and a three-volume work on President Franklin D. Roosevelt: The Crisis of the Old Order (1957), The Coming of the New Deal (1959) and The Politics of Upheaval (1960).

38. *Supra* note 36, at 1161.

39. Edward S. Corwin, The President: Office and Powers, 1787–1957 (4th ed., 1957).

A number of political scientists continue to study formal presidential powers.[40] Nonetheless, there has been a decline in the commitment of political scientists to public law.[41] Studies on behavioralism crowded out much of public law. Moreover, many political scientists see little incentive to publish in law reviews because their departments do not give credit (such as for promotion and tenure) for articles that appear in journals that are not peer-reviewed.[42] Top political science journals are not very receptive to articles that analyze constitutional aspects of the presidency. Beginning in 1999, however, *Presidential Studies Quarterly* created a section of the journal devoted to articles on "The Law."

As for lawyers, their approaches to studying presidential power vary a great deal, offering theories that directly contradict one another. Some publish careful studies that examine a range of presidential powers and how they are checked and shared with Congress.[43] Others promote broad presidential powers in times of emergencies, even to the extent of removing any legal and constitutional checks on the President and relying solely on the political constraints of elections and public opinion.[44]

# 12. INTERPRETIVE THEORIES

In its decisions on separation of powers, the Supreme Court adopts inconsistent principles. At times it embraces a functional and pragmatic approach, only to promote in a different case a strict, formalistic model. The functionalist approach was used in 1974 when the Court rejected President Nixon's claim of an absolute power to withhold the Watergate tapes. The Court chose

---

40. Mark J. Rozell, Executive Privilege: Presidential Power, Secrecy, and Accountability (3d ed., 2010); Christopher H. Pyle & Richard M. Pious, The Constitution Under Siege: Presidential Power Versus the Rule of Law (2010) (building on an earlier version by the two authors, The President, Congress, and the Constitution (1984)); Jeffrey Crouch, The Presidential Pardon Power (2009); Mitchel A. Sollenberger, The President Shall Nominate: How Congress Trumps Executive Power (2008); Louis Fisher, Constitutional Conflicts Between Congress and the President (6th ed. 2014); Louis Fisher, Presidential War Power (3d ed., 2013), Ryan C. Hendrickson, The Clinton Wars: The Constitution, Congress, and War Powers (2002); and Robert J. Spitzer, The Presidential Veto: Touchstone of the American Presidency (1988). Joseph Bessette & Jeffrey Tulis edited The Presidency in the Constitutional Order (1981) and The Constitutional Presidency (2009). Michael A. Geneovese & Robert J. Spitzer edited a casebook on The Presidency and the Constitution (2005).

41. Louis Fisher, *Political Scientists and the Public Law Tradition*, The Oxford Handbook of the American Presidency 797–815 (2009). For examples of many political scientists who remain active in the field of public law and testify before congressional committees on legal issues, see *Law and (Disciplinary) Order: A Dialogue about Louis Fisher, Constitutionalism, and Political Science*, 46 PS: Political Science & Politics 483 (2013).

42. For a critique of student-run law reviews, see Robert J. Spitzer, Saving the Constitution from Lawyers: How Legal Training and Law Reviews Distort Constitutional Meaning (2008).

43. Scott M. Matheson, Jr., Presidential Constitutionalism in Perilous Times (2009); James E. Baker, In the Common Defense: National Security Law for Perilous Times (2007); Harold J. Krent, Presidential Powers (2005); Peter M. Shane & Harold H. Bruff, The Law of Presidential Power: Cases and Materials (1988).

44. Eric A. Posner & Adrian Vermeule, The Executive Unbound: After the Madisonian Republic (2010); Eric A. Posner & Adrian Vermeule, Terror in the Balance: Security, Liberty, and the Courts (2007).

to emphasize checks and balances and the need for a "workable government."[45] Separation of powers entered the Court's analysis in the sense of preserving "the essential functions of each branch."[46] The Court made no effort to create rigid boundaries and prohibit the slightest intrusion of one branch over another.[47]

Three years later, in a case concerning ownership of Nixon's papers in the National Archives, the Court again adopted a practical understanding of separation of powers. It denied that the three branches of government must remain "entirely free from the control or coercive influence, direct or indirect, of either of the others."[48] It announced support for the "more pragmatic, flexible approach" of James Madison and Joseph Story.[49] This type of analysis allowed for some sharing and overlapping of powers.

A few years later, the Court promoted a strict interpretation of separated powers. In 1982, it upheld an absolute immunity for the President in civil cases and expressed concern about the "dangers of intrusion on the authority and functions of the Executive Branch."[50] When it struck down the legislative veto in *INS v. Chadha* (1983), the Court rejected arguments that the legislative veto might have been useful in settling issues between the legislative and executive branches: "Convenience and efficiency are not the primary objectives—or the hallmarks—of democratic government."[51] The Court concluded that government must be divided into "three defined categories, Legislative, Executive, and Judicial," and that it was a judicial duty to resist the "hydraulic pressures inherent within each of the separate Branches to exceed the outer limits of its power."[52] The Court's determination to eliminate the legislative veto once and for all failed to recognize that it offered important benefits to the elected branches. Despite the Court's ruling, the legislative veto survives because it satisfies executive and legislative needs (Chapter 5, section 6).

In justifying their positions, litigants, lawmakers, and executive officials will often seek support from the framers' intent. At times that effort takes the form of Originalism: the belief that the original public understanding is the only legitimate source of constitutional interpretation. According to this method of analysis, contemporary disputes should be settled by principles and values established by the founding generation. Framers' intent is certainly one source of guidance, but the record demonstrates that it does not guarantee clarity or consensus. When nine Justices do their historical homework and attempt to discern what the framers intended, as in the federalism case of *Alden v. Maine* (1999) or the Second Amendment case of *District of Columbia v. Heller* (2008), the Justices split 5-4.[53]

---

45. United States v. Nixon, 418 U.S. 683, 707 (1974).

46. Id.

47. Id. at 707–13.

48. Nixon v. Administrator of Gen. Serv., 433 U.S. 425, 441–42 (1977) (citing Humphrey's Executor v. United States, 295 U.S. 602, 629 (1935)).

49. Nixon v. Administrator of Gen. Serv., 433 U.S. at 442.

50. Nixon v. Fitzgerald, 457 U.S. 731, 754 (1982).

51. 462 U.S. 919, 944 (1983).

52. Id. at 951.

53. 527 U.S. 706 (1999); 554 U.S. 570 (2008). The spring 2009 issue of *Northwestern University Law Review*, Volume 103, Issue, 2, contains a series of articles devoted to Originalism.

Other theories have been advanced to decide constitutional disputes: Textualism, the Living Constitution, Minimalism, Moral Reading, Political Process, and Cost-Benefit Pragmatism. Initially, each approach promised unique advantages but none has emerged as a reliable or satisfactory method for analyzing constitutional issues.[54]

---

54. J. Harvie Wilkinson III, Cosmic Constitutional Theory: Why Americans Are Losing Their Inalienable Right to Self-Governance (2012).

# TWO

# Election and Removal
# of the President

DEBATED AND FRAMED IN 1787, THE U.S. CONSTITUTION BROKE WITH the monarchical model and moved toward republican government. The first three words of the document spoke clearly: "We the People." Yet the Framers were not prepared to support the direct election of the President or the Senate. Article I, section 2 selected that procedure for the House of Representatives, "to be composed of Members chosen every second Year by the People of the several States...." Under Article I, section 3, the Senate would be composed of "two Senators from each State, chosen by the Legislature thereof, for six Years." Not until the Seventeenth Amendment, ratified on April 8, 1913, were Senators directly elected by the people. The office of the President remains where it was in 1787, elected by an exceedingly complex and controversial system of Electors.

## 1. CHOOSING THE PRESIDENT BY ELECTORS

Article II, section 1 provides: "Each State shall appoint, in such Manner as the Legislature thereof may direct, a Number of Electors, equal to the whole Number of Senators and Representatives to which the State may be entitled in the Congress: but no Senator or Representative, or Person holding an Office of Trust or Profit under the Under State, shall be appointed an Elector." The Electors would meet in their respective states "and vote by Ballot for two Persons, of whom one at least shall not be an Inhabitant of the same State with themselves." Through that language the Framers hoped the Electors would look beyond their particular state to select a candidate with national appeal.

Voting by ballot "for two Persons" produced a political embarrassment in 1800. Thomas Jefferson and Aaron Burr, the two leading candidates for what became the Republican-Democratic Party, received an identical number of votes. An excruciating series of actions by the House of Representatives eventually determined who would be President and Vice President. That jolting experience led to the Twelfth Amendment, discussed in section 1B. Here the focus is on why the Framers decided on presidential Electors.

## A. Views of the Framers

The delegates at the Philadelphia convention considered several methods of selecting the President, including direct election by the people, by Congress, and by Electors chosen by the states. On May 29, 1787, Edmund Randolph proposed that the President be "chosen by the National Legislature."[1] His recommendation sparked substantial debate and even attracted unanimous support at times, before being discarded.[2] Elbridge Gerry raised one objection. He predicted that election by Congress would result in "constant intrigue," with Congress and the candidates willing to "bargain & play into one another's hands." Lawmakers would vote in return for "promises or expectations" by the candidates.[3]

On June 1, James Wilson ventured to say "at least that in theory he was for an election of the people." George Mason, without explaining why, regarded popular election as "impractical."[4] Gerry said he liked Wilson's proposal but feared it "would alarm & give a handle to the State partizans, as tending to supersede altogether the State authorities." He thought "the Community not yet ripe for stripping the states of their powers" and counseled "waiting till people <should> feel more the necessity of it."[5] To Roger Sherman, the people at large would "never be sufficiently informed of characters, and besides will never give majority of votes to any one man." They would "generally vote for some man in their own State, and the largest State will have the best chance for the appointment."[6] Sufficient support for popular election never emerged. A proposal to have the President appointed by state governors fared no better. It was voted down: 10 noes with Delaware divided.[7]

Part of what Mason regarded as "impractical" might have been the Framers' concern about the size of the country and the apprehension of smaller states, who could have concluded that "in a straight-out popular election the larger states would overwhelm them."[8] In 1787, how could citizens of the country effectively vote on a national candidate? The Framers may have decided "that the extent of the country and the difficulty of communication did not permit the informed selection of a national candidate."[9]

On June 1, Wilson moved that the Executive "consist of a single person." Charles Pinckney seconded the motion. Wilson said he preferred a single Executive "as giving most energy dispatch and responsibility to the office."[10] No doubt many of the delegates recalled the difficulty of three-man boards during the Continental Congress and the switch to single executives in 1781 to promote accountability (Chapter 1, section 6). On June 24, Hugh Williamson said he "did not like the Unity in the Executive." He wanted the executive power "lodged in three men taken

---

1. 1 Farrand 21.

2. For example, selection of the President by Congress passed 8 to 2 on June 2 (1 Farrand 77) and unanimously on July 23 (2 Farrand 22).

3. ·1 Farrand 80.

4. Id. at 68–69.

5. Id. at 80.

6. 2 Farrand 28.

7. 1 Farrand 181.

8. Shlomo Slonim, *Designing the Electoral College*, in Inventing the American Presidency 38 (Thomas E. Cronin, ed. 1989).

9. Id. at 55. Direct election of the President was voted down on July 17 (2 Farrand 32) and Aug. 24 (id. at 397).

10. 1 Farrand at 65.

from three districts into which the States should be divided."[11] There would be a President for the South, one for the North, and one for the middle states. His proposal attracted no support. The delegates agreed that a national Executive should consist of one person.

Essays by Alexander Hamilton, John Jay, and James Madison in the Federalist Papers supplement our understanding of the process used to elect a President. In Federalist No. 39, Madison asked whether the draft Constitution satisfied republican government: "It is evident that no other form would be reconcilable with the genius of the people of America; with the fundamental principles of the Revolution; or with that honorable determination which animates every votary of freedom, to rest all our political experiments on the capacity of mankind for self-government."[12] He defined a republic as "a government which derives all its powers directly or indirectly from the great body of the people, and is administered by persons holding their offices during pleasure, for a limited period, or during good behavior."[13] He conceded that the draft constitution provided for indirect selection of Senators and the President.

In Federalist No. 64, Jay concluded that because the system of appointing Senators and electing Presidents "will in general be composed of the most enlightened and respectable citizens, there is reason to presume that their attention and their votes will be directed to those men only who have become the most distinguished by their abilities and virtue, and in whom the people perceive just grounds for confidence."[14] Federalist No. 68 by Hamilton gave detailed attention to the method of electing the President. If the manner "be not perfect, it is at least excellent."[15] In choosing a President, it was "peculiarly desirable to afford as little opportunity as possible for tumult and disorder." The decision to rely on electors "will be much less apt to convulse the community with any extraordinary or violent movements, than the choice of *one* who was himself to be the final object of the public wishes."[16] Looking back on those who have served as President, we might find Hamilton a little too confident and optimistic: "It will not be too strong to say, that there will be a constant probability of seeing the station filled by characters preëminent for ability and virtue."[17]

At the Virginia ratifying convention, Patrick Henry expressed a decidedly different view about the President. For some, the Constitution "is said to have beautiful features; but when I come to examine these features, sir, they appear to me horribly frightful. Among other deformities, it has an awful squinting; it squints toward monarchy; and does not this raise indignation in the breast of every true American?" He warned that the President "may easily become king."[18]

The Framers reached other decisions about the President. Article II, section 1 provides that to be eligible the President shall "have attained to the Age of thirty five Years, and been fourteen Years a Resident within the United States." Presidents would be eligible for reelection. Compensation "shall neither be increased nor diminished during the Period for which he shall have been elected, and he shall not receive within that Period any other Emolument from the

11. 2 Farrand 100.
12. The Federalist 280.
13. Id. at 280–81.
14. Id. at 421.
15. Id. at 440.
16. Id. at 441 (emphasis in original).
17. Id. at 443.
18. 3 Elliot 58.

United States." The Framers wrestled with various terms of office, ranging from three to twenty years. Gerry preferred a lengthy term: "10, 15, or even 20" years.[19] A term of "good behavior" was considered.[20] Hamilton even suggested that the President serve "for life."[21] The Framers finally settled on a term of four years. Issues of citizenship and "natural born citizen" are handled in section 2 of this chapter.

## B. A tie vote in 1800

As ratified by the states, Article II, section 1 provided that Electors would meet in their respective states and vote by ballot "for two persons, of whom one at least shall not be an Inhabitant of the same State with themselves." The votes would be sent to the national government where the President of the Senate "shall, in the Presence of the Senate and House of Representatives, open all the Certificates, and the Votes shall then be counted." The person having the greatest number of votes would be President, if such number is a majority of the whole number of votes. If there is more than one who has a majority, and they have an equal number of votes, the House of Representatives "shall immediately chuse by Ballot one of them for President; and if no Person have a Majority, then from the five highest on the List the said House shall in like Manner chuse the President." Voting for President would be by states, with Representatives from each state having one vote. After choosing the President, the person having the greatest number of votes of the Electors "shall be the Vice President."

Although the Framers strongly endorsed the concept of a single Executive, they could not have anticipated what happened in the presidential election of 1796. The Federalist John Adams became President with 71 electoral votes. The Republican-Democrat Thomas Jefferson was first runner-up with 68 electoral votes and became Vice President. Thomas Pinckney, chosen by the Federalists to be Vice President, came in third. The nation now had "a divided executive branch."[22] Jefferson defeated Adams decisively for the presidency in 1800, but the Republican-Democrats faced an embarrassment. Jefferson and Burr tied at 73 electoral votes each. Burr might have urged the election of Jefferson, who was clearly the presidential candidate, and accepted the position of Vice President. Yet Burr remained silent. The matter therefore had to be resolved by the House of Representatives. After 35 ballots in February 1801, neither Jefferson nor Burr had a majority. With two weeks remaining in Adams's term, the House finally chose Jefferson on the 36th ballot.[23]

Congress now had to fix this problem of the Electoral College. The remedy: require Electors to designate one person for President and the other for Vice President. After several delays in the Senate, the Twelfth Amendment was submitted to the states and ratified on July 2, 1804. It provided that Electors "shall name in their ballots the person voted for as President, and in distinct ballots the person voted for as Vice-President."[24]

---

19. 2 Farrand 102.

20. Id. at 33.

21. 1 Farrand 289.

22. Richard B. Bernstein, Amending America 61–62 (1993).

23. Id. at 63.

24. Tadahisa Kuroda, The Origins of the Twelfth Amendment: The Electoral College in the Early Republic, 1787–1804 (1994).

## C. The election of 1876

Another constitutional problem surfaced with the presidential contest between Rutherford B. Hayes and Samuel Tilden. Hayes received 165 electoral votes. Tilden had 184, or one vote short of a majority of the Electoral College. Each claimed the remaining 20 disputed votes in South Carolina.[25] Both parties contributed to vote fraud. The number of votes cast in that state far exceeded the number of potential voters.[26] South Carolinians could vote repeatedly at different polling places because the unavailability of a list of registered voters prevented supervisors from challenging them. There was little doubt that blacks had been "forcibly prevented from getting anywhere near the polls, where the federal supervisors were stationed."[27]

Congress was divided. Democrats controlled the House and Republicans the Senate. Unable to resolve the matter, Congress passed legislation on January 29, 1877, to create an Electoral Commission consisting of five members of the House, five from the Senate, and five Justices of the Supreme Court. Four Justices were named in the statute. It was their duty to select the fifth Justice.[28] Because the House delegation was divided between three Democrats and two Republicans, the Senate between three Republicans and two Democrats, and with four Justices equally divided by their previous party affiliations, the fifth Justice would function as the tie breaker.[29]

The original plan was to select Justice David Davis, whose partisan leanings seemed sufficiently unclear that he might bring a measure of impartiality. Yet he became the Greenback candidate for a seat in the U.S. Senate. He was replaced by Justice Joseph P. Bradley, a Republican from New Jersey.[30] Republicans now had an 8-7 majority on the commission. A series of 8-7 votes awarded Hayes electoral votes from Florida, Louisiana, Oregon, and South Carolina, bringing his total to 185, enough to win the presidency.[31] House Democrats mounted a filibuster but Hayes eventually took office.[32]

## D. Electoral Count Act of 1887

The experience of the 1876 election, marred by fraud, voter intimidation, and the partisan result of the electoral commission, compelled Congress to search for a more credible process. Several principles guided lawmakers. First, they understood that at times the two houses would be controlled by different political parties, creating tie votes between the two chambers. Second, Congress believed that states should count electoral votes, provided they supplied authenticating documents. Third, Congress needed an expeditious process. Normal deliberative methods

---

25. Ari Hoogenboom, The Presidency of Rutherford B. Hayes 31 (1988).

26. Michael F. Holt, By One Vote: The Disputed Presidential Election of 1876, at 181 (2008).

27. Id. at 186.

28. 19 Stat. 227, 228, ch. 37 (1877).

29. Edward S. Corwin, The President: Office and Powers, 1787–1957, at 43 (4th ed. 1957).

30. Id. at 43–44.

31. Hoogenboom, *supra* note 25, at 41–50; Holt, *supra* note 26, at 233–35.

32. Holt, *supra* note 26, at 235–41.

were too slow and uncertain. Finally, Congress did not want to repeat the experience of 1886 and depend on the votes of Justices of the Supreme Court.[33]

This legislative effort produced the Electoral Count Act of 1887, fixing a day for the meeting of Electors of the President and Vice President to provide for and regulate the counting of votes. Certificates of the electoral votes would be submitted to Congress and acted upon in alphabetical order of the states. The President of the Senate could call for objections, if any. Objections had to be made in writing and signed by at least one Senator and one member of the House. Objections could also be made in the House. By concurrent action, the two houses were authorized to reject certain electoral votes. The joint meeting could not be dissolved until the count of electoral votes was completed and the results declared.[34]

Through this statute, it was the intention of Congress that future disputes over electoral votes should not be referred to outside commissions, including those that included participation by Justices of the Supreme Court. Disputes were to be settled by the legislative branch, without any involvement of the judiciary. As carried forth today in the U.S. Code, the 1887 statute is referred to as the "safe harbor" law. If any state provides to Congress, by law enacted prior to the day fixed for the appointment of Electors, a final determination of any controversy or contest concerning the appointment of all or any of its Electors, and such determination is made at least six days before the time set for the meeting of Electors, that determination "shall be conclusive."[35] Through those procedures, the selection of the President would remain in the hands of elected members of Congress.

## E. Supreme Court guidance

Until *Bush v. Gore* (2000), discussed in the next subsection, few rulings from the Supreme Court interpreted the use of Electors for Presidents and Vice Presidents. In *McPherson v. Blacker* (1892), a unanimous Court held that the system of Electors created by Article II was not amended by the Fourteenth and Fifteenth Amendments.[36] State legislatures retained exclusive power to direct the manner in which Electors of President and Vice President shall be appointed. The Court denied that all questions concerning Electors are "political in their nature" and the judiciary has no authority to dispose of them.[37] It further held that the appointment of Electors belongs "exclusively to the States."[38]

In 1952, the Court reviewed a requirement in Alabama that a candidate for Elector agree to pledge support for the party's nominee for President. It had been argued that the pledge violated the Twelfth Amendment and the intention of its Framers that Electors "should exercise their judgment in voting for President and Vice President."[39] The Court denied that the Twelfth

---

33. Stephen A. Siegel, *The Conscientious Congressman's Guide to the Electoral Count Act of 1887*, 56 FLA. L. REV. 542 (2004).

34. 24 Stat. 373 (1887).

35. 3 U.S.C. § 5. For an early analysis of the Electoral Count Act, see John W. Burgess, *The Law of the Electoral Count*, 3 POL. SCI. Q. 633 (1888).

36. 146 U.S. 1 (1892).

37. Id. at 23.

38. Id. at 35.

39. Ray v. Blair, 343 U.S. 214, 225 (1952).

Amendment "demands absolute freedom for the elector to vote his own choice, uninhibited by a pledge."[40] Justices Black and Frankfurter took no part in the case.

A dissent by Justice Jackson, joined by Douglas, disagreed with the majority's reliance on custom and practice to alter the apparent purpose of the Constitution and the Twelfth Amendment. Electors could operate as "free agents," at liberty to exercise an "independent and nonpartisan judgment as to the men best qualified for the Nation's highest offices."[41] In describing the original intent in this manner, Jackson punched holes in that expectation and said it had "miscarried." Electors, even those personally eminent and respectable, "became voluntary party lackeys and intellectual nonentities to whose memory we might justly paraphrase a tuneful satire: 'They always voted at their Party's call and never thought of thinking for themselves at all.'"[42] If the entire electoral system were to fail, Jackson said it "would not impress me as a disaster." To abolish it and substitute direct election of the President, "so that every vote wherever cast would have equal weight in calculating the result, would seem to me a gain for simplicity and integrity of our governmental processes."[43]

A decision by the Court in 1968 examined an Ohio law with heavy restrictions for a new political party to be placed on the state ballot to choose Electors pledged to particular candidates for President and Vice President. As in earlier cases, the Court rejected the argument that cases involving election law presented a political question doctrine that "precludes judicial consideration."[44] It also denied that Article II gave states unfettered discretion to appoint Electors. In this case, the Court held that the Ohio law violated the Equal Protection Clause of the Fourteenth Amendment by unconstitutionally tilting the advantage toward the two established political parties. In a dissent, Justice Stewart concluded that Ohio had the constitutional authority to enact its law.[45] Justices White and Chief Justice Warren offered other reasons in disagreeing with the majority.[46]

## F. The election of 2000

The constitutional problems of 1886 reappeared in the presidential race of 2000. Once again a disputed vote prevented the candidates—George W. Bush and Al Gore—from obtaining a majority of electoral votes. Initially, Bush received 246 electoral votes and Gore 267. They needed a majority: 270. The race focused on 25 electoral votes in Florida. From election day November 7 to December 12, the results remained uncertain. Various rulings were handed down by lower courts in Florida, federal district courts, the Eleventh Circuit, the Florida Supreme Court (four times), and the U.S. Supreme Court (twice). Sitting in the wings were other political institutions waiting to exercise their constitutional duties: the Florida Legislature and the U.S. Congress. On December 12, the U.S. Supreme Court ruled against a recount of Florida votes requested by

---

40. Id. at 228.
41. Id. at 232.
42. Id.
43. Id. at 234.
44. Williams v. Rhodes, 393 U.S. 23, 28 (1968).
45. Id. at 48–61.
46. Id. at 61–70.

Gore and the following day he gave his concession speech.[47] Once again someone with a majority of the popular vote would be the losing candidate. On January 6, 2001, a joint session of Congress officially tallied the electoral votes that made Bush the next President.

Judicial resolution of this political crisis left many unsatisfied, including Justices of the Court. The 5-4 ruling began with a brief per curiam followed by a concurrence by Rehnquist (joined by Scalia and Thomas), a dissent by Stevens (joined by Ginsburg and Breyer), and a dissent by Souter (joined by Breyer and by Stevens and Ginsburg in part). The fragmentation of the Court was broad and deep, with few clues about legal principles that might be applied in future presidential contests.

Why did the U.S. Supreme Court in *Bush v. Gore* decide the case instead of leaving it to established statutory procedures? Sections 5 and 15 of Title 3, drawn from the Electoral Count Act of 1887, directed states to take specified steps. If they did, their results would be treated as "conclusive" when Congress met to receive electoral votes. The purpose of the 1887 statute was to place the final decision with elected officials in the legislative branch, not with the judiciary. Because Gore won the popular vote and lost the election, there were calls for abolishing the Electoral College and electing Presidents directly by direct vote. Various reform proposals are analyzed in the next section.

A vast amount of literature has analyzed the decision of the U.S. Supreme Court in *Bush v. Gore*.[48] Here it is necessary only to examine a few key issues. Much of the scholarship has been taken to task as academic ranting. To David Ryden, "it is difficult to recall another instance in which the scholarly opinions and analysis appeared to derive directly from commentators' respective partisan or ideological dispositions."[49] Similarly, Jeff Polet remarked that for "all the charges of partisanship that have been leveled against the Court, one would be hard-pressed not to conclude that the same can be said of virtually all the commentary."[50]

Critics of the Court typically derided the positions of the majority while overlooking the unusual principles promoted by the minority. Both the conservative and liberal blocs in *Bush v. Gore* presented some strange configurations. As Ryden notes, the majority "exhibited a new-found fondness for the Equal Protection Clause, creatively manipulating it to stop the recounts," while the liberals "were transformed into the new caretakers of federalism and judicial restraint;

---

47. Bush v. Gore, 531 U.S. 98 (2000).

48. Charles L. Zelden, Bush v. Gore: Exposing the Hidden Crisis in American Democracy (2008); Louis Fisher, *Bush v. Gore: Too Political?*, in Nada Mourtada-Sabbah & Bruce E. Cain, eds., The Political Question Doctrine and the Supreme Court of the United States (2007); David K. Ryden, ed., The U.S. Supreme Court and the Electoral Process (2002); E. J. Dionne, Jr. & William Kristol, eds., Bush v. Gore: The Court Cases and the Commentary (2001); Howard Gillman, The Votes That Counted: How the Court Decided the 2000 Presidential Election (2001); Samuel Issacharoff, et al., When Elections Go Bad: The Law of Democracy and the Presidential Election of 2000 (2001); Richard A. Posner, Breaking Deadlock: The 2000 Election, the Constitution, and the Courts (2001); Jack N. Rakove, ed., The Unfinished Election of 2000: Leading Scholars Examine America's Strangest Election (2001); Cass R. Sunstein & Richard A. Epstein, eds., The Vote: Bush, Gore, and the Supreme Court (2001).

49. David K. Ryden, *Out of the Shadows*: Bush v. Gore, *the Court, and the Selection of a President*, in The U.S. Supreme Court and the Electoral Process 224 (David K. Ryden, ed., 2002).

50. Jeff Polet, *The Imperiousness of* Bush v. Gore, in The U.S. Supreme Court and the Electoral Process 263 (Ryden, ed., 2002).

their new best friends were legislatures rather than courts."[51] Critics who rebuked the Court for deciding a "political question" offered no objections to favorable rulings of the Florida Supreme Court in support of Gore.

Federal Judge Richard A. Posner defended the Court's decision in part because he lacked confidence in the capacity of Congress to handle this type of issue. In his judgment, Congress "is not a competent forum for resolving such disputes" because conflicts about the "lawfulness of competing slates of Presidential electors call for legal-type judgments rather than for raw exercises of political power."[52] He advised that "[w]e should endeavor to keep Congress out of the picture, so far as that is possible to do. It is a large, unwieldy, undisciplined body (actually two bodies), unsuited in its structure, personnel, and procedures to legal dispute resolution...."[53]

First, *Bush v. Gore* had more to do with the raw exercise of political power than "legal-type judgments." Second, Congress has long been a competent forum for resolving disputes about presidential elections. Both the Constitution and statutory law contemplate situations in which decisions about presidential elections are placed conclusively with Congress. Article I, section 5, clause 1 empowers each house of Congress to "be the Judge of the Elections, Returns and Qualifications of its own Members." Congress has rendered judgment on presidential elections in the past, including the Jefferson-Burr deadlock in 1800 and the Electoral Commission created by Congress in 1877 to resolve the Hayes-Tilden race. In 1824, electoral votes were divided among four candidates: Andrew Jackson, William Crawford, John Quincy Adams, and Henry Clay. The House picked Adams on the first ballot.[54]

The Electoral Vote Act of 1887, reflected today in Sections 5 and 15 of Title 3, provides that if states follow specified procedures their decisions will be treated as "conclusive" by Congress when it meets to receive electoral votes. Statutory procedures explain what will happen in disputes over the counting of votes. The two houses, acting separately, need to concur on a series of questions. If they cannot concur, the matter goes to the House of Representatives, with each state having one vote.[55] Through those processes, statutory and constitutional, Congress appropriately makes "legal-type judgments."

Cass Sunstein agreed with Posner that the Court needed to decide the matter because Congress was the wrong body to resolve the dispute. The Court's decision, according to Sunstein, "brought a chaotic situation to an abrupt end. From the standpoint of constitutional order, it is reasonable to speculate that any other conclusion would have been far worse. In all likelihood, the outcome would have been resolved in Congress, and here political partisanship might well have spiraled out of control."[56] There would have been no loss of control. The dispute would have gone to Congress, where a deadlock would have occurred initially between the Republican House and the Democratic Senate. Under established procedures, when the two chambers cannot concur, the matter goes to the House of Representatives. Because of Republican control over state delegations, the House would have selected Bush.

---

51. David K. Ryden, *What* Bush v. Gore *Does and Does Not Tell Us About the Supreme Court and Electoral Politics*, in The U.S. Supreme Court and the Electoral Process 251 (Ryden, ed., 2002).

52. Richard A. Posner, Breaking Deadlock: The 2000 Election, the Constitution, and the Courts 145 (2001).

53. Id. at 250.

54. Mary W. M. Hargreaves, The Presidency of John Quincy Adams 19–25, 36–40 (1988 ed.).

55. 3 U.S.C. § 15; U.S. Const., Amendment 12.

56. Cass R. Sunstein, *Order Without Law*, 68 U. Chi. L. Rev. 757, 772–73 (2001).

In reversing the Florida Supreme Court, the U.S. Supreme Court relied heavily on the December 12 deadline. Its analysis was strained. States could have forgone the "safe harbor" of 3 U.S.C. § 5 and submitted their results on December 18 or even later. It might have been more persuasive for the Court to say: "The standardless manual recount provisions in place in Florida for the presidential election violate fundamental principles of equal protection. We have no authority to create new standards in the middle of the game. Neither does the Florida Supreme Court, a Florida trial judge, or the Florida Legislature. The Florida Legislature has authority to create uniform standards that will satisfy equal protection guarantees, but those standards must necessarily govern future elections, not this one." Under those circumstances, the dispute would have gone to the House of Representatives and Bush would have been elected in accordance with existing law.

Courts have a legitimate right to participate in election contests to review accusations of misconduct, fraud, and other charges. In *Bush v. Gore*, however, the Court objected to standard-less procedures in Florida while issuing a ruling that lacked credible and applicable standards. The per curiam noted that "[o]ur consideration is limited to the present circumstances,..."[57] In other words, whatever constitutional principles were at play applied to that day only and were not to be relied on or cited in the future.

## G. Reform proposals

The number of Electors in 2013 stands at 538 (435 for each member of the House, 100 for each Senator, and 3 for the District of Columbia). It is possible for each presidential candidate to receive 269 votes, throwing the result into the House of Representatives. Changing the total to an odd number would avoid that complication.[58] In earlier years, the names of Electors appeared on ballots in the states at a time when Electors were supposed to be chosen as wise and learned. It is rare today for Electors to be named.[59] Also in earlier periods, there was the concept of Electors as independent actors, capable of choosing the individual they personally supported instead of mechanically registering the vote. Under that theory, "faithless electors" could bolt from election results. That freedom of action gradually declined, although examples are available in contemporary times from 1948 to 2000.[60]

The use of Electors to select the President and Vice President continues to attract strong opposition. A study in 2004, sparked in part by *Bush v. Gore*, referred to the reliance on Electors as "a totally arbitrary, largely irrational eighteenth-century counting system."[61] The use of Electors has triggered hundreds of constitutional amendments to abolish the Electoral College.[62] None has been successful. Other than the Twelfth Amendment, adopted to take care of the Jefferson-Burr tie in 1800, the only other constitutional amendment that modified the Electoral College is

---

57. 531 U.S. at 109.

58. Robert W. Bennett, Taming the Electoral College 86–94 (2006).

59. George C. Edwards III, Why the Electoral College Is Bad for America 4 (2004).

60. Id. at 19–27. In 2000, an Elector from the District of Columbia did not vote for Al Gore.

61. Foreword by Neal Pierce in Edwards, *supra* note 59, at ix.

62. David E. Kyvig, Explicit and Authentic Acts: Amendments the U.S. Constitution, 1776–1995, at 337–38, 370–71, 385-86-93 (1996); Bernstein, *supra* note 22, at 151–54, 267.

the Twenty-Third Amendment. Ratified on March 29, 1961, it awarded Electors for President and Vice President to the District of Columbia, "equal to the whole number of Senators and Representatives in Congress to which the District would be entitled if it were a State, but in no event more than the least populous State" (a total of three electoral votes).

Changes in electoral votes are possible without constitutional amendment. In 1969, Maine allowed for the determination of two of its four votes on the basis of the presidential popular vote in its two congressional districts.[63] The legislation applied to the presidential race in 1972. In 1992, Nebraska adopted district determination for three of its five electoral votes. These reforms therefore adopt a mix of the fixed electoral vote system and direct popular vote. Other states may move in that direction if they like.

A number of objections have been leveled at the Electoral College. A study by George Edwards regards this system as a violation of "political equality. It is not a neutral counting device. Instead, it favors some citizens over other others, depending solely upon the state in which voters cast their votes for president."[64] Also, it is possible for a presidential candidate to win the popular vote but lose to someone who had a majority of electoral votes. In 1876, Tilden had 251,746 more popular votes that Hayes. In 1888, Grover Cleveland had 95,096 more popular votes than William Henry Harrison, who became President with 233 electoral votes over Cleveland's 168. In 2000, Gore had a half million more popular votes than the winner, Bush.[65] The 1960 race between John F. Kennedy and Richard M. Nixon produced conflicting numbers on the popular vote. Kennedy won on electoral votes, 303 to 219. Depending on different counts, he may have had more or less popular votes.[66]

Why has it been so difficult to abolish the Electoral College? Although electing a President by direct popular vote may sound democratic and in keeping with the direct election for members of the House and the Senate, there are other factors to consider. Under the current system, presidential candidates are unlikely to devote time and resources to small states in search of a half dozen electoral votes to produce a victory.[67] With or without direct popular election, candidates will probably focus only on states with large populations or those seen as highly competitive. Small states may conclude, rightly or wrongly, that they will lose leverage with a direct election. In a close presidential contest with a popular vote system, it might be necessary to do a hand count throughout the entire country, and not simply for one state, as with Florida in 2000. There is some risk that a direct election could move the nation from a two-party system to a multi-party system, where no candidate wins a majority of votes and a runoff is necessary.[68]

---

63. Edwards, *supra* note 59, at 10.

64. Id. at 52.

65. Id at 45.

66. Id. at 45, 65.

67. Id. at 103–09.

68. For studies on the Electoral College and direct election, see Gary L. Gregg II, ed., Securing Democracy: Why We Have an Electoral College (2008 ed.); Robert W. Bennett, Taming the Electoral College (2006); Tara Ross, Enlightened Democracy: The Case for the Electoral College (2005); John C. Fortier, ed., After the People Vote: A Guide to the Electoral College (2004, 3d ed.); George Grant, The Importance of the Electoral College (2004); George C. Edwards III, Why the Electoral College is Bad for America (2004); Paul D. Schumaker & Burdett A. Loomis, eds.,Choosing a President: The Electoral College and Beyond (2002); Judith A. Best, The Choice of the People? Debating the Electoral College (1996); Michael J. Glennon, When No Majority Rules: The Electoral College and

## 2. ELIGIBILITY; "NATURAL BORN CITIZEN"

Article II, section 1 provides that no person "except a natural born Citizen, or a Citizen of the United States, at the time of the Adoption of this Constitution, shall be eligible to the Office of President." As explained in that section, no person shall be eligible to that office "who shall not have attained to the Age of thirty five Years, and been fourteen Years a Resident within the United States." The delegates heard proposals to require "certain qualifications of landed property" for the President, the judiciary, and members of Congress, for the purpose of "disqualifying all such persons as are indebted to, or have unsettled accounts with the United States." The word "landed" was struck out.[69]

The language about indebtedness and unsettled accounts did not survive. Gouverneur Morris thought that such restrictions "would be both odious & useless and in many instances unjust & cruel."[70] The lack of settlement "had been more the fault of the public than of the individuals."[71] What should be done, he asked, about "patriotic Citizens who have lent money, or services or property to their Country," without having been yet able to obtain a liquidation of their claims? Are they to be excluded?"[72] James Wilson agreed that reference to unsettled accounts "put too much power in the hands of the Auditors, who might combine with rivals in delaying settlements in order to prolong the disqualifications of particular men."[73] The language about unsettled accounts was deleted, with nine yeas and two noes.[74] Also rejected, by the same margin, was disqualification of public debtors.[75]

Setting the minimum age of the President at 35 was widely accepted by the delegates.[76] The requirement for being an inhabitant of the United States for a certain minimum of years encountered some debate, such as a proposal for 21 years.[77] That period of time was later reduced to 14.[78] The requirements of being a "natural born Citizen" and age 35 prompted no debate at Philadelphia.[79] Hamilton's draft constitution provided: "No person shall be eligible to the office of President of the United States unless he be now a Citizen of one of the States, or hereafter be born a Citizen of the United States."[80] On July 25, 1787, John Jay wrote to George Washington: "Permit me to hint, whether it would not be wise & seasonable to provide a strong

Presidential Succession (1992); Neal R. Peirce & Lawrence D. Longley, The People's President: The Electoral College in American History and the Direct Vote Alternative (1981 ed.; previously published in 1968); Lawrence D. Longley & Alan G. Braun, The Politics of Electoral College Reform (1972); Lucius Wilmerding, Jr., The Electoral College (1958).

69. 2 Farrand 117, 124.

70. Id. at 121.

71. Id.

72. Id.

73. Id. at 125.

74. Id. at 126.

75. Id.

76. Id. at 367.

77. Id.

78. Id. at 498.

79. Id. at 536 ("agreed to nem: con:").

80. 3 Farrand 629.

check to the admission of Foreigners into the administration of our national Government; and to declare expressly that the Command in chief of the American army shall not be given to, nor devolve on, any but a natural *born* Citizen."[81]

Joseph Story in his *Commentaries* elaborated on this theme about foreign influence on the presidency: "It is indispensable, too, that the president should be a natural born citizen of the United States.... [T]he general propriety of the exclusion of foreigners, in common cases, will scarcely be doubted by any sound statesman. It cuts off all chances of ambitious foreigners, who might otherwise be intriguing for the office; and interposes a barrier against those corrupt interferences of foreign governments in executive elections, which have inflicted the most serious evils upon the elective monarchies of Europe."[82]

The Constitution did not define "natural born Citizen." The phrase is generally associated with British precedents. For example, *Black's Law Dictionary* defines "Natural-born subject" in this manner: "In English law, one born within the dominions, or rather within the allegiance, of the king of England."[83] The phrase "natural born Citizen" applies exclusively to the President and the Vice President. The Twelfth Amendment provides that "No person constitutionally ineligible to the office of President shall be eligible to that of Vice-President of the United States." To qualify for the House of Representatives and the Senate, Article I stipulates that lawmakers need only be a "citizen." Members of the House must have "been seven Years a Citizen of the United States." For Senators, the requirement is "nine Years a Citizen of the United States."

The Naturalization Act of 1790 provided a uniform rule for the steps required for citizenship. Any alien, "being a free white person, who shall have resided within the limits and under the jurisdiction of the United States for the term of two years," may be admitted to become a citizen after applying to any common law court of record in any state.[84] The individual needed to reside in that state for "one year at least," provide proof to the court that "he is a person of good character," and take the oath or affirmation prescribed by law to support the Constitution.[85] The children of such persons so naturalized, "dwelling within the United States" and being under the age of 21 at time of the naturalization, "shall also be considered as citizens of the United States."[86] The statute concludes with this language:

> And the children of citizens of the United States, that may be born beyond sea, or out of the limits of the United States, shall be considered as natural born citizens: *Provided*, That the right of citizenship shall not descend to persons whose fathers have never been resident in the United States: *Provided also*, That no person heretofore proscribed by any state, shall be admitted a citizen as aforesaid, except by an act of the legislature of the state in which such person was proscribed.[87]

In defining citizen, the Fourteenth Amendment does not use the language "natural born citizen." Instead, Section 1 provides: "All persons born or naturalized in the United States, and

---

81. Id. at 61 (emphasis in original).

82. 3 Joseph Story, Commentaries on the Constitution of the United States 1473 (1833).

83. Black's Law Dictionary 925 (5th ed. 1979).

84. 1 Stat. 103 (1790).

85. Id.

86. Id. at 104.

87. Id.

subject to the jurisdiction thereof, are citizens of the United States and of the State wherein they reside." Any presidential candidate born in the United States is a citizen and meets the intent behind the phrase "natural born Citizen." Anyone born abroad to U.S. citizens is also a citizen and qualified to be President as a "natural born citizen."[88]

The eligibility of several presidential candidates has been challenged on the ground they were not a "natural born Citizen," either because of rumors they were born abroad or one parent was not a U.S. citizen. The names include Chester Arthur, George Romney, John McCain, and Barack Obama. Closer inspection reveals that some rumors lacked substance or inadequate attention was paid to the U.S. Constitution and federal law. Arthur's opponents in the early 1880s claimed he was born in Ireland. After that charge could not be documented, rumors surfaced he was born in Canada. No evidence was produced to substantiate either charge.[89]

Romney was born to American parents in Mexico. They had previously lived in the United States and the family returned there in 1912. Elected governor of Michigan in 1962, he was twice reelected and became a candidate for President in 1968, running as a Republican. Because he was born in Mexico, some regarded him as ineligible to be President. However, federal law provides that a person born outside the United States to parents who are U.S. citizens and who had resided in the United States prior to the birth is a U.S. citizen.[90] When John McCain ran for President in 2004 and 2008, his eligibility was questioned because he had been born in the Panama Canal Zone. A separate federal law states that any person born in the Republic of Panama on or after February 26, 1904, is a U.S. citizen if the father or mother, or both, were U.S. citizens at the time of the birth.[91]

Numerous legal challenges were filed against Barack Obama in 2008 regarding his eligibility to be President. He was born in Hawaii on August 4, 1961. His mother was a U.S. citizen; his father was from Kenya and a British subject. Issues were raised about her age and his nationality, but those issues were not relevant. Federal law is clear. Anyone born in Hawaii on or after April 30, 1900, is "a citizen of the United States at birth."[92] Various lawsuits were filed in state and federal court, contesting Obama's eligibility, but they failed on different grounds. The Supreme Court declined to hear any of them.[93]

---

88. Jack Maskell, *Qualifications for the Office of President of the United States and Legal Challenges to the Eligibility of a Candidate*, Congressional Research Service, April 3, 2009, at 5. See also William T. Han, *Beyond Presidential Eligibility: The Natural Born Citizen Clause as a Source of Birthright Citizenship*, 58 DRAKE L. REV. 457 (2010); Christina S. Lohman, *Presidential Eligibility: The Meaning of the Natural-Born Citizen Clause*, 36 GONZAGA L. REV. 349 (2000–01) Jill A. Pryor, *The Natural-Born Citizen Clause and Presidential Eligibility: An Approach to Resolving Two Hundred Years of Uncertainty*, 97 YALE L.J. 881 (1988); Michael Nelson, *Constitutional Qualifications for President*, 17 PRES. STUD. Q. 383 (1987); Charles Gordon, *Who Can Be President of the United States: The Unresolved Enigma*, 28 MD. L. REV. 1 (1968); Warren Freedman, *Presidential Timber: Foreign Born Children of American Parents*, 35 CORNELL L. Q. 357 (1950); Alexander Porter Morse, *Natural-Born Citizen of the United States*, 66 ALBANY L. J. 99 (1904).

89. ZACHERY KARABELL, CHESTER ALAN ARTHUR 53–54 (2004); THOMAS C. REEVES, GENTLEMAN BOSS: THE LIFE AND TIMES OF CHESTER A. ARTHUR 202–203 (1975).

90. 8 U.S.C. § 1401(c).

91. Id. at § 1403(b).

92. Id. at § 1405.

93. E.g., Berg v. Obama, 574 F. Supp. 2d 509 (E.D. Pa. 2008), cert. denied, 555 U.S. 1126, 1134 (2008); Wrotnowski v. Bysiewicz, 958 A.2d 709 (Conn. 2008), cert. denied, 555 U.S. 1083 (2008). For an unsuccessful challenge to

# 3. MULTIPLE TERMS; TWENTY-SECOND AMENDMENT

The Constitution placed no limit on the number of terms a President could serve. George Washington limited his service to two terms, a tradition continued by Jefferson. Several state legislatures urged Jefferson to run for a third term. He declined to do so, explaining to the Vermont legislature in 1807 that his decision to limit his presidency to eight years "is as much a duty as to have borne it faithfully."[94] He expressed concern that if the services of the President "be not fixed by the Constitution, or supplied by practice, his office, nominally for years, will, in fact, become for life."[95] History, he said, "shows how easily that degenerates into an inheritance."[96] He believed that a representative government, held to short periods of election, "is that which produces the greatest sum of happiness to mankind."[97]

The two-term tradition established by Washington and Jefferson continued under Madison, Monroe, Jackson, Grant, and Wilson. The second terms of Lincoln and McKinley were cut short by assassination. Cleveland served two terms but not consecutively. Theodore Roosevelt served out most of McKinley's term, won election in 1904 and tried unsuccessfully for an additional term in the 1912 campaign. The two-term tradition was shattered by Franklin D. Roosevelt, who was elected in 1932 and 1936, won a third term in 1940, and yet a fourth term in 1944. He died on April 12, 1945, succeeded by Harry Truman. In 1946, the Republicans gained control of Congress for the first time since 1928. One of the first orders of business was to consider a constitutional amendment to impose a two-term limit on Presidents.

Congress had acted in the past to require a maximum of two terms, but nothing was ever passed by both houses. As explained in a study by Alan Grimes, the Senate passed a resolution in 1824 by a vote of 36 to 3 in favor of a two-term limit.[98] The House in 1875, by a vote of 234 to 18, endorsed the two-term tradition. In 1896, the Democratic platform proclaimed that no President should be eligible for a third term. In 1928, the Senate passed language by a vote of 56 to 26 that was identical to the House resolution of 1875.[99] None of those measures cleared Congress to be considered by the states.

On February 6, 1947, the House Judiciary Committee reported a two-term amendment. Opponents regarded it as antidemocratic in limiting popular choice, but the measure passed largely along party lines, 285 to 121. The amendment gained the necessary two-thirds when 50 Democrats (most from southern or border states) voted for it.[100] The Senate passed the

---

John McCain's candidacy for President, see Robinson v. Bowen, 567 F. Supp. 2d 1144 (N.D. Cal. 2008). Other court challenges are discussed in Maskell, *supra* note 88.

94. Michael Nelson, ed., The Evolving Presidency: Landmark Documents, 1787–2010, at 75 (4th ed., 2012) (letter of Dec. 10, 1807).

95. Id.

96. Id.

97. Id.

98. Alan P. Grimes, Democracy and the Amendments to the Constitution 115 (1978).

99. Id. at 115.

100. Id. at 119.

amendment 59 to 23, again depending on Democrats from southern or border states.[101] The amendment was ratified on February 27, 1951. It states that no person shall be elected President more than twice. No person who has held the office of President for more than two years of a term to which another person had been elected could be elected more than once. The amendment had no application to the person holding office as President when it was proposed. Ironically, as a Republican amendment directed against Roosevelt's four terms, the individual to which the amendment first applied was Dwight D. Eisenhower, a popular Republican who served two terms from January 1953 to January 1961. There have been efforts to repeal the Twenty-Second Amendment, often by Republicans, but none has been successful.[102]

# 4. COMPENSATION AND EMOLUMENTS

Article II, section 1 provides that the President "shall, at stated Times, receive for his Services, a Compensation, which shall neither be increased nor diminished during the Period for which he shall have been elected, and he shall not receive within that Period any other Emolument from the United States, or any of them." The purpose was to protect the President's independence from legislative efforts to penalize him with salary cutbacks or for Presidents to attempt to curry favor by seeking a salary increase. In Federalist No. 73, Hamilton described the provision on fixed compensation as a way to protect "the vigor of the executive authority."[103] Congress, "with a discretionary power over the salary and emoluments of the Chief Magistrate, could render him as obsequious to their will as they might think proper to make him."[104] The choice would be to "reduce him by famine, or tempt him by largesses, to surrender at discretion his judgment to their inclinations."[105] Lawmakers "can neither weaken his fortitude by operating on his necessities, nor corrupt his integrity by appealing to his avarice."[106]

The President's salary began at $25,000 in 1789 and has been increased five times: to $50,000 in 1873, $75,000 in 1909, $100,000 in 1949, $200,000 in 1969, and $400,000 in 1999.[107] The salary is subject to income tax. Because of the constitutional prohibition against increases, a higher salary may apply only to the next President. Presidents also receive an expense allowance of $50,000, which is not taxable.[108] Upon leaving office, a President receives a pension that is equal to the salary of Level I of the Executive Schedule. As of January 2012, that came to $199,700.[109]

---

101. Id. at 120.

102. Richard B. Bernstein, Amending America: If We Love the Constitution So Much, Why Do We Keep Trying to Change It? 159–60 (1993). See also David E. Kyvig, Explicit and Authentic Acts: Amending the U.S. Constitution, 1775–1995, at 325–36 (1996).

103. The Federalist 467.

104. Id.

105. Id.

106. Id. at 468.

107. Barbara L. Schwemle, *President of the United States: Compensation*, Congressional Research Service, Oct. 17, 2012, RS20115, at 3.

108. Id. at 1.

109. Id. See also James F. Vivian, The President's Salary: A Study in Constitutional Declension, 1789–1990 (1993).

Article I, section 9 states that no person holding public office shall, "without the Consent of the Congress, accept of any present, Emolument, Office, or Title, of any kind whatever, from any King, Prince, or foreign State." On December 7, 2009, OLC released a memo concluding that President Obama's acceptance of the Nobel Peace Prize (worth approximately $1.4 million) did not conflict with the Emoluments Clause.[110] It reasoned that the Nobel Committee that awarded the prize is not a "King, Prince, or foreign State." OLC also concluded the Foreign Gifts and Decorations Act, 5 U.S.C. § 7342, did not apply either. OLC explained that the purpose of the Emoluments Clause is to protect Presidents and other public officers from foreign influence and corruption.[111] OLC noted that other federal officers had received the Nobel Peace Prize in past years: sitting Presidents Theodore Roosevelt and Woodrow Wilson, Senator Elihu Root, Vice President Charles Dawes, retired General George Marshall, and Secretary of State Henry Kisssinger.[112]

# 5. THE PRESIDENT'S OATH

The President's oath is set forth in Article II. Before he enters office he must take the following oath or affirmation: "I do solemnly swear (or affirm) that I will faithfully execute the Office of President of the United States, and will to the best of my Ability, preserve, protect and defend the Constitution of the United States."[113] The choice between oath and affirmation respects the views of Quakers and others who objected to invoking God for a secular purpose.[114] An oath of office signals a public commitment to carry out an office to the best of one's ability, without reservations or partial commitments.[115]

In his first inaugural address on April 30, 1789, George Washington added to his constitutional oath the words "so help me God," a custom followed by all Presidents.[116] His second inaugural address four years later reflected on the weightiness of the oath he took and was about to take again: "if it shall be found during my administration of the Government I have in any instance violated willingly or knowingly the injunctions thereof; I may, besides incurring constitutional punishment, be subject to the upbraidings of all who are now witnesses of the present solemn ceremony."[117]

---

110. Office of Legal Counsel, *Applicability of the Emoluments Clause and the Foreign Gifts and Decorations Act to the President's Receipt of the Nobel Peace Prize*, Dec. 7, 2009.

111. Id. at 3.

112. Id. at 4–6. See also Jack Maskell, *Gifts to the President of the United States*, Congressional Research Service, Aug. 16, 2012, R42662.

113. The history of this oath and presidential thoughts about it are covered in Robert F. Blomquist, *The Presidential Oath, the National Interest and a Call for Presiprudence*, 73 UMKC L. Rev. 1 (2004).

114. Steve Sheppard, I Do Solemnly Swear: The Moral Obligations of Legal Officials 106 (2009).

115. Id. at 107. For the views of a member of Congress toward the legislative oath, see Vic Snyder, *You've Taken an Oath to Support the Constitution, Now What? The Constitutional Requirement for a Congressional Oath of Office*, 23 UALR L. Rev. 897 (2001). See also Matthew A. Pauley, I Do Solemnly Swear the President's Constitutional Oath: Its Meaning and Importance in the History of Oaths (1999).

116. Nelson, *supra* note 94, at 41.

117. Arthur M. Schlesinger Jr. & Fred L. Israel, eds., My Fellow Citizens, The Inaugural Addresses of the Presidents of the United States, 1789–2009, at 5–6 (2010).

President James Buchanan, delivering his inaugural address on March 4, 1857, began by repeating the words of his oath, directing *him* to "preserve, protect, and defend the Constitution of the United States."[118] Yet on the issue of slavery, at that point being litigated, he said the issue "legitimately belongs to the Supreme Court" where it will "be speedily and finally settled."[119] The Court was indeed speedy. Two days later it issued its decision in *Dred Scott*.[120] Instead of the Court's ruling providing the final word on slavery, it helped propel the country toward civil war. President Buchanan and members of Congress, having taken oaths to preserve the Constitution, decided to transfer that solemn duty wholly to the Court.

In his first inaugural address, on March 4, 1861, President Abraham Lincoln explained what the oath meant to him. He had "no purpose, directly or indirectly, to interfere with the institution of slavery in the States where it exists. I believe I have no lawful right to do so, and I have no inclination to do so."[121] The Federal Union of States, however, he held to be "perpetual." No state had a constitutional right to leave the Union by issuing resolutions and ordinances. In view of the Constitution and the laws, "the Union is unbroken, and to the extent of my ability, I shall take care, as the Constitution itself expressly enjoins upon me, that the laws of the Union be faithfully executed in all the States."[122] He closed by saying that those who wanted to leave the Union had "no oath registered in heaven to destroy the Government, while I shall have the most solemn one to preserve, protect, and defend it."[123]

Presidents at times misstate their oath, claiming it is to defend *the nation*. In his speech at Oslo, Norway, on December 10, 2009, while accepting the Nobel Peace Prize, President Obama said: "as head of state sworn to protect and defend my nation...."[124] His oath under Article II, section 1 requires him to defend *the Constitution*, not the nation. Actions taken "in defense" of the nation may, and may not, defend the Constitution. At Oslo, he spoke of "just wars" and his belief that "force can be justified on humanitarian grounds."[125] He made no reference to securing authority from Congress when initiating military force against another nation. As explained in Chapter 8, section 9, he and other Presidents have gone to war in the last six decades without requesting or receiving congressional authority. No such actions were taken from 1789 to 1950.

# 6. DISABILITY AND DEATH

Article II, section 1 provides that in case of "the Removal of the President from Office, or of his Death, Resignation, or Inability to discharge the Powers and Duties of the said Office," those powers "shall devolve on the Vice President, and the Congress may by Law provide for the

---

118. Id. at 131.

119. Id. at 132.

120. Dred Scott v. Sandford, 60 U.S. (19 How.) 393 (1857).

121. SCHLESINGER & ISRAEL, *supra* note 117, at 141.

122. Id. at 143.

123. Id. at 148.

124. Remarks by the President at the Acceptance of the Nobel Peace Prize, Oslo, Norway, Dec. 10, 2009, http://www.whitehouse.gov/the-press-office/remarks-president-acceptance-nobel-peace-prize.

125. Id.

Case of Removal, Death, Resignation or Inability," both of the President and the Vice President. Congress could determine what officer shall act as President. Article II, section 1 specifies that officer would act "until the Disability be removed, or a President shall be elected." Delegates at the Philadelphia convention had little to say about this provision. In Federalist No. 68, Hamilton briefly noted that the Vice President "may occasionally become a substitute for the President, in the supreme executive magistracy."[126]

Congress passed legislation in 1792 to provide for the removal, death, resignation, or inability both of the President and Vice President.[127] The Succession Act designated the President pro tempore of the Senate first and the Speaker of the House of Representatives second.[128] They would serve temporarily until "the disability be removed or a President shall be elected."[129] The statute established procedures for those elections. The individuals who served as President and Vice President had to satisfy the constitutional requirements of age, residence, and natural-born citizenship.

In the years since 1789, Vice Presidents have succeeded to the presidency nine times, eight because of the death of a President and once because a President resigned. The latter refers to Gerald Ford becoming President after the resignation of Richard Nixon in 1974. Succession by death occurred first in 1841 when John Tyler succeeded William Henry Harrison. There was some question whether Tyler was Vice President "acting as President" or actually the President. He decided to take the presidential oath, fully authorized to exercise all powers and duties.[130] Presidential scholar Edward Corwin, after examining the debates at the constitutional convention, concluded: "it was the intention of the Framers that the Vice-President, for whatever reason he 'succeeded' the President, should remain Vice-President unless and until he was elected President."[131] That line of analysis has not prevailed. Constitutional meaning comes not from efforts to discern what the Framers might have meant about a Vice President succeeding to the President but from usage and custom.[132] Members of Congress referred to Tyler as "the President" and that precedent has been followed ever since.[133]

Millard Fillmore became President when Zachary Taylor died of natural causes. The next turnovers resulted from the assassinations of Abraham Lincoln, James A. Garfield, and William McKinley, succeeded by Andrew Johnson, Chester A. Arthur, and Theodore Roosevelt, respectively. A fourth assassination occurred in November 1963, when Lyndon B. Johnson succeeded John F. Kennedy. In two other cases, a Vice President became President because of an incumbent's death by natural causes: Calvin Coolidge replacing Warren G. Harding in 1923, and Harry Truman taking office as President after the death of Franklin D. Roosevelt. Those cases involved death or resignation, not disability.

---

126. The Federalist 443.

127. 1 Stat. 239 (1792).

128. Id.

129. Id.

130. Norma Lois Peterson, The Presidencies of William Henry Harrison and John Tyler 45–48 (1989); see Stephen W. Stathis, *John Tyler's Presidential Succession: A Reappraisal*, 8 Prologue 223 (1976).

131. Corwin, *supra* note 29, at 345.

132. Ruth C. Silva, Presidential Succession (1951).

133. Cong. Globe, 27th Cong. 3-5 (May 31 and June 1, 1841).

Garfield's death prompted Congress to pass the Succession Act of 1886. After being shot by an assassin on July 2, 1881, Garfield lingered for 79 days before succumbing to his wound on September 19. The offices of Speaker and President pro tempore were vacant throughout his illness. The House had yet to convene and the Senate failed to elect a President pro tempore. Legislation enacted in 1886 transferred succession after the Vice President from the President pro tempore and the House Speaker to cabinet officers, following the order in which they had been created: Secretary of State, Secretary of the Treasury, Secretary of War, Attorney General, Postmaster-General, etc.[134] That statute governed succession until 1947.

In 1945, after Truman succeeded Roosevelt as President, it was considered inappropriate in a democracy to have cabinet heads succeed to the Presidency instead of elected members of Congress. Under the Presidential Succession Act of 1947, if there is neither a President nor Vice President because of death, resignation, removal from office, inability, or failure to qualify, the Speaker shall "act as President."[135] If there is no Speaker, or if the Speaker fails to qualify as Acting President, the President pro tempore succeeds and shall "act as President."[136] If the Speaker and the President pro tempore are not available or decide they do not want to serve as President, the cabinet officers succeed under this order: Secretary of State, Secretary of the Treasury, Secretary of War, Attorney General, Postmaster General, Secretary of the Navy, Secretary of the Interior, Secretary of Agriculture, Secretary of Commerce, Secretary of Labor.[137] In every case, whether Speaker, President pro tempore, or cabinet officer, the individual serving as Acting President must be "eligible to the office of President under the Constitution."[138] Moreover, the cabinet officer must have been appointed "by and with the advice and consent of the Senate" and must not be "under impeachment in the House of Representatives at the time the powers and duties of the office of President devolve upon them."[139] The 1947 statute is regularly amended to reflect new cabinet-level departments or change of title, such as the change from Secretary of War to Secretary of Defense.

# 7. THE TWENTY-FIFTH AMENDMENT

Kennedy's assassination in 1963 set in motion the legislative activities that led to the Twenty-Fifth Amendment, establishing new procedures for presidential death and disability. Under the 1947 legislation, the two lawmakers in line to be President after Kennedy's death were 72-year-old House Speaker John McCormick and 86-year-old President pro tempore Carl Hayden.[140] Senator Birch Bayh took the lead in seeking a remedy for the disability and succession of a President. Pressure for a constitutional amendment was informed by Garfield's long incapacitation after he was shot, the lengthy illness of Woodrow Wilson after his stroke, and Dwight D. Eisenhower's

---

134. 24 Stat. 1 (1886).

135. 61 Stat. 380 (1947).

136. Id.

137. Id.

138. Id.

139. Id. See JOHN D. FERRICK, FROM FAILING HANDS: THE STORY OF PRESIDENTIAL SUCCESSION (1965).

140. BERNSTEIN, *supra* note 102, at 164.

heart attack in 1955 and a stroke in 1957. Bayh served as the driving force behind the amendment, which was quickly ratified on February 20, 1967. All states supported the amendment except for North Dakota, South Carolina, and Georgia.[141]

The Twenty-Fifth Amendment is long and complex. Section 1 clarifies that in case of the removal of the President by death or resignation, "the Vice President shall be President." If there is a vacancy in the office of the Vice President, the President shall nominate a Vice President who "shall take office upon confirmation by a majority vote of both Houses of Congress." Whenever a President transmits to the President pro tempore of the Senate and the Speaker of the House of Representatives his written declaration that he is unable to discharge the powers and duties of his office, and until he transmits to them a written declaration to the contrary, such powers and duties "shall be discharged by the Vice President as Acting President."

Section 4 of the amendment requires the Vice President and executive officials to make judgments about the President's capacity to perform the duties of his office. Whenever the Vice President and a majority of "either the principal officers of the executive departments or of such other body as Congress may by law provide," transmit to the President pro tempore and the House Speaker their written declaration that the President is unable to discharge the powers and duties of his office, the Vice President shall "immediately assume the powers and duties of the office as Acting President." Thereafter, when the President transmits to the President pro tempore and the House Speaker that no inability exists, he shall resume the powers and duties of his office unless the Vice President and a majority of either the principal officers of the executive department or of such other body as Congress may by law provide, transmit within four days to the President pro tempore and the House Speaker their written declaration that the President is unable to discharge his official powers and duties. At that point, Congress shall decide the issue by assembling within 48 hours if not already in session. If Congress determines by a two-thirds vote of each house that the President is unable to discharge his official duties and powers, the Vice President shall continue to discharge those duties and powers as Acting President. Otherwise, the President shall resume the powers and duties of his office.

The Twenty-Fifth Amendment was invoked in 1973 when Rep. Gerald R. Ford was nominated and approved to succeed Vice President Spiro T. Agnew, who had resigned. It was applied a year later when Nelson A. Rockefeller was nominated and approved to succeed Ford as Vice President, after Ford became President following Nixon's resignation. Implementation of the Twenty-Fifth Amendment depends on complex legal and political judgments by the White House Counsel, White House physician, agreements between Presidents and Vice Presidents, and other advisers.[142] The terrorist attacks of 9/11 heightened concerns about presidential succession, especially in the event the President and the Vice President were simultaneously killed or disabled.[143]

---

141. Kyvig, *supra* note 102, at 357–63; Bernstein, *supra* note 102, at 160–66.

142. Nancy Kassop, *When Law and Politics Collide: Presidents and the Use of the Twenty-Fifth Amendment*, 35 Pres. Stud. Q. 147 (2005).

143. Joel K. Goldstein, *Taking from the Twenty-fifth Amendment: Lessons in Ensuring Presidential Continuity*, 79 Fordham L. Rev. 959 (2010); Akhil Reed Amar, *Applications and Implications of the Twenty-fifth Amendment*, 47 Hous. L. Rev. 1 (2010); Joel K. Goldstein, *Akhil Reed Amar and Presidential Continuity*, 47 Hous. L. Rev. 67 (2010). For additional analysis on the impact of the Twenty-fifth Amendment on the Vice Presidency, see Joel K. Goldstein, *The New Constitutional Vice Presidency*, 30 Wake Forest L. Rev. 505 (1995); John D. Feerick, The Twenty-Fifth Amendment: Its Complete History and Applications (2d ed. 1992); Jules Witcover,

# 8. VICE PRESIDENT

The office of Vice President has followed an odd constitutional journey. Understood today as an executive officer and possible successor to a sitting President, the Vice President is only sketchily mentioned in Article II. The main reference appears in part of the Constitution set aside for Congress, Article I, section 3: "The Vice President of the United States shall be President of the Senate, but shall have no Vote, unless they be equally divided." Why would the Vice President be selected to preside over the Senate? In Article II, both the President and the Vice President are mentioned in the system of Electors. Article II, section 1 provides that in case the President is removed from office because of death, resignation, or inability to discharge official duties, "the Same shall devolve on the Vice President…." As explained in the previous section, there was some uncertainty from that language ("the Same") whether a Vice President in such circumstances became the President or an Acting President.

Article II states that impeachment applies to the President, Vice President, and all civil officers. The Constitution provides several details about the President: only a "natural born Citizen" is eligible, a minimum age of 35, 14 years residency requirement, a compensation that shall be neither increased nor diminished during his time in office, and an oath for the office. Such details are not specified for the Vice President. Four constitutional amendments (Twelfth, Twentieth, Twenty-fourth, and Twenty-fifth) apply to both President and Vice President.

To understand the duties of the Vice President and whether that office is located more in one branch than another, the text of the original Constitution is not helpful. Little elaboration appears in the debates at the Philadelphia Convention. Other than draft language making the Vice President the President of the Senate and a successor to the President, there was scant debate on the nature and purpose of the Vice President. Only toward the end of the convention, on September 7, did Elbridge Gerry speak against the Senate duty assigned to the Vice President. He protested: "We might as well put the President himself at the head of the Legislature. The close intimacy that must subsist between the President & vice-president makes it absolutely improper. He was agst. having any vice President."[144]

Roger Sherman defended the arrangement: "If the vice-President were not to be President of the Senate, he would be without employment"—a strange observation about a national officer who would receive the second highest number of electoral votes. Edmund Randolph concurred in Gerry's position. Hugh Williamson observed that "such an officer as vice-President was not wanted. He was introduced only for the sake of a valuable mode of election which required two to be chosen at the same time." George Mason regarded the office of Vice President as "an encroachment on the rights of the Senate; and that it mixed too much the Legislative & Executive, which as well as the Judiciary departments, ought to be kept as separate as possible." On the question of the Vice President serving as "ex officio President of the Senate," the motion

CRAPSHOOT: ROLLING THE DICE ON THE VICE PRESIDENCY (1992); Richard D. Friedman, *Some Modest Proposals on the Vice-Presidency*, 86 MICH. L. REV. 1703 (1988); BIRCH BAYH, ONE HEARTBEAT AWAY: PRESIDENTIAL DISABILITY AND SUCCESSION (1968); JOHN D. FEERICK, FROM FAILING HANDS: THE STORY OF PRESIDENTIAL SUCCESSION (1965).

144. 2 Farrand 536–37. See also Gerry's objections at 2 Farrand 635–36.

passed 8 to 2, with one state absent. The two states voting against were Massachusetts and New Jersey.[145]

In the Federalist Papers, Hamilton, Jay, and Madison said little about the Vice President. In Federalist No. 68, Hamilton explained that the Vice President "is to be chosen in the same manner with the President; with this difference, that the Senate is to do, in respect to the former, what is to be done by the House of Representatives, in respect to the latter."[146] He observed that the appointment of "an extraordinary person, as Vice-President, has been objected to as superfluous, if not mischievous."[147] Hamilton disagreed that it would have been better for the Senate to appoint one of its own as President. First, "to secure at all times the possibility of a definite resolution of the body, it is necessary that the President should have only a casting vote."[148] Second, to make a particular Senator President of the Senate "would be to exchange, in regard to the State from which he came, a constant for a contingent vote."[149]

Roger Sherman had made that point at the constitutional convention. If the Vice President did not serve as President of the Senate, "some member by being made President must be deprived of his vote, unless when an equal division of votes might happen in the Senate, which would be but seldom."[150] That is not a plausible argument. There is no reason why a Senator who serves as presiding officer cannot vote. They regularly do. For example, while Senator Mark Begich exercised the duties of presiding officer on October 12, 2011, he proceeded to vote on a bill.[151]

The first two Vice Presidents—John Adams and Thomas Jefferson—possessed impressive credentials. After ratification of the Twelfth Amendment, there were fears that the quality of Vice Presidents would decline. Attempts in Congress to abolish the office were defeated, 19 to 12 in the Senate and 85 to 27 in the House.[152] In the early decades, the individual in the administration most likely to be the next President was the Secretary of State, not the Vice President. That pattern is evident with Madison following Jefferson, Monroe coming after Madison, and John Quincy Adams the next President after Monroe. The caliber of Vice Presidents throughout the nineteenth century fell sharply. A few prominent men took the post, but the "credentials of some nominees were ludicrous."[153] Their service in office was "largely undistinguished."[154]

In which branch is the Vice President located? Legislative or executive? For much of its existence, the answer has been quite ambiguous. Harry Truman wrote that the Vice President "is not an officer of the executive branch of the government and therefore does not attend Cabinet sessions except at the invitation of the President."[155] During the presidency of Woodrow Wilson, Vice President Thomas Marshall presided over the cabinet while Wilson

---

145. Id. at 537–38.

146. The Federalist 443.

147. Id.

148. Id.

149. Id.

150. 2 Farrand 537.

151. 157 Cong. Rec. S6449, S6451 (daily ed. Oct. 12, 2011) (rollcall vote No. 161 Leg.).

152. Joel K. Goldstein, The Modern American Vice Presidency: The Transformation of a Political Institution 6–7 (1982).

153. Id. at 7.

154. Id.

155. Harry S. Truman, Year of Decisions 197 (1955).

was in Versailles. Vice President Calvin Coolidge was the first to attend cabinet meetings on a regular basis.[156] Dwight D. Eisenhower, in considering whether to pursue a second term, debated the merits of retaining Nixon as Vice President. He regarded the VP's constitutional duty to preside over the Senate "as not legally a part of the Executive branch and is not subject to direction by the President."[157] That position is overstated. Certainly in contemporary times, as in years past, the Vice President can be expected to preside and to vote in accordance with the objectives of the executive branch.

Activities of the Vice President in the twentieth and twenty-first centuries bear little resemblance to the record of the nineteenth century. Vice Presidents now serve regularly as a liaison to Congress, provide advice to the President, function as special envoy on trips abroad, chair various committees within the executive branch, serve on the National Security Council (by statutory designation), and speak publicly on political and policy matters, sometimes to the comfort (or discomfort) of the President.[158] Special attention has been directed to the influence of Vice President Dick Cheney in the George W. Bush administration.[159]

A number of constitutional issues about the Vice Presidency have emerged in recent years. May the Vice President conduct his office with full confidentially, thwarting investigations and inquiries by Congress and outside groups? In the past, the President has invoked "executive privilege" to shield certain documents and activities within the executive branch. Does the Vice President possess a similar privilege?[160] That issue arose prominently during the term of Vice President Cheney, particularly in response to efforts to explore his energy task force. He successfully fought off an investigation by the General Accounting Office (now the Government Accountability Office), but a lawsuit brought by a private organization produced more of a mixed picture.[161]

---

156. GOLDSTEIN, *supra* note 152, at 136.

157. DWIGHT D. EISENHOWER, WAGING PEACE, 1956–1961, at 6 (1965).

158. GOLDSTEIN, *supra* note 152, at 134–50, 151–76, 177–201. See the special issue on "The New Vice Presidency," 38 PRES. STUD. Q. 369 (2008). For the growth in power and prestige of the office of Vice President, see Harold C. Relyea, *Office of the Vice President*, THE EXECUTIVE OFFICE OF THE PRESIDENT 383–406 (Harold C. Relyea, ed. 1997); PAUL C. LIGHT, VICE-PRESIDENTIAL POWER: ADVICE AND INFLUENCE IN THE WHITE HOUSE (1984); IRVING G. WILLIAMS, THE RISE OF THE VICE PRESIDENCY (1956).

159. Joel K. Goldstein, *Cheney, Vice Presidential Power, and the War on Terror*, 40 PRES. STUD. Q. 102 (2010); Harold C. Relyea, *The Executive Office of the Vice President: Constitutional and Legal Considerations*, 40 PRES. STUD. Q. 327 (2010); BRUCE P. MONTGOMERY, RICHARD B. CHENEY AND THE RISE OF THE IMPERIAL VICE PRESIDENCY (2009); SHIRLEY ANNE WARSHAW, THE CO-PRESIDENCY OF BUSH AND CHENEY (2009); BARTON GELLMAN, ANGLER: THE CHENEY VICE PRESIDENCY (2008); STEPHEN F. HAYES, CHENEY: THE UNTOLD STORY OF AMERICA'S MOST POWERFUL AND CONTROVERSIAL VICE PRESIDENT (2007); LOU DUBOSE & JAKE BERNSTEIN, VICE: DICK CHENEY AND THE HIJACKING OF THE AMERICAN PRESIDENCY (2006).

160. In 1994, OLC held that the Office of the Vice President is not an "agency" for purposes of the Freedom of Information Act; 18 OP. O.L.C. 10 (1994).

161. Roy E. Brownell II, *Vice Presidential Secrecy: A Study in Comparative Constitutional Privilege and Historical Development*, 84 ST. JOHN'S L. REV. 423, 539–46 (2010); LOUIS FISHER, THE POLITICS OF EXECUTIVE PRIVILEGE 183–98 (2004); Walker v. Cheney, 230 F. Supp. 2d 51 (D.D.C. 2002); Cheney v. U.S. District Court, 542 U.S. 367 (2004). The second case was brought by two private groups, Judicial Watch and the Sierra Club. The D.C. Circuit rejected the administration's argument that the President and Vice President possess a broad immunity against any effort, through litigation, to determine how they formulate legislative proposals. It directed the two groups to narrow their request for documents. The Supreme Court declined to accept the administration's broad doctrine

Previous investigations of Vice Presidents, from Daniel Tomkins (who served under James Monroe) to Al Gore, were conducted vigorously at both the state and national level, with incumbents offering various levels of cooperation. Federal investigations included both Congress and the Federal Bureau of Investigation (FBI). At times, Vice Presidents actively encouraged such investigations to clear their name.[162]

Justice Department probes of Vice President Spiro Agnew led to his resignation after pleading no contest to income tax evasion.[163] Easing Agnew out of his position was delicate but essential. In the event that President Nixon were impeached and removed, or chose to resign, Agnew would advance to the Oval Office. Top officials in the executive and legislative branches were determined to prevent that from happening. Once Agnew left office, Congress replaced him with Gerald Ford. One of Ford's first actions, as President, was to issue a pardon for Nixon's activities as President, sparing him possible indictment and trial for criminal actions related to Watergate.[164] The pardon was so controversial that Ford decided to voluntarily testify before a House Judiciary subcommittee to explain the basis for his decision.[165]

One final issue. If the position of Vice President became vacant as a result of death, resignation, or impeachment, could the President use his recess appointment powers under Article II to select a new Vice President? Although the President has broad authority to "fill up all Vacancies that may happen during the Recess of the Senate,"[166] the exercise of that authority to put a Vice President in place encounters formidable hurdles. A major one is the Twenty-fifth Amendment, which specifies the procedures for nominating and approving a Vice President, including action by both houses of Congress by majority vote.[167]

# 9. IMPEACHMENT AND CENSURE

Under Article II, section 4, the President, Vice President, "and all civil Officers of the United States, shall be removed from Office on Impeachment for, and Conviction of, Treason, Bribery, or other High Crimes and Misdemeanors." The House of Representatives has the "sole Power of Impeachment." After House action, the Senate has the "sole Power to try all Impeachments." When sitting for that purpose, Senators shall be on oath or affirmation. If the President is tried, the Chief Justice shall preside. No person shall be convicted without the concurrence of two-thirds of the Senators present. Judgment in cases of impeachment shall not extend further than removal from office "and disqualification to hold and enjoy any Office of honor, Trust or Profit under the United

---

of executive immunity. It returned the case to the D.C. Circuit with instructions to seek an accommodation that protects the President from litigation that might distract from his constitutional duties.

162. Brownell, *supra* note 161, at 505–37.

163. Id. at 516–21. See Richard M. Cohen & Jules Witcover, A Heartbeat Away: The Investigation and Resignation of Vice President Spiro T. Agnew (1974). See also Michael Harwood, In The Shadow of Presidents: The American Vice-Presidency and Succession System (1966).

164. Jeffrey Crouch, The Presidential Pardon Power 66–85 (2009).

165. *Pardon of Richard M. Nixon, and Related Matters*, hearings before the Subcommittee on Criminal Justice of the House Committee on the Judiciary, 93d Cong., 2d Sess. 90-158 (1974); Brownell, *supra* note 161, at 521–24.

166. U.S. Const., art. II, sec. 2.

167. Roy E. Brownell II, *Can the President Recess Appoint a Vice President?*, 42 Pres. Stud. Q. 622 (2012).

States: but the Party convicted shall nevertheless be liable and subject to Indictment, Trial, Judgment and Punishment, according to Law."[168]

## A. Scope of impeachment

The Framers understood it was necessary to hold the President, Vice President, and executive officers accountable for misconduct. That procedure was basic to checks and balances and republican government. Gouverneur Morris expressed alarm at the impeachment clause. To him, one great object "of the Executive is to controul the Legislature. The Legislature will continually seek to aggrandize & perpetuate themselves."[169] The President "should be the guardian of the people, even of the lower classes, agst. Legislative tyranny, against the Great & the wealthy who in the course of things will necessarily compose—the Legislative body."[170] The President "ought to be so constituted as to be the great protector of the Mass of the people."[171]

Morris worried that if the President were impeachable, it "will hold him in such dependence that he will be no check on the Legislature, will not be a firm guardian of the people and of the public interest. He will be a tool of a faction, of some leading demagogue in the Legislature."[172] The proposal to remove the President and executive officers on impeachment "and conviction of malpractice or neglect of duty" passed by a vote of eight states to two.[173] Yet Madison thought it "indispensable that some provision should be made for defending the Community agst the incapacity, negligence or perfidy of the chief Magistrate."[174] The President might "lose his capacity" after his election.[175] He might "pervert his administration into a scheme of peculation or oppression. He might betray his trust to foreign powers."[176]

Charles Pinckney "did not see the necessity of impeachments."[177] He was sure that the Legislature would hold that "rod over the Executive and by that means effectively destroy his independence."[178] Elbridge Gerry defended impeachment procedures. A "good magistrate will not fear them. A bad one ought to be kept in fear of them."[179] Edmund Randolph agreed. The availability of impeachment "was a favorite principle with him; Guilt wherever found ought to be punished. The Executive will have great opportunities of abusing his power; particularly in time of war when the military force, and in some respects the public money will be in his hands."[180]

---

168. U.S. Const., art. I, sec. 2 and 3.

169. 2 Farrand 52.

170. Id.

171. Id.

172. Id. at 53.

173. Id. at 62.

174. Id. at 65.

175. Id.

176. Id. at 65–66.

177. Id. at 66.

178. Id.

179. Id.

180. Id. at 67.

After following the debate, Gouverneur Morris said his view had changed. He was "now sensible of the necessity of impeachments, if the Executive was to continue for any time in office."[181] The President "may be bribed by a greater interest to betray his trust; and no one would say that we ought to expose ourselves to the danger of seeing the first Magistrate in foreign pay without being able to guard agst it by displacing him."[182] The President therefore ought to be impeached "for treachery; Corrupting his electors, and incapacity."[183] For the latter, he should be punished "not as a man, but as an officer, and punished only by degradation from his office."[184] The President "is not the King but the prime-Minister. The people are the King."[185] On the question of removing the President by impeachment, eight states agreed. Massachusetts and South Carolina voted no.[186]

The Framers supported impeachment of the President for treason and bribery. Bribery was fairly well understood. Treason is defined in the Constitution. Treason against the United States "shall consist only in levying War against them, or in adhering to their Enemies, giving them Aid and Comfort. No Person shall be convicted of Treason unless on the Testimony of two Witnesses to the same overt Act, or on Confession in open Court."[187] George Mason regarded those grounds as insufficient: "Why is the provision restrained to Treason & bribery only? Treason as defined in the Constitution will not reach many great and dangerous offences. Hastings is not guilty of Treason. Attempts to subvert the Constitution may not be Treason as above defined—As bills of attainder which saved the British Constitution are forbidden, it is the more necessary to extend: the power of impeachments."[188] Mason moved to add "maladministration" as an impeachable offense. Madison objected: "So vague a term will be equivalent to a tenure during pleasure of the Senate."[189] Mason withdrew "maladministration" and substituted "other high crimes & misdemeanors" against the State. This change in language drew support, 8 to 3.[190] The key phrase "high crimes and misdemeanors" was not debated. Subsequent discussion in the Federalist Papers and the state ratification conventions clarifies that impeachment reaches actions that subvert the Constitution and endanger the republic.

Madison thought it was inappropriate to have the President tried by the Senate after being impeached by the House, particularly for "any act which might be called a misdemesnor [sic]."[191] The President in "these circumstances was made improperly dependent."[192] He preferred the Supreme Court for the trial of impeachments, "or rather a tribunal of which that should form a part."[193] Morris thought that "no other tribunal than the Senate could be trusted." Justices of the

---

181. Id. at 68.

182. Id.

183. Id. at 69.

184. Id.

185. Id.

186. Id. at 68–69.

187. U.S. Const., art. III, sec. 3.

188. 2 Farrand 550.

189. Id.

190. Id.

191. Id. at 551.

192. Id.

193. Id.

Supreme Court "were too few in number and might be warped or corrupted."[194] He was against "a dependence of the Executive on the Legislature, considering the Legislative tyranny the great danger to be apprehended." There could be "no danger that the Senate would say untruly on their oaths that the President was guilty of crimes or facts, especially as in four years he can be turned out."[195]

To Charles Pinckney, making the Senate the court of impeachment rendered the President "too dependent on the Legislature." If the President were to oppose "a favorite law, the two Houses will combine agst him, and under the influence of heat and faction throw him out of office."[196] Hugh Williamson countered: there was "more danger of too much lenity than of too much rigour towards the President, considering the number of cases in which the Senate was associated with the President."[197] Roger Sherman regarded the Supreme Court as an improper body to try the President, "because the Judges would be appointed by him."[198] Madison's motion to remove the Senate as the trial body for impeachment was defeated 9 to 2.[199]

In Federalist No. 64, Jay pointed to a number of qualities he hoped would limit government abuse and corruption: "honor, oaths, reputations, conscience, the love of country, and family affections and attachments."[200] He anticipated that the work of government would attract individuals of "talents, and integrity." If not, the motive of good behavior would be "amply afforded by the article on the subject of impeachments."[201]

Hamilton in Federalist No. 65 analyzed the meaning of "high crimes and misdemeanors." Did it apply only to a criminal action prosecuted in court? To him, impeachment need not result from something indictable under federal law. The subject of impeachment proceeds from "the misconduct of public men, or, in other words, from the abuse or violation of some public trust."[202] The actions meriting impeachment "are of a nature which may with peculiar propriety be denominated POLITICAL, as they related chiefly to injuries done immediately to the society itself."[203] The offense is political, not legal. When a government official endangers the nation, the individual must be removed. Hamilton raised another issue. A person impeached and removed would still be subject "to prosecution and punishment in the ordinary course of law."[204] For that reason the court of impeachment needed to be the Senate, not the Supreme Court or some other judicial tribunal. It would be improper for federal judges to sit both on an impeachment trial and in subsequent court proceedings.[205] Impeachment is a political activity handled by the two houses of Congress. Prosecution is a legal action left to the executive branch and the courts.

194. Id.
195. Id.
196. Id.
197. Id.
198. Id.
199. Id.
200. The Federalist 425.
201. Id.
202. Id. at 426.
203. Id.
204. Id. at 428.
205. Id.

James Iredell, who later served as Associate Justice on the Supreme Court, spoke at the North Carolina ratification convention about the impeachment provision. The power is lodged "in those who represent the great body of the people, because the occasion for its exercise will arise from acts of great injury to the community, and the objects of it may be such as cannot be easily reached by an ordinary tribunal."[206] Something short of an indictable crime, including a "great injury" to the community or the political system, can be sufficient to justify impeachment and removal. In the treaty process, the Senate might consent to a "pernicious" agreement with another country on the basis of misleading information supplied by the President. In such a situation, the President "must certainly be punishable for giving false information to the Senate."[207]

## B. Impeachment efforts

Three Presidents have faced impeachment proceedings: Andrew Johnson in 1868, Richard Nixon in 1974, and Bill Clinton in 1998. Johnson was impeached in large part because of his decision to remove Secretary of War Edwin Stanton. The Tenure of Office Act required that officers appointed with the advice and consent of the Senate would remain in place until their successors were similarly appointed. If the Senate was in recess and unable to act on the replacement, the President could suspend—but not remove—the official.[208] Johnson decided to challenge the constitutionality of the statute. The House impeached Johnson but the Senate failed to muster the two-thirds majority for his removal. Each of the three articles of impeachment fell short by a single vote.[209]

Nixon was impeached for various offenses related to the Watergate cover-up. The House Judiciary Committee supported three articles of impeachment: obstruction of justice, abuse of presidential power (including violating the constitutional rights of citizens), and refusal to produce tape recordings of his White House conversations that had been subpoenaed. A committee report explained that "high crimes and misdemeanors" need not be violations of criminal law.[210] Six days after the committee completed its deliberations, Nixon released some of the recordings. The Supreme Court, in *United States v. Nixon*, had unanimously ordered production of those materials.[211] One of the recordings provided clear evidence of obstruction of justice, with Nixon attempting to have the CIA close down the FBI investigation. He remarked at a March 22, 1973 meeting: "And, uh, for that reason, I am perfectly willing to—I don't give a shit what happens. I want you to stonewall it, let them plead the Fifth Amendment, cover-up or anything else, if it'll save the plan."[212] "Saving the plan" meant keeping Nixon in office. Release of the tapes, Nixon recognized, made impeachment "virtually a foregone conclusion."[213] He announced his resignation on August 8, 1974, effective the next day.

---

206. 4 Elliot 113.

207. Id. at 127.

208. 14 Stat. 430 (1867).

209. Michael Les Benedict, The Impeachment and Trial of Andrew Johnson (1973).

210. *Constitutional Grounds for Presidential Impeachment*, Report by the Staff of the Impeachment Inquiry, House Committee on the Judiciary, 93d Cong., 2d Sess. (Comm. Print, Feb. 1974).

211. 418 U.S. 683 (1974).

212. John J. Sirica, To Set the Record Straight 162 (1979).

213. Public Papers of the Presidents, 1974, at 622.

On December 19, 1998, the House adopted two articles of impeachment against President Clinton, one for perjury and the other for obstruction of justice.[214] The legislative inquiry examined his statements regarding an affair with White House intern Monica Lewinsky and how they might relate to a previous case brought by Paula Corbin Jones. She had sued Clinton for sexual harassment during his service as governor of Arkansas. The Supreme Court upheld her right to pursue this civil case.[215] One issue was whether Clinton's statements about Lewinsky were intended to protect his legal interests in the Jones case. Voting on February 12, 1999, the Senate "acquitted" Clinton of both articles.[216] On the perjury article, 45 Senators voted "guilty" and 55 voted "not guilty." The vote on obstruction of justice was 50 to 50, far short of the two-thirds needed for removal.

Placing quotes around "acquitted" is meant to signal procedural complexities about the votes. From 1789 to 1936, the Senate took two votes at an impeachment trial: the first for guilt and the next, if necessary, for removal. If Senators voted down all articles to find an accused not guilty, there was no need to vote on removal. If they found guilt on one or more articles, they proceeded to the next step: removal. This procedure allowed Senators to find that someone who was guilty did not merit removal for the particular offense. In 1936, the Senate decided that if someone was guilty the person should be removed from office. The two issues, previously distinct, now collapsed to a single vote.[217]

Many Senators who voted Clinton "not guilty" explained that he was indeed guilty of one or both counts but did not want him removed from office. For example, Senator Robert C. Byrd voted "not guilty" on both articles even though he regarded Clinton's behavior an "impeachable offense, a political high crime or misdemeanor against the state."[218] Not wanting to remove Clinton, he voted "not guilty." Other Senators decided that Clinton was guilty of one or both articles but voted "not guilty" because they thought removal was unwarranted. Senator John Breaux voted against both articles after saying that Clinton had "lied about it, tried to cover it up."[219] He explained: "I am voting not to convict and remove. But that is not a vote on the innocence of the President. He is not innocent."[220] Senator Fred Thompson, who voted "not guilty" on the perjury article, said that Clinton "lied, misled and helped conceal evidence both physical and testimonial in a court proceeding."[221] Senator Susan Collins, voting against both articles, stated her belief that Clinton "willfully lied to a federal grand jury, and that he wrongfully tried to influence testimony and to conceal evidence related to Paula Jones' lawsuit."[222] Senator James Jeffords voted against both articles, although he concluded that Clinton "obstructed justice by

214. 144 Cong. Rec. 28110-12 (1998). For details on Article I (perjury) and Article III (obstruction of justice): 144 Cong. Rec. D626-27 (1998).

215. Clinton v. Jones, 520 U.S. 681 (1997).

216. 145 Cong. Rec. 2376–77 (1999).

217. 80 Cong. Rec. 5606–07 (1936).

218. 145 Cong. Rec. 2570 (1999).

219. Id. at 2420.

220. Id. at 2421.

221. Id. at 2482.

222. Id. at 2499.

trying to influence the testimony of Bettie Currie" and "took at least one illegal action in an attempt to conceal the truth from Paula Jones."[223]

On January 19, 2001, his last day in office, Clinton admitted that he had provided—under oath—false responses to questions put to him about his relationship with Lewinsky. In a statement made to Independent Counsel Robert W. Ray to avoid further prosecution after he left office, Clinton acknowledged that in his deposition in the Jones case he had "knowingly violated Judge Wright's discovery orders" and that some of his responses to questions about Lewinsky "were false." In addition, he agreed to pay a fine of $25,000 to the Arkansas Bar Association, promised not to seek reimbursement of any legal fees from a federal court, and accepted a five-year suspension of his Arkansas law license.[224]

In 1993, the Supreme Court reviewed the Senate's practice of conducting an impeachment of federal judges in two stages: fact-finding by a 12-member committee followed by action by the full Senate. Federal judge Walter L. Nixon, Jr. sued on the ground that the Senate procedure violated Article I, section 3, which places upon the Senate, and not a committee of the Senate, "the sole Power to try all Impeachments." A district court and appellate court held that his claim was nonjusticiable. The Supreme Court concluded that the Senate had sole discretion to choose the procedures for impeachment, including use of a committee to take testimony and gather evidence.[225]

## C. Censure motions

On several occasions, the two houses of Congress have considered censuring a President as a substitute for full impeachment proceedings. The Constitution permits Congress to censure its own members. Under Article I, section 5, each house "may punish its Members for disorderly Behaviour, and, with the Concurrence of two thirds, expel a Member." Various terms are used in censuring lawmakers, including "condemned," "denounced," "reprimand," and "declared unworthy." May Congress censure individuals outside the legislative branch, including the President, a Supreme Court Justice, lower court judges, executive officials, and private individuals?

Article I, section 9 prohibits Congress from passing a bill of attainder (punishing individuals without judicial trial). In the 1946 *Lovett* case, the Supreme Court struck down language in an appropriations bill that withheld funds to pay the salaries of three federal employees considered by Congress to be "subversive" (Chapter 4, section 10). May Congress censure executive and judicial branch officials? In more than a dozen cases, Congress has done so. Most of those efforts involved a simple resolution adopted by one of the houses, falling short of the statutory condemnation in *Lovett*. Still, the decision of the House or the Senate to single out a federal official for misconduct, including misuse of funds, is extremely injurious to the individual. These

---

223. Id. at 2529. For additional studies on presidential impeachment, see Michael J. Gerhardt, The Federal Impeachment Process: A Constitutional and Historical Analysis (1996); William H. Rehnquist, Grand Inquests: The Historic Impeachments of Justice Samuel Chase and President Andrew Johnson (1992); John R. Labovitz, Presidential Impeachment (1978); and Irving Brant, Impeachment: Trials and Errors (1972).

224. Neil A. Lewis, *Exiting Job, Clinton Accepts Immunity Deal: Admits Testimony Was False—Long Legal Fight Ends*, N.Y. Times, Jan. 20, 2001, at A1.

225. Nixon v. United States, 506 U.S. 224 (1993).

resolutions commonly use the words "censure" and "condemn." At times Congress will refer to a federal official by title, not by name, but the identity of the individual is never in doubt. Most of these congressional actions occurred in the nineteenth century.[226]

In 1834, the Senate adopted a resolution rebuking President Jackson for assuming "upon himself authority and power not conferred by the Constitution and laws, but in derogation of both." The dispute arose from Jackson's decision to deposit federal funds in state banks instead of the national bank. Jackson attacked the Senate for censuring him on unspecified charges and charging him with an impeachable act before action by the House. Three years later the Senate expunged the censure resolution (Chapter 6, section 3). On January 3, 1848, the House censured President Polk for "unnecessarily and unconstitutionally" beginning the war with Mexico.[227] In 1860, the House adopted a resolution that former President Buchanan and his Secretary of the Navy deserved "reproof" for allowing campaign contributions to influence the awarding of government contracts. The resolution passed, 106 to 61.[228]

In some cases, the two houses consider censure resolutions but do not follow through. In 1800, the House debated censuring or impeaching President Adams for handing over to Great Britain a British subject charged with murder. The move came to a halt when Representative John Marshall in his "sole organ" speech explained that the President was not usurping power or violating the Constitution. He was exercising his authority under the Jay Treaty to extradite individuals charged with specified crimes. Under the Constitution, treaties are the "Law of the Land" and it is the duty of the President to "take Care that the Laws be faithfully executed" (Chapter 7, section 1B).

In 1862, the Senate considered a resolution to censure and condemn former President James Buchanan for failing to take "necessary and proper measures to prevent" the Civil War.[229] The sponsor of the resolution, Garrett Davis of Kentucky, asked for immediate consideration "with a view to take a vote, not to debate it."[230] He assumed that each Senator had already "made up his mind." Senator Lyman Trumbell objected that the resolution was "too important" to be passed without consideration.[231] The Senate took up the resolution the following day, with Davis again stating that he did not "desire to debate it, but simply to vote upon it."[232] Senator John Parker Hale of New Hampshire said he would vote against the resolution, not because he did not think Buchanan was worthy of censure, but because of a passage he recalled from the New Testament: "doth our law judge any man before it hear him?"[233] Hale believed that Congress should not destroy the reputation of private citizens in this manner. The resolution "will stamp Mr. Buchanan with infamy as long as he has a place in history."[234] He would vote against the censure "of any private citizen behind his back and unheard, where he has no chance to answer

---

226. Richard S. Beth, *Censure of Executive and Judicial Branch Officials: Past Congressional Proceedings*, CRS Report 98-983 GOV, Dec. 11, 1998.

227. CONG. GLOBE, 30th Cong., 1st Sess. 95 (1848).

228. CONG. GLOBE, 36th Cong., 1st Sess. 2951 (1860).

229. CONG. GLOBE, 37th Cong., 3d Sess. 83 (1862).

230. Id.

231. CONG. GLOBE, 37th Cong., 3d Sess. 83 (1862).

232. Id. at 101.

233. Id.

234. Id.

for himself."[235] If Buchanan were guilty of anything, the proper course to Hale was the impeachment process.[236]

Senator Willard Saulsbury of Delaware proposed to offer an amendment so that Buchanan would be notified that a resolution had been introduced against him and would have an opportunity to defend himself. The amendment read: "That a copy of the foregoing resolution be served upon the said James Buchanan, and that he be notified that he has liberty to defend himself before the Senate against the charges in said resolution contained, if he shall choose to do so." At that point there was a motion to lay the resolution and the amendment on the table. That motion passed, 38 to 3.[237]

In August 1974, Representative Paul Findley of Illinois offered a resolution to censure President Nixon. Although he objected to a number of actions by Nixon, he questioned whether the evidence was adequate to remove him through the impeachment process.[238] Findley's language illustrates the shortcomings of censure resolutions. It said that Nixon "(1) has shown insensitivity to the moral demands, lofty purpose and ideals of the high office he holds in trust, and (2) has, through negligence and maladministration, failed to prevent his close subordinates and agents from committing acts of grave misconduct [,] obstruction and impairment of justice, abuse and undue concentration of power, and contravention of the laws governing agencies of the Executive Branch."[239] Not only are the charges of moral insensitivity, negligence, and maladministration vague, but the resolution censured unnamed "close subordinates and agents." This resolution received no floor consideration.[240]

In 1998, members of Congress considered resolutions of censure against President Clinton as a substitute for impeachment. In a public statement on December 11, he said he was willing to agree to legislative censure. During House debate on impeachment, he told reporters: "I must also be at peace with the fact that the public consequences of my actions are in the hands of the American people and their Representatives in the Congress. Should they determine that my errors of word and deed require their rebuke and censure, I am ready to accept that."[241]

On December 19, 1998, the House debated a resolution stating that Clinton "made false statements concerning his reprehensible conduct with a subordinate; . . . wrongly took steps to delay discovery of the truth; . . . remains subject to criminal and civil penalties; and . . . by his conduct has brought upon himself, and fully deserves, the censure and condemnation of the American people and this House."[242] The Chair ruled that the censure resolution was not germane to the pending resolution of impeachment.[243] On a motion to appeal the ruling of the Chair, that motion was tabled, 230 to 204.[244]

---

235. Id.

236. Id. at 101–102.

237. Id. at 102.

238. 120 Cong. Rec. 26489 (1974).

239. Id. at 26820.

240. See Jack Maskell, *Censure of the President by the Congress*, CRS Report 98-843 A, Dec. 8, 1998.

241. Public Papers of the Presidents, 1998, II, at 2158; *President's Comments on the Impeachment Proceedings*, N.Y. Times, Dec. 12, 1998, at A9. See Dan Balz & Eric Pianin, *With Apology, An Open Plea for Censure*, Wash. Post, Dec. 12, 1998, at A1.

242. 144 Cong. Rec. 28100 (1998).

243. Id. at 28108.

244. Id. at 28108–09.

In February 1999, after the Senate had decided not to convict and remove President Clinton in the impeachment trial, some Senators offered a resolution to censure him for a "shameful, reckless and indefensible" relationship with "a subordinate employee in the White House."[245] The resolution further stated that he "deliberately misled and deceived the American people, and people in all branches of the United States government," conducting himself in an "unacceptable" manner that "creates disrespect for the laws of the land."[246] In explaining the intent of the resolution, Senator Dianne Feinstein said it "does not express legal conclusions in the court of impeachment. Rather, it is a legislative measure, expressing our conclusions regarding the President's conduct."[247]

Senator John Ashcroft opposed the censure resolution on several grounds: the impeachment trial was over, the Constitution "does not empower the Senate to punish a President," and censure "is an effort to end-run" the constitutional requirements of a two-thirds majority in the Senate for removal.[248] He pointed to inevitable tensions in drafting censure resolutions against a President: "any censure resolution will have to be weak. Even proponents of censure concede that a censure resolution that actually punished the President would be an unconstitutional bill of attainder."[249] The Senate voted to indefinitely suspend consideration of the censure resolution.[250]

There is another method of legislative rebuke: a vote of "no confidence" in a public official and presumably also the President. A Senate joint resolution, introduced on May 24, 2007, expressed the "sense of the Senate that Attorney General Alberto Gonzales no longer holds the confidence of the Senate and of the American people."[251] During debate on a cloture motion to permit a vote, several Senators described a vote of no confidence as being British or European, having few roots in American practice or law.[252] The vote to proceed to the joint resolution was 53 to 38, short of the three-fifths needed to close debate.[253]

# 10. EXECUTIVE IMMUNITY

Other than acting against the President through impeachment and censure motions, what remedies are available in court to sanction Presidents for legal and constitutional violations? May public employees and private citizens bring civil actions against Presidents, Cabinet heads, department officers, and White House aides? Article I, section 6 provides express immunity

---

245. 155 CONG. REC. 2590 (1999).

246. Id.

247. Id. at 2598.

248. Id. at 2379.

249. Id.

250. Id. at 2379–80; Edward Walsh, *Senate Puts Censure Resolution on Hold—Indefinitely*, WASH. POST, Feb. 13, 1999, at A32.

251. S. J. Res. 14, 110th Cong., 1st Sess. (May 24, 2007); 153 CONG. REC. S6927 (daily ed. May 25, 2007).

252. 153 CONG. REC. 15215 (Senator Lott), 15219 (Senator Sessions) (2007).

253. Id. at 15223. See Jack Maskell & Richard S. Beth, *"No Confidence" Votes and Other Forms of Congressional Censure of Public Officials*, CRS Report RL34037, June 11, 2007.

only for members of Congress, who "shall in all Cases, except Treason, Felony and Breach of the Peace, be privileged from Arrest during their Attendance at the Session of their respective Houses, and in going to and returning from the same; and for any Speech or Debate in either House, they shall not be questioned in any other Place." The purpose of this provision is to safeguard the independence of Congress from executive and judicial interference.[254]

Although the Constitution does not provide specific immunities for the other two branches, the courts have developed a doctrine of absolute immunity for officers "intimately associated with the judicial phase of the criminal process," including the decision of a state prosecutor to initiate and pursue a criminal prosecution.[255] Similarly, federal courts have granted judges absolute immunity in civil actions for their official duties.[256] Judges remain subject to impeachment and removal from office for actions unrelated to judicial duties, such as bribery, corruption, and criminal conduct. Investigating commissions and disciplinary proceedings at the federal and state level may lead to the resignation and disbarment of judges accused of misconduct and an inability to perform judicial duties.[257]

The Constitution does not contain an express immunity for the President or executive officers, but the courts have developed a doctrine of official immunity for the executive branch. Some of the cases date back to the nineteenth century.[258] A decision in 1838 explained the difference between the President's constitutional authority and the functions carried out by executive officers. The "executive power is vested in a President; and as far as his powers are derived from the constitution, he is beyond the reach of any other department, except in the mode prescribed by the constitution through the impeaching power. But it by no means follows, that every officer in every branch of that department is under the exclusive direction of the President."[259] Those issues are explored more fully in Chapter 3, section 6. The modern doctrine of executive immunity for Presidents, Cabinet officials, and White House aides took shape in several Supreme Court rulings after World War II.

A principal argument in favor of some level of immunity for executive officers is that unless they are protected from civil actions they cannot be expected to administer laws vigorously and effectively. Instead, they would be inclined to look over their shoulders, concerned about possible litigation by private parties determined to challenge their decisions and seek personal damages. That issue arose in a case decided by the Second Circuit in 1949. A lawsuit was brought against Attorney General Francis Biddle and officials within the Justice Department. Armand Gregoire was arrested as an enemy alien and kept in custody for nearly four years until a judge determined he was a Frenchman and not, as the government claimed, a German. Even though some government officials may act dishonestly and with personal ill-will, the court said it was necessary to provide broad immunity. To submit all officials, "the innocent as well as the guilty,

---

254. United States v. Helstoski, 442 U.S. 477, 491 (1979); United States v. Johnson, 383 U.S. 169, 177 (1966).

255. Imbler v. Pachtman, 424 U.S. 409, 430 (1976). This case involved an action under 42 U.S.C. § 1983, seeking damages caused by unlawful prosecution.

256. Pierson v. Ray, 386 U.S. 547 (1967); Bradley v. Fisher, 13 Wall. (80 U.S.) 335, 347 (1872).

257. WILLIAM THOMAS BRAITHWAITE, WHO JUDGES THE JUDGES: A STUDY OF PROCEDURES FOR REMOVAL AND RETIREMENT (1971); JOSEPH BOYKIN, THE CORRUPT JUDGE: AN INQUIRY INTO BRIBERY AND OTHER HIGH CRIMES AND MISDEMEANORS IN THE FEDERAL COURTS (1962).

258. Spalding v. Vilas, 161 U.S. 483, 498 (1896); Kendall v. Stokes, 3 How. (44 U.S.) 87 (1845); Kendall v. United States, 12 Pet. (37 U.S.) 524 (1838).

259. Kendall v. United States, 12 Pet. (37 U.S.) 524, 610 (1838).

to the burden of a trial and to the inevitable danger of its outcome, would dampen the ardor of all but the most resolute, or the most irresponsible, in the unflinching discharge of their duties."[260]

The Supreme Court divided 5 to 4 in an official immunity case in 1959. Several federal employees brought a libel action against the acting director of an office of rent stabilization. The Court weighed two considerations: oppressive and malicious actions on the part of federal officials versus the hazards of vindictive or ill-founded damage suits.[261] The majority, relying substantially on *Gregoire*, supported an absolute privilege against the alleged libel.[262] The dissenters objected that the majority created an artificial balancing test that tilted too much toward executive immunity and deprived individual employees of redress against malicious defamation.

Congress has passed legislation to permit lawsuits against the federal government. The Federal Tort Claims Act of 1946 authorized tort suits to be brought against federal agencies. With some exceptions, the United States is liable for injuries "caused by the negligent or wrongful act or omission of any employee of the Government while acting within the scope of his office or employment."[263] One exception is the *Feres* doctrine, which prohibits suits by military personnel for injuries sustained while on active duty or incident to service.[264]

## A. Filing a "Bivens action"

In 1971, the Supreme Court created what appeared to be an opportunity for private citizens to recover damages from federal agents who violated their constitutional rights. Agents of the Federal Bureau of Narcotics made a warrantless entry of an apartment, searched it, and arrested the owner on narcotics charges. Claiming the arrest was made without probable cause, Webster Bivens sought $15,000 from each of the agents to compensate him for personal humiliation, embarrassment, and mental suffering. A district court held that his suit failed to state a federal cause of action and that the agents were immune from suit because of their official position. The Second Circuit affirmed on the first ground alone. The Supreme Court held that the complaint stated a federal cause of action under the Fourth Amendment and that damages could be recovered under proof of injuries that resulted from the agents' violation of that amendment.[265]

The Court did not reach the immunity question directly, but under its ruling a federal agent could be successfully sued for unconstitutional conduct. From the opinion of Justice Brennan, writing for the majority, it appeared that Bivens was entitled to recover money damages for any injuries he suffered as a result of the agents' violation of the Fourth Amendment.[266] Although the agents would be held personally liable, the federal government would pay damages on their behalf. Much of the majority opinion, the concurrence by Justice Harlan, and the dissents by Chief Justice Burger and Justices Black and Blackmun focused on whether courts may provide

260. Gregoire v. Biddle, 177 F.2d 579, 581 (2d Cir. 1949), cert. denied, 339 U.S. 949 (1950).
261. Barr v. Matteo, 360 U.S. 564, 565 (1959).
262. Id. at 571–72.
263. 60 Stat. 843, sec. 403(a) (1946); 28 U.S.C. § 1346(b).
264. Feres v. United States, 340 U.S. 135 (1950).
265. Bivens v. Six Unknown Fed. Narcotics Agents, 403 U.S. 388 (1971).
266. Id. at 397.

judicial relief for litigants without express congressional authorization. While offering no view on the immunity defense in Bivens's case, Harlan thought that "at the very least such a remedy would be available for the most flagrant and patently unjustified sorts of police conduct."[267]

A dissent by Chief Justice Burger explained why the policy of excluding illegally obtained evidence from the courtroom has not been more effective in deterring improper and unconstitutional conduct by law enforcement officials. The exclusionary rule "does not apply any direct sanction to the individual official whose illegal conduct results in the exclusion of evidence in a criminal trial. With rare exceptions law enforcement agencies do not impose direct sanctions on the individual officer responsible for a particular judicial application of the suppression doctrine."[268] The federal government might be theoretically accountable, but the federal official is not.

*Bivens* offered a hope that rarely materializes in court. Time after time plaintiffs are advised that a *Bivens* action is not available to them, in part because courts decide an official is entitled to qualified immunity.[269] That pattern prevailed in the decades after 1971 and continued in the period after the terrorist attacks of September 11, 2001. Individuals sued the federal government for such violations as extraordinary rendition (taking individuals abroad for interrogation and torture), NSA warrantless surveillance, and cruel and inhumane treatment while detained overseas in such facilities as Abu Ghraib in Iraq. As detailed in Chapter 9, section 9, plaintiffs learned that efforts to hold federal officials personally accountable for illegal and unconstitutional actions could not prevail in the face of defenses mounted by the government, particularly the state secrets privilege.[270]

## B. Immunity for Presidents and executive officials

In *Nixon v. Fitzgerald* (1982), the Supreme Court held that the President is entitled to absolute immunity in civil suits for all official acts.[271] On that fundamental issue the Justices divided 5 to 4. The case arose when A. Ernest Fitzgerald, a management analyst with the Department of the Air Force, filed a civil action against President Richard Nixon for unlawfully retaliating against him for his congressional testimony. After identifying cost-overruns and unexpected technical difficulties with the C-5A transport plane at a congressional hearing on November 13, 1968, he lost his job. Some effort was made to find him another position in the executive branch, but a White House aide advised that he "must be given very low marks in loyalty; and after all, loyalty is the name of the game.... [w]e should let him bleed, for a while at least."[272]

The Court held that Nixon, as a former President of the United States, was "entitled to absolute immunity from damages liability predicated on his official acts." This immunity is "a

---

267. Id. at 411 (Harlan, J., concurring).

268. Id. at 416 (Burger, C.J., dissenting).

269. Saucier v. Katz, 533 U.S. 194 (2001).

270. James E. Pfander & David Baltmanis, *Rethinking* Bivens: *Legitimacy and Constitutional Adjudication*, 98 Geo. L. J. 117, 119 n.14 (2009), and Cornelia T. L. Pillard, *Taking Fiction Seriously: The Strange Results of Public Officials' Individual Liability Under* Bivens, 88 Geo. L. J. 65 (1999).

271. 457 U.S. 731 (1982).

272. Id. at 735–36.

functionally mandated incident of the President's unique office, rooted in the constitutional tradition of the separation of powers and supported by our history."[273] Given the visibility of the office and his effect on "countless people, the President would be an easily identifiable target for suits for civil damages."[274] The Court acknowledged that in a number of instances, including the Steel Seizure Case of 1952 and the Watergate Case of 1974, it decided it was appropriate to exercise jurisdiction and rule against the President.[275] In the case of Fitzgerald's "merely private suit for damages based on a President's official acts, we hold it is not."[276]

After granting the President absolute immunity in civil actions, the Court asked what kind of checks operate as "sufficient protection against misconduct." It first mentioned the "constitutional remedy of impeachment." Next it identified "formal and informal checks on Presidential action that do not apply with equal force to other executive officials," including "constant scrutiny by the press," "[v]igilant oversight by Congress," and "a desire to earn reelection, the need to maintain prestige as an element of Presidential influence, and a President's traditional concern for his historical stature."[277] Those may operate as constraints on Presidents capable of exercising good judgment for the nation, but the record over the last six decades inspires little confidence. During that period a number of Presidents acted unlawfully and unconstitutionally, doing serious damage to their personal reputations, their party, the nation, and countries subjected to U.S. military intervention and covert operations.

Justice White wrote a lengthy dissent in the Fitzgerald case, joined by Brennan, Marshall, and Blackmun. They objected that the majority cast the net of absolute immunity too broadly to cover all official duties of the President. Under this interpretation, a President may, "without liability, deliberately cause serious injury to any number of citizens even though he knows his conduct violates a statute or tramples on the constitutional rights of those who are injured."[278] A President could, without following statutory procedures on wiretapping, order "his subordinates to wiretap or break into a home for the purpose of installing a listening device." If the officer complied with his request, he "would be absolutely immune from suit." He would be immune "regardless of the damage he inflicts, regardless of how violative of the statute and the Constitution he knew his conduct to be, and regardless of his purpose."[279] The dissenters explained that their example was "not simply a hypothetical." The Court had recently decided precisely that kind of case.[280]

To White, the majority's decision to grant absolute immunity to actions taken by Presidents in their official duties, and to base that doctrine on the Constitution, was to prohibit Congress from providing any remedy against presidential misconduct. He did not agree that a President, to operate effectively and without fear of liability, may deliberately "inflict injury on others by conduct that he knows violates the law."[281] He recognized that members of Congress are absolutely

---

273. Id. at 749.

274. Id. at 753.

275. Id. at 754 (Youngstown Co. v. Sawyer, 343 U.S. 579 (1952); United States v. Nixon, 418 U.S. 683 (1974)).

276. Id. at 754.

277. Id. at 757.

278. Id. at 764 (White, J., dissenting, joined by Brennan, J., Marshall, J., and Blackmun, J.).

279. Id. at 765

280. Halperin v. Kissinger, 452 U.S. 713 (1981).

281. Nixon v. Fitzgerald, 457 U.S. at 765 (White, J., dissenting, joined by Brennan, J., Marshall, J., and Blackmun, J.).

immune under the Speech or Debate Clause, but that immunity applies only to their legislative acts. Lawmakers are subject to prosecution when some actions, including taking bribes, are not related to legislative activities. Similarly, federal judges are absolutely immune when they are performing a judicial function. If their actions fall outside judicial activity, they are subject to prosecution and sanctions as are members of Congress.[282]

On the same day the Court granted absolute immunity in civil suits for all official presidential acts, it supported a qualified immunity for presidential aides.[283] Eight Justices joined in the opinion or wrote concurring statements. Chief Justice Burger dissented. The case involved civil damages resulting from Fitzgerald losing his job with the Air Force. He sued two White House aides, Bryce Harlow and Alexander Butterfield, for possible involvement with his firing. The Court had to reconcile a number of its previous decisions on immunity. In 1972 it granted absolute immunity to congressional aides on the ground that they functioned as "alter egos" for members of Congress who were constitutionally protected by the Speech or Debate Clause.[284] Six years later, a sharply divided Court (5 to 4) granted qualified immunity to Cabinet heads and departmental assistants sued for civil damages.[285] The principle of qualified immunity requires public officials to demonstrate that, in light of clearly established law, there was reasonable ground to believe that their actions were lawful.[286]

On what constitutional principles did the Court treat congressional aides and departmental officials differently? For one, congressional immunity is specifically granted in the Constitution through the Speech or Debate Clause. Presidential and executive immunity are drawn from what courts have decided are protections implied in the system of separated powers. How would the Court now decide the immunity status of White House aides? One consideration are lawsuits authorized by federal law (42 U.S.C. § 1983) against state officials who violate constitutionally protected rights. The Court in 1974 reviewed the case of students killed on the campus of Kent State University in Ohio. It granted state officials, including the Governor, the Adjutant General, his assistant, members of the Ohio National Guard, and the president of Kent State University, qualified immunity. The ruling did not fully bless their actions. Further proceedings were necessary to determine the merits of the claims brought by plaintiffs.[287]

The Court in 1975 held that school officials are entitled to a qualified good-faith immunity from liabilities under Section 1983. They are not immune, however, if they knew or reasonably should have known that the actions they took within their sphere of official responsibility would violate the constitutional rights of students, or if they acted with malicious intent to deprive students of their rights. A district court defined "malice" to mean "ill will against a person—a wrongful act done intentionally without just cause or excuse."[288]

In the case of White House aides, the Court reasoned that having decided in *Butz* that members of the Cabinet "ordinarily enjoy only qualified immunity from suit, we conclude today that it would be equally untenable to hold absolute immunity an incident of the office of every

---

282. Id. at 765–66.
283. Harlow v. Fitzgerald, 457 U.S. 800 (1982).
284. Gravel v. United States, 408 U.S. 606 (1972).
285. Butz v. Economou, 438 U.S. 478 (1978).
286. Anderson v. Creighton, 483 U.S. 635, 641 (1987).
287. Scheuer v. Rhodes, 416 U.S. 232, 250 (1974).
288. Wood v. Strickland, 420 U.S. 308, 314 (1975).

Presidential subordinate based in the White House." Members of the Cabinet are "direct subordinates of the President, frequently with greater responsibilities, both to the President and to the Nation, than White House staff." The Court decided that the considerations that supported its ruling in *Butz* "apply with equal force to this case."[289] It suggested that executive aides involved in "such 'central' Presidential domains as foreign policy and national security" might merit absolute immunity, but it did not decide that question.[290]

This latter issue reached the Court in 1985. On November 6, 1970, Attorney General John Mitchell authorized a warrantless wiretap for the purpose of gathering intelligence regarding the activities of an antiwar group. In 1972, the Court ruled that the Fourth Amendment does not permit warrantless wiretaps in cases involving domestic threats to national security.[291] After years of litigation against Mitchell, a district court held he was not entitled to either absolute or qualified immunity and that he violated clearly established law. The Supreme Court agreed he was not absolutely immune but granted him qualified immunity because the wiretap occurred more than a year before the Court decided the Fourth Amendment issue.[292]

Subsequent cases involving the Attorney General granted broad immunity to charges of alleged constitutional violations. In 2009, the Supreme Court dismissed a lawsuit filed by Javaid Iqbal, a Pakistani Muslim arrested after 9/11 and subjected to harsh abuse at a Brooklyn detention center. He sued Attorney General John Ashcroft, FBI Director Robert Mueller, and other federal officials for those conditions. He accused Ashcroft and other executive officials of unconstitutionally fashioning a detention policy that discriminates on the basis of race, religion, and national origin. Five Justices held that Iqbal failed to establish a plausible link between the actions of federal officials and the abuses he suffered. The majority opinion, written by Justice Kennedy, referred to "harsh conditions" at the Brooklyn facility and noted that Iqbal alleged that the jailors "kicked him in the stomach, punched him in the face, and dragged him across" his cell without justification.[293]

Kennedy referred to an April 2003 report by the Inspector General in the Justice Department, who sharply criticized the abusive actions toward detainees in the Brooklyn facility. Both sides agreed that Ashcroft was entitled to qualified immunity. During oral argument on December 10, 2008, Justice Ginsburg referred to the IG report and asked whether it lent "plausibility" to Iqbal's claims. Solicitor General Gregory Garre did not think it did.[294] Iqbal's attorney told the Court he relied in part on the IG report.[295] Toward the end of oral argument, Garre made the point that the "higher up the chain of command you go, the less plausible it is that the high-level official like the Attorney General is going to be aware of and know about the sort of microscopic decisions here: mistreatment in the Federal detention facility in Brooklyn, alleged discriminatory applications made by FBI agents in the field."[296]

*Iqbal* was followed by a case that placed abusive actions much closer to the Attorney General. Abdullah al-Kidd was arrested at a Dulles International Airport ticket counter and confined in

289. Harlow v. Fitzgerald, 457 U.S. 800, 809 (1982).

290. Id. at 812 n.19.

291. United States v. United States District Court, 407 U.S. 297 (1972).

292. Mitchell v. Forsyth, 472 U.S. 511, 530–35 (1985).

293. Ashcroft v. Iqbal, 556 U.S. 662, 666, 668 (2009).

294. U.S. Supreme Court, oral argument, Ashcroft v. Iqbal, Dec. 10, 2008, at 25.

295. Id. at 30, 39.

296. Id. at 62.

high-security cells for 16 days. During that time he was strip-searched and shackled about his wrists, legs, and waist. After his release he was ordered to surrender his travel documents and report to a probation office for the next 15 months. He was fired from his job as a government contractor because he was denied a security clearance due to his arrest.[297] Unlike the distance between the Attorney General and conditions in a detention facility in Brooklyn, al-Kidd's case directly involved top Justice Department officials. While he was in jail in Idaho, FBI Director Mueller in testimony before Congress listed five "major successes" in the agency's effort toward "identifying and dismantling terrorist networks." The first was the capture of Khalid Sheikh Mohammed, identified as "a key planner and the mastermind of the September 11th attack." The second: al-Kidd.[298]

FBI arrested al-Kidd on inaccurate and misleading information. The agency stated in its affidavit that he was scheduled to take a one-way, first-class flight (costing approximately $5,000) to Saudi Arabia. In fact, he bought a round-trip, coach class ticket, priced at $1,700. The affidavit did not disclose (1) he was a U.S. resident and citizen, (2) his parents, wife, and two children were U.S. residents and citizens, and (3) he had previously cooperated when FBI agents asked to interview him.[299] Although al-Kidd was arrested as a material witness in the trial of Al-Hussayen, suspected of terrorist activities, he was never called as a witness in that trial or in any other criminal proceeding.[300] Al-Hussayen was not convicted of any of the charges brought against him. The government agreed not to retry Al-Hussayen and deported him to Saudi Arabia for visa violations.[301]

In March 2005, al-Kidd filed a "Bivens action" in federal district court, naming Ashcroft, two FBI agents, and other executive officials. The district court denied Ashcroft's claims of absolute and qualified immunity. It held that the allegations against him involved "more than vicarious liability but assert claims involving Mr. Ashcroft's own knowledge and actions relating to Mr. Kidd's alleged constitutional deprivations."[302] The Ninth Circuit affirmed those portions of the district court's decision, holding that Ashcroft was not entitled either to absolute or qualified immunity.[303] It said the Supreme Court "has never held that detention of innocent persons as material witnesses is permissible under the Fourth Amendment."[304] It cited from a Supreme Court opinion: "We do not believe that the security of the Republic will be threatened if its Attorney General is given incentives to abide by clearly established law."[305]

On May 31, 2011, the Supreme Court reversed the Ninth Circuit. A unanimous Court ruled that Ashcroft did not violate clearly established law and was thus entitled to qualified immunity.[306] On other issues, the Court split 4 to 4. Justice Kagan took no part in the consideration

---

297. Al-Kidd v. Ashcroft, 580 F.3d 949, 951–52 (9th Cir. 2009).

298. Id. at 955.

299. Id. at 953.

300. Id. at 954.

301. Id. at 953, n.4.

302. Id. at 956

303. Al-Kidd v. Ashcroft, 580 F.3d 949 (9th Cir. 2009).

304. Id. at 965.

305. Id. at 973, citing Mitchell v. Forsyth, 472 U.S. at 524. The Ninth Circuit states that the Court in *Forsyth* was quoting Harlow v. Fitzgerald, 457 U.S. at 819, but that is incorrect. The quoted language comes from *Forsyth*.

306. Ashcroft v. al-Kidd, 563 U.S. ___ (2011).

of this case. The Court determined that the affidavit accompanying the application for an arrest warrant "gave individualized reasons to believe that he was a material witness and that he would soon disappear."[307] It held that "an objectively reasonable arrest and detention of a material witness pursuant to a validly obtained warrant cannot be challenged as unconstitutional on the basis of allegations that the arresting authority had an improper motive."[308] However, the FBI agent falsely claimed that al-Kidd had purchased a one-way ticket, which was not objective or a valid reason for the arrest warrant.

The Justices who concurred in the Court's decision agreed that the Ninth Circuit "disregarded the purposes of the doctrine of qualified immunity."[309] In a separate concurrence, three Justices objected that the Court "assumes at the outset the existence of a *validly obtained* material witness warrant," a characterization they found "puzzling."[310] They asked: "Is a warrant 'validly obtained' when the affidavit on which it is based fails to inform the issuing Magistrate Judge that 'the Government has no intention of using [al-Kidd as a witness] at [another's] trial'... and does not disclose that al-Kidd had cooperated with FBI agents each of the several times they had asked to interview him?"[311] The affidavit "misrepresented that al-Kidd was about to take a one-way flight to Saudi Arabia."[312] They also agreed that al-Kidd's treatment "presents serious questions, unaddressed by the Court, concerning 'the [legality of] the Government's use of the Material Witness Statute in this case.'"[313] Even if the initial material witness classification had been proper, "what even arguably legitimate basis could there be for the harsh custodial conditions to which al-Kidd was subjected...."?[314]

If a civil action against an Attorney General fails because of the doctrine of qualified or absolute immunity, a plaintiff may nonetheless prevail against subordinate government employees who were responsible for abusive actions. Al-Kidd was able to reach a settlement with the government for his treatment in detention. In addition, the use of falsehoods and misrepresentations in the affidavit prepared by two FBI agents "could negate any claim of immunity" on their part. Al-Kidd sued them in a separate case Idaho.[315] On September 27, 2012, a federal district judge held that FBI agent Michael Gneckow was "reckless" in the preparation of an affidavit to the magistrate who issued an arrest warrant on al-Kidd and that Gneckow was not entitled to qualified immunity in his defense.[316]

The ruling against this FBI agent contrasts to the nearly unbroken record in recent decades of executive officials not being held accountable for abusive and criminal actions. In the Watergate scandal, top officials in the Nixon administration (including Attorney General John Mitchell) were prosecuted, convicted, and sent to prison. Since that time, presidential pardons

---

307. Id. at ___.

308. Id. at __.

309. Id. at ___ (Kennedy, J., Ginsburg, J., Breyer, J., and Sotomayor, J., concurring).

310. Id. at ___ (Ginsburg, J., Breyer, J., and Sotomayor, J., concurring) (italics in original).

311. Id. at ___ (brackets in original).

312. Id. at __.

313. Id. at __.

314. Id. at __.

315. Robert Barnes, *Ashcroft Not Liable in Man's Detention*, N.Y. Times, June 1, 2011, at A2.

316. Al-Kidd v. Gonzales, Case No. 1:05-cv-093-EJl-MHW (D. Idaho 2012).

(Iran-Contra), court rulings on executive immunity, and judicial acquiescence to executive claims of state secrets (Chapter 9, section 9) have provided regular shelter for executive officials accused of abusive and criminal actions.[317]

## C. Presidential immunity for unofficial acts

A separate issue is whether the President is entitled to absolute immunity in civil suits for *unofficial* acts: those committed in a personal capacity rather than as President. That issue crystallized when Paula Corbin Jones brought a lawsuit against Bill Clinton for an incident that allegedly occurred before he became President. She claimed that in 1991, at a conference held at a hotel in Little Rock, Clinton, who was then Governor of Arkansas, sexually harassed and assaulted her. Clinton's attorneys argued that the President should have a temporary immunity while serving in office, and that the case should proceed only after he left office. In 1997, a unanimous Court decided that the Constitution did not afford the President temporary immunity in this case.[318] The lawsuit was later dismissed when a district judge held that there were "no genuine issues for trial in this case." After Jones appealed, Clinton agreed to settle the case by giving her $850,000 and acknowledged that he had given false answers under oath.[319]

The Court's prediction in 1997 that the case could move forward without substantially burdening President Clinton has been much maligned, with the Court heavily criticized for political naiveté. However, the resulting burden on Clinton had less to do with the Jones case than to new allegations about his relationship with White House intern Monica Lewinsky and substantial charges that he made false statements and obstructed justice (covered earlier in this chapter, in section 9B).

HAVING COVERED BASIC issues about the election and removal of the President and Vice President, including questions of impeachment, censure, and executive immunity, the next chapter focuses on selected powers of the President. It is understood that the President has access to both enumerated and implied powers. What about "inherent" powers and the executive prerogative? How is the distinction drawn between ministerial and discretionary powers? Other topics covered in Chapter 3 include the removal and pardon powers, the Opinion Clause, the Take Care Clause, executive orders and proclamations, and presidential commissions.

---

317. Stephen I. Vladeck, *The National Security Canon*, 61 Am. U. L. Rev. 1295 (2012); Stephen I. Vladeck, *National Security and Bivens after Iqbal*, 14 Lewis & Clark L. Rev. 255 (2010).

318. Clinton v. Jones, 520 U.S. 681 (1997).

319. Neely Tucker & Susan Schmidt, *Lewinsky Case Report Released*, Wash. Post, March 7, 2002, at A1, A5; *Correspondence and Agreed Order in the Settlement of Clinton's Case*, N.Y. Times, Jan. 20, 2001, at A14.

# THREE

# The Powers of the President

PRESIDENTIAL POWER HAS MANY SOURCES: PROVISIONS EXPRESSLY STATED in the Constitution, authorities reasonably implied in those provisions, statutory grants from Congress, judicial decisions, national emergencies (real and contrived), and attempts by Presidents to exercise powers that are not expressly stated or reasonably implied. This chapter begins by analyzing three concepts that go beyond powers expressly stated: "implied," "inherent," and "prerogative." It is important to understand how they differ. Subsequent sections focus on specific presidential powers, such as the power to remove executive officials and to issue pardons. Presidential powers wax and wane depending on who occupies the Oval Office, initiatives urged by advisers and supporters, national and international pressures, popular support (and lack thereof), and actions taken by the legislative and judicial branches to encourage or curb executive power.

## 1. ENUMERATED AND IMPLIED POWERS

Chapter 1 touched briefly on "inherent" powers and how they differ from constitutionally legitimate "implied" powers. They have fundamentally different meanings. On occasion, members of Congress, executive officials, federal courts, and scholars refer to the U.S. Constitution as one of "enumerated powers." Those statements suggest that *every power* granted to the national government is expressly stated in the Constitution, and anything beyond powers specifically enumerated lacks legitimacy. In *McCulloch v. Maryland* (1819), Chief Justice John Marshall made this claim: "This government is acknowledged by all, to be one of enumerated powers. The principle, that it can exercise only the powers granted to it … is now universally admitted."[1]

All governments require more than enumerated powers, and yet some scholars conclude: "A necessary corollary (and one that leaps from the Constitution) is that Congress is limited to its enumerated powers."[2] Congress is not restricted to enumerated powers nor is the President or the judiciary. All three branches have access to a number of implied powers that can be legitimately drawn from their express powers.

---

1. 17 U.S. (4 Wheat.) 316, 404 (1819).
2. Saikrishna Prakash, *Regulating Presidential Powers*, 91 CORNELL L. REV. 215, 241 (2005).

In *McCulloch*, Chief Justice Marshall had to decide whether Congress possessed authority to create a national bank (the U.S. Bank). Nothing in the Constitution specifically grants Congress that power. Marshall admitted: "Among the enumerated powers, we do not find that of establishing a bank or creating a corporation."[3] He found it necessary to jettison his model of enumerated powers by reasoning: "there is no phrase in the instrument which, like the articles of confederation, excludes incidental or implied powers; and which requires that everything granted shall be expressly and minutely described."[4] He upheld the Bank's creation on the basis of implied powers and by interpreting in broad fashion the Necessary and Proper Clause of Article I.[5] Marshall counseled: "Let the end be legitimate, let it be within the scope of the constitution, and all means which are appropriate, which are plainly adapted to that end, which are not prohibited, but consist with the letter and spirit of the constitution, are constitutional."[6] Details of the U.S. Bank dispute are covered later in this section.

Marshall did not write on a clean slate. His grasp of implied powers benefited from principles developed by the Framers. They understood the need for implied powers. Madison wrote in Federalist No. 44: "No axiom is more clearly established in law, or in reason, than that wherever the end is required, the means are authorized; wherever a general power to do a thing is given, every particular power necessary for doing it is included."[7] During the First Congress, Madison successfully defeated an effort to limit the national government to powers expressly delegated. The Articles of Confederation, which became effective in 1781, gave broad protection to the states. They retained all powers except those "expressly delegated" to the national government.[8]

When the members of the First Congress debated the Bill of Rights, someone proposed that the Tenth Amendment include the words "expressly delegated." The constitutional language would read: "The powers not expressly delegated to the United States by the Constitution, nor prohibited by it to the States, are reserved to the States respectively, or to the people." Madison objected to the word "expressly" because the functions and duties of the federal government could not be delineated with such precision. It was impossible, he said, to confine a government to the exercise of express or enumerated powers, for there "must necessarily be admitted powers by implication, unless the Constitution descended to recount every minutiae."[9] Madison's argument prevailed. The word "expressly" was deleted.

Another constitutional dispute in the First Congress concerned the President's authority to remove executive officials. The Constitution makes no express mention of that power. From May 19 through June 24, 1789, lawmakers debated the existence of a removal power.[10] Key to that discussion was the President's express duty under Article II to "take Care that the Laws be faithfully executed." What would happen if a department head interfered with the execution

---

3. 17 U.S. (4 Wheat.) at 404.

4. Id.

5. "To make all Laws which shall be necessary and proper for carrying into Execution the foregoing Powers, and all other Powers vested by this Constitution in the Government of the United States, or in any Department or Officer thereof." U.S. Const., art. I, sec. 8, cl. 18.

6. 17 U.S. (4 Wheat.) at 421.

7. The Federalist 322.

8. Merrill Jensen, The Articles of Confederation 263 (1963 ed.) (Article 2).

9. 1 Annals of Cong. 761 (Aug. 18, 1789).

10. A summary of the congressional argument on the President's removal power appears in Louis Fisher, Constitutional Conflicts Between Congress and the President 57–62 (6th ed. 2014).

of law? Could the President remove that individual? As recounted in section 7 of this chapter, Madison led the debate and both houses of Congress agreed that the President possesses an implied power to remove department heads. Interestingly, lawmakers also recognized that certain officials within a department should not serve at the pleasure of the President or take direction from the President. That point is underscored throughout this chapter, especially section 6 on ministerial and discretionary powers.

The issue of implied powers resurfaced in 1791 when Congress decided to create a national bank. The Continental Congress had formed a national bank ten years earlier to deal with the crisis of the Revolutionary War,[11] but delegates at the Philadelphia convention gave little attention to the authority of Congress to create a national bank. While debating a section granting Congress authority to establish post offices and post roads, the delegates discussed the legislative power "to grant charters of incorporation where the interest of the U.S. might require & the legislative provisions of individual States may be incompetent."[12] On September 14, 1787, Rufus King of Massachusetts expressed concern that Congress might use the power to establish a national bank, sparking new tensions between banking interests in Philadelphia and New York. The delegates decided to omit language on incorporation.[13]

When the House debated a national bank in 1791, Madison objected that the power of creating a national bank was not among the enumerated powers listed in Article I. He also said a national bank would interfere with the rights of the states.[14] His colleagues pointed to the inconsistency of his constitutional analysis. Two years earlier he had defended the President's implied power to remove department heads. Why support implied powers for the President but not for Congress?[15] During debate on the Bill of Rights, Madison had argued persuasively that the national government required not merely enumerated powers but implied powers as well.

The bill for a national bank passed the House 39 to 20.[16] The Senate had already supported the measure. President George Washington turned to his Cabinet for advice on whether the bill was constitutional. Attorney General Edmund Randolph and Secretary of State Thomas Jefferson concluded that Congress lacked authority to create a bank.[17] However, Jefferson suggested that congressional judgment in favor of constitutionality could weigh against strict legal reasoning. He advised Washington that if "the pro and con hang so even as to balance his judgment, a just respect for the wisdom of the legislature would naturally decide the balance in favour of their opinion."[18]

Secretary of the Treasury Alexander Hamilton strongly defended the constitutionality of a national bank. When Chief Justice Marshall later upheld the bank in *McCulloch*, he depended

---

11. 20 Journals of the Continental Congress 519, 530–31, 545–48 (Hunt ed., 1912).

12. 2 Farrand 615.

13. Id. at 615–16.

14. 2 Annals of Cong. 1945–52 (1791).

15. Id. at 1960 (remarks of Rep. Sedgwick).

16. Id. at 2012.

17. Walter Dellinger & H. Jefferson Powell, *The Constitutionality of the Bank Bill: The Attorney General's First Constitutional Law Opinions*, 44 Duke L. J. 110 (1994).

18. 19 The Papers of Thomas Jefferson 280 (Boyd, ed., 1974). For Randolph's evaluation, see 31 The Writings of George Washington 215–16 (Fitzpatrick, ed., 1939).

not merely on Hamilton's reasoning about implied powers but his very language. Like Hamilton, Marshall read the Necessary and Proper Clause broadly. Compare the structure and words used by Hamilton in advising Washington: "If the end be clearly comprehended within any of the specified powers, & if the measure have an obvious relation to that end, and is not forbidden by any particular provision of the constitution—it may safely be deemed to come within the compass of the national authority."[19] Marshall's version: "Let the end be legitimate, let it be within the scope of the constitution, and all means which are appropriate, which are plainly adapted to that end, which are not prohibited, but consist with the letter and spirit of the constitution, are constitutional."[20]

Although implied powers were recognized during the debates over the Constitution and in the early years of the national government, judicial rulings continued to describe the Constitution as one of "enumerated powers." In 1821, the Supreme Court decided whether Congress possessed authority to hold individuals in contempt. No such authority is granted in the Constitution. A unanimous Court cautioned: "It is true, that such a power, if it exists, must be derived from implication, and the genius and spirit of our institutions are hostile to the exercise of implied powers."[21] Yet the Court dealt amicably with these hostile forces, admitting that in the Constitution there is not "a grant of powers which does not draw after it others, not expressed, but vital to their exercise."[22] Without the power of contempt, Congress would be "exposed to every indignity and interruption that rudeness, caprice, or even conspiracy, may meditate against it."[23]

Implied powers are regularly acknowledged by federal courts.[24] Nevertheless, the doctrine of "enumerated powers" remains on prominent display. In 1995, while striking down a congressional effort to regulate guns in schoolyards, the Supreme Court announced: "We start with first principles. The Constitution creates a Federal Government of enumerated powers."[25] That is not a first principle. If it were, the Court would not have the power of judicial review to invalidate actions by Congress, the President, and the states. Judicial review is not enumerated in the Constitution. In 1997 the Court again stated: "Under our Constitution, the Federal Government is one of enumerated powers."[26] In supporting the Affordable Care Act in 2012, Chief Justice Roberts made this claim: "If no enumerated power authorizes Congress to pass a certain law, that Law may not be enacted…."[27] Congressional power has never been defined or restricted in that manner. Some powers are enumerated, but the federal government is more than that.

19. 8 The Papers of Alexander Hamilton 107 (Syrett, ed., 1965). For documents on the U.S. Bank: 1 Goldsmith 193–229.

20. McCulloch v. Maryland, 17 U.S. (4 Wheat.) at 421.

21. Anderson v. Dunn, 6 Wheat. (19 U.S.) 204, 225 (1821).

22. Id. at 225–26.

23. Id. at 228. For the implied power of federal courts to hold individuals in contempt, see Michaelson v. United States, 266 U.S. 42 (1924).

24. Inland Waterways Corp. v. Young, 309 U.S. 517, 525 (1940); United States v. Midwest Oil Co., 236 U.S. 459, 475 (1915); Michael J. Glennon, *The Use of Custom in Resolving Separation of Powers Disputes*, 64 Boston U. L. Rev. 109 (1984).

25. United States v. Lopez, 514 U.S. 549, 552 (1995).

26. Boerne v. Flores, 521 U.S. 507, 516 (1997).

27. National Federation of Independent Business v. Sebelius, 567 U.S. ___, ___ (2012).

All three branches have numerous implied powers, provided they are reasonably drawn from enumerated powers.

# 2. THE VESTING CLAUSE

Scholars differ on the breadth of what is called the Vesting Clause. Article II, section 1 begins: "The executive Power shall be vested in a President of the United States of America." Are those powers the ones specifically identified in the Constitution, augmented by implied powers, necessarily drawn from them? Or is the "executive Power" a source of power that goes beyond enumerated and implied powers? Some studies, including by Steven Calabresi and Kevin Rhodes, read the Vesting Clause to empower the President to exercise exclusive control over the executive branch, creating a "Unitary Executive" that cannot be limited by Congress, such as creating statutory limitations on the President's power to remove executive officials.[28]

This doctrine encounters two problems: one historical, the other theoretical. As explained in section 7 of this chapter, the President's removal power was restricted by Congress in 1789 when it created the office of Comptroller in the Treasury Department as an executive official who did not serve at the pleasure of the President, but exercised an independent capacity to ensure the legality of expenditures. Many members of the First Congress were delegates at the Philadelphia convention and had recent experience with and understanding of constitutional principles. A broad reading of the Vesting Clause also has a theoretical hurdle. If the President's power under Article II is subject to no limitations by Congress (or by the judiciary), such a power could recreate part of the executive authority that William Blackstone fashioned for the British king—a system of government the Framers clearly rejected.

Research by Calabresi and Rhodes stimulated a series of articles in 1994 in the *Northwestern University Law Review*.[29] In justifying their conclusions, Calabresi stated that the federal government "is one of limited and enumerated powers (even if some of those enumerated powers sometimes seem pretty sweeping)."[30] But all three branches have access to both enumerated and implied powers.

In a 2001 study, Saikrishna Prakash and Michael Ramsey advocated a "residual" presidential power that incorporates broad executive prerogatives developed by Locke and Blackstone from British practice.[31] Claims of residual power open the door to Blackstone's prerogative that gave the executive exclusive control over external affairs, which the Framers explicitly rejected. The President possesses certain implied powers needed to carry out the enumerated powers of

---

28. Steven G. Calabresi & Kevin H. Rhodes, *The Structural Constitution: Unitary Executive, Plural Judiciary*, 105 HARV. L. REV. 1153 (1992).

29. A. Michael Froomkin, *The Imperial Presidency's New Vestments*, 88 Nw. U. L. REV. 1346 (1994); Steven G. Calabresi, *The Vesting Clauses as Power Grants*, 88 Nw. U. L. REV. 1377 (1994); Kevin H. Rhodes, *A Structure Without Foundation*, 88 Nw. U. L. REV. 1406 (1994); and A. Michael Froomkin, *Still Naked After All These Words*, 88 Nw. U. L. REV. 1420 (1994).

30. Calabresi, *supra* note 29, at 1379.

31. Saikrishna B. Prakash & Michael D. Ramsey, *The Executive Power over Foreign Affairs*, 111 YALE L.J. 231, 234–36, 253–57, 265–72 (2001).

Article II. In a separate study, Ramsey rejected the notion that the President possesses "inherent powers in foreign affairs."[32] Curtis Bradley and Martin Flaherty observed that "there is not a single reference to the Vesting Clause Thesis in all of the records of the Federal Convention." The repeated opposition of most delegates to creating a President that "resembled the British monarch further weighs against the Thesis."[33] Other studies conclude that presidential power must be based not from broad theories of the Vesting Clause but from powers expressly stated and those that may be reasonably drawn as implied powers.[34]

# 3. THE "HEREIN-GRANTED" DEBATE

Propenents of broad presidential power often distinguish between the powers granted by Article I for Congress and Article II for the President. Article I begins: "All legislative Powers herein granted shall be vested in a Congress of the United States...." Was the intent to limit Congress to those powers specifically enumerated? Article II appears to provide greater breadth: "The executive Power shall be vested in a President of the United States of America." What authorities might be included in the "executive power"? The executive power originally granted to the British king? Such a theory runs counter to the text of the Constitution, America's rejection of royal power, and its commitment to republican principles, separation of powers, and checks and balances.

Is it possible to crisply delineate between "legislative powers herein granted" and presidential powers not subject to that limitation? That effort might have some appeal if the Constitution limited the national government—and its three branches—to enumerated powers. But it does not. The Framers clearly rejected that form of government. Notwithstanding the different vesting clauses, Congress, the President, and the judiciary all have access to an array of implied powers.

During oral argument in the Steel Seizure Case of 1952, Holmes Baldridge of the Justice Department advised District Judge David Pine about the difference between Articles I and II, with "herein granted" supposedly providing a narrower grant of power than the Vesting Clause for the President. To Baldridge, it was "obvious that the legislative powers are limited to those specifically enumerated, whereas all executive power, whether or not enumerated, is vested in the Chief Executive. Hence, the executive power is broader." Building on that theory, Baldridge concluded that the President in a time of national emergency possesses whatever power is needed to meet the emergency.[35] Judge Pine was unimpressed with that argument and rejected the claim of inherent and emergency presidential powers. The Supreme Court affirmed his opinion (Chapter 8, section 6).

32. Michael D. Ramsey, *The Myth of Extraconstitutional Foreign Affairs Power*, 42 Wm. & Mary L. Rev. 379, 442 (2001).

33. Curtis A. Bradley & Martin S. Flaherty, *Executive Power Essentialism and Foreign Affairs*, 102 Mich. L. Rev. 545, 592 (2004).

34. Robert J. Reinstein, *The Limits of Executive Power*, 59 Am. U. L. Rev. 259 (2009).

35. H. Doc. No. 534 (Part I), 82d Cong., 2d Sess. 382–83 (1952).

## A. *Pacificus-Helvidius*

One of the first attempts to limit the powers of Congress under Article I and to expand presidential power under Article II was by Alexander Hamilton, writing under the name "Pacificus" in 1793. He came to the defense of President Washington for issuing a proclamation of neutrality in the war between England and France. Critics protested that Washington had overstepped his constitutional authority. Hamilton disagreed, pointing to the broad language of Article II: "the EXECUTIVE POWER shall be vested in a President of the United States of America."[36] Although Article II proceeded to identify specific powers for the President, including the power to nominate and grant pardons, he said it "would not consist with the rules of sound construction, to consider this enumeration of particular authorities as derogating from the more comprehensive grant in the general clause, further than as it may be coupled with express restrictions or limitations."[37]

To Hamilton, Article II vests in the President the full "executive power" subject to certain express limits, such as the power of Congress to override a veto or the requirement that the Senate agree to treaties by a two-thirds vote. He compared the general grant of executive power to what might appear to be narrower authority for Congress: "In the article which gives the legislative powers of the government, the expressions are: 'All legislative powers herein granted shall be vested in a Congress of the United States.' "[38] Hamilton concluded that this language was adopted to limit Congress to the powers specifically enumerated in Article I.

Madison, using the pseudonym "Helvidius," published a number of articles to rebut Hamilton. From what source, he asked, did Hamilton borrow in creating this broad scope of presidential power in foreign affairs? To Madison, there "is but one answer to this question. The power of making treaties and the power of declaring war, are *royal prerogatives* in the *British government*, and are accordingly treated as *executive prerogatives* by British commentators."[39] Madison charged that Hamilton was not analyzing the language of Articles I and II. He was going outside the Constitution to incorporate British doctrines of unchecked executive power.

Madison had some fun by quoting from a published work that defended the draft Constitution. The author of that work said this about the treaty power: "Though several writers on the subject of government placed that power [*of making treaties*] in the class of *executive authorities*, yet this is *evidently* an *arbitrary disposition*. For if we attend *carefully* to its operation, it will be found to partake *more* of the *legislative* than of the *executive* character, though it does not seem strictly to fall within the definition of either of them."[40] The language comes from Federalist No. 75, written by Hamilton. Madison predicted that if Hamilton's broad theory of "executive power" were ever adopted, "no citizen could any longer guess at the character of the government under which he lives; the most penetrating jurist would be unable to scan the extent of constructive prerogative."[41] That point is further developed in sections 4 and 5 of this chapter, dealing with inherent powers and the prerogative.

---

36. 4 THE WORKS OF ALEXANDER HAMILTON 437 (Lodge, ed., 1904).

37. Id. at 438.

38. Id. at 438–39.

39. 6 THE WRITINGS OF JAMES MADISON 150 (Hunt ed., 1900–10) (emphasis in original).

40. Id. at 150–51 (Madison added this emphasis and the bracketed words).

41. Id. at 152.

## B. Roosevelt-Taft models

Some of the flavor of the *Pacificus-Helvidius* debate reappears in the works of Theodore Roosevelt and William Howard Taft. Roosevelt said he regarded himself as "a steward of the people bound actively and affirmatively to do all he could for the people, and not to content himself with the negative merit of keeping his talents undamaged in a napkin."[42] He disagreed with the view that what was "imperatively necessary for the Nation could not be done by the President unless he could find some specific authorization to do it."[43] Roosevelt advanced a highly simplistic and shallow understanding of the Constitution. No President before him felt confined to powers particularly authorized. It was well understood that the Constitution grants the President a combination of express and implied powers, the latter including the power to remove department officials and to withhold from Congress certain documents.[44]

Roosevelt believed "it was not only his right but his duty to do anything that the needs of the Nation demanded unless such action was forbidden by the Constitution or the laws." Under that interpretation, he said, "I did and caused to be done many things not previously done by the President and the heads of the departments."[45] In making that statement, Roosevelt seemed to go outside express and implied powers and claim a broader authority, perhaps some type of prerogative or inherent power. But he offered no examples of exercising executive power in such a bold and ambitious manner. Roosevelt's rhetoric regularly exceeded his performance in office.[46]

Roosevelt created two presidential models: one covering Andrew Jackson and Abraham Lincoln, the other for James Buchanan, who took the "narrowly legalistic view that the President is the servant of Congress rather than of the people, and can do nothing, no matter how necessary it be to act, unless the Constitution explicitly commands the action."[47] No President read the Constitution that narrowly, not even Buchanan.[48] Nevertheless, Roosevelt charged that his successor to the White House, William Howard Taft, "took this, the Buchanan, view of the President's powers and duties."[49] There is nothing to Roosevelt's accusation other than personal spite and animosity. One of Roosevelt's biographers made this observation about his views about Taft in later years: "The violence of Roosevelt's denunciations of the man he had loved and admired approached hysteria."[50] The two models created by Roosevelt marked a self-serving effort to associate himself with Jackson and Lincoln while assigning Taft to the ranks of Buchanan. With a light touch of humor, Taft remarked that the "identification of Mr. Roosevelt with Mr. Lincoln might have otherwise escaped notice, because there are many

---

42. THEODORE ROOSEVELT: AN AUTOBIOGRAPHY 389 (1919).

43. Id.

44. HAROLD J. KRENT, PRESIDENTIAL POWERS 36–48, 173–87 (2005).

45. ROOSEVELT, *supra* note 42, at 389.

46. LEWIS L. GOULD, THE PRESIDENCY OF THEODORE ROOSEVELT 300 (1991) ("Roosevelt accepted the constraints of legality and precedent as necessary conditions of political life during his presidency.").

47. ROOSEVELT, *supra* note 42, at 395.

48. Buchanan took a number of initiatives in foreign policy and in dispatching U.S. troops abroad to protect American interests; ELBERT B. SMITH, THE PRESIDENCY OF JAMES BUCHANAN 68–71 (1975).

49. ROOSEVELT, *supra* note 42, at 395.

50. HENRY F. PRINGLE, THEODORE ROOSEVELT: A BIOGRAPHY 392 (1955).

differences between the two, presumably superficial, which would give the impartial student of history a different impression."[51]

In the Steel Seizure Case of 1952, Holmes Baldridge of the Justice Department described for Judge Pine the "stewardship theory of the Presidency" and how Theodore Roosevelt believed that the President "can do what is imperatively necessary for the good of the nation without specific authorization."[52] Judge Pine repudiated the stewardship model, regarding it as "a theory with which our government of laws and not of men is constantly at war."[53] The Supreme Court also found no merit to the stewardship model (Chapter 8, section 6).

Taft explained in his book that he did not confine himself to powers specifically authorized in statutes or in the Constitution: "the President can exercise no power which cannot be fairly and reasonably traced to some specific grant of power *or justly implied* and included within such express grant as proper and necessary to its exercise."[54] He exercised both enumerated and implied powers. In Taft's judgment, Lincoln's "claim of right to suspend the writ of habeas corpus...was well founded."[55] Executive power, Taft said, "is sometimes created by custom, and so strong is the influence of custom that it seems almost to amend the Constitution."[56] Limits could be placed on executive power "so far as it is possible to limit such a power consistent with that discretion and promptness of action that are essential to preserve the interests of the public in times of emergency, or legislative neglect or inaction."[57] Taft's model is drawn from the Constitution and precedents. Roosevelt's model is intended to inflate his status and denigrate Taft, often with misconceptions and exaggerations.

## C. Contemporary analysis of "herein granted"

Hamilton's reasoning about Article I's "herein granted" language has been adopted by some public officials and legal scholars. John Yoo, during his service with the Justice Department from 2001 to 2003, wrote a series of memos that broadly interpreted presidential power in the field of war-making and foreign affairs. In a memo dated September 25, 2001, he concluded that "any ambiguities in the allocation of a power that is executive in nature—such as the power to conduct military hostilities—must be resolved in favor of the executive branch."[58] The reason: "Article II, section 1 provides that '[t]he executive Power shall be vested in a President of the United States.'"[59] Article I, Yoo noted, "gives Congress only the powers 'herein granted.'"[60] To Yoo, the "difference in language indicates that Congress's legislative powers are limited to the list enumerated in Article I, section 8, while the

---

51. William Howard Taft, Our Chief Magistrate and His Powers 144 (1925, originally published in 1916).

52. H. Doc. No. 534 (Part I), 82d Cong., 2d Sess. 384 (1952).

53. Youngstown Co. v. Sawyer, 103 F. Supp. 569, 575–76 (D.D.C. 1952).

54. Taft, *supra* note 51, at 139–40 (emphasis added).

55. Id. at 147.

56. Id. at 135.

57. Id. at 156.

58. Memorandum opinion from John C. Yoo, Deputy Assistant Attorney General, to Timothy Flanagan, Deputy Counsel to the President, Sept. 25, 2001, at 4; http://www.usdoj.gov/olc/warpowers925.htm.

59. Id.

60. Id.

President's powers include inherent executive powers that are unenumerated in the Constitution."[61] Yoo relied on Hamilton for his analysis.[62]

Congress is not limited to the powers enumerated in Article I, section 8. It has a range of powers that are implied in its express duty to legislate. To legislate in an informed manner and to oversee the laws that are enacted, it has the implied powers to investigate, to issue subpoenas, and to hold individuals in contempt.[63] With regard to Yoo's dependence on "inherent" powers for the President, that subject is analyzed in section 4 of this chapter.

In their writings on the "unitary executive," Steven Calabresi and Christopher Yoo similarly read Article II expansively while pointing to the supposedly more restrictive "herein granted" language in Article I. They note that Hamilton's principal thesis is that the "executive power" of the nation is vested in the President, "subject only to the *exceptions* and *qualifications* which are expressed in the instrument."[64] Hamilton, they say, "bolstered" his analysis by comparing the Vesting Clauses of Article I and II, with Congress receiving powers "herein granted" and the President the "executive power." They add that this construction of Article II is made "all the more authoritative" by Hamilton's observation: "this mode of construing the Constitution has indeed been recognized by Congress in formal acts upon full consideration and debate; of which *the power of removal from office is an important instance.*"[65]

Hamilton confused two concepts. The President's authority to remove Cabinet heads is an *implied* power, reasonably drawn from the President's express power to see that the laws are faithfully carried out. If the head of a department is unwilling or unable to carry out a law, the President needs power to remove that individual and put in place someone capable of honoring both the statute and the Constitution. Furthermore, the President's removal power is limited and Madison recognized those limits, as explained in section 7 of this chapter. Section 6, which discusses the difference between ministerial and discretionary duties in the executive branch, makes clear that the rule of law places definite limits on a President's constitutional authority to interfere with or in any way direct the decisions reached by subordinates within executive departments and agencies. Those limits have been recognized both by federal courts and by Attorneys General.

In recent years, Congress has debated a bill called the Enumerated Powers Act. It is actually something else. The bill would merely require that each statute of Congress "shall contain a concise explanation of the specific constitutional authority relied upon for the enactment of each portion of that Act."[66] The bill is not confined to express or enumerated authority but rather to "specific constitutional authority." That phrase could include something as broad as the Necessary and Proper Clause, the Commerce Clause, or the taxing power. It could include a

61. Id.

62. Regarding Yoo's analysis of Hamilton, see David Gray Adler, *Presidential Power and Foreign Affairs in the Bush Administration: The Use and Abuse of Alexander Hamilton*, 41 PRES. STUD. Q. 531 (2010), and Louis Fisher, *John Yoo and the Republic*, 41 PRES. STUD. Q. 177 (2011).

63. MORTON ROSENBERG, WHEN CONGRESS COMES CALLING: A PRIMER ON THE PRINCIPLES, PRACTICES, AND PRAGMATICS OF LEGISLATIVE INQUIRY (2009).

64. STEVEN G. CALABRESI & CHRISTOPHER S. YOO, THE UNITARY EXECUTIVE: PRESIDENTIAL POWER FROM WASHINGTON TO BUSH 55 (2008) (emphasis in original).

65. Id. (emphasis added by Calabresi and Yoo).

66. S. 1319, 111th Cong., 1st Sess. (2009), sec. 2 (§ 102a).

range of implied powers, such as the implied congressional power to investigate, issue subpoenas, and hold witnesses in contempt.

On January 5, 2011, the House of Representatives adopted a rule (Clause 7 of Rule XII) that requires members, when introducing a bill or joint resolution, to indicate how their legislation is justified by specific powers granted to the Congress in the Constitution. Members vary in the details included in their "Constitutional Authority Statement." In introducing H.R. 603 in 2011, Rep. Gregg Harper provided this information: "Congress has the power to enact this legislation pursuant to the following: Article I, Section 8, Clauses 1 and 3 of the Constitution of the United States."[67] A statement by Rep. Erik Paulsen in introducing H.R. 605 that year was even briefer: "Congress has the power to enact this legislation pursuant to the following: Article I, Section 8."[68]

In supporting the Enumerated Powers Act, Senator Orrin Hatch stated that Article I gives Congress "only 'legislative powers herein granted.' Those powers are listed, or enumerated, in article I, section 8."[69] However, Congress also has powers that are implied. Hatch continued: "The 10th amendment affirms that the Federal Government has only powers that are affirmatively delegated to it."[70] That is a misconception, suggesting that the national government is limited to powers expressly delegated to it. The word "expressly" does not appear in the Tenth Amendment. Hatch further noted: "James Madison agreed in Federalist No. 45 that the powers delegated to the Federal Government are 'few and defined.'"[71] In using those words, Madison never meant that Congress was restricted to enumerated powers. As explained in the section on implied power at the start of this chapter, Madison vigorously denied in the *Federalist Papers* and in the debates on the Tenth Amendment that a government could be limited to powers expressly identified. To survive and function, all three branches of government require implied powers.

# 4. INHERENT POWERS

Scholars at times refer to "inherent" presidential power when the more accurate word is *implied*. For example, in a study on treaties and international agreements, Oona Hathaway stated that the President "has the power to make international agreements entirely on his own inherent constitutional authority. Yet that power is not unlimited."[72] The limits, she explained, are not supplied

---

67. 157 Cong. Rec. H681 (daily ed., Feb. 10, 2011). Clause 1 provides: "The Congress shall have Power to lay and collect Taxes, Duties, Impost and Excises, to pay the Debts and provide for the common Defence and general Welfare of the United States; but all Duties, Imposts and Excises shall be uniform throughout the United States." Clause 3 provides: "To regulate Commerce with foreign Nations, and among the several States, and with the Indian Tribes."

68. Id. Section 8 consists of 18 clauses, covering domestic and military powers and ending with the Necessary and Proper Clause. See Kenneth R. Thomas, *Sources of Constitutional Authority and House Rule XII, Clause 7(c)*, CRS Report R41548, Jan. 18, 2011.

69. 155 Cong. Rec. S9548 (daily ed., Sept. 17, 2009).

70. Id.

71. Id.

72. Oona A. Hathaway, *Presidential Power over International Law: Restoring the Balance*, 119 Yale L.J. 140, 210 (2009).

by international law but by domestic law, and in the United States "the central source to which we must turn is the U.S. Constitution, which is the source of both the President's unilateral international lawmaking authority and the limits thereon."[73] In other words, the authority is a mix of express and implied powers, not inherent, which as invoked by Presidents and their advisers means powers not subject to checks by the legislative and judicial branches.

A study by Jack Goldsmith and John Manning explored the President's "completion" power. They state that "each of the three branches has some degree of inherent power to carry into execution the powers conferred upon it."[74] They correctly note that President Truman "relied not on express statutory authority" to seize the steel mills in 1952, "but rather on inherent executive authority emanating from the Clause vesting 'the executive Power' in the President, the Commander in Chief Clause, and the Clause enjoining the President to 'take Care that the Laws be faithfully executed.' "[75] Expressed in that manner, it seems that Truman pointed to enumerated and implied powers, but in fact he went beyond those sources and claimed inherent powers not subject to the control of the other branches. As explained in this section and in Chapter 8, section 6, he lost that constitutional argument because it represented a direct attack on the concept of limited government and the American system of checks and balances.

When read in full, the article by Goldsmith and Manning does not argue for inherent presidential power. Instead, they refer to powers expressly stated (the Commander in Chief Clause, the Take Care Clause, and the Executive Vesting Clause) plus powers that are "reasonably incidental" to a statutory command[76]—that is, a mix of express and implied powers. Importantly (and contrary to those who claim inherent presidential power), the type of power they describe "does not permit the President to act *contra legem*."[77] They find much of merit in the dissent by Chief Justice Vinson in the Steel Seizure Case, but Vinson did not advocate inherent presidential power. He defended Truman on the basis of legislatively approved policies, treaty obligations (the UN Charter), and military appropriations.[78]

An express commitment to inherent presidential power comes from John Yoo, who during his service in the Justice Department supported "inherent executive powers that are unenumerated in the Constitution."[79] Some scholars treat implied powers and inherent powers as the same.[80] They are quite different. Implied powers are drawn reasonably from express powers. They are therefore anchored in the Constitution. Inherent powers, by definition, are not drawn from express powers. As the word suggests, these powers "inhere" in a person or an office. *Black's Law Dictionary* has defined inherent power in this manner: "An authority possessed without its being derived from another.... [P]owers over and beyond those explicitly granted in the

73. Id. at 210–11.

74. Jack Goldsmith & John F. Manning, *The President's Completion Power*, 115 Yale L.J. 2280, 2282 (2006).

75. Id. at 2283.

76. Id. at 2302, 2308.

77. Id. at 2309.

78. Id. at 2284.

79. Yoo, *supra* note 58, at 4.

80. Calabresi & Yoo, *supra* note 64, at 20, 430. In *The President's Completion Power*, 115 Yale L.J. 2280, 2282 (2006), Jack Goldsmith and John F. Manning state: "each of the three branches has some degree of inherent power to carry into execution the powers conferred upon it." More precisely: Each of the three branches has certain *implied* powers.

Constitution or reasonably to be implied from express grants."[81] As a concept, inherent power is clearly set apart from express and implied powers.

The Constitution is protected when Presidents act under express and implied powers. It is in danger when they claim inherent powers. John Yoo consistently treats inherent powers as so central to presidential power and national security that they cannot be limited by statutes or treaties. According to his analysis, any power "that is executive in nature" must be vested solely in the executive branch.[82] The President, he argues, possesses "complete discretion in exercising the Commander-in-Chief power."[83] Congress's power to declare war "does not constrain the President's independent and plenary constitutional authority over the use of military force."[84] The President exercises "plenary authority in foreign affairs."[85] Congress may not by statute "place any limits on the President's determinations as to any terrorist threat, the amount of military force to be used in response, or the method, timing, and nature of the response. These decisions, under our Constitution, are for the President alone to make."[86] The scope and limits of the Commander in Chief Clause are analyzed in Chapter 8.

A constitution safeguards individual rights and liberties by specifying and limiting government. Express and implied powers serve that purpose. Inherent powers invite claims of power that have no limits, other than those voluntarily accepted by the President. What "inheres" in the President? The word "inherent" is sometimes cross-referenced to "intrinsic," which can be something "belonging to the essential nature or construction of a thing."[87] What is in the "nature" of a political office? Nebulous words and concepts invite political abuse and unconstitutional actions. They threaten individual liberties. Presidents who assert inherent powers move the nation from one of limited powers to boundless and ill-defined authority, undermining republican government, the doctrine of separation of powers, and the system of checks and balances.[88] When this type of authority is asserted, as Madison noted in his *Helvidius* article, "no citizen could any longer guess at the character of the government under which he lives; the most penetrating jurist would be unable to scan the extent of constructive prerogative."[89]

Presidents have at times declined to exercise powers that are not expressly granted or reasonably implied. In 1851, President Fillmore was asked by the marshal of the southern district of New York to provide him with counsel "at the public expense to advise, protect, and defend him" in cases arising under the Fugitive Slave Law. Attorney General Crittenden advised Fillmore "to forbear from interference with the functions of subordinate public officers, and to leave them to the discharge of their proper duties under all their legal responsibilities, and subject also, to removal from office for every neglect or abuse of their official trust." This principle of non-intervention did not apply to "employment of counsel in cases to which the United

81. BLACK'S LAW DICTIONARY 703 (5th ed., 1979).

82. Yoo, *supra* note 58, at 4.

83. Id. at 2.

84. Id. at 3.

85. Id. at 5.

86. Id. at 16.

87. MERRIAM-WEBSTER'S COLLEGIATE DICTIONARY 614 (10th ed., 1965).

88. Louis Fisher, *The Unitary Executive and Inherent Executive Power*, 12 U. PA. J. CONST. L. 569, 586–90 (2010); Louis Fisher, *Invoking Inherent Powers: A Primer*, 37 PRES. STUD. Q. 1 (2007).

89. Madison, *supra* note 41.

States are parties." To Crittenden, the cases alluded to by the New York marshal "are not of that description." He concluded that "in this instance, you have no proper authority to comply with the request made by the marshal, and that it would be inexpedient, also, to do so."[90]

A different result occurred in 1890, when the Supreme Court supported President Benjamin Harrison's assignment of David Neagle, a U.S. deputy marshal, to ride circuit to offer protection to Justice Stephen Field.[91] Field's life had been threatened by two people he had sent to jail, David and Sarah Terry. One morning during breakfast, David Terry assaulted Field. Neagle, after identifying himself as a public officer, shot and killed Terry. Attorneys defending Neagle acknowledged that no specific statute made it a duty to furnish protection to a Supreme Court Justice, but argued that whatever was "necessarily implied is as much a part of the Constitution and statutes as if it were actually expressed therein."[92] The Court, divided 6 to 2, agreed: "In the view we take of the Constitution of the United States, any obligation fairly and properly inferrible from that instrument, or any duty of the marshal to be derived from the general scope of his duties under the laws of the United States, is 'a law' within the meaning of this phrase."[93]

Two Justices dissented. They agreed with the proposition that "whatever is necessarily implied in the Constitution and laws of the United States is as much a part of them as if they were actually expressed."[94] But the implied powers they recognized were in Article I under the Necessary and Proper Clause. Finding no such law passed by Congress specifically authorizing the President's decision, and therefore no power of the national government to try a man charged with murder, they would have had Neagle placed in the custody of the sheriff of San Joaquin, California, to be tried in the courts of that state.[95]

In 1895, a unanimous Court upheld the decision of President Grover Cleveland to send troops to Chicago to break a railroad strike. The railroads were under contract to carry, and did carry, the mails of the United States. Cleveland did not exercise inherent power. Instead, he acted under the implied power of the national government to protect its enumerated interests. At issue for the Court was whether the responsibility of the federal government over interstate commerce and the transportation of the mails authorized direct action to prevent obstruction.[96] In describing the system of federalism that divides political power between the nation and the states, the Court claimed that the nation "is properly styled a government of enumerated powers."[97] Implied powers had been recognized for more than a century, but here again is a fixation on enumerated powers for the national government. Still, the Court reasoned: "within the limits of such enumeration it has all the attributes of sovereignty, and, in the exercise of those enumerated powers, acts directly upon the citizen, and not through the intermediate agency of the State."[98]

90. 5 OP. ATT'Y GEN. 287, 288 (1851).

91. HOMER E. SOCOLOFSKY & ALLAN N. SPETTER, THE PRESIDENCY OF BENJAMIN HARRISON 186–87 (1987); HARRY J. SIEVERS, BENJAMIN HARRISON: HOOSIER PRESIDENT 93–101 (1968).

92. In re Neagle, 135 U.S. 1, 27 (1890).

93. Id. at 59.

94. Id. at 77–78 (Lamar, J. and Fuller, C.J., dissenting).

95. Id. at 80–81, 83, 99.

96. In re Debs, 158 U.S. 564, 577 (1895).

97. Id. at 578.

98. Id.

The Court agreed with previous rulings that the national government possessed authority to use physical force to carry out the powers belonging to it.[99] Among those powers are the control of interstate commerce and the creation of a post office system for the nation. In exercising those powers, Congress had passed many legislative acts, including the operation of interstate railroads.[100] The Court had no doubt that the national government could prevent any unlawful and forcible interference with interstate commerce and the mails. Those who interfered could be prosecuted in the courts. The Court asked: "But is that the only remedy?" If it were, states could regularly frustrate legitimate national interests.[101] The Court refused to see such "impotency" on the part of the national government laws.[102]

Several Presidents have claimed the right to exercise inherent powers. On each occasion they were rebuffed by Congress, the courts, or both: Truman trying to seize steel mills in 1952 to prosecute the war in Korea (Chapter 8, section 6), Nixon impounding appropriated funds (Chapter 6, section 6), Nixon conducting warrantless domestic surveillance (next paragraph), and Bush after the 9/11 terrorist attacks creating military tribunals without first obtaining authority from Congress (Chapter 9, section 8C).

On June 5, 1970, President Nixon met with the heads of several intelligence agencies, including the National Security Agency (NSA), to initiate a program designed to monitor what the administration considered radical individuals and groups in the United States. Joining others at the meeting was Tom Charles Huston, a young attorney working at the White House. He drafted a 43-page top-secret memorandum that became known as the Huston Plan. Huston put the matter bluntly to Nixon: "Use of this technique is clearly illegal; it amounts to burglary."[103] His plan directed NSA to use its technological capacity to intercept—without judicial warrant—the communications of U.S. citizens using international phone calls or telegrams.[104]

Although Nixon, under pressure from FBI Director J. Edgar Hoover, withdrew the Huston Plan, NSA had been targeting domestic groups for several years and continued to do so. Huston's blueprint, kept in a White House safe, became public in 1973, after Congress investigated the Watergate affair, and provided documentary evidence that Nixon has ordered NSA to illegally monitor American citizens. To conduct its surveillance operations, NSA entered into agreements with U.S. companies, including Western Union and RCA Global. U.S. citizens, expecting that their telegrams would be handled with utmost privacy, learned that American companies had been turning over telegrams to NSA.[105]

In 1971, a district court expressly dismissed the claim of a broad "inherent" presidential power to conduct domestic surveillances without a warrant.[106] The Sixth Circuit affirmed, unimpressed by the government's sweeping argument that the power at issue "is the inherent power of the President to safeguard the security of the nation."[107] Unanimously, the Supreme Court

---

99. Id. at 578–79.

100. Id. at 579–80.

101. Id. at 581–82.

102. Id. at 582.

103. Keith W. Olson, Watergate: The Presidential Scandal That Shook America 16 (2003).

104. James Bamford, Body of Secrets: Anatomy of the Ultra-Secret National Security Agency 430 (2002).

105. Id. at 431–39.

106. United States v. Sinclair, 321 F. Supp. 1074, 1077 (E.D. Mich. 1971).

107. United States v. United States Dist. Ct. for E.D. of Mich., 444 F.2d 651, 658 (6th Cir. 1971).

affirmed the Sixth Circuit and held that the Fourth Amendment required prior judicial approval for surveillances of domestic organizations.[108] The executive branch asserted that the surveillance "was lawful, though conducted without prior judicial approval, as a reasonable exercise of the President's power (exercised through the Attorney General) to protect the national security."[109] A unanimous Court disagreed. Fourth Amendment freedoms "cannot properly be guaranteed if domestic security surveillances may be conducted solely within the discretion of the Executive Branch." The Fourth Amendment "does not contemplate the executive officers of Government as neutral and disinterested magistrates."[110]

Following these decisions, Congress passed legislation to provide statutory guidelines for the President's power to conduct surveillance over foreign powers. The result was the Foreign Intelligence Surveillance Act (FISA) of 1978.[111] In congressional hearings, Attorney General Edward H. Levi testified in support of legislation that would require "independent review at a critical point by a detached and neutral magistrate."[112] The theory of independent and inherent presidential power would be replaced by a judicial check. FISA established a special court, the Foreign Intelligence Surveillance Court (FISC) to ensure outside supervision on the exercise of executive power. FISA made clear that the statutory procedures for electronic surveillance within the United States for intelligence purposes "shall be the exclusive means" for conducting such surveillance.[113]

# 5. PREROGATIVE POWERS

Inherent power is at times identified with the prerogative power. They have very different meanings. Under inherent power, the President claims authority to act independently without any interference from the other branches. Prerogative accepts that the executive may take the initiative, but only with the understanding that the legislative branch must act later: approving or modifying the executive's decision or even punishing and removing the executive for illegal and unconstitutional conduct. In exercising the prerogative, the President recognizes that he is not acting under the law.

In 1690, John Locke defined prerogative as the power of the executive "to act according to discretion for the public good, without the prescription of the law and sometimes even against it."[114] William Blackstone, writing in 1765, regarded the king's prerogative as "those rights and

---

108. United States v. United States District Court, 407 U.S. 297 (1972).

109. Id. at 301.

110. Id. at 317.

111. 92 Stat. 1788 (1978).

112. *Electronic Surveillance Within the United States for Foreign Intelligence Purposes*, hearings before the Subcommittee on Intelligence and the Rights of Americans of the Senate Committee on Intelligence, 94th Cong., 2d Sess. 76 (1976).

113. 92 Stat. 1788, 1797, sec. 201(f) (1978).

114. John Locke, Second Treatise of Civil Government § 160 (1690). See Thomas S. Langston & Michael E. Lind, *John Locke & the Limits of Presidential Prerogative*, 24 Polity 49 (1991); Larry Arnhart, "*The God-Like Prince*": *John Locke Executive Prerogative, and the American Presidency*, 9 Pres. Stud. Q. 121 (1979).

capacities which the king enjoys alone."[115] At the Philadelphia convention, the delegates recognized that the President was authorized to "repel sudden attacks," especially when Congress was not in session to take legislative action.[116] There are no grounds, however, for believing that the Framers embraced the British model of Locke and Blackstone, who put *all* of external affairs with the executive (Chapters 7 and 8).

Presidents have at times gone beyond express and implied powers to unilaterally announce and decide national policy. Generally they discover they need legislative support, either by statute or by treaty. An early example is the neutrality proclamation issued by President Washington in 1793. As explained in section 11B of this chapter, he was embarrassed to discover that his initiative was ineffective in prosecuting those who failed to comply with the proclamation. The reason: jurors refused to find defendants guilty because he lacked statutory authority, a deficiency he proceeded to remedy by requesting what became the Neutrality Act of 1794. President Jefferson exercised the prerogative when he decided to go beyond the instructions of Congress in purchasing territory from France. After receiving legislative authority to pay as much as $10 million for New Orleans and the Floridas, he learned that Napoleon Bonaparte was willing to sell all of Louisiana because he needed money to fight Great Britain. On April 30, 1803, France ceded the vast territory of Louisiana for $15,000,000. The Senate approved the Louisiana treaties and the United States took possession of 828,000 square miles, doubling the size of the nation.[117]

Jefferson recognized that he lacked authority to act as he did. He wondered whether a constitutional amendment might be required.[118] Instead of fabricating a strained constitutional theory to justify his action, he asked Congress for support, which it granted. Particularly because of the "constitutional difficulty," he thought it might be best for Congress to engage in "as little debate as possible."[119] To his Attorney General, Levi Lincoln, Jefferson decided that a constitutional amendment was not necessary or advisable: "the less that is said about any constitutional difficulty, the better; and that it will be desirable for Congress to do what is necessary, *in silence*."[120]

For certain military actions, Jefferson believed he had authority to act first in defensive operations and seek congressional approval later. After Congress recessed in 1807, a British

115. WILLIAM BLACKSTONE, COMMENTARIES ON THE LAWS OF ENGLAND 232 (1765). Also on the prerogative: Richard M. Pious, *Franklin D. Roosevelt and the Destroyer Deal: Normalizing Prerogative Power*, 42 PRES. STUD. Q. 190 (2012); George Thomas, *As Far as Republican Principles Will Admit: Presidential Prerogative and Constitutional Government*, 30 PRES. STUD. Q. 534 (2000); Henry P. Monaghan, *The Protective Power of the Presidency*, 93 COLUM. LAW REV. 1 (1993); Robert Scigliano, *The President's "Prerogative Power*," in INVENTING THE AMERICAN PRESIDENCY, at 236–56 (Thomas E. Cronin, ed., 1989); Robert L. Borosage, *Para-Legal Authority and Its Perils*, 40 LAW & CONTEMP. PROB. 166 (1976); James R. Hurtgen, *The Case for Presidential Prerogative*, 7 U. TOLEDO L. REV. 59 (1975); Lucius Wilmerding, *The President and the Law*, 67 POL. SCI. Q. 321 (1952).

116. 2 Farrand 318.

117. ALEXANDER DECONDE, THIS AFFAIR OF LOUISIANA (1976); MARSHALL SPRAGUE, SO VAST SO BEAUTIFUL A LAND: LOUISIANA AND THE PURCHASE (1974). Also: Richard J. Daugherty, *Thomas Jefferson and the Rule of Law: Executive Power and American Constitutionalism*, 28 N. KY. L. REV. 513 (2001); Barry J. Balleck, *When the Ends Justify the Means: Thomas Jefferson and the Louisiana Purchase*, 22 PRES. STUD. Q. 679 (1992); and Eberhard P. Deutsch, *The Constitutional Controversy Over the Louisiana Purchase*, 53 AM. BAR ASS'N J. 50 (1967).

118. 10 THE WRITINGS OF THOMAS JEFFERSON 410–11 (Bergh ed., 1903); letter from Jefferson to John Breckinridge, Aug. 12, 1803.

119. Id. at 418; letter from Jefferson to Wilson C. Nicholas, Sept. 7, 1803.

120. Id. at 417; letter dated Aug. 30, 1803 (emphasis in original). For documents on Louisiana Purchase:1 Goldsmith 438–50.

vessel fired on the American ship *Chesapeake*. Without specific appropriations for that purpose, Jefferson ordered military purchases for the emergency and reported to Congress after it convened. "To have awaited a previous and special sanction by law," he said, "would have lost occasions which might not be retrieved."[121] Objections were raised by some lawmakers, but Congress voted overwhelmingly to support Jefferson's initiative.[122]

After leaving the presidency, Jefferson wrote to John B. Colvin on September 20, 1810, responding to the question whether "circumstances do not sometimes occur, which make it a duty in officers of high trust, to assume authorities beyond the law."[123] Jefferson warned that the question "is easy of solution in principle, but sometimes embarrassing in practice."[124] He explained: "A strict observance of the written laws is doubtless *one* of the high duties of a good citizen, but it is not *the highest*. The laws of necessity, of self-preservation, of saving our country when in danger, are of higher obligation. To lose our country by a scrupulous adherence to written law, would be to lose the law itself, with life, liberty, property and all those who are enjoying them with us; thus absurdly sacrificing the end to the means."[125]

Jefferson cautioned Colvin about legal and political hazards. A President who acts outside the law "does indeed risk himself on the justice of the controlling powers of the constitution, and his station makes it his duty to incur that risk."[126] Jefferson did not invite "persons charged with petty duties" to exercise the prerogative. Political risks are reserved to higher authorities.[127] The prerogative is thus limited by a crucial check: the executive needs to seek and obtain legislative authority.

Nothing in Jefferson's career in public office reveals a careless or cavalier attitude about the law. His service as Secretary of State in the Washington administration and his eight years as President demonstrate a conscientious effort to ensure the responsible exercise of executive power.[128] Examples are offered in Chapter 8 with regard to military actions against the Barbary pirates and possible conflict with Spain. On each occasion he recognized that the institution authorized to take the country from a state of peace to a state of war was Congress, not the President.

President James Monroe exercised a form of prerogative in 1823 by issuing what became known as the "Monroe Doctrine." It declared the "new world" of the Americas to be off-limits to any attempts by foreign powers to exert their control over neighboring countries. His message to Congress on December 2, 1823, stated that the "American continents" are "henceforth not to be considered as subjects for future colonization by any European powers."[129] Congress could

---

121. 1 Richardson 377.

122. Abraham D. Sofaer, War, Foreign Affairs and Constitutional Power: The Origins, at 172–73 (1976).

123. 5 The Writings of Thomas Jefferson 542 (Washington ed., 1861).

124. Id.

125. Id. (emphasis in original).

126. Id. at 544.

127. Id. See Jeremy David Bailey, *Executive Prerogative and the "Good Officer" in Thomas Jefferson's Letter to John B. Colvin*, 34 Pres. Stud. Q. 732 (2004).

128. Gary J. Schmitt, *Thomas Jefferson and the Presidency*, Inventing the American Presidency, 326–46 (Thomas E. Cronin, ed., 1989); Caleb Perry Patterson, The Constitutional Principles of Thomas Jefferson (1953).

129. Michael Nelson, ed., The Evolving Presidency: Landmark Documents, 1787–2010, at 75–79 (4th ed., 2010).

have modified or reversed his doctrine, but Monroe captured a position widely accepted by law-makers and citizens. In 1904, President Theodore Roosevelt warned that nations in the Western Hemisphere need not fear U.S. interference in their internal affairs, provided that they act with "reasonable efficiency and decency in social and political matters ... [and] if it keeps order and pays its obligations...."[130] Implied in his announcement was that the United States might feel compelled to intervene militarily when mismanagement prevents nations from meeting their foreign and financial obligations. This policy became known as the "Roosevelt Corollary" to the Monroe Doctrine.[131]

Presidents have frequently intervened in the Caribbean, Central America, and South America by using military force to pursue U.S. interests: Panama in 1903; the Dominican Republic in 1904; Taft's interventions in Nicaragua, Honduras, and Cuba; Wilson in Veracruz, the Dominican Republic, and Haiti; Kennedy in Cuba; Reagan in Nicaragua and Grenada; Bush I in Panama; and Clinton in Haiti.[132]

President Barack Obama has referred to the term "prerogative" to defend what he considered to be his constitutional authority, but his remarks misuse the word. In an April 15, 2011, signing statement, he raised objections to a bill that defunded certain "czar" positions.[133] He spoke of the President's "well-established authority to supervise and oversee the executive branch" and the President's "prerogative to obtain advice that will assist him in carrying out his constitu-tional responsibilities."[134] Yes, the President has authority to supervise the executive branch and obtain advice, but he has no authority to create and fund White House positions. That authority belongs to Congress, which can increase and decrease the number of White House officials and increase or decrease their salaries.[135] His signing statement claimed that the statutory restric-tions "violate the separation of powers by undermining the President's ability to exercise his constitutional responsibilities and take care that the laws be faithfully executed."[136] The statute did not violate separation of powers. Congress acted within its constitutional authority to decide how many aides a President may have and how much they will be paid. Obama referred to a prerogative that did not exist. The only advice a President is entitled to, without limit, is advice from individuals in the private sector.

# 6. MINISTERIAL AND DISCRETIONARY POWERS

*Marbury v. Madison* (1803) is incorrectly praised for the doctrine of judicial supremacy. The author of that opinion, Chief Justice John Marshall, did not believe that judicial rulings were

---

130. 14 Richardson 6923.

131. Louis Fisher, Presidential War Power 57–60 (3d ed., 2013).

132. Id. at 58–62, 124–26, 161–63, 165–68, 178–81, 280–82.

133. Mitchel A. Sollenberger & Mark J. Rozell, The President's Czars: Undermining Congress and the Constitution 170–72 (2012).

134. Statement by the President on H.R. 1473; http://www.whitehouse.gov/the-press-office/2011/04/15/statement-president-hr-1473.

135. 3 U.S.C. § 105; 92 Stat. 2445 (1978).

136. *Supra* note 134.

necessarily preeminent over the other branches and controlling on them. He knew that any effort by him to order President Jefferson or Secretary of State Madison to deliver the disputed commission to William Marbury would have been ignored. The legal and political issues of *Marbury* are covered in Chapter 9, section 1. Of interest here is the valuable distinction that Marshall drew between ministerial and discretionary duties.

Marshall explained that the heads of executive departments function in part as political agents of the President. At the same time, they receive legal duties assigned to them by Congress. Focusing on the Secretary of State, Marshall said the office exercised two types of duties: ministerial and discretionary. The first duty extends to the nation and the law. By statutory command, Congress may direct executive officers to carry out certain activities. When a Secretary of State performs "as an officer of the United States," he or she is "bound to obey the laws."[137] Functioning in that capacity, the Secretary acts "under the authority of law, and not by the instructions of the president. It is a ministerial act which the law enjoins on a particular officer for a particular purpose."[138]

Marshall recognized that the President under the Constitution "is invested with certain important political powers, in the exercise of which he is to use his own discretion, and is accountable only to his country in his political character and to his own conscience."[139] To assist him in the performance of those duties, "he is authorized to appoint certain officers, who act by his authority, and in conformity with his orders."[140] In such cases, "their acts are his acts; and whatever opinion may be entertained of the manner in which executive discretion may be used, still there exists, and can exist, no power to control that discretion. The subjects are political. They respect the nation, not individual rights, and being intrusted to the executive, the decision of the executive is conclusive.... The acts of such an officer, as an officer, can never be examinable by the courts."[141]

At times the Secretary of State conforms to the President's will. On other occasions Congress by statute may direct the Secretary of State to carry out specified ministerial acts. Marshall underscored that point: "But when the legislature proceeds to impose on that officer other duties; when he is directed peremptorily to perform certain acts; when the rights of individuals are dependent on the performance of those acts; he is so far the officer of the law; is amenable to the laws for his conduct; and cannot, at his discretion sport away the vested rights of others."[142]

## A. Attorney General opinions

The distinction between ministerial/legal and discretionary/political has been the subject of many opinions issued by Attorneys General and federal courts. In 1823, Attorney General William Wirt analyzed for President James Monroe the extent of his control over agency accounting officers. The laws regulating the settlement of public accounts required Auditors in the Treasury Department to

---

137. Marbury v. Madison, 5 U.S. (1 Cr.) 137, 157 (1803).

138. Id.

139. Id. at 165.

140. Id.

141. Id.

142. Id. at 165–66.

receive and examine accounts and certify them to the Comptrollers, who then examined and passed judgment on them. Although the Constitution requires the President to "take Care that the Laws be faithfully executed," he is not expected to execute each law by himself. If officers under his supervision fail to carry out their duties, the President needs to see that they are "displaced, prosecuted, or impeached."[143] It "could never have been the intention of the constitution, in assigning this general power to the President to take care that the laws be executed, that he should in person execute the laws himself." Such a burden would be "an impossibility."[144]

It is not the President's duty to audit public accounts. If Auditors and Comptrollers "continue to discharge their duties faithfully," Wirt advised Monroe, "the President has no authority to interfere."[145] Any person dissatisfied with the Comptroller's decision may, under law, appeal within six months. At that point "the right of appeal stops; there is no proviso for an appeal to the President."[146] Wirt reminded Monroe of his constitutional duties over foreign and domestic relations, as Commander in Chief, exercise of the pardon power, and handling appointments, including the filling of vacancies during a Senate recess.[147] How could the President perform those duties, and others, "if he is also to exercise the appellate power of revising and correcting the settlement of all the individual accounts which pass through the hands of the accounting officers?"[148]

Over the next few years, Wirt had frequent occasion to instruct Monroe that he had no business being involved in the settlement of accounts.[149] Interference by the President "in any form would, in my opinion, be illegal."[150] It "would be an unauthorized assumption of authority for you to interfere in the case in any manner whatever."[151] Two more opinions by Wirt in 1825 drove home the same point.[152] In 1831, Attorney General Roger Taney advised President Andrew Jackson that a dispute over the decision of the Treasury Department about a government contractor had to be left to Congress. An appeal could not be submitted "to the President. The power to give relief resides in Congress; and to them, in my opinion, the application must be made."[153]

Attorney General John Mason offered similar advice to President James Polk in 1846. An appeal had been forwarded to the President following a decision by the Commissioner of Pensions, later approved by the Secretary of War. The Constitution, Mason said, "assigns to Congress the power of designating the duties of particular subordinate officers," and the power of removal does not include "the power of correcting, by his own official act, the errors of judgment

143.  1 Op. Att'y Gen. 624, 625 (1823).

144.  Id.

145.  Id. at 624.

146.  Id. at 627.

147.  Id. at 628.

148.  Id. at 629.

149.  1 Op. Att'y Gen. 636 (1824).

150.  1 Op. Att'y Gen. 678, 680 (1824).

151.  Id. at 681.

152.  1 Op. Att'y Gen. 705, 706 (1825).

153.  2 Op. Att'y Gen. 480, 482 (1831). For similar opinions by Taney, see 2 Op. Att'y Gen. 507 (1832); 2 Op. Att'y Gen. 544 (1832).

of incompetent or unfaithful subordinates."[154] Moreover, the President could not discharge "the high constitutional duties of the President" if he were to "undertake to review the decisions of subordinates on the weight or effect of evidence in cases appropriately belonging to them."[155] If someone wanted to appeal a decision of the Commissioner, they were entitled to "apply for relief to Congress, whose power cannot be doubted."[156]

In 1850, Attorney General John Crittenden advised President Millard Fillmore that a decision by the Comptroller of the Treasury on a claim was "final and conclusive" on all branches of the executive government. Presidents had no business exercising an appellate jurisdiction in the settlement of claims. Their duties were of a higher order: "*the settlement & adjustment of accounts have been left to accountants.*"[157] In a memo to President Franklin Pierce in 1854, Attorney General Caleb Cushing distinguished between ministerial and discretionary acts: "Where the laws define what is to be done by a given head of department, and how he is to do it, there the President's discretion stops; but if the law require an executive act to be performed, without saying how or by whom, it must be for him to supply the direction, in virtue of his powers under the Constitution, he remaining subject always to that, to the analogies of statute, and to the general rules of law and of right."[158] Presidents Abraham Lincoln, Ulysses S. Grant, Chester A. Arthur, and Benjamin Harrison received similar advice from their Attorneys General.[159]

## B. Amos Kendall case

Through litigation, federal courts developed their own understanding of ministerial and discretionary duties. A major case involved a private contract entered into with William T. Barry, Postmaster General of the United States. The contractors were entitled to certain credits and allowances for transporting mail. In 1835, Barry resigned and Amos Kendall took his place. Kendall reexamined the contracts and ordered that the allowances and credits be withdrawn. Congress passed legislation on July 2, 1836, directing the Solicitor of the Treasury Department to settle and adjust the claims brought by the contractors.[160] The Solicitor completed his assignment and awarded the contractors the amount of $161,563.89 in principal and interest. Instead, Kendall awarded them $122,101.46.[161]

The contractors requested President Andrew Jackson to comply with the statute and award them the full amount. He advised them to take their grievance to Congress, which would be "the best expounder of the intent and meaning of their own law."[162] The Senate Judiciary Committee, after reviewing the matter, concluded that Congress intended the Solicitor's award to be final

154. 4 Op. Att'y Gen. 515, 516 (1846).

155. Id.

156. Id. at 518.

157. 5 Decisions of the First Comptroller in the Department of the Treasury of the United States 412, 413 (1884) (by William Lawrence) (emphasis in original).

158. 6 Op. Att'y Gen. 326, 341 (1854).

159. 10 Op. Att'y Gen. 526 (1863); 10 Op. Att'y Gen. 527 (1863); 11 Op. Att'y Gen. 14 (1864); 13 Op. Att'y Gen. 28 (1869); 18 Op. Att'y Gen. 31 (1884); 19 Op. Att'y Gen. 685 (1890).

160. Kendall v. United States, 12 Pet. (37 U.S.) 524, 528 (1838).

161. Id. at 530.

162. Id. at 531.

and that Congress need take no further action. A district court and circuit court ruled against Kendall, issuing a mandamus requiring him to credit the contractors with the full amount as decided by the Solicitor.[163]

In arguments before the Supreme Court, the administration protested that the "judiciary has assumed a power which the executive department resists. It is a power hitherto unknown to the judiciary—hitherto exercised by the executive alone, without question."[164] Intervention by the judiciary "annihilates one great department in one of its appropriate functions, if not all the departments."[165] The executive power "is vested in the President, and cannot be vested else-where.... [I]t cannot be given to the courts, because it is not judicial power."[166] The attorney representing the contractors summarized the administration's position in these terms: "Substantially, this Court is asked...to expunge the act of congress from the statute book; and to treat the proceedings of the solicitor as a nullity."[167]

Attorney General Benjamin Butler told the Court that when Congress passes legislation "in matters properly concerning the executive department, it belongs to the President to take care that this law be faithfully executed; and we apply to such a case the remark of Gen. Hamilton, in Pacificus, that 'he who is to execute the laws, must first judge for himself of their meaning.'"[168] Butler parted company with Attorneys General before him who regularly counseled Presidents not to involve themselves in the settlement of accounts because it was impracticable and inappropriate for them to function as an accountant.

The Court rejected the administration's legal and constitutional arguments. Justice Smith Thompson, writing for the Court, denied that the case interfered "in any respect whatever" with the rights and duties of the President. The mandamus ordered the performance "of a mere ministerial act, which neither he nor the President had any authority to deny or control."[169] To Thompson, the vesting of the executive power in the President did not mean "that every officer in every branch of that department is under the exclusive direction of the President." Certain political duties imposed on executive officers are under the direction of the President, "[b]ut it would be an alarming doctrine, that congress cannot impose upon any executive officer any duty they may think proper, which is not repugnant to any rights secured and protected by the constitution; and in such cases, the duty and responsibility grow out of and are subject to the control of the law, and not to the direction of the President. And this is emphatically the case, where the duty enjoined is of a mere ministerial character."[170]

The statute directed the Postmaster General to credit the contractors with whatever sum the Solicitor decided was due them. No one in the executive branch could exercise discretion or control over the Solicitor's decision.[171] In the words of Justice Thompson: "To contend that the obligation imposed on the President to see the laws faithfully executed, implies a power to

163. Id. at 531–35, 609.
164. Id. at 535
165. Id.
166. Id. at 546–47.
167. Id. at 566.
168. Id. at 600.
169. Id. at 610.
170. Id.
171. Id. at 611.

forbid their execution, is a novel construction of the constitution, and entirely inadmissible."[172] Chief Justice Taney differed with Thompson only on the authority of the circuit court to issue a writ of mandamus in this case.[173] Justice Barbour also dissented from the majority opinion with regard to the circuit court's mandamus authority.[174] Justice Catron concurred in the opinions of Taney and Barbour.[175]

Kendall's case was cited by the Supreme Court in 1840 when it decided the case of Susan Decatur, widow of Captain Stephen Decatur. Congress had passed two laws: a general one for widows of any officer who died in the naval service, and a second one specifically for Susan Decatur. She wanted compensation under both laws. The Secretary of the Navy, supported by the Attorney General, advised her to select one. She chose the general law. After the Secretary of the Navy retired and was replaced by James K. Paulding, she asked for compensation under both laws and took the dispute to court. The Supreme Court held it had no jurisdiction to second-guess the Secretary's decision.[176] Some of the Justices wondered why the Court would even take a case where it had to sit in judgment of the Secretary of the Navy backed by the President and the Attorney General.[177]

Within a few years, Amos Kendall was back in court. The contractors sued him for damages resulting from the delay in payment and costs in court. A jury found malice in Kendall's conduct and awarded damages of $11,000. The allegation of malice was later dropped but Kendall was again found liable.[178] To Chief Justice Taney, a public officer is not liable when "it is his duty to exercise judgment and discretion; even although an individual may suffer by his mistake."[179] Taney said that Kendall "committed an error in supposing that he had a right to set aside allowances for services rendered upon which his predecessor in office had finally decided." But Kendall acted "from a sense of public duty and without malice," and his action in a matter properly belonging to his department could give no cause for a second lawsuit against him.[180]

Taney denied that a private party may bring two lawsuits for the same cause of action. The contractors in the mandamus suit recovered "the full amount of the award."[181] The second suit was an effort to recover damages resulting from the detention of the money. Taney found that procedure impermissible: "The law does not permit a party to be twice harassed for the same cause of action; nor suffer a plaintiff to proceed in one suit to recover the principal sum of money, and then support another to recover damages for the detention."[182] Had Kendall refused to obey the mandamus, "then indeed an action on the case might have been maintained against

---

172. Id. at 613.

173. Id. at 627–41 (Taney, C.J., dissenting).

174. Id. at 641–53 (Barbour, J., dissenting).

175. Id. at 653 (Catron, J., dissenting).

176. Decatur v. Paulding, 14 Pet. (39 U.S.) 497 (1840).

177. E.g., Justice Catron, at 519. See also Reeside v. Walker, 11 How. (52 U.S.) 272 (1850).

178. LEONARD D. WHITE, THE JACKSONIANS: A STUDY IN ADMINISTRATIVE HISTORY, 1829–1861, at 278 (1954). White says "about $12,000" but the Supreme Court put the amount at $11,000; Kendall v. Stokes, 3 How. (44 U.S.) 87, 89 (1845).

179. Kendall v. Stokes, 3 How. at 98.

180. Id. at 98–99.

181. Id. at 100.

182. Id.

him. But the present suit is not brought on that ground."[183] Taney found another point objectionable. The largest item in the amount of $11,000 consisted of interest of more than $9,000, but the record showed that the contractors had earlier requested interest from the Solicitor, who granted them $6,893.93 for that purpose. To allow this claim in the second suit "was to enable the plaintiffs to recover twice for the same thing."[184]

In a dissenting opinion, Justice McLean disagreed about giving immunity to an executive officer who is said to act in good faith.[185] It seemed immaterial to McLean whether an officer does or does not act in good faith. The issue was "the character of the act and its consequences," not "the intent with which it was done."[186] If a public officer injured an individual in an action that did not come within the exercise of discretion, the officer "may be held legally responsible."[187] A year after the Court's decision, Congress passed a private bill providing Kendall with counsel fees and other expenses in this second lawsuit.[188]

## C. Other court rulings

Federal courts frequently explored the distinction between ministerial and discretionary duties. In 1880, the Supreme Court reviewed the case of an individual who appeared to be entitled to 160 acres in Utah. The title for the property had been prepared with instructions to deliver it to him. When he appeared at the local land-office in Salt Lake City, he learned that the title had been returned to the Department of the Interior, subject to the control of Secretary of the Interior Carl Schurz. Could a court issue a mandamus ordering Schurz to deliver the title to the individual?[189] The Court reviewed the principles that had been developed under *Marbury v. Madison* and *Kendall v. United States*, distinguishing between executive acts that require judgment and discretion versus those that are merely ministerial.[190]

The Court turned to the Article IV authority of Congress "to dispose of and make all needful rules and regulations respecting the territory or other property belonging to the United States."[191] Under this statutory structure of the case, the Court decided that once a title for property of public lands is granted to a citizen, the President signs the title and it is countersigned by the recorder of the land-office and recorded in the record book kept for that purpose, the public act of the government is complete. Delivery of the title is not necessary.[192] The land "has ceased to be the land of the government."[193] There "remains the duty, simply ministerial, to deliver the patent to the owner,—a duty which, within all the definitions, can be enforced by the writ

---

183. Id. at 101.
184. Id. at 103.
185. Id. at 792 (McLean, J., dissenting).
186. Id.
187. Id. at 793.
188. 9 Stat. 657 (1846).
189. United States v. Schurz, 102 U.S. 378, 379–80 (1880).
190. Id. at 392–95.
191. Id. at 395–96.
192. Id. at 397.
193. Id. at 402.

of *mandamus*."[194] In their dissent, Chief Justice Waite and Justice Swayne agreed that when all steps of granting public land to an individual are complete, actions after that point are ministerial. Actual delivery is not necessary. But the record convinced Waite and Swayne that a dispute pending before the department required judgment and discretion. Only after resolving that dispute in the individual's favor, they said, would the action in granting title be considered ministerial.[195]

A Supreme Court decision in 1884 analyzed competing theories of executive control. In one, the Secretary has ultimate control over every action within the department.[196] In the other, the Secretary's control depends on the nature of the duties entrusted to subordinates and the statutory policy adopted by Congress.[197] A unanimous Court held that legislative policy for the Department of the Interior created a system of tribunals and judicial proceedings, including authority by the Commissioner of Patents to award a patent to an inventor. The Court concluded: "to whatever else supervision and direction on the part of the head of the department may extend, in respect to matters purely administrative and executive, they do not extend to a review of the action of the Commissioner of Patents in those cases in which, by law, he is appointed to exercise his discretion judicially." The statutory scheme convinced the Court that the Commissioner of Patents was expected to exercise "quasi-judicial functions" and those decisions were final and conclusive over the Secretary.[198] If the Commissioner decided erroneously, the appeal is not to the Secretary but to the agency tribunals created to provide that review.[199]

A unanimous decision by the Supreme Court in 1885 concluded that when Congress directs the head of an executive department to pay a specified sum to a named person for a specific purpose, the matter allows for no discretion. It is a ministerial duty, to be put into effect without any individual judgment.[200] Similarly, a unanimous Court in 1898 ruled there was no power on the part of Treasury Department officers to reexamine the correction of a claim paid by virtue of a congressional statute. Instead, it was the duty of executive officers to pay the money as directed by the statute.[201] A decision by the D.C. Circuit in 1954 concerned a congressional statute that directed the Secretary of the Interior to place certain moneys in a special account. It concluded that the Secretary was "specifically and unequivocally directed by the Congress to cause the distribution of that balance according to the terms of the statute." That decision was later vacated as moot.[202]

These cases were generally directed at the heads of executive departments. They can also be aimed at the President. Federal courts invoked the ministerial-discretionary distinction on a regular basis during the Nixon administration to force the release of funds the President refused to spend (the "impoundment" dispute, analyzed in Chapter 6, section 6).[203] These cases reached

---

194. Id. at 403.

195. Id. at 405–07.

196. Butterworth v. Hoe, 112 U.S. 50, 55 (1884).

197. Id. at 56–57.

198. Id. at 67.

199. Id. at 68–69.

200. United States v. Price, 116 U.S. 43 (1885).

201. United States v. Louisville, 169 U.S. 249 (1898).

202. Clackamas County, Ore. v. McCay, 219 F.2d 479 (D.C. Cir. 1954), vacated as moot, 349 U.S. 909 (1955).

203. Berends v. Butz, 357 F. Supp. 143 (D. Minn. 1973); Train v. City of New York, 420 U.S. 35 (1975).

the President indirectly through department heads. Lawsuits can also specifically target the President. In 1974, an appellate court held that President Nixon had violated the law by refusing to carry out a statute on federal pay. It was his obligation to either submit to Congress a pay plan recommended by the salary commission or offer his own alternative proposal. Nixon had done neither. He was required, said the court, to do one or the other. There was no constitutional authority to ignore the law.[204]

# 7. REMOVAL POWER

Law professor and former Justice Department official John Yoo has written: "From the time of George Washington, presidents have understood Article II to grant them the authority to hire and fire all subordinate officers of the United States, and hence command their activities, even though the Constitution mentions only the power to appoint, not to remove."[205] That claim is too broad. It is true that in 1789, during debate on the new executive departments, Congress agreed to recognize an implied power of the President to remove Cabinet heads who interfered with his constitutional duty to "take Care that the Laws be faithfully executed." But Congress also recognized limits on the removal power.

This debate, frequently referred to as the "Decision of 1789,"[206] occupies almost 200 pages of the legislative record. James Madison precipitated the debate by proposing three executive departments: Foreign Affairs, Treasury, and War. At the head of each department would be a Secretary appointed by the President with the advice and consent of the Senate "and to be removable by the President."[207] William Smith of South Carolina immediately objected to giving the President the sole power of removal. Madison countered by saying the removal power would make the President responsible for the conduct of department heads.[208] Theodorick Bland wanted the removal power shared with the Senate to make it consistent with the appointment process. The House rejected his motion.[209]

The debate continued from May 19 through July 1, representing one of the most thorough expositions on the nature of implied power and an excellent example of lawmakers taking seriously their duty to shape constitutional meaning.[210] As the debate continued, members wondered whether they should delete the words "to be removable by the President." They finally decided to acknowledge the President's removal power by implication, not by explicit declaration. The Senate encountered tie votes on the President's power to remove the Secretary of Foreign Affairs. Vice President John Adams broke the tie to preserve the President's power. Other votes in the Senate were quite close, such as 9 to 10 on a motion to strike the President's power to remove

---

204. National Treasury Employees Union v. Nixon, 492 F.2d 587 (D.C. Cir. 1974).

205. John Yoo, *An Executive Without Much Privilege*, N.Y. Times, May 26, 2010, at A23.

206. Saikrishna Prakash, *New Light on the Decision of 1789*, 91 Cornell L. Rev. 1021 (2006).

207. 1 Annals of Cong. 371 (1789).

208. Id. at 371–72.

209. Id. at 373–74, 381–82.

210. The House debate appears in 1 Annals of Cong. 368–83 (May 19), 384–96 (May 20), 396 (May 21), 455–79 (June 16), 479–512 (June 17), 512–52 (June 18), 552–77 (June 19), 578–85 (June 22), 590–91 (June 24),

the Secretary of War.[211] Congress eventually passed legislation to adopt the same approach for all three departments. The subordinate officers would have charge and custody of all records whenever the Secretary "shall be removed from office by the President of the United States."[212]

The fact that Congress recognized the President's freedom to remove department heads did not mean the President was at liberty to remove *all* subordinate executive officials. When Madison turned his attention to the Comptroller of the Treasury, he said it was necessary "to consider the nature of this office." To Madison, its properties were not "purely of an Executive nature." It seemed to him "they partake of a Judiciary quality as well as Executive; perhaps the latter obtains to the greatest degree." Because of the mixed nature of the office, "there may be strong reasons why an officer of this kind should not hold his office at the pleasure of the Executive branch of the Government."[213]

How did Madison know so much about a Comptroller's office being created in 1789? The answer is that in 1781 the Continental Congress created the positions of a Superintendent of Finance, auditors, and a Comptroller to function as a semi-judicial officer. The Comptroller was responsible for the settlement of public accounts. On all appeals it was his duty to openly and publicly hear the parties. His decision after the hearing was final and conclusive. As pointed out in the last section on ministerial and discretionary actions, those types of accounting judgments convinced Attorneys General to advise Presidents to stay out of them. Perhaps ironically, the President had more control over a department head than subordinate officers.

## A. Confrontations with Andrew Jackson and Andrew Johnson

President Andrew Jackson collided with Congress in 1833 when he removed the Secretary of the Treasury for refusing to carry out his policy toward the U.S. Bank. Congress had been comfortable in treating the Departments of Foreign Affairs and War as executive departments, but lawmakers regarded Treasury with proprietary interest, often treating the Secretary as *its* agent. It had, for example, delegated to the Secretary—not the President—responsibility for placing public funds either in national banks or state banks. As explained in Chapter 2, section 9C, and Chapter 6, section 3, this dispute ripened into a Senate resolution of censure, an action that Jackson deeply resented. Three years later the Senate expunged the resolution from its record.

Enactment of the Tenure of Office Act in 1867 set the stage for another poisonous dispute between Congress and the President. Under the statute, every person holding civil office with the advice and consent of the Senate was entitled to hold office until the President appointed a successor, with the advice and consent of the Senate. With regard to the Secretaries of State, Treasury, War, Navy, and Interior, the Postmaster General, and the Attorney General, those individuals would hold office during the term of the President who appointed them and for one

---

592–607 (June 25), 611–14 (June 27), 614–15 (June 30), and 615 (July 1). Senate debate was substantial. For a summary of the leading arguments and the votes taken, see Louis Fisher, Constitutional Conflicts Between Congress and the President 57–62 (6th ed. 2014). For documents on removal power: 1 Goldsmith 178–92, 2 Goldsmith 1018–1124.

211. 1 Journal of the First Session of the Senate 51 (1820) (action on Aug. 4, 1789). Adams broke another tie vote on the issue of the removal power; id. at 50, 62–63.

212. 1 Stat. 29, 50, 67 (1789).

213. 1 Annals of Cong. 611–12 (June 27, 1789).

month thereafter, "subject to removal by and with the advice and consent of the Senate." During recesses the President could suspend an official but would have to report to the Senate, upon its return, the evidence and reasons for the suspension. If the Senate concurred in his action, the suspended officer would be removed. If the Senate did not concur, the suspended officer would resume the functions of his office. Johnson vetoed the bill, providing reasons why it violated the Constitution and the construction placed upon it by the debates in 1789, but both houses promptly overrode his veto.[214]

Johnson hoped the disruptive voice in his Cabinet, Secretary of War Edwin Stanton, would resign. He did not. After Johnson suspended Stanton, the Senate refused to concur. Johnson escalated the dispute by *removing* Stanton, hoping the constitutionality of the Tenure of Office Act would be tested in the courts and he would prevail. His tactic failed because Ulysses S. Grant, whom Johnson had installed as War Secretary ad interim, and Grant's successor, Lorenzo Thomas, enabled Stanton to regain his office. The crisis led to Johnson's impeachment in the House and trial in the Senate, where the effort to remove him fell one vote short.[215]

President Grant, in his first annual message in 1869, recommended the repeal of the Tenure of Office Act, arguing that the law was inconsistent with efficient and accountable administration. Congress revised the act that year, softening the suspension session but retaining the Senate's involvement in the removal process.[216] Congress continued to expand the Senate's role. Legislation in 1872 required the Postmaster General and his three assistants be appointed by the President, by Senate advice and consent, and provided that they might be "removed in the same manner." Four years later, Congress required the Senate's advice and consent for the removal of all first-, second-, and third-class postmasters.[217]

Conflicts over the removal power deepened from 1885 to 1886, when President Grover Cleveland suspended several hundred officials and refused to deliver papers and documents to the Senate, as required by law. He insisted that the power to remove or suspend executive officials was vested solely in the President by the Constitution, particularly by the "Executive Power" and "Take Care" Clauses. He argued that the law governing suspensions, as amended in 1869, did not justify the Senate's request for documents. Under these pressures, Congress repealed the Tenure of Office Act in 1887.[218]

## B. Court interpretations

In 1839, the Supreme Court directed its first full attention to the scope of the removal power. After a new federal district judge decided to remove his clerk, the clerk requested a writ of

---

214. 8 Richardson 3690–94 (March 2, 1867); 14 Stat. 430 (1867).

215. Raoul Berger, Impeachment 252–96 (1973); Lately Thomas, The First President Johnson 484–618 (1968); Harold M. Hyman, *Johnson, Stanton, and Grant: A Reconsideration of the Army's Role in the Events Leading to Impeachment*, 66 Am. Hist. Rev. 85 (1960).

216. 9 Richardson 3992 (Dec. 6, 1869); 16 Stat. 6 (1869).

217. 17 Stat. 284, sec. 2 (1872); 19 Stat. 80, sec. 6 (1876).

218. 10 Richardson 4960–68 (March 1, 1886); 16 Stat. 7, sec. 2 (1869); 24 Stat. 500 (1887). This incident is described in detail in Grover Cleveland, Presidential Problems 19–76 (1904), and Louis Fisher, *Grover Cleveland Against the Senate*, 7 Cong. Stud. 11 (1979).

mandamus to restore him to office. Although the Court was briefed extensively on the "Decision of 1789" and the various positions that had been debated and decided by Congress, it refused to get involved. It ruled unanimously that the power to appoint or remove the clerk had been vested exclusively in the lower court. The Court held that it lacked any jurisdiction over the appointment or removal of clerks in the lower courts. If the judge had acted improperly or without authority, the Court advised the plaintiff to look elsewhere for relief. Precisely how or where, the Court did not disclose.[219]

In 1854, the Court reviewed the President's authority to remove Aaron Goodrich as Chief Justice of the Supreme Court of the territory of Minnesota. This was no mere case of a federal district judge removing a clerk. It was now the President exercising control over the judiciary. Attorney General Crittenden advised President Fillmore that he possessed the power to remove territorial judges "for any cause that may, in your judgment, require it."[220] Unlike federal judges, territorial judges did not serve for life. In Minnesota they served for a term of four years.[221] Territorial judges did not sit on constitutional courts, as with Article III courts. They sat on legislative courts, created by statute under Article I and subject to the conditions imposed by Congress.[222]

Writing for the majority, Justice Daniel said the key question did not relate to the tenure of office or the powers and functions of the President. Instead: could a court command the withdrawal of money from the Treasury to settle Goodrich's claim? Daniel regarded the President's action as executive in nature, requiring judgment and discretion, and could not therefore be reviewed and countermanded by the courts.[223] In a dissent, Justice McLean agreed that the President's removal power over executive officers had been well established, but extending it to judicial officers presented a unique matter. The President's responsibility over administrators related to political, not judicial, officers. Subjecting judicial power to executive control would put an end to the "independence and purity" of the courts. To McLean, paying money to Goodrich represented a ministerial act subject to mandamus proceedings.[224]

A unanimous Court in 1886 held that a naval cadet, discharged by the Secretary of Navy, remained in office and entitled to the pay attached to it. The Court ruled that when Congress vests in the head of a department the appointment of inferior officers, it may limit and restrict the power of removal as it considers best for the public interest.[225] Another unanimous Court, in 1903, recognized that Congress may, by statute, specify the cause for removing executive officials. Congress had identified "inefficiency, neglect of duty, or malfeasance in office" as the statutory grounds for removing a customs official. President McKinley removed a customs official without relying on any of those reasons. The Court acknowledged that Congress can limit

---

219. Ex parte Hennen, 13 Pet. (38 U.S.) 230 (1839).

220. 5 Op. Att'y Gen. 288, 291 (1851).

221. Id. at 289.

222. Id. at 289–90.

223. United States v. Guthrie, 17 How. (58 U.S.) 284, 304 (1854).

224. Id. at 310. For a decision upholding the right of the President to suspend a territorial judge and replace him with someone else before the completion of his term of office, see McAllister v. United States, 141 U.S. 175 (1891). In 1897, the Court unanimously concluded that President Cleveland could legitimately remove a U.S attorney "when in his discretion he regards it for the public good, although the term of office may have been limited by the words of the statute creating the office." Parsons v. United States, 167 U.S. 324, 343 (1897).

225. United States v. Perkins, 116 U.S. 483 (1886).

the President to specified causes, but only if the statute uses "plain language" to restrict the President's general power of removal.[226] Other cases during this period concerned the authority of Congress to limit presidential removals to causes prescribed by law.[227]

## C. From Myers to Humphrey's Executor

The celebrated case of Myers v. United States (1926) appeared to mark a broad endorsement of independent presidential power to remove subordinates. A close reading of this lengthy opinion yields a more modest grant of executive authority. The case began with the appointment of Frank S. Myers, postmaster at Portland, Oregon, to a four-year term in 1917. Prior to the expiration of his term, the Postmaster General removed him, an action concurred in by President Wilson. Legislation required the Senate's advice and consent for the removal of all first-, second-, and third-class postmasters, which covered Myers. He sued to recover his salary. His attorneys argued the appointment of postmasters derived from a statute based on specific constitutional powers given to Congress ("to establish post offices and post roads"), enabling Congress to attach certain conditions to an appointment. In response, Solicitor General James M. Beck maintained that the legislative condition requiring Senate advice and consent for removals could be struck down "without assuming the absolute power of the President to remove any executive officer."[228]

Chief Justice Taft, writing for a 6-3 majority, decided on a broader interpretation of presidential power—too broad to withstand scholarly scrutiny and subsequent Court holdings. Taft rejected his earlier position in Wallace (1922), where he had held that "at least in absence of restrictive legislation, the President, though he could not appoint with the consent of the Senate, could remove without such consent in the case of any officer whose tenure was not fixed by the Constitution."[229] He now claimed a presidential power to remove even in the presence of statutory limitations. From the congressional debates of 1789 he concluded there was not the "slightest doubt" that the power to remove officers appointed by the President and the Senate is "vested in the President alone."[230] The record from 1789 in fact revealed deep divisions among lawmakers and extremely close (even tie) votes in the Senate. Lawmakers certainly supported presidential removal of department heads. There was no reason to automatically extend that principle to first-, second-, and third-class postmasters.

Taft necessarily acknowledged that the Court in Shurtleff (1903) agreed that Congress might restrict the President's removal power by specifying causes of removal. He was also aware that Congress, in establishing regulatory agencies (such as the Interstate Commerce Committee in 1887), had specified causes for removal: inefficiency, neglect of duty, and malfeasance in office. In a significant passage—frequently overlooked by those who parse this 71-page opinion—Taft admitted that "there may be duties so peculiarly and specifically committed to the discretion of

226.  Shurtleff v. United States, 189 U.S. 311, 316 (1903).

227.  Blake v. United States, 103 U.S. (13 Otto.) 227 (1881), Reagan v. United States, 182 U.S. 491 (1901), Bernap v. United States, 252 U.S. 512 (1920). A 1922 case focused on President Wilson's dismissal of an officer from the Quartermaster Corps and concluded that the legislative restrictions imposed on the President's power to remove an Army officer did not apply. Wallace v. United States, 257 U.S. 541, 545–46 (1922).

228.  Myers v. United States, 272 U.S. 52, 61, 98 (1926).

229.  Wallace v. United States, 257 U.S. 541, 544 (1922) (emphasis added).

230.  Myers v. United States, 272 U.S. at 114.

a particular officer as to raise a question whether the President may overrule or revise the officer's interpretation of his statutory duty in a particular instance."[231] Here he referred to executive, not adjudicatory, duties, because in the next sentence he identified a second limitation on presidential removals: "Then there maybe duties of a quasi-judicial character imposed on executive officers and members of executive tribunals whose decisions after hearing affect interests of individuals, the discharge of which the President can not in a particular case properly influence or control."[232] Attorneys General had been flagging those issues ever since 1823.

In a dissent, Justice Holmes described Taft's arguments as "spider's webs inadequate to control the dominant facts."[233] A dissent by Justice McReynolds identified many of the statutes that set forth restrictions on removals.[234] In a third dissent, Justice Brandeis agreed that the power to remove or suspend a high political officer "might conceivably be deemed indispensable to democratic government and, hence, inherent in the President."[235] But he strongly rejected the idea that the workings of government required presidential removal of an inferior administrative officer appointed for a fixed term, such as a postmaster.[236]

Taft's decision aroused strong criticism from the academic community. The most devastating rebuke came from political scientist Edward S. Corwin. He did not object that the President could remove someone he had appointed with the advice and consent of the Senate. Such a position, although "decidedly vulnerable on both historical and logical grounds, is not improbably supported by practical considerations."[237] What Corwin found indefensible was the claim that the President could remove *any* executive officer. He believed a balance had to be found between two competing constitutional principles: the President's removal authority and the power of Congress to create an office under the Necessary and Proper Clause. In analyzing that balance, Corwin emphasized the nature of a political office. He pointed to employees in the civil service who could not be removed "except for such cause as will promote the efficiency of said service and for reasons given in writing, and the person whose removal is sought shall have notice of the same and of any charges preferred against him." Congress has passed many statutes that specified the causes to remove commissioners from regulatory agencies.[238]

The issue that split the Court in *Myers* returned less than a decade later in *Humphrey's Executor v. United States* (1935). William E. Humphrey, nominated by President Hoover for the Federal Trade Commission (FTC) in 1931, had been confirmed by the Senate. Under the FTC Act, the President could remove a commissioner only for "inefficiency, neglect of duty, or malfeasance in office." On July 25, 1933, President Roosevelt asked Humphrey to resign: "I do not feel that your mind and my mind go along together on either the policies or the administering of the Federal Trade Commission." Humphrey's response described unnamed enemies with "slanderous and polluted

---

231. Id. at 135.

232. Id.

233. Id. at 177 (Holmes, J., dissenting)

234. Id. at 178–239 (McReynolds, J., dissenting)

235. Id. at 247 (Brandeis, J, dissenting).

236. Id.

237. EDWARD S. CORWIN, THE PRESIDENT'S REMOVAL POWER UNDER THE CONSTITUTION vi (1927).

238. Corwin's study was reproduced with little change as *Tenure of Office and the Removal Power Under the Constitution*, 27 COLUM. L. REV. 353 (1927).

lips and spew their putrid filth upon you under the pledge of secrecy."[239] Confronted by someone who refused to resign, Roosevelt removed Humphrey for purely policy reasons rather than those specified in the statute.

A unanimous opinion by Justice Sutherland went against Roosevelt. The Court described FTC as charged with the enforcement of "no policy except the policy of the law. Its duties are neither political nor executive, but predominantly quasi-judicial and quasi-legislative." Sutherland distinguished between the executive duties of a postmaster (*Myers*) and those of an FTC commissioner. The FTC, he said, "cannot in any proper sense be characterized as an arm or an eye of the executive."[240] If would be a stretch to call even a postmaster an arm or an eye of the President.

Roosevelt's removal of Arthur E. Morgan, chairman of the Board of Directors of the Tennessee Valley Authority (TVA), led to another round of courts cases, this time with the agency regarded as predominantly an administrative arm of the executive branch and therefore distinguishable from the FTC.[241] More analogous to *Humphrey's* was President Eisenhower's removal of a member of the War Claims Commission in 1953. A unanimous Supreme Court held that the President possessed no authority under the Constitution or a statute to remove a member of the commission. The agency's task, said the Court, had an "intrinsic judicial character."[242] Important cases involving the removal power for independent commissions, boards, and the independent counsel continue to be decided, raising questions about the continued force of *Humphrey's Executor* (Chapter 4, sections 8 and 12).

A number of important dismissals for disloyalty reached the courts, some raising a bill of attainder issue (Chapter 4, section 10). Others involved removals of federal employees on national security grounds (Chapter 7, section 10). A Supreme Court removal case in 1987 turned on First Amendment rights of federal employees.[243] Several cases focused on patronage dismissals at the state and local levels.[244] President Clinton's firing of seven employees of the White House Travel Office ("Travelgate") caused severe political damage to the administration.[245] A long simmering dispute over appointment and removal of members of the Civil Rights Commission was resolved in 2002 in favor of President Bush.[246]

Congress has a significant role in the removal process. It may remove an individual by abolishing the office. Either house of Congress can use different methods in attempting to dislodge federal employees, ranging from passing simple (non-binding) resolutions or concurrent

---

239. William E. Leuchtenburg, *The Case of the Contentious Commissioner: Humphrey's Executor v. U.S.*, FREEDOM AND REFORM: ESSAYS IN HONOR OF HENRY STEEL COMMAGER 289 (Harold M. Hyman & Leonard W. Levy, eds., 1967).

240. Humphrey's Executor v. United States, 295 U.S. 602, 624, 627–28 (1935).

241. Morgan v. TVA, 115 F.2d 990 (6th Cir. 1940), cert. denied, 312 U.S. 701 (1941). For background on Morgan's removal, see C. HERMAN PRITCHETT, THE TENNESSEE VALLEY AUTHORITY 203–15 (1943). A transcript of White House hearings, conducted by President Roosevelt in the presence of Chairman Morgan and the other two directors of the TVA, is reprinted in S. Doc. No. 155, 75th Cong., 3d Sess. (1938). Acting Attorney General Robert H. Jackson had advised FDR that the TVA was an executive agency and its members could be removed by the President; 39 OP. ATT'Y GEN. 145 (1938).

242. Wiener v. United States, 357 U.S. 349, 355 (1958).

243. Rankin v. McPherson, 483 U.S. 378 (1987).

244. Rutan v. Republican Party of Illinois, 497 U.S. 62 (1990); Branti v. Finkel, 445 U.S. 507 (1980); Elrod v. Burns, 427 U.S. 347 (1976).

245. FISHER, *supra* note 210, at 74–78.

246. Id. at 78–79.

resolutions (also non-binding) and conducting investigative hearings, using a variety of tactics for the purpose of driving out federal employees. Congress can also use legislative tools to *protect* federal employees from removal.[247] The abolishment of Article III judges is treated in Chapter 9, section 2.

# 8. PARDON POWER

Article II, section 2 empowers the President to grant "Reprieves and Pardons for Offenses against the United States, except in Cases of Impeachment." The authority is limited to offenses against the United States, not against individual states and localities. At the Philadelphia Convention, Luther Martin proposed adding the words "after conviction" following "reprieves and pardons." James Wilson objected that granting a pardon before conviction "might be necessary in order to obtain the testimony of accomplices," and this might "particularly happen" in the case of forgeries. Martin withdrew his motion.[248] Another substantive discussion concerned adding the language "except cases of treason." Edmund Randolph feared that the President "may himself be guilty. The Traytors may be his own instruments." James Wilson countered that if the President were a party to the guilt "he can be impeached and prosecuted." Randolph's motion failed, 2 to 8, with one state divided.[249]

In Federalist No. 74, Hamilton described the pardon power as essential because the "criminal code of every country partakes so much of necessary severity, that without an easy access to exceptions in favor of unfortunate guilt, justice would wear a countenance too sanguinely and cruel."[250] Placing the pardon power in one person, he said, would permit prompt and timely action. In time of insurrection or rebellion, "there are often critical moments, when a well-timed offer of pardon to the insurgents or rebels may restore the tranquillity of the commonwealth."[251] Exercising this power may take various forms: a full pardon, conditional pardon, clemency for a class of people (amnesty), commutation (reduction of a sentence), and remission of fines and forfeitures.[252]

Through its appropriations and taxing powers, Congress may also remit fines, penalties, and forfeitures. Congress has vested that authority in the Secretary of the Treasury and other executive officials.[253] Congress may legislate a general pardon or amnesty by repealing a law that had imposed criminal liability. Congress derives this power not by "sharing" the President's pardon power but through its authority to legislate and to repeal legislation. Certain statutory provisions have been struck down by the Supreme Court as impermissible interferences with the

247. Id. at 79–83; Louis Fisher, *Congress and the Removal Power*, in Divided Democracy: Cooperation and Conflict Between the President and Congress 255–74 (James A. Thurber, ed., 1991).

248. 2 Farrand 426.

249. Id. at 626–27.

250. The Federalist 473.

251. Id. at 475.

252. Harold J. Krent, Presidential Powers 189–214 (2005).

253. The Laura, 114 U.S. 411 (1885); 8 Op. Att'y Gen. 281, 282 (1857).

pardon power.[254] When a proviso in an appropriations statute attempts to control the President's power to pardon and to prescribe for the judiciary the effect of a pardon, the statutory provision is invalid.[255] After the Civil War, several conflicts developed between presidential pardons and legislation passed by Congress regarding Southern sympathizers.[256]

The Office of the Pardon Attorney in the Justice Department provides assistance to the President. The general procedure is to have petitioners seeking a pardon submit their applications to the Office, where they are screened and evaluated, and comments are received from the law enforcement community before the Office makes a recommendation to the President. Most petitioners go through that process. Others, with the support of influential and powerful interests, go directly to the President. As explained below, some of these petitioners prevail but only at the cost of damaging the reputation of the President.

Judicial Watch, a non-profit public interest organization, requested documents concerning pardon applications considered or granted by the Pardon Office during the Clinton administration. The Justice Department released thousands of pages of documents but withheld 4,865 pages, citing two exemptions in the Freedom of Information Act (FOIA). The materials were withheld on the grounds that they were protected by the presidential communications and deliberative process privileges. A district court held that the documents were legitimately withheld because they were intended to advise the President on a "quintessential" matter of executive power expressly stated in the Constitution.[257] The D.C. Circuit reversed, pointing out that the Pardon Office did not involve the President or close White House advisers. The appeals court also noted that the Office of the President is distinct from the Executive Office of the President (EOP). Although the EOP is an agency subject to FOIA, the Office of the President is not.[258]

Controversial pardon decisions over the last half century have circumvented the Office of the Pardon Attorney, with petitioners seeking relief directly from the President and a small circle of White House advisers. These decisions include the pardon of Richard Nixon, the Iran-Contra pardons in the Bush I administration, the FALN commutation and Marc Rich pardon in the Clinton administration, and the Scooter Libby commutation in the Bush II administration.[259]

On September 8, 1974, President Ford granted a full pardon "for all offenses against the United States which Richard Nixon has committed or may have committed or taken part in during the period from January 20, 1969, through August 9, 1974." To allay the concerns of some lawmakers that he might have entered into a deal with Nixon to secure the nomination as

---

254. Ex parte Garland, 71 U.S. 333, 380 (1867). See 12 Stat. 502 (1862) and 13 Stat. 424 (1865).

255. United States v. Klein, 80 U.S. (13 Wall.) 128 (1872). See Louis Fisher, United States v. Klein: *Judging Its Clarity and Application*, 5 J. Nat'l Security L. & Pol'y 237 (2011).

256. Krent, *supra* note 252, at 194–97.

257. Judicial Watch, Inc. v. United States DOJ, 259 F. Supp. 2d 86 (D.D.C. 2003).

258. Judicial Watch, Inc. v. Department of Justice, 365 F.3d 1108 (D.C. Cir. 2004).

259. Jeffrey Crouch, The Presidential Pardon Power 21–22 (2009). For other analyses of the pardon power, see Jeffrey Crouch, *Presidential Misuse of the Pardon Power*, 38 Pres. Stud. Q. 722 (2008); Margaret Colgate Love, *Of Pardons, Politics, and Collar Buttons: Reflections on the President's Duty to be Merciful*, 27 Fordham Urban L.J. 1483 (2000); Brian C. Kalt, *Pardon Me? The Constitutional Case Against Presidential Self-Pardons*, 106 Yale L.J. 779 (1996); Mark J. Rozell, *President Ford's Pardon of Richard M. Nixon: Constitutional and Political Considerations*, 24 Pres. Stud. Q. 121 (1994); Peter M. Shane, *Presidents, Pardons, and Prosecutors: Legal Accountability and the Separation of Powers*, 11 Yale L. & Policy R. 361 (1993); David Gray Adler, The President's Pardon Power, Inventing the American Presidency 209–35 (Thomas E. Cronin, ed., 1989); William F. Duker, *The President's Power to Pardon: A Constitutional History*, 18 Wm. & Mary L. Rev. 475 (1977). An insightful analysis of the

Vice President, Ford agreed to appear before a House Judiciary subcommittee to explain why he granted the pardon.[260] Some critics regarded it as improper for Ford to grant a pardon before formal charges had been lodged and without a formal admission of guilt from Nixon. However, it is established that a pardon may be granted before conviction and even before indictment.[261] There are, nonetheless, substantial political risks. Without access to facts produced through the normal trial procedure, a President may grant a pardon that looks ill-considered after new evidence comes to light. For that reason, Attorneys General have generally cautioned against issuing a pardon before trial.[262]

In 1977, President Carter clashed with Congress over two appropriations acts that prohibited him from using funds to carry out his amnesty order. With certain exceptions, his order granted an unconditional pardon for Vietnam-era violators of the selective service laws. Some of his actions, such as canceling indictments and terminating investigations, did not depend on appropriations. He particularly objected to a statutory prohibition concerning the exclusion of aliens because of possible violations of selective service law. Carter considered these provisions an unconstitutional interference with his pardon power, a bill of attainder, and a denial of due process.[263]

The Iran-Contra affair involved the sending of arms to Iran and the supply of military assistance to the Contra rebels in Nicaragua. The former violated the announced policy of the Reagan administration; the latter violated statutory law. A number of mid-level and low-level officials in the administration were convicted for their participation, as were several individuals from the private sector. The legal and constitutional issues were so serious that officials within the administration recognized that President Reagan could be impeached. To forestall that prospect, Reagan took the extraordinary step of completely waiving executive privilege. He directed Cabinet members and other officials to testify fully before Congress and disclose matters that on other occasions would have been withheld (Chapter 6, section 9).[264]

On December 24, 1992, in one of his last actions in office, President George H. W. Bush pardoned six individuals for their conduct in the Iran-Contra affair: former Secretary of Defense Caspar Weinberger, former Assistant Secretary of State Elliot Abrams, former National Security Adviser Robert McFarland, and three officials from the Central Intelligence Agency: Duane Clarridge, Alan Fiers, and Clair George. Several of these individuals faced prosecution and possible conviction. The pardon of Weinberger was criticized because Bush had a direct and

Pardon Office appeared in the *Washington Post*: Dafna Linzer & Jennifer LaFleur, *A Racial Gap for Criminal Seeking Mercy*, Dec. 4, 2011, at A1, and Dafna Linzer, *A Lawmaker's Good Word Improves the Odds*, Dec. 5, 2011, at A1.

260. *Pardon of Richard M. Nixon, and Related Matters*, hearings before the Subcommittee on Criminal Justice of the House Committee on the Judiciary, 93d Cong., 2d Sess. 90–158 (1974).

261. Ex parte Garland, 71 U.S. 333, 380 (1867); 1 Op. Att'y Gen. 341, 343 (1820); Murphy v. Ford, 390 F. Supp. 1372 (W.D. Mich. 1975). For close analysis of the Nixon pardon, see Crouch, *supra* note 259, at 1–2, 66–85, 129–36, 137–39, 143.

262. 2 Op. Att'y Gen. 275 (1825); 6 Op. Att'y Gen. 20 (1853).

263. Public Papers of the Presidents, 1977, II, at 1409–10. See 91 Stat. 114, sec. 306 (1977); 91 Stat. 444, sec. 706 (1977).

264. Lawrence E. Walsh, Firewall: The Iran-Contra Conspiracy and Cover-up (1997); Theodore Draper, A Very Thin Line: The Iran-Contra Affairs (1991).

apparent conflict of interest. The defense in the Weinberger prosecution indicated that it might call Bush and subject him to cross-examination for his role in the Iran-Contra affair.[265]

Although Presidents possess exclusive authority to grant pardons, misuse of that power has damaged many occupants of the Oval Office. On August 11, 1999, Bill Clinton offered clemency to 16 members of a Puerto Rican terrorist group, the FALN (Armed Forces of Puerto Rican National Liberation). Fourteen accepted the conditions attached to the clemency (such as renouncing violence). They had been convicted and imprisoned for seditious conspiracy for planting more than 130 bombs in public places in the United States, including shopping malls and restaurants. At least six people were killed and approximately 70 injured. The FALN operation marked the biggest terrorist campaign within U.S. borders, and yet Clinton's clemency released individuals from prison after serving less than 20 years of terms running from 55 to 90 years.[266]

Clinton's action was criticized for a number of reasons. It did not receive the formal review of the Pardon Attorney, the Deputy Attorney General, or the Attorney General. Some Justice Department officials met several times with advocates for FALN clemency but did not solicit the views of victims or law enforcement officials. Background checks by the FBI were not requested. The White House knew that the FBI was on record as opposed to clemency for the FALN members. The clemency provoked bipartisan condemnation from members of Congress. Democrats were either silent on the clemency decision or issued public rebukes. Both houses passed resolutions condemning Clinton's pardons. The House resolution passed 311 to 41. Republicans voted 218 to 0; the Democratic vote was 93 to 41. A Senate resolution deploring the clemency passed five days later, 95 to 2.[267]

In his remaining hours in office, Clinton issued pardons to 140 people and commuted 36 prison sentences. Pardon Attorney Roger Adams said that many of the people on the list had not applied for pardons and that there was often no time to conduct record checks with the FBI. The lion's share of attention fell on Clinton's pardon of Marc Rich and Pincus Green, charged in 1983 with conducting the largest tax-evasion scheme in U.S. history. Rather than stand trial, they fled to Switzerland. Rich's ex-wife, Denise Rich, met with President Clinton, contributed more than a million dollars to the Democratic Party over the years, and donated $450,000 to Clinton's presidential library in Little Rock. Beth Dozoretz, a close friend of Denise Rich, met with Clinton and pledged to raise $1 million for the Clinton library.[268]

In a lengthy op-ed piece for the *New York Times*, Clinton defended his pardons of Rich and Green. He said the case for the pardons was reviewed and advocated not only by his former White House Counsel Jack Quinn but also by "three distinguished Republican attorneys: Leonard Garment, a former Nixon White House official; William Bradford Reynolds, a former high-ranking official in the Reagan Justice Department; and Lewis Libby, now Vice President Cheney's chief of staff."[269] Within hours, Garment, Reynolds, and Libby denied

---

265. James J. Brosnahan, *Pardoning Weinberger Belittles Democracy*, NAT'L L. J., Jan. 18, 1993, at 17–18. See CROUCH, *supra* note 259, 101–07, 136–39.

266. Louis Fisher, *When Presidential Power Backfires: Clinton's Use of Clemency*, 32 PRES. STUD. Q. 586, 589–90 (2002).

267. Id. at 590–91. Also on the FALN clemencies, see CROUCH, *supra* note 259, at 3–4, 21–22, 25–26, 95, 108–11, 140–42.

268. Fisher, *supra* note 266, at 594.

269. William Clinton, *My Reasons for the Pardons*, N.Y. TIMES, Feb. 18, 2001, at 13.

Clinton's account. At that point, Clinton's office acknowledged that none of the three lawyers had reviewed the pardon applications for Rich and Green or lobbied for them.[270] What did Clinton have in mind? That he could shift blame to Republicans?

A more recent firestorm about a pardon concerned the decision of President George W. Bush to commute the sentence of I. Lewis "Scooter" Libby, who had served as chief of staff to Vice President Dick Cheney. Libby was investigated by a special counsel for the leak of classified information regarding the decision to go to war against Iraq. Found guilty of obstruction of justice and perjury before a grand jury, he was sentenced to 30 months in prison, fined $250,000, and given two years' probation. The district judge decided that Libby would have to begin serving his prison sentence while pursuing an appeal. Within a month after the sentence, Bush signed a grant of clemency for Libby, reducing the 30-month sentence to zero and leaving in place the fine and probation.[271] Bush explained that the prison sentence was "excessive."[272]

Public reaction to the commutation was critical for a number of reasons. Thirty months was within the range of sentences for obstruction of justice.[273] If the sentence was "excessive," why not reduce it to 20 months or 15 months, rather than zero? More fundamental, the Bush administration (as with past administrations) took a firm stand against any leaks of classified information, especially in the field of national security. Subordinate executive branch employees, including agency "whistleblowers," could expect heavy sanctions for releasing confidential documents to the public. Libby, as chief counsel to the Vice President, had his sentence fully commuted. The commutation had some analogies to high-ranking officials in the Reagan administration involved in Iran-Contra. They received pardons from Bush I. Cheney's effort to pressure Bush II to grant Libby a full pardon was unsuccessful.

# 9. OPINION CLAUSE

Article II, section 2 provides that the President "may require the Opinion, in writing, of the principal Officer in each of the executive Departments, upon any Subject relating to the Duties of their respective Offices." It is a curious provision. Had this language not been placed in the Constitution, surely a President would have the right to seek the opinion of the heads of each department. Why did the Framers include these words?

There is little in the Philadelphia debates, the Federalist Papers, or the ratification debates to guide us. On August 20, 1787, the following proposition was referred to the Committee of Five, which was designated to draft the final language: "Each Branch of the Legislature, as well as the supreme Executive shall have authority to require the opinions of the supreme Judicial Court upon important questions of law, and upon solemn occasions."[274] The Supreme Court agreed to

---

270. Joseph Kahn, *Clinton's Defense of Pardons Brings Even More Questions*, N.Y. TIMES, Feb. 19, 2001, at A1, A15. For further analysis on the Marc Rich pardon, see CROUCH, *supra* note 259, at 4, 22, 26, 96, 111–12, 112–17, 140.

271. CROUCH, *supra* note 259, at 117–26, 142–46.

272. Id. at 123.

273. Id. at 124.

274. 2 Farrand 334, 341.

engage in "advisory opinions" for the first few years, but quickly discontinued them as inappropriate (Chapter 9, section 4).

In late July, the Committee of Detail offered this power for the President: "He shall have a Right to advise with the Heads of the different Departments as his Council."[275] On August 20, Gouverneur Morris and Charles Pinckney submitted a plan for a Council of State to assist the President. It would be composed of the heads of various executive departments and the Chief Justice of the Supreme Court, who would preside over the Council in the absence of the President. At any time the President could submit "any matter" to the Council for discussion and "may require the written opinions of any one or more of the members." But the President "shall in all cases exercise his own judgment."[276]

Not until September 4, toward the end of the convention, was language reported to add the following presidential power: "and may require the opinion in writing of the principal officer in each of the executive departments, upon any subject relating to the duties of their respective offices." The language was accepted, with only New Hampshire voting no. The Opinion Clause was later adopted unanimously.[277] This modest language about receiving the opinions of department heads was a substitute for a more ambitious idea of having a Council of State or an Executive Council advise the President. The Council proposal was voted down, 3 to 8.[278]

In Federalist No. 74, Hamilton regarded the constitutional language about the President seeking opinions from department heads as "a mere redundancy." The Constitution, he said, clearly meant to include that authority as implied.[279] Justice Jackson, in the Steel Seizure Case of 1952, challenged the Solicitor General's claim that the Vesting Clause in Article II grants "all of the executive powers of which the Government is capable." It that were true, Jackson said, "it is difficult to see why the forefathers bothered to add several specific items, including some trifling ones."[280] His footnote 9 cited the Opinion Clause.

At the North Carolina ratification convention in 1788, James Iredell regarded the Opinion Clause as, "in some degree, substituted for a council." The President may consult with department heads only "if he thinks proper." The requirement of offering their opinion in writing "will render them more cautious in giving them, and make them responsible should they give advice manifestly improper."[281] Iredell expressed concern that the council model, as drawn from Great Britain, could result in a lack of accountability, making it difficult "to know whether the President or counsellors were most to blame." The Opinion Clause avoided that problem. The President "will personally have the credit of good, or the censure of bad measures; since, though he may ask advice, he is to use his own judgment in following or rejecting it."[282]

275. Id. at 135.

276. Id. at 343.

277. Id. at 495, 499, 541–43.

278. Id. at 541–42. For background on the Council idea and opposition to it, see HENRY BARRETT LEARNED, THE PRESIDENT'S CABINET 74–94 (1912).

279. The Federalist 473.

280. Youngstown Co. v. Sawyer, 343 U.S. 579, 640–41 (1952) (Jackson, J., concurring).

281. 4 Elliot 108.

282. Id. at 110. See Akhil Reed Amar, *Some Opinions on the Opinion Clause*, 82 VA. L. REV. 647 (1996).

The scope of the Opinion Clause was litigated in the late 1970s. President Carter had requested his Water Resources Council to prepare a report on future water resource policy matters. The Council began preparing the report without an Environmental Impact Statement (EIS), as required by law. North Dakota filed suit to enjoin the report's transmission to Carter until completion of an EIS. The Justice Department argued that Carter's access to the Council's report was protected by the Opinion Clause. The case was resolved without reaching the constitutional issue.[283]

# 10. TAKE CARE CLAUSE

Article II, section 3 directs the President to "take Care that the Laws be faithfully executed." On June 1, 1787, Madison moved that the national executive be empowered "to carry into execution the national laws." His motion was agreed to.[284] That language remained until August 6, when the Committee of Detail changed it to "he shall take care that the laws of the United States be duly and faithfully executed."[285] The Committee of Style preserved that language but deleted "duly and."[286] In Federalist No. 70, Hamilton emphasized the need for "energy in the Executive" to protect the community from foreign attacks and "the steady administration of the laws." "A feeble Executive," he said, "is but another phrase for a bad execution; and a government ill executed, whatever it may be in theory, must be, in practice, a bad government."[287] Unlike some who read his language to justify independent presidential action in national security matters, Hamilton believed that a "vigorous Executive" was consistent with "the genius of republican government."[288]

## *A. Scope of presidential control*

Elements of the Take Care Clause were treated earlier in this chapter. Section 6 distinguished between "ministerial" (legal) and "discretionary" (political) powers. For ministerial duties, Congress by statute may vest certain responsibilities with subordinate officers in a department, such as making final judgment on individual claims. As Attorneys General have advised from the start, the President's responsibility is not to personally carry out those laws, which would be impractical and in conflict with statutory directives. Rather, the President must see that

---

283. Neil Thomas Proto, *The Opinion Clause and Presidential Decision-Making*, 44 Mo. L. Rev. 185, 187–90 (1979). Also exploring the Opinion Clause: Lawrence Lessig & Cass R. Sunstein, *The President and the Administration*, 94 Colum. L. Rev. 1, 32–38, 72 (1994).

284. 1 Farrand 63, 67.

285. 2 Farrand 185

286. Id. at 574, 600.

287. The Federalist 451.

288. Id. For interpretations of Hamilton that endorse an expansive view of presidential power, see John Yoo, Crisis and Command: A History of Executive Power from George Washington to George W. Bush 3–4, 10–11, 22–23, 37–49, 84–91, 114, 394, 402, 420, 425–26 (2009). For a challenge to Yoo's analysis of Hamilton, see David Gray Adler, *Presidential Power and Foreign Affairs in the Bush Administration: The Use and Abuse of Alexander Hamilton*, 40 Pres. Stud. Q. 531 (2010).

the agency officer assigned the statutory duty carries out the law faithfully. If so, presidential interference and intervention are impermissible. Section 7 on the removal power covers similar issues. The President's power to remove a departmental or agency official is at its highest level with executive duties. It is at its lowest with agency adjudication.

## B. The "Unitary Executive" debate

In recent decades, scholars traded divergent views on the Take Care Clause. To some, the nature of government from the very beginning placed certain agency actions outside the direct control of the President. That was especially true with ministerial duties, agency adjudication, and the rise of independent agencies.[289] Other scholars insisted on full presidential control of *all* execution of the laws. For them, the granting of the "executive power" to the President is exclusive and Congress may not create administrative units that are independent of presidential control.[290]

When these studies interpret the Philadelphia debates, the ratification conventions, and administrative practice over the last two centuries, they find little common ground. The unitary executive model, if reasonably applied, has a certain amount to commend it. The Framers experienced first-hand the administrative inefficiencies of the Continental Congress from 1774 to 1787 and were determined at the Philadelphia convention to create a national government better structured for accountability and efficiency. A single executive in the form of the President was seen as a key step toward improved management. When Congress created three executive departments in 1789, it expressed a similar commitment to accountability by placing authority in a single secretary, not in a multi-person board.

At the same time, the principle of a unitary executive contradicted other values. One is the exception Madison made during the "Decision of 1789" to have the Comptroller in the Treasury Department function in an independent manner because of the "judicial" nature of his duties. That precedent was later extended to cover other types of adjudicatory work performed by federal agencies, including decisions by administrative law judges and executive officials who handle various claims and benefits.

In their book, *The Unitary Executive* (2008), Steven Calabresi and Christopher Yoo make this claim: "[A]ll forty-three presidents, from George Washington to George W. Bush, have insisted on the view that the Constitution gives them the power to remove and direct subordinates as to law execution. All forty-three presidents have refused to acquiesce in repeated congressional efforts to sabotage the unitary executive bequeathed to us by the framers."[291] That claim reaches

289. Lawrence Lessig & Cass R. Sunstein, *The President and the Administration*, 94 COLUM. L. REV. 1 (1994); A. Michael Froomkin, *The Imperial Presidency's New Vestments*, 88 NW. U. L. REV. 1346 (1994); Morton Rosenberg, *Congress's Prerogative over Agencies and Agency Decisionmakers: The Rise and Demise of the Reagan Administration's Theory of the Unitary Executive*, 57 GEO. WASH. L. REV. 627 (1989); and Peter L. Strauss, *The Place of Agencies in Government: Separation of Powers and the Fourth Branch*, 84 COLUM. L. REV. 573 (1984).

290. Steven G. Calabresi & Saikrishna B. Prakash, *The President's Power to Execute the Laws*, 104 YALE L.J. 541 (1994); Saikrishna B. Prakash, *Hail to the Chief Administrator: The Framers and the President's Administrative Powers*, 102 YALE L.J. 991 (1993); Steven G. Calabresi & Kevin H. Rhodes, *The Structural Constitution: Unitary Executive, Plural Judiciary*, 105 HARV. L. REV. 1153 (1992); Stephen L. Carter, *The Independent Counsel Mess*, 102 HARV. L. REV. 105 (1988); and Geoffrey P. Miller, *Independent Agencies*, 1986 SUP. CT. REV. 41.

291. STEVEN G. CALABRESI & CHRISTOPHER YOO, THE UNITARY EXECUTIVE: PRESIDENTIAL POWER FROM WASHINGTON TO BUSH 418 (2008).

too far. Not only have Presidents "acquiesced" in statutory limits on their power to execute the law, Attorneys General regularly advised Presidents not to interfere in some agency decisions. As explained in Chapter 5, section 6, agencies often share administrative decisions with committees and subcommittees of Congress. Agency manuals specifically require budget officials to seek prior approval in certain instances from designated committees before shifting funds to new purposes.[292]

The Constitution does not empower the President to carry out the laws. That would impose an impossible assignment. It is the duty of the President to see that laws are faithfully carried out. The great bulk of that work is done by agency employees at various levels. Many remain legitimately outside the President's direct control, provided they discharge their statutory tasks.[293] A separate issue, discussed next, is whether the President may decline to carry out statutory provisions he regards as unconstitutional, even if he or a predecessor signed them into law or they became law over his veto.

## *C. Nonenforcement of the law*

In a memo dated November 2, 1994, OLC analyzed the President's constitutional authority to decline to execute what the administration considers to be an unconstitutional statute. It reasoned that the President is required to act in accordance with the laws, including the Constitution, "which takes precedence over other forms of law. This obligation is reflected in the Take Care Clause and the President's oath of office."[294] The memo states that, "as a general matter, if the President believes that the Court would sustain a particular provision as constitutional, the President should execute the statute, notwithstanding his own beliefs about the constitutional issue." Why should a President surrender his independent constitutional judgment by anticipating how a court might decide? The memo continued: "If, however, the President, exercising his independent judgment, determines both that a provision would violate the Constitution and that it is probable that the Court would agree with him, the President has the authority to decline to execute the statute."[295] In each case, according to OLC, the President should look to the court for guidance and reassurance.

The memo acknowledges that a dispute might not be litigated or that a court could refuse to take a case: "Some legislative encroachments on executive authority, however, will not be justiciable or are for other reasons unlikely to be resolved in court." In such a case, the President "must shoulder the responsibility of protecting the constitutional role of the presidency."[296] Why not shoulder that responsibility from the start, rather than attempting to predict how a court might or might not decide and whether it would even take the case?

The memo states that the "fact that a sitting President signed the statute in question does not change this analysis."[297] If a President determines that a bill presented to him is unconstitutional,

---

292. Louis Fisher, *Committee Controls of Agency Decisions,* Congressional Research Service, Report No. RL33151, Nov. 16, 2005, http://www.loufisher.org/docs/lv/2626.pdf.

293. Louis Fisher, *The Unitary Executive and Inherent Executive Power,* 12 U. PA. J. CONST. L. 569 (2010).

294. 18 OP. O.L.C. 199, 200 (1994).

295. Id. at 200.

296. Id. at 201.

297. Id. at 202.

or would likely be held unconstitutional by a court, why not veto the bill, publicly explain the constitutional defects, and have Congress correct it? Why sign what the executive branch regards as an unconstitutional bill? The memo does identify an option available to the President: sign what he considers to be an unconstitutional bill, but, in a signing statement, publicly identify the provision that is unconstitutional and offer reasons to support that judgment.[298] Examples of these signing statement disputes are included in Chapter 5, section 5.

An earlier OLC memo, issued in 1980, concludes that the President in rare cases would be justified in not enforcing a statute. At the same time, it denies that the President possesses what was called in English constitutional history the "dispensing power": the freedom of executives to dispense with and ignore certain laws.[299] The memo concedes that there is no specific evidence that the Framers intended to give the President a constitutional privilege to disregard statutes deemed to be inconsistent with the Constitution.[300] Yet in "rare cases the Executive's duty to the constitutional system may require that a statute be challenged; and if that happens, executive action in defiance of the statute is authorized and lawful if the statute is unconstitutional."[301] The opinion closed with this statement: "Altogether, there have been very few occasions in our history when Presidents or Attorneys General have undertaken to defy, or to refuse to defend, an Act of Congress."[302]

Acts of executive defiance became frequent during the administration of Richard Nixon, who repeatedly refused to spend appropriated funds, sometimes cutting programs in half or eliminating them entirely. A series of court rulings and the Impoundment Control Act of 1974 put an end to that practice (Chapter 6, section 6). Beginning in 1979, Congress directed the Attorney General to issue a report to both houses in any case in which the Attorney General refrained from enforcing a statutory provision because the Justice Department has determined "that such provision of law is not constitutional." Also, the department must report to Congress when it decides to "contest, or will refrain from defending, any provision" of statutory law in any judicial or administrative proceedings because of constitutional objections.[303] President Obama and Attorney General Holder complied with this statute in 2011 when reporting to Congress that the administration could no longer defend the Defense of Marriage Act (DOMA).[304] The constitutionality of DOMA has been contested in a number of lower courts. On June 26, 2013, the Supreme Court in *United States v. Windsor* struck down a key part of DOMA and declared that gay couples married in states where it is legal must receive the same federal benefits (including tax, health, and Social Security) that heterosexual couples receive.

---

298. Id.

299. 4A Op. O.L.C. 55, 57–58 (1980).

300. Id. at 5.

301. Id. at 59.

302. Id. at 61. For other OLC opinions supporting the President's authority not to carry out certain statutes or statutory provisions, see 16 Op. O.L.C. 18, 31–36 (1992); 14 Op. O.L.C. 37, 46–52 (1990). Studies that analyze the President's constitutional power not to enforce statutes include Dawn E. Johnsen, *Presidential Non-Enforcement of Constitutionally Objectionable Statutes*, 63 Law & Contemp. Prob. 7 (2000); Christopher N. May, Presidential Defiance of "Unconstitutional" Laws (1998); Gary Lawson & Christopher D. Moore, *The Executive Power of Constitutional Interpretation*, 81 Iowa L. Rev. 1267 (1996); and Christine E. Burgess, *When May a President Refuse to Enforce the Law?*, 72 Texas L. Rev. 631 (1994).

303. 98 Stat. 1040, 1049–50, sec. 21 (1979), revised by 116 Stat. 1771, sec. 202 (2002); 28 U.S.C. § 530D.

304. U.S. Department of Justice, Letter from the Attorney General to Congress on Litigation Involving the Defense of Marriage Act, Feb. 23, 2011, http://www.justice.gov/opa/pr/2011/February/11-ag-223.html

President Reagan provoked a lengthy court battle in 1984 when he signed the Competition in Contracting Act (CICA), which gave the General Accounting Office new powers to monitor contract disputes in executive agencies. Attorney General William French Smith and Office of Management and Budget (OMB) Director David Stockman instructed agencies not to comply with that part of the statute. A series of court rulings in the Third Circuit and the Ninth Circuit upheld the constitutionality of the statutory provision. The Ninth Circuit ruled that under Article I, section 7, the President "must either sign or veto a bill presented to him. Once signed by the President, as CICA was on July 18, 1984, the bill becomes part of the law of the land and the President must 'take care that [it] be faithfully executed.'" Article I, section 7 "does not empower the President to revise a bill, either before or after signing. It does not empower the President to employ a so-called 'line item veto' and excise or sever provisions of a bill with which he disagrees."[305]

A controversy in 2004 involved the Chief Actuary for the Centers for Medicare and Medicaid Services in the Department of Health and Human Services. By law, he was required to provide independent and professional cost estimates to Congress. With regard to a controversial prescription drug benefit bill, his estimates were substantially higher than those given to Congress by the administration. He was advised by his supervisor that if he provided his estimates to Congress he could be fired. That dispute is analyzed in Chapter 5, section 8C.

# 11. EXECUTIVE ORDERS AND PROCLAMATIONS

To carry out the laws, executive agencies issue rules and regulations and Presidents rely on executive orders and proclamations. Although "making laws" is generally associated with Congress, studies also analyze the "ordinance making" and "decree making" authority of Presidents. Often these executive instruments are used to implement statutory policy; at times they represent purely presidential initiatives.[306] Increasingly, Presidents have become involved in monitoring and controlling agency regulations. Congress has enacted a number of provisions to provide public notice of these forms of executive-branch lawmaking.

## A. Statutory policy

By law, substantive agency policies are published in the *Federal Register* and the *Code of Federal Regulations*, not in internal agency manuals.[307] Presidential executive orders and proclamations

---

305. Lear Siegler, Inc., Energy Products Div. v. Lehman, 842 F.2d 1102, 1124 (9th Cir. 1988), withdrawn in part on other grounds, 893 F.2d 205 (9th Cir. 1989, as amended on Jan. 10, 1990). For other CICA cases, see the series of rulings at Ameron, Inc. v. U.S. Army Corps of Engineers, 607 F. Supp. 962 (D. N.J. 1985); Ameron, Inc. v. U.S. Army Corps of Engineers, 610 F. Supp. 750 (D. N.J. 1985); Ameron, Inc. v. U.S. Army Corps of Engineers, 787 F.2d 875 (3d Cir. 1986); and Ameron, Inc. v. U.S. Army Corps of Engineers, 809 F.2d 979 (3d Cir. 1986). On the CICA litigation, see Eugene Gressman, *Take Care, Mr. President*, 64 N.C. L. Rev. 381 (1986).

306. John M. Carey & Matthew Soberg Shugart, eds., Executive Decree Authority (1998); James Hart, The Ordinance Making Powers of the President of the United States (1925).

307. Morton v. Ruiz, 415 U.S. 199 (1974).

that have general applicability and legal effect are also published in the *Federal Register*. Based partly on statutory authority vested in him by the Federal Register Act of 1935, President Roosevelt issued an executive order in 1936 that gave the Bureau of the Budget (now the Office of Management and Budget) the responsibility for reviewing all proposed executive orders and proclamations.[308]

The Administrative Procedure Act (APA) of 1946 requires an opportunity for interested parties to submit comments on proposed rules and regulations during a period before their effective date. Judicial review is available. Courts may find unlawful any agency action that is "arbitrary, capricious, an abuse of discretion, or otherwise not in accordance with law" and "contrary to constitutional right, power, privilege, or immunity."[309] Although executive orders and proclamations are published in the *Federal Register*, their announcement is not expected to be preceded by formal notice, hearings, and opportunity for public comment. Draft copies are sometimes made available to Congress and the public for notice and comment, but such initiatives are voluntary on the part of the President.[310]

Case law in the early 1980s suggested that Congress may impose notice and comment requirements on presidential executive orders and proclamations that are issued to implement statutory policy, provided Congress does so explicitly.[311] In 1982, a district court remarked that statutes enacted by Congress "are not subjected to notice and comment periods and no reason appears why the same should not be true for presidential proclamations."[312] This analogy ignores the explicit constitutional grant of legislative power to Congress and the checks that operate on that power, including bicameralism and the presidential veto. Those constraints do not operate on executive orders and proclamations.

No one knows how many executive orders have been issued. By August 6, 2013, the numbered series had reached 13,651. That total is understated. When some executive orders were discovered from prior decades, they had to be shoehorned into the existing series by using letters or fractions: e.g., Executive Order 106½ and Executive Order 103A. Estimates of the unnumbered executive orders range from 15,000 to 50,000.[313] On August 9, 2013, President Obama issued Proclamation 9002. There is no clear distinction between executive orders and

---

308. 49 Stat. 500, sec. 5 (1935). Roosevelt's Executive Order 7298, Feb. 18, 1936, appeared too early for the first volume of the *Federal Register*. It is reprinted in James Hart, *The Exercise of Rule-Making Power*, THE PRESIDENT'S COMMITTEE ON ADMINISTRATIVE MANAGEMENT 355 (1937).

309. 60 Stat. 237, sec. 10(e) (1946); 5 U.S.C. § 706.

310. A rare, if not unprecedented, example of an executive order published in draft form in the *Federal Register* for notice and comment was an order by President Carter to improve federal regulations. It was printed at 42 FED. REG. 59740 (1977) and 43 FED. REG. 12661 (1978), including an analysis of public comments. It was published in final form as Executive Order 12044 four months after its original publication.

311. In United States v. Wayte, 549 F. Supp. 1376, 1389–91 (C.D. Cal. 1982), a district court held that President Carter's Proclamation 4771 on draft registration was invalid for failing to comply with notice and comment requirements of the Military Selective Service Act. Although reversed in United States v. Wayte, 710 F.2d 1385, 1388–89 (9th Cir. 1983), both decisions recognized the authority of Congress to make such a requirement.

312. United States v. Martin, 557 F. Supp. 681, 690 (N.D. Iowa 1982).

313. On numbering of executive orders, see PRESIDENTIAL EXECUTIVE ORDERS, compiled by WPA Historical Records survey (2 vols., 1944), at viii. On estimates, see *Executive Orders and Proclamations: A Study of a Use of Presidential Power*, printed for the House Committee on Government Operations, 85th Cong., 1st Sess. 37 (1957). A partial list of unnumbered orders appears in *List and Index of Presidential Executive Orders (Unnumbered Series)*, 1789–1941, New Jersey Historical Records Survey, Work Projects Administration (1943).

proclamations. Many proclamations are merely declaratory in effect, such as those issued to designate Earth Week, Law Day, National Farm Safety Week, and other issues of general interest. Some proclamations have substantive impact.

# B. Presidential lawmaking

The first venture into unilateral presidential lawmaking occurred in 1793 when the Washington administration debated the merits of proclaiming America's neutrality in the war between England and France. Would the proclamation encroach on the power of Congress to decide questions of war and peace? President Washington asked his Cabinet whether he should consult with Congress by calling it back in special session. They advised against it.[314] Relying for authority on the "law of nations," Washington warned Americans to avoid any involvement in the war and instructed law officers to prosecute all persons who violated his proclamation.[315]

Washington discovered that his foray into executive lawmaking contained a built-in check. Enforcement of his proclamation required the consent and cooperation of jurors. When Gideon Henfield was prosecuted for violating the proclamation, jurors refused to convict anyone simply on the basis of a proclamation. That might have sufficed in England, where kings could issue proclamations and have them nailed on trees, but not in republican America. The creation of U.S. criminal law, jurors insisted, required a statute passed by Congress. With no statute in hand, the administration dropped other prosecutions.[316] At that point Washington sought the support of Congress. When it returned in December 1793, he told the two houses that it rested with "the wisdom of Congress to correct, improve, or enforce" the policy his proclamation had established.[317] The Neutrality Act of 1794 gave the administration the firm legal footing it needed to prosecute violators.[318] Washington's proclamation sparked the public exchange between "Pacificus" (Alexander Hamilton) and "Helvidius" (James Madison) regarding the scope of independent presidential power (section 3A of this chapter).

Lincoln's Emancipation Proclamation is often described as a purely presidential initiative in lawmaking, but he acted only after Congress had passed a number of supportive statutes. His proclamation progressed through three stages: the July 22, 1862 draft presented to the Cabinet, the revised proclamation of September 22, 1862, and the final, official version released on January 1, 1863.[319] Congress had already passed two confiscation acts of August 6, 1861 and July 17, 1862, establishing national policy to seize all property (including slaves) of southern

---

314. 32 THE WRITINGS OF GEORGE WASHINGTON 420–21, note 14 (Fitzpatrick ed. 1939).

315. For the confused process followed in drafting the Neutrality Proclamation, see Robert J. Reinstein, *Executive Power and the Law of Nations in the Washington Administration*, 46 U. RICH. L. REV. 373, 409–33 (2012). Also: Jules Lobel, *The Rise and Decline of the Neutrality Act: Sovereignty and Congressional War Powers in United States Foreign Policy*, 24 HARV. INT'L L. J. 1 (1983).

316. FRANCIS WHARTON, STATE TRIALS OF THE UNITED STATES DURING THE ADMINISTRATIONS OF WASHINGTON AND ADAMS 84–85, 88 (1849); 2 JOHN MARSHALL, THE LIFE OF GEORGE WASHINGTON 273 (1832).

317. ANNALS OF CONG., 3d Cong., 1-2 Sess. 11 (1793).

318. 1 Stat. 381–84 (1794). See Robert J. Reinstein, *An Early View of Executive Powers and Privilege: The Trial of Smith and Ogden*, 2 HASTINGS CONST. L. Q. 309 (1975).

319. HAROLD HOLZER, EMANCIPATING LINCOLN: THE PROCLAMATION IN TEXT, CONTEXT, AND MEMORY 34–35, 88, 129 (2012). See JOHN HOPE FRANKLIN, THE EMANCIPATION PROCLAMATION (1995 ed.).

states that had taken up arms against the Union.[320] On March 13, 1862, it prohibited military and naval officers from returning fugitive slaves to their masters.[321] On April 10, 1862, it declared that the United States should cooperate with states willing to gradually abolish slavery by offering financial aid to compensate them.[322] On April 16, 1862, it abolished slavery in the District of Columbia.[323]

Looking to more contemporary times, a number of executive orders and proclamations have proven to be costly for Presidents, private citizens, and the country's reputation. During his first 15 months in office, President Roosevelt signed 674 executive orders as part of the administration's effort to stimulate the economy. In its first year, the National Recovery Administration (NRA) approved hundreds of codes and released 2,998 administrative orders that approved or modified the codes. Almost 6,000 NRA press releases, some with legislative effect, were issued during this period.[324] So many orders were issued that department officials were often unaware of their own regulations. At one point the government discovered that it had brought an indictment and taken an appeal to the Supreme Court without realizing that the portion of the regulation on which the proceeding was based had been eliminated by an executive order.[325]

Congress created the NRA to obtain from industrial and trade associations a variety of regulations designed to minimize competition, raise prices, and restrict production. If the President regarded the codes as unacceptable, he could prescribe his own and enforce them as law. The drafting of the NRA statute was dominated by industries and trade associations; executive officials appeared to have little interest in constitutional questions or procedural safeguards.[326] In an early case, the Supreme Court struck down a section of the NRA statute governing controls on petroleum production because it failed to establish a "criterion to govern the President's course." The Court said that Congress "has declared no policy, has established no standard, has laid down no rule."[327] The rest of the NRA was invalidated that same year.[328] These decisions also struck down the executive orders that Roosevelt had issued to implement the NRA. In 1935, the House Judiciary Committee condemned the "utter chaos" regarding the publication and distribution of administrative rules and pronouncements.[329] The legislative result was a requirement

---

320. 12 Stat. 319 (1861); 12 Stat. 589 (1862). See SILVANA R. SIDDALI, FROM PROPERTY TO PERSON: SLAVERY AND THE CONFISCATION ACTS, 1861–1862 (2005).

321. 12 Stat. at 354 (1862).

322. Id. 617 (1862).

323. Id. at 376 (1862). See Sanford Levinson, *The David C. Baum Memorial Lecture: Was the Emancipation Proclamation Constitutional? Do We/Should We Care What the Answer Is?*, 2001 U. ILL. L. REV. 1135; Michael Stokes Paulsen, *The Emancipation Proclamation and the Commander in Chief Power*, 40 GA. L. REV. 807 (2006); Paul Finkelman, *Lincoln, Emancipation, and the Limits of Constitutional Change*, 2008 SUP. CT. REV. 349 (2009); and Paul Finkelman, *Lincoln and the Preconceptions for Emancipation: The Moral Grandeur of a Bill of Lading*, in LINCOLN'S PROCLAMATION: RACE, PLACE, AND THE PARADOXES OF EMANCIPATION 13–44 (William A. Blair & Karen Fisher Younger, eds., 2009).

324. 59 A.B.A. REP. 553–54 (1934).

325. Panama Refining Co. v. Ryan, 293 U.S. 388, 412–13 (1935). The discovery by administration officials that an executive order had inadvertently deleted penalties is discussed in PETER H. IRONS, THE NEW DEAL LAWYERS 70–71 (1982).

326. IRONS, *supra* note 325, at 22–107.

327. Panama Refining Co. v. Ryan, 293 U.S. at 430.

328. Schechter Corp. v. United States, 295 U.S. 495 (1935).

329. H. Rep. No. 280, 74th Cong., 1st Sess. 1-2 (1935).

that a *Federal Register* be created to publish all presidential and agency documents having the effect of law.[330]

In 1942, President Roosevelt issued Executive Order 9066, requiring the transfer of more than 110,000 Americans of Japanese descent (about two-thirds of them natural-born U.S. citizens) from their homes to "relocation centers." Roosevelt acted in part on "the authority vested in me as President of the United States, and Commander in Chief of the Army and Navy."[331] With no evidence of disloyalty or subversive activity, and without the benefit of any form of hearing, these individuals were imprisoned solely because of their ancestry and race. Congress enacted legislation ratifying the executive order and two Supreme Court decisions in 1943 and 1944 sustained both a curfew and detention against the Japanese Americans. The constitutional deficiencies of these policies are discussed in Chapter 9, section 8B.

In 1947, President Truman issued Executive Order 9835, requiring a loyalty investigation of every employee in the federal executive branch. There was no opportunity to confront and cross-examine secret accusers (Chapter 7, section 10). In 1952, Truman faced a nationwide strike of steelworkers, jeopardizing his ability to prosecute the war against North Korea. He reacted by issuing Executive Order 10340, directing the Secretary of Commerce to take possession of and operate the plants and facilities of major steel companies. Although Truman cited his authority as Commander in Chief, the Supreme Court struck down the executive order (Chapter 8, section 6).

Congress created the Subversive Activities Control Board (SACB) in 1950 to investigate communist activities.[332] The board required the public registration of "communist-action" and "communist-front" organizations. A series of court decisions held that the registration feature violated the Fifth Amendment prohibition against self-incrimination.[333] Facing extinction, the board gained a new lease on life in 1971 when President Nixon issued Executive Order 11605 to expand the board's power and field of inquiry.[334] Efforts were made to prohibit the use of any appropriated funds to implement the order.[335] House and Senate conferees compromised by providing the board with $350,000 but expressly prohibited it from using any of those funds to carry out the executive order.[336] Beginning with the fiscal 1974 budget, the administration did not even bother requesting funds for the SACB.

Many other executive orders and proclamations have been controversial because they involved unilateral presidential decisions concerning tariff duties, tariff surcharges, fees on imported oil, and other parts of the taxing power.[337] A proclamation by President Clinton in 1996 illustrates how the President can independently accomplish what Congress was considering doing by legislation. Congress debated a bill to designate as wilderness 1.8 million acres owned by the federal government in Utah. The proposal cleared House and Senate committees but was

---

330. 49 Stat. 500 (1935).

331. 7 Fed. Reg. 1407 (1942).

332. 64 Stat. 997 (1950).

333. Boorda v. SACB, 421 F.2d 1142 (D.C. Cir. 1969), cert. denied, 397 U.S. 1042 (1970); United States v. Robel, 389 U.S. 258 (1967); Albertson v. SACB, 382 U.S. 70 (1965); Communist Party of the United States v. SACB, 367 U.S. 11 (1961).

334. 36 Fed. Reg. 12831 (1971).

335. 117 Cong. Rec. 25898-902, 27305-12 (1971); 118 Cong. Rec. 21053-74 (1972).

336. 86 Stat. 1134, sec. 706 (1972).

337. Louis Fisher, *Executive Orders and Proclamations, 1933–99: Controversies with Congress and the Courts*, Congressional Research Service, report RL30264, July 23, 1999, at 7, 11, 12–13, 14.

not enacted. Clinton then issued Proclamation 6920 to establish the Grand Staircase-Escalante National Monument in Utah. Acting under the Antiquities Act of 1906, as amended, he set aside approximately 1.7 million acres.[338] In response, legislation was introduced to provide that for any national monument in excess of 5,000 acres, the President would need an act of Congress and the concurrence of the governor and the state legislature. The House passed this legislation but the Senate did not.[339] Congress can retaliate against executive orders and proclamations it finds objectionable, but moving remedial legislation through both chambers can be an uphill struggle.[340]

A current example of overreliance on executive orders, as though they present a surefire way to accomplish presidential policy, is the executive order issued by President Obama in January 2009 to close down the Guantánamo detention facility within a year.[341] Because of inadequate political preparation by the administration, both to Congress and the public, the executive order proved feckless and the facility remained open. It has been reported that Obama "admitted that he had never devised a plan to persuade Congress to shut down the prison."[342] He seemed to have "a sense that if he sketches a vision, it will happen."[343] (Guantánamo is further discussed in Chapter 9, section 8C).

## C. Presidential control over agency rulemaking

Over the last four decades, Presidents have tried to gain closer control over agency rulemaking, responding in part to objections that the federal government was issuing burdensome and unnecessary regulations. A major step came in 1981 with President Reagan's Executive Order 12291, which required agencies to send a copy of each proposed rule to the Office of Information and Regulatory Affairs (OIRA) in OMB. Agencies had to prepare a cost-benefit analysis for each "major" rule (e.g., those with a $100 million impact on the economy).[344] A series of executive orders have established White House policy over agency rules: Ford's Executive Order 11821 in 1974, Carter's Executive Order 12044 in 1978, Reagan's Executive Order 12498 in 1985, Clinton's

338. 61 FED. REG. 50223-27 (1996).

339. Fisher, *supra* note 337, at 18–19.

340. Many studies on executive orders and proclamations have appeared in recent years: ADAM L. WARBER, EXECUTIVE ORDERS AND THE MODERN PRESIDENCY: LEGISLATING FROM THE OVAL OFFICE (2006); WILLIAM G. HOWELL, POWER WITHOUT PERSUASION: THE POLITICS OF DIRECT PRESIDENTIAL ACTION (2003); PHILLIP J. COOPER, BY ORDER OF THE PRESIDENT: THE USE AND ABUSE OF EXECUTIVE DIRECT ACTION (2002); and KENNETH R. MAYER, WITH THE STROKE OF A PEN: EXECUTIVE ORDERS AND PRESIDENTIAL POWER (2001). The scope of executive orders and proclamations attracted two congressional hearings in 1999: *Congressional Limitation of Executive Orders*, hearing before the Subcommittee on Commercial and Administrative Law of the House Committee on the Judiciary, 106th Cong., 1st Sess. (1999); and *Executive Orders*, hearing before the Subcommittee on Legislative and Budget Process of the House Committee on Rules, 106th Cong., 1st Sess. (1999).

341. The White House, Office of the Press Secretary, *Review and Disposition of Individuals Detained at the Guantánamo Bay Naval Base and Closure of Detention Facilities*, Executive Order, Jan. 22, 2009.

342. Jo Becker & Scott Shane, *Secret 'Kill List' Proves a Test of Obama's Principles and Will*, N.Y. TIMES, May 29, 2012, at A10.

343. Id. See Louis Fisher, *Closing Guantánamo: President Obama Must Do It Right This Time*, Nat'l L. J., July 1, 2103, at 42.

344. 46 FED. REG. 13193 (1981).

Executive Order 12866 in 1993, Bush's Executive Order 13422 in 2007, and Obama's Executive Order 13563 in 2011.[345]

Some researchers objected that OMB review delayed and in some cases permanently blocked agency efforts to issue rules for their statutorily assigned programs. Cost-benefit analysis can be easily manipulated to artificially inflate costs and minimize benefits. What is presented as OMB oversight can equally serve as a "conduit" to promote the interests of private industry. These off-the-record ex parte contacts between agency and White House officials depart from APA's model of public knowledge and participation. A natural tension exists between OMB review and the statutory values and purposes that Congress places in agency experts.[346] An article published in 1997 acknowledged the increased role of the President in agency rulemaking but expressed concern that it pushed the activity too much from legal obligations to mere politics.[347]

A study by Elena Kagan in 2001 concluded that active presidential involvement need not be hostile to agency regulations. It may serve pro-regulatory objectives. Presidents who assert personal ownership of agency regulations can add transparency to the regulatory process. She admitted, however, that President Clinton's control "did not show itself in all, or even all important, regulation; no President (or his executive office staff) could, and presumably none would wish to, supervise so broad a swath of regulatory activity."[348] If Presidents and their staff can only select a few rules to monitor, what competence do they bring to that task? No doubt the regulatory process is political—whether within the agency or the White House—but how is public policy improved by having a President and his aides devote time trying to understand the details of a pending regulation?

Clinton seemed to appreciate that regulations calling for "significant levels of scientific expertise," such as hazardous substances in the environment and workplace, were not appropriate for presidential intervention.[349] With regard to environmental regulation, Kagan said that Clinton was reluctant to intervene "for fear" that his involvement would "appear excessively to politicize administrative action thought to rest on neutral competence."[350] Kagan also identified another area of agency activity that would be off-limits to the President: adjudication of individual rights and benefits.[351] On the whole, however, she argued that any delegation of rulemaking authority to an agency is an implicit delegation to the President unless Congress specifically provides otherwise.

---

345. 39 Fed. Reg. 41501 (1974), 43 Fed. Reg. 12661 (1978), 50 Fed. Reg. 1036 (1985), 58 Fed. Reg. 51735 (1993), 72 Fed. Reg. 2763 (2007), 76 Fed. Reg. 3821 (2011). See Curtis W. Copeland, *Federal Rulemaking: The Role of the Office of Information and Regulatory Affairs*, Congressional Research Service, Report RL32397, June 9, 2009.

346. Curtis W. Copeland, *Executive Order 13422: An Expansion of Presidential Influence in the Rulemaking Process*, 37 Pres. Stud. Q. 531 (2007); Christopher C. DeMuth & Douglas H. Ginsburg, *White House Review of Agency Rulemaking*, 99 Harv. L. Rev. 1097 (1986); Morton Rosenberg, *Beyond the Limits of Executive Power Presidential Control of Agency Rulemaking Under Executive Order 12,291*, 80 Mich. L. Rev. 193 (1981); and Paul R. Verkuil, *Jawboning Administrative Agencies: Ex Parte Contacts by the White House*, 80 Colum. L. Rev. 943 (1980).

347. Peter L. Strauss, *Presidential Rulemaking*, 72 Chicago-Kent L. Rev. 965 (1997).

348. Elena Kagan, *Presidential Administration*, 114 Harv. L. Rev. 2245, 2250 (2001).

349. Id. at 2308.

350. Id. at 2356.

351. Id. at 2306, 2358, 2363.

Kagan conceded that if an agency agreed to change a proposed regulation, it may have nothing to do with the President and White House aides possessing superior analytical and scientific skills. Other factors can come into play: "Agency officials may accede to his preferences because they feel a sense of personal loyalty and commitment to him; because they desire his assistance in budgetary, legislative, and appointments matters; or in extreme cases because they respect and fear his removal power."[352] Those reasons, while understandable, are unrelated to the statutory and legal duties assigned to agencies.

The Congressional Review Act (CRA) of 1996 established procedures to permit Congress to review and disapprove agency regulations. The statute offered Congress expedited procedures for passing a joint resolution of disapproval. Under CRA, before any final rule could take effect it had to be filed with each house of Congress and the General Accounting Office (now the Government Accountability Office).[353] The sponsors of this legislation were concerned that Congress's legislative functions were being increasingly exercised by agencies and the White House, but there has been little use of this statutory procedure. From April 1996 to September 2011, 57,897 rules were reported to Congress, including 1,029 major rules. A total of 72 resolutions of disapproval concerning 47 rules were introduced.[354] Only one was enacted, affecting an ergonomics rule in 2001.[355] Congress has been more effective in using its power of the purse against agency regulations. Congress can add language to appropriations bills that deny funds for a rule or place restrictions and conditions on it.[356]

# 12. PRESIDENTIAL COMMISSIONS

Presidents have created commissions to study national problems. These commissions typically include individuals selected from outside the executive branch. During the Whiskey Rebellion in western Pennsylvania in 1794, President Washington created a commission in an effort to mediate an end to the insurrection. He selected Attorney General William Bradford, Pennsylvania Supreme Court Justice Jasper Yeates, and Senator James Ross. They were empowered to grant an amnesty to the rebels for all past criminal actions in return for assurances they would no longer obstruct the law. The commission made some progress, but Washington decided it was necessary to send in state militias to restore order.[357]

---

352. Id. at 2298.

353. 110 Stat. 868 (1996), 5 U.S.C. §§ 801–08.

354. Statistics compiled by Morton Rosenberg, former attorney for Congressional Research Service.

355. 115 Stat. 7 (2001). For analysis of the statute overturning the ergonomics rule, see Note, *The Mysteries of the Congressional Review Act*, 122 HARV. L. REV. 2162 (2009). For the general ineffectiveness of the CRA, see Morton Rosenberg, *Whatever Happened to Congressional Review of Agency Rulemaking?: A Brief Overview, Assessment, and Proposal for Reform*, 51 ADMIN. L. REV. 1051 (1999), and Daniel Cohen & Peter L. Strauss, *Congressional Review of Agency Rulemaking*, 49 ADMIN. L. REV. 95 (1996).

356. Curtis W. Copeland, *Congressional Influence on Rulemaking and Regulation Through Appropriations Restrictions*, Congressional Research Service, report RL34354, Aug. 5, 2008. See PHILLIP J. COOPER, THE WAR AGAINST REGULATION FROM JIMMY CARTER TO GEORGE W. BUSH (2009).

357. THOMAS P. SLAUGHTER, THE WHISKEY REBELLION: FRONTIER EPILOGUE TO THE AMERICAN REVOLUTION 196–203 (1986).

In 1842, President Tyler created a commission to study the New York Customs House. A House resolution asked him "under what authority," "for what purposes and objects," and "out of what fund" the commission functioned. Tyler said he created the commission under his constitutional authority to "take care" that the laws be faithfully executed, to give Congress "from time to time information on the state of the Union," and to "recommend to their consideration such measures as he shall judge necessary and expedient."[358] Congress has at times denied public funds for these commissions, forcing the President to seek private contributions.

## A. Congressional support

Many study committees and commissions have been established and funded by Congress to analyze government programs. The Cockrell Committee (1887–1889) exposed some of the reasons for huge backlogs in administrative work: time-consuming and duplicative routines, unnecessary recordkeeping, and the use of copyists who transcribed by hand rather than using typewriters and duplicating machines. The Cockrell-Dockery Commission (1893–1895) conducted investigations into agency operations, resulting in new accounting procedures for the Treasury Department.[359] For much of the nineteenth century, Congress remained active in overseeing the operations of executive departments and agencies.[360]

By the turn of the century, students of public administration and activists from the progressive movement urged Presidents to devote more of their efforts to this oversight function.[361] The federal civilian workforce had grown markedly since the Civil War and new agencies had been created. In accepting a leadership role, President Theodore Roosevelt appointed five federal officials in 1905 to serve on what was called the Keep Commission. He directed them to determine how the executive branch might more economically and effectively discharge its duties.[362] Roosevelt developed a pattern of appointing volunteer, unpaid commissioners to study social and economic issues. To publish the findings of one of his commissions, he asked Congress to appropriate $25,000. Not only did Congress refuse but in 1909 it enacted a prohibition against the use of public funds to pay for the compensation or expenses of any commission, council, board, "or other similar body" unless authorized by law. Roosevelt protested that Congress had no right to pass such legislation and threatened to ignore the proscription, but he did not receive

---

358. Carl Marcy, Presidential Commissions 8 (1945).

359. Oscar Kraines, *The Cockrell Committee, 1887–1889: First Comprehensive Congressional Investigation into Administration*, 4 West. Pol. Q. 583 (1951). For the Cockrell-Dockery Commission, see Fred W. Powell, comp., Control of Federal Expenditures: A Documentary History, 1775–1894, at 706–915 (1939); Lloyd Milton Short, The development of National Administrative Organization in the United States 278–80 (1923); and Gustavus A. Weber, Organized Efforts for the Improvement of Methods of Administration in the United States 67–70 (1919).

360. Peri I. Arnold, Making the Managerial Presidency: Comprehensive Reorganization Planning, 1905–1996, at 3–21 (1998).

361. Id. at 13–18; Herbert Croly, The Promise of American Life (1909).

362. Louis Fisher, Presidential Spending Power 28 (1975). See also Oscar Kraines, *The President Versus Congress: The Keep Commission, 1905–1909: First Comprehensive Presidential Inquiry into Administration*, 23 West. Pol. Q. 5 (1970); Lewis L. Gould, The Presidency of Theodore Roosevelt 220–21 (1991).

congressional funds. He had to seek the support of a private organization, which agreed to publish the study.[363]

In 1910, President Taft asked Congress to authorize an investigation into more efficient and economical ways of conducting the public business. Congress appropriated $100,000 to fund that project and Taft used the money to set up a five-member Commission on Economy and Efficiency.[364] In June 1912, he submitted to Congress the commission's proposal for a national budget. The President would be made responsible for reviewing departmental estimates and organizing them into a coherent document.[365] On June 10, 1912, Taft directed departmental heads to prepare two sets of estimates: one for the fragmented "Book of Estimates" that had been submitted in the past, and the second for the national budget recommended by the commission.

Congress blocked his plans by passing legislation to require agencies to prepare estimates and submit them to Congress "only in the form and at the time now required by law, and in no other form and at no other time."[366] Taft regarded the form in which he transmitted recommendations to Congress as purely an executive matter. He proceeded with his plans to submit two budgets, but the model budget proposed by the commission was almost completely ignored by Congress. After leaving office, Taft lamented that dust was accumulating on the commission's report.[367] Taft's leadership, however, prepared the way for congressional action that culminated in the Budget and Accounting Act of 1921, a significant milestone in fixing budgetary responsibilities on the President (Chapter 6, section 5).

## B. Presidential reorganization

Private commissions have contributed to the institutional strengthening of the President's office. In 1936, President Franklin D. Roosevelt named three public administration scholars— Louis Brownlow, Charles E. Merriam, and Luther Gulick—to form the President's Committee on Administrative Management. They were supported by a research director and a staff of 26. Roosevelt planned to use emergency funds to support the committee, but Comptroller General J. Raymond McCarl regarded that as an illegal use of appropriated funds, forcing Roosevelt to seek $100,000 from Congress. The appropriation came with a restriction: to identify agency activities that overlapped with other agencies and to recommend that the duplication be abolished and personnel reduced. The administration objected to the condition, but it was enacted.[368] The Senate and the House had taken their own initiatives to study executive reorganization. As a result, the Brownlow Committee agreed to part with $10,000 of its appropriation to support the congressional study.[369]

363. 20 The Works of Theodore Roosevelt 552–53, 416–17 (1926); 35 Stat. 1027, sec. 9 (1909).

364. 36 Stat. 703 (1910). Congress subsequently granted the commission supplement amounts of $75,000 (36 Stat. 1364), $10,000 (37 Stat. 643), and $75,000 (37 Stat. 417). For progress reports and comments on the commission, see 15 Richardson 7698–7719, 7736–45, and 16 Richardson 7829–35.

365. *The Need for a National Budget*, H. Doc. 854, 62d Cong., 2d Sess. (1912).

366. 37 Stat. 415, sec. 9 (1912).

367. William Howard Taft, Our Chief Magistrate and His Powers 64–65 (1916). For the model budget, see 49 Cong. Rec. 3985 (1913). For details on Taft's experience, see Arnold, *supra* note 360, at 26–51.

368. 49 Stat. 1600 (1936).

369. Arnold, *supra* note 360, at 94–95, 98–99.

The committee based its findings on the premise that "managerial direction and control of all departments and agencies of the Executive Branch...should be centered in the President." Its recommendations and studies eventually led to the creation of an Executive Office of the President (EOP) to house federal agencies immediately serving the President. It began with such units as the White House Office, the National Resources Planning Board, and the Central Statistical Board. Agencies added later included the Bureau of the Budget, Council of Economic Advisers, the National Security Council, and other organizations responsible to the President.[370] The committee also recommended the appointment of six presidential assistants who would have a "passion for anonymity."[371]

These proposals encountered strong opposition from Congress in part because they coincided with Roosevelt's court-packing plan (Chapter 9, section 7). The combination of these executive initiatives signaled too much of an effort to aggrandize presidential power. Legislative action had to await 1939, when Congress gave Roosevelt limited reorganization powers and the six assistants. Roosevelt used the reorganization authority to create the EOP and to move the Bureau of the Budget from the Treasury Department to the EOP.

World War II created a huge national debt and the need for managerial competence within the executive branch. In 1947, Congress created a 12-member Commission on Organization of the Executive Branch of the Government to promote economy, efficiency, and improved service by federal agencies. It authorized the President to appoint four commissioners, two from the executive branch and two from private life. The same ratio existed for the four commissioners appointed by the President pro tempore of the Senate and the House Speaker: two from the Senate, two from the House, and two each by the Senate and the House from private life.[372] House Speaker Joseph Martin made the most important appointment: former President Herbert Hoover. In accordance with the statute, the commission elected a chairman. It selected Hoover. Republican leaders hoped the commission would push back against New Deal programs and the size of the White House staff, but Hoover generally supported a strengthened presidential office and additional White House staff.[373] A second Hoover Commission, with reports issued in 1955, also sought ways to augment presidential control of the executive branch.[374]

Subsequent administrations pursued a number of managerial reforms, with promises and goals generally exceeding accomplishments. The idea of a President actually managing the executive branch, in the sense of being personally involved, is wholly impractical.[375] At best the President might attempt to manage through White House aides, but such efforts defeat the constitutional principle of a single executive and confirmed agency officials. Moreover, even operating through surrogates the President can only target a few agency programs. There are too many other pressing obligations.

---

370. Harold C. Relyea, *The Executive Office of the President: An Historical Overview*, Congressional Research Service, Report 98-606 GOV, Nov. 26, 2008. See also Harold C. Relyea, ed., The Executive Office of the President: A Historical, Biographical, and Bibliographical Guide (1997).

371. Arnold, *supra* note 360, at 103. See Louis Brownlow, A Passion for Anonymity (1958), and Report of the President's Committee on Administrative management (1937).

372. 61 Stat. 247 (1947).

373. Arnold, *supra* note 360, at 122–59.

374. Id. at 160–227.

375. See id. at 361–64.

## C. Pearl Harbor and Kennedy's assassination

Presidential commissions that include Supreme Court Justices have received substantial criticism. In December 1941, President Roosevelt named Justice Owen Roberts to chair a commission to investigate the Japanese attack on Pearl Harbor. Although Roberts had prior experience as a prosecutor, he was uncertain about the steps needed for a credible investigation. Several generals had to insist that he put witnesses under oath and have their remarks transcribed to create a record.[376] Also, the commission focused on whether Army or Navy leaders at Pearl Harbor were at fault for being insufficiently unprepared for an attack. Errors of judgment and performance by high civilian officials in Washington, D.C., were not pursued. The commission condemned Admiral Husband E. Kimmel and General Walter C. Short, the top military officers at Pearl Harbor, for dereliction of duty.[377] The investigation took little more than a month. The executive order creating the commission is dated December 18; Justice Roberts handed the report to President Roosevelt on January 23.[378] Other critiques have been directed at the commission, including ex parte contacts between commission members and top officials in Washington, D.C.[379]

The adequacy of the Roberts investigation remained in dispute. In addition to poor performances by Kimmel and Short, were errors committed by civilian officials in the Roosevelt administration? Legislation enacted by Congress on June 13, 1944 ordered separate investigations by the War and Navy Departments.[380] Those reports called into question the findings of the Roberts Commission, especially in the allocation of blame. A joint congressional committee conducted hearings from November 1945 to May 1946, uncovering additional errors of judgment by officials in Washington.[381]

Carl Marcy, author of an early study on presidential commissions, offered a harsh appraisal of congressional efforts to investigate national problems. He said congressional committees "are not reliable fact-finders" and referred to the "general ineffectiveness" of congressional committees in finding facts.[382] A "political body" like Congress "cannot hope to find the real facts."[383] But when he turned his attention to the Roberts Commission, he found no deficiencies at all.[384]

Also subject to criticism is the commission created by President Johnson in November 1963 to investigate the assassination of President Kennedy. Johnson, concerned about reports that linked the killing to other countries, including Cuba and Russia, decided a national commission was essential. It could not be, he said, "an agency of the Executive branch. The commission

---

376. Kenneth Kitts, Presidential Commissions and National Security: The Politics of Damage Control 25–26 (2006).

377. Id. at 26–32.

378. Id. at 26, 32.

379. Id. at 35–36. Another harsh appraisal of the Roberts Commission: Gordon W. Prange, At Dawn We Slept: The Untold Story of Pearl Harbor 592–604 (1981). The commission report is published as S. Doc. No. 159, 77th Cong., 2d sess. (1942).

380. 58 Stat. 276, ch. 247 (1944).

381. Martin V. Melosi, The Shadow of Pearl Harbor: Political Controversy Over the Surprise Attack, 1941–1946, at 97–98, 101, 108, 117, 121, 145–47, 156–57 (1977).

382. Marcy, supra note 358, at 103.

383. Id. at 106.

384. Id. at 91–92, 96, 97.

had to be composed of men who were known to be beyond pressure and above suspicion." He wanted a "Republican chairman whose judicial ability and fairness were unquestioned." The choice: Chief Justice Earl Warren, even though Johnson knew "it was not a good precedent to involve the Supreme Court in such an investigation." Warren reached the same conclusion and "was vigorously opposed to it." He objected "on constitutional grounds."[385]

When Warren arrived at the White House, Johnson insisted that when the country "is confronted with threatening divisions and suspicions" and "its foundation is being rocked, and the President of the United States says that you are the only man who can handle the matter, you won't say 'no,' will you?" He recalled that Warren "swallowed hard and said, 'No, sir.' "[386] Johnson told Warren that given the rumors circulating around the world, a result might be war, including nuclear war, with a first strike against the United States leading to "the loss of forty million people."[387] Given his duties on the Court, Warren could not possibly participate as an active member of the commission in the investigation or even provide close supervision. His function was to provide prestige and credibility to the commission's efforts. Warren later gave three excellent reasons why federal judges should not serve on this type of presidential commission.[388]

Hundreds of books on the Kennedy assassination offer conflicting claims that the case is "closed" or still "open."[389] Edward Jay Epstein, a graduate student at Cornell University, offered an early evaluation. His major focus was not on the assassination but rather on the professional quality of the Warren Commission report. He found that all five senior lawyers on the commission returned to their private practice and made no contribution to the writing of the final report.[390] The members who served on the commission—Senators, Representatives, high executive officials—were "almost invariably men occupied by other important responsibilities."[391]

What was the commission's principal assignment? To objectively and independently assess evidence? Or to dismiss "assassination rumors" about the possible roles of Cuba and Russia? If the latter, as Johnson's claim of 40 million potential U.S. casualties indicated, leads might have to be ignored or discredited no matter the weight of evidence.[392] When Chief Justice Warren's book was published, an editor said that Norman Redlich, an attorney on the commission, claimed that Epstein had "grossly falsified" information that Redlich provided him and refuted "key parts"

---

385. Lyndon Baines Johnson, The Vantage Point: Perspectives of the Presidency, 1963–1969, at 25–27 (1971).

386. Id. at 27.

387. Earl Warren, The Memoirs of Earl Warren 358 (1977).

388. "First, it is not in the spirit of constitutional separation of powers to have a member of the Supreme Court serve on a presidential commission; second, it would distract a Justice from the work of the Court, which had a heavy docket; and, third, it was impossible to foresee what litigation such a Commission might spawn, with resulting disqualification of the Justice from sitting in such cases." Warren, supra note 387, at 356. For additional reasons why federal judges should not serve on presidential commissions, see Wendy E. Ackerman, *Separation of Powers and Judicial Service on Presidential Commissions*, 53 U. Chi. L. Rev. 993 (1986). Exceptions may apply to judges sitting on commissions that involve judicial administration and judicial rulemaking.

389. E.g., Gerald Posner, Case Closed: Lee Harvey Oswald and the Assassination of JFK (1993); and Harold Weisberg, Case Open: The Omissions, Distortions and Falsifications of Case Closed (1994).

390. Edward Jay Epstein, Inquest: The Warren Commission and the Establishment of Truth 23 (1966 paperback edition).

391. Id. at 53.

392. Id. at 30.

of Epstein's book. However, the editor provided no details to substantiate or explain Redlich's objections.[393]

David Belin, one of the attorneys on the commission, agreed with the report's main conclusion that Lee Harvey Oswald was the sole assassin of Kennedy. Yet Belin identified a number of mistakes committed in the course of the investigation: an "overzealous" top-secret designation of investigative material and the exclusion of vital evidence, including photographs and X-rays taken during the autopsy of Kennedy. Belin says the investigation was hampered by inaccurate reports from a number of agencies: the FBI, the Secret Service, the Dallas Police Department, and the Dallas Sheriff's Office.[394]

Some presidential commissions are intended to prevent or limit independent congressional inquiries. In December 1974, newspaper reports revealed a number of illegal CIA operations, including domestic spying and attempts to assassinate foreign leaders. President Ford decided to create the Rockefeller Commission to investigate these agency activities and make recommendations. Of the eight commissioners, one was Governor Ronald Reagan, who was able to attend only 10 of the 26 meetings.[395] Notwithstanding Ford's intent, both houses of Congress conducted their own investigations of CIA illegalities. Recent studies have analyzed the effectiveness of other commissions in the field of national security.[396]

The success of presidential commissions depends on their stated purpose. Is the inquiry well defined? Is the objective likely to be attained, particularly within the four years (or less) of a President's term? Who serves on the commission? Competent, experienced individuals who have the time to devote to a lengthy, complex study? Busy public officials and private citizens who can, at most, lend their prestigious names? Is the commission so weighted with special interests that its report will lack credibility and usefulness?[397]

This chapter has focused on powers exercised mainly or exclusively by the President: removals, pardons, the Opinion Clause, the Take Care Clause, executive orders and proclamations, and presidential commissions. The next chapter turns to powers that regularly involve Congress, including appointments, delegated power, and the creation of independent agencies. Jointly held powers are also analyzed in Chapter 5, which is devoted to vetoes and access to information.

393. WARREN, *supra* note 387, at 363.

394. DAVID W. BELIN, NOVEMBER 22, 1963: YOU ARE THE JURY 3, 16–17, 345–49, 361–62, 422 (1973).

395. Kenneth Kitts, *Commission Politics and National Security: Gerald Ford's Response to the CIA Controversy of 1975*, 26 PRES. STUD. Q. 1081, 1089 (1996).

396. JORDAN TAMA, TERRORISM AND NATIONAL SECURITY REFORM: HOW COMMISSIONS CAN DRIVE CHANGE DURING CRISES (2011); and KENNETH KITTS, PRESIDENTIAL COMMISSIONS AND NATION SECURITY: THE POLITICS OF DAMAGE CONTROL (2006).

397. See Amy B. Zegart, Blue Ribbons, Black Boxes: Toward a Better Understanding of Presidential Commissions, 34 PRES. STUD. Q. 366 (2004); DAVID FLITNER, JR., THE POLITICS OF PRESIDENTIAL COMMISSIONS (1986); TERRENCE R. TUCHINGS, RHETORIC AND REALITY: PRESIDENTIAL COMMISSIONS AND THE MAKING OF PUBLIC POLICY (1979); MIRRA KOMAROVSKY, ed., SOCIOLOGY AND PUBLIC POLICY: THE CASE OF PRESIDENTIAL COMMISSIONS (1975); THOMAS R. WOLANIN, PRESIDENTIAL ADVISORY COMMISSIONS: TRUMAN TO NIXON (1975); and FRANK POPPER, THE PRESIDENT'S COMMISSIONS (1970). For a study of riot commissions from 1917 to 1970, see ANTHONY M. PLATT, ed., THE POLITICS OF RIOT COMMISSIONS: A COLLECTION OF OFFICIAL REPORTS AND CRITICAL ESSAYS (1971).

# FOUR

# The President and Congress

PREVIOUS CHAPTERS ANALYZED POWERS ALLOCATED PRIMARILY TO THE President, although congressional involvement can be significant in directing "ministerial" actions and placing statutory limits on the President's removal power. Many of the commissions discussed at the end of Chapter 3 were created both by Congress and the President. This chapter examines powers that routinely call for presidential-congressional interactions: the legislative process, appointments, independent counsels, delegation of authority, and independent commissions.

## 1. INAUGURAL ADDRESS

Article II, section 1 requires the President, before he enters "on the Execution of his Office," to take an oath or affirmation to preserve, protect, and defend the Constitution. Taking this oath marks a public commitment in full view of federal officials and the public (Chapter 2, section 5). It is the custom for the retiring President to be present at the inauguration ceremony to signify the peaceful transfer of power. There are some exceptions. In 1801, President John Adams decided to leave the nation's capital at an early hour and did not appear at Jefferson's inauguration.[1] In 1829, John Quincy Adams decided not to participate in the inauguration of Andrew Jackson.[2] In 1869, President-elect Ulysses S. Grant refused to ride to the inaugural ceremony with outgoing President Andrew Johnson, reflecting a dispute between the two on Johnson's effort to remove Edwin Stanton as his Secretary of War (Chapter 3, section 7A).[3]

The Constitution does not require an inaugural address, but it has been the practice of Presidents to offer some remarks to convey general principles, plans, and values.[4] There is general agreement that the nature of the inaugural address—and other presidential speeches—has changed fundamentally from practices of the nineteenth century. President George Washington seldom delivered more

---

1. JOSEPH E. KALLENBACH, THE AMERICAN CHIEF EXECUTIVE: THE PRESIDENCY AND THE GOVERNORSHIP 275 (1966).

2. Id.

3. Id. at 275–76.

4. ARTHUR M. SCHLESINGER, JR. & FRED L. ISRAEL, eds., MY FELLOW CITIZENS: THE INAUGURAL ADDRESSES OF THE PRESIDENTS OF THE UNITED STATES, 1789–2009 (2010).

than a major speech a year.[5] Presidents now have access to a large number of speechwriters capable of grinding out hundreds of products for public consumption, all made easier with the rise of the modern media.[6] Beyond the sheer volume of speeches is concern about their quality. Instead of functioning as the head of the administration to carry out constitutional duties, presidential rhetoric is aimed less at Congress than at the general public. These speeches often create false expectations and feed public skepticism.[7]

It is often assumed that presidential speeches are effective methods of building support for White House objectives. They might be effective in gaining nomination and winning primaries and the general election, but use of the same kind of rhetoric once in office does not ensure political success. In a study released in 2003, George Edwards found little evidence that "going public" had much influence in building public support for a President's agenda. He points out that campaigns "are waged in either/or terms," while governing "involves deliberation, cooperation, negotiation, and compromise over an extended period."[8] Going public is likely to contribute to gridlock, incivility, and public cynicism.[9]

The inaugural address is not used to announce specific legislative recommendations. Those proposals are set forth in the State of the Union Message and other public statements. In the first inaugural address, President Washington chose to omit the listing of "a recommendation of particular measures" and instead paid tribute to members of Congress. He spoke of "the talents, the rectitude, and the patriotism which adorn the characters selected to devise and adopt them."[10]

Vice Presidents typically give short inaugural statements, usually not on the same day or the same place as the President. They also take different oaths. The President's oath appears in Article II, section 1. The Vice President's oath, as with other public officials, is provided by statute.[11] Short statements by Vice Presidents when they are inaugurated are likely to take place in the Senate chamber.[12] Vice President Andrew Johnson gave a lengthy inaugural address in 1865,

---

5. James W. Ceaser, Glen E. Thurow, Jeffrey Tulis & Joseph M. Bessette, *The Rise of the Rhetorical Presidency*, 11 PRES. STUD. Q. 158, 159 (1981).

6. ROBERT SCHLESINGER, WHITE HOUSE GHOSTS: PRESIDENTS AND THEIR SPEECHWRITERS (2008).

7. Ceaser et al., *supra* note 5. See also J. Richard Broughton, *The Inaugural Address as Constitutional Statesmanship*, 28 QUINNIPIAC L. REV. 265 (2010); SAMUEL KERNELL, GOING PUBLIC: NEW STRATEGIES FOR PRESIDENTIAL LEADERSHIP (4th ed. 2007); Elvin T. Lim, *Five Trends in Presidential Rhetoric: An Analysis of Rhetoric from George Washington to Bill Clinton*, 32 PRES. STUD. Q. 328 (2002); RICHARD J. ELLIS, ed., SPEAKING TO THE PEOPLE: THE RHETORICAL PRESIDENCY IN HISTORICAL PERSPECTIVE (1998); JEFFREY K. TULIS, THE RHETORICAL PRESIDENCY (1987); Karlyn Kohrs Campbell & Kathleen Hall Jamieson, *Inaugurating the Presidency*, 15 PRES. STUD. Q. 394 (1985); and Edward W. Chester, *Beyond the Rhetoric: A New Look at Presidential Inaugural Addresses*, 10 PRES. STUD. Q. 571 (1980).

8. GEORGE C. EDWARDS III, ON DEAF EARS: THE LIMITS OF THE BULLY PULPIT 247 (2003).

9. Id. at 254.

10. MICHAEL NELSON, ed., THE EVOLVING PRESIDENCY: LANDMARK DOCUMENTS, 1787–2008, at 44 (4th ed., 2012). See Charles O. Jones, *The Inaugural Address: Ceremony of Transitions*, in MICHAEL NELSON & RUSSELL L. RILEY, eds., THE PRESIDENT'S WORDS: SPEECHES AND SPEECHWRITING IN THE MODERN WHITE HOUSE 87–110 (2010). The views of speechwriters of inaugural addresses are found at id., 111–46. Also on inaugural addresses, the State of the Union Message, and farewell addresses: WAYNE FIELDS: UNION OF WORDS: A HISTORY OF PRESIDENTIAL ELOQUENCE (1996).

11. 5 U.S.C. § 3331.

12. Stephen W. Stathis & Ronald C. Moe, *America's Other Inauguration*, 10 PRES. STUD. Q. 550, 557 (1980).

remembered for its rambling and incoherent quality.[13] Vice President Spiro Agnew's address in 1969 amounted to 80 words.[14] Some Vice Presidents choose to give no inaugural address at all.[15]

## 2. STATE OF THE UNION MESSAGE

Article II, section 3, directs the President "from time to time" to give Congress "Information on the State of the Union, and recommend to their Consideration such Measures as he shall judge necessary and expedient." The latter is known as the Recommendation Clause, and is treated next in section 3. Nothing in the constitutional text defines "from time to time," but it has been taken to mean an annual address. Initially, the Philadelphia convention anticipated that the President would propose to the legislature such measures as concern the Union "by Speech or Messg."[16] A later draft directed the President "to inform" the legislature "of the Condition of U.S. so far as may respect his Department."[17] The choice between speech or message was replaced by the more general duty to "give" Congress information on the state of the Union.[18]

Presidents George Washington and John Adams met personally with Congress to present their State of the Union messages. That practice was not followed by Thomas Jefferson, perhaps because of some discomfort or dislike about public speaking. He submitted his annual messages in writing.[19] With a style much more informal than Washington and Adams, Jefferson may have objected that their appearances in Congress were too close to the British monarchical model. Another factor was the move of the national government to Washington, D.C. Jefferson had to travel a mile through swampy land in the nation's capital from the White House to Congress, and lawmakers several weeks later had to make the same trip to deliver their response to his special message. Jefferson preferred to send written messages without requiring a formal legislative reply. As he explained in a letter accompanying his first annual message:

> The circumstances under which we find ourselves placed rendering inconvenient the mode heretofore practiced of making by personal address the first communication between the legislative and executive branches, I have adopted that by message, as used on all subsequent occasions through the session. In doing this, I have had principal regard to the convenience of the legislature, to the economy of their time, to their relief from the embarrassment of immediate answers on subjects not yet fully before them, and to the benefits thence resulting to the public affairs.[20]

Jefferson concluded that his political strengths lay not in speaking to large assemblies but in meeting privately with a small number of lawmakers at a dinner party, which became a

---

13. Id. at 557–58.

14. Id. at 559.

15. Id. at 557.

16. 2 Farrand 145.

17. Id. at 158. See also id. at 171, 185, 398, 404–05.

18. Id. at 574, 600.

19. Tulis, *supra* note 7, at 56.

20. Gerhard Casper, *Executive-Congressional Separation of Power During the Presidency of Thomas Jefferson*, 47 Stan. L. Rev. 473, 479 (1995), citing 8 The Writings of Thomas Jefferson 108, n. 2 (Ford ed. 1899).

regular practice.[21] His precedent of not personally delivering remarks to Congress lasted until Woodrow Wilson, who decided to present his remarks publicly to a joint session of Congress.[22] Every President since Wilson has done the same. With television, the presentation is not merely to members of Congress but to the general public.[23] Lyndon Johnson changed the time of the speech to the evening to attract a larger viewing audience.[24]

# 3. RECOMMENDATION CLAUSE

Article II, section 3 provides that the President "shall" recommend to Congress for "their Consideration such Measures as he shall judge necessary and expedient." At the Philadelphia convention, the Committee of Detail agreed that the President "shall propose to the Legisle. from Time to Time by Speech or Messg such Meas[ures] as concern this Union."[25] Presidential recommendations may be submitted at any time, not only in the State of the Union message. That language was later altered: "It shall be his Duty to inform the Legislature of the Condition of U.S. so far as may respect his Department—to recommend Matters to their Consideration."[26] By August 6 the language included the words "necessary" and "expedient."[27]

The delegates debated whether the President "may" or "shall" recommend measures to Congress. The latter was adopted on August 6.[28] Apparently "may" crept back in, because on August 24, Gouverneur Morris successfully struck out "may" and returned to "shall."[29] The purpose: "in order to make it the *duty* of the President to recommend, & thence prevent umbrage or cavil at his doing it."[30] Apparently some delegates thought it might seem intrusive of the President to make recommendations to Congress. A specific command would give the President some cover. But what is the difference between "may" and "shall"? Wouldn't the former provide sufficient cover? What does the latter add? Would a President violate the Constitution if he made no recommendations? In Federalist No. 77, Hamilton mentions the Recommendation Clause but does not elaborate on it. He does note that this provision, along with several others,

21. FORREST McDONALD, THE PRESIDENCY OF THOMAS JEFFERSON 38–39 (1976).

22. DONNA R. HOFFMAN & ALISON D. HOWARD, ADDRESSING THE STATE OF THE UNION: THE EVOLUTION AND IMPACT OF THE PRESIDENT'S BIG SPEECH 34–37 (2006).

23. For an evaluation of the impact of the state of the union message on public opinion, see Kathryn Dunn Tenpas, *The State of the Union Address: Process, Politics, and Promotion*, in NELSON & RILEY, *supra* note 10, at 147–66.

24. Colleen J. Shogan & Thomas H. Neale, *The President's State of the Union Address: Tradition, Function, and Policy Implications*, Congressional Research Service, R40132, Nov. 17, 2010, at 3. See also DEBORAH KALB, GERHARD PETERS & JOHN T. WOOLEY, STATE OF THE UNION: PRESIDENTIAL RHETORIC FROM WOODROW WILSON TO GEORGE W. BUSH (2007), and Ryan L. Teten, *Evolution of the Modern Rhetorical Presidency: Presidential Presentation and Development of the State of the Union Address*, 33 PRES. STUD. Q. 333 (2003).

25. 2 Farrand 145.

26. Id. at 158.

27. Id. at 185.

28. Id.

29. Id. at 405.

30. Id. (emphasis in original).

produced "no objection."[31] In Federalist No. 69, he again refers to the Recommendation Clause, but only in listing a number of enumerated presidential powers without further analysis.[32]

Initially, when a President submitted a recommendation to Congress, each house provided a written reply. In 1794, President Washington advised Congress that the growth of "democratic societies" (citizens who met privately to discuss public policies) posed a threat to the national government.[33] He did not want citizens attending these meetings, especially to oppose government policy, such as the challenges that led to the Whiskey Rebellion in western Pennsylvania. Washington's sixth annual address, issued on November 19, 1794, took aim at these private groups. He urged Congress "to turn the machinations of the wicked to the confirming of our constitution: to enable us at all times to root out internal sedition, and put invasion to flight."[34] The Senate rushed to his defense. The House over a period of five days, in considering his message, refused to support a broadside against democratic societies. Members of the House insisted that private citizens had every right to debate national policy. Madison advised his colleagues in the House: "If we advert to the nature of Republican Government, we shall find that the censorial power is in the people over the Government, and not in the Government over the people."[35]

It has been argued that the Recommendation Clause entered a decline after Presidents Washington and Adams. In 1801, President Jefferson "discontinued this short-lived custom of presenting recommendations to Congress through speeches."[36] Jefferson might have acquiesced to members of his party who regarded presidential messages to Congress as too close to the British monarch addressing Parliament.[37] However, Jefferson did not keep himself at arm's length from members of Congress. Although he did not make recommendations in person, he did so in private writing. In addition, he met regularly with lawmakers over dinner to build a legislative base for public policies. Jefferson drafted bills and gave them to friendly members of Congress to introduce and promote. On one occasion, he told Secretary of the Treasury Albert Gallatin about a proposed draft on embargo enforcement: "If you will prepare something on these and other ideas you like better... Mr. Newton [of Virginia]...will push them through the House."[38] Other lawmakers, including William B. Giles, John Randolph, and Wilson Cary Nicolas, all from Jefferson's state of Virginia, served as Jefferson's link to Congress.[39]

Jefferson had maintained close ties with Congress during his previous service as Vice President. He lived in a large boardinghouse on Capitol Hill, sharing company and political insights with members of Congress.[40] The messages he wrote to lawmakers as President were

---

31. The Federalist 488.

32. Id. at 445.

33. 1 Richardson 116–17.

34. 34 THE WRITINGS OF GEORGE WASHINGTON 37 (Fitzpatrick ed.).

35. ANNALS OF CONG., 3d Cong., 1-2 Sess. 934 (1794). For further details: LOUIS FISHER, THE CONSTITUTION AND 9/11: RECURRING THREATS TO AMERICA'S FREEDOMS 66–72 (2008); Robert M. Chesney, *Democratic-Republican Societies, Subversion, and the Limits of Legitimate Dissent in the Early Republic*, 82 N.C. L. REV. 1525 (2004); and EUGENE PERRY LINK, DEMOCRATIC-REPUBLICAN SOCIETIES, 1790–1800 (1942).

36. J. Gregory Sidak, *The Recommendation Clause*, 77 GEO. L.J. 2079, 2093 (1989).

37. Id. at 2093 n.61.

38. 1 THE WRITINGS OF ALBERT GALLATIN 380 (Adams, ed., 3 vols., 1960 ed.).

39. RALPH VOLNEY HARLOW, THE HISTORY OF LEGISLATIVE METHODS IN THE PERIOD BEFORE 1825, at 168 (1917).

40. JAMES STERLING YOUNG, THE WASHINGTON COMMUNITY, 1800–1828, at 16, 162 (1966).

closely coordinated with Cabinet heads and supporters in the legislative branch. His messages received "considerable coverage in the press, the text being printed in newspapers and broadsides."[41] He did not mechanically send written statements to Congress. They were carefully designed to promote specific legislative objectives.

It has been argued that Congress cannot use its appropriations power "to override the President's constitutional duty to recommend policy measures to Congress."[42] Yet this same study acknowledges that the President, in the absence of appropriations, "cannot hire consultants in the private sector to study a panoply of subjects, obligating the federal government to millions of dollars in debts."[43] Chapter 3, section 12 provides examples of Congress denying the President public funds to finance studies completed by outside consultants, forcing the President to locate private funds. Congress often resorts to riders in appropriation bills to limit what agencies (and therefore Presidents) may do.[44]

On occasion, the Justice Department will object to a legislative proposal that "purports to *require* the President to submit legislative recommendations," arguing that the Recommendation Clause "vests the President with discretion to do so when he sees fit."[45] This objection is highly theoretical and of little practical application. Nevertheless, in recent times Presidents George W. Bush and Barack Obama raised Recommendation Clause objections to bills that required the executive branch to submit budget requests to Congress in particular forms.[46] In the past, Presidents regularly complied with statutory duties to report on different matters, such as the requirement to submit an annual budget and comply with the format established by law (Chapter 6, section 5).

# 4. CONVENING AND ADJOURNING CONGRESS

Article II, section 3, provides that the President "may, on extraordinary Occasions, convene both Houses, or either of them, and in Case of Disagreement between them, with Respect to the Time of Adjournment, he may adjourn them to such Time as he shall think proper." At the Philadelphia convention, the Committee of Detail included language to empower the President "to convene the Legislature on extraordinary Occasions—to prorogue [suspend or terminate]

---

41. Noble E. Cunningham, Jr., The Process of Government Under Jefferson 85 (1978). For further details on the use of annual messages by Jefferson to promote his legislative agenda, see also 72–86.

42. Sidak, *supra* note 36, at 2101.

43. Id. at 2098. For additional analysis of the State of the Union Clause and the Recommendation Clause, see Vasan Kesavan & J. Gregory Sidak, *The Legislator-in-Chief*, 44 Wm. & Mary L. Rev. 1 (2002).

44. Neal Devins, *Appropriations Redux: A Critical Look At the Fiscal Year 1988 Continuing Resolution*, 1988 Duke L.J. 389; Neal Devins, *Regulation of Government Agencies Through Limitation Riders*, 1987 Duke L.J. 456.

45. Statement by John P. Ellwood, Deputy Assistant Attorney General, Office of Legal Counsel, U.S. Department of Justice, statement before the House Committee on the Judiciary, concerning presidential signing statements, Jan. 31, 2007, at 8 (emphasis in original).

46. Statement by President George W. Bush on H.R. 2673, Jan. 23, 2004; http://georgewbush-whitehouse. archives.gov/news/releases/2004/01/print/20040123-10.html; statement by President Barack Obama on H.R. 1105, March 11, 2009.

them, provided such Prorogation shall not exceed      Days in the space of any."[47] (The delegates would fill in the blank later.) This language changed somewhat in subsequent drafts, but there was no dispute on the need to grant those powers to the President. In Federalist No. 69, Hamilton referred to the powers of convening and adjournment but did not discuss them.[48]

Congress has its own constitutional authority to decide when to meet. Under Article I, Section 4, Congress "shall assemble at least once in every Year, and such Meeting shall be [on the first Monday in December] unless they shall by Law appoint a different Day." The language in brackets was changed by section 2 of the Twentieth Amendment: "The Congress shall assemble at least once in every year, and such meeting shall begin at noon on the 3d day of January, unless they shall by law appoint a different day." With both branches possessing power to call Congress into session, conflicts could arise between special sessions called by the President and regular sessions called by Congress. President John Adams called a special session for 1797.[49] Presidents Jefferson and Madison announced special sessions on October 17, 1803, and September 19, 1814.[50]

Legislation passed by Congress in 1836, to appoint a day for the annual meeting of Congress, encountered a veto from President Jackson.[51] He did not doubt the power of Congress to "fix by law a day for the regular annual meeting of Congress" but objected that the concluding part of the bill was intended to "fix the adjournment of every succeeding Congress to the second Monday in May after the commencement of the first session."[52] To Jackson, the language on adjournment conflicted with the Constitution. He pointed to language in Article I, section 7, which states that every order, resolution, or vote to which the concurrence of the two houses may be necessary (except on a question of Adjournment) shall be presented to the President. He noted his own powers of adjournment in Article II, section 3.

According to Jackson's interpretation, "the day of the adjournment of Congress is not the subject of legislative enactment."[53] The question of adjournment could be decided "by each Congress for itself, by the separate action of each House for the time being." That is, for a particular Congress. But it "is one of those subjects upon which the framers of that instrument did not intend one Congress should act, with or without the Executive aid, for its successors."[54] The purpose of the bill was "to fix a day by law to be binding in all future time unless changed by consent of both Houses of Congress, and to take away the contingent power of the Executive which in anticipated cases of disagreement is vested in him."[55] His veto was sustained. The Senate's effort to override failed on a vote of 16 to 23.[56]

Under subsequent administrations, Presidents frequently called Congress into special session to deal with legislative matters. Lincoln called Congress back in session on July 4, 1861, to

---

47. 2 Farrand 158.

48. The Federalist 445–46.

49. KALLENBACH, *supra* note 1, at 325.

50. Everett S. Brown, *The Time Meetings of Congress*, 25 AM. POL. SCI. REV. 955, 956–58 (1931).

51. 4 Richardson 1450.

52. Id. at 1451.

53. Id.

54. Id.

55. Id.

56. S. JOURNAL, 24th Cong., 1st Sess., at 485–86 (1836).

respond to his emergency measures after the start of the Civil War. President William Howard Taft called Congress back in session in 1909 to deal with tariff matters.[57] President Harry Truman assembled Congress in an extraordinary session in 1947 to act on a series of domestic programs.[58]

Statutes may provide procedures for emergency sessions. The War Powers Resolution of 1973 states that when the President introduces U.S. forces into hostilities or into situations where imminent hostilities are clearly indicated by the circumstances, and if Congress has adjourned sine die (without a date designated for resumption) or has adjourned for any period in excess of three calendar days, the two chambers "shall jointly request the President to convene Congress in order that it may consider the [President's] report and take appropriate action."[59]

# 5. APPOINTMENTS CLAUSE

Article II, section 2 provides that the President "shall nominate, and by and with the Advice and Consent of the Senate, shall appoint Ambassadors, other public Ministers and Consuls, Judges of the supreme Court, and all other Officers of the United States, whose Appointments are not herein otherwise provided for, and which shall be established by Law." Congress "may by Law vest the Appointment of such inferior Officers, as they think proper, in the President alone, in the Courts of Law, or in the Heads of Departments." Finally, the President "shall have Power to fill up all Vacancies that may happen during the Recess of the Senate, by granting Commissions which shall expire at the End of their next Session."[60]

The President's appointment power extends to "Officers of the United States," a term given clearer meaning by several court decisions. The Supreme Court has defined an office as "a public station or employment, conferred by the appointment of government. The term embraces the ideas of tenure, duration, emoluments, and duties."[61] The functions of an officer are "continuing and permanent, not occasional or temporary."[62] Occasional or intermittent duties are carried out by agents, not officers.[63] Unless someone holds a position by virtue of a presidential appointment, or by an appointment from the courts or department heads as authorized by law, that

---

57. Stanley D. Solvick, *William Howard Taft and the Payne-Aldrich Tariff,* 50 Miss. Valley Hist. Rev. 424 (1963).

58. Kallenbach, *supra* note 1, at 327–28.

59. 87 Stat. 555, 556, sec. 5(a) (1973).

60. For additional analysis of the Appointments Clause: Mitchel A. Sollenberger, Judicial Appointments and Democratic Controls (2011); *Congressional Restrictions on the President's Appointment Power and the Role of Longstanding Practice in Constitutional Interpretation,* 120 Harv. L. Rev. 1914 (2007); Lee Epstein & Jeffrey A. Segal, Advice and Consent: The Politics of Judicial Appointments (2005); Harold J. Krent, Presidential Powers 24–36 (2005); Michael J. Gerhardt, The Federal Appointments Process: A Constitutional and Historical Analysis (2000); Cheryl A. Marquardt, *The Appointments Clause: A Battle Between Formalism and Pragmatism,* 40 U. Kan. L. Rev. 1043 (1992); and Joseph P. Harris, The Advice and Consent of the Senate: A Study of the Confirmation of Appointments by the United States Senate (1968).

61. United States v. Hartwell, 73 U.S. (6 Wall.) 385, 393 (1868).

62. Id.

63. United States v. Germaine, 99 U.S. (9 Otto.) 508, 511–12 (1879); Auffmordt v. Hedden, 137 U.S. 310, 316–27 (1890).

person is not an officer of the United States.[64] Any appointee exercising "significant authority" pursuant to a federal statute is an officer of the United States.[65]

Five issues are analyzed in this section: the President's nomination power, participants in that process, senatorial courtesy, the definition of "inferior" officers, and statutory controls. Sections 6 and 7 focus on recess appointments and presidential "czars." The appointment of ambassadors, subject to Senate advice and consent, is sometimes skirted by Presidents who name "special envoys" (Chapter 7, section 7A). Treated separately in the last chapter are presidential nominations of federal judges and recess appointments to federal courts (Chapter 9, sections 5 and 6).

## A. The President "shall nominate"

The British monarch not only appointed officers but created the positions. The Framers rejected that concentration of power and its potential for abuse. It was necessary for Congress to create offices and for the Senate to confirm the President's nominees. Confirmation was not required for certain "inferior" officers. Under Article II, section 2, the power of appointment may be placed directly in the President, the courts, or department heads.

The initial draft constitution submitted at Philadelphia (the Virginia Plan) lodged in Congress the responsibility for choosing an executive and members of a national judiciary.[66] The executive would have been empowered "to appoint to offices in cases not otherwise provided for" by the Constitution.[67] James Wilson objected to the appointment of judges by a legislature: "Experience shewed the impropriety of such appointmts. by numerous bodies. Intrigue, partiality, and concealment were the necessary consequences. A principal reason for unity in the Executive was that officers might be appointed by a single, responsible person."[68] John Rutledge feared that vesting such power in a single person would be "leaning too much toward Monarchy."[69]

James Madison suggested a compromise: Let the Senate (with fewer members than the House) appoint the judges. His plan was tentatively agreed to in mid-June 1787.[70] Some delegates worried that the executive, armed with the power to appoint, might favor one region of the country over another. Luther Martin insisted that the Senate would be "best informed of characters & most capable of making a fit choice."[71] Madison offered another proposal: allow the executive to appoint judges with the concurrence of some fraction of the Senate. He thought his idea joined the responsibility of the executive with the security afforded by Senate opposition to "incautious or corrupt" nominations.[72] Yet on July 21 the convention voted to have judges

---

64. United States v. Mouat, 124 U.S. 303, 307 (1888).

65. Buckley v. Valeo, 424 U.S. 1, 126 (1976).

66. 1 Farrand 21.

67. Id. at 63.

68. Id. at 119.

69. Id.

70. Id. at 119–28, 232–33.

71. 2 Farrand 41.

72. Id. at 42–43. See also 41–44, 80–83.

appointed solely by the Senate. The President would retain power "to appoint to offices in cases not otherwise provided for" in the Constitution.[73]

As the debate continued, delegates dropped the idea of allowing Congress to choose judicial officers. In early September, the convention gave the President authority to nominate, by and with the advice and consent of the Senate, ambassadors, other public ministers and consuls, Justices of the Supreme Court, and all other federal officers.[74] A few days later the convention authorized the President to fill all vacancies that "may happen" during the Senate's recess.[75] It reserved to Congress the right to vest the appointment of inferior officers in the President, the courts, or department heads.[76]

## B. Who participates?

Hamilton discussed in Federalist No. 66 the roles of the President in making nominations and the Senate in confirming. He spoke confidently about a division of power: "There will, of course, be no exertion of *choice* on the part of the Senate. They may defeat one choice of the Executive, and oblige him to make another; but they cannot themselves *choose*—they can only ratify or reject the choice of the President."[77] From the start, that has not been the practice. President Washington not only sought the advice of Senators on nominations but also depended on judgments by advisers in other quarters. Recommendations from members of the House of Representatives, although constitutionally excluded from the confirmation process, also carried considerable weight.[78]

In *Marbury v. Madison*, Chief Justice Marshall called the nomination process the "sole act of the president" and "completely voluntary."[79] Technically that is true. Only the President may nominate executive officials and federal judges. Read literally, the Constitution seems to make the act of nomination fully within presidential control: "he shall nominate." In a concurring opinion in 1989, Justice Kennedy stated that the Constitution "divides the appointment power into two separate spheres: the President's power to 'nominate,' and the Senate's power to give or withhold its 'Advice and Consent.' No role whatsoever is given either to the Senate or to Congress as a whole in the process of choosing the person who will be nominated for appointment."[80] An OLC opinion that year concluded that attempts by members of Congress to nominate a particular person "are an unconstitutional attempt to share in the appointment authority which is textually committed to the President alone."[81]

---

73. Id. at 83, 121.

74. Id. at 498–99.

75. Id. at 533.

76. Id. at 627–28.

77. The Federalist 434 (emphasis in original).

78. Roy Swanstrom, *The United States Senate, 1789–1801*, S. Doc. No. 64, 87th Cong., 1st Sess. 93-95, 101-02 (1962), and Dorothy Gansfield Fowler, *Congressional Dictation of Local Appointments*, 7 J. Pol. 25 (1945).

79. 5 U.S. (1 Cr.) 137, 155 (1803).

80. Public Citizen v. Department of Justice, 491 U.S. 440, 483 (1989).

81. 13 Op. O.L.C. 248, 250 (1989). That position was not repeated when OLC released an opinion in 1996 that supersedes the 1989 memo; 20 Op. O.L.C. 124 (1996).

Practice departs considerably from text. Senators often submit to the President names for district judges, U.S. attorneys, and marshals who serve in their states. When Senator John Warner presented three names to the Bush administration in 1989 for a vacant federal judgeship in Virginia's Western District, plus two names for a vacancy in the Eastern District, a newspaper dutifully reported: "Warner Nominates 5 for judgeships."[82] Under this procedure, it is the President who finds himself giving "advice and consent" to a Senate recommendation. The President and his advisers may object to certain proposals and ask for names more acceptable. Teddy Roosevelt entered the White House by declaring: "The Senators and Congressmen shall ordinarily name the *man*, but I shall name the *standard*; and the men have to come up to it."[83]

Nominations are generally shared with members of the executive branch, lawmakers and judges, and participants from the private sector. Presidents who insisted on some type of monopoly over nominations quickly learned that political reality compelled them to share that decision with others. Attempts to exclude others, particularly members of Congress, could result in the Senate not acting at all on a President's nominee.[84]

Once an office is authorized by Congress it must be filled. The President cannot refuse to nominate. Presidents may attempt to frustrate the statutory purpose for a time, such as waiting a lengthy period before submitting a nominee, but at some point a name must go forward. That principle was underscored in 1973 by court rulings against President Nixon. His budget recommended the deletion of $18 million in American Indian education funds.[85] The administration impounded the money pending congressional action on his rescission request. Private parties sued to require him to appoint members of the National Advisory Council on Indian Education. Federal courts decided that whatever discretion the President possessed to appoint to the Council, there was no discretion on whether the Council should or should not be constituted. Nixon appointed 15 individuals to the Council and, under court order, released the $18 million.[86]

Nixon's failure to nominate ignored his constitutional duty to "take care that the laws be faithfully executed." Making no appointments effectively nullified the law. When an agency consists of several members at the top (such as commissioners of federal regulatory bodies), precedents exist for not filling every office. Although the Interstate Commerce Commission (ICC) was authorized to have eleven commissioners, President Carter kept it to seven by not filling all the vacancies. The reduced size did not prevent the agency from functioning. Several trucking companies filed a lawsuit, objecting that the ICC was illegally constituted and had reached decisions without a quorum. In 1980, an appellate court ruled that a quorum under the statute

82. WASH. POST, March 12, 1989, at B3.

83. 2 GEORGE H. HAYNES, THE SENATE OF THE UNITED STATES 741, n.1 (1938) (emphasis in original).

84. MITCHEL A. SOLLENBERGER, THE PRESIDENT SHALL NOMINATE: HOW CONGRESS TRUMPS EXECUTIVE POWER (2008), and Mitchel A. Sollenberger, *The President 'Shall Nominate': Exclusive or Shared Constitutional Power?*, 36 PRES. STUD. Q. 714 (2006).

85. BUDGET OF THE UNITED STATES GOVERNMENT, Fiscal Year 1974, Appendix, at 1074.

86. Minnesota Chippewa Tribe v. Carlucci, 358 F. Supp. 973, 975 (D.D.C. 1973); Minnesota Chippewa Tribe v. Carlucci, Civ. Action No. 628-73 (D.D.C. 1973), memorandum form. See Anne Joseph O'Connell, *Vacant Offices: Delays in Staffing Top Agency Positions*, 82 S. CAL. L. REV. 913 (2009) and Note, *Constitutional Law Separation of Powers—Mandatory Injunction to President—Minnesota Chippewa Tribe v. Carlucci, 358 F. Supp. 973 (D.D.C. 1973)*, 1974 WIS. L. REV. 198 (1974).

consisted of a majority of the existing commissioners, not a majority of the full complement of eleven.[87]

To what extent may Congress participate in the appointment of officers? In 1976, the Supreme Court reviewed a lower court decision that upheld the authority of Congress to nominate four members to the Federal Election Commission (FEC). By statute, the President nominated two. All voting members of the commission required confirmation by the majority of *both* houses of Congress. A lower court reasoned that Congress drew constitutional authority from the Necessary and Proper Clause to appoint members who carried out appropriate legislative functions, even if the commission also performed "quasi-executive" and "quasi-judicial" duties.[88]

The Supreme Court agreed that the Necessary and Proper Clause empowered Congress to create the commission, but that language could not be interpreted to permit Congress to appoint its members. Constitutional clauses must be read in concert with other constitutional provisions. For example, Congress could not invoke the Necessary and Proper Clause to pass a bill of attainder or an ex post facto law, both of which the Constitution expressly prohibits (this chapter, section 10). The Necessary and Proper Clause could not be used to transfer the appointment power to Congress, especially when a commission discharges more than legislative functions. The powers conferred on the FEC could be exercised only by "Officers of the United States" appointed pursuant to Article II, section 2, clause 2. To the Court, Congress had two options: nomination by the President, subject to the advice and consent of the Senate, or vesting the appointment power in the President alone, in the courts of law, or in department heads.[89] Congress chose the first option when it rewrote the statute in 1976.[90]

The Supreme Court acknowledged that if an agency's powers are "essentially of an investigative and informative nature," Congress may appoint the agency officials.[91] When Congress reauthorized the Civil Rights Commission in 1983, it gave itself the right to appoint four of the eight members. The remaining four would be appointed by the President. In signing the bill, President Reagan acknowledged that Congress operated within its authority because the essential functions of the commission were investigative.[92]

Although Congress may not appoint agency officials who discharge executive functions, it may authorize private parties to select members of federal policymaking agencies. The Federal Open Market Committee exercises important powers of monetary policy. It consists of seven members of the Board of Governors (presidential appointees) and five representatives of the Federal Reserve Banks. The latter are elected annually by the boards of directors of the banks. Members of Congress and private citizens who have challenged the constitutionality of this procedure have been denied standing by courts to have their case heard and decided.[93]

---

87. Assure Comp. Transp., Inc. v. United States, 629 F.2d 467 (7th Cir. 1980), cert. denied, 449 U.S. 1124 (1981).

88. Buckley v. Valeo, 519 F.2d 821, 890–92 (D.C. Cir. 1975).

89. Buckley v. Valeo, 424 U.S. 1, 133–43 (1976).

90. 90 Stat. 475, sec. 101 (1976).

91. Buckley v. Valeo, 424 U.S. at 137.

92. 97 Stat. 1301 (1983); PUBLIC PAPERS OF THE PRESIDENTS, 1983, II, at 1634–35.

93. E.g., Melcher v. FOMC, 836 F.2d 561 (D.C. Cir. 1987), cert. denied, 486 U.S. 1042 (1988); Committee for Monetary Reform v. Board of Governors, 766 F.2d 538 (D.C. Cir. 1985); Riegle v. FOMC, 656 F.2d 873 (D.C. Cir.

In 1987, the Supreme Court struck down a district court's action in appointing private attorneys to prosecute criminal contempt actions.[94] Although courts have an inherent right to hold individuals in contempt as a means of protecting the dignity and authority of the judiciary, the private attorney appointed should be as disinterested as a public prosecutor. In this case, the two private attorneys had a direct involvement with the plaintiffs, who pursued a trademark infringement of their line of leather goods.[95] Several issues of the appointment power, including the role of the American Bar Association in advising on potential nominees for judgeships, are treated in Chapter 9, section 5.

In 2010, the Court decided an important case involving both the appointment and removal powers. The Sarbanes-Oxley Act of 2002 created the Public Company Accounting Oversight Board (PCAOB), a title so challenging that at times it is referred to as "Peekaboo." Possessing broad powers over the accounting industry, the board is composed of five members appointed by the Securities and Exchange Commission (SEC). They are not subject to Senate confirmation. The SEC cannot remove Board members at will, but only "for good cause shown," in accordance with specified procedures. The commissioners themselves cannot be removed by the President except for cause (inefficiency, neglect of duty, or malfeasance in office). The Board existed at two levels of for-cause removal from the President.

Divided 5 to 4, the Court upheld the SEC's appointment powers but found the double for-cause removal procedure to be unconstitutional.[96] It held that the Board members are "inferior" officers whose appointment Congress may permissibly vest in the head of a department, pursuant to Article II. It doing so, it treated the SEC as a "department," even if not in the same sense as other executive departments. Moreover, it saw no reason why the chairman of the multimember SEC cannot be regarded as the "head" of the agency.[97] As for the removal power, the Court reasoned that the President cannot "take care" that the laws be faithfully executed "if he cannot oversee the faithfulness of the officers who execute them." It concluded that the "multilevel protection" from removal is contrary to Article II's vesting of the executive power in the President.[98] Left unsaid in the decision is how close the Court is to overturning *Humphrey's Executor*. The addition of one more conservative Justice might push the Court in that direction.[99]

## C. Senatorial courtesy

During the first year of Washington's administration, the Senate rejected his nomination of Benjamin Fishbourn to be naval officer at Savannah, Georgia. It was rumored that the two

1981), cert. denied, 454 U.S. 1082 (1981); Reuss v. Balles, 584 F.2d 461 (D.C. Cir. 1978), cert. denied, 439 U.S. 997 (1978).

94. Young v. U.S. ex rel. Vuitton et Fils S.A., 481 U.S. 787 (1987).

95. Id.

96. Free Enterprise Fund v. Public Company Accounting Oversight Bd., 561 U.S. 407 (2010).

97. Id. at 484, 512–13.

98. Id. at 484–514.

99. For evaluations of *Free Enterprise Fund* at the D.C. Circuit and Supreme Court levels: Julian Helisek, *The Fault, Dear PCAOB, Lies Not in the Appointments Clause, but in the Removal Power, That You Are Unconstitutional*, 77 G.W. L. Rev. 1063 (2009), and Neomi Rao, *A Modest Proposal: Abolishing Agency Independence in Free Enterprise Fund v. PCAOB*, 79 Fordham L. Rev. 2541 (2011).

Senators from that state opposed the nomination because they had someone else in mind for that position.[100] Washington, stung by the rebuff, advised Senators that before voting down a nominee they should first inquire as to the individual's qualifications and the President's reasons for selecting the person: "Whatever may have been the reasons which induced your dissent, I am persuaded they were such as you deemed sufficient. Permit me to submit to your consideration whether, on occasions where the propriety of nominations appear questionable to you, it would not be expedient to communicate that circumstance to me, and thereby avail yourselves of the information which led me to make them, and which I would with pleasure lay before you."[101]

It has become an accepted custom for Senators to defer to a colleague's judgment about a nomination affecting their state. The practice is consistent with the Framers' expectation that Senators would be well suited to determine the fitness of candidates from their constituencies. In the First Congress, Madison pointed out that Senators had been joined with the President in the appointment process because they were, "from their nature, better acquainted with the character of the candidate than an individual [the President]."[102] Several weeks later, Representative Benjamin Goodhue made the same point, noting that it was "more probable that the Senate may be better acquainted with the characters of the officers that are nominated than the President himself."[103]

To come within the scope of senatorial courtesy, a nominee must be from the state of the Senator and the appointment must be to a position within the state, rather than to a national office, such as the Cabinet. The custom can be further refined by insisting that the objecting Senator be from the same party as the President. Although many nominations have been defeated because they were "personally offensive" to a Senator, not every use of senatorial courtesy has prevailed.[104]

The leverage of an individual Senator can reach beyond the formal dimensions of senatorial courtesy. In 1970, Senator Barry Goldwater advised the Secretary of State that an individual nominated to a national office (within the State Department) was "personally obnoxious" because he had written an article in 1964 linking Goldwater—at the time the Republican candidate for President—with right-wing elements in Germany. The Nixon administration, warned by Goldwater that there would be "trouble," withdrew the nomination.[105] Moreover, Senators who are not from the President's party may successfully bargain for power over nominations. During the Nixon years, Senators Alan Cranston and John Tunney of California (both Democrats) worked out an agreement that gave them the right to name every third federal district judgeship in their state.[106]

100. MITCHEL A. SOLLENBERGER, THE PRESIDENT SHALL NOMINATE: HOW CONGRESS TRUMPS EXECUTIVE POWER 24–27 (2008), and Mitchel A. Sollenberger, *Georgia's Influence on the U.S. Senate: A Reassessment of the Rejection of Benjamin Fishbourn and the Origin of Senatorial Courtesy*, 93 GA. HIST. SOC. 182 (2009).

101. 1 ANNALS OF CONG. 59 (1789).

102. Id. at 380 (May 19, 1789).

103. Id. at 534 (June 18, 1789).

104. RIDDICK'S SENATE PROCEDURE: PRECEDENTS AND PRACTICES, S. Doc. No. 101-28, 101st Cong., 2d Sess. 951-52 (1992); see also JOSEPH P. HARRIS, THE ADVICE AND CONSENT OF THE SENATE 215–37 (1953).

105. WASH. POST, Aug. 31, 1970, at A1, and Sept. 1, 1970, at A2.

106. John Tunney, *The Judicial Appointment Process*, 34 PEPP. L. REV. 275, 278–79 (2007); Nina Totenberg, *Will Judges Be Chosen Rationally?*, 60 JUDICATURE 93, 95 (1976). See also MITCHEL A. SOLLENBERGER, JUDICIAL

Senatorial courtesy, in the sense of Senators announcing that a nominee from their state is "personally obnoxious," is not followed as in the past. It has been replaced by other techniques similarly effective. An individual Senator can block a nominee by threatening a filibuster, by indicating opposition through the "blue slip" procedure used by the Senate Judiciary Committee, and by placing a "hold" on a nomination. Using a hold to block action on a nominee may have nothing to do with the credentials of the appointee. Senators may invoke a hold for unrelated purposes, such as forcing the administration to release documents previously requested. For holds, the objecting Senator does not have to be from the state of the nominee.[107]

## D. *"Inferior" officers*

In 1988, the Supreme Court clarified the meaning of "inferior offices" when it upheld the constitutionality of the independent counsel. Congress had created this position to investigate and prosecute high-level executive officials (discussed later in this chapter, section 8). If the Attorney General concluded that an independent counsel was necessary, he or she could go to a special panel of judges to have the officer appointed. Opponents of the law argued that the independent counsel was not an "inferior officer" to be appointed by the courts, but rather a "principal officer" who must be selected by the President with the advice and consent of the Senate.

Writing for a 7-to-1 Court, Chief Justice Rehnquist acknowledged that the line between inferior and principal officers "is far from clear" and that the Framers provided little guidance.[108] Without attempting a precise definition of the two officers, Rehnquist decided that the independent counsel was an inferior officer for several reasons: the independent counsel could be removed from office by the Attorney General, implying that the office was to some degree inferior in rank and authority; the independent counsel had statutory authority to perform only certain, limited duties; the office of independent counsel was restricted in jurisdiction by statute and by the grant of authority conferred by the special federal court; and the independent counsel was limited in tenure, even though the "temporary" nature of the office could last for several years.[109] After reauthorizing the independent counsel a number of times, Congress allowed the position to expire in 1999.

In *Freytag v. Commissioner* (1991), the Court was asked to examine the constitutionality of the appointing authority of the Chief Judge of the U.S. Tax Court, who had been empowered to select special trial judges to hear a case and prepare proposed findings and an opinion.[110] The actual decision would be rendered by a Tax Court judge. Could complex tax cases be initially assigned to a special trial judge without violating the Appointments Clause? The Court held that statutory authority permitted the Chief Judge to assign *any* tax court proceeding, regardless

---

APPOINTMENTS AND DEMOCRATIC CONTROLS 91–94 (2011), and G. CALVIN MACKENZIE, THE POLITICS OF PRESIDENTIAL APPOINTMENTS 121–24 (1981).

107.  SOLLENBERGER, *supra* note 106, at 99–104, 129–45, 149–53; SOLLENBERGER, *supra* note 100, at 153, 155, 174, 176; and Madeleine Scinto & Elana Schor, *Sens. Still Hold Out Over Holds*, THE HILL, Sept. 27, 2006, at 1.

108.  Morrison v. Olson, 487 U.S. 654, 671 (1988).

109.  Id. at 671–72.

110.  501 U.S. 868 (1991).

of complexity, to a special trial judge for preliminary work.[111] The Court ruled that "Courts of Law" under the Appointments Clause were not limited to Article III judges confirmed by the Senate. The Clause covered Article I legislative courts as well.[112] Tax Court judges are appointed to 15-year terms, not lifetime terms, by the advice and consent of the Senate. The special trial judges were inferior officers subject to the control of the Chief Judge of the Tax Court.[113] A concurrence by Scalia, joined by O'Connor, Kennedy, and Souter, often read like a dissent.[114]

In 1997, in *Edmond v. United States*, the Court again addressed the issue of "inferior officers."[115] The Coast Guard Court of Criminal Appeals hears appeals from the decisions of courts martial. Judges assigned to the Court of Criminal Appeals must be members of the bar, but they may be commissioned officers or civilians. During the time of this litigation, the court had two civilian members. Both were assigned to the court by the General Counsel of the Department of Transportation. Anticipating that those assignments might be invalidated under the Appointments Clause, the Secretary of Transportation issued a memorandum "adopting" the General Counsel's assignments as appointments of his own. In *Ryder v. United States* (1995), a unanimous Supreme Court had overturned a conviction prior to the Secretary's action. The Court ruled that the judges had not been validly appointed pursuant to the Appointments Clause.[116]

In *Edmond*, the Court held that the judicial appointments from the Secretary of Transportation were valid. The decision was unanimous, with a concurrence from Justice Souter. The Court admitted that its cases "have not set forth an exclusive criterion for distinguishing between principal and inferior offices for Appointment Clause purposes."[117] It reasoned that whether one is an inferior officer "depends on whether he has a superior."[118] Inferior officers are those whose work is directed and supervised by those appointed by the President with the advice and consent of the Senate, in this case the Secretary of Transportation.[119] In the case already discussed, *Free Enterprise Fund* in 2010, the Court held that the members of the Public Company Accounting Oversight Board were "inferior officers" under the SEC.[120] The position of inferior office, as defined in *Morrison v. Olson* (1988), is further analyzed in the section on independent counsels in section 8 of this chapter.

111. Id. at 877.

112. Id. at 889–90.

113. Id. at 881.

114. Id. at 892–922 (Scalia, J., concurring, joined by O'Connor, J., Kennedy, J., and Souter, J.). In Weiss v. United States, 510 U.S. 163, 169–70 (1994), the Supreme Court relied on *Freytag* in part in holding that military trial and appellate judges may legitimately carry out their judicial duties under the Appointments Clause because they have been appointed by the President with the advice and consent of the Senate.

115. 520 U.S. 651 (1997).

116. Ryder v. United States, 515 U.S. 177 (1995).

117. Edmond v. United States, 520 U.S. 651, 661 (1997).

118. Id. at 662.

119. Id. at 663.

120. Free Enterprise Fund, *supra* note 96, at 477.

## *E. Statutory controls*

The Supreme Court in 1852 held that although Congress creates offices, it cannot, "by law, designate the person to fill those offices."[121] That principle was buttressed in 1871 by Attorney General Akerman, who reviewed a proposal that permitted a civil service board to designate a single person for appointment. To Ackerman it was "inadmissible" to have a method of selection that left no room for the exercise of judgment by the President. To require the President to appoint a person judged by examiners as the fittest was no different in constitutional principle than insisting that "he shall appoint John Doe to that office."[122] In 1947, the Supreme Court noted that Congress may not violate the Bill of Rights by enacting legislation to provide that "no Republican, Jew or Negro shall be appointed to federal office."[123]

The Civil Service Act of 1883 allowed the President some latitude by restricting appointments to those "among" the highest grades in competitive examinations. The first rules promulgated by President Arthur provided that four names would be considered for each vacancy. In 1888 that number was lowered to three.[124] Present law provides that a nominating or appointing official will be furnished at least three names from the top of the list of those eligible for each vacancy.[125] When a vacancy occurs in the office of Comptroller General or Deputy Comptroller General, a commission of members of Congress recommends at least three individuals to the President, who may also ask the commission to recommend additional names.[126]

In creating an office, Congress may stipulate the qualifications of appointees. The Judiciary Act of 1789 specified that the Attorney General and U.S. Attorneys must be "a meet person learned in the law."[127] No one in congressional debate raised any constitutional objection to that qualification.[128] It would be an extreme argument to regard that kind of statutory standard as a congressional encroachment on presidential power. In a 1926 decision, Justice Brandeis prepared a lengthy list of requirements that Congress has imposed on the President's selection of nominees: citizenship; being a resident of the United States, a state, a particular state, a particular district, a particular territory, the District of Columbia, or a particular foreign country; specific professional attainments or occupational experience; test by examinations; requirements of age, sex, race, property, or habitual temperance in the use of intoxicating liquors; selection on a nonpartisan basis; and representation by industrial or geographic criteria.[129]

On October 4, 2006, while signing an appropriations bill, President Bush objected to the following statutory qualifications for the Administrator of the Federal Emergency Management Agency

121. United States v. Ferreira, 54 U.S. (13 How.) 39, 50–51 (1852). See also Myers v. United States, 272 U.S. 52, 128 (1926).

122. 13 Op. Att'y Gen. 516, 523 (1871).

123. United Public Workers v. Mitchell, 330 U.S. 75, 100 (1947).

124. 22 Stat. 404 (1883); Civil Service Commission, Biography of an Ideal: A History of the Federal Civil Service 47 (1973).

125. 5 U.S.C. §§ 3317–18.

126. 31 U.S.C. § 703(a)(3).

127. 1 Stat. 73, sec. 35, at 92–93 (1789).

128. The Senate debated the bill at length but its debate is not recorded; 1 Annals of Cong. 48, 49 (1789). For House debate on the bill, see id. at 782–85, 796–820, 820–34, 899–903.

129. Myers v. United States, 272 U.S. at 265–74 (dissenting opinion). For the position that Congress may not specify statutory qualifications for positions that require Senate confirmation, see Hanah Metchis Volokh, *The*

(FEMA): the Administrator "shall be appointed from among individuals who have (A) a demonstrated ability in and knowledge of emergency management and homeland security; and (B) not less than 5 years of executive leadership and management experience in the public or private sector."[130] The legislative intent was to avoid a recurrence of the amateurish leadership of FEMA officials during the Hurricane Katrina disaster in New Orleans. Bush insisted that the statutory qualifications ruled out "a large portion of those persons best qualified by experience and knowledge to fill the office" and announced that the executive branch would construe the bill language "in a manner consistent with the Appointments Clause of the Constitution."[131]

What does this constitutional argument imply? That Congress may not require that an individual nominated for the position of Surgeon General be a medical doctor? That Congress is prohibited from stipulating that people nominated to serve on the Council of Economic Advisers actually be economists? What is the practical effect of Bush's challenge? Could Bush or his successors nominate someone for FEMA Administrator with less than five years of relevant professional experience? Certainly they could, but the Senate could then peremptorily reject the nominee, or not even hold hearings, creating a political stalemate, an empty office, and presidential embarrassment.

Senate inaction is especially likely toward the end of a President's term. In 1976, dozens of nominations sent to Congress by President Ford were sidetracked in committee, left there to die quietly. The positions included judges, U.S. attorneys, U.S. marshals, and regulatory commissioners.[132] President Carter received the same treatment in 1980 when Republicans sensed (correctly) they would soon have their own man in the White House.[133] Every President, toward the end of his term, experiences the same limitations on the appointing power.

# 6. RECESS APPOINTEES

The Framers understood that the Senate would not always be in session to give advice and consent to a presidential nomination. They therefore empowered the President "to fill up all Vacancies that may happen during the Recess of the Senate by granting Commissions which shall expire at the End of their next Session." The delegates at the Philadelphia convention accepted this language without a dissenting vote.[134] There is little in the record to fix the intent and scope of this presidential power in Article II.[135]

Two words in the Recess Clause produce the most controversy: "happen" and "recess." Does "happen" mean "happen to take place" during the recess (the literal meaning)? A long list of

---

*Two Appointment Clauses: Statutory Qualifications for Federal Officers*, 10 U. PA. J. CONST. L. 745, 746 (2008) ("statutory requirements are unconstitutional for all appointments that require the advice and consent of the Senate.")

130. Section 503(c)(2) of H.R. 5441, 109th Congress.

131. PUBLIC PAPERS OF THE PRESIDENTS, 2006, II, at 1775.

132. WASH. POST, Aug. 26, 1976, at A5, and Oct. 3, 1976, at A8.

133. Id., Oct. 16, 1980, at A4.

134. 2 Farrand 540.

135. Id. at 574, 600, 660; 3 Farrand 421. Federalist No. 67, written by Hamilton, adds little to explain the intent of the Recess Clause.

opinions by Attorneys General has interpreted the language more broadly to mean "happen to exist" at the time of a recess, including vacancies that occur while the Senate is in recess and capable of giving its advice and consent. Attorney General Wirt in 1823 concluded that the second and broader meaning satisfied the reason, spirit, and purpose of the Constitution, which to Wirt meant keeping offices filled.[136] Through various statutes, discussed in this section, Congress acted to limit the reach of his opinion.

The word "recess" requires interpretation. It means more than final adjournment at the end of the first session of a Congress or at the end of a Congress (which ends every two years because of the two-year limit for Representatives). A temporary recess of the Senate, "protracted enough to prevent that body from performing its functions of advising and consenting to executive nominations," permits the President to make recess appointments.[137] A Senate adjournment from July 3 to August 8, 1960, constituted a "Recess of the Senate" as interpreted by the Justice Department.[138] When the Senate temporarily adjourned in the middle of that session and reconvened, it continued the same session. It did not begin the "next session" in the meaning of the Recess Clause.[139]

There is general acceptance that a Senate recess of a month, or more, constitutes a recess of sufficient length to permit a recess appointment.[140] What of shorter periods: two weeks, a week, or less than a week? According to an Attorney General opinion in 1921, brief adjournments "for 5 or even 10 days" do not "constitute the recess intended by the Constitution."[141] A Justice Department brief in 1993 suggested that recess appointments might be valid for recesses in excess of three days, but the litigation that prompted that analysis was not decided on that ground.[142] There are examples of recess appointments made during what the administration of Theodore Roosevelt called a "constructive recess," a matter of minutes between the end of an

---

136. 1 Op. Att'y Gen. 631 (1823). For other Attorney General opinions consistent with this view: Taney at 2 Op. Att'y Gen. 525 (1832); Mason at 4 Op. Att'y Gen. 523 (1846); Bates at 10 Op. Att'y Gen. 356 (1862); Stanbery at 12 Op. Att'y Gen. 32, 38 (1866); Evarts at 12 Op. Att'y Gen. 455, 457 (1868); Devans at 16 Op. Att'y Gen. 522, 524 (1880); Brewster at 18 Op. Att'y Gen. 29 (1884); Miller at 19 Op. Att'y Gen. 261, 262 (1889); Gregory at 30 Op. Att'y Gen. 314, 315 (1914); Daugherty at 33 Op. Att'y Gen. 20, 23 (1921); and Walsh at 41 Op. Att'y Gen. 463, 465–66 (1960). A federal district court concurred with the Attorney General opinions from 1823 to 1880; In re Farrow, 3 F. 112, 113–15 (C.C.N.D. Ga. 1880).

137. 41 Op. Att'y Gen. 463, 466 (1960).

138. Id. The Comptroller General has adopted a similar interpretation; 28 Comp. Gen. 30 (1948).

139. 41 Op. Att'y Gen. 463, 477 (1921); see also 23 Op. Att'y Gen. 599, 604 (1901). For further legal analysis: Blake Denton, *While the Senate Sleeps: Do Contemporary Events Warrant a New Interpretation of the Recess Appointments Clause?*, 58 Cath. U. L. Rev. 751 (2009); Anne Joseph O'Connell, *Vacant Offices: Delays in Staffing Top Agency Positions*, 82 S. Cal. L. Rev. 913 (2009); Michael B. Rappaport, *The Original Meaning of the Recess Appointment Clause*, 52 UCLA L. Rev. 1487 (2005); Michael A. Carrier, *When is the Senate in Recess for Purposes of the Recess Appointments Clause?*, 92 Mich. L. Rev. 2204 (1994); and Stuart J. Chanen, *Constitutional Restrictions on the President's Power to Make Recess Appointments*, 79 Nw. U. L. Rev. 191 (1984).

140. 13 Op. O.L.C. 271 (1989), stating that a Senate intrasession recess of 33 days permitted the President to make a recess appointment.

141. 33 Op. Att'y Gen. 20, 25 (1921). See also 3 Op. O.L.C. 311, 314 (1979).

142. Memorandum of Points and Authorities in Support of Defendants' Opposition to Plaintiffs' Motion for Partial Summary Judgment, at 24–26, Mackie v. Clinton, Civ. Action No. 93-0032-LFO (D.D.C. 1993).

extraordinary session and the quick merger into the regular session.[143] The controversy led to extensive Senate debate and a report from its Judiciary Committee highly critical of the notion of "constructive recess." To the committee, the time between the end of the extraordinary session and the beginning of a regular session did not create a "recess" within the "letter or spirit of the Constitution."[144]

## A. Pro forma sessions; Obama's initiative

In November 2007, the Senate began holding pro forma sessions every three business days to prevent recess appointments by President George W. Bush.[145] One Senator calls the Senate into session and then adjourns, usually in less than a minute. An example is the action of Senator Patrick J. Leahy, who called the Senate to order on October 27, 2011, at ten seconds after 11:00 a.m. After assuming the chair as Acting President pro tempore, he ordered the Senate to stand adjourned until 3 p.m. on Monday, October 31, 2011. The Senate adjourned at 33 seconds after 11:00 a.m. Leahy's action consumed 23 seconds.[146]

Beginning on October 17, 2011 and projected to end on January 23, 2012, the Senate held a series of these pro forma sessions, intended this time to prevent recess appointments by President Obama. However, on January 4, 2012, after a pro forma session, he made four recess appointments: Richard Cordray to be Director of the Consumer Financial Protection Bureau (CFPB) and three members of the National Labor Relations Board (NLRB).[147] In a memo dated two days later, OLC concluded that the holding of pro forma sessions in which no business is to be conducted does not have the legal effect of interrupting what OLC called a functional recess of 20 days. Under that interpretation, President Obama possessed authority to make the recess appointments.[148]

The constitutional issue is complicated by several factors. Under the President's constitutional obligation to take care that the laws be faithfully executed, if a position is vacant and the Senate is unavailable to confirm, a recess appointment is understandable. Yet designating

---

143. "Constructive Recess," a letter from Secretary of War Elihu Root to Senator Redfield Proctor, Acting Chairman of the Senate Committee on Military Affairs, S. Doc. No. 147, 58th Cong., 2d Sess. (1904), reprinted at 38 CONG. REC. 1604 (1904).

144. S. Rep. No. 4389, 58th Cong., 3d Sess. 1, 3 (1905). The controversy began with President Roosevelt convening Congress in extraordinary session on Nov. 9, 1903: 37 CONG. REC. 145 (1903). The Senate adjourned the extraordinary session on Dec. 7, 1903 "without day." Id. at 544. It immediately began its regular session. Roosevelt and his advisers argued that there was a period of time that permitted recess appointments. For debate on these recess appointments: 38 CONG. REC. 113, 1017–23, 1432–39, 1603–09 (1903–04); 39 CONG. REC. 3823–24 (1905). See also Henry B. Hogue & Richard S. Beth, *Efforts to Prevent Recess Appointments through Congressional Scheduling and Historical Recess Appointments During Short Intervals Between Sessions*, Congressional Research Service, Oct. 24, 2011, at 14–20.

145. SOLLENBERGER, *supra* note 106, at 42–43.

146. 157 CONG. REC. S6895 (daily ed. Oct. 27, 2011).

147. Helene Cooper & Jennifer Steinhauer, *Bucking Senate, Obama Appoints Consumer Chief*, N.Y. TIMES, Jan. 5, 2012, at A1; David Nakamura & Felicia Sonmez, *Obama Defies Senate, Puts Cordray in Consumer Post*, WASH. POST, Jan. 5, 2012, at A1.

148. Office of Legal Counsel, *Lawfulness of Recess Appointments During a Recess of the Senate Notwithstanding Periodic Pro Forma Sessions*, Jan. 6, 2012, http://www.justice.gov/olc/2012/pro-forma-sessions-opinion.pdf.

a Director of the CFPB did not seem an urgent matter to President Obama. The Dodd-Frank statute created the CFPB position on July 21, 2010. Obama did not submit Cordray's name until almost a year later, on July 18, 2011.[149] OLC reasoned that the Senate is not in session during pro forma periods because party leaders announce "in advance that there is to be 'no business conducted' at such sessions."[150] It concluded that "the President may determine that pro forma sessions at which no business is to be conducted do not interrupt a Senate recess for purposes of the Recess Appointment Clause."[151]

OLC chose to rely on what party leaders *said* rather than on what the Senate *did*. In fact, business was conducted during these pro forma sessions, including Senate action on a temporary payroll tax bill on December 23, 2011.[152] When Obama signed the bill into law, the administration understood that the Senate in pro forma session has the capacity to conduct business. If the Senate can pass legislation during a pro forma session, it could confirm appointees if it wished to do so. OLC's memo raises two other issues. Article I, section 5 of the Constitution provides that neither house of Congress may adjourn "for more than three days" without the consent of the other house. The House of Representatives did not consent to a Senate adjournment beyond three days. Furthermore, Article I, section 5 stipulates that each house "may determine the Rules of its Proceedings." The Senate determines its rules, not the President or OLC.[153]

OLC acknowledged that Obama's actions presented "novel" issues and "substantial arguments on each side create some litigation risk for such appointments."[154] Shortly after he made the recess appointments, several lawsuits were filed. If the administration lost a legal challenge, decisions taken by the NLRB and CFPB could be nullified. In 2010, the Supreme Court voided more than 500 decisions by the NLRB because it attempted to operate with a two-person quorum in an agency authorized to have five board members.[155]

The Senate has full constitutional authority to withhold confirmation over a particular nominee because of qualifications and many other factors. The issue with Cordray was unique. In mounting a filibuster against his nomination,[156] it was clear from the debate on the cloture motion Republican Senators did not block confirmation because he was unqualified. Senate Minority Leader Mitch McConnell explained that the Republicans were opposed to *any* nominee for the position unless and until President Obama and Congress rewrote the underlying statute to satisfy three conditions: "replace the single Director with a board of directors," subject the Bureau "to the congressional appropriations process" (the Bureau depends on funds transferred to it from the Federal Reserve), and "allow other financial regulators to provide a check on CFPB rules."[157]

---

149. 157 CONG. REC. S4646 (daily ed. July 18, 2011).

150. Office of Legal Counsel memo, *supra* note 148, at 2.

151. Id. at 13.

152. 157 CONG. REC. S8789 (daily ed. Dec. 23, 2011), unanimous consent request by Senate Majority Leader Harry Reid on H.R. 3765.

153. Some Senate rules are impermissible, such as the Senate "reconsidering" a nominee who has been confirmed, taken the oath, and entered into the duties of office. United States v. Smith, 286 U.S. 6 (1932).

154. Office of Legal Counsel memo, *supra* note 148, at 4.

155. New Process Steel, L.P. v. NLRB, 560 U.S. 674 (2010).

156. 157 CONG. REC. S8347 (daily ed. Dec. 6, 2011) and S8428-29 (daily ed. Dec. 8, 2011).

157. Id. at S8422 (daily ed. Dec. 8, 2011).

In no previous instance has a group of Senators refused to confirm a nominee unless the authorizing statute was rewritten in accordance with their specifications. Senator Sherrod Brown asked Senate Historian Donald Ritchie if, in the past, "one political party tried to block the nomination of a Presidential appointee based on wanting to change the agency." Ritchie could locate no precedent.[158] Could this legislative tactic be used against any nominee chosen to head an executive department, agency, or bureau? Under this interpretation, a minority of Senators could prevent confirmation of a Secretary of Defense, Attorney General, EPA Administrator, and other nominees until enabling statutes were revised to satisfy their instructions. Such actions have the potential for crippling government.

On January 25, 2013, the D.C. Circuit ruled that Obama's recess appointees to the NLRB were unconstitutional.[159] In an exceptionally broad ruling, the court held that recess appointments may be made only between sessions of Congress, not in the middle of a session. Under that reading, a recess appointment would be permissible between sessions even if the break is a matter of days, but would be impermissible in the middle of a session even if the Senate were gone for a month or two. Moreover, according to the D.C. Circuit, the vacancy would have to "arise" between two sessions, not before. The ruling by the D.C. Circuit, if upheld, might nullify more than 300 decisions made by the NLRB.[160] Were the administration to lose this case, decisions reached by Cordray with Consumers Financial Protection Bureau could also be nullified. On different grounds, the Third Circuit on May 16, 2013, in *NLRB v. New Vista Nursing and Rehabilitation*, found Obama's recess appointments to the NLRB to be unconstitutional. Other appellate courts have received challenges to Obama's actions. The Supreme Court agreed to review the D.C. Circuit decision and rule on the constitutional issues, including the question of pro forma sessions.

## B. Funding restrictions

For more than a century, Congress has experimented with funding limits to curb the President's power to make recess appointments. When lawmakers decide that the President has abused that power, they can prohibit the use of public funds to pay the salaries of recess appointees. Senator Fessenden remarked in 1863: "It may not be in our power to prevent the [recess] appointment, but it is in our power to prevent the payment; and when payment is prevented, I think that will probably put an end to the habit of making such appointments."[161] The Senate Judiciary Committee was asked this question: Did the practice of appointing offices to fill vacancies that existed *prior* to a recess—while the Senate was in session—violate the Constitution? The committee rejected the position of Attorney General Wirt that a recess appointee can fill a vacancy that occurred during a session. To the committee, a reading of the constitutional words "may

158. Id. at S8428.

159. Noel Canning v. NLRB, No. 12-115 (D.C. Cir. 2013); Charlie Savage & Steven Greenhouse, *Court Rejects Obama Move to Fill Posts*, N.Y. Times, Jan. 16, 2013, at A1; Robert Barnes & Steven Mufson, *Obama Recess Picks Invalid*, Wash. Post, Jan. 26, 2013, at A1.

160. Steven Greenhouse, *More Than 300 Labor Board Decisions Could Be Nullified*, N.Y. Times, Jan. 26, 2013, at A10.

161. Cong. Globe, 37th Cong., 3d Sess. 565 (1863).

happen during the Recess of the Senate" to include what happened before the recess was "a perversion of language." That analysis tilted power toward the President and placed excessive emphasis on the filling of a vacancy. It denied an opportunity to the Senate to pass judgment on the qualifications of an officeholder. Unless Congress placed constraints on the power to make recess appointments, an "ambitious, corrupt, or tyrannical executive" could nullify the Senate's constitutional authority.[162]

Legislation in 1863 prohibited the use of funds to pay the salary of anyone appointed during a Senate recess to fill a vacancy that existed "while the Senate was in session and is by law required to be filled by and with the advice and consent of the Senate, until such appointee shall have been confirmed by the Senate."[163] Because of this statute, an officer would have to serve without pay (relying on savings or loans) until the Senate consented to the nomination. For example, George Rublee, nominated to the Federal Trade Commission in March 1915, served for more than a year as a recess appointee and received no federal salary during that period. After the Senate voted to reject him, he continued to serve the balance of his recess appointment until September 1916. In this case, Congress passed a special appropriation that paid his salary for 14 months, from the date his service began to the date the Senate rejected him.[164]

By 1940, Congress concluded that the 1863 statute was excessively burdensome and took steps to make the law "more flexible."[165] Three exceptions were permitted. First, payments to recess appointees are allowed if a vacancy arose within 30 days before the end of Senate's session. Nominations submitted during that period are unlikely to receive the Senate's approval. Second, payments are allowed if, at the end of the session, a nomination is pending before the Senate (other than for someone appointed during a preceding recess). This exception has two purposes: it protects the Senate from successive recess appointees, and it protects nominees whose names went forward in a timely manner. Third, payments are allowed if a nomination is rejected by the Senate within 30 days before the end of a session and an individual (other than the one rejected) receives a recess appointment. The purpose is to take care of nominees rejected on the eve of a recess. The statute adds this limitation: a nomination to fill a vacancy referred to in the three exceptions must be submitted to the Senate no later than 40 days after the Senate's next session begins.[166] "Next session" has been interpreted in a nontechnical way to mean the return of the Senate from its recess, not the next session of Congress.[167]

This statute can be manipulated to promote executive interests. Presidents may let a position remain unfilled for months without submitting a name to the Senate. Just before a recess, he can forward a name and have it covered under the second exception. As an example, the office of OMB Deputy Director became vacant on March 24, 1978. President Carter did not submit the name of John White until October 7, making it "pending" at the time of the recess. By resubmitting White's name within 40 days after the Senate convened, Carter stayed within the letter of

162. S. Rep. No. 80, 37th Cong., 3d Sess. 5–6 (1863).

163. 12 Stat. 646 (1863). For the restrictive effect of this statute, see 16 OP. ATT'Y GEN. 522, 531 (1880); 26 OP. ATT'Y GEN. 234, 235 (1907); 32 OP. ATT'Y GEN. 271, 272 (1920); 41 OP. ATT'Y GEN. 463, 473–74 (1960).

164. 39 Stat. 801 (1916). See HAYNES, *supra* note 83, at 776–77.

165. H. Rep. No. 2646, 76th Cong., 3d Sess. (1940); S. Rep. No. 1079, 76th Cong., 1st Sess. (1939).

166. 54 Stat. 751 (1940); 5 U.S.C. § 5503. For commentary on hardships experienced by appointees who served without compensation: 28 COMP. GEN. 30, 37 (1948) and 41 OP. ATT'Y GEN. 463, 479–80 (1960).

167. 41 OP. ATT'Y GEN. 463, 477 (1960).

the law, but his initial delay of six months helped circumvent the statutory effort to protect the Senate's authority to confirm. That step did not occur until April 10, 1979.

## C. Holdover clauses

The scope of recess appointments is complicated by the presence of "holdover" clauses in federal statutes. For example, a member of the Federal Election Commission may serve after the expiration of that member's term in office "until his successor has taken office as a member of the Commission."[168] The statute does not define *how* the successor assumes office: by Senate confirmation (required for new members) or as a recess appointee. The statute says that any vacancy in the membership of the commission "shall be filled in the same manner as in the case of the original appointment" (presumably by Senate confirmation).[169] Nevertheless, on October 25, 1978, President Carter made John McGarry a recess appointee to the seat held by Neil Staebler, who was serving in a holdover capacity.[170] Staebler refused to leave office, arguing that McGarry had not been confirmed by the Senate and therefore no vacancy existed for Carter to fill.

A federal district court, deciding against Staebler, pointed to many inconsistencies in the statute. If a vacancy existed only at the point of confirmation of a successor, would that place an unmanageable task on the President? How could he recruit someone for the office and submit a nomination if, in theory, no vacancy existed? Moreover, if the existing commissioner left before the end of the individual's term, that would disrupt the statutory design of staggered six-year terms for the six commissioners. The court asked whether Staebler's interpretation would require the statutory dates for those terms to shift to take account of holdovers, creating a "baggage of peculiar practical difficulties."[171] The court discovered no clear evidence that Congress tried to restrict the President's power to make recess appointments.[172] If it was the intent of the Senate to protect its right to advise and consent, it could have rejected McGarry's nomination when Carter first submitted it on September 27, 1977, and then again on April 10, 1978. Only after two sessions of Senate inaction on those nominations did Carter make the recess appointment.[173]

The district court's decision raises several questions. There should be little doubt that a President may search for a candidate to replace someone serving in a holdover capacity and have the candidate confirmed by the Senate. A President need not wait for a vacancy to begin that search. Moreover, it does not follow that holdovers disrupt the statutory design of staggered six-year terms. The terms would not change. Once a nominee had been confirmed, that person would serve out the remainder of the six-year term.

The tension between the two elected branches is illustrated by President Reagan's action in 1984, giving a recess appointment to Martha Seger to the Federal Reserve Board.[174] He acted

---

168. 2 U.S.C. § 437c(a)(2)(B) (1976).

169. Id. at § 437c(a)(2)(D).

170. Mary Russell, *John McCarry Sworn In As Member of the FEC*, WASH. POST, Oct. 26, 1978, at A15.

171. Staebler v. Carter, 464 F. Supp. 585, 589 (D.D.C. 1979). On appeal, the D.C. Circuit dismissed the case as moot on May 17, 1979, remanding it to the district court.

172. Id. at 592.

173. Id. at 601. For the Senate's record on McGarry, see id. at 587.

174. PUBLIC PAPERS OF THE PRESIDENTS, 1984, II, at 777.

a few days after Congress began a three-week recess. The Senate Banking Committee had approved her nomination by the narrow margin of 10 to 8. Following Reagan's action, Senator Robert C. Byrd introduced a Senate resolution to limit the power to make recess appointments to two conditions: in situations where the Senate has formally terminated a session or when the Senate would be in recess for longer than 30 days.[175] That resolution was never put to a vote. A year later, the Senate passed another Byrd resolution, this one expressing that recess appointments should not be made to the Federal Reserve Board except under unusual circumstances and only for the purpose of fulfilling "a demonstrable and urgent need" to consider nominations to the board in an expeditious manner.[176] When President Reagan continued to use his recess appointment power, Senator Byrd retaliated late in 1985 by holding up action on all presidential nominations.[177] White House actions that offend a Senate party leader, especially someone as skilled and determined as Byrd, can come at heavy cost to the executive branch.

Congress can force a recess appointee to resign by rejecting the nomination. Because of language placed each year in the Treasury Department appropriations bill, a rejection can have the effect of eliminating the appointee's compensation. The language: "Hereafter, no part of any appropriation contained in this or any other Act shall be paid to any person for the filling of any position for which he or she has been nominated after the Senate has voted not to approve the nomination of said person."[178] This type of language has been added to appropriations bills for more than a half century. In an opinion in 1979, the Office of Legal Counsel acknowledged that, "as a practical matter, Congress can force the recess appointee to resign by rejecting his nomination. Pursuant to an annual appropriation rider, a rejection has the effect of cutting off his compensation."[179]

The power to make recess appointments has been a major issue in the life of the Legal Services Corporation (LSC). Through the use of holdover provisions and recess appointments, Presidents Reagan and Bush I were able to largely circumvent the Senate's power of confirmation. Some court decisions restricted the President's power to make recess appointments, not only to the LSC but also to other agencies.[180] An important use of the recess appointment power is placing federal judges on the bench for a brief period, rather than the constitutionally assigned lifetime appointment. That issue is analyzed in Chapter 9, section 6.

## D. Temporary appointments

In addition to recess appointments, Presidents make other temporary or interim appointments. When the head of an executive department dies, resigns, or is sick or absent, the next in

175. 130 CONG. REC. 23234–36, 23341 (1984).

176. 131 CONG. REC. 17622–24, 17679 (1985).

177. Helen Dewar, *Recess Appointments Raise Senators' Anger*, WASH. POST, Sept. 26, 1985, at A23; PUBLIC PAPERS OF THE PRESIDENTS, 1985, II, at 1209; Ira R. Allen, *White House Asks End of Appointee 'Backlog,'* WASH. POST, Oct. 9, 1985, at A17.

178. E.g., 121 Stat. 2021, sec. 709 (2007).

179. 3 OP. O.L.C. 314, 317 (1979).

180. Wilkinson v. Legal Services Corp., 865 F. Supp. 891 (D.D.C. 1994), reversed on other grounds, Wilkinson v. Legal Services Corp., 80 F.3d 535 (D.C. Cir. 1996); Mackie v. Clinton, 827 F. Supp. 56 (D.D.C. 1993); McCalpin v. Durant, 766 F.2d 535 (D.C. Cir. 1985); McCalpin v. Dana, No. 85-542 (D.D.C. October 5, 1982). Also: *An LSC*

command may perform official duties until a successor is appointed or the absence ceases. As an alternative, the President may direct someone else (previously appointed *with the advice and consent of the Senate*) to perform the duties. These acting officials were at one time restricted by law to a period not to exceed 30 days. That limit was violated with such frequency that in 1988 Congress increased it to 120 days. Even that appeared to be insufficient. In 1998, Congress lifted it once again, to 210 days.[181]

As an example of earlier conflicts under the 30-day rule, L. Patrick Gray was named Acting Director of the Federal Bureau of Investigation in May 1972, following the death of Director J. Edgar Hoover. Gray continued to serve in that capacity for almost a year. President Nixon did not submit his name to the Senate for confirmation until February 21, 1973. In a letter to Senator William Proxmire the next day, Comptroller General Elmer Staats concluded that Gray was subject to the 30-day limit and his continued service violated the law.[182] The Justice Department maintained that Gray became Acting Director under a different law.[183] With the Senate clearly opposed to Gray, Nixon withdrew the nomination on April 17 and Gray resigned shortly thereafter.

Congress tolerated temporary appointees who exceeded the 30-day limit if the President promptly sent the person's name to the Senate for confirmation. To do otherwise threatened the Senate's role in the appointment process. In 1973, President Nixon planned to dismantle the Office of Economic Opportunity (OEO). Instead of nominating a Director and seeking the advice and consent of the Senate, he appointed Howard J. Phillips as Acting Director. The administration asserted that the President possessed constitutional authority to appoint temporary officers without Senate confirmation, drawing that power from the President's authority under Article II to "take Care that the Laws be faithfully executed." The argument seems bizarre on its face: the President was willing to violate the law on vacancies.

A district court denied that the President possesses an inherent (or derivative) power to make interim appointments unless in an emergency. The court found no emergency in this situation. The appointment was invalid because it did not satisfy the statute (requiring Senate advice and consent) nor was the appointment made during a Senate recess.[184] The D.C. Circuit denied Phillips's motion for a stay, pending appeal, because he failed to show sufficient likelihood of success on the merits.[185] Other cases during this period challenged acting officials who exceeded the 30-day limit.[186]

---

*Dispute May Take Power from President*, NAT'L LAW J., Feb. 19, 1996, at A1. These decisions often turn on statutory issues. In *Mackie*: Is the holdover limited to one year? In *Wilkinson*: Does the statute say the holdover "shall" or "may" continue to serve?

181. 5 U.S.C. §§ 3345–48, 112 Stat. 2681-611, sec. 151 (1998). For an earlier version: 102 Stat. 988, sec. 7 (1988). Previous statutes on temporary appointments: 12 Stat. 656 (1863), 15 Stat. 168 (1868), and 26 Stat. 733 (1891). For the difficulties in finding a sufficient number of "interim appointees" with previous Senate confirmation to serve in the newly created Department of Energy, see 2 OP. O.L.C. 405 (1978).

182. Staats to Proxmire, letter no. B-150136, Feb. 22, 1973.

183. The Justice Department relied on 28 U.S.C. §§ 508–10.

184. Williams v. Phillips, 360 F. Supp. 1363 (D.D.C. 1973).

185. Williams v. Phillips, 482 F.2d 669 (D.C. Cir. 1973). For further details on this case: Lois Reznick, *Temporary Appointment Power of the President*, 41 U. CHI. L. REV. 146 (1973).

186. United States v. Halmo, 386 F. Supp. 593 (E.D. Wis. 1974); United States v. Lucido, 373 F. Supp. 1142 (E.D. Mich. 1974).

Disputes over temporary appointments continued. In 1997, President Clinton weighed the politics of making Bill Lann Lee a recess appointee to be Assistant Attorney General for the civil rights division.[187] Instead, he chose to designate him an Acting Assistant Attorney General over that division, citing authority under various statutes but not the Vacancies Act.[188] This action bypassed a Senate confirmation hearing that would have focused on the issue of affirmative action, not only leading to lengthy delays but also a possible rejection of Lee.[189] The question then turned on whether Lee would be limited in his acting capacity to the time period specified in the Vacancies Act at that time (120 days).[190] The dispute involved more than Lee. A report issued by the Congressional Research Service on March 11, 1998, pointed out that at least 64 officials in 14 executive departments were serving in an acting capacity in positions that required Senate confirmation. At least 43 of those officials served beyond the 120-day limit of the Vacancies Act, and they occupied 20 percent of high-level department positions.[191]

Lee's designation as acting head of the Civil Rights Division put pressure on Congress to revisit the Vacancies Act. Legislation enacted on October 21, 1998, extended the period from 120 days to at least 210 days. Under some circumstances, as explained in this complex statute, the period could exceed 210 days.[192] The generous expansion of the time limit was intended to make the statute the exclusive vehicle for temporarily filling vacant positions that require Senate confirmation.[193]

# 7. PRESIDENTIAL "CZARS"

The word "czar" has been added—sometimes fairly, sometimes not—to certain presidential aides. The term should be reserved to executive branch officials who exercise significant duties over federal programs, control staff and funds, and have not been confirmed by the Senate. This type of aide is generally unavailable to testify before Congress. The term is used improperly when applied to executive officials who have been confirmed by the Senate and appear regularly before legislative committees.

---

187. Dan Carney, *Battle Over Lee Could Escalate With Recess Appointment*, Cong. Q. Weekly Rept., Nov. 29, 1997, at 2955.

188. In Order No. 2134-97, Dec. 15, 1997, signed by Attorney General Janet Reno, the legal authorities were these: 28 U.S.C. §§ 509–10, 5 U.S.C. § 301, and 28 C.F.R. § 0.132(d).

189. John F. Harris & Helen Dewar, *President Bypasses Congress, Appoints Lee on 'Acting' Basis*, Wash. Post, Dec. 16, 1997, at A1; John M. Broder, Clinton, *Softening Slap at Senate, Names 'Acting' Civil Rights Chief*, N.Y. Times, Dec. 16, 1997, at A1.

190. Helen Dewar, *Senators Question How Long Lee Can Stay in Rights Post*, Wash. Post, Dec. 20, 1997, at A8; David Stout, *Senator Asks How Long Rights Choice Will Remain*, N.Y. Times, Dec. 20, 1997, at A9.

191. Rogelio Garcia, *Acting Officials in Positions Requiring Senate Confirmation in Executive Departments, As of February 1998*, Congressional Research Service, Report 98-252 GOV, March 11, 1998. See also Kirk Victor, *Executive Branch End Run*, Nat'l J., May 16, 1998, at 1112, which cites this report.

192. 112 Stat. 2681–611 (1998).

193. Morton Rosenberg, *The New Vacancies Act: Congress Acts to Protect the Senate's Confirmation Prerogative*, Congressional Research Service, 98-892 A, Oct. 27, 1998; Brannon P. Denning, *Article II, the Vacancies Act and the Appointment of "Acting" Executive Branch Officials*, 76 Wash. U. L. Q. 1039 (1998).

Activities by unconfirmed officials raise several constitutional issues. A republican form of government depends on voters who select individuals to represent them in Congress. Lawmakers authorize and fund programs, create offices to run them, and assure that top officials are confirmed by the Senate and remain available to testify at congressional hearings. Those steps are essential in maintaining accountability to the voters and adherence to the law. Popular government requires that programs operate through statutes enacted by elected members of Congress. To have unconfirmed White House aides participate in the shaping and execution of federal programs adds an activity that competes with officials confirmed to do precisely that. Concerns are also justified by the rapid growth of White House staff. Unlike the six assistants recommended by the Brownlow Committee in the late 1930s, operating with a "passion for anonymity," presidential aides are in much greater number today and more deeply involved in the details and implementation of programs.[194]

Concerns about presidential aides precipitated two Senate hearings in 2009. On October 6, the Senate Committee on the Judiciary heard testimony from a number of experts. Statements at the hearing clarified the meaning of czars, applying it to unconfirmed rather than confirmed officials. Testimony also distinguished between aides who work directly under a confirmed official and those assigned to the White House. Further, there should be little dispute about the President's right to obtain advice, whether from White House aides or private citizens. However, the question is quite different when those aides exercise authority that Congress has vested in confirmed officials. A second Senate hearing on October 22, 2009, by the Committee on Homeland Security and Governmental Affairs, covered similar ground.[195]

Two examples illustrate the broad scope of activity by what has been called presidential czars. On January 29, 2001, President Bush announced a new White House office responsible for allocating federal funds for the needy through faith-based organizations. The office was created by executive order and its director was not subject to Senate confirmation.[196] In June 2010, after the massive oil spill in the Gulf of Mexico, President Obama directed Kenneth Feinberg to oversee a $20-billion victims' fund that had been established by British Petroleum. The previous year, Obama had appointed Feinberg under the auspices of the Treasury Department. His duties included establishing and enforcing pay guidelines for companies that received federal bailout money from the Troubled Asset Relief Program (TARP). Feinberg exercised those powers without being subject to Senate confirmation. The administration could not answer a number of basic questions about his legal basis for administering the victims' fund.[197]

The growing number of White House aides has reached the point where some seem to argue that the President possesses independent authority to create these positions. He does not. On April 15, 2011, while signing a bill, President Obama objected to language that denied

194. For analysis of constitutional issues dealing with these presidential aides, see MITCHEL A. SOLLENBERGER & MARK J. ROZELL, THE PRESIDENT'S CZARS: UNDERMINING CONGRESS AND THE CONSTITUTION (2012), and PRESIDENT OBAMA'S CZARS, a Judicial Watch Special Report, Sept. 15, 2011.

195. *Examining the History and Legality of Executive Branch "Czars,"* hearing before the Senate Committee on the Judiciary, 111th Cong., 1st Sess. (Oct. 6, 2009); *Presidential Advice and Senate Consent: The Past, Present, and Future of Policy Czars,* hearing before the Senate Committee on Homeland Security and Governmental Affairs, 111th Cong., 1st Sess. (Oct. 22, 2009).

196. SOLLENBERGER & ROZELL, *supra* note 194, at 138–39.

197. Id. at 1–2. See also Justin S. Vaughn & José D. Villalobos, *The Policy Czar Debate,* in THE OBAMA PRESIDENCY: A PRELIMINARY ASSESSMENT 315–41 (Robert P. Watson, Jack Covarrubias & Tom Lansford, eds. 2012).

appropriated funds for the salaries and expenses of the "czars" of energy, health reform, auto recovery, and urban affairs. He stated that as President he "has well-established authority to supervise and oversee the executive branch, and to obtain advice in furtherance of this supervisory authority."[198] Obama claimed it is the President's "prerogative to obtain advice that will assist him in carrying out his constitutional responsibilities." Legislative efforts, he warned, "that significantly impede the President's ability to exercise his supervisory and coordinating authorities or to obtain the views of the appropriate senior advisers violate the separation of powers by undermining the President's ability to exercise his constitutional responsibilities and take care that the laws by faithfully executed." He said he would construe the bill language "not to abrogate these Presidential prerogatives."[199]

As explained Chapter 3, section 5, the President has a "prerogative" to seek advice, including from those in the private sector. He has no prerogative to create and fund positions in the executive branch. For that he needs statutory authority. In 1978, Congress revised existing language to clarify the availability of assistance and services for the President. The statute specifies the number and pay of White House aides.[200] The President has access to that assistance, as provided by law. Congress can revise that law at any time, increasing or reducing the number of presidential aides and changing the salary levels. In terms of these publicly paid employees, the matter is settled by law, not by presidential prerogative. There is no issue of separation of powers. The question is solely one of what Congress decides to authorize and fund.

# 8. INDEPENDENT COUNSELS

At times a President has agreed to rely on prosecutors not within the Justice Department but from the private sector. In such situations, corruption within the administration is typically so pervasive that it cannot credibly investigate itself. One example concerned oil leases on federal property, including the site at Teapot Dome, Wyoming. A congressional investigation uncovered evidence of illegalities, including by Cabinet officials. On February 27, 1924, Congress passed legislation directing President Coolidge to obtain private counsel, subject to Senate advice and consent.[201] Through that process the Senate confirmed Atlee Pomerene, former Democratic Senator from Ohio, and Owen J. Roberts, a Republican lawyer from Philadelphia, to direct the prosecution. Several Cabinet officials resigned, including Navy Secretary Edwin Denby and Attorney General Harry Daugherty. Interior Secretary Albert Fall, found guilty of accepting a bribe, served a jail term.[202]

In 1973, President Nixon agreed to establish a special prosecutor in the Justice Department to investigate crimes relating to the break-in of the Democratic National Committee headquarters

---

198. Statement by the President signing H.R. 1473, April 15, 2011.

199. Id.; James Risen, *Obama Takes On Congress Over Policy Czar Positions*, N.Y. TIMES, April 17, 2011, at 16.

200. 3 U.S.C. § 105. See Mitchel A. Sollenberger & Mark J. Rozell, *Prerogative Power and Executive Branch Czars: President Obama's Signing Statement*, 41 PRES. STUD. Q. 819 (2011).

201. 43 Stat. 16, ch. 42 (1924).

202. KATY J. HARRIGER, THE SPECIAL PROSECUTOR IN AMERICAN POLITICS 15–17 (2d ed., 2000); Hasia Diner, *Teapot Dome*, in CONGRESS INVESTIGATES, 1792–1974, at 199–217 (Arthur M. Schlesinger, Jr. & Roger Bruns, eds., 1975).

at the Watergate building in Washington, D.C. The Justice Department issued a regulation on May 31, 1973, stating that the Attorney General would not "countermand or interfere with the Special Prosecutor's decisions or actions. The Special Prosecutor will determine whether and to what extent he will inform or consult with the Attorney General about the conduct of his duties and responsibilities. The Special Prosecutor will not be removed from his duties except for extraordinary improprieties on his part."[203]

When Archibald Cox was selected to be Special Prosecutor, he appeared at a Senate Judiciary Committee hearing with Elliot Richardson, who had been nominated to be Attorney General. Richardson underscored the complete independence of Cox to conduct the investigation. The committee asked what Cox would do if Richardson demanded information he did not want to give up. Cox offered this scenario: "Well, I guess...I would revert to the role of professor and say, 'Look, Elliot, that isn't the way we understood it.'" If Cox thought the information should not be shared, he would tell Richardson: "The only way to exercise your final statutory authority is to fire me. It is your move."[204]

Later that year, when Cox pursued the investigation, he insisted that the White House make available to him the actual tapes of presidential recordings, rather than the tape summaries proposed by Nixon. At that point Nixon sought to remove Cox. Richardson, citing his commitment at the confirmation hearing to provide complete independence for Cox, decided he had no alternative but to resign, which he did. Deputy Attorney General William Ruckelshaus, asked to discharge Cox, also resigned. Robert Bork, now Acting Attorney General, removed Cox. A district court ruled that Cox's removal was in clear violation of the regulation issued by the Justice Department. The court noted, "[i]t is freely admitted that he was not discharged for an extraordinary impropriety."[205] As explained in Chapter 5, section 7, the Supreme Court denied Nixon's claim to withhold the tapes. The resulting release of incriminating information led to his resignation.

## A. Statutory support

In 1978, Congress passed legislation to create an independent counsel (later called special prosecutor) to investigate charges against the President, the Vice President, and specified high-level executive branch employees, including those in the Executive Office of the President, the Justice Department, the Central Intelligence Agency, and the Internal Revenue Service. The pattern here is of interest. Presidents supported the initial legislation and subsequent efforts to reauthorize the position, even though at times they voiced constitutional objections. Yet in every case they signed the bills instead of vetoing them.

On several occasions the Justice Department offered legal challenges. At a Senate hearing in 1975, Assistant Attorney General Michael Uhlmann of the Office of Legislative Affairs focused on the proposal to authorize federal judges to appoint the special prosecutor: "A portion of the executive branch would thereby be placed under the control of the judiciary." He insisted

---

203. 38 Fed. Reg. 14688 (1973).

204. *Nomination of Elliot L. Richardson to be Attorney General*, hearings before the Senate Committee on the Judiciary, 93d Cong., 1st Sess. 149 (1973).

205. Nader v. Bork, 366 F. Supp. 104, 107 (D.D.C. 1973).

that the appointment be made either by the President or the Attorney General.[206] During hearings a year later, Attorney General Edward Levi testified that this kind of legislation was "of highly questionable constitutionality" because it permitted a court to appoint the special prosecutor.[207] The appointment issue was analyzed in 1977 by John Harmon, head of the Office of Legal Counsel. He said that "because of the extraordinary cases that we are dealing with, we support the appointment of a special prosecutor. In those circumstances, it is proper for the judiciary to participate in the appointment of a special prosecutor."[208] He was asked: "Well, is it the Department's understanding that the public perception of justice at this time is at an all-time low and that there is a need for some outside prosecutor to be appointed to overlook and oversee the affairs of the executive department of Government?" Harmon replied: "Yes; it is."[209]

On May 3, 1977, President Carter announced his support for legislation to authorize the appointment of a temporary Special Prosecutor to handle cases "of misconduct by high-ranking Executive Branch officials."[210] The Special Prosecutor "would be appointed by a specially empaneled court" and could be removed only upon a finding of "extraordinary impropriety or incapacity."[211] Legislation with those features became law on October 26, 1978, creating a special counsel for a period of five years.[212] In the first year of the Reagan administration, Attorney General William French Smith expressed "serious reservations" about the 1978 law, stating that it "appears fundamentally to contradict the principle of separation of powers erected by the Constitution."[213] Nevertheless, Congress reauthorized the law in 1983 for an additional five years, changing the name of the position from special prosecutor to independent counsel.[214] President Reagan offered no statement when he signed the bill.

In Reagan's second term, when an independent counsel investigated the Iran-Contra affair, administration officials became more critical of the law. In July 1987, Assistant Attorney General John Bolton attacked a number of independent counsels, including Lawrence E. Walsh (Iran-Contra), Whitney North Seymour, Jr. (who subpoenaed the Canadian ambassador), and Alexia Morrison (investigating Assistant Attorney General Theodore Olson). Bolton, who regarded the independent counsel as unconstitutional and objected to the expense of these investigations, urged Reagan to veto a reauthorization bill.[215] When the bill cleared Congress in

206. *Watergate Reorganization and Reform Act of 1975*, hearings before the Senate Committee on Government Operations, 94th Cong., 1st Sess. 5 (1975).

207. *Provision for Special Prosecutor*, hearings before the Subcommittee on Crime of the House Committee on the Judiciary, 94th Cong., 2d Sess. 34 (1976).

208. *Special Prosecutor Legislation*, hearing before the Subcommittee on Criminal Justice of the House Committee on the Judiciary, 95th Cong., 1st Sess. 3 (1977).

209. Id. at 4.

210. Public Papers of the Presidents, 1977, I, at 786.

211. Id. at 788.

212. 92 Stat. 1824, 1867–74 (1978).

213. Thomas O'Toole, *Attorney General Questions Special Prosecutor Law*, Wash. Post, April 21, 1981, at A3. See also Charles R. Babcock, *Attorney General Urges Repeal of Prosecutor Act*, Wash. Post, May 22, 1981, at A4.

214. 96 Stat. 2039 (1983). For constitutional analysis during this early period: Charles Tiefer, *The Constitutionality of Independent Officers as Checks on Abuses of Executive Power*, 63 Boston U. L. Rev. 59 (1983).

215. George Lardner, Jr., *Justice Dept. Attacks Special Counsels*, Wash. Post, June 17, 1987, at A1.

December, there were expectations that the Justice Department and the Office of Management and Budget would recommend a veto.[216]

Yet the bill, reauthorizing the independent counsel for another five years, became law.[217] In signing the bill, Reagan expressed "profound concern" over the constitutionality of the legislation, pointing to "disregard for the carefully crafted restraints spelled out in the Constitution." He said he had "very strong doubts about its constitutionality." Instead of vetoing the bill and protecting presidential powers, he noted that the constitutional issues were before the D.C. Circuit, where the administration would continue to express its constitutional objections. He signed the bill to "ensure that public confidence in government not be eroded while the courts are in the process of deciding these questions."[218]

## B. The office is upheld

On June 29, 1988, the Supreme Court upheld the independent counsel statute, ruling that it did not violate the Appointments Clause or interfere impermissibly with the President's authority under Article II.[219] Writing for a 7-to-1 majority, Chief Justice Rehnquist turned first to the Appointments Clause. Acknowledging that the line between "inferior" and "principal" offices is "far from clear" and that little guidance comes from the Framers, he decided that an independent counsel is an inferior officer for these reasons: (1) the independent counsel may be removed by the Attorney General, (2) is empowered to perform only certain, limited duties, (3) the office is limited in jurisdiction, and (4) the office is limited in tenure.[220] As to the role of the special panel of judges (the "Special Division") in appointing the independent counsel, Rehnquist interpreted Article II to confer "significant discretion" to Congress. The Constitution provides that Congress "may by Law vest the Appointment of such inferior Officers, *as they think proper*, in the President alone, in the Courts of Law, or in the Heads of Departments."[221]

The Court determined that the duties assigned to the Special Division were not incompatible with the powers provided in Article III for the judiciary. First, Congress decided under the Appointments Clause to place those duties with the Special Division, "a source of authority for judicial action that is independent of Article III."[222] Although the Court expressed some doubts about the Special Division's power to terminate the office of an independent counsel, because such duties are not typically "judicial," it did not view this provision "as a significant judicial encroachment upon executive power or upon the prosecutorial discretion of the independent counsel."[223] The Court regarded the termination provision as "basically a device for

---

216. George Lardner, Jr., *House Passes Special-Counsel Bill: Reagan Aides to Recommend a Veto*, WASH. POST, Dec. 3, 1987, at A8.

217. 101 Stat. 1293 (1987).

218. PUBLIC PAPERS OF THE PRESIDENTS, 1987, II, at 1524.

219. Morrison v. Olson, 487 U.S. 654 (1988).

220. Id. at 670–71.

221. Id. at 673 (emphasis added, citing U.S. CONST., Art. II, section 2).

222. Id. at 678–79.

223. Id. at 682.

removing from the public payroll an independent counsel who has served his or her purpose, but is unwilling to acknowledge the fact."[224]

The Court analyzed whether the statute was invalid under the constitutional principle of separation of powers. Did the restriction on the Attorney General to remove the independent counsel only for "good cause" impermissibly interfere with the President's exercise of his constitutional appointed functions? Also: did the statute violate separation of powers by reducing the President's ability to control the prosecutorial powers of the independent counsel? The Court pointed to previous cases where Congress had placed limits on executive power: restrictions on the President's removal power (*Myers v. United States* in 1926) and the Gramm-Rudman deficit control act (*Bowsher v. Synar* in 1986). Unlike those examples, the independent counsel statute did not involve "an attempt by Congress itself to gain a role in the removal of executive officials other than its established powers of impeachment and conviction."[225]

Those who challenged the constitutionality of the independent counsel statute relied on previous decisions by the Court that distinguished between "purely executive" officials and those who exercised "quasi-legislative" and "quasi-judicial" powers.[226] Rehnquist answered that "our present considered view" is that the determination of whether the Constitution allows Congress to impose a "good cause" restriction on the President's removal power does not turn on whether or not that official is classified as "purely executive."[227] He decided the Court could not say the good-cause standard "by itself unduly trammels on executive authority."[228] No independent counsel could be appointed without a specific request from the Attorney General, and the decision not to request appointment if the Attorney General finds "no reasonable grounds to believe that further investigation is warranted" is left solely to the Attorney General.[229]

A dissent by Justice Scalia emphasized that the Framers viewed the principle of separation of powers "as the absolutely central guarantee of a just government." Without a secure structure of separated powers, "our Bill of Rights would be worthless."[230] In language that is often cited, Scalia remarked that frequently an issue comes to the Court "in sheep's clothing: the potential of the asserted principle to effect important change in the equilibrium of power is not immediately evident, and must be discerned by a careful and perceptive analysis. But this wolf comes as a wolf."[231] He found it "frightening" that an independent counsel could assemble a staff "for an indeterminate period of time, in order to investigate and prosecute the President or a particular named individual in his administration."[232] He referred to the substantial budgetary resources to support these investigations.[233]

---

224. Id. at 683.

225. Id. at 686.

226. E.g., Humphrey's Executor v. United States, 295 U.S. 602 (1935) and Wiener v. United States, 357 U.S. 349 (1958).

227. Morrison v. Olson, 487 U.S. at 689.

228. Id. at 691.

229. Id. at 696.

230. Id. at 697.

231. Id. at 699.

232. Id. at 712.

233. Id. at 714.

## C. Termination of the office

Because of growing opposition to the work of some independent counsels, the law was scheduled to expire on December 15, 1992.[234] What helped bring it back to life were several scandals in the Clinton administration. Some Republicans realized it might be politically beneficial to have independent counsels investigate those matters. In June 1994, Congress once again reauthorized the independent counsel.[235] Over the next few years, substantial criticism was directed at several independent counsels, ranging from Kenneth Starr's investigation of President Clinton to lengthy inquiries of Clinton cabinet members Mike Espy and Henry Cisneros.[236] On February 8, 1999, the American Bar Association voted 384 to 49 to oppose reauthorization "in any form."[237] The basic objection was that an independent counsel, assigned to investigate a single person, would lose perspective and indulge in an open-ended investigation with neither time nor budgetary limitations.[238] When the office of independent counsel expired in 1999, Congress did not renew it.

The performance of independent counsels from 1978 to 1999 does not support the general claim that these individuals inevitably target a particular person and use unlimited funds to indict them. Over this period of time, independent counsels conducted 20 investigations. No indictments were brought in twelve of them. When indictments and convictions were obtained, as with probes into corruption in executive departments (Housing and Urban Development, Agriculture) or the Iran-Contra affair, the abuses were substantial and needed attention. Complaints were made about the time and expenditures taken (especially Lawrence Walsh's investigation of Iran-Contra and Kenneth Starr's inquiry into Watergate and related matters), but much of the delay and cost came from the complexity of the issues and the decision of administrations to withhold key documents.

Some kind of independent counsel (statutory or not) is needed. Many activities by the President and White House officials cannot be credibly investigated by the Justice Department. On December 30, 2003, Acting Attorney General James Comey appointed Patrick Fitzgerald as special counsel to investigate the leak from the Bush White House of the name of a CIA employee, Valerie Plame. In 2005, a grand jury indicted I. Lewis "Scooter" Libby, aide to Vice President Cheney, for perjury and making false statements. Two years later a jury found him guilty. Later that year President Bush commuted Libby's prison sentence but left in place his conviction (Chapter 3, section 8). Although Fitzgerald had been appointed by the executive branch, not by a panel of judges, he was criticized in a manner similar to previous independent counsels.[239]

---

234. Joan Biskupic, *Hill Signs Point to Peril for Independent Counsel Law*, Cong. Q. Weekly Report, Sept. 5, 1992, at 2634.

235. 108 Stat. 732 (1994).

236. For analysis of criticism directed at the independent counsel office: Katy J. Harriger, The Special Prosecutor in American Politics (2d ed., 2000), and Charles Tiefer, *The Specially Investigated President*, 5 U. Chi. L. Sch. Roundtable 143 (1998).

237. George Lardner, Jr., *ABA Advocates End to Independent Counsel*, Wash. Post, Feb. 9, 1999, at A3.

238. Id.

239. Katy J. Harriger, *Executive Power and Prosecution: Lessons from the Libby Trial and the U.S. Attorney Firings*, 38 Pres. Stud. Q. 491 (2008).

## D. Presidents safeguarding their office?

A study on executive power argued that President Carter "had little choice" but to sign the special prosecutor law, despite "the severe misgivings of senior Carter administration officials about the act's constitutionality."[240] Yet all Presidents have a choice in protecting their office. If Carter capitulated because of a range of political calculations, that is understandable. His performance, however, undermines the notion of a unitary executive model that operates as a reliable lodestar to guide all Presidents.

This same study points out the constitutionality of the independent counsel "was opposed (albeit- not with complete consistency) by every president that followed Carter."[241] Of what value is it for Presidents to "oppose" and "object" to incursions into their office if, in the end, they throw in the towel? There were plenty of analyses in the Ford, Carter, and Reagan administrations that found serious constitutional deficiencies in this type of independent prosecutor, even after the Supreme Court in *Morrison* found it constitutional.[242] Yet Reagan chose to sign the independent counsel bill in 1983 and 1987, and Clinton signed another extension in 1994. Nothing in this record provides any evidence of Presidents upholding the unitary executive (see Chapter 3, section 10B). Certainly it is an overstatement to claim that the "historical record thus shows Ronald Reagan to be a steadfast proponent and supporter of the unitary executive."[243] Steadfast means firm in belief, determination, and adherence (someone who is *unfaltering*). A different word is needed to describe the presidential record on the independent counsel.

# 9. INELIGIBILITY AND INCOMPATIBILITY CLAUSES

Although the Framers did not intend a pure separation of powers, they added to the Constitution two provisions to keep the executive and legislative branches at a certain distance. Both provisions affect the Appointments Clause. Article I, section 6 provides: "No Senator or Representative shall, during the Time for which he was elected, be appointed to any civil Office under the Authority of the United States, which shall have been created, or the Emoluments whereof shall have been increased during such time" (the Ineligibility Clause). Section 6 continues: "and no Person holding any Office under the United States shall be a Member of either House during his Continuance in Office" (the Incompatibility Clause).

## A. Ineligibility

The Framers included these two clauses to prevent the Executive from using the appointment power to corrupt legislators. At the same time, the Framers wanted fit and qualified individuals

---

240. Steven G. Calabresi & Christopher S. Yoo, The Unitary Executive: Presidential Power from Washington to Bush 426 (2008).

241. Id.

242. Id. at 359, 365–66, 376–77, 386.

243. Id. at 383.

available for public office. The tension between those two values was vigorously debated. At the Philadelphia convention, the initial version of the Ineligibility Clause excluded members of Congress from positions outside the legislative branch "during the term of their membership & for one year after." Nathanial Gorham considered the language "unnecessary & injurious," although he admitted there had been abuses of public offices in Great Britain.[244] Pierce Butler, insisting that the "precaution agst. intrigue was necessary," referred to examples of men gaining seats in the British Parliament to "get offices for themselves."[245] Gorham moved that the one-year limitation be deleted. James Wilson agreed: "Strong reasons must induce me to disqualify a good man from office."[246] Members of Congress "ought to be excluded from any other office, but no longer."[247]

James Madison interpreted the issue differently. It was his opinion "that no office ought to be open to a member, which may be created or augmented while he is in the legislature."[248] After the one-year limitation was removed,[249] the debate focused on Madison's proposal. The word "augmented" was clarified to mean emoluments, or an increase in salary. He concluded that "the unnecessary creation of offices, and increase of salaries, were the evils most experienced, & that if the door was shut agst. them, it might properly be left open for the appointt. of members to other offices as an encouragmt. to the Legislative service."[250] Later, after much debate, the convention returned to Madison's proposal and agreed to make a member of Congress ineligible for any civil office that had been created, or had its emoluments increased, during that lawmaker's term in office.[251]

Interpretations of the Ineligibility Clause by Congress and the executive branch have far outweighed judicial contributions. Opinions by Attorneys General from 1882 to 1895 held that members of Congress were ineligible under the Constitution to accept appointments to executive positions.[252] However, in several instances the executive branch was willing to accept for civil office a member of Congress who was ineligible under a literal reading of the Constitution. The first exception occurred in 1909. President Taft wanted Senator Philander Knox to serve as Secretary of State, even though the salary of that office had been increased during Knox's term as Senator. As a way of addressing part of the constitutional problem, the Senate passed legislation to reduce the compensation of the Secretary of State to the previous level.[253] That did not satisfy the literal meaning of the Constitution, but Congress tried to eliminate the appearance of personal gain and corruption.

The bill passed the Senate without debate and without a recorded vote, but substantial opposition developed in the House. Representative James B. Clark, who would serve as Speaker from

---

244. 1 Farrand 375.

245. Id. at 376.

246. Id. at 379.

247. Id. at 380.

248. Id.

249. Id. at 384.

250. Id. at 386.

251. 2 Farrand 492. For earlier debate, largely against Madison's proposal, see 1 Farrand 386–90, 2 Farrand 283–84, 488–91.

252. 17 Op. Att'y Gen. 365 (1882), 17 Op. Att'y Gen. 522 (1883), and 21 Op. Att'y Gen. 211 (1895).

253. 43 Cong. Rec. 2205 (1909).

1911 to 1919, strongly objected: "we all know that this bill is an attempt to make a man eligible as Secretary of State who is ineligible under the Constitution of the United States. [Applause.] This bill is simply an effort to override the Constitution by statute. We are asked to stultify ourselves, for that is exactly what it amount to, for fear that we will be personae non gratae at the White House. [Applause.] . . . It is a question of the construction of the Constitution. It is a question of understanding plain English. . . ."[254] The House passed the bill by a vote of 173 to 116, largely on the ground that the President has a right to select individuals he wants for the cabinet and that the legislative remedy satisfied the spirit, if not the letter, of the Ineligibility Clause.[255]

A similar situation developed in 1973. President Nixon wanted to nominate William Saxbe to be Attorney General, even though the salary of that office had been increased during Saxbe's term as Senator. The Justice Department supported the nomination, provided that Congress pass legislation setting Saxbe's salary to the level established before the increase: "Neither the public, the Executive Branch, nor the Legislative branch is well-served by a prohibition so broad that it overcorrects and needlessly deprives members of Congress of opportunities for public service in appointive civil offices."[256] After lengthy debate, the remedial bill passed the Senate, 75 to 16.[257] With less debate, the House passed the bill 261 to 129 and it became law.[258]

The courts have done little to clarify the meaning or boundary of the Ineligibility Clause. Senator Hugo Black was nominated to the Supreme Court in 1937. A retirement system for the judiciary had been enacted that year while Black served in the Senate. The court avoided the constitutional issue by holding that the individual who brought the case lacked standing.[259] Later, the nomination of Congressman Abner Mikva to the D.C. Circuit was challenged because salaries of federal judges had been increased while he served in the House. Once again, a lawsuit was dismissed because of lack of standing.[260] The court said that Mikva's opponents had an opportunity to defeat the nomination. Senators on the losing side could not then ask the judiciary to reverse the Senate's action.[261] The Justice Department held that Mikva's appointment to the D.C. Circuit was not barred by the Ineligibility Clause. It reasoned that the scheduled salary increase had not taken effect at the time of Mikva's nomination, and that if it had he could be given the same statutory relief as Senators Knox and Saxbe.[262]

Building on those precedents, Congress passed legislation in 1980 and 1993 to permit Senator Ed Muskie to become Secretary of State and Senator Lloyd Bentsen to become Secretary

---

254. Id. at 2392.

255. Id. at 2414; 35 Stat. 626 (1909). For subsequent Justice Department opinions on the Ineligibility Clause, see 33 Op. Att'y Gen. 88 (1922) and 42 Op. Att'y Gen. 381 (1969).

256. 119 Cong. Rec. 37689 (1973) (statement of Robert G. Dixon, Assistant Attorney General, Office of Legal Counsel, Nov. 19, 1973).

257. Id. at 38315–48.

258. Id. at 39234–45; 87 Stat. 697 (1973). See Daniel H. Pollitt, *Senator/Attorney-General Saxbe and the "Ineligibility Clause" of the Constitution: An Encroachment Upon Separation of Powers*, 53 N.C. L. Rev. 111 (1974).

259. Ex parte Levitt, 302 U.S. 633 (1937). See D. O. McGovney, *Is Hugo L. Black a Supreme Court Justice De Jure?*, 26 Cal. L. Rev. 1 (1937).

260. McClure v. Carter, 513 F. Supp. 265 (D. Idaho 1981), aff'd sub nom., McClure v. Reagan, 454 U.S. 1025 (1981).

261. McClure v. Carter, 513 F. Supp. at 270.

262. 3 Op. O.L.C. 298 (1979).

of the Treasury. Both men had their salaries reduced to the level before it was increased during their service in the Senate.[263] Similar legislation was enacted in 2008 to permit Senator Hillary Clinton to be Secretary of State in the Obama administration.[264] An effort to challenge the constitutionality of her appointment as a violation of the Ineligibility Clause was dismissed for lack of standing.[265]

## B. Incompatibility

The Incompatibility Clause has also been difficult to litigate. When the clause reached a district court in 1971, plaintiffs objected to the right of members of Congress to simultaneously hold a commission in the armed forces reserves. The judge remarked that the "meaning and effect of this constitutional provision have never before been determined by a court."[266] The court held that the plaintiffs had standing and were entitled to a declaratory judgment that the Incompatibility Clause prohibits any member of Congress from holding a commission in the armed forces reserve during his term in office. However, the court noted several factors that impelled it to deny injunctive relief. It explained that it "must take into account the importance of its action to persons not before the Court, and the fact that any resolution of the matter must necessarily involve coordinate branches of the Government."[267]

In 1974, the Supreme Court denied standing to plaintiffs who challenged the right of members of Congress to hold a commission in the armed forces reserves.[268] In response to the objection that if courts fail to resolve the meaning of this clause, as a practical matter no one can, the Court replied: "Our system of government leaves many crucial decisions to the political processes."[269] In 1977, when the Justice Department examined the issue whether members of Congress may hold commissions as officers in the armed forces reserves, it concluded that the "exclusive responsibility for interpreting and enforcing the Incompatibility Clause rests with Congress."[270]

---

263. 94 Stat. 343 (1980); 107 Stat. 4 (1993). See Michael Stokes Paulsen, *Is Lloyd Bentsen Unconstitutional?*, 46 STAN. L. REV. 907 (1994), and John F. O'Connor, *The Emoluments Clause: An Anti-Federalist Intruder in a Federalist Constitution*, 24 HOFSTRA L. REV. 89 (1995).

264. 122 Stat. 5036 (2008).

265. Rodearmel v. Clinton, 666 F. Supp. 2d 123 (D.D.C. 2009), dismissed by the Supreme Court on June 7, 2010 for want of jurisdiction, 560 U.S. ___ (2010). For further details on the Ineligibility Clause: SOLLENBERGER, *supra* note 106, at 43–48.

266. Reservists Committee to Stop War v. Laird, 323 F. Supp. 833, 834 (D.D.C. 1971), aff'd without published opinion, 495 F.2d 1075 (D.C. Cir. 1972), reversed and remanded, 418 U.S. 208 (1974). For additional information on incompatible offices, see 1 HINDS' PRECEDENTS, ch. 16; 6 CANNON'S PRECEDENTS, ch. 158; 40 OP. ATT'Y GEN. 301 (1943); and 1 OP. O.L.C. 242 (1977).

267. Reservists Committee to Stop War v. Laird, 323 F. Supp. at 842.

268. Schlesinger v. Reservists to Stop the War, 418 U.S. 208 (1974).

269. Id. at 227.

270. 1 OP. O.L.C. 242 (1977).

# 10. BILL OF ATTAINDER CLAUSE

Article I, section 9 provides: "No Bill of Attainder or ex post facto Law shall be passed." A bill of attainder is legislative punishment without judicial process. Article I, section 10 prohibits states from passing "any Bill of Attainder" or ex post facto law. When those restrictions on Congress were first presented to the Philadelphia convention on August 22, no one questioned the need to prohibit bills of attainder.[271] After differences were expressed about the language on ex post facto, the clause passed with seven states in support and three against.[272] Hamilton in Federalist No. 78 singled out legislative actions as appropriately subject to invalidation by judicial review, including bills of attainder.[273] In 1802, one year before the Supreme Court announced that it possessed the power of judicial review, Representative James Bayard explained the necessity for a judicial check over legislative action. He said if Congress passed a bill of attainder, the courts "are bound to decide."[274]

In *Fletcher v. Peck* (1810), the Supreme Court referred to a bill of attainder as something that "may affect the life of an individual, or may confiscate his property, or both."[275] It faced this constitutional provision more squarely in the 1867 Civil War cases of *Cummings v. the State of Missouri* and *Ex parte Garland*. Congress and some of the states passed "test oaths" that required individuals to swear they had never borne arms against the United States or given any aid or encouragement to persons engaged in that effort. The oath covered attorneys who practiced before the federal courts and other professions, including the clergy and teachers. Failure to take the oath could result in the loss of privileges, such as the right to vote. The penalties applied not just to actions taken in the future but also in the past, raising issues about bills of attainder and ex post facto laws.[276]

Both cases were decided 5 to 4. In *Cummings*, the Court held that the states could not, in effect, inflict a punishment for a past act that was not punishable at the time it was committed.[277] It explained that bills of attainder may be directed against individuals by name or against a whole class, and they may inflict punishment absolutely or conditionally. The Constitution intended to secure the rights of the citizen against deprivation for past conduct by legislative enactment under any form and however disguised.[278] The dissenters referred to their positions in the next case, *Ex parte Garland*, which covered attorneys practicing in federal court.[279] Congress required individuals to take a federal or state oath to support the Union. Failure to do so could cost the

---

271. 2 Farrand 376.

272. Id. The vote of 7 to 3 was repeated on August 28; id. at 440.

273. The Federalist 491.

274. 11 Annals of Cong. 645 (1802).

275. 10 U.S. (6 Cr.) 87, 138 (1810).

276. For background on these two cases: Paul Kens, Justice Stephen Field: Shaping Liberty from the Gold Rush to the Gilded Age 11–17 (1997), and Carl Brent Swisher, Stephen J. Field: Craftsman of the Law 138–54 (1930).

277. 71 U.S. (4 Wall.) 277 (1867).

278. Id.

279. Id. at 332 (Chase, C.J., dissenting, joined by Swayne, J., Davis, J., and Miller, J.)

individual his profession, including being a priest or an attorney. The Court struck down the statutory provision.[280]

A bill of attainder case that directly involved the President concerned language placed in an appropriations bill in 1943. Earlier that year the House of Representatives created a special subcommittee to investigative "subversives."[281] The chairman of the subcommittee, John Kerr, later acknowledged: "We discovered after organization the fact that there had never been declared judicially or by any legislative body what constituted subversive activities in respect to this Government."[282] Yet Congress passed legislation denying funds to pay the salaries of three named federal employees: Goodwin B. Watson, William E. Dodd, Jr., and Robert Morss Lovett.[283] President Roosevelt signed the bill "reluctantly" because of the urgent need for agency funds. Had it been possible to veto the amendment "without delaying essential war appropriations, I should unhesitatingly have done so."[284] He condemned the bill for removing federal employees for their "political opinions," an action he considered "not only unwise and discriminatory, but unconstitutional" as a bill of attainder.[285]

The Court of Claims, without reaching the constitutional issue, ruled that the three men were entitled to recover the salaries they had lost.[286] The Supreme Court went directly to the constitutional question, concluding that legislative acts, whatever their form, that apply either to named individuals or to easily ascertainable members of a group in such a way as to inflict punishment on them without judicial trial are bills of attainder prohibited by the Constitution.[287] A concurrence by Justices Frankfurter and Reed denied that a bill of attainder existed, which they said required that an individual be deemed guilty and that a punishment be imposed.[288] They pointed to the legislative history, which included repeated opposition by the Senate to the language covering the three men and the objections raised by President Roosevelt when he signed the bill. They would have avoided the constitutional question by simply affirming the ruling of the Court of Claims, returning to the men their lost salaries.[289]

In 1965, the Supreme Court split 5 to 4 in deciding that language in a 1959 statute constituted a bill of attainder. Congress had made it a crime for a Communist Party member (or one who had been a member during the preceding five years) to serve as a member of the executive

---

280. Ex parte Garland, 71 U.S. (4 Wall.) 333 (1867).

281. 89 Cong. Rec. 734 (1943).

282. Id. at 4582.

283. 57 Stat. 450, sec. 304 (1943).

284. The Public Papers and Addresses of Franklin D. Roosevelt, 1943 volume, at 385 (1950).

285. Id. at 386.

286. Lovett v. United States, 66 F. Supp. 142, 148 (Ct. Cl. 1945). In their concurrences, Judges Whitaker and Madden concluded that the statute constituted a forbidden bill of attainder. Id. at 148, 151.

287. United States v. Lovett, 328 U.S. 303 (1946).

288. Id. at 322–23 (Frankfurter, J., concurring, joined by Reed, J.).

289. Id. at 330. For further analysis, see Louis Fisher, The Constitution and 9/11: Recurring Threats to America's Freedoms 138–43 (2008); John Hart Ely, United States v. Lovett: Litigating the Separation of Powers, 10 Harv. Civil Rights-Civil Liberties L. Rev. 1 (1975); Gerald J. Norville, Bill of Attainder—A Rediscovered Weapon Against Discriminatory Legislation, 26 Ore. L. Rev. 78 (1947); Frederick L. Schuman, "Bill of Attainder" in the Seventh-Eighth Congress, 37 Am. Pol. Sci. Rev. 819 (1943).

board of a labor organization.[290] In 1977, when the Court reviewed statutory policy to preserve the presidential papers of Richard Nixon, it denied that singling him out for special treatment constituted a bill of attainder. As the Court pointed out, Nixon alone among Presidents had entered into an agreement calling for the destruction of certain materials. He was thus "a legitimate class of one."[291]

Litigation in the 1980s concerned language in a federal statute governing the Comprehensive Employment Training Act. Funds were denied to the participation of individuals who "publicly advocate the violent overthrow of the Federal Government, or who have within the past five years, publicly advocated the violent overthrow of the Federal Government." The statute did not name an individual, but during litigation it was determined that it was aimed at Dorothy Blitz. The courts decided that the statutory provision offended the First Amendment, not the Bill of Attainder Clause.[292]

Over the next few decades, litigation expanded the application of bills of attainder to include petitions of habeas corpus, the invalidation of regulatory schemes, housing ordinances, the constitutionality of a DNA database, and constitutional amendments directed at gays, lesbians, bisexuals, and transsexuals.[293] In 2009, Congress passed legislation denying federal funds to ACORN, a national community organizing group. The provision was attacked in court as a prohibited bill of attainder.[294] The Second Circuit ruled that the denial of funds was not comparable to other congressional acts of punishment and there was no congressional finding of guilt as in past cases.[295]

# 11. DELEGATION OF POWER

In one of the most restrictive opinions ever written on the President's legislative role, Justice Black in 1952 concluded that the President's power "to see that the laws are faithfully executed refutes the idea that he is to be a lawmaker. The Constitution limits his functions in the lawmaking process to the recommending of laws he thinks wise and the vetoing of laws he thinks bad."[296] Even in the early years of the Washington administration, presidential powers were never defined

---

290. United States v. Brown, 381 U.S. 437 (1965). For an analysis of *Brown* and historical background on bills of attainder: Charles H. Wilson, Jr., *The Supreme Court's Bill of Attainder Doctrine: A Need for Clarification*, 54 Cal. L. Rev. 212 (1966).

291. Nixon v. Administrator of General Services, 433 U.S. 425, 472 (1977).

292. Blitz v. Donovan, 538 F. Supp. 1119 (D.D.C. 1982), remanded to district court by Donovan v. Blitz, 459 U.S. 1095 (1983), and decided in Blitz v. Donovan, 569 F. Supp. 58 (D.D.C. 1983).

293. Jacob Reynolds, *The Rule of Law and the Origins of the Bill of Attainder Clause*, 18 St. Thomas L. Rev. 177 (2005).

294. Andrew Kim, *Falling from the Legislative Grace: The ACORN Defunding and the Proposed Restraint of Congress' Appropriations Power Through the Bill of Attainder Clause*, 60 Am. U. L. Rev. 643 (2011); Anthony Dick, *The Substance of Punishment Under the Bill of Attainder Clause*, 63 Stan. L. Rev. 1177 (2011); Note, *Constitutional Law—Separation of Powers—Second Circuit Holds that Law Barring ACORN from Receiving Federal Funding is Not a Bill of Attainder.—ACORN v. United States, 618 F.3d 125 (2d Cir. 2010)*, 124 Harv. L. Rev. 859 (2011).

295. ACORN v. United States, 618 F.3d 125 (2d Cir. 2010), cert. denied, 564 U.S. __ (2011).

296. Youngstown Co. v. Sawyer, 343 U.S. 579, 587 (1952).

that strictly. Congress delegated substantial legislative power to the President, executive agencies, and later to independent commissions. To maintain some semblance of control, Congress evolved a sophisticated system of legislative oversight, often informal and decentralized.

## A. Nondelegation doctrine

It is a fundamental principle of constitutional government that the legislature may not delegate its power to another branch. John Locke said the legislature "cannot transfer the power of making laws to any other hands, for it being but a delegated power from the people, they who have it cannot pass it over to others."[297] This concept finds expression in the ancient maxim *delegata potestas non potest delegari* (delegated power cannot be delegated).[298] Although Congress may not surrender its basic legislative power entrusted to it by the Constitution, it regularly gives substantial discretionary authority to executive agencies to implement the law.

The natural tension between these two competing values is relieved by adroit judicial tightrope walking. One expert suggested a humorous but perceptive syllogism: *Major Premise*: Legislative power may not be constitutionally delegated by Congress. *Minor Premise*: It is essential that certain powers be delegated to administrative officers and regulatory commissions. *Conclusion*: Therefore, the powers thus delegated are not legislative powers.[299] This kind of circular logic is used regularly in judicial rulings on delegation.

Typically the Supreme Court declares that it would be a breach of the Constitution for Congress to transfer its legislative power to the President. After paying homage to the theory of separation of powers, courts generally uphold the delegation in question.[300] The judiciary typically insists on some "intelligible principle" expressed in the statute, though it is generally easy to satisfy that threshold. Legislative language is sanctioned even when the general guideline is protecting the "public interest" and avoiding "unfair method of competition."[301]

The courts tolerate this kind of legislation not because it is specific, which it is not, but because Congress sets forth procedures to guide agency officials in administering the statute. Agencies are required to give notice and a hearing prior to issuing a rule or regulation that is legislative in effect. Findings of fact are supplied for the record by the agency; opportunities exist for appeal. Through the Administrative Procedure Act (APA), Congress requires that agencies take actions that are not arbitrary, capricious, an abuse of discretion, in excess of statutory authority, or contrary to constitutional right, power, privilege, or immunity.[302]

297. JOHN LOCKE, SECOND TREATISE OF CIVIL GOVERNMENT, § 141 (1690).

298. Patrick W. Duff & Horace E. Whiteside, *Delegata Potestas Non Potest Delegari: A Maxim of American Constitutional Law*, 14 CORNELL L. Q. 168 (1929); Horst P. Ehmke, *"Delegata Potesta Non Potest Delegari," A Maxim of American Constitutional Law*, 47 CORNELL L. Q. 50 (1961).

299. ROBERT E. CUSHMAN, THE INDEPENDENT REGULATORY COMMISSIONS 429 (1941).

300. E.g., Field v. Clark, 143 U.S. 649, 692 (1891); Hampton & Co. v. United States, 276 U.S. 394, 406 (1928).

301. The "public interest" guideline was upheld in ICC v. Goodrich Transit Co., 224 U.S. 194, 214–15 (1912). For "unfair method of competition," see FTC v. Gratz, 253 U.S. 421, 427–28 (1920).

302. 60 Stat. 237, 243–44, sec. 10(e) (1946); 5 U.S.C. § 706.

## *B. Reasons for delegation*

From the very start, Congress found it necessary to set general goals and give executive officials discretion to carry out statutory policy. In 1789, the House of Representatives debated a bill to appoint a certain number of commissioners to make recommendations on the best location for the new national government. With the President's advice, they would propose the property to be purchased and the buildings to be constructed for Congress and the rest of government. Representative Thomas Tucker found this delegation "totally admissible" because it permitted a discretionary power "which no body of men ought to exercise but ourselves with the other branch of the Legislature.... Were we sent here to give such powers to any men?"[303] He proposed that the commissioners report to Congress, not the President, and require Congress at a later session to pass legislation for the nation's capital. His motion lost, 21 to 29.[304] A year later, Congress delegated the task to the President and his commissioners.[305]

Delegation may recognize the unpredictability of future events. Contingent (or conditional) legislation has a long tradition in America and elsewhere. An early legal test involved trade legislation directed at Great Britain. After the statute lapsed in 1810, Congress empowered the President to renew the trade restrictions at his discretion by proclamation. A merchant complained that these presidential actions had the force of law and thus were legislative in nature, violating the nondelegation and separation of power doctrines. In 1825 the Supreme Court saw "no sufficient reason, why the legislature should not exercise its discretion in reviving the act of March 1st, 1809, either expressly or conditionally, as their judgment should direct."[306] The nature of government, said the Court, often requires Congress to pass general legislation and "commit something to the discretion of the other departments, and the precise boundary of this power is a subject of delicate and difficult inquiry, into which a Court will not enter unnecessarily."[307] In enacting law, Congress may empower "those who are to act under such general provisions to fill up the details."[308] Courts accept statutory broadness and generality as understandable features of legislative drafting.[309]

Vague legislative formulations may meet the needs of Congress and the executive branch. Specificity can undermine the consensus needed to pass a bill. Adopting a ban on "sex discrimination" is easier to attract majority support in each house. Defining exactly what the term means with regard to father-son banquets or boy choirs might fracture the coalition needed for passage. In the early decades of the twentieth century, general tariff-making for each industry exposed Congress to such ridicule and rebuke that it decided to shift that task to the executive branch and the Tariff Commission (later named the International Trade Commission).[310] As

303. 1 ANNALS OF CONG. 879 (1789).

304. Id. at 880.

305. 1 Stat. 130 (1790).

306. Brig Aurora v. United States, 11 U.S. (7 Cr.) 382, 388 (1813).

307. Wayman v. Southard, 23 U.S. (10 Wheat.) 1, 46 (1825).

308. Id. at 43.

309. E.g., Buttfield v. Stranahan, 192 U.S. 470, 496 (1904), Union Bridge Co. v. United States, 204 U.S. 364, 386 (1907), Monongahela Bridge Co. v. United States, 216 U.S. 177 (1910), and United States v. Grimaud, 220 U.S. 506, 516 (1911).

310. RAYMOND A. BAUER et al., AMERICAN BUSINESS & PUBLIC POLICY 37 (1972). For studies on the delegation of legislative power: GEORGE I. LOVELL, LEGISLATIVE DEFERRALS: STATUTORY AMBIGUITY, JUDICIAL POWER,

explained in one study: "every favor which can be conferred is also a danger, because it must sometimes be refused. Responsibility involves blames. And, if the demands exceed what the congressman can effectively handle, then he may happily yield up a significant portion of his power. That is what happened with the tariff."[311]

## C. Judicial invalidations: the NRA

On two occasions in 1935, the Supreme Court struck down a delegation of congressional power to the executive branch. Both decisions involved the National Industrial Recovery Act (NIRA), which authorized industrial and trade associations to draft codes to minimize competition, raise prices, and restrict production. If the President found the codes unacceptable, he could prescribe his own and enforce them as law. Here was delegation not merely to the executive branch but to private parties. Those who drafted the NIRA gave little thought to constitutional questions of delegation or procedural safeguards. Under the pressure of the Great Depression, the bill went through Congress with insufficient scrutiny. General Hugh Johnson, administrator of the National Recovery Administration (NRA), demonstrated little interest in matters of due process. The attorneys operating under him had to compete with industry and trade association officials who were present at the drafting sessions. There was great difficulty in producing coherent and responsible codes in the midst of conflicts among NRA attorneys, U.S. attorneys, Interior Department lawyers, the Antitrust Division of the Justice Department, and private parties.[312]

In the first NRA case, *Panama Refining*, the Court struck down a section of the statute governing controls on petroleum production because it failed to establish a "criterion to govern the President's course. It does not require any finding by the President as a condition of his action.... it gives to the President an unlimited authority to determine the policy and to lay down the prohibition, or not to lay it down, as he may see fit. And disobedience to his order is made a crime punishable by fine and imprisonment."[313] The Court concluded that Congress "has declared no policy, has established no standard, has laid down no rule."[314] Justice Cardozo dissented, finding that Congress had supplied adequate standards.[315]

Cardozo's tolerance vanished in the second case, in which he exclaimed: "This is delegation running riot."[316] Chief Justice Hughes, writing for a unanimous Court in *Schechter*, struck down a "Live Poultry Code" as an unconstitutional delegation by Congress of legislative power. Congress "is not permitted to abdicate or to transfer to others the essential legislative functions with which it is vested."[317] The Court did not deny to Congress "the necessary resources

AND AMERICAN DEMOCRACY (2003); DAVID SCHOENBROD, POWER WITHOUT RESPONSIBILITY: HOW CONGRESS ABUSES THE PEOPLE THROUGH DELEGATION (1993); D. RODERICK KIEWIET & MATHEW D. MCCUBBINS, THE LOGIC OF DELEGATION: CONGRESSIONAL PARTIES AND THE APPROPRIATIONS PROCESS (1991); and SOTIRIOS A. BARBER, THE CONSTITUTION AND THE DELEGATION OF CONGRESSIONAL POWER (1975).

311. BAUER, et al., *supra* note 310, at 37.

312. PETER H. IRONS, THE NEW DEAL LAWYERS 22–107 (1982).

313. Panama Refining Co. v. Ryan, 293 U.S. 388, 415 (1935).

314. Id. at 430.

315. Id. at 434.

316. Schechter Corp. v. United States, 295 U.S. 495, 553 (1935).

317. Id. at 529.

of flexibility and practicality" in performing its legislative duties, but Congress must enact the standards to be followed and not attempt to transfer that basic function to others.[318] A year later, an appellate court struck down an emergency appropriations bill because it unconstitutionally delegated legislative power to the President.[319]

The decisions in *Panama Refining* and *Schechter* were handed down in a climate increasingly hostile to agency rulemaking. A Committee on Administrative Law, established by the American Bar Association in May 1933, viewed with anxiety the creation of New Deal agencies, objected to the "haphazard bedlam" of administrative practice, and urged more uniformity and due process.[320] During his first 15 months in office, President Roosevelt issued 674 executive orders. In its first year, NRA approved hundreds of codes and released 2,998 administrative orders that approved or modified the codes. Almost six thousand NRA press releases, some of them having legislative effect, were issued during this period.[321] In *Panama Refining*, the Court learned that the government had brought an indictment and took an appeal to the Court before discovering that the regulation on which the proceeding was based had been eliminated by an executive order.[322]

The "Schechter Rule," with its insistence on statutory standards, was seldom applied after 1935. Standardless delegations were upheld for many reasons, including the accumulated customs of a regulated industry and the practices developed by states that helped narrow the discretion of a federal agency.[323] Standardless delegations were found acceptable if the legislative history supplied guidelines for administrative action.[324]

A separate question involves not the delegation of legislative power to the executive branch but to *private parties*. In 1936 the Supreme Court struck down a statute in part because it delegated power to representatives of the coal industry to set up a code of mandatory regulations: "This is legislative delegation in its most obnoxious form; for it is not even delegation to an official or an official body, presumptively disinterested, but to private persons whose interests may be and often are adverse to others in the same business."[325] The Court considered such statutes an unconstitutional interference with personal liberty and private property and a denial of rights safeguarded by the Due Process Clause of the Fifth Amendment. A few years later, however, the Court allowed Congress to give farmers a veto power over marketing proposals by the Secretary of Agriculture. In subsequent years it upheld the delegation of legislative power to private associations that possess attributes of sovereignty over their members.[326]

318. Id. at 530.

319. Franklin Tp. in Somerset County, N.J. v. Tugwell, 85 F.2d 208, 218–20 (D.C. Cir. 1936).

320. 58 A.B.A. Rep. 201 (1933).

321. 59 A.B.A. Rep. 553–54 (1934).

322. Panama Refining, 293 U.S. at 412–13.

323. Fahey v. Mallonee, 332 U.S. 245, 250, 253 (1947), concerning the Home Owner's Loan Act of 1933 and the Federal Home Loan Bank Board.

324. Carl McGowan, *Congress, Court, and Control of Delegated Powers*, 77 Colum. L. Rev. 1119, 1128 n.33 (1977), citing Amalgamated Meat Cutters & Butcher Workmen v. Connolly, 337 F. Supp. 737 (D.D.C. 1971).

325. Carter v. Carter Coal Co., 298 U.S. 238, 311 (1936).

326. Currin v. Wallace, 306 U.S. 1 (1939). United States v. Mazurie, 419 U.S. 544 (1975), permitted a delegation of legislative power to Indian tribal councils. In Larkin v. Gendel's Den, Inc., 459 U.S. 116 (1982), the Court declared unconstitutional the delegation of state power to churches to veto liquor-license applications in their vicinity. For the broad scope of participation by private groups in the administration of federal law: George W. Liebmann, *Delegation to Private Parties in American Constitutional Law*, 50 Ind. L. Rev. 650 (1975).

In 1989, eight of nine Justices rejected a claim that Congress had delegated excessively in creating the U.S. Sentencing Commission; only Justice Scalia dissented.[327] Unanimous decisions in 1991 and 1996 dismissed the argument that Congress had unconstitutionally delegated its legislative power.[328] In two cases in the 1990s, the Supreme Court explored the relationship between the President and the Administrative Procedure Act (APA). In the first, the Court held that a judgment by the Secretary of Commerce and the President affecting the census and reapportionment was not reviewable under the APA.[329] The President is not "an agency within the meaning of the Act."[330] A concurrence by four Justices (Stevens, Blackmun, Kennedy, and Souter) read more like a dissent. They concluded that the census report prepared by the Secretary of Commerce was "final agency action" subject to judicial review under the APA, and that the Secretary's actions "were not arbitrary or capricious."[331]

Two years later, the Court decided a case requiring interpretation of a statute for the closing of military bases. It held that presidential actions for base closure are not subject to judicial review under the APA because he is not an "agency" under that statute.[332] A concurrence by Justice Blackmun agreed that the base closure statute precluded judicial review.[333] A separate concurrence by Justice Souter, joined by Justices Blackmun, Stevens, and Ginsburg, reached the same conclusion that Congress did not provide for judicial review of presidential actions under the base closure statute.[334]

In 1999, the D.C. Circuit held that language in the Clean Air Act represented an unconstitutional delegation of legislative power to the Environmental Protection Agency (EPA).[335] After the EPA issued final rules, the D.C. Circuit could not yet determine whether the nondelegation doctrine had been satisfied.[336] Two years later the Supreme Court unanimously decided that the transfer of this authority to the EPA to promulgate national ambient air quality standards did not violate the nondelegation doctrine.[337] Concurrences by Justices Thomas, Stevens, Souter, and Breyer agreed there had been no invalid delegation. A concurrence by Stevens and Souter noted that "legislative" powers are exercised by executive agencies. By their logic (defining legislation as prescribing rules for the future), the judicial branch also legislates.[338]

In the midst of the financial crisis of 2008, Congress passed the Emergency Economic Stabilization Act of 2008, which included a "bailout" of the financial industry through TARP

---

327. Mistretta v. United States, 488 U.S. 361 (1989).

328. Touby v. United States, 500 U.S. 160 (1991); Loving v. United States, 517 U.S. 748 (1996).

329. Franklin v. Massachusetts, 505 U.S. 788 (1992).

330. Id. at 796.

331. Id. at 807 (Stevens, J., concurring, joined by Blackmun, J., Kennedy, J., and Souter, J.).

332. Dalton v. Specter, 511 U.S. 462 (1994).

333. Id. at 477 (Blackmun, J., concurring).

334. Id. at 478–84 (Souter, J., concurring, joined by Blackmun, J., Stevens, J., and Ginsburg, J.).

335. American Trucking Associations v. U.S. E.P.A., 175 F.3d 1027 (D.C. Cir. 1999).

336. American Trucking Associations, Inc. v. E.P.A., 195 F.3d 4 (D.C. Cir. 1999).

337. Whitman v. American Trucking Assns., Inc. 531 U.S. 457, 472–76 (2001).

338. Id. at 488–89 (Stevens, J., concurring, joined by Souter, J.). See also Gary Lawson, *Discretion as Delegation: The "Proper" Understanding of the Nondelegation Doctrine*, G.W. L. Rev. 235 (2005), Gary Lawson, *Delegation and Original Meaning*, 88 Va. L. Rev. 327 (2002), and Cass R. Sunstein, *Nondelegation Canons*, 67 U. Chi. L. Rev. 325 (2000).

(Troubled Assets Relief Program).[339] Substantial delegation was placed in the executive branch to implement the program. Critics objected that Congress failed to provide any "intelligible principle" to guide executive officials in carrying out the program. The Department of the Treasury submits monthly reports to Congress on TARP, and on October 11, 2012, the Congressional Budget Office released a report on the program. A number of recent studies have analyzed the delegation doctrine.[340]

## D. Subdelegation

The problem of delegation is compounded when the agent of Congress transfers the statutory duty to a subordinate. The Supreme Court has been as accepting of subdelegation as delegation. It recognizes that the President and department heads cannot personally discharge all the statutory responsibilities assigned to them. It would be unreasonable to assume that every statute imposed upon the President a personal and nondelegable duty to review the decisions of subordinates. Such an interpretation would place "a burdensome, if not impossible, personal duty on the President" and could not be accepted as legislative intent unless Congress so stated.[341]

After World War II, Congress enacted legislation to specifically recognize the President's need to subdelegate some of the functions vested in him by law. A survey disclosed that President Truman had to act, expressly or by implication, under more than 1,100 statutes.[342] In 1950, on the basis of that study, Congress authorized the President to subdelegate statutory functions to his department heads or agency officials on the condition that the officer discharging those duties be someone who had been confirmed by the Senate. In that way, Congress chose to maintain a system of accountability to elected representatives.[343]

# 12. INDEPENDENT AGENCIES

Independent commissions exercising "quasi-judicial" and "quasi-legislative" powers were discussed in Chapter 3, section 7, with regard to presidential removals. This section treats commissions more fully. When Congress looked at the industries to be regulated after the Civil War, it saw turbulent, even revolutionary, changes in progress. Acting by legislation alone would

---

339. 122 Stat. 3765, 3767 (2008).

340. Curtis A. Bradley, *International Delegations, the Structural Constitution, and Non-Self-Execution*, 55 STAN. L. REV. 1557 (2003); Eric A. Posner & Adrian Vermeule, *Nondelegation: A Post-mortem*, 70 U. CHI. L. REV. 1331 (2003); Larry Alexander & Saikrishna Prakash, *Reports of the Nondelegation Doctrine's Death Are Greatly Exaggerated*, 70 U. CHI. L. REV. 1297 (2003); and Eric A. Posner & Adrian Vermeule, *Interring the Nondelegation Doctrine*, 69 U. CHI. L. REV. 1721 (2002).

341. French v. Weeks, 259 U.S. 326, 332 (1922). As noted in United States v. Chemical Foundation, 272 U.S. 1, 13 (1926): "Obviously all the functions of his great office cannot be exercised by the President in person."

342. 95 CONG. REC. 11395 (1949) (statement of Rep. McCormack).

343. 64 Stat. 419 (1950), 31 U.S.C. § 301. See NATHAN GRUNDSTEIN, PRESIDENTIAL DELEGATION OF AUTHORITY IN WARTIME (1961); Eli G. Nobleman, *The Delegation of Presidential Functions: Congressional and Legal Aspects*, 307 THE ANNALS 134 (1956); Glendon A. Schubert, Jr., *The Presidential Subdelegation Act of 1950*, 13 J. POL. 647

require substantial amendments almost every year to keep pace with shifting industrial conditions. It was decided that utilizing multi-member commissions run by experts offered a more practical approach than having members of Congress constantly revise statutes. Operating under a general charter, commissions could respond more effectively to economic and technological changes.

Independent commissions differ from conventional executive agencies in several ways. They operate under a group of administrators, with essentially equal powers, rather than under a single executive. As the Hoover Commission explained in 1949, independent commissions are multi-member (or "collegial") bodies for a reason: "Just as we want appellate courts to be made up of plural members, to protect against the idiosyncracies of a single individual, we want agencies that exercise judicial power to be collegial."[344] Second, the President may remove a commissioner only for purposes identified in the enabling statute. Third, commissioners have staggered terms to insulate them from presidential transitions. Fourth, statutory provisions specify the number of commissioners who may belong to the same political party. The latter restriction may be avoided by selecting nominal members of a political party whose political affiliation is more likely to be independent or even sympathetic to the other party.

The Interstate Commerce Commission (ICC), created by Congress in 1887, became the forerunner and prototype for independent commissions.[345] The ICC was modeled after railroad commissions that had been operating in more than 20 states. Reformers believed that commissions could accumulate more easily than lawmakers the expert knowledge needed to effectively supervise railroad corporations. With the railroad industry undergoing rapid change, a new type of administrative structure was needed.[346]

Initially, state railroad commissions functioned as fact-finding and advisory bodies, operating as agents of the legislative branch. They were not part of the executive branch. Over time, the commissions evolved into an agency within the executive branch but with some autonomy from the governor.[347] After the financial panics of 1873 and 1885, a number of small railroad lines went into bankruptcy. Upon consolidation, they began forming interstate, not intrastate, systems, requiring regulation by Congress rather than state legislatures. In 1886, the Supreme Court struck down an Illinois railroad statute because it affected, even for the part of the journey within the state, commerce among the states.[348] That decision required Congress to pass legislation to regulate railways.

The statute creating the ICC prohibited railroad practices such as rate discrimination, rebating, drawbacks, and the charging of unjust and unreasonable rates.[349] The commission was not empowered to establish railroad rates, but it could issue orders against the rates set by railroads and enforce its orders in the courts. Members of Congress considered two approaches to

(1951); and Glendon A. Schubert, Jr., *Judicial Review of the Subdelegation of Presidential Power*, 12 J. Pol. 668 (1950).

344. Kenneth Culp Davis, Administrative Law of the Seventies 15 (1976).

345. 24 Stat. 379 (1887).

346. Elihu Root, *Public Service By the Bar*, address in 1916; reprinted in Separation of Powers and the Independent Agencies: Cases and Selected Readings, prepared for the Subcommittee on Separation of Powers of the Senate Judiciary Committee, S. Doc. No. 91-49, 91st Cong., 1st Sess. 4-16 (1969).

347. Robert E. Cushman, The Independent Regulatory Commissions 21–34 (1941).

348. Wabash &c., Railway Co. v. Illinois, 118 U.S. 557 (1886).

349. 24 Stat. 379, sec. 2 (1887).

regulation: allowing the Justice Department to enforce the railroad policy established by statute, or rely on a commission to carry out legislative policy. It favored the latter because it would provide for more flexible and expert administration and build on the model of state commissions. There were concerns that "flexibility" would end up undermining statutory policy and that the ICC could not successfully compete with the expertise and political influence of railroads.[350]

The ICC was followed by other independent regulatory commissions: the Federal Reserve System in 1913, the Federal Trade Commission in 1914, the Federal Power Commission in 1920, and several agencies created in the 1930s: the Securities and Exchange Commission, the Federal Communications Commission, the Civil Aeronautics Board, the National Labor Relations Board, and the Federal Maritime Commission.[351] Other independent regulatory commissions were added later.

## A. Evaluating commissions

One of the harshest indictments of independent commissions came from the Brownlow Committee in 1937, which attacked them as "a headless 'fourth branch' of the Government, a haphazard deposit of irresponsible agencies and uncoordinated powers."[352] The committee claimed that independent agencies violated the "basic theory of the American Constitution that there should be three major branches of the Government and only three."[353] It further charged that although the commissions "enjoy power without responsibility, they also leave the President with responsibility without power."[354] Placed by the Constitution "at the head of unified and centralized Executive Branch" and charged with the duty to see that laws are faithfully executed, the President "must detour around powerful administrative agencies which are in no way subject to his authority and which are, therefore, both actual and potential obstructions to his effective over-all management of the national administration."[355]

The committee's language is overwrought. Although there existed "one" executive branch in the past, there were numerous examples of executive employees operating with substantial independence from presidential control, starting with the Comptroller in 1789 and the many occasions on which Attorneys General instructed Presidents they had no business interfering with ministerial duties entrusted by statute to agency personnel (Chapter 3, section 6). To the extent that independent commissions performed adjudicatory duties, those activities would not be subject to any greater presidential control if they were reassigned to an executive department.

More supportive of independent commissions was a task force of the 1949 Hoover Commission. It described the independent regulatory commission as a "useful and desirable agency where constant adaptation to changing conditions and delegation of wide discretion

---

350. Cushman, The Independent Regulatory Commissions, *supra* note 347, at 45–54.

351. Louis Fisher, The Politics of Shared Power: Congress and the Executive 149 (4th ed., 1998).

352. President's Committee on Administrative Management, Administrative Management in the Government of the United States 36 (1937).

353. Id.

354. Id.

355. Id.

in administration are essential to effective regulation."[356] Commissions provided a means of "insulating regulation from partisan influence or favoritism, for obtaining deliberation, expertness and continuity of attention, and for combining adaptability of regulation with consistency of policy so far as practical."[357] The task force found that conflict and inadequate coordination between the commissions and other executive agencies, although a potential problem, had been "limited in extent and generally avoided by cooperation."[358]

A third evaluation came from the Ash Council in 1971, which concluded that independent commissions "are not sufficiently accountable" to either Congress or the President. According to the Council, they are not responsive to changes in industry structure, technology, economic trends, and public needs; are unable to attract consistently high-quality commissioners and professional staff; and are over-judicialized through their reliance on formal procedures. The Council proposed that most of the commissions be transferred to four new regulatory agencies.[359] Their reorganization proposal was never adopted.

Independent commissions are sometimes criticized for being unresponsive to popular pressures, but they were created to avoid abrupt policy swings that might occur from one administration to the next. It is difficult to conceive of a commission being both independent and politically responsive. For agencies that make judicial rulings on licensing and ratemaking, independence is consistent with the standards and values associated with courts. Commissions are not created or structured to accommodate each shift in political winds.

A more serious concern is whether these commissions are eventually "captured" by the industries they are charged to regulate. That can happen, just as with regular executive departments. However, business, agriculture, labor, and other interests from the private sector are not monoliths capable of controlling a commission. Those private interests consist of many subsets competing for dominance. Some of the independent commissions had their origin as an executive department. The Federal Power Commission (FPC), created in 1920, consisted of the Secretary of War, the Secretary of the Interior, and the Secretary of Agriculture.[360] The President named the head of the commission.[361] A decade later, the FPC acquired its independence. A reorganization statute in 1930 changed the FPC to an agency of five commissioners with staggered terms.[362] After the original term of the commissioner designated as chair by the President had expired, future heads were named by the commission itself. In 1977, the FPC was renamed the Federal Energy Regulatory Commission (FERC) and placed within the newly created Department of Energy.[363] Despite this change in location, FERC retained its status as an independent regulatory commission. The Secretary of Energy has very limited control over the operations and decisions of FERC.

---

356. COMMISSION ON ORGANIZATION OF THE EXECUTIVE BRANCH OF THE GOVERNMENT [HOOVER COMMISSION], TASK FORCE REPORT ON REGULATORY COMMISSIONS (1949), reprinted in SEPARATION OF POWERS, *supra* note 346, at 816.

357. Id.

358. Id.

359. PERI E. ARNOLD, MAKING THE MANAGERIAL PRESIDENCY: COMPREHENSIVE REORGANIZATION PLANNING, 1905–1996, at 288 (1998 ed.)

360. 41 Stat, 1063 (1920).

361. Id.

362. 46 Stat. 797 (1930).

363. 91 Stat. 582 (1977).

Most independent agencies are able to conduct litigation in lower courts using their own agency attorneys. Over the years, the Solicitor General in the Justice Department has tightened its control over Supreme Court litigation, both for executive departments and independent agencies. Some independent agencies may represent themselves before the Supreme Court if the Solicitor General refuses to defend their positions.[364] Control over litigation by independent agencies depends on the willingness of Congress to protect the agencies and decisions by the Justice Department to cede some of its litigating authority.[365]

## B. Presidential control

Independent commissions are subject to the control of Congress, the President, and the courts. Congress creates the commissions, defines their authorities, specifies the qualifications for commissioners, and provides funding. Statutory provisions severely limit the President's ability to remove commissioners. The appointment of commissioners is formally shared by the President and the Senate, and yet members of Congress have shown a capacity to have their own staff selected as commissioners.[366] Through their power to nominate commissioners, Presidents are generally able to alter the composition and orientation of independent agencies. Within a matter of a couple of years, Presidents can be expected to have majorities of their own choosing.

By the time of Nixon's resignation in August 1974, after five and half years in office, he had nominated *every* commissioner of these agencies: the Civil Aeronautics Board (five commissioners), Federal Communications Commission (seven), Federal Maritime Commission (five), Federal Power Commission (five), National Labor Relations Board (five), Securities and Exchange Commission (five), and Consumer Products Safety Commission (five).[367] Presidential control over these commissions depends on the extent to which opposition-party commissioners are determined to serve out their term, thus decreasing the new President's ability to place a personal stamp on commissions. Also, opposition party Senators may insist on the "batching" of nominees to include a mix of the President's party and the opposition party.[368]

In 1975, Lloyd Cutler and David Johnson advocated legislation to empower the President to modify or direct certain actions by the regulatory agencies, subject to a one-house legislative veto and expedited judicial review.[369] A study commission of the American Bar Association

---

364. Neal Devins, *Unitariness and Independence: Solicitor General Control over Independent Agency Litigation*, 82 CAL. L. REV. 255, 269, 275 (1994).

365. Neal Devins, *Political Will and the Unitary Executive: What Makes an Independent Agency Independent?*, 15 CARDOZO L. REV. 273 (1993).

366. FISHER, *supra* note 351, at 155–59.

367. CONGRESSIONAL QUARTERLY, GUIDE TO CONGRESS 186 (1976). See also William E. Brigman, *The Executive Branch and the Independent Regulatory Agencies*, 11 PRES. STUD. Q. 244 (1981); Glen O. Robinson, *On Reorganizing the Independent Regulatory Agencies*, 57 VA. L. REV. 947, 951 n.14 (1971); David M. Welborn, *Presidents, Regulatory Commissioners and Regulatory Policy*, 15 J. PUBLIC L. 3 (1966); and Seymour Scher, *Regulatory Agency Control through Appointment: The Case of the Eisenhower Administration and the NLRB*, 23 J. POL. 667 (1961).

368. Neal Devins & David E. Lewis, *Not-so Independent Agencies: Party Polarization and the Limits of Institutional Design*, 88 BOSTON U. L. REV. 459 (2008).

369. Lloyd N. Cutler & David R. Johnson, *Regulation and the Political Process*, 84 YALE L.J. 1395, 1414–17 (1975).

considered this proposal and suggested a similar approach in 1979, but without the legislative veto. The commission recommended that Congress enact a statute to authorize the President to direct certain regulatory agencies, both within and outside the executive branch, to consider or reconsider the issuance of certain regulations. Before the presidential order could take effect, Congress would have a specified number of days to review the order and react to it. The President could then modify or withdraw the order and issue a new one.[370] Those reforms were not adopted. In *INS v. Chadha* (1983), the Supreme Court declared the legislative veto to be unconstitutional (Chapter 5, section 6C).

*Chadha*, followed by the Gramm-Rudman case of *Bowsher v. Synar* (1986),[371] emboldened the Reagan administration to make a concerted effort to eliminate independent commissions. In its brief in *Bowsher*, the Justice Department attacked the status of independent commissions. The brief argued that they are inconsistent with the Framers' deliberate choice of "a unitary Executive in order to promote a sense of personal responsibility and accountability to the people in the execution of the laws—and thereby to ensure vigorous administration of the laws and protection of the liberty, property, and welfare of the people."[372] Yet from the creation of an independent Comptroller in 1789 to the concept of ministerial duties within executive agencies, strict hierarchical values have been regularly ignored.

When the Gramm-Rudman case was argued before the Supreme Court, attorneys defending the statute warned the Justices that the Reagan administration wanted to invalidate all the independent regulatory agencies. Solicitor General Charles Fried dismissed these claims as just "scare tactics." The courtroom filled with laughter when Justice Sandra Day O'Connor remarked: "Well, Mr. Fried, I'll confess you scared me with it."[373]

Chief Justice Warren Burger assigned himself the task of writing the majority opinion in *Bowsher*. His colleagues on the Court advised him not to cast any doubt about the constitutionality of independent commissions. Yet his first draft did precisely that, prompting Justices to insist that he steer clear of that issue or any challenge to the 1935 case of *Humphrey's Executor*.[374] When *Bowsher* was issued, a footnote specifically stated that some of the litigants were "wide of the mark" in arguing that the Court's decision "requires casting doubt on the status of 'independent' agencies because no issues involving such agencies are presented here."[375]

Theodore Olson, former head of the Office of Legal Counsel in the Reagan administration, filed a suit that challenged the constitutionality of the Federal Trade Commission. He argued that the commission's enforcement functions must be carried out by officers who are subject to the supervisory control of the President and who serve at his pleasure.[376] The constitutional challenge centered on Article II of the Constitution, vesting the "executive power" in the President

---

370. Commission on Law and the Economy of the American Bar Association, Federal Regulation: Roads to Reform, Final Report 79–82, 88–91 (1979).

371. 478 U.S. 714 (1986).

372. Brief for the United States, Bowsher v. Synar, Supreme Court of the United States, October Term, 1985, at 21.

373. 160 Landmark Briefs and Arguments of the Supreme Court of the United States: Constitutional Law 604 (1987).

374. Bernard Schwartz, *An Administrative Law "Might Have Been"—Chief Justice Burger's* Bowsher v. Synar *Draft*, 42 Admin. L. Rev. 221 (1990).

375. Bowsher v. Synar, 478 U.S. 714, 725 n.4 (1986). See William H. Hardie III, *The Independent Agency After* Bowsher v. Synar *—Alive and Kicking*, 40 Vand. L. Rev. 903 (1987).

376. Complaint, Ticor Title Ins. Co. v. FTC (D.D.C. Sept. 16, 1985), at 6.

and directing the President to take care that the laws be faithfully executed.[377] Those issues were not reached because of the failure of plaintiffs to exhaust available administrative remedies.[378]

In a subsequent challenge to independent commissions, a federal appellate court upheld the Securities Exchange Commission against the claim that its exercise of civil enforcement actions violated separation of powers. The litigants argued that the President is given sole and exclusive control over the execution of the laws. The court firmly rejected that proposition: "It is a matter of fundamental law that the Constitution assigns to Congress the power to designate duties of particular officers. The President is not obligated under the Constitution to exercise absolute control over our government executives. The President is not required to execute the laws; he is required to take care they be executed faithfully."[379]

A NUMBER OF issues concerning executive-legislative relations remain. Several are addressed in the next chapter: the presidential veto and congressional opportunities to override; the pocket veto and "hybrid" vetoes; the item veto; presidential signing statements; the judicial invalidation of legislative vetoes and their survival; the collision between the President's executive privilege and the need of Congress to obtain executive documents and testimony as part of legislative oversight; and the legislative dependence on information from agency employees, including whistleblowers.

377. Ticor Title Ins. Co. v. F.T.C., 814 F.2d 731, 732 (D.C. Cir. 1987).

378. Id. at 741. See also Ticor Title Ins. Co. v. F.T.C., 625 F. Supp. 747 (D.D.C. 1986).

379. S.E.C. v. Blinder, Robinson & Co., Inc., 855 F.2d 677, 682 (10th Cir. 1988), cert. denied, 489 U.S. 1033 (1989). See also Geoffrey P. Miller, *Independent Agencies*, 1986 Sup. Ct. Rev. 41.

# FIVE

# Vetoes and Access to Information

MANY DISPUTES BETWEEN CONGRESS AND THE PRESIDENT INVOLVE enumerated powers, such as the President's authority to veto bills submitted to him. The Framers provided for a qualified, not an absolute, veto, but many unresolved questions about the veto power persist. The elected branches press competing interpretations; federal courts issue theirs. Added to this mix is the "legislative veto," a mechanism often described as congressional encroachment on executive power. In fact, Presidents encouraged it long ago and understood its benefits for the executive branch. Invalidated by the Supreme Court in *INS v. Chadha* (1983), the legislative veto nevertheless survives for reasons quite understandable. This chapter concludes by analyzing conflicts between the elected branches over access to information. Here the disagreement is not over enumerated powers but is rather a struggle between two implied powers: a claim of "executive privilege" by the President versus the congressional need for information to exercise its powers in an informed manner.

## 1. PRESIDENTIAL VETO

At the time of the Philadelphia convention, advocates of an absolute executive veto recalled this first charge against King George III in the Declaration of Independence in 1776: "He has refused his Assent to Laws, the most wholesome and necessary for the common good." Some of the Framers, including Alexander Hamilton and James Wilson, urged an absolute veto. Not one state supported their cause. Before deciding what kind of veto to adopt, the delegates debated whether to create a council consisting of the Executive and federal judges to review bills before they took effect.

### A. Council of revision

At the Philadelphia convention on May 29, 1787, a proposal joined the President with "a convenient number of the National Judiciary" to form a council of revision to examine "every act of the National Legislature before it shall operate, & every act of a particular [i.e., state] Legislature before a Negative thereon shall be final."[1] The council would thus possess a veto not only over Congress but state legislatures as well. The council's decision would prevail "unless the Act of the National Legislature be again passed, or that of a particular Legislature be again negatived by        of the members of each branch."[2] The blank was to be filled in later by a fraction. Some delegates wanted a veto by Congress over "all laws, passed by the several States, contravening, in the opinion of the national legislature, the articles of union."[3] Support for the latter power never developed.[4]

Delegates debated the council of revision on June 4. Elbridge Gerry doubted whether judges should be part of the council. Anticipating the power of judicial review, he thought that judges would have "a sufficient check agst. encroachments on their own department by their exposition of the laws, which involved a power of deciding on their Constitutionality."[5] Rufus King raised another objection. Judges "ought to be able to expound the law as it should come before them, free from the bias of having participated in its formation."[6] The proposal to include judges in a council of revision was rejected, three states voting in favor, eight against.[7]

## B. Qualified, not absolute

James Wilson argued that without an absolute veto the legislative branch could "at any moment sink" the Executive into "non-existence." Hamilton joined Wilson in urging an absolute negative.[8] Benjamin Franklin, recalling his experience in Pennsylvania, objected that the governor had used his absolute veto to "extort money." No bill, regardless of its merits, "could be passed without a private bargain with him. An increase of his salary, or some donation, was always made a condition."[9] Roger Sherman was against "enabling any one man to stop the will of the whole. No one man could be found so far above all the rest in wisdom."[10] On the question of giving the Executive an absolute negative, ten states votes against. Not one state voted in favor.[11]

The presidential veto is qualified by enabling Congress to override by a certain margin. Initially a two-thirds vote in each house was required. Later the fraction was moved up to three-fourths.[12] Still later the delegates returned to two-thirds. Hugh Williamson, who had earlier proposed three-fourths instead of two-thirds, announced on September 12 that he had changed his mind. He was now "convinced that the latter proportion was the best. The former

---

1. 1 Farrand 21.
2. Id.
3. Id. at 47, 54.
4. Id. at 164–68, 169–73, 293, 337; 2 Farrand 21–22, 27–28.
5. 1 Farrand 97.
6. Id. at 98.
7. Id. at 131, 140.
8. Id. at 98.
9. Id. at 99.
10. Id.
11. Id. at 103.
12. 1 Farrand 94, 104; 2 Farrand 71, 295, 298–301, 569, 582.

puts too much in the power of the President."[13] The delegates supported two-thirds by six states in favor and four opposed, with one state divided.[14]

Article I, section 7 provides that every bill that passes Congress "shall, before it becomes a Law, be presented to the President of the United States" (the Presentment Clause). If he approves, "he shall sign it." If he disapproves, "he shall return it, with his Objections to that House in which it shall have originated, who shall enter the Objections at large on their Journal, and proceed to reconsider it." If the house to which the bill is returned agrees to pass the bill by a two-thirds margin, it is sent to other house. If approved by two-thirds of that house "it shall become a Law." The votes cast by both houses "shall be determined by yeas and Nays," and the names of the persons voting "shall be entered on the Journal of each House respectively." If any bill is not returned by the President "within ten Days (Sundays excepted)" after being presented to him, "the Same shall be a Law, in like Manner as if he had signed it, unless the Congress by their Adjournment prevent its Return, in which Case it shall not be a Law." This latter language invited "pocket vetoes" by the President, analyzed in this chapter in section 2.

The Presentment Clause is clarified by language at the end of Article I, section 7. "Every Order, Resolution, or Vote to which the Concurrence of the Senate and House of Representatives may be necessary (except on a question of Adjournment) shall be presented to the President of the United States." Before those specified measures take effect, they shall be approved by him or, if disapproved, repassed by two-thirds of each house, "according to the Rules and Limitations prescribed in the Case of a Bill." Resolutions passed by a single chamber (simple resolutions) are not presented to the President. They have no legal significance. Even resolutions passed by both chambers (concurrent resolutions) are not presented to the President. Questions about simple and concurrent resolutions are taken up later in the section on legislative vetoes.

## C. Hamilton's analysis

In Federalist No. 69, Hamilton explained that the qualified veto of the President "differs widely from the absolute negative of the British sovereign."[15] He elaborated more fully in Federalist No. 73, warning about the "propensity of the legislative department to intrude upon the rights, and to absorb the powers, of the other departments."[16] Were he writing today, he might have been concerned about the propensity of the President and the Supreme Court to intrude upon the rights of other branches. He implied that by discussing "the insufficiency of a mere parchment delineation of the boundaries of each" branch and the "necessity of furnishing each with constitutional arms for its own defence."[17]

Hamilton identified another issue. Was the veto to be used only against bills the President considered unconstitutional, or used more broadly against bills poorly designed and drafted? In Federalist No. 73, he defended the veto against both kinds of measures. The veto "not only serves as a shield to the Executive, but it furnishes an additional security against the enaction

---

13. 2 Farrand 585.

14. Id. at 587.

15. The Federalist 445.

16. Id. at 468.

17. Id. at 468–69.

of improper laws."[18] Used for that purpose, it "establishes a salutary check upon the legislative body, calculated to guard the community against the effects of faction, precipitancy, or of any impulse unfriendly to the public good, which may happen to influence a majority of that body."[19] The veto was necessary to guard against "the passing of bad laws, through haste, inadvertence, or design."[20]

Having lost the battle for an absolute veto, Hamilton in No. 73 continued to reject arguments leveled against it. He referred to those who said "it was not to be presumed a single man would possess more virtue and wisdom than a number of men."[21] He found that observation as "rather specious than solid."[22] The veto was necessary not because of "the supposition of superior wisdom and virtue" in the Executive, but upon the supposition that Congress "will not be infallible" and that the "love of power" may sometimes dispose it to encroach upon other branches.[23] Fair enough, but the love of power in the President and the Supreme Court can also invite encroachments. Fallibility is a characteristic of all three branches. The veto operates as a check on legislative fallibility; the congressional override is a check on executive fallibility; judicial review functions as a check on legislative and executive fallibility. The elected branches and popular opinion check judicial fallibility.

Hamilton reviewed the recent history of England to conclude that the king, "with all his train of sovereign attributes, and with all the influence he draws from a thousand sources, would, at this day, hesitate to put a negative upon the joint resolutions of the two houses of Parliament."[24] He noted that a "very considerable period has elapsed since the negative of the crown has been exercised."[25] If the British king was reluctant to exercise the veto, Hamilton asked: "how much greater caution may be reasonably expected in a President of the United States, clothed for the short period of four years with the executive authority of a government wholly and purely republican?"[26] The greater danger, Hamilton said, was in the President "not using his power when necessary, than of his using it too often, or too much."[27] He reasoned that although Presidents might have been very reluctant to use an absolute veto, they would be more willing to use a qualified one. By taking the latter action, he was simply returning a bill for reconsideration and possible override.[28]

## *D. Use of the veto*

In an article in 1976, Charles L. Black, Jr. argued that President Ford had misused the veto power, which Black said may be applied "only rarely, and certainly not as a means of systematic policy

18. Id. at 469.

19. Id. at 469.

20. Id. at 470.

21. Id. at 469.

22. Id.

23. Id

24. Id. at 470.

25. Id. at 470–71.

26. Id. at 471.

27. Id.

28. Id. at 471.

control over the legislative branch, on matters constitutionally indifferent and not menacing the President's independence."[29] No such restriction applies to the veto. According to Black, the early vetoes were mainly intended to protect the integrity of the President's office. However, the Framers could not have anticipated the volume of legislation that would come from Congress. On a single day in 1886, President Cleveland received nearly 240 private bills granting new pensions for veterans, increasing their benefits, and restoring old names to the list. He did not hesitate to offer policy reasons why those bills were indefensible.[30]

From the start, Presidents used a mix of policy and constitutional reasons when exercising the veto power. President Washington vetoed two bills, the first on constitutional grounds (an apportionment bill). With the second, he thought it so carelessly drafted and so unwise in substance that it should not become law.[31] Neither bill affected the President's office. Black suggested that the second bill, involving the military, "may have been seen as a dangerous weakening of the country's military force, connected with the Commander-in-Chief power, so that the veto may well be thought to fall within the category of defense of the presidential office."[32] That analysis depends on too many "mays." The evidence is that Washington thought it a bad bill.

Presidents John Adams and Thomas Jefferson did not use the veto power. Their record should not imply they were weak leaders, failed to protect their office, or did not care about policy and constitutional issues. Rather, they and their supporters in Congress had sufficient influence on the legislative process that a veto was unnecessary. During the first 28 years, covering four Presidents and seven administrations, there were only seven regular vetoes: five for constitutional reasons. One affected the independence of the executive, a district courts bill that Madison vetoed in part because he thought it usurped his appointment power.[33]

Increased use of the veto power by Presidents Jackson and Tyler triggered objections from lawmakers. In 1841, under the influence of Whig (pro-legislative) theories, President William Henry Harrison recommended a restrained use of the veto, for it was "preposterous" to believe that the President could better understand the wishes of the people than their own representatives. He explained that the veto was necessary to oppose legislation of a strongly local nature, to protect the Constitution, defend the people from hasty legislation, and preserve the rights of minorities from the effects of combinations.[34] Harrison's successor, John Tyler, exercised the veto with such frequency that his opponents in Congress introduced a resolution to impeach him. Among the grounds: "I charge him with the high crime and misdemeanor of withholding his assent to laws undispensable [sic] to the just operations of government, which involved no constitutional difficulty on his part."[35]

---

29. Charles L. Black, Jr., *Some Thoughts on the Veto*, 40 LAW & CONTEMP. PROB. 87, 90 (1976).

30. 10 Richardson 5001–02 (May 8, 1886) and 5020–40 (June 21-23, 1886). Details of Cleveland's vetoes of private pension bills: LOUIS FISHER, PRESIDENTIAL SPENDING POWER 25–27 (1975). For the growth of private bills: Clarence A. Berdahl, *The President's Veto of Private Bills*, 52 POL. SCI. Q. 505 (1937).

31. 1 Richardson 116, 203.

32. Black, *supra* note 29, at 90.

33. 2 Richardson 496.

34. 3 Richardson 1866. For Whiggish opposition to the veto: ROBERT J. SPITZER, THE PRESIDENTIAL VETO: TOUCHSTONE OF THE AMERICAN PRESIDENCY 39–59 (1988). For documents on vetoes and Whig attacks: 1 Goldsmith 329–60; 2 Goldsmith 597–721.

35. CONG. GLOBE, 27th Cong., 3d Sess. 144 (1843) (Rep. John Minor Botts).

Exceptionally controversial was the decision by President Jackson to veto a bill recreating the U.S. Bank. He was urged to sign the legislation because it had been supported by previous Presidents, previous Congresses, and the Supreme Court in *McCulloch v. Maryland* (1819). He disagreed, insisting that precedents alone did not prevent him from making an independent judgment about the merits and constitutionality of bills presented to him. Each public official, he said, takes an oath to support the Constitution "as he understands it, and not as it is understood by others."[36] It is as much the duty of lawmakers in the House and Senate and the President "to decide upon the constitutionality of any bill or resolution which may be presented to them for passage or approval as it is of the supreme judges when it might be brought them for judicial decision."[37] A judicial ruling "has no more authority over Congress than the opinion of Congress has over the judges, and on that point the President is independent of both."[38]

The Constitution recognizes three forms of presidential action in exercising the veto power: sign a bill, veto it, or allow it to lapse by using a "pocket veto." A fourth option emerged: letting a bill become law without a President's signature. President Cleveland took that course in 1894 as a means of dissociating himself from the Wilson-Gorman Tariff Act. A veto risked offending his party (in control of both houses of Congress and therefore responsible for the bill). Still, Cleveland did not want his name on the legislation. He believed it contained provisions "which are not in line with honest tariff reform, and it contains inconsistencies and crudities which ought not to appear in tariff laws or laws of any kind."[39]

President Clinton took a similar course in 1995, letting a defense appropriations bill become law without his signature. Although the bill contained $7 billion more than he had requested, a result that might please many Presidents, he regarded the amount as so excessive that he planned to ask Congress to rescind (terminate) some of the funds. Yet he also planned to use some of the excess funds to finance his deployment of U.S. troops to Bosnia, a commitment that Congress had not authorized or approved.[40]

## E. Constitutional procedures

Many procedures for the veto process have been settled by the two elected branches, with their interpretations later accepted by the courts. If the President decides to exercise the veto, he is directed by Article I, section 7 to return the bill with his objections to the house that originated the bill, which "shall … proceed to reconsider it." Must Congress, as this language seems to imply, *immediately* proceed to reconsider? That was the practice during the early years, when

---

36. 3 Richardson 1145.

37. Id.

38. Id. See Gerald N. Magliocca, *Veto! The Jacksonian Revolution in Constitutional Law*, 78 Neb. L. Rev. 205 (1999).

39. 2 Robert McElroy, Grover Cleveland 116 (1923).

40. Public Papers of the Presidents, 1995, II, at 1813. For general studies on the presidential veto: Richard A. Watson, Presidential Vetoes and Public Policy (1993); Robert J. Spitzer, The Presidential Veto: Touchstone of The American Presidency (1989); Carlton Jackson, Presidential Vetoes, 1792–1945 (1967); and Edward Campbell Mason, The Veto Power: Its Origin, Development and Function in the Government of the United States, 1789–1889 (1890).

vetoes were infrequent. But Congress eventually began to delay a vote to permit committees of jurisdiction to report their recommendations. If Congress decides not to contest a veto, it need not be reconsidered at all. It is established today that if a President vetoes a bill, Congress may schedule an override vote anytime during the two years of a Congress.[41]

Article I, section 7 provides that if during reconsideration each house musters a two-thirds majority, the vetoed bill "shall become a Law." What is meant by two-thirds: two-thirds of the total membership of each house, or two-thirds of the lawmakers present? The House of Representatives decided on two-thirds of the members present, provided they formed a quorum.[42] This ruling was liberalized in 1912 when Speaker Champ Clark held that an override required two-thirds of the members present and *voting*.[43] This particular override attempt produced 174 yeas, 80 nays, and 10 present but not voting. The affirmative votes did not represent two-thirds of the 264 present, but it did constitute two-thirds of those who voted. Under Clark's ruling, the override therefore prevailed.[44] In 1919 the Supreme Court, referring to these precedents of Congress, decided that two-thirds of a quorum sufficed for an override.[45] Two-thirds of "that House" meant a house organized and empowered to perform legislative duties (a quorum).[46] The practice of Congress has been to require two-thirds of the members present and voting.

Another issue: may a President sign a bill after Congress has recessed? If presidential approval of a bill is not strictly an executive function but legislative in nature, must approval occur only when both houses are actually sitting for legislative business? The Court in 1899 rejected that construction.[47] If a President decides to sign a bill, no further action by Congress is needed and there is no reason for it to be in session to act.[48] A related question: may a President sign a bill after final adjournment of a Congress? At an early date, Presidents regarded themselves as so connected to Congress with respect to lawmaking that they could sign legislation only while Congress was in session. They would come to a special room in the Capitol for that purpose.[49]

President Cleveland broke with that practice and refused to visit the Capitol for bill-signing. Under the advice of his Attorney General, however, he decided to make the trip.[50] In 1920 and again in 1931, two Attorneys General concluded that a President has constitutional authority to sign a bill after the final adjournment of Congress.[51] In 1932, the Court accepted those interpretations.[52] Important for the Court was the constitutional right of the President to take up to

---

41. Louis Fisher, *When Must Congress Reconsider Vetoes?*, Congressional Research Service, Sept. 14, 1988, reprinted in *Pocket Veto Legislation*, hearing before the House Committee on the Judiciary, 101st Cong., 2d Sess. 95–114 (1990).

42. 4 HINDS' PRECEDENTS §§ 3537–3538 n.2.

43. Id. at § 1111.

44. Id.

45. Missouri Pac. Ry. Co. v. Kansas, 248 U.S. 276 (1919).

46. Id. at 285.

47. La Abra Silver Mining Co. v. United States, 175 U.S. 423 (1899).

48. Id. at 451–55.

49. Lindsay Rogers, *The Power of the President to Sign Bills After Congress has Adjourned*, 30 YALE L.J. 1, 1 (1920).

50. E. I. Renick, *The Power of the President to Sign Bills After the Adjournment of Congress*, 32 AM. L. REV. 208, 212 (1898).

51. 32 OP. ATT'Y GEN. 225 (1920) and 36 OP. ATT'Y GEN. 403 (1931); Rogers, *supra* note 49.

52. Edwards v. United States, 286 U.S. 482 (1932).

ten days (Sundays excepted) to consider the merits of bills presented to him. The Court noted that during the last 24 hours of the 71st Congress, 184 bills were presented to President Hoover, a burden that required the full ten days for him to act with requisite care.[53] Furthermore, the Court's prior holding in the 1899 *La Abra* case, that no action by Congress was required for the signing of a bill after a recess, applied equally well to a signing after final adjournment.[54]

What does the Constitution mean when it requires that bills be "presented" to the President? The answer might seem obvious but is not. Must Congress present a bill to him personally? Language in Article I, section 7 refers to "presented to him." May it leave a bill with an agent at the White House? Even the answer to that is not simple. If the President is traveling outside Washington, D.C. but within the United States, presentation either to the President or the White House should not be that difficult. What if the President is traveling abroad?

To handle these problems, the two elected branches agreed to some accommodations. In a letter to Congress on November 10, 1943, President Roosevelt noted he would be absent from the nation's capital "for some time in the near future" and asked that "insofar as possible the transmission of completed legislation be delayed until my return."[55] In cases of emergency legislation, the White House Office was authorized to forward the bills to him "at once by the quickest means."[56] He insisted that the ten-day period for presidential consideration would not begin when the materials reached the White House. Rather, the White House Office "will not receive bills or resolutions on behalf of the President but only for the purpose of forwarding them."[57] As soon as the bills reached him, "their presentation to the President will have been completed in accordance with the terms of the Constitution."[58] President Eisenhower received similar advice from Attorney General Brownell in 1955.[59]

The issue of "presenting" bills to a President when he travels abroad reached the Court of Claims in 1964. Congress sent a bill to the White House on August 31, 1959, after President Eisenhower had left for a trip to Europe. He returned on September 7 and vetoed the bill on September 14. Congress did not attempt an override. Did the bill become law because he failed to veto it within the ten-day period? The court identified three options for Presidents when they travel abroad. A President could (1) insist that Congress personally present bills to him while abroad, (2) ask that they be delayed until his return, or (3) direct that bills be accepted at the White House as though the President was there. If Congress disliked the second option, it could send the bill abroad and present it to the President ("who has to make himself reasonably available for that purpose").[60] Under the circumstances, the court held that Eisenhower's veto was timely. Congress knew of the White House procedure before he departed on his trip. It could have sent the legislation to Eisenhower in Europe but did not.[61]

---

53. Id. at 493.

54. Id. at 490.

55. 2 Op. Att'y Gen. 383, 385 (1977).

56. Id.

57. Id.

58. Id.

59. Id. at 386.

60. Eber Bros. Wine & Liquor Corporation v. United States, 337 F.2d 624, 630 (Ct. Cl. 1964).

61. Id. at 633; cert. denied, 380 U.S. 950 (1965).

An opinion by the Office of Legal Counsel in 1977 reviewed these political and constitutional principles. It said that when the President is in the United States, "presentation does not require delivery to him personally; rather it is done by delivery of the bill to one of the legislative clerks on the White House staff."[62] The same procedure exists with vetoed bills. Congressional clerks are available to receive a returned bill when Congress is not in session. The fact that Congress is not in session does not prohibit the bill's "return" and justify a pocket veto. One can compare the leniency of presidential absences when bills are submitted to the White House with the treatment of pocket vetoes and recess appointments. Administrations have argued that if the Senate is in recess for as little as three days, the President may resort to his recess appointment power.[63] Consider this statement in the OLC analysis: "the President normally withdraws the legislative clerks' authority to accept enrolled bills on his behalf when he travels abroad and so advises the Congress."[64] The President basically announces: "You cannot 'present' bills to me because I am not here." Should similar opportunities be available to Congress to create fictions that protect it from pocket vetoes and recess appointments?

An OLC opinion in 2005 added a new twist to the veto power. Article I, section 7 states that when a bill is submitted to the President "he shall sign it" or return it with his veto message. Does that mean he must personally sign the bill? Drawing from English cases dating back to 1614, OLC concluded that signing could be done with an autopen. The President may sign a bill or direct "a subordinate to affix the President's signature to it."[65] While traveling in Europe in 2011, President Obama exercised that option by directing that his signature be placed on a bill extending the Patriot Act.[66]

## F. Statements of Administration Policy (SAPs)

In 1817, President Monroe alarmed some members of Congress by signaling in advance his opposition to contemplated legislation. He expressed his "settled conviction" that Congress lacked the constitutional authority to appropriate money for projects at the state and local level ("internal improvements").[67] A House committee, established to review and comment on his message, reacted with indignation that a President would attempt to influence Congress while it is legislating. It insisted that nothing should restrain in any way the ability of Congress to express its independent will. If Congress, influenced by the President's intervention, refrained from action, "it might happen that the opinion of the President would prevent the enaction of a law, even though there should be the Constitutional majority of two-thirds of both Houses in its

---

62. 2 Op. O.L.C. 383, 383 (1977).

63. Memorandum of Points and Authorities in Support of Defendants' Opposition to Plaintiffs' Motion for Partial Summary Judgment, at 24–26, Mackie v. Clinton, Civ. Action No. 93-0032-LFO (D.D.C. 1993). The litigation that prompted that analysis was not decided on that ground.

64. 2 Op. O.L.C. at 384.

65. Office of Legal Counsel, *Whether the President May Sign a Bill by Directing that His Signature Be Affixed to It*, July 7, 2005, at 2.

66. Michael D. Shear, *Making Legislative History, With Nod from Obama and Stroke of an Autopen*, N.Y. Times, May 28, 2011, http://www.nytimes.com/2011/05/28/us/politics/28sign.html?_r=1.

67. Annals of Cong., 15th Cong.,1st Sess. 18 (1817).

favor."[68] The committee objected to this presidential influence, objecting that it "would acquire a force unknown to the Constitution, and the legislative body would be shorn of its powers from a want of confidence in its strength, or from indisposition to exert it."[69]

In contemporary times, such "interference" by the President is commonplace. Administrations release a Statement of Administration Policy (SAP) prepared by the Office of Management and Budget after a bill passes either house or is in conference committee for final adjustments. A SAP identifies specific provisions of a bill that the administration warns is an invitation to a veto unless changed in accordance with instructions set forth by the President. Of course during the entire period of considering legislation the President and other executive officials are at liberty to critique different provisions of a draft bill they find unacceptable for both policy and constitutional reasons. That type of feedback can be shared at congressional hearings, in meetings with lawmakers and their staff, and in public comments issued by the administration.[70]

## 2. POCKET VETO

Article I, section 7 provides that any bill not returned by the President "within ten Days (Sundays excepted)" shall become law "unless the Congress by their Adjournment prevent its Return, in which Case it shall not be a Law." A "pocket veto" was first used in 1812 by President Madison.[71] He used it again in 1816. President Jackson resorted to the pocket veto seven times, provoking congressional rebukes for acting in an "arbitrary and unconstitutional manner."[72] From Madison through Andrew Johnson, Presidents who used the pocket veto generally prepared a memorandum explaining the basis for their disapproval. That practice lapsed from Grant through Hoover but was reinstated by Franklin D. Roosevelt.[73]

The constitutionality of the pocket veto did not reach the Supreme Court until 1929. In this and all other cases, the question was whether Congress by an adjournment had "prevented" the President from returning a bill. Congress submitted a bill to President Coolidge on June 24, 1926, less than ten days before it adjourned at the end of its first session. Congress adjourned on July 3 and did not return until the first Monday in December.[74] A unanimous Court concluded that the length of the adjournment prevented the President from returning the bill. The key issue was not whether the adjournment was final or interim but whether it prevented a return. The Court also decided that "ten Days" meant calendar days, not legislative days.[75]

---

68. Id. at 452.

69. Id.

70. For some contemporary views of presidential vetoes: J. Richard Broughton, *Rethinking the Presidential Veto*, 42 Harv. J. on Legis. 91 (2005), and Michael B. Rappaport, *The President's Veto and the Constitution*, 87 Nw. U. L. Rev. 735 (1993).

71. Jackson, *supra* note 40, at 8–9.

72. Spitzer, *supra* note 40, at 107. For presidential vetoes divided between regular and pocket: Kevin R. Kosar, *Regular Vetoes and Pocket Vetoes: An Overview*, Congressional Research Service, RS22188, Nov. 18, 2010, at 3–4.

73. Clement E. Vose, *The Memorandum Pocket Veto*, 26 J. Pol. 397 (1964).

74. The Pocket Veto Case, 279 U.S. 655, 672 (1929).

75. Id. at 679. The term "legislative days" refers to the days during which Congress is in legislative session and excludes calendar days that are not legislative days. The Court held that words in the Constitution are to be taken

The next case, in 1938, involved a pocket veto during a brief period in which Congress had not adjourned. The Senate alone had recessed for three days. The Court regarded the time as so short that the Senate could act with "reasonable promptitude" on the veto.[76] Also, the Secretary of the Senate was present during the recess and was able to receive (and did receive) the bill. To the Court, the veto serves two fundamental purposes: (1) to give the President an opportunity to consider a bill presented to him, and (2) to give Congress an opportunity to review presidential objections and override them. Both constitutional purposes require protection. Permitting the pocket veto to expand without limit would produce the absolute veto emphatically rejected by the Framers.[77] An Attorney General opinion in 1943 supported a pocket veto after Congress had adjourned for two months.[78]

## A. Efforts at political accommodation

Three decades elapsed before the pocket veto was again litigated. On December 14, 1970, the Family Practice of Medicine Bill was presented to President Nixon. It had passed by such overwhelming majorities (64 to 1 in the Senate, 346 to 2 in the House) that a veto would have met an almost instant override. Both houses adjourned on December 22 for the Christmas holidays. The Senate returned on December 28. The House met the next day. Not counting December 27, a Sunday, the Senate was gone for four days, the House for five. During the recess, the Senate designated an officer to receive messages from the President. Yet Nixon pocket vetoed the bill on December 24.[79]

Nixon's action differed markedly from the 1929 case, which involved a short recess during a session rather than a lengthy adjournment as the end of a session. A district court held that the Christmas recess did not prevent Nixon from returning the bill to Congress as a regular bill. It ruled that the bill became law on December 25, 1970.[80] An interesting feature of the case is that it was brought by Senator Ted Kennedy. Members of Congress are rarely able to demonstrate standing in court. In this case, however, the court reasoned that the pocket veto rendered Kennedy's vote in the Senate for the bill "ineffective and deprived him of his constitutional right to vote to override the Presidential Veto in an effort to have the bill passed without the President's signature."[81]

When the D.C. Circuit affirmed this ruling the following year, it cast doubt on pocket vetoes during *any* intrasession adjournment, no matter the length.[82] It concluded that an intrasession adjournment "does not prevent the President from returning a bill which he disapproves so long as appropriate arrangements are made for the receipt of presidential messages during the

---

in their natural and obvious sense. See Abram R. Serven, *The Constitution and the "Pocket Veto,"* 7 N.Y.U. L. Q. REV. 495 (1929).

76. Wright v. United States, 302 U.S. 583, 590 (1938).

77. Id. at 589–90, 596–97.

78. 40 OP. ATT'Y GEN. 274 (1943).

79. PUBLIC PAPERS OF THE PRESIDENTS, 1970, at 1156. The pocket veto, dated December 24, was released two days later. See Note, *The Presidential Veto Power: A Shallow Pocket*, 70 MICH. L. REV. 148 (1971).

80. Kennedy v. Sampson, 364 F. Supp. 1075, 1087 (D.D.C. 1973).

81. Id. at 1978.

82. Kennedy v. Sampson, 511 F.2d 430 (D.C. Cir. 1974).

adjournment."[83] After the Nixon administration decided not to contest the appellate ruling, the bill became law and was backdated to December 25, 1970.[84]

Kennedy's litigation resulted in a political accommodation. On December 19, 1975, just as the House was about to adjourn sine die for the session, Congressman Bob Eckhardt suggested the only way to prevent a pocket veto was to adjourn for a period no longer than 3 days. House Minority Leader John Rhodes said that would not be necessary. He announced that President Ford told him "when legislation is sent down to him, he will either sign it or veto it in the ordinary way, which would preserve the right of this House and of the other body to either sustain or override those vetoes when we come back after the sine die adjournment."[85]

Kennedy's determination yielded an accommodation by the Justice Department on April 13, 1976. It stated that President Ford would use the regular veto rather than the pocket veto during both intrasession and intersession recesses and adjournments of Congress, provided that Congress specifically authorized an officer to receive return vetoes during those periods. The pocket veto would be used only during the sine die adjournment of Congress at the end of its second session.[86]

Ford's decision was honored during the four years of Carter's term. It ended with the Reagan administration. On December 29, 1981, after Congress had adjourned at the end of the first session of the 97th Congress, to return in about six weeks, Reagan pocket vetoed a special relief bill for a bankrupt Florida firm.[87] At the end of the 98th Congress, he issued a pocket veto again, this time for a bill to require the certification of human rights practices in El Salvador as a precondition for sending military aid.[88] The House adjourned sine die on November 18, 1983 and did not return until January 23, 1984—nine weeks later. Those pocket vetoes were issued between sessions, not in the middle of one.

After the second pocket veto, a bipartisan group of 33 members of the House filed suit to require the bill be issued as a public law. A district court in *Barnes v. Carmen* upheld Reagan's action.[89] The court reasoned that the case most relevant was the Pocket Veto Case of 1929, which also involved a multi-month sine die adjournment between the first and second sessions. Although the 1929 decision had been shaken by *Wright* in 1938 and the *Kennedy* cases, the court felt an obligation to follow the holding that seemed most on point.[90] In these disputes, Reagan was willing to abide by *Kennedy v. Sampson* to the extent that he would not exercise a pocket veto *during* a session.[91]

The *Barnes* decision was overturned by the D.C. Circuit, which noted that both the House and the Senate had authorized an agent to receive veto messages from the President.[92] It was

---

83. Id. at 437. See Note, *The Veto Power and* Kennedy v. Sampson: *Burning a Hole in the President's Pocket*, 69 Nw. U. L. Rev. 587 (1974).

84. Arthur John Keefe, with John Harry Jorgenson, *Solicitor General Pocket Vetoes the Pocket Veto*, 61 Am. Bar Ass'n J. 755 (1975); Pub. L. 91-696, 84 Stat. 2080-1 (1970).

85. 121 Cong. Rec. 41884 (1975).

86. 122 Cong. Rec. 11202 (1976); Kennedy v. Jones, 412 F. Supp. 353 (D.D.C. 1976).

87. Public Papers of the Presidents, 1981, at 1208.

88. Public Papers of the Presidents, 1983, II, at 1636.

89. Barnes v. Carmen, 582 F. Supp. 163 (D.D.C. 1984).

90. Id.

91. Public Papers of the Presidents, 1984, II, at 1205.

92. Barnes v. Kline, 759 F.2d 21 (D.C. Cir. 1985).

difficult to understand, said the court, "how Congress could be said to have prevented return of H.R. 4042 simply by adjourning. Rather, by appointing agents for receipt of veto messages, Congress affirmatively *facilitated* return of the bill in the eventuality that the President would disapprove it."[93] The D.C. Circuit also noted that "the line that divides the first session of a Congress from the second has ceased to have any practical significance."[94] A dissent by Judge Robert Bork urged the court "to renounce outright the whole notion of congressional standing."[95] Following the appellate court decision, President Reagan on January 17, 1986, agreed not to exercise a pocket veto on a federal employee benefits bill and instead returned it to the House for possible override.[96]

The Supreme Court agreed to hear the *Barnes* case, creating the expectation it would resolve once and for all the pocket veto question.[97] Instead, it sidestepped the constitutional issue by holding that the case was moot because the bill at issue had expired by its own terms on September 30, 1984, a few weeks after the D.C. opinion.[98] John Paul Stevens, joined by Byron White, dissented. They said the Senate and the bipartisan leadership group in the House "retain the same sort of interest in obtaining a ruling on the merits as they did prior to September 30, 1984."[99] Prior to that date, the bill "was either a 'dead letter' because it had been killed by a valid pocket veto, or it was a valid law because the President's attempt to veto it was ineffective."[100] The issue was a live case in the sense that the pocket veto exercised by Reagan was "capable of repetition" and therefore appropriate for the Court to decide. The Court might have relied on mootness to duck the controversial issue whether members of Congress have standing to sue in court.[101]

## B. A statutory solution?

The mootness ruling pushed the dispute back to the elected branches for possible resolution, which may have been another reason for the Court's decision. In 1989 and 1990, the House Rules and Judiciary Committees held hearings on legislation to clarify the President's pocket veto authority.[102] The Rules Committee reported legislation on March 12, 1990, to restrict the

---

93. Id. at 30 (emphasis in original).

94. Id. at 38.

95. Id. at 41 (Bork, J., dissenting). See Benson K. Whitney, Barnes v. Kline: *Picking the President's Pocket?*, 70 Minn. L. Rev. 1149 (1986), and John Houston Pope, *The Pocket Veto Reconsidered*, 72 Iowa L. Rev. 163 (1986).

96. Public Papers of the Presidents, 1986, I, at 64; 132 Cong. Rec. 2-5 (1986).

97. David Sellers, *High Court to Settle Argument over Legality of 'Pocket Veto,'* Wash. Times, March 4, 1986, at 2A.

98. Burke v. Barnes, 479 U.S. 361, 363 (1987). The D.C. Circuit decided the case on Aug. 29, 1984, but later issued an amended ruling on April 12, 1985.

99. Id. at 365 (Stevens, J., dissenting, joined by White, J.).

100. Id. at 365.

101. Id. at 366. For analysis of the *Barnes* case: Benson K. Whitney, Barnes v. Kline: *Picking the President's Pocket?*, 70 Minn. L. Rev. 1149 (1986) and John Houston Pope, *The Pocket Veto Reconsidered*, 72 Iowa L. Rev. 163 (1986).

102. *H.R. 849*, hearing before the Subcommittee on the Legislative Process of the House Committee on Rules, 101st Cong., 1st Sess. (1989); *Pocket Veto Legislation*, hearing before the Subcommittee on Economic and Commercial Law, House Committee on the Judiciary, 101st Cong, 2d Sess. (1990)

pocket veto to the end of a Congress (adjournment sine die at the end of the second session).[103] The bill was referred to the House Judiciary Committee, which favorably reported the bill later that year.[104] The House took no further action.

At the hearing before the Rules Committee, the Justice Department argued that the President may pocket veto a bill anytime Congress adjourns for more than three days, which is the period of time in Article I, section 5, that requires either house to obtain the consent of the other when it adjourns for more than three days.[105] However, there is no constitutional relationship between the three-day rule specified for the two houses when they plan to adjourn and the pocket veto power of the President.[106]

The framers placed their emphasis on the regular veto over the pocket veto. The regular veto may be used at any time and is subject to a legislative override. The pocket veto is restricted to adjournments that prevent the return of a bill. It operates as an absolute, not a qualified, veto. Pocket vetoes are incompatible with the Constitution when a return veto is available.[107]

# 3. A HYBRID VETO

Following Senator Kennedy's successful litigation on the pocket veto, the Ford administration changed its procedures. Instead of pocket vetoing a bill and keeping it at the White House, President Ford claimed a pocket veto but then returned the bill to the house of origination. Surely that is a bizarre procedure. Under the Constitution, a President may exercise a pocket veto if an adjournment of Congress "prevents" the return of a bill. What would justify a pocket veto of a bill that is indeed returned to Congress?

On October 17, 1974, Congress presented to Ford a bill on vocational rehabilitation. On that same day it adjourned for 31 days for congressional elections. On October 29, Ford exercised a pocket veto on H.R. 14225 but returned the bill to the House. He said he was advised by the Attorney General that the absence of his signature on the bill "prevents it from becoming law." He then stated: "[w]ithout in any way qualifying this determination," he was returning the bill "without my approval to those designated by Congress to receive messages at this time."[108] Not only was he returning the bill but he did so with the understanding that the House authorized an agent to receive bills during a congressional adjournment. On November 20, the House voted 398 to 7 to override his veto; the Senate voted 90 to 1 the next day for the override. However,

---

103. H. Rep. No. 417 (Part 1), 101st Cong., 2d Sess. (1990).

104. H. Rep. No. 417 (Part 2), 101st Cong., 2d Sess. (1990). See Congressman Butler C. Derrick, Jr., *Stitching the Hole in the President's Pocket: A Legislative Solution to the Pocket-Veto Controversy*, 31 Harv. J. on Legis. 371 (1994).

105. *H.R. 849*, hearing before the House Committee on Rules, 101st Cong., 1st Sess. 57-58 (1989) (William P. Barr, Office of Legal Counsel).

106. See Barnes v. Kline, 759 F.2d 21, 39–41 (D.C. Cir. 1985).

107. Robert J. Spitzer, *The "Protective Return" Pocket Veto: Presidential Aggrandizement of Constitutional Power*, 31 Pres. Stud. Q. 720 (2001).

108. Public Papers of the Presidents, 1974, Ford, at 504–05.

the administration refused to publish the bill as a law. Congress passed an identical bill on November 26 and Ford signed it into law on December 7.[109]

In October 1974, Ford repeated this identical procedure on four other bills: H.R. 11541, H.R. 6624, H.R. 7768, and H.R. 13342. On each occasion he claimed to exercise a pocket veto to prevent the bill from becoming law but returned the bill to Congress for a possible override. On November 18, he delivered a message to Congress on legislative priorities, stating that during the adjournment "it was necessary for me to pocket veto five bills." He used the same language that his actions prevented the bills from becoming law but had returned them to those authorized in Congress to receive presidential messages during an adjournment period.[110]

The motivation behind this hybrid veto is explained, in part, by a *New York Times* editorial on January 15, 1975, and the response to it by Solicitor General Robert Bork. The editorial rebuked Bork's role in the five Ford pocket vetoes as lacking respect for the rule of law and a repeat of the attitude that led to the Watergate scandal. The *Times* said that in a letter to Kennedy, Bork had expressed doubt that the Senator possessed standing to bring his lawsuit.[111] Bork dismissed the *Times* editorial as "fatuous."[112] He thought the D.C. Circuit ruling in the Kennedy case had been correctly decided, but saw no comparison between Nixon's pocket veto that provoked the Kennedy lawsuit and the five pocket vetoes exercised by Ford. Nixon's action "came during a five-day recess (including a weekend). President Ford acted during a recess of more than thirty days."[113]

Bork elaborated on his position in a lengthy memo to Attorney General Levi on January 26, 1976. He recommended that Levi make a public announcement on behalf of Ford that he "will use the return veto rather than the pocket veto during intra-session and inter-session recesses and adjournments of Congress," provided the two houses designated an officer to receive return vetoes during such periods.[114] He recommended that the Justice Department accept the judgment of the district court in *Kennedy v. Jones*, which upheld Kennedy's argument that two bills passed by Congress and subsequently pocket vetoed should have been published by the administration as public laws. The district court rejected the administration's argument that Kennedy lacked standing to bring the case and that the case was moot because Congress later passed identical bills and they were signed into law.[115] To Bork, the debates at the Philadelphia convention shed "little further light on this matter, [but] it is apparent that the Framers intended the President to exercise only a qualified negative over legislation and did not contemplate an expansive reading of the Pocket Veto Clause."[116]

Strangely, Bork's memo proceeds to discredit the five "pocket vetoes" issued by Ford during the 31-day intrasession adjournment. (Bork referred to it as 32 days.)[117] He denied that "the

---

109. 88 Stat. 1617 (1974); Derrick, *supra* note 104, at 382. On the first bill not becoming law but the second being signed and enacted into law, see PUBLIC PAPERS OF THE PRESIDENTS, 1974, FORD, at 506, note.

110. PUBLIC PAPERS OF THE PRESIDENTS, 1974, FORD, at 624.

111. *The Rule of Law* (editorial), N.Y. TIMES, Jan. 15, 1975, at 42.

112. *Solicitor General Bork: The Pocket-Veto Issue*, N.Y. TIMES (letter to the editor), Jan. 24, 1975, at 30.

113. Id.

114. Bork's letter is reprinted in *H.R. 849*, hearing before the House Committee on Rules, 101st Cong., 1st Sess. 125–39 (1989).

115. Kennedy v. Jones, 412 F. Supp. 353 (D.D.C. 1976).

116. *H.R. 849*, *supra* note 114, at 126.

117. Id.

length of the intra-session adjournment can be constitutionally significant under modern conditions," so long as Congress designates officials to receive presidential messages during recesses and adjournments.[118] He added: "it follows that the use of a pocket veto is improper whenever a return veto is possible."[119] Then why did Ford "pocket veto" five bills when it was not only possible to return the bills but he actually did so?

Bork does make an important point about the capacity of Congress to protect itself from pocket vetoes. There is no time limit for the period between passing a bill and presenting it to the President. If Congress were concerned about the prospect of a pocket veto, it "could defeat the power by leaving a bill with an officer instructed to present it to the President nine days before the end of any recess or adjournment."[120] That fact, Bork argued, reduces the claim of pocket vetoes "during intra-session or inter-session recesses or adjournments to the level of constitutional triviality."[121]

Regarding the D.C. Circuit opinion in *Kennedy v. Sampson*, Bork explained why the administration decided not to petition the Supreme Court for a writ of certiorari. First, the result of the case "seemed to us to be unquestionably correct."[122] Had the administration sought further review it would have been in the "untenable position" of agreeing with the decision and much of its reasoning. Moreover, Bork considered the case "to be a particularly inappropriate vehicle for presenting to the Supreme Court the question of congressional standing to sue."[123] Almost a decade later, in his dissent in *Barnes v. Kline* (1985), Bork offered lengthy reasons for fully rejecting congressional standing.[124]

Three days after receiving Bork's memo, Attorney General Levi wrote a short memo to President Ford, offering his view that continued use of the pocket veto during intrasession and intersession recesses or adjournments, when a congressional officer is available to receive return vetoes, "cannot be justified as consistent with the provisions of the Constitution."[125] For that reason, he recommended that the administration accept the merits of the district court decision in *Kennedy v. Jones*.[126] The administration publicly disclosed that position on April 13, 1976.[127] As explained in this chapter in section 2A, the political accommodation over the pocket veto in the Ford and Carter administration was reversed by the Reagan administration.

The hybrid veto returned in 1989. On November 30, 1989, President Bush exercised what seemed to be a pocket veto providing emergency relief for Chinese immigration. He said the adjournment of Congress "prevented my return of H.R. 2712 within the meaning of Article

118. Id.

119. Id. at 127.

120. Id. at 128.

121. Id. at 129.

122. Id. at 134.

123. Id.

124. 759 F.2d at 41–71 (Bork, J., dissenting).

125. *H.R. 849, supra* note 114, at 140 (memo from Attorney General Edward H. Levi to President Ford, Jan. 29, 1976).

126. Id.

127. John P. MacKenzie, *Ford Changes Mind, Vetoes Pocket Veto*, Wash. Post, April 14, 1976, at A2; 122 Cong. Rec. 11202 (1976). See also Edward M. Kennedy, *Congress, the President, and the Pocket Veto*, 63 Va. L. Rev. 355 (1977)

I, section 7, clause 2 of the Constitution," citing the Pocket Veto Case as controlling law.[128] However, because of questions raised by *Kennedy v. Sampson*, he sent the bill with his objections to the Clerk of the House of Representatives.[129] On January 23, 1990, the House published his veto message in the *Congressional Record* and treated it as a regular veto subject to congressional override.[130] On the following day, the House voted 390 to 25 to override the veto. A day later, by a vote of 62 to 37, the Senate failed to override.[131] The Senate Library recorded the veto as a regular veto, not a pocket veto.[132]

On May 17, 1990, OLC released a legal analysis on the Pocket Veto Clause. How can a President purport to pocket veto a bill but return it to Congress? To OLC, the President "cannot choose whether to use a return veto or a pocket veto; by definition, the Pocket Veto Clause operates only when a return veto is impossible."[133] However, a return veto is impossible only if Congress fails to designate an officer to receive bills during a recess or adjournment. The OLC analysis argued that the Framers, in drafting the "structural provisions" of the Constitution, "sought to establish brightline rules that are capable of mechanical operation.... Clarity is all-important with respect to the law-making process itself."[134] At a House hearing on July 26, 1989, OLC had promoted a brightline rule by referring to another clause in Article I that when one house plans to adjourn for more that 3 days, it must obtain the consent of the other house.[135] OLC asserted: "the Constitution implies that any adjournment by the Congress—that is, any adjournment of either house for longer than three days—gives occasion for a pocket veto."[136] If bright lines and clarity are important objectives, why not a rule that restricts pocket vetoes to the end of a two-year Congress?

Hybrid vetoes continued under the administrations of George H. W. Bush, Bill Clinton, and George W. Bush. Several times they exercised what they called a pocket veto while returning bills to Congress for possible override.[137] On December 28, 2007, Bush II issued a pocket veto on H.R. 1585 but returned the bill to Congress, which did not attempt an override.[138] The following January, Congress passed the bill again with one change: it allowed the President to waive certain rights of American citizens to sue Iraq for recovery of damages related to torture at the hands of the Iraqi army in 1991.[139] In litigation that reached the Supreme Court in 2009, the Court chose to avoid the issue of a return pocket veto: "We need not inquire into that point,

128. PUBLIC PAPERS OF THE PRESIDENTS, 1989, II, at 1612.

129. Id.

130. 136 CONG. REC. 4–5 (1990).

131. Id. at 444–45, 563.

132. PRESIDENTIAL VETOES, 1789–1996, S. PUB. 105–22, at 2.

133. 14 OP. O.L.C. 103, 106 (1990).

134. Id. at 104.

135. *H.R. 849, supra* note 114, at 57. U.S. CONST., art. I, section 5: "Neither House, during the Session of Congress, shall, without the Consent of the other, adjourn for more than three days, nor to any other Place than that in which the two Houses shall be sitting."

136. *H.R. 849, supra* note 114, at 61.

137. Robert J. Spitzer, *Growing Executive Power: The Strange Case of the 'Protective Return' Pocket Veto*, 42 PRES. STUD. Q. 637 (2012).

138. Id. at 649.

139. Id. at 649–50.

since Congress (evidently thinking the veto effective) enacted a new bill that was identical in all material aspects but for the addition of Presidential waiver authority."[140]

President Obama has continued the practice of hybrid vetoes. On December 30, 2009, he signed a "memorandum of disapproval" (signaling a pocket veto) but added: "To leave no doubt that the bill is being vetoed as unnecessary legislation, in addition to withholding my signature, I am also returning H.J. Res. 64 to the Clerk of the House of Representatives, along with this Memorandum of Disapproval."[141] Congress treated it as a regular veto, subject to override.[142] Another hybrid veto appeared on October 8, 2010.[143] The House, after receiving the bill (H.R. 3808), took a vote to override the veto. The effort failed, 185 to 235.[144]

# 4. ITEM VETOES

It has been argued in recent decades that the President needs an item veto to protect his authority from "omnibus" bills that contain unrelated "riders." Critics of this type of legislation insist that the Constitution expected Congress to pass bills for specific subjects, giving the President maximum opportunity to sign or veto legislation. As a bill increases in size, a President may feel compelled to tolerate unacceptable provisions in order to receive provisions he wants. Hence the need, according to this argument, for an item veto—granted either by statute, constitutional amendment, or by recognizing that the President possesses an "inherent" item veto.

## A. Omnibus bills and riders

Part of the stimulus for an "inherent" item veto came from an article by Stephen Glazier in the *Wall Street Journal* in 1987.[145] His argument gained prominence by frequent reprints in the *Congressional Record*.[146] Glazier called attention to the practice of Congress "bunching bills together" instead of passing them separately. Actually, when Presidents submit draft bills they do the same, hoping that a suspect provision might glide to safety in the company of popular sections. "Taken to its extreme," Glazier argued, Congress could at the end of the second session put all legislation into "one huge bill," placing the President in the position of "forgoing the veto or vetoing two complete years of legislation and perhaps destroying our government in the process." Acting in self-defense, the President should "unbunch such bills by vetoing line items

---

140. Republic of Iraq v. Beaty, 556 U.S. 848, 862–63 n.2 (2009).

141. 156 CONG. REC. H11 (daily ed. Jan. 12, 2010).

142. Id. at H48-49, H104-05 (daily ed. Jan. 13, 2010); Meghan McCarthy, *House Tests President on Pocket Veto*, CONG. Q. WEEKLY REP., Jan. 18, 2010, at 179.

143. 156 CONG. REC. H7402 (daily ed. Nov. 15, 2010).

144. Id. at H7506-07 (daily ed. Nov. 17, 2010).

145. Stephen Glazier, *Reagan Already Has Line-Item Veto*, WALL ST. J., Dec. 4, 1987, at 14.

146. E.g., 133 CONG. REC. 34208, 38287 (1987).

and riders." For Glazier, presidential use of an inherent item veto "offers everything to gain and nothing to lose." If the administration met defeat in court, the result would be "no worse than the status quo."

Part of this argument appeared earlier in a law review article by Richard Givens, published in 1965, offering support for an inherent item veto over nongermane riders. Brief in length (four and a quarter pages), the article concludes that a President's selective veto of a rider "might well be upheld by the courts if the rider bore no relation to the remainder of the legislation."[147] Relying on a secondary source, Givens states that there "is no evidence that the practice of attaching riders was foreseen at the time of the writing or adoption of the Constitution."[148] Without any documentation, he claimed the "general practice" of Congress "has been to enact separate bills, each dealing with a separate subject, and not to enact omnibus legislation covering entirely diverse matters dealt with by different committees of Congress."[149] However, the American Framers were quite familiar with riders and the early statutes enacted by Congress were clearly omnibus in nature.

At the Philadelphia convention on June 13, 1787, Pierce Butler spoke about the capacity of the Senate "of tacking other clauses to money bills."[150] On August 13, the delegates debated the procedure for passing tax bills in the House and allowing the Senate to offer amendments. George Mason expressed concern that the Senate might follow "the practice of tacking foreign matter to money bills."[151] Thomas Jefferson's *Manual of Parliamentary Practice*, prepared during his years as Vice President from 1797 to 1801, referred to the practice of adding nongermane amendments to bills: "Amendments may be made so as totally to alter the nature of the proposition; and it is a way of getting rid of a proposition by making it bear a sense different from what it was intended by the movers, so that they vote against it themselves."[152]

If the framers wanted to control tacking, riders, and nongermane amendments, they knew how to do it. They could have stipulated, as in some state constitutions, that legislation shall not be added to appropriation bills,[153] each bill shall embrace but one subject,[154] and the general funding bill shall contain nothing but appropriations.[155] The Framers declined to place those restrictions on Congress. Implicit in the arguments of Glazier and Givens is the belief that the early Congresses passed separate bills for discrete subjects, thereby maximizing the President's veto power. A review of the statutes enacted during that period demonstrates that this impression is incorrect.

---

147. Richard A. Givens, *The Validity of a Separate Veto of Nongermane Riders to Legislation*, 39 Temple L. Q. 60 (1965).

148. Id., citing "C. Zinn. The Veto Power of the President 34 (Comm. Print 1951)."

149. Givens, *supra* note 147, 39 Temple L. Q. at 63.

150. 1 Farrand 233.

151. 2 Farrand 273. For further details on the Framers' familiarity with legislative "riders," see Robert J. Spitzer, Saving the Constitution from Lawyers: How Legal Training and Law Reviews Distort Constitutional Meaning 73–77 (2008).

152. H. Doc. No. 109-157, 109th Cong., 2d Sess. § 467 (2007).

153. *Item Veto: State Experience and Its Application to the Federal Situation*, prepared by the House Committee on Rules, 99th Cong., 2d Sess. 255–57 (1986).

154. Id. at 258–64.

155. Id.

The first appropriation bill passed by Congress was an omnibus measure, including many items. On September 29, 1789, Congress passed legislation appropriating $216,000 for the "civil list," $137,000 for the Department of War, $190,000 to discharge the warrants issued by the previous Board of Treasury, and $96,000 to pay the pensions for invalids.[156] Four lump-sum amounts, covering 13 lines in the U.S. Statutes, funded the entire government. President Washington received the bill, take it or leave it. He signed it. A similar omnibus bill was enacted on March 26, 1790, this time covering two pages.[157] In addition to lump-sums for the categories listed above, the bill provided funds for smaller specified amounts. Again, one appropriation bill for the entire government. Congress passed other omnibus bills during those early years.[158]

Actions by the First Congress are highly significant. Many of the lawmakers had been delegates to the Philadelphia convention. Their legislative work for the First Congress represents "contemporaneous construction" by the Framers and commands great respect by the Supreme Court and other branches of government. Lawmakers in 1789 recognized no constitutional problems in "bunching up" a number of subjects and combining them to form a single bill. President Washington never protested that his veto power was eviscerated by omnibus bills and riders. Writing to Edmund Pendleton on September 23, 1793, he offered his view of the veto power: "From the nature of the Constitution, I must approve all the parts of a Bill, or reject it in toto."[159]

Although it can be argued that the President's veto is weakened with massive continuing resolutions passed in a crisis atmosphere at the end of a fiscal year, this urgency can strengthen the President's hand. A threat to veto the bill can pressure lawmakers to remove many unwanted items from the draft considered in conference committee. Whatever frustrations the modern President experiences, the Framers would be astonished at the President's current role in the legislative process, the institutional apparatus of the White House and the Executive office of the President (including the Office of Management and Budget), and the vast size and influence of the executive branch.[160]

## B. OLC's analysis in 1988

The availability of an inherent item veto has been the subject of many congressional hearings and academic scrutiny. On July 8, 1988, the Office of Legal Counsel released a detailed 54-page analysis, finding not the slightest merit to the idea that the President possesses inherent authority to delete items from bills submitted to him. The study was later released as part of the OLC series of legal memoranda.[161] OLC looked particularly at the meaning of the term "Bill" in Article I. It found no constitutional requirement that a "Bill" must be limited to one subject and noted that the framers foresaw the possibility that Congress might "tack" foreign matter onto money

---

156. 1 Stat. 95 (1789).

157. Id. at 104–06.

158. E.g., 1 Stat. 190 (1791); 1 Stat. 226 (1791).

159. 33 The Writings of George Washington 96 (Fitzpatrick ed., 1940).

160. For a close critique of the inherent item veto, see Robert J. Spitzer, *The Constitutionality of the Presidential Line-Item Veto*, 112 Pol. Sci. Q. 261 (1997).

161. 12 Op. O.L.C. 128 (1988).

bills. When presented with a bill, the President "has two, but only two, options with respect to the instrument presented: to 'approve... it' or 'not.'"[162] The Constitution "does not suggest that the President may approve 'parts of it' or indicate any presidential prerogative to delete or alter or revise the bill presented."[163]

OLC reviewed the arguments presented by Stephen Glazier and found them unpersuasive. How could the Framers reject an absolute veto for the President (other than pocket vetoes) but allow an absolute veto over items?[164] OLC identified a number of actions that Presidents may take when presented with a single omnibus bill covering all of government. The President "should inform Congress that if it engages in its now-routine practice of presenting the President with an omnibus appropriations bill upon adjourning, then he will not only veto the measure, but also exercise his constitutional authority to call Congress back into special session."[165] If Presidents receive bills with wasteful expenditures and riders unrelated to the bill, they can veto those bills and insist that Congress remove objectionable items.[166]

Following release of the OLC memo, there were reports in October 1989 that President Bush might exercise an inherent item veto and let courts decide whether the authority exists.[167] Senator Kennedy asked two law professors, Laurence H. Tribe and Philip B. Kurland, to share their views about an inherent item veto. In a letter dated October 31, 1989, they concluded that any attempt by a President "to exercise such a 'line-item veto' would clearly be unconstitutional."[168] The issue stayed alive in 1990 when White House Counsel C. Boyden Gray indicated he was looking through bills to find the right target to test the inherent item veto.[169] In May 1991, 52 members of Congress introduced resolutions to encourage President Bush to exercise an item veto to provoke litigation.[170]

On March 20, 1992, President Bush finally announced that Attorney General William Barr had convinced him that an inherent item veto does not exist. Bush said that Barr, "in whom I have full confidence, and my trusted White House Counsel [C. Boyden Gray], backed up by legal opinions from most of the legal scholars, feel that I do not have that line-item veto authority. And this opinion was shared by the Attorney General in the previous administration."[171] Even with Bush's concession, there remained advocates for an inherent item veto. A Senate

---

162. Id. at 129.

163. Id. at 130.

164. Id. at 131–32.

165. Id. at 169.

166. Id. For conference proceedings on the inherent item veto, including a presentation by the author of the OLC memo, Charles J. Cooper, see Pork Barrels and Principles: The Politics of the Presidential Veto (1988).

167. *A Bush Line-Item Veto?*, Cong. Q. Weekly Rep., Oct. 28, 1989, at 2848; Gerald F. Seib, *If Bush Tests Constitutionality of Line-Item Veto, Reverberations Could Transform Government*, Wall St. J., Oct. 30, 1989, at A12.

168. 135 Cong. Rec. 26608–09 (1989); see J. Gregory Sidak & Thomas A. Smith, *Four Faces of the Item Veto: A Reply to Tribe and Kurland*, 84 Nw. U. L. Rev. 437 (1990).

169. Marshall Ingwerson, *Line-Item Veto: Bush, Congress Resume Battle*, Christian Sci. Mon., Jan. 17, 1990, at 7.

170. Timothy J. Burger, *Resolution Urges President to Try Line-Item Veto as a Test of Power*, Roll Call, May 20, 1991, at 3.

171. Public Papers of the Presidents, 1992–93, I, at 479; see J. Gregory Sidak & Thomas A. Smith, *Why Did President Bush Repudiate the "Inherent" Line-Item Veto?*, 9 J. Law & Policy 39 (1992).

hearing on June 15, 1994, evaluated a Senate resolution to express the sense of the Senate that the President currently has constitutional authority to veto individual items of appropriations and the President should exercise that power without waiting for statutory authority.[172] The Senate took no action on the resolution.

## *C. Line Item Veto Act*

From 1985 to 1995, members of Congress explored different ways of granting the President some type of statutory item-veto. The purpose was to give the President the power to "rescind" (terminate) funds to a degree greater than permitted under the Impoundment Control Act of 1974 (Chapter 6, section 6). One concept was called "expedited rescission." It would authorize the President to identify items to be rescinded and ensure that at least one house voted on his recommendations. "Enhanced rescission" would give the President greater power. His recommendations would automatically become law unless Congress passed a resolution of disapproval, which could be vetoed by the President. To restore legislative priorities, Congress would need a two-thirds majority in each chamber for the override.

In 1996, Congress passed enhanced rescission in the form of the Line Item Veto Act.[173] Although the apparent purpose was to give the President power to cut wasteful spending, the bill was drafted to delay its effectiveness until January 1, 1997. The objective: to prevent President Clinton from using it in the middle of a presidential election year. In 1997, a district court held the statute was unconstitutional by violating the legislative procedures set forth in Article I. The court concluded that presidential cancellations were equivalent to repeal and that repeal can be accomplished only through the regular legislative process: passage by both houses and presentment of a bill to the President.[174] Through expedited appeal, the Supreme Court ruled that the plaintiffs (members of Congress) lacked standing to bring the case.[175]

The following year, a district court in a separate case found standing for private plaintiffs and held the statute unconstitutional for failing to follow the procedures of Article I. The Supreme Court affirmed.[176] Budgetary savings from the statute were extremely modest. Over a five-year period, savings came to less than $600 million.[177] The anticipated use of the item veto to cut spending to balance the budget had been greatly oversold.[178]

There were efforts after 1998 to enact some other type of item-veto authority. After the Court invalidated enhanced rescission, the likely alternative focused largely on expedited rescission. In 2006, Congress debated legislation to give the President that authority (S. 2381 and H.R. 4890).

---

172. *Line Item Veto: The President's Constitutional Authority*, hearing before the Subcommittee of the Constitution of the Senate Committee on the Judiciary, 103d Cong., 2d Sess. (1994).

173. 110 Stat. 1200 (1996); Neal E. Devins, *In Search of the Lost Chord: Reflections on the 1996 Item Veto Act*, 47 CASE W. RES. L. REV. 1605 (1997).

174. Byrd v. Raines, 956 F. Supp. 25 (D.D.C. 1997).

175. Raines v. Byrd, 521 U.S. 811 (1997).

176. Clinton v. City of New York, 524 U.S. 417 (1998), aff'g City of New York v. Clinton, 985 F. Supp. 168 (1998).

177. *The Line Item Veto*, hearing before the House Committee on Rules, 105th Cong., 2d Sess. 13 (1998).

178. For analysis of the fiscal effects of Clinton's actions, see Robert J. Spitzer, *The Item Veto Dispute and the Secular Crisis of the Presidency*, 28 PRES. STUD. Q. 799, 800–02 (1998).

The Budget Committees in each house held hearings. The legislation authorized the President to send Congress a special message proposing the cancellation of specified items that had been enacted into law. Unlike the Impoundment Control Act of 1974, Congress could not ignore his recommendations. The bills required committee and floor action. If the committee of jurisdiction failed to act, the President's proposals would be automatically discharged from committee for floor action. No legislative amendments were permitted, either in committee or on the floor. The house to which the proposals were sent would be required to vote, either for or against. If one house rejected the proposals, the other house would not have to act. Support for the President's recommendations needed the approval of both houses in a bill returned to the President for his signature. H.R. 4890 passed the House on June 22, 2006. The Senate did not act on that bill or its own version.

In 2009 and 2010, with deficits climbing because of tax cuts, the deep recession, the expense of two wars in Iraq and Afghanistan, entitlement programs for individuals (including social security and Medicare), and the financial bailout, hearings were held on expedited rescission in the House and the Senate. President Obama asked for expedited rescission authority.[179] The bills did not pass. Legislative interest continued into 2011 and the election year of 2012. On February 8, 2012, the House passed legislation to provide expedited rescission for the President.[180] The Senate took no action on the bill.

Congressional resistance has been tied in part to institutional concerns. Passage of this legislation would communicate to the public that Congress is irresponsible on the budget and needs to trust in the President as the better guardian of the purse. But presidential actions, ranging from tax cuts to spending commitments, have been major contributors to budget deficits. At the aggregate level, Presidents are more likely to advocate expensive projects like social security, the space program, Medicare, Medicaid, and the wars in Korea, Vietnam, Iraq, and Afghanistan. Under expedited rescission, once the President submitted a list of proposed items to be cut, he or she would automatically receive public acclaim for combating waste, even if few in the general public could distinguish between "justified" and "unjustified" programs. If Congress failed to support the rescissions, it would invite public rebuke. It had authorized the President to identify wasteful programs and now refused to support him. If Congress agreed with his recommendations, it would confirm that it had included poorly conceived programs in its legislation and needed the President to find those items, spotlight them, and excise them.

There is one other institutional concern. Expedited rescission would provide the President with a tool to coerce lawmakers and weaken their independence. He or executive officials could alert a member of Congress that a particular project in his or her district or state has been included in a draft bill for rescission. During the phone call or visit, the member would learn that the administration now concluded that the project has merit and every effort would be made to remove it from the rescission bill. The conversation could then shift ever so slightly to a new topic. The President would like the lawmaker's support for a particular bill, treaty, or nomination. That type of horse-trading would push spending up, not down.

179. Jackie Calmes, *Obama Asks for Authority to Cut Items for Spending*, N.Y. TIMES, May 25, 2010, at A18; Walter Alarkon, *President Asks Congress for More Power to Cut Spending*, THE HILL, May 25, 2010, at 3.

180. Rachel Bade, *Bill Would Restore Line-Item Veto for Appropriations; Opponents Say Measure Violates Separation of Powers*, CONG. Q. WEEKLY REP., Dec. 22, 2011, at 2674; 158 CONG. REC. H593-615 (daily ed. Feb. 8, 2012).

The issue of quid pro quos was raised earlier in 1992 when the GAO issued a study estimating that had President Reagan possessed an item veto, he could have saved up to $70 billion over a six-year period.[181] Senator Robert C. Byrd asked me to evaluate the report. Using the same data available to the GAO, my analysis estimated potential savings to be not $70 billion but $2–3 billion at most and probably less. I pointed out that Presidents could use the item veto to coerce lawmakers to support executive spending programs, pushing spending up.[182] In response, Comptroller General Charles Bowsher wrote to Senator Byrd, apologizing for defects in the methodology of the GAO report and conceding that savings over the six-year period would not be $70 billion but could be "close to zero." He agreed that Presidents could use the item veto to increase spending by securing legislative support for executive priorities.[183]

# 5. SIGNING STATEMENTS

While signing a bill, Presidents will often make statements about the merits and constitutionality of certain provisions. Some of these statements, as explained below, can be constructive. In other cases they represent a type of item veto. In 1830, President Jackson signed a bill and simultaneously sent to Congress a message that restricted the reach of the statute.[184] Later, in 1842, a House report protested that his message constituted, in effect, an item veto of one provision.[185] In that same year, President Tyler signed a bill but deposited with the Secretary of State "an exposition of my reasons for giving to it my sanction." The document included objections about the constitutionality of the entire statute.[186] A House committee insisted that the Constitution restricts a President to three actions when receiving a bill: sign it, veto it, or issue a pocket veto if a congressional recess prevents the veto's return. To sign a bill and add extraneous matter in a separate document could be regarded "in no other light than a defacement of the public records and archives."[187]

Some studies deny that signing statements are the equivalent of an item veto. Curtis Bradley and Eric Posner conclude that when a President relies on a signing statement he "is not purporting to use the presidential authority to block enactment of the law, which is what happens with a veto." After a President issues a signing statement, they point out, "the statute remains on the books."[188] Quite true, but the President may intend to block implementation of a provision he signed into law. The challenged provision could become a nullity or substantially changed, at least for the President. It is further argued that when the President makes a statement while

---

181. General Accounting Office, *Line Item Veto: Estimating Potential Savings*, GAO/AFMD-92-7, Jan. 1992.

182. Louis Fisher, *GAO's Report on "Line Item Veto" (January 1992)*, Congressional Research Service, memo to Senator Robert C. Byrd, March 23, 1992, reprinted at 138 Cong. Rec. 9981–92 (1992).

183. 142 Cong. Rec. 6513 (1996); Bowsher's letter is dated July 23, 1992.

184. 3 Richardson 1046 (May 30, 1830).

185. H. Rep. No. 909, 27th Cong., 2d Sess. 5–6 (1842).

186. 5 Richardson 2012 (June 25, 1842).

187. H. Rep. No. 909, 27th Cong., 2d Sess. 2 (1842).

188. Curtis A. Bradley & Eric A. Posner, *Presidential Signing Statements and Executive Power*, 23 Const. Comm. 307, 338 (2006).

signing a bill, "he is not purporting to use any executive authority to cancel all or part of a stat-ute."[189] In effect he does. Although the provision technically remains in the statute, the adminis-tration may decide not to enforce it.

## A. Contemporary disputes

The constitutionality and effectiveness of signing statements are resolved almost exclusively out-side the courts. A rare case of judicial involvement occurred in 1972. President Nixon, while sign-ing a military authorization bill, objected that the Mansfield Amendment—related to the military commitment to Southeast Asia—did not represent the policy of his administration and was "without binding force or effect."[190] A district court disagreed: "No executive statement denying efficacy to the legislation could have either validity or effect."[191] The court advised Nixon that the Mansfield Amendment became the policy of his administration when he signed the bill into law.

Similarly, in 1984 President Reagan in a signing statement said that a provision in the bill presented to him marked an unconstitutional attempt to empower the Comptroller General to perform executive duties. He instructed his Attorney General to inform all executive branch agencies not to comply with what he considered to be unconstitutional.[192] Extensive litigation forced the administration to implement the provision. The Ninth Circuit ruled that the President must either sign or veto a bill. He may not "revise a bill, either before or after signing. It does not empower the President to employ a so-called 'line item veto' and excise or sever provisions of a bill with which he disagrees."[193]

A less controversial use of a signing statement is the action by President Roosevelt in 1943 in signing an emergency appropriation bill to meet military needs in World War II. As explained in Chapter 4, section 10, his signing statement objected that a provision was unconstitutional because it represented a bill of attainder. Congress in the bill had denied funds to pay the sal-aries of three executive officials because of their "subversive" views. Three years later, when the Supreme Court struck down the legislative provision as a bill of attainder, it referred to Roosevelt's signing statement.[194]

A signing statement binds only the President who made it. His successor has no obligation to adopt the same policy. In 1999, Congress passed legislation to criminalize the commercial creation, sale, or possession of certain depictions of animal cruelty. Although legislative debate centered on what is known as "crush videos" (videos showing women crushing small animals to death with their bare feet or while wearing high-heeled shoes), the bill language was so broad that it could criminalize hunting and fishing magazines. Instead of vetoing the bill because of its overbreadth, President Clinton in a signing statement said he would direct the Justice

---

189. Id. at 339.

190. Public Papers of the Presidents, 1971, at 1141.

191. DaCosta v. Nixon, 55 F.R.D. 145, 146 (E.D. N.Y. 1972).

192. Public Papers of the Presidents, 1984, II, at 1053.

193. Lear Siegler, Inc., Energy Products Div. v. Lehman, 842 F.2d 1102, 1124 (9th Cir. 1988), modified as to attorney fees, 893 F.2d 205 (9th Cir. 1989) (en banc). For other cases involving this provision, see the series of *Ameron* rulings: 607 F. Supp. 962 (D. N.J. 1985), 610 F. Supp. 750 (D. N.J. 1985), 787 F.2d 875 (3d Cir. 1986), and 809 F.2d 979 (3d Cir. 1986).

194. United States v. Lovett, 328 U.S. 303 (1946).

Department to prosecute only depictions of "wanton cruelty to animals designed to appeal to a prurient interest in sex" (crush videos).[195]

His position did not bind his successor, George W. Bush. Instead of prosecuting someone for trafficking in crush videos, the Bush Justice Department brought criminal charges against an individual who sold dogfighting videos. When the Third Circuit struck down the statute in 2008 as facially unconstitutional,[196] the market for crush videos quickly revived. In 2010, the Supreme Court held the statute to be substantially overbroad and therefore invalid under the First Amendment.[197] Congress rewrote the statute to focus solely on crush videos and it was enacted on December 9, 2010.[198] Litigation could have been avoided had Clinton vetoed the bill, directed Congress to fix it, and not attempt to "make law" with a signing statement.

Signing statements attracted public attention in 2005 when Congress passed language against torture. The bill provided that no one in the custody of the U.S. government, "regardless of nationality or physical location, shall be subject to cruel, inhuman, or degrading treatment or punishment."[199] That policy had supposedly been settled by earlier statutes and treaties. Yet in signing the bill, President Bush said he would interpret it "in a manner consistent with the constitutional authority of the President to supervise the unitary executive branch and as Commander in Chief and consistent with the constitutional limitations on the judicial power."[200]

In other words, whatever Congress passes and is enacted into law may be rewritten or nullified by the President, even though he is directed by the Constitution to "take Care that the Laws be faithfully executed."

An objection to this type of signing statement is its vague and broad-brush nature. Unlike Roosevelt's signing statement in 1943, directed against a specific provision of the Constitution (the Bill of Attainder), the signing statement by Bush was couched in vague references to the "unitary executive branch," the Commander in Chief Clause, and supposed constitutional constraints on judicial power. The "unitary executive" is a fiction created by advocates of executive power, as explained elsewhere (Chapter 3, sections 3C and 10B, and Chapter 4, section 8D). Federal courts have been involved in war power cases from 1800 forward (Chapter 8, section 1). Other signing statements rely on highly generalized references to the Appointments Clause (Chapter 4, section 5), the Recommendation Clause (Chapter 4, section 3), and other concepts without explaining or analyzing them.[201]

---

195. Public Papers of the Presidents, 1999, II, at 2245; 113 Stat. 1732 (1999).

196. United States v. Stevens, 533 F.3d 218 (3d Cir. 2008).

197. United States v. Stevens, 559 U.S. 460 (2010).

198. 124 Stat. 3177 (2010). For legislative history, see Louis Fisher, Defending Congress and the Constitution 324–26 (2011).

199. 119 Stat. 2739, sec. 1003(a) (2005).

200. 41 Weekly Comp. Pres. Doc. 1919 (2005).

201. For studies placing signing statements in historical, legal, and political context, see Christopher S. Kelley & Bryan W. Marshall, *The Last Word: Presidential Power and the Role of Signing Statements*, 38 Pres. Stud. Q. 248 (2008); Louis Fisher, *Signing Statements: Constitutional and Practical Limits*, 16 Wm. & Mary Bill Rts. J. 183 (2007); Note, *Context-Sensitive Deference to Presidential Signing Statements*, 120 Harv. L. Rev. 597 (2006); Phillip J. Cooper, *George W. Bush, Edgar Allan Poe, and the Use and Abuse of Presidential Signing Statements*, 35 Pres. Stud. Q. 515 (2005); Kristy L. Carroll, *Whose Statute Is It Anyway?: Why and How Courts Should Use Presidential Signing Statements When Interpreting Federal Statutes*, 46 Cath. U. L. Rev. 475 (1997); Mark R. Killenbeck, *A Matter of Mere Approval? The Role of the President in the Creation of Legislative History*, 48 Ark. L. Rev. 239 (1995); Frank B. Cross, *The Constitutional Legitimacy and Significance of Presidential "Signing Statements,"* 40

Similarly, President Obama in a signing statement claimed a "prerogative" that did not exist (Chapter 3, section 5). Later, in a signing statement on January 2, 2013, he stated the Constitution "does not afford the President the opportunity to approve or reject statutory sections one by one."[202] However, he asserted that part of the bill represented "an unnecessary and ill-advised provision," raised "constitutional concerns," and threatened to "interfere with my ability as Commander as Chief to make time-sensitive determinations about the appropriate disposition of detainees in an active area of hostilities." Other sections of the bill, he said, "could" interfere with his constitutional authority "to conduct the foreign relations of the United States" and "threaten to interfere with my constitutional duty to supervise the executive branch." This latter comment implied some type of "unitary executive," which does not exist. For more than two centuries, Congress has regularly placed constraints on presidential control over executive officials, including the area of ministerial duties (Chapter 3, section 6).[203]

## B. Searching for boundaries

In 1993, OLC prepared a memo on signing statements, indicating how they "may on appropriate occasions perform useful and legally significant functions."[204] Three benefits were identified: (1) explaining what the President believes to be the likely effects of the law's adoption, (2) instructing executive officials how to interpret and administer the law, and (3) informing Congress and the public that a particular provision will be unconstitutional in certain applications or is unconstitutional on its face and will not be given effect by the executive branch. OLC concluded: "In light of our constitutional history, we do not believe the President is under any duty to veto legislation containing a constitutionally infirm provision, although of course it is entirely appropriate for the President to do so."[205]

A year later, OLC released a memo on "Presidential Authority to Decline to Execute Unconstitutional Statutes."[206] It gave a number of examples where Presidents, by refusing to carry out a law, triggered litigation that helped clarify the reach and meaning of a statute. The standoff between Congress and the President over the Tenure of Office Act and its limitation on the President's removal power led to *Myers v. United States* (1926), which upheld the President's authority to remove officials who carry out purely executive duties.[207] OLC also underscored

---

ADM. L. REV. 209 (1988); Brad Waites, *Let Me Tell You What You Mean: An Analysis of Presidential Signing Statements*, 21 GA. L. REV. 755 (1987); and Marc N. Garber & Kurt A. Wimmer, *Presidential Signing Statements as Interpretations of Legislative Intent: An Executive Aggrandizement of Power*, 24 HARV. J. ON LEGIS. 363 (1987). A symposium dedicated to "The Last Word? The Constitutional Implications of Presidential Signing Statements," appears in 16 WM. & MARY BILL RTS. J. (2007).

202. Statement on H.R. 4310, Jan. 2, 2013, http://www.whitehouse.gov/the-press-office/2013/01/03/statement-president-hr-4310.

203. Peter Finn, *Activists Blast Obama for Signing Defense Bill*, WASH. POST, Jan. 4, 2013, at A2; Charlie Savage, *Obama Disputes Detainee Limits in Defense Bill*, N.Y. TIMES, Jan. 4, 2013, at A1.

204. 17 OP. O.L.C. 131, 131 (1993).

205. Id. at 135.

206. 18 OP. O.L.C. 199 (1994).

207. Id. at 201–02, 209.

the obligation of the executive branch to identify unconstitutional provisions in pending bills in an effort to have the legislation corrected.[208] On nonenforcement of the law, see also Chapter 3, section 10C.

Congressional hearings in 2006 and 2007 explored possible statutory remedies for signing statements. The hearings were provoked in large part by legislation enacted in 2005, providing that no one in the custody of the U.S. government, "regardless of nationality or physical location, shall be subject to cruel, inhuman, or degrading treatment or punishment."[209] Congress passed this legislation in response to reports of abuse of detainees at Abu Ghraib in Iraq and in CIA "black sites" abroad. In signing the bill, President Bush said he would interpret it "in a manner consistent with the constitutional authority of the President to supervise the unitary executive branch and as Commander in Chief and consistent with the constitutional limitations on the judicial power."[210]

Members of Congress found this signing statement objectionable because of its broad-brush nature. It was unlike President Roosevelt's signing statement in 1943 that singled out a specific provision that violated express language in the Constitution: the Bill of Attainder Clause (Chapter 4, section 10). Instead, Bush's statement relied on vague and ill-defined concepts, including the unitary executive, the Commander in Chief Clause, and supposed constitutional limits that restrain judicial control. Claims of a "unitary executive" embrace many misconceptions (Chapter 3, section 10B). The Commander in Chief Clause is not a source of limitless presidential power (Chapter 8). Federal courts have been involved in war power cases from 1800 forward (Chapter 8, section 2B).

On June 27, 2006, during hearings before the Senate Judiciary Committee, Michelle Boardman of OLC testified that signing statements "are not an attempt to cherrypick parts of the law that the President can choose to follow or an attempt to redefine an established law."[211] Yet that is precisely what President Bush did with his remarks on coercive interrogations. Congress had established national policy to restrict and limit executive branch actions. Bush said he would not implement the language of the statute but rather his interpretation of it to protect and maximize presidential power. Boardman also testified that the emphasis should not be on the Take Care Clause. Instead, emphasis should be on the President's responsibility to "preserve, protect, and defend the Constitution," making Presidents "responsible for ensuring that the manner in which they enforce acts of Congress is consistent with America's founding document."[212]

However, part of the President's responsibility to defend the Constitution is to "take Care that the Laws be faithfully executed." Boardman called attention to signing statements that object to committee vetoes that violate the Supreme Court's decision in *INS v. Chadha*. She said that Presidents ordered executive officials to merely notify committees rather than seek their approval.[213] As explained in the next section on legislative vetoes, agencies continue to

208. Id. at 200.

209. 119 Stat. 2739, sec. 1003(a) (2005).

210. 41 WEEKLY COMP. PRES. DOC. 1919 (2005).

211. *The Use of Presidential Signing Statements*, hearing before the Senate Committee on the Judiciary, 109th Cong., 2d Sess. 6 (2006).

212. Id. at 98.

213. Id. at 106.

seek committee approval regardless of what Presidents say in signing statements. Government is often a choice between theory and practice. In the case of post-*Chadha* activity, practice largely prevails.[214]

Boardman denied that signing statements were a "power grab" by the President: "the statements do not augment presidential power." If Congress exceeded its own power in violation of the Constitution, "the President is bound to defer to the Constitution." The effort by Congress in 2005 to place limits on coercive methods of interrogation did not raise such clear questions of constitutionality that President Bush was forced to subordinate statutory language to his own interpretation. The bill language was not obviously "unconstitutional," nor can it be argued that Bush was "bound to defer to the Constitution" instead of to the statute. Moreover, his remarks in the signing statement did "augment presidential power" and were intended to do that. In 2007, the House Judiciary Committee also held hearings on signing statements.[215]

Several bills were introduced in an effort to place limits on presidential statements. H.R. 5486, dated May 25, 2006, invoked the power of the purse: "None of the funds made available to the Executive Office of the President, or to any Executive agency...from any source may be used to produce, publish, or disseminate any statement made by the President contemporaneously with the signing of any bill or joint resolution presented for signing by the President."[216] What is "contemporaneous"? Within a day of the bill's enactment? A week or so later? Would this language prevent the President, in a signing statement, from praising the bill's sponsors? Even if the funding restriction worked, the Justice Department, the Office of Management and Budget, and other agencies could prepare memos that challenged the constitutionality of certain provisions in a law and direct agencies not to comply.

S. 3731, introduced on July 26, 2006, was designed to regulate the judicial use of signing statements. The bill stated that judicial use of the statements "is inappropriate, because it in effect gives these statements the force of law." However, when courts look to legislative history, no one argues that what a member says on the floor or in a committee force has the force of law. The bill prohibited "judicial reliance on presidential signing statements as a course of authority in the interpretation of Acts of Congress." Congress has no authority to dictate to courts how they shall interpret federal statutes. This bill was reintroduced on June 29, 2007, as S. 1747, and on April 23, 2009, as S. 875. These bills were not enacted. Some Presidents may prefer to rely more on SAPs than on signing statements.[217]

---

214. Louis Fisher, *Obama's Objections to Committee Veto Misguided*, Roll Call, Jan. 19, 2012, at 14–15; Louis Fisher, *Committee Controls of Agency Decisions*, Congressional Research Service, RL33151, Nov. 16, 2005, http://www.loufisher.org/docs/lv/2626.pdf.

215. *Presidential Signing Statements Under the Bush Administration: A Threat to Checks and Balances and the Rule of Law?*, hearing before the House Committee on the Judiciary, 110th Cong., 1st Sess. (2007).

216. H.R. 5486, 109th Cong., 2d Sess. (2006). Reintroduced as H.R. 264, 110th Cong., 1st Sess. (2007) and H.R. 258, 111th Cong.,1st Sess. (2009).

217. Todd Garvey, *The Obama Administration's Evolving Approach to the Signing Statement*, 41 Pres. Stud. Q. 393 (2011).

# 6. LEGISLATIVE VETOES

In an effort to control delegated authority, Congress experimented with what are called "legislative vetoes." They do not become public law because they are not presented to the President. Controls are exercised by both houses (a concurrent resolution), by either house (a simple resolution), and even by committees and subcommittees. Concurrent resolutions merely express the opinion of Congress. They are not legally binding. In a formal sense the legislative veto was struck down by the Supreme Court in the 1983 *Chadha* decision, but it survives in part because the Court did not adequately understand what it was dealing with. It tried to resolve a complex issue with abstract and impractical principles.

Article I, section 7 provides that "Every Order, Resolution, or Vote to which the Concurrence of the Senate and House of Representatives may be necessary (except on a question of Adjournment)" shall be presented to the President. Fundamental to this process are two principles: bicameralism (both houses must act) and presentment. At the Philadelphia convention, Madison expressed concern that if the President's veto power "was confined to *bills*; it would be evaded by acts under the name of Resolutions, votes &c."[218] An exception to that process is the adoption of constitutional amendments. They go directly to the states for ratification rather than to the President. That procedure, sanctioned by Article V, was upheld by the Supreme Court in 1798.[219]

From an early date, Congress passed simple resolutions and concurrent resolutions for internal housekeeping matters. Because they were not considered "legislative in effect," there was no need to present them to the President. They were adopted pursuant to congressional power under Article I to determine procedural rules and to punish or expel members. A Senate report in 1897 explained that "legislative in effect" depended not merely on form but substance. If a resolution contained matter "legislative in its character and effect," it had to be submitted to the President.[220]

Several departures from that principle permitted Congress by simple resolution, concurrent resolution, or committee action to determine legislative policy. The executive branch found many of those departures acceptable. Legislative vetoes have a complex history and cannot be described solely as congressional encroachments on executive power. Presidents and Attorneys General did more than tolerate them and acquiesce. They often invited and encouraged their growth.

## A. Early history

Simple and concurrent resolutions evolved into instruments to control executive actions. Committee and subcommittee vetoes came later. An important conceptual breakthrough occurred in the mid-nineteenth century when executive officials realized that the legislative effect of such resolutions could be changed fundamentally by having their use sanctioned in a

---

218. 2 Farrand 301 (emphasis in original).
219. Hollingsworth v. Virginia, 3 Dall. 378 (1798).
220. S. Rep. No. 1335, 54th Cong., 2d Sess. 8 (1897).

public law. In 1854, Attorney General Caleb Cushing reasoned that a simple resolution could not coerce a department head "unless in some particular in which a law, duly enacted, has subjected him to the direct action of each; and in such case it is to be intended, that, by approving the law, the President has consented to the exercise of such coerciveness on the part of either House."[221]

A committee veto obligates an executive agency to submit a recommendation to designated committees to seek their approval. Legislation in 1867 placed the following restriction on appropriations for public buildings and grounds: "To pay for completing the repairs and furnishing the executive mansion, thirty-five thousand dollars: *Provided*, That no further payments shall be made on any accounts for repairs and furnishing the executive mansion until such accounts shall have been submitted to a joint committee of Congress, and approved by such committee."[222] Why allow such bills to become law? Why not veto them? The answer: Presidents and their advisers recognized an important advantage. If the administration reached the statutory limit of $35,000 and wanted to exceed it, it was not necessary to seek additional funds by passing another law and obtaining the approval of both houses. Securing approval from the joint committee would suffice.

Some of the legislative vetoes during this period were modest in scope. An appropriations bill in 1899 for rivers and harbor projects provided that after a regular report is submitted, "no supplemental or additional report or estimate for the same fiscal year shall be made unless ordered by a concurrent resolution of Congress."[223] In 1903, Congress resorted to simple resolutions to direct the Secretary of Commerce to make investigations and issue reports.[224] Two years later Congress relied on concurrent resolutions to direct the Secretary of War to submit additional reports on rivers and harbors projects.[225]

Committee vetoes faced opposition from President Wilson. A bill in 1920 provided that no government publication could be printed, issued, or discontinued unless authorized under regulations prescribed by the Joint Committee on Printing. To Wilson, Congress had no right to endow a joint committee or a committee of either house "with power to prescribe 'regulations' under which executive departments may operate."[226] In that same year, he vetoed a bill that allowed Congress to remove by concurrent resolution the Comptroller General and the Assistant Comptroller General. He objected not merely to the concurrent resolution but to any interference with the removal power, which he regarded "as an essential incident" to the President's appointment power. The House failed to override his veto.[227] When enacted a year later as the Budget and Accounting Act, the concurrent resolution was changed to a joint resolution.[228]

In 1933, Attorney General William D. Mitchell regarded as unconstitutional a bill that authorized the Joint Committee on Internal Revenue Taxation to make the final decision on

221. 6 Op. Att'y Gen. 680, 683 (1854).

222. 14 Stat. 469 (1867).

223. 30 Stat. 1121, 1149, sec. 2 (1899).

224. 32 Stat. 829, sec. 8 (1903).

225. 33 Stat. 1147, sec. (1905). For a comprehensive review of legislative vetoes in these early years and their growth later: H. Lee Watson, *Congress Steps Out: A Look at Congressional Control of the Executive*, 63 Cal. L. Rev. 983 (1975).

226. H. Doc. No. 764, 66th Cong., 2d Sess. 2 (1920).

227. 59 Cong. Rec. 8609–14 (1920).

228. 42 Stat. 20, 23–24, sec. 303 (1921).

any tax refund in excess of $20,000.[229] Previously, Congress had examined all tax refunds over $75,000.[230] Executive officials accepted that procedure. Lowering the dollar amount seemed to precipitate a constitutional dispute. Acting on the advice of his Attorney General, President Hoover vetoed the bill with the committee control. The House voted 193 to 158 to override the veto, short of the required two-thirds majority.[231] Under contemporary law, the joint tax committee conducts a review of tax refunds in excess of $2 million.[232]

## B. Presidential encouragement

Far from being a steadfast opponent of the legislative veto, President Hoover became one of its ardent champions. In 1929, facing the Great Depression, he wanted to reorganize the executive branch to achieve "economy and efficiency." Yet he doubted that his proposals would survive the hurdles of the legislative process, including amendments and presidential proposals never acted on. As a shortcut, he recommended that Congress give him authority to reorganize the executive branch. Under his proposal, he could act only "upon approval of a joint committee of Congress or with the reservation of power of revision by Congress within some limited period adequate for its consideration."[233]

In 1932, Congress granted Hoover reorganization authority. Under the statutory procedure, after reorganization plans were submitted to Congress they would become law within 60 days unless either house disapproved. Hoover recognized several benefits. His recommendations could not be amended by Congress, buried in committee, or filibustered in the Senate. If lawmakers failed to block his proposals within that period of time, they would become law even though Congress had never acted.[234] In December, after being defeated overwhelmingly for reelection, he issued eleven executive orders consolidating some 58 governmental activities.[235] Deciding to leave reorganization to his successor, Franklin D. Roosevelt, the House took a single vote to reject all of his proposals.[236]

Because of greater trust in the new President, Congress in 1933 passed legislation to give Roosevelt broad-ranging powers of reorganization without the check of a legislative veto. That authority lasted two years.[237] In 1937, Roosevelt asked Congress to renew his authority to reorganize the executive branch, this time subject to a joint resolution of disapproval, satisfying the twin principles of bicameralism and presentment. He advised Congress the next year that any legislative action short of a bill or joint resolution, such as a simple resolution or a concurrent

229. 37 Op. Att'y Gen. 56 (1933).

230. 76 Cong. Rec. 2448 (1933).

231. Id. at 2449.

232. 26 U.S.C. § 6405.

233. Public Papers of the Presidents, 1929, at 432.

234. 47 Stat. 382, 413–15 (1932).

235. 76 Cong. Rec. 233–53 (1932).

236. Id. at 2103–26.

237. 47 Stat. 1518, sec. 403 (1933); 48 Stat. 16 (1933).

resolution, would be merely "an expression of congressional sentiment" and could not "repeal Executive action taken in pursuance of a law."[238]

The Senate passed a bill incorporating his constitutional principles, but members of the House rejected Roosevelt's request. Disapproval by joint resolution meant that if he exercised the veto power each house would need a two-thirds majority for the override. In effect, lawmakers would have delegated authority to the President by majority vote but could recapture it only with an extraordinary majority. Realizing his legislative proposal was dead in the House, Roosevelt reversed his constitutional principles within a matter of days. He now agreed that Congress could disapprove a reorganization plan by a majority vote of both houses: a concurrent resolution.

Arguments were hastily concocted to rationalize Roosevelt's switch. The President would be acting as an "agent" of Congress, subject to the conditions established by the legislative branch. The legislative veto would serve as the vehicle to permit Congress to announce that the President had violated or misused his power of agency. Administration officials distinguished between the use of a concurrent resolution applied to past laws (in their view unconstitutional) to those applied to laws "in the making" (which they considered constitutionally acceptable). In acting to reorganize the executive branch, the President "will exercise legislative rather than executive powers."[239]

By 1939, both branches agreed that a reorganization plan would become law within 60 days unless during that period Congress passed a concurrent resolution of disapproval.[240] The House Select Committee on Government Organization defended the concurrent resolution by pointing to a recent Supreme Court decision, *Currin v. Wallace*, which upheld a delegation of authority to the Secretary of Agriculture to designate tobacco markets. No market could be designated, however, unless two-thirds of the growers voting in a referendum favored it.[241] To the committee, it seemed absurd "to believe that the effectiveness of action legislative in character may be conditioned upon a vote of farmers but may not be conditioned on a vote of the two legislative bodies of the Congress."[242] When Congress extended reorganization authority in 1949, it changed the two-house veto to one-house.[243] The one-house veto was retained by a reorganization statute in 1977.[244]

Whatever constitutional misgivings Presidents and Attorneys General had about other legislative vetoes, they acquiesced in the case of executive reorganization. They understood that Congress would not delegate the authority without attaching strings to it. The constitutional issue was thus mixed with practical calculations. Another example is President Roosevelt's attitude toward the Lend Lease Act of 1941. He regarded it as unconstitutional because the statute permitted Congress to terminate presidential authority by concurrent resolution. However, he did not want to make his position publicly known. Political opponents had opposed the

---

238. 83 Cong. Rec. 4487 (1938).

239. Id. at 5004–05.

240. 53 Stat. 562, sec. 5 (1939); John D. Millett & Lindsay Rogers, *The Legislative Veto and the Reorganization Act of 1939*, 1 Pub. Adm. Rev. 176 (1941).

241. Currin v. Wallace, 306 U.S. 1 (1939).

242. H. Rep. No. 120, 76th Cong., 1st Sess. 6 (1939).

243. 63 Stat. 203 (1949).

244. 91 Stat. 29 (1977).

two-house veto as unconstitutional; to reveal his objections would associate him with enemies and alienate supporters. Signing the bill without revealing his objections, Roosevelt directed Attorney General Robert Jackson to make his legal position public at a later date. Jackson published Roosevelt's views in an article in the *Harvard Law Review* in 1953. Jackson explained: "to make public his views at that time would confirm and delight his opposition and let down his friends. It might seriously alienate some of his congressional support at a time when he would need to call on it frequently."[245]

Committee vetoes flourished in the 1940s in response to emergency conditions during World War II. Because of the volume of wartime construction, it was impractical to continue the regular practice of having Congress authorize each defense installation or public works project. Beginning with an informal system in 1942, proposals for the acquisition of land and leases were submitted in advance to the Naval Affairs Committees in each house for their approval.[246] With that procedure acceptable to both branches, Congress passed general authorization statutes in lump sums without specifying individual projects. By 1944, Congress had written that understanding into law.[247] Additional "coming into agreement" provisions were added in 1949 and 1951, requiring the executive branch to obtain the approval of the Armed Services Committees for the acquisition of land and real estate transactions.[248]

That political accommodation began to unravel. On May 15, 1951, President Truman vetoed a bill relating to real estate transactions because it required the military departments and the Federal Civil Defense Administration to "come into agreement" with the Armed Services Committees for properties valued in excess of $10,000.[249] He objected that the procedure imposed "a severe and unnecessary burden" on the Defense Department and would create delays in trying to secure congressional approval.[250] He added: "Under our system of Government it is contemplated that the Congress will enact the laws and will leave their administration and execution to the executive branch."[251] The House overrode his veto by a substantial margin, 312 to 68, but the Senate took no action.[252] Congress rewrote the bill by raising the dollar threshold from $10,000 to $25,000 but retained the "coming into agreement" procedure. Truman, perhaps anticipating an override by both houses, let the bill become law.[253]

The dispute over "coming into agreement" is illuminating. Preventing Congress from using one method to control the executive branch may prompt it to find an equally effective substitute. During the Eisenhower administration, Attorney General Brownell issued an opinion that the committee

---

245. Robert H. Jackson, *A Presidential Legal Opinion*, 66 HARV. L. REV. 1353, 1356–57 (1953). For the use of concurrent resolutions during this period: Howard White, *Executive Responsibility to Congress via Concurrent Resolution*, 36 AM. POL. SCI. REV. 895 (1942). A review of concurrent resolutions and other forms of legislative vetoes is by an attorney who worked in the Office of Solicitor General: Robert W. Ginnane, *The Control of Federal Administration by Congressional Resolutions and Committees*, 66 HARV. L. REV. 569 (1953).

246. 89 CONG. REC. 1217–29 (1943).

247. 58 Stat. 7–8, 189–90 (1944).

248. 63 Stat. 66 (1949), 65 Stat. 365 (1951).

249. PUBLIC PAPERS OF THE PRESIDENTS, 1951, at 280.

250. Id. at 281.

251. Id. at 282.

252. 97 CONG. REC. 5435–45, 5490 (1951).

253. 65 Stat. 336, 365, sec. 601 (1951). For the growth of the use of the legislative veto during this period: Joseph & Ann Cooper, *The Legislative Veto and the Constitution*, 30 G.W. L. REV. 467 (1962).

veto represented an unconstitutional infringement of executive duties.[254] So advised, Congress adopted another procedure that yielded precisely the same legislative control. It drafted a bill to prohibit appropriations for certain real estate transactions unless the Public Works Committees first approved the contracts. If committees could not directly control the administration, they could do it indirectly. Eisenhower signed the bill after being assured by Brownell that this procedure, based on the separate legislative stages of authorization and appropriation, was fully within the constitutional authority of Congress to adopt its own rules.[255] The form had changed; the committee veto remained.

In a speech to Congress in 1961, President Kennedy asked for legislative authority over agricultural programs. He suggested that the administration would submit proposals to Congress 60 days before they took effect. If either house during that period disapproved, "the program will not go into effect." No agricultural program would be adopted if "regarded adversely by a majority of either House of the Congress."[256] Kennedy regularly supported committee vetoes, raising an objection only on one occasion.[257]

## C. Legislative veto struck down

These political accommodations came to an end (for the most part) in 1978 when President Carter issued a broad critique of the legislative veto. He explained that the procedure had grown rapidly in recent years from its initial use for reorganization plans to cover many new areas. Over the past four years at least 48 new legislative vetoes "have been enacted—more than in the preceding twenty years."[258] Legislative vetoes were now being used to control agency regulations, federal salaries, presidential papers, arms sales, war powers, national emergencies, and other areas of government.[259]

To Carter, the legislative veto over reorganization plans did not pose a constitutional issue: "This kind of legislative veto does not involve Congressional intrusion into the administration of on-going substantive programs, and it preserves the President's authority because he decides which proposals to submit to Congress. The Reorganization Act jeopardizes neither the President's responsibilities nor the prerogatives of Congress."[260] The reasoning here is strained. According to Carter's logic, he should not object to legislative vetoes whenever the President decides which proposals to submit to the Congress. But that would justify legislative vetoes for

---

254. 41 Op. Att'y Gen. 230 (1955), reprinted at Herbert Brownell, Jr., *Separation of Powers: Executive and Legislative Branches*, 60 Dick. L. Rev. 1 (1955). See also 41 Op. Att'y Gen. 300 (1957).

255. Joseph P. Harris, Congressional Control of Administration 230–31 (1964). For a statute prohibiting the appropriation of funds for public buildings involving expenditures above a certain amount if construction "has not been approved by resolutions" adopted by the Committees on Public Works, see 73 Stat. 479, 480, sec. 7 (1959).

256. Public Papers of the Presidents, 1961, at 196.

257. Watson, *Congress Steps Out*, *supra* note 225, at 1026.

258. Public Papers of the Presidents, 1978, I, at 1146.

259. Barbara Hinkson Craig, The Legislative Veto: Congressional Control of Regulation (1983); Harold H. Bruff & Ernest Gellhorn, *Congressional Control of Administrative Regulation: A Study of Legislative Vetoes*, 90 Harv. L. Rev. 1369 (1977).

260. Public Papers of the Presidents, 1978, I, at 1147.

arms sales and many other matters. His justification seems more political than constitutional. He and his administration wanted reorganization authority and agreed to take the legislative veto that came with it. The executive branch was prepared to make other accommodations. At a news conference on the day that Carter issued his critique of legislative vetoes, Attorney General Griffin Bell and White House adviser Stuart Eizenstat told the press they were willing to abide by legislative vetoes over arms sales, military commitments, and other areas in which Congress "has a legitimate interest."[261]

Legislative vetoes faced challenges in the lower courts. Federal judges approached the cases cautiously, focusing on the specific statutory provision being challenged and avoiding grand pronouncements. In some cases the Supreme Court decided not to rule on legislative vetoes, such as the one-house veto over regulations proposed by the Federal Election Commission (FEC).[262] In a separate case, an appellate court ruled that the dispute over FEC regulations was not ripe for judicial determination.[263] Another court saw no constitutional infirmity regarding a one-house veto in the Federal Salary Act.[264] The Supreme Court reviewed a case involving a one-house veto over Nixon's presidential papers but did not invalidate it.[265]

The case decided by the Supreme Court in 1983, *INS v. Chadha*, had been handled with circumspection by the Ninth Circuit. Acting under statutory authority, the House disapproved 6 of 340 requests by the Attorney General to suspend the deportation of aliens. The Ninth Circuit held that the legislative veto violated the doctrine of separated powers and intruded impermissibly into executive and judicial powers. But it carefully limited the reach of its decision, confining it to legislative vetoes that affect individual, adjudicative determinations. It specifically avoided commenting on other types of legislative vetoes, such as those over agency regulations.[266]

This incremental, case-by-case approach ended abruptly in 1982 when the D.C. Circuit struck down a one-house veto over regulations by the Federal Energy Regulatory Commission (FERC), a two-house veto over Federal Trade Commission (FTC) regulations, and a committee veto over reorganizations by the Department of Housing and Urban Development (HUD). The broad thrust of those decisions suggested that all legislative vetoes were unconstitutional for failing to comply with bicameralism and presentment.[267] In the HUD case, two judges urged the court to rehear the case en banc "because vitally important issues of executive-legislative relations are articulated too broadly and explored inadequately in the panel opinion." They warned about the danger of lumping all legislative vetoes together, ranging from rulemaking to war powers.[268]

261. Office of the White House Secretary, Briefing by Attorney General Griffin B. Bell, Stuart E. Eizenstat, Assistant to the President for Domestic Affairs and Policy, and John Harmon, Office of Legal Counsel, June 21, 1978, at 4. For someone who served in OLC in the mid-1970s and saw the issue from the inside: Robert G. Dixon, Jr., *The Congressional Veto and Separation of Powers: The Executive on a Leash?*, 56 N.C. L. Rev. 423 (1978).

262. Buckley v. Valeo, 424 U.S. 1, 140 n.176 (1976).

263. Clark v. Valeo, 559 F.2d 642 (D.C. Cir. 1977), aff'd sub nom., Clark v. Kimmitt, 431 U.S. 950 (1977).

264. Atkins v. United States, 556 F.2d 1028, 1063–65 (Ct. Cl. 1977), cert. denied, 424 U.S. 1009 (1978).

265. Nixon v. Administrator of General Services, 433 U.S. 425, 444–45 (1977).

266. Chadha v. INS, 634 F.2d 408, 433 (9th Cir. 1980).

267. Consumer Energy Council of America v. FERC, 673 F.2d 425 (D.C. Cir. 1982), Consumers Union, Inc. v. FTC, 691 F.2d 575 (D.C. Cir. 1982), and AFGE v. Pierce, 697 F.2d 303 (D.C. Cir. 1982).

268. AFGE v. Pierce, 697 F.2d at 308–09 (Judges Abner Mikva and Patricia Wald).

The immigration case from the Ninth Circuit was argued twice before the Supreme Court. On its face, the one-house veto over deportation decisions may appear to be congressional intrusion into executive decisions over aliens who faced potential abuse if returned to their country. The issue is more complicated, however. The legislative veto over deportations originated during the FDR administration. The only available relief for aliens about to be deported was passage of a private bill, satisfying both bicameralism and presentment. Delays in the legislative process meant deportation.

To lessen hardship on aliens of good character and increase the discretionary authority of the executive branch, Congress passed legislation in 1940 to empower the Attorney General to suspend deportations. Congress reserved the right to disapprove suspensions by a two-house veto.[269] The executive branch was pleased to receive this authority and uttered no constitutional objections. In 1952, Congress adopted a two-house resolution of approval for some aliens and a one-house disapproval for others.[270] These statutes marked a standard accommodation between the two branches.

The Supreme Court ruled that the one-house veto used for Jagdish Chadha was unconstitutional because it violated the requirements of bicameralism and presentment. Chief Justice Burger, joined by five Justices, held that whenever congressional action has the "purpose and effect of altering the legal rights, duties, and relations of persons" outside the legislative branch, Congress must act through both houses in a bill submitted to the President.[271] That principle is far too broad. As the Justice Department acknowledges, each house of Congress may alter the legal rights and duties of individuals outside the legislative branch without resorting to bicameral action and presentation. The issuance of committee subpoenas is one method.[272] The Court itself has recognized the power of either house to issue subpoenas and hold uncooperative executive officials and private citizens in contempt.[273] Impeachment is another way the House of Representatives can affect someone outside the legislative branch without bicameralism and presentment.

In a concurrence, Justice Powell expressed preference for a more narrowly drawn holding. A dissent by Justice White dissected the majority's reasoning. Justice Rehnquist dissented on the question of severability. The legislative history seemed persuasive to him that Congress delegated the authority to suspend deportations only on the condition that it retain a one-house veto. If the legislative veto fell, so should the suspension authority. To Rehnquist they were inseverable. The majority opinion, by deciding that the legislative veto could be severed, gave a one-sided advantage to the executive branch. The statutory accommodation from 1940 to 1983 had tried to balance legislative and executive interests.[274]

---

269. 54 Stat. 670, 671–73, sec. 20 (1940); Harvey C. Mansfield, *The Legislative Veto and the Deportation of Aliens*, 1 PUB. ADM. REV. 281 (1940).

270. 66 Stat. 163, 214–17, sec. 244 (1952).

271. INS v. Chadha, 462 U.S. 919, 952 (1983). A few weeks later the Court affirmed the opinions of the D.C. Circuit striking down the FERC and FTC legislative vetoes; 463 U.S. 1216 (1983).

272. 20 OP. O.L.C. 124, 138 (1996).

273. Subpoena power: Eastland v. United States Servicemen's Fund, 421 U.S. 491, 505 (1975); contempt power: Anderson v. Dunn, 6 Wheat. 204 (1821).

274. See BARBARA HINKSON CRAIG, CHADHA: THE STORY OF AN EPIC CONSTITUTIONAL STRUGGLE (1988).

Chief Justice Burger's opinion for the majority claimed that the Framers wanted congressional power exercised "in accord with a single, finely wrought and exhaustively considered, procedure." The records of the Philadelphia convention and ratification debates, he said, provide "unmistakable expression of a determination that legislation by the national Congress be a step-by-step, deliberate and deliberative process."[275] This account of Framer intent and the legislative process is highly abstract and far removed from actual procedures. Both houses of Congress are at liberty to suspend their rules, operate by unanimous consent, place legislative riders on appropriations bills, attach unrelated amendments to bills, and even pass bills that have never been sent to committee.

The majority opinion insisted the Constitution did not allow Congress "to repeal or amend laws by other than legislative means pursuant to Art. I."[276] By exercising the one-house veto in the deportation case, Congress was not repealing or amending the law. It was following it. The law was effectively amended when the Court deleted the legislative veto but allowed the remainder of the statute that empowered the Attorney General to remain in force. That was contrary to the intent and expectation of the elected branches when they reached agreement on the statute.[277]

## D. They survive

The Court in *Chadha* attempted to invalidate every type of legislative veto being litigated in the lower courts, hoping to eliminate in one fell swoop all legal disputes. But its theory of government was too much at odds with practices developed over the years by the elected branches. Neither agency officials nor lawmakers wanted the static, artificial model developed by the Court. The conditions that spawned the legislative veto in the past did not disappear. Executive officials still wanted substantial latitude in administering delegated authority; lawmakers still insisted on maintaining control without having to pass another statute. The elected branches began to develop substitutes that could serve as the functional equivalent of the legislative veto.[278]

The majority in *Chadha* demonstrated little understanding of the lawmaking process. Denying Congress the legislative veto need not benefit the President. Instead of a one-house

---

275. INS v. Chadha, 462 U.S. at 951, 959.

276. Id. at 954 n.18

277. Laurence H. Tribe, *The Legislative Veto Decision: A Law by Any Other Name?*, 21 Harv. J. on Legis. 1 (1984); Peter L. Strauss, *Was There a Baby in the Bathwater? A Comment on the Supreme Court's Legislative Veto Decision*, 1983 Duke L.J. 789; E. Donald Elliott, *INS v. Chadha: The Administrative Constitution, the Constitution, and the Legislative Veto*, 1983 Supreme Ct. Rev. 125.

278. Several cases after *Chadha* refined its meaning. An appellate court in 1984 emphasized that there is nothing unconstitutional about executive officials meeting frequently with congressional committees to discuss pending decisions: "indeed, our separation of powers makes such informal cooperation much more necessary than it would be in a pure system of parliamentary government." City of Alexandria v. United States, 737 F.2d 1022, 1026 (Fed. Cir. 1984). It cited a concurrence by Justice Jackson from 1952 explaining that the "actual art of governing under our Constitution does not and cannot conform to judicial definitions of the power of any of its branches based on isolated clauses or even single Articles torn from context." Id., citing Youngstown Co. v. Sawyer, 343 U.S. 579, 635 (1952). Citing the principles of *Chadha*, the Court in 1991 held that a review board that includes members of Congress violated separation of powers principles. Wash. Airports v. Noise Abatement Citizens, 501 U.S. 252 (1991).

veto over executive reorganization proposals, Congress could switch to a joint resolution of approval. In terms of *Chadha*, it satisfies bicameralism and presentment. But now the President would have to gain the approval of both houses within a specified number of days. Previously, a President's plan took effect unless one house disapproved within a fixed period of time. A joint resolution of approval reverses the burden. If one house decided to withhold support, the practical effect is a one-house veto. In 1984, Congress passed legislation requiring a joint resolution of approval for reorganization plans.[279] The Reagan administration found the new procedure so onerous that it never requested a renewal of reorganization authority when the statute expired. Congress could adopt the joint resolution of approval to other areas of delegated authority, including arms sales, national emergencies, and specific agency regulations.

In 1984, President Reagan signed an appropriations bill for HUD. His signing statement objected to seven provisions that required executive agencies to seek the prior approval of the Appropriations Committees. He vowed to implement the bill "in a manner consistent with the *Chadha* decision."[280] The clear message: executive agencies would regard committee-approval provisions as having no legal effect. Agencies would merely notify committees, get their feedback, and do as they liked. That policy might have seemed reasonable to the White House and the Justice Department, but it made little sense to agency officials who have to work daily with congressional committees and maintain constructive relationships.

The House Appropriations Committee immediately responded to Reagan's challenge by reviewing a procedure that had worked well with the National Aeronautics and Space Administration (NASA). Statutory ceilings were placed on various NASA programs. If the agency wanted to exceed those caps it needed to obtain the approval of the Appropriations Committees. Because of Reagan's statement, House Appropriations said it would repeal not only the committee veto but NASA's authority to exceed the caps.[281] In short, if NASA wanted to spend beyond the caps, it would have to do what the Court mandated in *Chadha*: pass a bill through both houses and have it presented to the President.

NASA officials did not want to seek a public law every time it found it necessary to exceed a spending cap. NASA Administrator James Beggs wrote to the Appropriations Committees and proposed a remedy. Instead of putting caps in a public law, place them in a conference report. He then pledged, in his letter, never to exceed a ceiling without first obtaining the prior approval of the Appropriations Committees.[282] This agreement, incorporated in a private letter rather than a statute, is permissible under *Chadha*. Informal or not, NASA officials knew that any violation of trust would provoke the Appropriations Committees to put caps in public law and compel the agency to obtain a new law every time it needed to exceed spending ceilings.

This type of political accommodation, understood by agencies but not by the Supreme Court, applies to other areas. Some statutes required written prior approval from the Appropriations Committees before funds could be transferred from one appropriations account to another.

---

279. 98 Stat. 3192 (1984).

280. Public Papers of the Presidents, 1984, II, at 1057.

281. H. Rep. No. 916, 98th Cong., 2d Sess. 48 (1984).

282. Letter from James M. Beggs, NASA Administrator, to Congressman Edward P. Boland, chairman of the Subcommittee on HUD-Independent Agencies of the House Committee on Appropriations, Aug. 9, 1984, printed in part in Louis Fisher, *The Legislative Veto: Invalidated, It Survives*, 56 Law & Contemp. Prob. 273, 289 (1993). Also on the continuation of legislative vetoes after 1983: Darren A. Wheeler, *Implementing INS v. Chadha: Communication Breakdown?*, 52 Wayne L. Rev. 1185 (2006).

To the Reagan administration, that procedure violated *Chadha*. Initially it agreed to accept the committee veto, but when it later refused to do so, Congress deleted both the committee veto and the transfer authority.[283] An unwillingness to work jointly with congressional committees can come at substantial cost to the executive branch.

Presidents continue to object to committee vetoes in bills presented to them. In their signing statements, they consider the procedures contrary to *Chadha* and instruct agencies to ignore requirements for committee prior-approval. Executive officials are directed to notify committees of their need to move money to new requirements, receive their input, and then do whatever the agencies decide. But agency budget manuals explicitly require committee approval for certain movement of funds. Agencies have both a moral and legal duty to comply with their written regulations. Eliminating committee vetoes would deprive executive agencies of the flexibility to carry out complex duties. The federal government needs to perform effectively. Committee vetoes serve that purpose.[284]

To lessen the chance of self-inflicted wounds, the Supreme Court supposedly follows the prudential course of not formulating a rule of constitutional law "broader than is required by the precise facts to which it is to be applied."[285] The Court ignored that fundamental principle in *Chadha* by issuing a decision that reached beyond the immigration statute to exceed the Court's understanding of executive-legislative relations and the system of separated powers. In some cases, the Court's decision drove underground a set of legislative vetoes that used to operate in plain sight. Committees and agency officials find it necessary and desirable to fashion political accommodations and to honor those agreements over the impractical rules of *Chadha*.

From the standpoint of presidential power, one of the casualties of the legislative veto decision was the loss of reorganization authority, previously subject to one-house or two-house vetoes. After *Chadha*, Congress passed legislation in 1984 requiring a joint resolution of approval to comply with bicameralism and presentment. This procedure was measurably more difficult for the President, forcing the administration to secure the approval of both houses within a set amount of time. On February 16, 2012, President Obama submitted legislation to restore presidential reorganization authority, based on the joint resolution of approval adopted in 1984.[286]

# 7. EXECUTIVE PRIVILEGE

Discovering limits to enumerated powers is often difficult. Article II, section 2 states quite clearly that the President "shall nominate," but that decision is often shared with members of Congress,

---

283. Fisher, *supra* 282, at 290.

284. For details on agency budget manuals that require agencies to seek committee approvals for certain types of actions, see Louis Fisher, *Committee Controls of Agency Decisions*, Congressional Research Service, Report RL33151, Nov. 16, 2005; http://loufisher.org/docs/lv/2626.pdf.

285. Ashwander v. TVA, 297 U.S. 288, 347 (1936), citing Liverpool, N.Y. v. Phila. Steamship Co. v. Emigration Comm'r, 113 U.S. 33, 39 (1885).

286. Letter from Jeffrey D. Zients, Acting Director, Office of Management and Budget, to Speaker John Boehner, Feb. 16, 2012; http://www.whitehouse.gov/sites/default/files/omb/legislative/letters/reorg-authority-letter-and-legislation-to-speaker-of-the-house.pdf. See also Henry B. Hogue, *Presidential Reorganization Authority: History, Recent Initiatives, and Options for Congress*, Congressional Research Service, Dec. 11, 2012, R42852.

Justices, and other participants. A similar complexity applies to implied powers, especially when they are in competition. The Constitution makes no mention of a presidential privilege to withhold information from Congress, but some capacity to act in that manner has existed from the beginning. Although the Constitution says nothing about congressional access to documents in the executive branch, Congress needs information to legislate in an informed manner and ensure that statutory policy is being properly carried out.

The Supreme Court has recognized that the elected branches possess those implied powers. In 1927, it stated that a legislative body "cannot legislate wisely or effectively in the absence of information respecting the conditions which the legislation is intended to affect or change."[287] In 1974, it affirmed a presidential power to withhold information to protect confidentiality: "To the extent this interest relates to the effective discharge of a President's powers, it is constitutionally based."[288] What the Court cannot do is predict the result when one implied power collides with another. Which one must yield? The answer generally depends more on political factors than judicial principles. Antonin Scalia, while serving as head of the OLC, crystallized the issue during a Senate hearing in 1975. When presidential and congressional interests clash, the resolution is likely to lie in "the hurly-burly, the give-and-take of the political process between the legislative and the executive.... [W]hen it comes to an impasse the Congress has means at its disposal to have its will prevail."[289] The key word here is *will*. Lawmakers need the staying power to cope with what is often a long and frustrating battle against executive resistance.[290]

## A. Some early lessons

Raoul Berger in a 1974 book referred to executive privilege as a "myth."[291] He observed: "The very words 'executive privilege' were conjoined only yesterday, in 1958."[292] While that was true, it is insufficient to discover when a term appears. More important is the executive *practice* of withholding information from Congress, which dates back to the administration of George Washington. Scholarly studies have recognized some discretion on the part of the President to withhold documents and testimony.[293] In a rare move in 1987, President Reagan fully waived executive privilege in the midst of the congressional investigation of the Iran-Contra affair (Chapter 6, section 9). Executive officials were at liberty to publicly disclose what they said to President Reagan and what he said to them. On all other occasions, congressional and

---

287. McGrain v. Daugherty, 273 U.S. 135, 175 (1927).

288. United States v. Nixon, 418 U.S. 683, 711 (1974).

289. *Executive Privilege—Secrecy in Government*, hearings before the Subcommittee on Intergovernmental Relations of the Senate Committee on Government Operations, 94th Cong., 1st Sess. 87 (1975).

290. Louis Fisher, *Congressional Access to Information: Using Legislative Will and Leverage*, 52 Duke L.J. 323 (2002).

291. Raoul Berger, Executive Privilege: A Constitutional Myth (1974).

292. Id. at 1.

293. Mark J. Rozell, Executive Privilege: Presidential Power, Secrecy, and Accountability (3d ed., 2010). For some commentary on Berger's scholarship: Louis Fisher, *Raoul Berger and Public Law*, 9 Pol. Sci. Rev. 173 (1978); Joseph K. Smaha, *In Defense of Raoul Berger*, 27 Pres. Stud. Q. 362 (1997); and Louis Fisher & Mark J. Rozell, *Raoul Berger on Executive Privilege*, 28 Pol. Sci. Q. 687 (1998).

judicial demands for executive documents have produced various types of accommodations and compromises.

During the First Congress, the House debated a request from Robert Morris to review his record as Superintendent of Finance during the period of the Continental Congress. The House created a committee of five to investigate the matter.[294] Some lawmakers objected that Congress had no authority to evaluate the conduct of executive officers, and the issue should be left to the President or specially appointed commissioners.[295] However, the House committee pursued its inquiry and issued a report on February 16, 1791.[296]

A request from Treasury Secretary Hamilton to Congress in 1790 triggered a dispute over legislative access to documents held by the executive branch. He asked Congress to compensate Baron von Steuben for his military assistance to America during the Revolutionary War. Hamilton recommended a lump sum of $7,396.74, an annuity for life, and "a moderate grant of land."[297] Committees of both houses looked into the request. When Hamilton resisted handing over a number of documents, the leverage was with Congress. It could simply take no action on the bill. After much hard feeling between the two branches, Congress deleted the lump sum (having discovered that the Continental Congress had given Steuben $7,000), deleted the grant of land, and settled on an annuity of $2,500 for life.[298]

More familiar is the 1792 congressional investigation into heavy military losses suffered by the troops of Maj. Gen. Arthur St. Clair to Indian tribes. The House sought testimony from executive officials and access to papers and records. According to the account of Secretary of State Jefferson, President Washington convened the Cabinet to consider the House request. They agreed that the House "was an inquest, and therefore might institute inquiries" and call for papers. President Washington "ought to communicate such papers as the public good would permit, and refuse those, the disclosure of which would injure the public: consequently were to exercise a discretion." The Cabinet concluded "there was not a paper which might not be properly produced."[299] The House committee examined papers furnished by the executive branch, listened to explanations from department heads and other witnesses, and received a written statement from General St. Clair.[300] However, the general principle of executive privilege had been established. The President could refuse to release papers "the disclosure of which would injure the public." The language here is significant. Injury has to be to the *public*, not to the President, his associates, or his political party. Information should not be withheld because it might embarrass the administration or reveal improper and illegal activities.

In 1794, the Senate launched an investigation into the conduct of Gouverneur Morris as American minister to France. It requested his official correspondence with the French and American governments. Once again President Washington turned to his Cabinet for guidance.

294. 1 ANNALS OF CONG. 1168, 1204, 1233 (Feb. 8, 10, and 11, 1790); 2 ANNALS OF CONG. 1514 (March 19, 1790).

295. 2 ANNALS OF CONG. 1515 (March 19, 1790).

296. Id. at 2017 (Feb. 16, 1791).

297. 6 THE PAPERS OF ALEXANDER HAMILTON 326–27 (Syrett ed. 1962).

298. 6 Stat. 2 (1790). For details on this investigation: LOUIS FISHER, THE POLITICS OF EXECUTIVE PRIVILEGE 7–10 (2004).

299. 1 THE WRITINGS OF THOMAS JEFFERSON 304–05 (Bergh ed. 1903).

300. 3 ANNALS OF CONG. 1106–13 and Appendix, 1052–59, 1310–17 (1792).

On this occasion the administration decided to release the correspondence but only after deleting certain passages.[301]

Well known is the refusal of President Washington to give Jay Treaty documents to the House. This was not an exercise of executive privilege in the sense of denying Congress information. The papers affecting the negotiation with Great Britain had been given to the Senate. Washington offered two arguments for withholding documents from the House: it could not be trusted with secret communications, and treaty-making was a matter for the Senate, not the House. As explained in Chapter 7, section 3B, neither argument is persuasive. Washington did not trust the Senate with confidential documents either, and members of the House did not need instruction from the President that the Constitution excludes them from treaty-making. They knew that. The House asked for information about the *post*-treaty process: whether to pass authorizations and appropriations to implement the treaty. To vote in an informed manner, the House needed documents.

The confrontation with the administration produced some close votes, with the House eventually supporting the treaty. Had one or two votes changed, the House could have told President Washington: "Without additional documents from you, we have inadequate grounds to debate and pass the necessary legislation." The choice then would have been to let the treaty sink or release documents to the House. Washington's position was weak on constitutional principles and a precedent he had established in 1793. In order to ensure that the Algerine Treaty pass and be implemented (to pay bribes to the Dey of Algiers), Washington agreed to give the House the identical documents he gave the Senate, including confidential letters. For several days the House met in secret session to debate the documents entrusted to them (also covered in Chapter 7, section 3B).[302]

When President Washington denied the House papers on the Jay Treaty, he said the only ground on which the House might have legitimately requested documents was as part of an impeachment process, "which the resolution has not expressed."[303] Had Congress requested the documents on that basis, presumably Washington would have complied. President Polk said in 1846 that the power of impeachment gives the House "the right to investigate the conduct of all public officers under the Government. This is cheerfully admitted. In such a case the safety of the Republic would be the supreme law, and the power of the House in the pursuit of this object would penetrate into the most secret recesses of the Executive Department."[304]

## B. Congressional leverage

Several examples will illustrate that withholding documents from Congress can work against executive interests. If the Washington administration had denied lawmakers access to papers about Baron von Steuben, Congress could have easily retaliated by putting the private bill on a shelf and

---

301. DANIEL N. HOFFMAN, GOVERNMENTAL SECRECY AND THE FOUNDING FATHERS: A STUDY IN CONSTITUTIONAL CONTROLS 104–18 (1981); 4 ANNALS OF CONG. 34, 37–38, 55–56 (Jan. 17, Jan. 23–24, Feb. 24, Feb. 26, 1794).

302. FISHER, *supra* note 298, at 30–32.

303. ANNALS OF CONG., 4th Cong., 1st Sess. 759 (1796).

304. 5 Richardson 2284 (April 20, 1846).

taking no further action. Similar issues arose with the Algerine and Jay Treaties. Refusing to pro-vide documents to the House under an artificial constitutional argument could have resulted in no legislation to authorize and fund the treaties. Presidents over the years have frequently accom-modated congressional and judicial requests for executive documents and testimony.[305]

The appointment process requires the executive branch to provide documents—often quite sensitive ones—to committees of jurisdiction. Documents that might have been withheld under the doctrine of executive privilege, such as FBI reports and private details about an individual's medical record, are released. Senate committees routinely request an administration to send all papers and information related to a particular nomination. Committees gain access to this information because a candidate approves release of the material and the executive branch is confident that the nomination will not produce embarrassments either for the nominee or the administration.[306] Attorney General Robert Jackson explained in 1941: "I have taken the posi-tion that committees called upon to pass on the confirmation of persons recommended for appointment by the Attorney General would be afforded confidential access to any informa-tion that we have—because no candidate's name is submitted without his knowledge and the Department does not intend to submit the name of any person whose entire history will not stand light."[307]

On July 31, 1986, President Reagan refused to release certain documents to the Senate Judiciary Committee, which was reviewing the nomination of William Rehnquist to be Chief Justice. The committee wanted memos that Rehnquist had written while serving as head of OLC from 1969 to 1971. Rehnquist did not object to releasing the documents, but the administration wanted to assert a familiar strand of the doctrine of executive privilege: protecting the confiden-tiality and candor of legal advice submitted to Presidents and executive officials.[308] Whatever the merits of that legal reasoning, it ran into a cold political fact: the committee might decide not to act on the nomination unless it received the memos. The dispute threatened not only Rehnquist's nomination but that of Antonin Scalia to be Associate Justice. The Senate planned to vote on both nominees on August 14. Bipartisan support existed for a committee subpoena demanding the OLC documents: eight Democrats and two Republicans. To break the impasse, Reagan allowed six Senators and six staff members to read some of the memos. The Senate then proceeded to confirm Rehnquist and Scalia on September 17.[309]

When administrations withhold documents or refuse to testify, Congress can issue subpoe-nas and hold executive officials in contempt. Invoking those two powers will usually provide committees the materials they need.[310] The contempt power requires the Justice Department to take the matter to a grand jury for possible criminal action. The law provides that when either house votes for contempt, the President of the Senate or the Speaker of the House shall certify

305. Stephen W. Stathis, *Executive Cooperation: Presidential Recognition of the Investigative Authority of Congress and the Courts*, 3 J. Law & Pol. 183 (1986).

306. Mitchel A. Sollenberger, Judicial Appointments and Democratic Controls 109–11 (2011).

307. 40 Op. Att'y Gen. 45, 51 (1941).

308. Al Kamen & Ruth Marcus, *Reagan Uses Executive Privilege to Keep Rehnquist Memos Secret*, Wash. Post, Aug. 1, 1986, at A1.

309. Fisher, *supra* note 298, at 76–77. For other nominees caught up in document fights, with the administra-tion compelled to surrender more documents than it wanted to, see id. at 71–88.

310. Id. at 91–134.

the facts to the appropriate U.S. Attorney, "whose duty it shall be to bring the matter before the grand jury for action."[311]

Despite the mandatory nature of that statutory duty, on three occasions the Justice Department refused to take contempt citations to a grand jury. The first precedent came in 1982, following the decision of the Reagan administration to withhold materials concerning the "Superfund" program. The House voted 259 to 105 to hold Anne Gorsuch, Administrator of the Environmental Protection Agency (EPA), in contempt. Fifty-five Republicans joined 204 Democrats to build the top-heavy majority.[312] The Justice Department, refusing to prosecute the case, asked a district court to declare the House action an unconstitutional intrusion into presidential authority. The court dismissed the government's suit on the ground that judicial intervention in executive-legislative disputes "should be delayed until all possibilities for settlement have been exhausted."[313] The court urged both parties to devote their energies to compromise and cooperation, not confrontation.

The administration, choosing not to appeal, eventually agreed to release documents to Congress.[314] A casualty in this confrontation: former EPA official Rita M. Lavelle. The House Energy and Commerce Committee voted unanimously to find her in contempt for defying a committee subpoena to testify. The House voted 413 to zero to hold her in contempt.[315] She was sentenced in 1984 to six months in prison, five years' probation, and a fine of $10,000 for lying to Congress about her management of the Superfund program. More than 20 other top officials, including Gorsuch, left the EPA amid allegations of perjury, conflict of interest, and political manipulation.[316]

An OLC memo of May 30, 1984, concluded that a U.S. attorney is not required to refer a contempt citation to a grand jury. It interpreted the word "shall" in 2 U.S.C. § 194 to include some "discretion" on the part of the executive branch to determine whether a violation of law had occurred.[317] Second, it held that the contempt statute "was not intended to apply and could not constitutionally be applied to an Executive Branch official who asserts the President's claim of executive privilege" in the context of the Gorsuch case.[318]

The second challenge to the contempt power occurred during the administration of George W. Bush. In 2008, the House Judiciary Committee investigated the forced resignation of nine U.S. attorneys. It voted to hold two executive officials in contempt: White House Counsel Harriet Miers for refusing to testify, and White House Chief of Staff Joshua Bolten for withholding

---

311. 2 U.S.C. § 194; Todd D. Peterson, *Prosecuting Executive Branch Officials for Contempt of Congress*, 66 N.Y.U. L. Rev. 563 (1991).

312. 128 Cong. Rec. 31746–76 (1982).

313. United States v. U.S. House of Representatives, 556 F. Supp. 150, 152 (D.D.C. 1983).

314. *EPA Document Agreement*, Cong. Q. Weekly Rep., March 26, 1983, at 635; Stanley M. Brand & Sean Connelly, *Constitutional Confrontations: Preserving a Prompt and Orderly Means by Which Congress May Enforce Investigative Demands Against Executive Branch Officials*, 36 Cath. U. L. Rev. 71 (1986); Ronald L. Claveloux, *The Conflict Between Executive Privilege and Congressional Oversight: The Gorsuch Controversy*, 1983 Duke L.J. 1333 (1983).

315. 129 Cong. Rec. 12717–25 (1983).

316. *Burford Resigns From EPA Post Under Fire*, 1983 Cong. Q. Almanac, at 442–35; Al Kamen, *Lavelle Gets Prison Term, $10,000 Fine*, Wash. Post, Jan. 10, 1984, at A2.

317. 8 Op. O.L.C. 101, 102 (1984).

318. Id.

requested documents. The House held each in contempt, but the Justice Department decided not to comply with the statutory requirement to take the cases to grand jury. The House filed suit in district court to require compliance with the statute. The court held that Miers was required to appear to testify before the committee and found no valid reason for Bolten to withhold non-privileged documents.[319]

On October 6, 2008, the D.C. Circuit noted that the 110th House of Representatives would cease to exist on January 3, 2009, and the subpoenas it issued would expire. It decided to leave the dispute to the new President and the new House.[320] On March 4, 2009, the House Judiciary Committee reached an agreement with the Obama White House to have Miers and former White House official Karl Rove testify in transcribed depositions under penalty of perjury and to receive Bush White House documents relevant to the inquiry.[321]

The third example of the Justice Department declining to take a contempt action to a grand jury occurred during the Obama administration. On January 27, 2011, Senator Charles E. Grassley wrote to Kenneth E. Melson, Acting Director of the Alcohol, Tobacco, and Firearms (ATF) agency, asking if the agency had allowed assault weapons to leave the United States and enter Mexico.[322] The House Committee on Oversight and Government Reform also conducted a vigorous investigation into what became known as "Operation Fast and Furious." The dispute deepened when the Justice Department replied to Grassley that his allegations were "false."[323] In fact, what was false was the Department's letter. Grassley's allegations were well founded, which the Department later acknowledged. The Department's letter of apology was not issued until ten months later.[324]

On June 20, 2012, the House committee voted Attorney General Eric Holder in contempt.[325] On that same day, Deputy Attorney General James M. Cole wrote to the committee that President Obama had asserted executive privilege over documents involved in Fast and Furious.[326] Eight days later the House voted 255 to 67 to support a resolution finding Attorney General Eric Holder in contempt.[327] Deputy Attorney General Cole advised Congress that U.S. Attorney Ronald C. Machen, Jr. for the District of Columbia would not take the contempt action to grand jury because of President Obama's assertion of executive privilege.[328] The House has

---

319. Committee on Jud., U.S. House of Repre. v. Miers, 558 F. Supp. 2d 53 (D.D.C. 2008). For details on the contempt actions in this case and the EPA case in 1983, see Morton Rosenberg, When Congress Comes Calling: A Primer on the Principles, Practices, and Pragmatics of Legislative Inquiry 15–18 (The Constitution Project, 2009).

320. Committee on Judiciary v. Miers, 542 F.3d 909, 911 (D.C. Cir. 2008). For details on the Miers-Bolten dispute: Rozell, *supra* note 293, at 71–78, and Josh Chafetz, *Executive Branch Contempt of Congress*, 76 U. Chi. L. Rev. 1083 (2009).

321. The White House, Agreement Concerning Accommodation: Committee on the Judiciary, U.S. House of Representatives v. Harriet Miers et al. Civil Action No. 08-0409 (JDB), March 4, 2009. Mark J. Rozell & Mitchel A. Sollenberger, *Executive Privilege and the U.S. Attorneys Firings*, 38 Pres. Stud. Q. 315 (2008).

322. Louis Fisher, *Obama's Executive Privilege and Holder's Contempt: "Operation Fast and Furious,"* 43 Pres. Stud. Q. 167, 168 (2013); http://www.loufisher.org/docs/ep/fast2.pdf.

323. Id. at 169–71.

324. Id. at 171–75.

325. Jordy Yager, *Issa's Panel Finds Holder in Contempt*, The Hill, June 21, 2012, at 1.

326. Fisher, *supra* note 322, at 179.

327. 158 Cong. Rec. H4417 (daily ed. June 28, 2012).

328. Fisher, *supra* note 322, at 181.

filed a civil action to compel compliance with a subpoena issued by the House Committee on Oversight and Government Reform.[329]

## C. Judicial leverage

Federal courts seek documents that a President may wish to withhold. Similar to the nomination process, the result may turn less on superior legal doctrines than political weaknesses of the President. In the midst of congressional investigations into the Watergate scandal, President Nixon argued in 1973 that the release of presidential conversations would undermine the independence of the executive branch and jeopardize the operations of the White House. He objected to Congress seeking testimony from his White House Counsel, John Dean. No President, Nixon insisted, "could ever agree to allow the Counsel to the President to go down and testify before a committee."[330]

Under political pressure, Nixon abandoned his arguments. A number of White House aides, including Dean, began testifying at congressional hearings. Investigation by the Senate disclosed the existence of listening and recording devices in the Oval Office. Some of those tapes wound up in the hands of Judge John Sirica, revealing evidence of a cover-up.[331] The House Judiciary Committee reported three articles of impeachment. The first charged that Nixon "prevented, obstructed, and impeded the administration of justice." Article I of the impeachment referred to "withholding relevant and material evidence or information from lawfully authorized investigative officers." Article II focused on Nixon's use of the IRS, the FBI, and the CIA to violate the constitutional rights of citizens. In Article III, the committee stated that Nixon had failed to produce "papers and things as directed by duly authorized subpoenas" issued by the committee, and that he had "willfully disobeyed such subpoenas."[332]

In response to the subpoenas, Nixon produced edited transcripts of some conversations in the White House but withheld the tapes. The committee concluded that edited transcripts were untrustworthy and unreliable. When the committee compared the edited transcripts with some recordings it possessed, it discovered omissions, material added, attributions of statements by one speaker when they were made by another, statements the White House had described as unintelligible when the committee could hear the words, and other errors and misrepresentations.[333]

During these struggles with Congress, Nixon threatened to defy any judicial effort to gain access to the Watergate tapes. Congress wanted documents as part of its impeachment inquiry. The courts wanted documents and tapes as part of the effort to prosecute Watergate crimes. The Special Prosecutor investigating the Watergate affair subpoenaed certain tapes and documents relating to conversations between Nixon and others. Nixon, claiming executive privilege, filed a motion to quash the subpoena. To permit Nixon absolute control over the information would have prevented the judiciary from carrying out its duties. A unanimous Supreme Court rejected

329. Id. at 181–82.

330. Public Papers of the Presidents, 1973, at 160. He subsequently offered other arguments for prohibiting testimony by White House staff; id. at 185, 203, 211. For congressional access to the testimony of White House officials: Fisher, *supra* note 298, at 199–227.

331. John J. Sirica, To Set the Record Straight 162 (1979).

332. H. Rep. No. 93-1305, 93d Cong., 2d Sess. 1–4 (1974).

333. Id. at 203.

Nixon's argument that the final decision to release such documents is for the President, not the courts.[334] The Court's leverage was heightened by the impeachment proceedings. An effort by Nixon to stonewall the Court would have accelerated his impeachment and removal from office. With release of the tapes, Nixon recognized that a House vote of impeachment "is, as a practical matter, virtually a foregone conclusion."[335] He announced his resignation on August 8, 1974, effective the next day.

The Court was on strong ground in protecting the rights of litigants and judges to obtain relevant evidence in criminal cases. A grand jury had returned an indictment charging seven individuals with various offenses, including conspiracy to defraud the United States and obstruct justice. The Court explained that in the U.S. adversary system of criminal justice the need to develop all relevant facts is "both fundamental and comprehensive."[336] The ends of criminal justice "would be defeated if judgments were to be founded on a partial or speculative presentation of the facts."[337] The integrity of the judicial system and the public's confidence in that system "depend on full disclosure of all the facts, within the framework of the rules of evidence."[338] Compulsory process must be available for the production of evidence needed by the prosecution and the defense.[339] On that note the Court's decision safeguarded essential values of law.

Unfortunately, the Court decided to add conflicting and irrelevant themes. It suggested that the outcome of the case might have been different had there been "a claim of need to protect military, diplomatic, or sensitive national security secrets."[340] Did it mean under those circumstances the government may prosecute individuals and they have no right to see and contest the evidence? Would it have made a difference had Nixon used national security arguments in withholding the tapes? The Court seemed to say so: "To read the Art. II powers of the President as providing an absolute privilege as against a subpoena essential to enforcement of criminal statutes on no more than a generalized claim of the public interest in confidentiality of *non-military and nondiplomatic* discussions would upset the constitutional balance of 'a workable government' and gravely impair the role of the courts under Art. III."[341]

Several years after the *Nixon* decision, the D.C. Circuit illustrated how federal judges can actively guide contesting parties in a national security case to reach an accommodation satisfactory to both sides. A House subcommittee issued a subpoena to obtain from the American

334. United States v. Nixon, 418 U.S. 683 (1974).

335. PUBLIC PAPERS OF THE PRESIDENTS, 1974, at 622. During this period, the D.C. Circuit held that it would not enforce a Senate subpoena for production of tape recordings of conversations between Nixon and John Dean. Senate Select Committee on Pres. Cam. Act v. Nixon, 498 F.2d 725 (D.C. Cir. 1974). The litigation trail is complex, but the court might have concluded that House impeachment proceedings and pending criminal actions brought by the Special Prosecutor were sufficient for the moment.

336. United States v. Nixon, 418 U.S. at 709.

337. Id.

338. Id.

339. Id.

340. Id. at 706. For Justice Department reliance on this dicta: 8 Op. O.L.C. 101, 116 (1984).

341. Id. at 707 (emphasis added). For analysis of the *Nixon* case: Archibald Cox, *Executive Privilege*, 122 U. PA. L. REV. 1383 (1974); Paul A. Freund, *The Supreme Court, 1973 Term. Foreword: On Presidential Privilege*, 88 HARV. L. REV. 13 (1974); Louis Henkin, *Executive Privilege: Mr. Nixon Loses but the Presidency Largely Prevails*, 22 UCLA L. REV. 40 (1974); Leonard G. Ratner, *Executive Privilege, Self Incrimination, and the Separation of Powers Illusion*, 22 UCLA L. REV. 92 (1974); and William Van Alstyne, *A Political and Constitutional Review of* United States v. Nixon, 22 UCLA L. REV. 116 (1974).

Telephone and Telegraph Company information on national security wiretaps by the administration. A district court, after attempting to balance the investigative power of Congress against
the President's executive privilege in foreign affairs, announced in 1976 that "if a final determination as to the need to maintain the secrecy of this material, or as to what constitutes an
acceptable risk of disclosure, must be made, it should be made by the constituent branch of government to which the primary role in these areas is entrusted. In the areas of national security
and foreign policy, that role is given to the Executive."[342]

The D.C. Circuit remanded that decision five months later. The election of Jimmy Carter as
President created new possibilities for resolving the matter out of court. In returning the case
to district court, the D.C. Circuit recommended that the two branches try to negotiate a settlement: "A compromise worked out between the branches is most likely to meet their essential
needs and the country's constitutional balance."[343] The D.C. Circuit supplied additional guidance, putting pressure on both parties to clarify their major concerns and reach an accommodation. The case was dismissed on December 21, 1978, after the Justice Department and the
subcommittee resolved their differences.[344]

## D. Clarifying Nixon

Contemporary cases have further defined the scope of the President's executive privilege, helping to clarify the broad and often vague principles announced in *United States v. Nixon*. Does the
privilege apply particularly to the President's personal involvement or does it extend to all staff
throughout the executive branch who might have had some role in the policymaking process?
Those questions surfaced during the Clinton years and involved Agriculture Secretary Mike
Espy, who was being prosecuted by an independent counsel. President Clinton asked the White
House to conduct its own inquiry. A grand jury issued a subpoena for documents and served
it on the White House Counsel. The subpoena requested notes of any meetings in the White
House concerning Espy and any conversations between Espy or his counsel and White House
employees. The White House withheld 84 documents on grounds of the deliberative process
privilege, as recognized in *Nixon*. A district court, after reviewing the documents *in camera*,
upheld the White House claims of privilege.[345]

The D.C. Circuit unanimously reversed, drawing a distinction between the President's
communications privilege and the broader doctrine of deliberative process privilege throughout the executive branch. Constitutional support for the former is greater than the latter. The
President's communications privilege, said the court, applies only to direct decision making
by the President.[346] "Not every person who plays a role in the development of presidential
advice, no matter how remote and removed from the President, can qualify for the privilege. In

---

342. United States v. AT&T, 419 F. Supp. 454, 461 (D.D.C. 1976).

343. United States v. AT&T, 551 F.2d 384, 394 (D.C. Cir. 1976).

344. United States v. AT&T, 567 F.2d 121 (D.C. Cir. 1977). For the settlement, see *Court Proceedings and Actions
of Vital Interest to the Congress, Current to December 31, 1978*, prepared by the House Select Committee on
Congressional Operations, 95th Cong., 2d Sess. 50 (1978).

345. The district court's decision is not reported; the summary of its action comes from the D.C. Circuit decision, cited next.

346. In re Sealed Case, 121 F.3d 729, 752 (D.C. Cir. 1997).

particular, the privilege should not extend to staff outside the White House in executive branch agencies."[347] None of the 84 documents withheld by the administration "was actually reviewed by the President."[348]

Building on the Espy case, federal courts continued to place limits on the presidential communications privilege. President Clinton claimed that executive privilege protected his conversations with two White House aides, Bruce Lindsey and Sidney Blumenthal. They refused to answer certain questions put to them before a grand jury that investigated issues involved in the Monica Lewinsky and Paula Jones litigation. A district judge ordered both men to testify.[349] When Secret Service officers refused to answer certain questions during depositions conducted by an independent counsel, as part of grand jury proceedings on Monica Lewinsky, a district judge and the D.C. Circuit declined to recognize any privilege and ordered their testimony.[350]

Of major interest is a decision by the D.C. Circuit in 2004 involving a presidential communication privilege over pardon documents. The court decided whether the Freedom of Information Act (FOIA) protects internal documents in the Office of the Pardon Attorney and the Office of the Deputy Attorney General. The Justice Department invoked the deliberative process privilege and the presidential communications privilege to withhold documents related to pardon decisions by President Clinton. The D.C. Circuit held that the presidential communications privilege applies only to pardon documents solicited and received by a President or his immediate advisers in the Office of the President.[351] A dissenting judge concluded that all documents originated for the sole purpose of advising the President on his pardon power are protected by the presidential communications privilege.[352]

# 8. EMPLOYEE ACCESS TO CONGRESS

Members of Congress depend on information given them directly by employees in the executive branch. At times these employees are called "whistleblowers." Presidents and agency supervisors frequently attempt to block such communications and express concern about the release of classified documents. On other occasions an administration fears that lawmakers will learn of waste, misconduct, corruption, and illegality within the executive branch. Publicly, Presidents and members of Congress typically praise federal employees who reveal problems within their agency. Privately the employees can expect little but retaliation and punishment for their conduct, even though whistleblower statutes supposedly grant them protection.

---

347. Id.

348. Id. at 746.

349. In re Grand Jury Proceedings, 5 F. Supp. 2d 21 (D.D.C. 1998).

350. In re Sealed Case, 148 F.3d 1073 (D.C. Cir. 1998).

351. Judicial Watch, Inc. v. Dept. of Justice, 365 F.3d 1108, 1123 (D.C. Cir. 2004).

352. Id. at 1136–39 (Randolph, J., dissenting). For analyses of the cases involving Espy and the pardon power: Rozell, *supra* note 293, at 129–31, 167–69; Rosenberg, *supra* note 319, at 26–29.

## A. Lloyd-LaFollette Act

In 1902, a "gag order" from President Roosevelt prohibited agency employees from seeking to influence legislation "individually or through associations" other than through the head of their department. Failure to abide by the order could lead to dismissal from federal service.[353] Seven years later, President Taft issued another gag order. He prohibited any bureau chief or subordinate in an executive agency from communicating with either house of Congress, any committee of Congress, or any member of Congress, with regard to legislation, appropriation, or congressional action of any kind, "except with the consent and knowledge of the head of the department; nor shall any such person respond to any request for information from either House of Congress, or any committee of either House of Congress, or any Member of Congress, except through, or as authorized by, the head of the department."[354]

In response, Congress in 1912 added to an appropriation bill language known as the Lloyd-LaFollette Act. It provided procedural safeguards for the review and removal of federal employees, including notice, time to respond in writing, and limiting removals "for such cause as will promote the efficiency of said service."[355] The language ended with this provision: "The right of persons employed in the civil service of the United States, either individually or collectively, to petition Congress, or any Member thereof, or to furnish information to either House of Congress, or to any committee or member thereof, shall not be denied or interfered with."[356]

Lawmakers in 1912 objected that a committee "only gets one side of a case [testimony from Cabinet officials and agency heads] unless the members of the committee assume to themselves the responsibility of making a personal investigation or personal inquiry among the employees of their acquaintance." They refused to be "at the mercy of the whims" of executive officials and insisted on access to agency rank and file.[357] Part of the legislative debate singled out the First Amendment rights to free speech, peaceable assembly, and to petition the government for a redress of grievances.[358]

The Civil Service Reform Act of 1978 carried forward and supplemented Lloyd-LaFollette, codifying it as permanent law.[359] The conference report in 1978 encouraged agency employees to disclose information to Congress and underscored the need for procedural safeguards to protect them from reprisal or retaliation by supervisors.[360] The Whistleblower Protection Act (WPA) of 1989 stated that disclosures by federal employees "serve the public interest by assisting in the elimination of fraud, waste, abuse and unnecessary Government expenditures." Protecting federal employees who reveal government "illegality, waste, and corruption is a major step toward a more effective civil service."[361] When President Bush signed the bill, he praised the whistleblower

---

353. The 1902 order is reprinted at 48 CONG. REC. 4513 (1912).

354. Id.

355. 37 Stat. 539, 555, sec. 6 (1912).

356. Id.

357. 48 CONG. REC. 4657 (1912) (statement by Rep. Reilly).

358. Id. at 5201 (Rep. Prouty), 5637 (Rep. Wilson), 10674 (Senator Reed).

359. 5 U.S.C. § 7211.

360. S. Rep. No. 95-1272, 95th Cong., 2d Sess. 132 (1978).

361. 103 Stat. 16, sec. 2(a) (1989).

as "a public servant of the highest order.... [T]hese dedicated men and women should not be fired or rebuked or suffer financially for their honesty and good judgment."[362]

## B. Treatment of whistleblowers

Notwithstanding this public appreciation for agency whistleblowers, the record demonstrates that they are routinely fired, rebuked, and suffer financially for disclosing problems within their departments and bureaus. Political institutions designed to protect employees from retaliation (the Office of Special Counsel, the Merit Systems Protection Board (MSPB), and the Federal Circuit) have rarely provided support. At a House hearing in 1985, the presiding officer observed: "There is no dispute—whistleblowers have no protection. We urge them to come forward, we hail them as the salvation of our budget trauma, and we promise them their place in heaven. But we let them be eaten alive."[363] The WPA and amendments to it in 1994 did little to protect agency employees who disclosed agency abuse. A House committee in 1994 concluded: "The WPA has created new reprisal victims at a far greater pace than it is protecting them."[364] The committee noted that the MSPB and Federal Circuit Court of Appeals had not been favorable to federal whistleblowers. The Court of Appeals had been even more hostile than the MSPB.[365]

Congress passed legislation in 1998 in an effort to provide whistleblower rights for employees in the Central Intelligence Agency, the Defense Intelligence Agency, the National Security Agency, and other parts of the Intelligence Community. The statute recognized that Congress "is empowered by the Constitution to serve as a check on the executive branch; in that capacity, it has a 'need to know' of allegations of wrongdoing within the executive branch, including allegations of wrongdoing in the Intelligence Community."[366] The statute expressed concern that "the risk of reprisal perceived by employees and contractors of the Intelligence Community for reporting serious or flagrant problems to Congress may have impaired the flow of information needed by the intelligence community to carry out oversight responsibilities."[367]

From 2008 to 2010, Congress developed legislation to strengthen whistleblower rights. At a House hearing in 2009, the Justice Department testified that the administration "strongly supports protecting the rights of whistleblowers."[368] It recognized that "the best source of information about waste, fraud, and abuse in government is often a government employee committed

---

362. Public Papers of the Presidents, 1989, I, at 391.

363. Comments by Rep. Pat Schroeder, *Whistleblower Protection*, hearings before the House Committee on Post Office and Civil Service, 99th Cong., 1st Sess. 237 (1985).

364. H. Rep. No. 103-769, 103d Cong., 2d Sess. 12 (1994).

365. Id. at 17. See Robert G. Vaughn, *Whistleblower Protection and the Challenge to Public Employment*, in Public Sector Employment in the Twenty-First Century (Marilyn Pittard & Phillipa Weeks eds., 2007), and Bruce D. Fong, *Whistleblower Protection and the Office of Special Counsel: The Development of Reprisal Law in the 1980s*, 40 Am. U. L. Rev. 1015 (1991).

366. 112 Stat. 2396, 2413, sec. 701(b) (1998).

367. Id. at 2414.

368. *Protecting the Public from Waste, Fraud and Abuse: H.R. 1507, the Whistleblower Protection Enhancement Act of 2009*, Statement of Rajesh De, Deputy Assistant Attorney General, Office of Legal Policy, Department of Justice, before the House Committee on Oversight and Government Reform, May 14, 2009, at 1.

to public integrity and willing to speak out. Empowering whistleblowers is a keystone of the President's firm commitment to ensuring accountability in government."[369] The executive official explained that, under current law, "a whistleblower is not protected if she informs her boss of wrongdoing, only to discover that her boss was the one responsible for the wrongdoing."[370] With regard to whistleblowers in the national security agencies, the official proposed that their disclosures go not to Congress but to an agency within the executive branch.[371] The administration opposed any judicial remedy for national security whistleblowers.[372]

On October 10, 2012, President Obama issued a policy directive covering whistleblowers with access to classified information. The purpose of the directive is to ensure that employees serving the Intelligence Community or who are eligible for access to classified information "can effectively report waste, fraud, and abuse while protecting classified national security information." The directive prohibits "retaliation against employees for reporting waste, fraud, and abuse."[373] The following month, on November 27, he signed into law the Whistleblower Protection Enhancement Act of 2012.[374] The legislation, designed to clarify the disclosure of information, had been under consideration for many years. An important provision permits appeals to go to other federal courts, ending the sole jurisdiction of the Court of Appeals for the Federal Circuit.

## C. Appropriation controls

At times lawmakers are denied information from agency officials created and funded by Congress. In 1997, Congress created a Chief Actuary in the Health Care Financing Administration (HCFA) to ensure reliable and expert calculations in determining the cost of medical care. The statute stipulated that the individual "shall be appointed from among individuals who have demonstrated, by their education and experience, superior expertise in the actuarial sciences."[375] Those duties were to be exercised "in accordance with professional standards of actuarial independence." The person could be removed only "for cause."[376] Congress created the office to provide reliable forecasts to both branches when considering legislation and oversight. Richard S. Foster, in his service as Chief Actuary, appeared at congressional hearings to provide testimony.[377]

On March 16, 2004, Secretary of Health and Human Services (HHS) Tommy Thompson ordered an internal investigation into accusations that the Bush administration had threatened to fire Foster if he gave data to Congress showing the high cost of pending legislation to create prescription drug benefits for the elderly. Foster estimated the benefits would cost $500 billion

369. Id.

370. Id. at 4.

371. Id. at 7–9.

372. Id. at 9–10.

373. President Barack Obama, Presidential Policy Directive/PPD-19, *Protecting Whistleblowers with Access to Classified Information*, Oct. 10, 2012, at 1.

374. 126 Stat. 1465 (2012).

375. 111 Stat. 251, 488, sec. 4643 (1997); 42 U.S.C. § 1317,

376. Id. The statute does not elaborate on the meaning of "for cause."

377. E.g., testimony before the Subcommittee on Health of the House Committee on Energy and Commerce, April 9, 2003, http://www.hhs.gov/asl/testify/t030409a.html.

to $600 billion over a period of ten years. The administration claimed the cost would not exceed $400 billion. Some lawmakers said had they known of Foster's higher estimates, the bill would not have passed.[378]

An attorney for Congressional Research Service (CRS) released an analysis on April 26, 2004, concluding that the "gag order" on Foster to prevent him from communicating directly with members of Congress "would appear to violate a specific and express prohibition of federal law," 5 U.S.C. § 7211 (Lloyd-LaFollette). The CRS attorney added: "Congress has a clear right and recognized prerogative, pursuant to its constitutional authority to legislate, to receive from officers and employees of the agencies and departments of the United States accurate and truthful information regarding the federal program and policies administered by such employees and agencies."[379]

A memo by OLC, dated May 21, 2004, relied on the "Unitary Executive" model to argue that the President's relationship with his subordinates must be free from interference by other branches to permit the President to carry out his constitutional duties. OLC reasoned that statutes such as Lloyd-LaFollette could not be applied to Foster's situation.[380] On July 6, 2004, the Office of Inspector General in HHS completed its investigation of the threats made against Foster. It found that the department had withheld certain estimates requested by members of Congress but found no evidence that this conduct violated criminal statutes. Although there was evidence that Thomas Scully, former Administrator of the Centers for Medicare and Medicaid Services (CMS), had advised a congressional staffer that he would fire Foster for releasing information, Scully did not take disciplinary action against Foster. Had Scully remained at CMS, the IG's office would have referred the matter to the department for possible administrative action; a referral was not made because Scully left government.[381]

On September 7, 2004, the Government Accountability Office (GAO) released a legal analysis of Foster's communications with Congress. It looked particularly at statutory language that prohibits the use of appropriated funds to pay the salary of a federal official who prevents another federal employee from communicating with Congress. It held that the information that Foster wanted to share with Congress was not classified information and had nothing to do with the deliberative process privilege. It further noted that HHS and OLC had overstated the President's constitutional powers and had failed to recognize Congress's need for information to carry out its legislative and oversight responsibilities. It concluded that payments for Scully's salary,

378. Robert Pear & Sheryl Gay Stolberg, *Inquiry Ordered on Medicare Official's Charge*, N.Y. TIMES, March 17, 2004.

379. Jack Maskell, Legislative Attorney, American Law Division, Congressional Research Service, memo to Rep. Charles Rangel, House Committee on Ways and Means, April 26, 2004, at 9. This memo was publicly released by Rep. Rangel. See Robert Pear, *Agency Sees Withholding of Medicare Data from Congress as Illegal*, N.Y. TIMES, May 4, 2004.

380. Jack L. Goldsmith III, Assistant Attorney General, Office of Legal Counsel, *Letter Opinion for the General Counsel Department of Health and Human Services*, May 21, 2004, at 3, http://www.justice.gov/olc/crsmemoresponsese.htm.

381. Statement of Dara Corrigan, Acting Principal Deputy Inspector General, Department of Health and Human Services, on Thomas Scully and Richard Foster Investigation, July 6, 2004, http://oig.hhs.gov/publications/docs/press/2004/070704igstatement.pdf.

beginning with the pay period when his initial threat to Foster was made until his departure from CMS, were improper under law and that HHS should take steps to recover those funds.[382]

MANY OF THE documents and expert testimony needed by lawmakers are located within executive agencies that are created, authorized, and funded by Congress. In both a legal, constitutional, and practical sense, agencies are creatures of Congress and must serve both the executive and legislative branches. With greater portions of executive power flowing to the President's office, Congress and the courts have a heightened need to obtain agency and White House documents and require presidential aides to testify. Congress also has a need to hear from employees within agencies about operations and programs that the administration may want to keep secret, in part because release of such information could be embarrassing to the President and his team. Whether lawmakers actually receive the information they request depends on their political skills and determination to overcome the bureaucratic hurdles that are likely to be placed in their way. Members of Congress, assigned specific constitutional duties, have no reason to automatically defer to presidential claims of exclusive and overriding power.

382. Government Accountability Office, Department of Health and Human Services—Chief Actuary's Communications with Congress, B-302911, Sept. 7, 2004, http://www.gao.gov/decisions/appro/302911.pdf.

# SIX

# Budgetary Duties

WHEN THE FRAMERS DRAFTED AND DEBATED THE CONSTITUTION, THE POWERS over war and spending were considered essential to legislative prerogatives and republican government. As explained in Chapter 8, much of the war power has drifted to the President. The spending power remains with Congress, if it chooses to exercise it. At times it has been willing to surrender it as well, such as when it gave the President an item veto (Chapter 5, section 4). After the Supreme Court in *INS v. Chadha* struck down the legislative veto, Congress retained a committee veto over agency spending adjustments during a fiscal year (Chapter 5, section 6D). This chapter focuses on basic principles of the spending power, confidential and covert spending, the President's duty to submit a national budget, presidential refusal to spend appropriated funds (impoundment), the Budget Act of 1974, President Reagan and the Gramm-Rudman Act, the Iran-Contra affair, and the failure of the elected branches to control national deficits.

## 1. POWER OF THE PURSE

In Federalist No. 58, James Madison called the power of the purse "the most complete and effectual weapon with which any constitution can arm the immediate representatives of the people, for obtaining a redress of every grievance, and for carrying into effect every just and salutary measure."[1] He understood the essential link between this power and republican government. In that same essay he explained the evolution of the spending power in the British Constitution: "an infant and humble representation of the people gradually enlarging the sphere of its activity and importance, and finally reducing, as far as it seems to have wished, all the overgrown prerogatives of the other branches of the government."[2]

After a centuries-long struggle, the British Parliament used the power of the purse to gradually place limits on the monarch. English kings tried to circumvent Parliament by reaching to outside sources to finance military expeditions and other initiatives. Some of those funds came from private parties and foreign governments. Fueled by those transgressions, England lurched into a bloody civil war and Charles I lost both his office and his head.[3] With Iran-Contra,

---

1. The Federalist 391.

2. Id.

3. PAUL EINZIG, THE CONTROL OF THE PURSE 57–62, 100–06 (1959).

President Reagan also decided to pursue executive policies by relying on private and foreign money. He managed to escape impeachment (section 9 in this chapter).

Madison spoke plainly in Federalist No. 58: "the legislative department alone has access to the pockets of the people."[4] Language in Article I, section 9 reflects that principle: "No Money shall be drawn from the Treasury, but in Consequence of Appropriations made by Law." Other provisions in Article I, section 9 underscore legislative control over the purse. Congress is empowered to lay and collect taxes, duties, imposts, and excises; borrow money on the credit of the United States; and coin money and regulate its value.[5] Madison argued against placing the power of Commander in Chief in the same hands as the power to go to war: "Those who are to *conduct a war* cannot in the nature of things, be proper or safe judges, whether *a war ought* to be *commenced, continued,* or *concluded.* They are barred from the latter functions by a great principle in free government, analogous to that which separates the sword from the purse, or the power of executing from the power of enacting laws."[6]

Notwithstanding the clarity of Article I, section 9, Presidents have attempted to wrest the spending power from Congress by entering into financial obligations not authorized by law. Some of those initiatives have been discussed, including President Jefferson and the Louisiana Purchase and his commitment of funds following the British firing on the *Chesapeake* (Chapter 3, section 5). In each case he knew he needed authorization from Congress. Other presidential actions pose much graver threats to constitutional government, such as initiating wars (Chapter 8, section 1), refusing to spend money that Congress has appropriated (this chapter, section 6), and seeking funds from foreign governments and private citizens in violation of statutory policy (this chapter, section 9).

# 2. STATEMENT AND ACCOUNT CLAUSE

Underscoring the power of the purse, the Framers added language to Article I, section 9: "A regular Statement and Account of the Receipts and Expenditures of all public Money shall be published from time to time." This provision, although essential to republican government, democratic budgeting, and financial accountability, did not appear in the draft constitution until the final few days. On September 14, 1787, George Mason proposed that "an Account of the public expenditures should be annually published."[7] Gouverneur Morris objected that publication would be "impossible in many cases."[8] A strong supporter of executive authority, Morris

4. The Federalist 345.

5. David E. Engdahl, *The Spending Power*, 44 DUKE L.J. 1 (1994); Kate Stith, *Congress' Power of the Purse*, 97 YALE L.J. 1343 (1988); and Kenneth W. Dam, *The American Fiscal Constitution*, 44 U. CHI. L. REV. 271 (1977). For a rebuttal to Prof. Stith, arguing that Presidents may obligate Treasury funds without an appropriation: J. Gregory Sidak, *The President's Power of the Purse*, 1989 DUKE L.J. 1162 (1989). Judicial decisions in such areas as mental institutions and prisons exercise part of the spending power; Gerald E. Frug, *The Judicial Power of the Purse*, 126 U. PA. L. REV. 715 (1978).

6. 6 THE WRITINGS OF JAMES MADISON 148 (Hunt ed., 1906) (emphasis in original).

7. 2 Farrand 618.

8. Id.

might have believed in some level of secrecy and confidentiality. He regarded the President as the "guardian of the people, even of the lower classes, agst. Legislative tyranny."[9] He warned that Congress would "continually seek to aggrandize & perpetuate themselves."[10]

Rufus King faulted Mason's proposal: "the term expenditures went to every minute shilling. This would be impracticable. Congs. might indeed make a monthly publication, but it would be in such general Statements as would afford no satisfactory information."[11] Unlike Morris, King seemed more concerned about impractical detail and frequency of publications than the need for secrecy and confidentiality. James Madison proposed to delete "annually" and insert "from time to time," giving Congress some discretion over public disclosure.[12] Other statements during the debate point to the need for secrecy. James Wilson remarked that many operations of finance "cannot be properly published at certain times."[13] Thomas Fitzsimons insisted it was "absolutely impossible to publish expenditures in the full extent of the term."[14] The convention accepted Madison's amendment without a dissenting vote. Mason's proposal, as amended, included an accounting for receipts as well as expenditures and applied the requirement for publication to "all public Money."[15]

At the Virginia ratifying convention, Mason said the Framers added "from time to time" because "there might be some matters which might require secrecy."[16] He seemed to have in mind a delay in publication: "In matters relative to military operations, and foreign negotiations, secrecy was necessary sometimes. But he did not conceive that the receipts and expenditures of the public money ought ever to be concealed. The people, he affirmed, had a right to know the expenditures of their money."[17] After some period of time, the cost of secret operations would be made public.

An exception to public access appeared in 1790. Congress provided the President with $40,000 to be used for foreign intercourse, leaving to his judgment the extent to which the expenditure would be made public.[18] Legislation three years later authorized the President to make a certificate of the amount of expenditures in foreign intercourse "he may think it advisable not to specify."[19] A certificate states that funds have been spent without providing any details. It is referred to as unvouchered funds. When the House in 1848 insisted on information about confidential funds in foreign intercourse for the period from March 4, 1841 to May 8, 1843, President Polk refused by pointing to the statutory authority available to the President to decide the extent to which such funds should be made public.[20]

---

9. Id. at 52.

10. 1 Diary and Letters of Gouverneur Morris 12 (Anne Cary Morris ed., 1888).

11. 2 Farrand 618.

12. Id. at 618–19.

13. Id. at 619.

14. Id.

15. Id.

16. 3 Elliot 459. That language also appears at 3 Farrand 326.

17. Id.

18. 1 Stat. 129 (1790).

19. Id. at 300 (1793). Codified today at 31 U.S.C. § 3526(e).

20. 5 Richardson 2281–86.

In 1811, Congress passed a secret statute giving President Madison $100,000 to take temporary possession of territory south of Georgia. The law was not published until 1818.[21] Throughout the nineteenth century, the only annual exception to the Statement and Account Clause was the President's contingency account in foreign intercourse. By 1899, the yearly amount had reached $63,000.[22] A second exception emerged in 1916, authorizing the Secretary of the Navy to make a certificate of expenses for "obtaining information from abroad and at home."[23] A third example became law in 1935, giving the FBI a confidential fund of $20,000 (later raised to an amount specified in an appropriations bill).[24] For the first 146 years, Congress departed from the Statement and Account Clause on only rare occasions and for relatively modest amounts of money.

With World War II, the magnitude of confidential funds increased dramatically. Congress provided billions of dollars to develop and produce the atomic bomb. Only a few lawmakers knew that secret funds had been tucked away in two appropriation accounts: "Engineer Service, Army" and "Expediting Production."[25] After World War II, a number of agencies received confidential and unvouchered funds, including the White House, the Defense Department, the District of Columbia, the Attorney General, the Bureau of Narcotics and Dangerous Drugs, the Secret Service, the Coast Guard, the Bureau of Customs, and the Immigration and Naturalization Service.[26]

Overshadowing those funds in dollar amounts are the agencies that make up the U.S. intelligence community: the Central Intelligence Agency, the Defense Intelligence Agency, the National Security Agency, and many others. Money could be spent on a confidential basis, using certificates rather than vouchers. Appropriations accounts made no mention of these agencies. Instead, their funds were included in different accounts in the appropriation bills covering other departments of government. After the bills became law, OMB transferred the funds to the particular intelligence agencies.[27]

William Richardson, an attorney in Pennsylvania, asked the judiciary in the 1960s to declare this method of secret funding a violation of the Statement and Account Clause. A district court in 1968 ruled that he failed to establish standing to raise a justiciable controversy.[28] The Third

---

21. 3 Stat. 471–72 (1818); see David Hunter Miller, Secret Statutes of the United States (1918). For background on the secret statute: Stephen F. Knott, Secret and Sanctioned: Covert Operations and the American Presidency 87–104 (1996).

22. 30 Stat. 826 (1899) (Emergencies Arising in the Diplomatic and Consular Service). The margin refers to R.S., sec. 291, which calls for certificates, not vouchers.

23. 39 Stat. 557 (1916), 10 U.S.C. § 7231.

24. 49 Stat. 78 (1935), 28 U.S.C. § 537.

25. Louis Fisher, Presidential Spending Power 214 (1975); Leslie R. Groves, Now It Can Be Told 360–61 (1962).

26. Louis Fisher, *Confidential Spending and Governmental Accountability*, 47 G.W. L. Rev. 347 (1979).

27. Douglas P. Elliott, *Cloak and Ledger: Is CIA Funding Constitutional?*, 2 Hastings Const. L. Q. 717 (1975); Note, *The CIA's Secret Funding and the Constitution*, 84 Yale L.J. 608 (1975); and Robin Herman Schwartzman, *Fiscal Oversight of the Central Intelligence Agency: Can Accountability and Confidentiality Coexist?*, 7 N.Y.U. J. Int'l L. & Pol. 493 (1974).

28. Richardson v. Sokol, 285 F. Supp. 866 (W.D. Pa. 1968).

Circuit affirmed, deciding that courts lack jurisdiction to hear such cases.[29] The Supreme Court denied certiorari, with only Justice Douglas insisting the case be heard.[30]

Richardson initiated a new suit in 1970, this time asking that a three-judge court be convened to determine the constitutionality of the CIA budget. Once again a district court decided he lacked standing but added that the subject matter raised "political questions in a governmental sense and the subject is not open to a United States District Court for adjudication in any manner."[31] Up to that point, he had been blocked by three procedural hurdles: standing, jurisdiction, and justiciability.

This time the Third Circuit saw merit to his lawsuit. On July 20, 1972, by a 6 to 3 vote, the appellate court vacated the district court ruling and directed that a three-judge court be designated to adjudicate the issue. Judge Max Rosenn, writing the opinion, underscored the importance and purpose of the Statement and Account Clause:

> A responsible and intelligent taxpayer and citizen, of course, wants to know how his tax money is being spent. Without this information he cannot intelligently follow the actions of the Congress or of the Executive. Nor can he properly fulfill his obligation as a member of the electorate. The Framers of the Constitution deemed fiscal information essential if the electorate was to exercise any control over its representatives and meet their new responsibilities as citizens of the Republic.[32]

The Supreme Court agreed to review the procedural aspect of the case: whether Richardson had standing to request a three-judge court.[33] A separate writ of certiorari by Richardson, urging the Court to examine the substance and constitutionality of the issue, was rejected.[34] On June 25, 1974, a divided Court (5 to 4) dismissed the case for lack of standing.[35] The majority suggested that "the subject matter is committed to the surveillance of Congress, and ultimately to the political process."[36] Of course the matter had been in the hands of Congress, which thus far chose not to comply with the Statement and Account Clause. Justice Douglas, in a dissent, insisted that the Framers inserted the Clause "to give the public knowledge of the way public funds are expended."[37] He agreed that Congress "has discretion; but to say that it has the power to read the clause out of the Constitution when it comes to one or two or three agencies is astounding."[38] He added: "The sovereign in this Nation is the people, not the bureaucracy."[39] It is not unusual, or inappropriate, for the Court to return constitutional disputes to the elected branches to resolve.

29. Richardson v. Sokol, 409 F.2d 3 (3d Cir. 1969).

30. Richardson v. Sokol, 396 U.S. 949 (1969).

31. Richardson v. United States, C.A. No. 7023 (W.D. Pa. 1970). Not reported, but reprinted at United States v. Richardson, *Petition for a Writ of Certiorari to the United States Court of Appeals for the Third Circuit*, U.S. Supreme Court Docket No. 72-885, at 55a–58a.

32. Richardson v. United States, 465 F.2d 844, 853 (3d Cir. 1972).

33. United States v. Richardson, 410 U.S. 953 (1973) (No. 72-885).

34. Richardson v. United States, 410 U.S. 955 (1973) (No. 72-894).

35. United States v. Richardson, 418 U.S. 166, 170 (1974).

36. Id. at 179.

37. Id. at 200.

38. Id. at 200–01.

39. Id. at 201.

In other court actions, in 1976 a district court held that the Freedom of Information Act exempted disclosure of the CIA budget.[40] A year later, the D.C. Circuit decided that Representative Michael Harrington lacked standing to bring suit against the use of public funds for what he claimed to be illegal CIA activities.[41] It also remarked that the Statement and Account Clause "is not self-defining and Congress has plenary power to give meaning to the provision."[42] The court said that Harrington "has suffered no injury in a constitutional sense" and was asking the judiciary "to usurp the legislative function and to grant him the relief which his colleagues have refused him."[43] It was evident that the judiciary would not interpret the Statement and Account Clause to require publication of the budgets of the intelligence community.[44] Disclosure (and compliance with the Constitution) would require action by the elected branches.

House and Senate committees held hearings on whether to publicly disclose the aggregate amount of the intelligence budget. At various times the two chambers moved in that direction, but never at the same time.[45] Steven Aftergood of the Federation of American Scientists filed a number of FOIA requests and lawsuits to uncover the aggregate budget. His efforts prompted the CIA in 1997 to release the figure of $26.6 billion (with the CIA accounting for about $3 billion) and $26.7 billion the following year. Aftergood and other researchers disclosed CIA budget information for some earlier years.[46] In 2005, a top U.S. intelligence official inadvertently revealed at a public meeting what she thought to be the annual intelligence budget: $44 billion.[47]

In 2004, the 9/11 Commission recommended the disclosure of the aggregate budget of the intelligence community. Three years later Congress passed legislation to implement that proposal. The statute required the Director of National Intelligence (DNI) to disclose the aggregate budget, but it authorized the President by fiscal 2009 to waive the disclosure requirement if he deemed it necessary.[48] On October 30, 2007, DNI Mike McConnell released the aggregate amount of $43.5 billion for fiscal 2007.[49] That figure was only part of the picture. News reports pointed out that his aggregate did not include funds for military intelligence (Defense Department) operations. Including those amounts pushed the total well beyond $50 billion.[50] An estimate in July 2010 put the total at approximately $75 billion.[51] In October 2010, the

40. Halperin v. Colby, Civ. Action No. 75-676 (D.D.C. June 4, 1976).

41. Harrington v. Bush, 553 F.2d 190 (D.C. Cir. 1977).

42. Id. at 194.

43. Id. at 215.

44. For other unsuccessful lawsuits to seek documents from the CIA: Halperin v. Central Intelligence Agency, 629 F.2d 144 (D.C. Cir. 1980); Goland v. Central Intelligence Agency, 607 F.2d 339 (D.C. Cir. 1978); Ray v. Turner, 587 F.2d 1187 (D.C. Cir. 1978); and Baker v. Central Intelligence Agency, 580 F.2d 664 (D.C. Cir. 1978).

45. LOUIS FISHER, CONSTITUTIONAL CONFLICTS BETWEEN CONGRESS AND THE PRESIDENT 212–13 (5th ed. 2007).

46. Id. at 213–14. I filed a declaration in court to support Aftergood's efforts.

47. Scott Shane, Official Reveals Budget for U.S. Intelligence, N.Y. TIMES, Nov. 11, 2005, at A24.

48. 121 Stat. 335 (2007).

49. Office of the Director of National Intelligence, Public Affairs Office, News Release, DNI Releases Budget Figure for National Intelligence Program, Oct. 30, 2007.

50. Mark Mazzetti, $43.5 Billion Spying Budget for Year, Not Including Military, N.Y. TIMES, Oct. 31, 2007, at A16; Walter Pincus, 2007 Spying Said to Cost $50 Billion, WASH. POST, Oct. 30, 2007, at A4.

51. Clapper: Military Intel Budget to Be Disclosed, included in the July 21, 2010 issue of Secrecy News, available at http://www.fas.org/blog/secrecy.

government announced it had spent $80.1 billion for intelligence activities.[52] Two years later, the aggregate had declined to $75.4 billion.[53]

# 3. CONTROLLING THE TREASURY

Members of Congress in 1789 needed to create the executive departments. They regarded the Departments of Foreign Affairs and War as executive in nature and assigned them directly to the President.[54] Those departmental heads had no regular obligation to come to Congress and present reports. Both departments retained their identity as administrative agencies during the transition from the Articles of Confederation to the Constitution. The continuity is remarkable. Robert Livingston and John Jay held the post of Secretary for Foreign Affairs from 1781 to 1790. Henry Knox served as Secretary of War from 1785 to 1794.[55]

A different attitude applied to the Treasury Department. Robert Morris had been Superintendent of Finance from 1781 to 1784, at which point the management of finances fell back to the previous Board of Treasury. Lawmakers viewed the Treasury Department as close to Congress because of the spending power. In 1789, members in the House debated whether the Secretary of the Treasury should not only *digest* plans for the improvement and management of the revenue but also *report* them. John Page of Virginia regarded this authority as a "dangerous innovation upon the Constitutional privilege of this House" and would "create an undue influence within these walls."[56] Members might defer to executive officials "even against their own judgment."[57] He feared it would create a precedent "which might be extended, until we admitted all the ministers of the Government on the floor, to explain and support the plans they have digested and reported: thus laying a foundation for an aristocracy or a detestable monarchy."[58]

Benjamin Goodhue rejected this suspicion and jealousy toward the new Treasury Department: "We certainly carry our dignity to the extreme, when we refuse to receive information from any but ourselves."[59] It was his expectation that the Treasury Secretary "will, from the nature of his office, be better acquainted with the subject of improving the revenue or curtailing expense, than any other person; if he is thus capable of affording useful information, shall we reckon it hazardous to receive it?"[60] Thomas Fitzsimons recommended that the bill be amended

---

52. Walter Pincus, *Intelligence Spending at Record $80.1 Billion Overall*, Wash. Post, Oct. 29, 2010, at A2.

53. *Secrecy News*, Oct. 31, 2012, http://www.fas.org/blog/secrecy/2012/10/fy2012_intelbud.html.

54. Statutes creating the Departments of Foreign Affairs and War: 1 Stat. 28, 49 (1789).

55. For studies that closely trace and explain the continuity of executive departments from 1781 to the First Congress and beyond: William B. Michaelsen, Creating the American Presidency, 1775–1789 (1987); Jennings B. Sanders, The Presidency of the Continental Congress, 1774–1789: A Study in American Institutional History (1971); Harry M. Ward, The Department of War, 1781–1795 (1962); and E. James Ferguson, The Power of the Purse: A History of American Public Finance, 1776–1790 (1961).

56. 1 Annals of Cong. 592 (June 25, 1789).

57. Id.

58. Id. at 592–93.

59. Id. at 594.

60. Id.

by striking the word "report" and inserting "prepare."[61] The bill that became law reflected that change: "it shall be the duty of the Secretary of the Treasury to digest and prepare plans for the improvement and management of the revenue, and for the support of the public credit; to prepare and report estimates of the public revenue, and the public expenditures."[62] The statute also required him to "make report, and give information to either branch of the legislature, in person or in writing (as he may be required), respecting all matters referred to him by the Senate or House of Representatives, or which shall appertain to his office."[63] Leonard White, a specialist in public administration, concluded that Hamilton played a significant role in drafting the bill.[64]

Relationships between Hamilton and Congress soured over the years. When he asked to come before Congress in 1792 to answer questions concerning the public debt, some lawmakers objected to the practice of mixing the two branches. They did not want the heads of departments to originate legislation or even voice an opinion that might influence Congress.[65] Attacks on Hamilton continued. A House resolution in 1793 claimed he had violated appropriation laws, ignored presidential instructions, failed to discharge essential duties, and committed an indecorum against the House.[66] On each count he was exonerated. A new charge in 1794, regarding a pension claim, was later dismissed by Congress as "wholly illiberal and groundless." Legislative investigations persisted until December 1794, when Hamilton announced his intention to resign.[67]

President Andrew Jackson's opposition to the Second U.S. Bank opened a new chapter in the struggle over the spending power. Congress often treated the Secretary of the Treasury as its agent, delegating to him—rather than the President—the responsibility for placing public funds either in the national bank or in state banks. Jackson wanted the funds deposited in state banks and had to remove two Secretaries of the Treasury before finding a third willing to carry out his orders. On March 28, 1834, the Senate passed a resolution censuring Jackson for assuming "upon himself authority and power not conferred by the Constitution and laws, but in derogation of both."[68] Senator Henry Clay led the attack on Jackson, arguing that "although the heads of the State, War, and Navy Department were emphatically the mouth-pieces of the President, yet the Treasury was one over which the control of Congress was complete, and therefore the President had no right to interpose his authority over the head of that department."[69]

Outraged that the Senate would censure him on the basis of unspecified charges and without an opportunity to defend himself, Jackson accused the Senate of violating the Constitution by charging him with an impeachable act without first waiting for the House to act: "Without notice, unheard and untried, I thus find myself charged on the records of the Senate, and in a form hitherto unknown in our history, with the high crime of violating the laws and Constitution of my

61. Id. at 604.

62. 1 Stat. 65, sec. 2 (1789).

63. Id. at 66; 1 Annals of Cong. 604, 607.

64. Leonard D. White, The Federalists: A Study in Administrative History, 1789–1801, at 118, n. 3 (1948).

65. Annals of Cong., 2d Cong., 1–2 Sess. 703–08 (Nov. 20, 1792).

66. Id. at 899–963 (Feb. 28 to March 1, 1793).

67. Annals of Cong., 3d Cong., 1–2 Sess. 458 (Feb. 19, 1794). Id. at 463–66 (Feb. 24, 1794) and 954 (Dec. 2, 1794); Louis Fisher, The Politics of Executive Privilege 11–13 (2004).

68. 1 Cong. Globe 271 (1834).

69. Id. at 269.

country.”[70] Jackson regarded the Secretary as "wholly an executive officer" subject to removal whenever the President was no longer willing to be responsible for his actions.[71] He regarded the safekeeping of public funds as an executive, not a legislative, responsibility.[72]

In the 1836 elections, Jacksonians gained a majority in the Senate and began a lengthy debate to expunge the censure resolution. They argued that the resolution was "irregularly and illegally adopted . . . in violation of the rights of defence which belongs to every citizen, and in subversion of the fundamental principles of law and justice." Jackson had been "adjudged and pronounced to be guilty of an impeachable offence, and a stigma placed upon him as a violator of his oath of office . . . without going through the forms of an impeachment, and without allowing to him the benefits of a trial, or the means of defence."[73] The vote to expunge, taken on January 16, 1837, was 24 to 19.[74]

In an article published in 2000, James C. Ho stated that the Senate "did not actually censure Jackson" and "did not condemn him with words of censure."[75] Yet this article acknowledges that the Senate resolved that Jackson "assumed upon himself authority and power not conferred by the constitution and laws, but in derogation of both."[76] According to this study, the Senate resolution "merely described what the President had done."[77] In fact, it condemned Jackson for acting in violation of both the Constitution and the law.

In 1840, the Whigs won the White House. President William Henry Harrison in his inaugural address of March 4, 1841, warned of the "unhallowed union of the Treasury with the executive department."[78] The essential difference between monarchy and the American presidency, he said, was the former's control over public finances. He believed it was "a great error" on the part of the Framers "not to have made the officer at the head of the Treasury Department entirely independent of the Executive."[79] Those Whiggish sentiments did not last long in the presidency. The next section covers the efforts of Presidents to review agency budget requests to Congress before that duty was formally placed upon them by the Budget and Accounting Act of 1921.


# 4. SUBMITTING A BUDGET

In budgetary circles, the year 1921 is often identified as a point of origin for presidential budgetary duties. In that year Congress passed the Budget and Accounting Act, directing the President to formulate and present a national budget. Congress created a Bureau of the Budget—later

---

70. 3 Richardson 1289 (April 15, 1834). See also 1292ff for further details on the impeachment argument.

71. Id. at 1301.

72. Id.

73. 13 Reg. of Debates, 24th Cong., 2d Sess. 380–81 (1837). Full debate: 380–417, 428–505.

74. Id. at 504; the vote is recorded at S. Journal, 24th Cong., 2d Sess. 123–24 (1837).

75. James C. Ho, *Misunderstood Precedent: Andrew Jackson and the Real Case Against Censure*, 24 Harv. J. L. & Public Pol. 282, 285 (2000).

76. Id.

77. Id.

78. 3 Richardson 1867 (March 4, 1841).

79. Id. at 1868.

the Office of Management and Budget—to provide technical assistance. Given this development, it might seem that Presidents and Treasury Secretaries had been largely bystanders from 1789 to 1921, passively forwarding budget estimates to Congress without revision or comment.[80] A closer look demonstrates that they were not so barren of leadership. Presidents and Treasury Secretaries took an active hand in revising agency budget estimates before they were sent to Congress.

Jefferson's Secretary of the Treasury, Albert Gallatin, demanded close scrutiny of budget estimates. His principal goals included reduction of the national debt and elimination of excise taxes.[81] Recommendations by Gallatin, who had previously served on the House Ways and Means Committee, were routinely accepted by the Cabinet and by Congress. John Randolph, chairman of the committee, was a close personal friend of Gallatin and helped control federal expenditures.[82] President Monroe complained on several occasions that Treasury reports were being sent to Congress without first being shared with him. Relationships with his Secretary of the Treasury, William Crawford, were severely strained.[83] President John Quincy Adams stayed well informed about budget estimates. When his Secretary of the Treasury pressed for reductions in departmental budget estimates to the lowest possible level, Adams recommended a little padding. Congressional committees felt an obligation to "retrench something from the estimates presented to them; and if some superfluity be not given them to lop off, they will cut into the very flesh of the public necessities."[84]

The financial panic of 1837 called for presidential leadership of the budget. President Van Buren's first annual message stated that the condition of the country made it necessary to keep budget estimates as low as possible. His last annual message, on December 5, 1840, referred to the need to reduce expenditures because of the recession.[85] As mentioned earlier, William Henry Harrison promoted a strict separation between the President and the Treasury. His successor, John Tyler, reiterated that sentiment:

> ...I deem it of the most essential importance that a complete separation should take place between the sword and the purse. No matter where or how the public moneys shall be deposited, so long as the President can exert the power of appointing and removing at his pleasure the agents selected for their custody the Commander in Chief of the Army and Navy is in fact the treasurer.[86]

Despite this plea for a complete separation between sword and purse, Tyler quickly discovered that the nation's business slump required executive leadership. His second annual message on December 6, 1842 stated that department heads had paid "every proper attention" to the

---

80. For that impression, see the works cited in FISHER, *supra* note 25, at 268–70.

81. 1 HENRY ADAMS, HISTORY OF THE UNITED STATES OF AMERICA 238–40 (1889–1891); 1 THE WRITINGS OF ALBERT GALLATIN 25 (Adams ed., 1879).

82. RAYMOND WALTERS, JR., ALBERT GALLATIN 148 (1957); 1 HENRY ADAMS, HISTORY OF THE UNITED STATES OF AMERICA 241–42, 272; 4 ADAMS, HISTORY OF THE UNITED STATES 156–67, 366–67; 6 id. at 126–27, 157–58; HENRY ADAMS, LIFE OF ALBERT GALLATIN 167–75 (1879).

83. 4 MEMOIRS OF JOHN QUINCY ADAMS 500–01 (Charles Francis Adams ed., 1874–1877); 6 id.439; 7 id. 81.

84. 7 id. 359. See also id. at 195, 247.

85. 4 Richardson 1554 (Sept. 4, 1837), id. at 1596 (Dec. 5, 1837), id. at 1826 (Dec. 5, 1840).

86. Id. at 1890–91 (April 9, 1841).

interest of the nation and that the "reduction in the annual expenditures of the Government already accomplished furnishes a sure evidence that economy in the application of the public moneys is regarded as a paramount duty."[87] A year later, reporting on the Navy, he told Congress that "every effort has been and will continue to be made to retrench all superfluities and lop off all excrescences which from time to time may have grown up."[88]

Executive budget leadership increased in 1844 with the election of James K. Polk as President. Drawing upon his legislative experience as chairman of the House Ways and Means Committee, he participated actively in exercising control over agency estimates and the level of federal expenditures. He directed his Cabinet to pay close attention to the estimates submitted by bureau chiefs, who were "favourable to large expenditures, and in some instances included objects which were unconstitutional, especially in regard to internal improvements."[89] Polk reviewed agency estimates with Cabinet members and even with bureau chiefs. If budget cuts by his Cabinet seemed insufficient, he intervened to reduce items or eliminate them altogether.[90]

In the years following the Civil War, some Presidents developed a reputation as guardians of the purse, especially when compared to Congress. In vetoing a rivers and harbors bill in 1882, President Arthur explained the peculiar deficiency of this kind of legislation. Citizens from one state, learning that public revenues were being spent for projects elsewhere, insisted on projects for themselves. "Thus," Arthur noted, "as the bill becomes more objectionable it secures more support."[91] After Congress overrode his veto, a cartoon by Thomas Nast showed the President armed with a rifle, watching an oversized vulture perched upon the Capitol, consuming his veto message. The bottom of the cartoon supplied words of encouragement: "President Arthur, hit him again! Don't let the vulture become our national bird."[92]

Another drain on the Treasury came from the military pension system. Fraudulent claims followed the Revolutionary War and the War of 1812, but the full measure of chicanery by pension claimants and their agents emerged after the Civil War. Federal outlays for military pensions rose from $29 million in 1870 to $139 million at the turn of the century.[93] Veterans met slight resistance from Congress. During the first term of President Cleveland, from 1885 to 1889, he vetoed 414 bills (304 regular vetoes and 110 pocket vetoes)—more than twice the number of all vetoes before him. A full 345 of the vetoes were leveled at private and general pension bills.[94] On a single day in 1886 Cleveland received nearly 240 private bills granting new pensions, increasing their benefits, or restoring old names to the list. Some disabilities existed before the claimant's enlistment to military service; others were not incurred in the line of duty; still others had their origin after discharge.[95]

---

87. 5 Richardson 2056 (Dec. 6, 1842).

88. Id. at 2122 (Dec. 1843).

89. 1 The Diary of James K. Polk 48 (Quaife ed., 4 vols., 1910).

90. 3 id. 213–21; 4 id. 165–81.

91. 10 Richardson 4708 (Aug. 1, 1882).

92. *Harper's Weekly*, Aug. 12, 1882.

93. William H. Glasson, Federal Military Pensions in the United States 123 (1918). For references to earlier pension frauds, see Leonard D. White, The Jacksonians 413 (1954); Talcott Powell, Tattered Banners (1933); and 17 Cong. Rec. 7764–65 (1886).

94. Presidential Vetoes, 1789–1988, compiled by the Senate Library 65–137 (1992).

95. 10 Richardson 5001–02 (May 8, 1886).

Cleveland's veto messages earned a reputation for their sarcastic quality. One claimant, who enrolled in the Army on March 25, 1865, entered a post hospital a week later with the measles. He returned to duty on May 8 before being mustered out of the service three days later. Cleveland observed that 15 years after this "brilliant service and this terrific encounter with the measles," the claimant discovered that the measles somehow affected his eyes and spinal column. Cleveland found no merit to the claim. He bristled at another pension request from a widow whose husband had joined the service but deserted several days later. "Those who prosecute claims for pension," he said, "have grown very bold when cases of this description are presented for consideration."[96] A Thomas Nast cartoon captures Cleveland in his role as protector of the purse. He is shown manfully blocking the door to the Treasury while thwarted pension agents slink from his presence.[97]

# 5. BUDGET AND ACCOUNTING ACT

Federal expenditures increased sharply at the end of the nineteenth century. On top of pension bills and rivers and harbors projects, outlays rose because of the Spanish-American War and construction of the Panama Canal. After 28 uninterrupted years of budget surpluses, from 1866 to 1903, the nation encountered deficits for the next six years. Congress initiated a number of inquiries into work methods of the executive departments, including the Cockrell Committee (1887–1889) and the Cockrell-Dockery Commission (1893–1895). In 1905, President Roosevelt appointed the Keep Commission to determine how the executive branch might more efficiently conduct its business. President Taft in 1910 secured $100,000 from Congress to set up a five-member Commission on Economy and Efficiency. Those initiatives are discussed in Chapter 3, section 12.

In June 1912, Taft submitted to Congress the Commission's proposals for a national budget. The President would be made responsible for reviewing departmental estimates and organizing them into a coherent document. The Commission concluded that the budget was the "only effective means whereby *the Executive* may be made responsible for getting before the country a definite, well-considered, comprehensive program with respect to which *the legislature* must also assume responsibility either for action or inaction."[98] Several factors blocked action on Taft's proposals. Passage of the Sixteenth Amendment, proposed in 1909 and ratified in 1913, promised larger revenues from an income tax. It took the financial shock of expenditures for World War I to precipitate action on budget reform. The war pushed federal expenditures to record levels—from about $700 million before the war to upwards of $12.7 billion and $18.5 billion by 1918 and 1919. Deficits reached unprecedented magnitudes. The total national debt, slightly over one billion in 1916, soared beyond $25 billion by 1919. Debt management problems after

---

96. Claimant with measles: id. at 5028 (June 23, 1886); deserter: id. at 5033–34 (June 23, 1886).

97. *Harper's Weekly*, July 3, 1886, at 421. The merits of Cleveland's pension vetoes are evaluated by EDWARD CAMPBELL MASON, THE VETO POWER 87–93 (1890).

98. *The Need for a National Budget*, H. Doc. 854, 62d Cong., 2d Sess. 138 (1912) (emphases in original).

the war called for modernization of the budget process and an increased financial responsibility for the executive branch.

Several reform proposals placed the President in a superior position. John J. Fitzgerald, chairman of the House Appropriations Committee, met with the New York constitutional convention in 1915 to discuss changes in national budgeting. He supported a process that made it as difficult as possible for lawmakers to increase estimates submitted by the President. He believed it was necessary to prohibit Congress from appropriating any funds "unless it had been requested by the head of the department, unless by a two-thirds vote, or unless it was to pay a claim against the government or for its own expenses."[99]

An article by Charles Wallace Collins, published in 1916, advocated adoption of the British parliamentary system. "Our institutions," he argued, "being more nearly akin to those of England, it is to the English budget system that we more naturally look for the purpose of illustration."[100] He noted that the British Parliament had long ago yielded the initiative in financial legislation to the Cabinet. The budget in England was generally ratified as introduced by executive officials. To Collins, an essential feature of a national budget system in America was "the relinquishing of the initiative in financial legislation to the executive by the Congress."[101] The President would "possess the functions of a Prime Minister in relation to public finance" by taking responsibility for preparation of the budget.[102] Congress would surrender its power to amend the presidential budget "by way of increasing any item in the budget, and also its power to introduce any bill making a charge upon the Treasury, without the consent of the executive."[103]

In March 1918, Representative Medill McCormick introduced a number of bills and resolutions calling for unification of agency estimates by the Secretary of the Treasury, creation of a House budget committee to replace the Committees on Appropriations and Ways and Means, establishment of an independent audit of departmental accounts, and reorganization of the Treasury Department. The budget committee would have jurisdiction over both appropriations and revenue, with power to reduce but not add, unless requested by the Secretary of the Treasury upon the President's authority, or unless the committee could muster a two-thirds majority. Members of the House would not be permitted to add to the budget on the floor, except to restore what the President had originally submitted. This budget system, heavily dependent on the British model of parliamentary government, largely subordinated Congress to the President and the Secretary of the Treasury.[104]

William McAdoo, President Wilson's first Secretary of the Treasury, recommended a budget system to prohibit Congress from increasing the President's requests: "Let us be honest with ourselves and honest with the American people. A budget which does not cover the initiation or increase of appropriations by Congress will be a semblance of the real thing."[105] When Secretary

---

99. *Budget Systems*, Municipal Research, No. 62 (June 1915), at 312, 322, 327, 340. See also William Franklin Willoughby, The Problem of a National Budget 146–49 (1918).

100. Charles Wallace Collins, *Constitutional Aspects of a National Budget System*, 25 Yale L.J. 376, 376 (1916).

101. Id. at 380.

102. Id.

103. Id.

104. *Plan for a National Budget System*, H. Doc. No. 1006, 65th Cong., 2d Sess. (1918).

105. *Annual Report of the Secretary of the Treasury*, 1918–19, at 121 (from his testimony of Oct. 4, 1919, to the House Select Committee on the Budget).

of the Treasury Carter Glass submitted budget estimates in 1919, he said that the budget "as thus prepared for the President and on his responsibility should not, as such, be increased by the Congress."[106] David Houston, the next Secretary of the Treasury, urged Congress in 1920 not to add to the President's budget unless recommended by the Secretary of the Treasury or approved by a two-thirds majority.[107]

Critics of this executive-centered model considered it a diminution of the congressional power of the purse and a threat to republican government. "Uncle Joe" Cannon, Speaker of the House from 1903 to 1911, warned that if Congress consented to an executive budget "it will have surrendered the most important part of a representative government."[108] His advice: "I think we had better stick pretty close to the Constitution with its division of powers well defined and the taxing power close to the people."[109] Edward Fitzpatrick, author of a budget study in 1918, described the British budget model as a step toward autocracy and a Prussian-style military state.[110]

In June 1919, the House passed a resolution to create a Select Committee on the Budget. Its report criticized the lack of internal executive checks on departmental estimates: "The estimates are a patchwork and not a structure. As a result, a great deal of the time of the committees of Congress is taken up in exploding the visionary schemes of bureau chiefs for which no administration would be willing to stand responsible."[111] Economy and efficiency, said the committee, could be secured only by making an officer responsible for receiving and scrutinizing requests for funds by bureau and departmental chiefs: "In the National Government there can be no question but that the officer upon whom should be placed this responsibility is the President of the United States."[112] A newly created Bureau of the Budget would provide technical assistance to the President.

The bill that passed the House on October 21, 1919, did not provide for an "executive budget" patterned after the British model. It was executive only in the sense that the President became responsible for the estimates. It was legislative thereafter, giving Congress full power to increase or reduce the estimates. Increases could be made in committee or on the floor by simple majority vote, not the two-thirds margin earlier proposed by some reformers and certainly not by requiring Congress to seek permission from the President and the Secretary of the Treasury. The report from the House Select Committee on the Budget set forth its constitutional principles: "The budget under this plan will be an Executive budget only to the extent that the Executive initiates the budget. It is a congressional budget after it has been considered and acted upon by Congress. The responsibility of the Executive and Congress will be clearly defined, and each branch will be held to a strict accountability for the part it has played."[113]

President Wilson vetoed the bill because it provided for removal of the Comptroller General and Assistant Comptroller General by concurrent resolution, a measure that requires approval by both houses but is not submitted to the President for his signature or veto. Wilson regarded

---

106. Id. at 117.

107. David Houston, Eight Years with Wilson's Cabinet 88 (1926).

108. *The National Budget*, H. Doc. No. 264, 66th Cong., 1st Sess. 28 (1919).

109. Id. at 28–29.

110. Edward Fitzpatrick, Budget Making in a Democracy viii–ix, 117 (1918).

111. H. Rep. No. 362, 66th Cong., 1st Sess. 4 (1919).

112. Id. at 5.

113. *National Budget System*, H. Rep. No. 362, 66th Cong., 1st Sess. 7 (1919).

the removal power as an "essential incident" to the appointing power of the President.[114] The House vote to override the veto was 178 to 103, short of the necessary two-thirds.[115] Congress passed a new bill early in 1921, signed into law by President Harding. The bill created a Bureau of the Budget to be located in the Treasury Department. Removal of the Comptroller General and Assistant Comptroller would be by joint resolution, requiring action by both houses and submission of the resolution to the President. To protect the independence of the legislative and judicial branches, estimates for Congress and the Supreme Court were to be included in the President's budget "without revision."[116]

# 6. IMPOUNDING FUNDS

From the days of George Washington forward, Presidents were not required to spend every dollar that Congress appropriated. Some appropriation accounts were purely discretionary, such as contingency funds. Presidents had no obligation to spend all the money. A highly publicized account, cited by the Nixon administration to justify its impoundment policy, was the decision by President Jefferson in 1803 to withhold $50,000 for gunboats. However, there was no dispute with Congress. He explained to lawmakers that the Louisiana Purchase made it unnecessary to immediately spend the money. He took time to study the most recent models of gunboats and informed Congress when he was proceeding with the program.[117]

As Attorney General Harmon noted in 1896, an appropriation was not mandatory "to the extent that you are bound to expend the full amount if the work can be done for less…."[118] These decisions were routine managerial functions, in no sense representing a threat to legislative prerogatives. Federal courts recognized that "the head of an executive department of the government, in the administration of the various and important concerns of his office, is continually required to exercise judgment and discretion."[119] The Supreme Court observed in 1840 that judicial interference "with the performance of the ordinary duties of the executive departments of the government, would be productive of nothing but mischief; and we are quite satisfied that such a power was never intended to be given them."[120]

Some impoundments encroached on the ability of Congress to set national policy and decide budget priorities. House Appropriations chairman George Mahon observed in 1949 that members of Congress did not object to any reasonable economies in government: "But economy

---

114. H. Doc. No. 805, 66th Cong., 2d Sess. 2 (1920).

115. 59 Cong. Rec. 8609–14 (1920).

116. 42 Stat. 20, sec. 201(a) (1921).

117. 1 Richardson 348, 360. For discussion of the historical background to Jefferson's action, see the study by Joseph Cooper placed in *Impoundment of Appropriated Funds by the President*, joint hearings before the Senate Committee on Government Operations and the Senate Committee on the Judiciary, 93d Cong., 1st Sess. 676-77 (1973) (hereafter Ervin hearings).

118. 21 Op. Att'y Gen. 414, 415 (1896); similar statements appear at 21 Op. Att'y Gen. 391, 392 (1896) and 21 Op. Att'y Gen. 420, 422 (1896).

119. Brashear v. Mason, 47 U.S. (6 How.) 92, 102 (1848).

120. Decatur v. Paulding, 39 U.S. (14 Pet.) 497, 516 (1840).

is one thing, and the abandonment of a policy and program of the Congress another thing."[121] From 1940 through the 1960s, Presidents collided with Congress by refusing to spend appropriated funds. On January 3, 1941, President Roosevelt in his budget message announced the postponement of construction projects that would interfere with the defense program.[122] President Truman impounded Air Force funds and canceled a supercarrier.[123] Many of these impoundments and subsequent withholdings of funds affected military programs.[124] Impoundments continued during the Eisenhower, Kennedy, and Johnson administrations.[125] In each case the political system made the necessary political accommodations. A constitutional crisis did not emerge. There was no need for litigation.

Matters changed dramatically with the Nixon administration.[126] During a news conference on January 31, 1973, President Nixon asserted that the "constitutional right for the President of the United States to impound funds—and that is not to spend money, when the spending of money would mean either increasing prices or increasing taxes for all the people—that right is absolutely clear."[127] He vowed not to spend money "if the Congress overspends."[128] Officials in his administration claimed that impoundment was consistent with the President's "constitutional authority in the area of foreign affairs, his role as Commander in Chief, and his constitutional duty to 'take care that the laws be faithfully executed.'"[129] They further maintained that impoundment was authorized by the constitutional provisions that vest the executive power with the President.[130]

Deputy Attorney General Joseph Sneed doubted whether Congress could legislate against impoundment even in the domestic area: "To admit the existence of such power deprives the President of a substantial portion of the 'executive power' vested in him by the Constitution...."[131] With regard to national defense and foreign relations, he argued that the President's constitutional powers to impound funds find their source not only in the Take Care Clause and his "express status as Commander-in-Chief" but as the "sole organ of the Nation in the conduct of its foreign affairs."[132] Misconceptions about the sole-organ doctrine are addressed in Chapter 7, section 1B.

Officials in the Nixon administration cited Jefferson's withholding of funds for gunboats as a guiding precedent. Questioned by a Senate committee on impoundment actions, HUD

---

121. 95 Cong. Rec. 14922 (1949).

122. J.D. Williams, The Impounding of Funds by the Bureau of the Budget, Inter-University Case Program #28 5, 8–20 (1955).

123. Louis Fisher, The Politics of Impounded Funds, 15 Adm. Sci. Q. 361, 366–68 (1970).

124. Roy E. Brownell II, The Constitutional Status of the President's Impoundment of National Security Funds, 12 Seton Hall Const. L.J. 1 (2001).

125. Fisher, supra note 123, at 368–69, 370–72.

126. Louis Fisher, Funds Impounded by the President: The Constitutional Issue, 38 G.W. L. Rev. 124 (1969); Louis Fisher, Impounded Funds: Uses and Abuses, 23 Buff. L. Rev. 141 (1973); and James P. Pfiffner, The President, the Budget, and Congress: Impoundment and the 1974 Budget Act (1979).

127. Public Papers of the Presidents, 1973, at 62.

128. Id.

129. Testimony by OMB Director Roy Ash, Ervin hearings, supra note 117, at 271.

130. Id. at 270, 272.

131. Id. at 369.

132. Id.

Secretary George Romney replied: "I guess Thomas Jefferson started this."[133] OMB Director Casper Weinberger told another Senate committee that it all started "in the days of Thomas Jefferson. Every President since Thomas Jefferson has done precisely the same thing...." After sharing some statistics with the committee, Weinberger claimed that "we are doing not only nothing different than any other President since Thomas Jefferson has done; we are doing it in no greater degree."[134] The differences between the actions of Jefferson and Nixon were worlds apart. Jefferson, after explaining to Congress how circumstances had changed, delayed spending money but eventually purchased gunboats to carry out statutory policy. Nixon claimed the constitutional right to cut programs in half and eliminate them altogether. The severity of those reductions prompted about 80 lawsuits, with the administration losing almost all of them.[135]

Before discussing some of those cases, it is appropriate to note that President Nixon was not using impoundment merely to combat inflation and avoid public debt. In announcing plans to cut research health grants, Model Cities funds, grants for urban renewal, and funds for the clean-water program, he sponsored such costly projects as the supersonic transport, a manned landing on Mars, general revenue sharing, a larger Merchant Marine fleet, and the Safeguard Anti-ballistic Missile (ABM) system. Impoundment was thus a means of shifting spending from congressional priorities to executive priorities.

During December 1972, the Nixon administration ordered wholesale reductions in farm programs, including the $225.5 million Rural Environmental Assistance Program (REAP) and the $10 million Water Bank Program. It terminated the disaster loan program of the Farmers Home Administration, the rural electrification program, and the water and sewer grant program. The legal justification for terminating and curtailing those programs: they had been *authorized* by Congress but not *mandated*. Under that legal theory, unless Congress stripped the executive branch of all discretion and flexibility, statutory programs could be axed. The response by Congress was predictable. It began rewriting laws to make them mandatory.[136] A district court, after reviewing the actions of Secretary of Agriculture Earl Butz, declared that he had acted in excess of his authority, violated several regulations promulgated by his agency, and conducted himself in a manner that was arbitrary and capricious.[137] In another case, a district court held that Butz lacked statutory authority to terminate a direct loan program and use those funds for a different loan program favored by the administration.[138] In 1974, a district court ruled that the Secretary of HUD had an "affirmative obligation" to administer a water and sewer grant program. While discretion existed there was no statutory authority to entirely suspend the program. The Secretary's failure to carry out the program constituted an "abuse of discretion."[139]

133. *Department of Housing and Urban Development; Space, Science, Veterans, and Certain Other Independent Agencies Appropriations, Fiscal Year 1973*, hearings before the Senate Committee on Appropriations, 93d Cong., 2d Sess. 565 (1972).

134. *Caspar W. Weinberger to Be Secretary of Health, Education, and Welfare* (Part 1), hearings before the Senate Committee on Labor and Public Welfare, 93d Cong., 1st Sess. 29 (1973).

135. FISHER, *supra* note 25, at 175–201.

136. Id. at 171–84.

137. Berends v. Butz, 357 F. Supp. 143, 148 (D. Minn. 1973).

138. Sioux Valley Empire Electric Association v. Butz. 367 F. Supp. 686 (D.S.D. 1973).

139. Rooney v. Lynn, Civil Action No. 201-73 (D.D.C. 1974). See Nile Stanton, *History and Practice of Executive Impoundment of Appropriated Funds*, 53 NEB. L. REV. 1 (1974); Louis Fisher, *Impoundment of Funds: Uses and Abuses*, 23 BUFF. L. REV. 141 (1973); Nile Stanton, *The Presidency and the Purse: Impoundment 1803–1973*, 45 U. COLO. L. REV. 25 (1973).

Impoundment of funds for the clean-water program reached the Supreme Court. Congress provided $18 billion in contract authority over a three-year period to provide for waste treatment. The statute provided for administrative flexibility. For each year, the dollar amounts were described as "not to exceed." They were thus ceilings rather than mandatory levels for obligation and expenditure. Instead of using this flexibility to implement the program within a scheduled period of time, Nixon cut it in half.[140] Federal courts had to decide whether a statutory commitment existed. If it did, could the President use impoundment to undermine that commitment?

A number of federal courts concluded that although some discretion existed as to final expenditures, the statute required the administration to make full allotments to the states to assure them of federal funding.[141] On February 18, 1975, the Supreme Court ruled that the Clean Water Act required *full* allotment. A unanimous Court decided that the addition of phrases such as "not to exceed" did not alter the "entire complexion and thrust of the Act." The statute was intended to provide a firm commitment of substantial sums within a fixed period of time.[142]

These decisions, combined with congressional hearings, committee studies, and floor debate, discredited the legal and constitutional arguments offered by the Nixon administration. Both houses worked on impoundment control bills. Instead of passing legislation to deal specifically with this issue, lawmakers decided to add impoundment as one title of a much larger package: the Budget Act of 1974. The impoundment title has been effective in curbing executive abuses. The rest of the statute, by weakening presidential responsibility under the 1921 act, produced even less capacity to control deficits.

# 7. BUDGET ACT OF 1974

In 1972, President Nixon blamed Congress for the level of federal deficits. He said they resulted from the "hoary and traditional procedure of the Congress, which now permits action on the various spending programs as if they were unrelated and independent actions."[143] Because of its decentralized process, he explained, Congress "arrives at total Federal spending in an accidental, haphazard manner."[144] Yet lawmakers were regularly informed of the larger picture by

---

140. FISHER, *supra* note 25, at 184–89.

141. City of New York v. Ruckelshaus, 358 F. Supp. 669 (D.D.C. 1973); City of New York v. Train, 494 F.2d 1033, 1042 (D.C. Cir. 1974); Minnesota v. Fri, No. 4-73 Civ. 133 (D. Minn. 1973); Florida v. Train, Civ. No. 73-156 (N.D. Fla. 1974); Texas v. Ruckelshaus, C.A. No. A-73-CA-38 (W.D. Tex. 1973); Martin-Trigona v. Ruckelshaus, No. 72-C-3044 (N.D. Ill. 1973); Ohio v. Environmental Protection Agency, Nos. C73-1061 and C74-104 (N.D. Ohio 1974); Maine v. Train, No. 14-51 (D. Maine 1974). The nearest the administration came to "victory" in these clean-water cases was a decision by Judge Hauk in California, who dismissed the case for reasons of standing. In dicta he indicated that the statute "does not require that the EPA allot every authorized dollar." Brown v. Ruckelshaus, 364 F. Supp. 258, 266 (D. Cal. 1973).

142. Train v. City of New York, 420 U.S. 35 (1975). Other legislative action and litigation on Nixon impoundments appear in FISHER, *supra* note 25, at 175–201. See also *Court Challenges to Executive Branch Impoundments of Appropriated Funds*, Special Report of the Joint Committee on Congressional Operations, 93d Cong., 2d Sess. (committee print, 1974), cumulative to March 15, 1974.

143. PUBLIC PAPERS OF THE PRESIDENTS, 1972, at 742.

144. Id.

their Joint Committee on Reduction of Federal Expenditures. "Scorekeeping reports," printed in the *Congressional Record* from month to month, told members of Congress how congressional actions compared to the President's budget. The results revealed a systematic and responsible pattern, not chaos. Congressional totals generally remained within the President's budget aggregates.

The premise of legislative irresponsibility led to the creation of a Joint Study Committee on Budget Control. In its final report of April 18, 1973, the joint committee basically agreed with Nixon that the increasing size of budget deficits resulted from congressional deficiencies: "The constant continuation of deficits plus their increasing size illustrates the need for Congress to obtain better control over the budget. The Joint Study Committee has concluded that the failure to arrive at congressional budget decisions on an overall basis has been a contributory factor in this picture."[145]

As to the source of those deficits, statistics in the committee report did not support its claim of legislative irresponsibility. In pointing out that the federal budget had been in a deficit position 37 times since 1920, the report acknowledged that in 32 of those years Presidents submitted budgets to Congress with a deficit.[146] For the Nixon years, table 6 in the report showed the net effect of congressional action on the deficit was near zero. From fiscal years 1969 through 1973, Congress reduced Nixon's appropriation requests by $30.9 billion.[147] During that same period, it increased spending authority on legislative bills (backdoor spending and mandatory programs) by $30.5 billion.[148] As for actual outlays, table 6 indicated that Congress had added $6.8 billion to the deficit over the five-year period. However, the total deficit over that period exceeded $100 billion. The problem was not solely legislative action; high deficits were regularly incorporated in budgets submitted to Congress. What was missing was a responsible presidential budget promised by the 1921 statute.

Each house drafted legislation to control presidential impoundment. The general idea was to divide impoundments into two categories: "rescissions" (actions to terminate funds) and "deferrals" (proposals to delay spending). Lawmakers agreed to prohibit Presidents from canceling a program unless Congress specifically approved by statute. The President would have to submit a rescission proposal to Congress and have it approved within a designated period of days. Congress could ignore the request if it so chose. Legislative inaction required the funds to be spent. For deferrals, lawmakers agreed that Congress could disapprove by something short of a public law. The choice was a one-house veto.[149] Members of Congress worried that action on a separate impoundment bill would be interpreted as pro-spending because its purpose was to release impounded funds to be spent. In 1974, an election year, lawmakers wanted impoundment

---

145. H. Rep. No. 93-147, 93d Cong., 1st Sess. 1 (1973).

146. Id. at 7. Detailed statistics from the committee report appear in Louis Fisher, *Congress, the Executive and the Budget*, 411 THE ANNALS 102, 105 (1974).

147. H. Rep. No. 93-147, *supra* note 145, at 39.

148. Id.

149. 88 Stat. 297, 334–35, sec. 1013 (1974). The Supreme Court's decision in *INS v. Chadha* (1983), striking down the legislative veto, invalidated the one-house veto for deferrals. The D.C. Circuit determined that the one-house veto was tied inextricably to the deferral authority. If one fell, so did the other. The President's authority to make policy deferrals thus disappeared. Only routine, non-policy deferrals are permitted. Congress promptly converted the judicial ruling into statutory policy. City of New Haven, Conn. v. United States, 809 F.2d 900 (D.C. Cir. 1987); 101 Stat. 785, sec. 206 (1987).

control combined with legislation that promised control over spending and deficits. As a result, impoundment control became Title X of the Budget Act of 1974.

The nine other titles radically revamped congressional procedures. Congress created budget committees in each house and directed them to draft budget resolutions to set totals for aggregates: total spending, total revenues, and the resulting deficit or surplus. The budget resolution divided spending into broad functional categories such as national defense, agriculture, transportation, and other sectors. The objective was to facilitate debate on budget priorities. The statute established a new Congressional Budget Office (CBO) to provide analytical support to lawmakers.[150]

The 1974 statute assumed that members of Congress would behave more responsibly if they voted on budget aggregates, facing up to totals rather than voting in "piecemeal" fashion on separate authorization, appropriation, and revenue bills. One result of this statute was to weaken the central purpose of the 1921 statute: to place a personal and nondelegable duty on the President to prepare a responsible budget, particularly with regard to aggregates. The 1974 statute generated multiple budgets: one submitted by the President, the House budget resolution, the Senate budget resolution, and the final resolution agreed to by both chambers. From 1921 to 1974, the President's budget provided a fixed and visible benchmark, making it easy for the public to know if congressional action was above or below the President's estimates. That reference point disappeared in 1974. Instead of keeping within the President's aggregates, lawmakers could vote on generous ceilings in budget resolutions and tell their constituents they had "stayed within the budget," even if their actions exceeded the President's budget.

When Representative Tom Steed managed an appropriation bill for fiscal 1977, he explained: "Although we are over the President's budget, we are under the legislative budget.... [T]his particular bill will be well within the limits set by the Committee on the Budget."[151] In 1983, after lawmakers asked whether a pending bill was below or above budget, House Majority Leader Jim Wright assured them: "This bill is not over the budget; the amounts proposed in this amendment are well within budgeted figures. The amounts that we have agreed to and have discussed are not in excess of the congressional budget resolution. That, of course, is the budget." He admitted, however, that the amounts might exceed the President's budget, but "that, of course, is not the budget. Congress makes the budget; the President does not."[152]

President Reagan was more than willing to step aside and let Congress make the budget. He found many political benefits to the new procedure. In 1985, he announced his acceptance of appropriations bills "even if above my budget, that were within the limits set by Congress's own budget resolution."[153] If Presidents ducked their duty under the 1921 statute to present a responsible budget and submitted one with high deficits, Congress was institutionally incapable of converting an irresponsible presidential budget to a responsible one. To do so would require drastic cuts in spending and sharp increases in taxes. Politically that was extremely unlikely.

---

150. 88 Stat. 297 (1974). For excellent analyses of this statute, see PHILIP G. JOYCE, THE CONGRESSIONAL BUDGET OFFICE: HONEST NUMBERS, POWER, AND POLICYMAKING (2011); ALLEN SCHICK, CONGRESS AND MONEY: BUDGETING, SPENDING, AND TAXING (1980); JAMES P. PFIFFNER, THE PRESIDENT, THE BUDGET, AND CONGRESS: IMPOUNDMENT AND THE 1974 BUDGET ACT (1979); and JOEL HAVEMANN, CONGRESS AND THE BUDGET (1978).

151. 122 CONG. REC. 17843 (1976).

152. 129 CONG. REC. 25417 (1983).

153. PUBLIC PAPERS OF THE PRESIDENTS, 1985, II, at 1401.

The 1974 statute also weakened the Appropriations Committees, which had previously functioned as guardian of the purse. It had been their custom to keep appropriations under the President's requests. Under the new procedure, they found it difficult to resist amendments for greater spending. If their draft bill fell below the amount allocated to them in a budget resolution, lawmakers would pressure the Appropriations Committees to spend "up to" the figure in the budget resolution. A chief clerk in an appropriations committee complained that spending limits in a budget resolution had been set at far too generous a level, forcing the committee to "spend up to the full budget allocation."[154] In 1979, Rep. Bob Giaimo as chairman of the House Budget Committee admitted that budget resolutions up to that time had given "a sizeable incremental funding increase, almost regardless of its effectiveness."[155]

Most budget reformers in 1974, including lawmakers and outside experts, believed that centralization of Congress was better than decentralization, comprehensive action superior to fragmentation, and large legislative vehicles (budget resolutions) more productive of responsible action than smaller vehicles. After seeing the damage done by the 1974 process, especially in the Reagan years, former CBO Director Rudolph Penner offered insightful analysis during a House hearing in 1990. He concluded that Congress operating under its former decentralized and informal system had been more coherent and responsible. Both elected branches performed reasonably well under the older and now discredited legislative process. He now observed: "I have always been struck by the fact in looking at the history of the [budget] process that it appeared chaotic in the late 19th century and early 20th century, but the results were very good in terms of budget discipline, yielding balanced budgets and surpluses most of the time, unless there was really a good reason to run a deficit." Although the 1974 statute created a process that "looks very elegant on paper," it had led to "very dishonest and disorderly results." He noted that those who criticized the Budget Act as "too complex and too time consuming, are right on the mark."[156]

# 8. REAGAN AND GRAMM-RUDMAN

Those who drafted the Budget Act of 1974 believed that centralizing the legislative process would strengthen Congress and weaken the President. The first year of the Reagan presidency proved them wrong. By attracting votes from conservative Democrats and loyal Republicans, President Reagan gained control of the budget resolution and used it to promote White House objectives: tax cuts, increased military spending, and reduction of some domestic programs. He used the reconciliation process, created by the 1974 statute, to ensure that spending and tax bills remained consistent with his budget resolution. The House Appropriations Committee explained how reconciliation played into the hands of the President: "It is much easier for the Executive Branch to gain support for its program when it is packaged in one bill rather than

---

154. Schick, *supra* note 150, at 313. See also Havemann, *supra* note 150, at 152–53.

155. 125 Cong. Rec. 9028 (1979).

156. *Budget Process Reform*, hearing before the House Committee on the Budget, 101st Cong., 2d Sess. 20–21 (1990).

pursuing each and every authorization and appropriation measure to insure [sic] compliance with the Executive's program. The device tends to aid the Executive Branch in gaining additional control over budget matters and to circumvent the will of Congress."[157]

The results of 1981 exposed serious weaknesses within Congress and the Budget Act. Instead of following CBO's projections or substituting an economic forecast of its own, Congress accepted the administration's flawed assumptions. The 1974 statute had been praised for giving Congress an independent analytical capacity. In 1981, however, it chose to embrace the President's false premises and calculations. When Reagan's theory of supply-side economics failed to generate anticipated revenues, the nation did not experience annual deficits of $25 billion, as during the Nixon years. They now exploded to more than $200 billion a year. The 1974 procedures, supposedly far better at dealing with budget aggregates, proved wholly ineffective.

Could the political and economic errors of 1981 have occurred without budget resolutions and the reconciliation process? Not likely. Reagan, as with any President, would have faced almost insurmountable hurdles had he presented his economic plan to a decentralized Congress. White House proposals would have undergone independent scrutiny by a series of committees and subcommittees, each one capable of substantially altering the President's budget. Incremental actions (or inactions) by a series of legislative actors would have fundamentally altered presidential objectives.[158]

The whole purpose of the 1974 statute was to force Congress to vote on an overall budget plan. If the White House gained control of that plan, the process would serve presidential ends. David Stockman, OMB Director from 1981 to 1985, explained how the centralized process created in 1974 furthered executive goals. The constitutional prerogatives of Congress "would have to be, in effect, suspended. Enacting the Reagan administration's economic program meant rubber stamp approval, nothing less. The world's so-called greatest deliberative body would have to be reduced to the status of a ministerial arm of the White House."[159] For Reagan's budget plan to succeed, Congress had to "forfeit its independence."[160] The effect of the Budget Act of 1974 was to replace the constitutional system of separation of powers and checks and balances with a British-style parliamentary government, with the executive branch very much in control.

The damage done by President Reagan and the 1974 budget process is evident in the deficits accumulated over his eight years. The total national debt from 1789 to 1981 stood at one trillion dollars when he entered office. It reflected various wars, fiscal crises, and the Great Depression over a period of almost two centuries. By the end of Reagan's first term the national debt had *doubled* to $2 trillion. Four years later, at the end of his second term, it climbed to $3 trillion. The architects of the 1974 statute thought they had build a process to control aggregates, especially deficits. What developed were a remarkable series of miscalculations: political, economic, institutional, and constitutional.

In this climate of uncontrolled deficits, the two branches decided in 1985 to make things much worse by passing the Gramm-Rudman-Hollings (GRH) statute. It was designed to control

---

157. *Views and Estimates on the Budget Proposed for Fiscal Year 1983*, House Committee on Appropriations, 97th Cong., 2d Sess. 12 (committee print, 1982).

158. Rudolph G. Penner, *An Appraisal of the Congressional Budget Process*, in ALLEN SCHICK, CRISIS IN THE BUDGET PROCESS 69 (1986), and Allen Schick, *How the Budget Was Won and Lost*, PRESIDENT AND CONGRESS: ASSESSING REAGAN'S FIRST YEAR 25 (Norman J. Ornstein ed., 1982).

159. DAVID A. STOCKMAN, THE TRIUMPH OF POLITICS: HOW THE REAGAN REVOLUTION FAILED 59 (1986).

160. Id. at 200.

deficits. It failed utterly in that regard. What Gramm-Rudman did was to announce, very plainly, that the 1974 process could not be counted on to handle budget aggregates and deficits. Gramm-Rudman established a statutory schedule to eliminate deficits by fiscal 1991. Beginning with a deficit of $171.9 billion for fiscal 1986, the deficit was supposed to decline by $36 billion a year over five years until it reached zero. The President with his budget and Congress with its budget resolutions were obliged to honor these statutory mandates. If in any fiscal year the projected deficit exceeded the statutory allowance by more than $10 billion, another mechanical solution kicked in. A "sequestration" process required across-the-board cuts to protect the statutory targets. Half of the reductions would come from national defense. Designated social programs were exempt from these automatic cuts.

Draft legislation relied on two congressional offices (CBO and GAO) to carry out what seemed clearly to be executive duties. One bill required the CBO and OMB Directors to estimate the levels of total revenues and budget outlays to determine whether the deficit for a particular year would exceed the statutory limit. These two agencies had to specify the degree to which agency spending had to be cut to eliminate the excess deficit.[161] Upon receiving the joint CBO-OMB report, it was the duty of the President to issue an order to eliminate the excess deficit. The President could exercise no discretion. It was his duty to sign his name to the sequestration order prepared by CBO and OBM.

The Senate held no hearings on the constitutionality of this process. The House Committee on Government Operations held a hearing on October 17, 1985. Comptroller General Charles Bowsher, OMB Director Jim Miller, and CBO Director Rudolph Penner testified but not did comment on constitutional issues. I was the fourth to testify and proceeded to state that the bill was unconstitutional because it gave CBO and GAO "substantive enforcement responsibilities."[162] My testimony relied in part on the Supreme Court's decision in *Buckley v. Valeo* (1976), which prohibited Congress from vesting substantive and enforcement responsibilities in legislative officers.[163]

The bill that emerged from conference committee authorized the Comptroller General to certify the results submitted by CBO and OMB. Senator Bob Packwood concluded that the addition of GAO, "which indeed is an executive agency…cures the allegation of unconstitutionality."[164] GAO is not an executive agency. It functions as a research and investigative arm of Congress. Instead of resolving the constitutional issue, Congress chose to punt to the judiciary. It authorized any member of Congress to adjudicate the question, following an expedited process that would begin with a three-judge court and go from there directly to the Supreme Court.[165]

The three-judge court held the delegation of executive powers to the Comptroller General to be unconstitutional and the Supreme Court affirmed.[166] Recognizing that the process was constitutionally vulnerable, Congress provided for a "fallback" procedure in the event the courts

161. *The Balanced Budget and Emergency Deficit Control Act of 1985*, hearing before the House Committee on Government Operations, 99th Cong., 1st Sess. 26–27 (1985).

162. Id. at 200. See also 198–200 and 207–12.

163. Buckley v. Valeo, 424 U.S. 1 (1976).

164. 131 Cong. Rec. 30274 (1985).

165. 99 Stat. 1098, sec. 274 (1985).

166. Synar v. United States, 626 F. Supp. 1374, 1391–93 (D.D.C. 1986) (three-judge court), aff'd, Bowsher v. Synar, 478 U.S. 714 (1986).

invalidated the statute. Under the substitute process, the OMB and CBO reports would go to a specially created Temporary Joint Committee on Deficit Reduction consisting of the full membership of both budget committees. The joint committee would report the sequestration bill for floor action, and, if passed by both houses, would go to the President to be signed or vetoed.

If Congress failed to pass the appropriations bills, the national government had to rely on stopgap continuing resolutions, creating further uncertainty in executive agencies. With the regular legislative process at a standstill, both branches decided to hold "budget summits" at the White House and other locations. The result: a further weakening of representative and democratic government. Many senior lawmakers from substantive committees were excluded from those summits and had no way to participate in "the normal give and take of congressional deliberations."[167] Those who did attend were likely to be congressional party leaders without the expertise and experience of committee members.

Gramm-Rudman allowed deficits to climb while the elected branches sought refuge in dishonest projections, budget manipulation, escapism, and new forms of accounting ingenuity. By focusing on a particular fiscal year to project a deficit result, the two branches could indulge in different types of budgetary games. Costs were shifted to the next year or even the previous one. Items could be moved off budget. Improbable estimates of higher revenue were devised to satisfy the projected deficit number even if they never materialized.[168]

Representative Marty Russo, member of the House Budget Committee, explained in 1990 how the two branches practiced deceit with budget deficits: "The President submits a budget that relies on very optimistic economic and technical assumptions and questionable savings proposals to meet the Gramm-Rudman deficit target. Congress attacks the assumptions and proposals as phony, but uses them in the budget resolution anyway."[169] Congress accepted the President's phony figures because honest figures (which were available) would have increased the projected deficit and made Congress look like the "big spender." Once the President ducked responsibility by submitting a deceptive budget, politics led Congress to embrace the same mistaken and misleading numbers.

Budget analyst Allen Schick summarized the result: "GRH started out as a process for reducing the deficit and has become a means of hiding the deficit and running away from responsibility."[170] Gramm-Rudman never met any of its deficit targets. When it became obvious that the targets could not be met, Congress enacted a revision in 1986 known as GRH II. It projected a deficit of zero by fiscal 1993. The actual deficit for that year: $255 billion.[171]

Presidents and Congresses continue to sidestep responsibility for federal deficits. The national debt, having jumped from $1 trillion to $3 trillion by the end of Reagan's presidency, climbed to $4 trillion after four years of President George H. W. Bush. A political settlement

167. Raphael Thelwell, *Gramm-Rudman-Hollings Four Years Later: A Dangerous Illusion*, 50 Pub. Admin. Rev. 190, 197 (1990).

168. *Budget Reform Proposals*, joint hearings before the Senate Committee on Governmental Affairs and the Budget, 101st Cong., 1st Sess. 3 (1989); Allen Schick, The Capacity to Budget 204 (1990).

169. *Budget Process Reform*, hearing before the House Committee on the Budget, 101st Cong., 2d Sess. 1 (1990).

170. Schick, *supra* note 168, at 205.

171. For analysis of the enactment and implementation of GRH, see Jasmine Farrier, Passing the Buck: Congress, the Budget, and Deficits 82–128 (2004).

during the Clinton years gave hope controlling deficits, even promising surpluses. The decision by President George W. Bush to fight two wars without paying for them, the economic collapse in 2008, and slow recovery under President Barack Obama pushed the national debt beyond $16 trillion. That story is pursued in the last section, but here it is necessary to turn to another budgetary issue that emerged under President Reagan. After Congress prohibited the use of any appropriated funds for rebels in Nicaragua, the Reagan administration decided to seek funds not from Congress but from private citizens and foreign governments. The scandal, known as Iran-Contra, came close to his impeachment, a threat that was alleviated in part when Reagan waived executive privilege to permit a full congressional investigation.

# 9. SEEKING OUTSIDE FUNDS: IRAN-CONTRA

Beginning in 1982, Congress adopted statutory provisions to restrict the Reagan administration's effort to support the Contra resistance in Nicaragua. Executive officials hoped the rebel force would overthrow the Sandinista government. Despite imposing statutory restrictions, Congress learned that the administration continued to supply various forms of assistance. Some executive officials believed it was impermissible for Congress to use funding restrictions to limit the President's constitutional powers over foreign policy. That attitude led the administration to consciously violate statutory limitations and destroy documents.[172]

There was nothing novel about Congress using its power of the purse to control foreign policy.[173] Even in recent years, officials in the Reagan administration could recall that Congress adopted the Cooper-Church Amendment in 1971 to prohibit the use of any funds to introduce U.S. ground combat troops into Cambodia.[174] In 1973, Congress cut off all funds for military operations in Southeast Asia.[175] Three years later, with the Clark Amendment, Congress prohibited all U.S. assistance for conducting military or paramilitary operations in Angola.[176]

## A. The Boland amendments

In response to Reagan administration policy in Nicaragua, Congress added language to a continuing resolution in 1982 to prohibit the CIA and the Defense Department from furnishing

---

172. A valuable compilation of facts and documents on Iran-Contra was compiled by the National Security Archive to assist Congress and the Iran-Contra special prosecutor. THE CHRONOLOGY: THE DOCUMENTED DAY-BY-DAY ACCOUNT OF THE SECRET MILITARY ASSISTANCE TO IRAN AND THE CONTRAS (1987).

173. Thomas A. Balmer, *The Use of Conditions in Foreign Relations Legislation*, 7 DENVER J. INT'L L. & POLICY 197 (1978); Michael J. Glennon, *Strengthening the War Powers Resolution: The Case for Purse-Strings Restrictions*, 60 MINN. L. REV. 1 (1975); Garry J. Wooters, *The Appropriations Power as a Tool of Congressional Foreign Policy Making*, 50 BOSTON U. L. REV. 34 (1970); and Eli E. Nobleman, *Financial Aspects of Congressional Participation in Foreign Relations*, 289 THE ANNALS 145 (1953).

174. 84 Stat. 1942, 1953, sec. 7(a) (1971).

175. 87 Stat. 99, 129, sec. 307 (1973); 87 Stat. 130, 134, sec. 108 (1973).

176. 90 Stat. 729, 757, sec. 404 (1976).

military equipment, military training or advice, or other support for military activities "to any group or individual, not part of a country's armed forces, for the purpose of overthrowing the Government of Nicaragua or provoking a military exchange between Nicaragua and Honduras."[177] A House report issued on May 13, 1983, described the statutory curb as ineffective. The insurgents in Nicaragua "openly acknowledged" their goal of overthrowing the Sandinistas and provoking a "military confrontation."[178] Congress discovered early in 1984 that the administration, operating through the CIA, had mined the harbors of Nicaragua. It passed statutory language specifically prohibiting that activity.[179]

In response to this pattern of executive officials skirting statutory limitations, Congress decided on October 12, 1984, to adopt strict language to prohibit any kind of U.S. military assistance to the Contras. The statutory language (at times referred to as Boland II) was meant to put a halt to further evasion and circumvention by the executive branch:

> During fiscal year 1985, no funds available to the Central Intelligence Agency, the Department of Defense, or any other agency or entity of the United States involved in intelligence activities may be obligated or expended for the purpose or which would have the effect of supporting, directly or indirectly, military or paramilitary operations in Nicaragua by any nation, group, organization, movement, or individual.[180]

Congress drafted this elaborate language to prevent the administration from continuing to evade statutory policy. With this provision, Congress intended to close all further executive efforts to ignore legislative intent. Senator Christopher Dodd suspected in early 1985 that the administration might still be finding ways to assist the Contras. During Senate hearings, he spoke about rumors and newspaper stories that the administration might try the fund the Contras "through private groups or through funneling funds through friendly third nations, or possibly through a new category of assistance and asking the Congress to fund the program openly."[181] Ambassador Langhorne Motley, appearing as the administration's spokesman, assured Dodd that the executive branch understood the meaning of Boland II and had no intention of trying to evade it with tricks: "Nobody is trying to play games with you or any other Member of Congress. That resolution stands, and it will continue to stand; and it says no direct or indirect. And that is pretty plain English; it does not have to be written by any bright, young lawyers. And we are going to continue to comply with that."[182]

Motley provided similar assurances to the House Appropriations Committee during testimony on April 18, 1985. He said the administration would not attempt to solicit funds from

---

177. 96 Stat. 1830, 1865, sec. 793 (1982).

178. H. Rep. No. 122 (Part 1), 98th Cong., 1st Sess. 11 (1983).

179. 98 Stat. 494, 1210, sec. 2908 (1984).

180. 98 Stat. 1837, 1935, sec. 8066(a) (1984). Details on this Boland Amendment and others are set forth in *Report of the Congressional Committee Investigating the Iran-Contra Affair*, H. Rep. No. 100-433 and S. Rep. No. 100-216, 100th Cong., 1st Sess. 395–410 (November 1987) (hereafter *Iran-Contra Affair*). See Louis Fisher, *How Tightly Can Congress Draw the Purse Strings?*, 83 Am. J. Int'l L. 758 (1989).

181. *Security and Development Assistance*, hearings before the Senate Committee on Foreign Relations, 99th Cong., 1st Sess. 908 (1985).

182. Id. at 910.

outside sources to assist the Contras.[183] When President Reagan signed the bill containing the strict language of Boland II, he did not claim that Congress had overstepped its constitutional authority or imply he would continue to assist the Contras. The constitutionality of Boland II was not challenged by the Attorney General or the Office of Legal Counsel. Yet while Motley testified and offered assurances that the administration would comply with Boland II, executive officials were actively soliciting funds from private parties and foreign governments to assist the Contras.

Following enactment of Boland II, Congress continued to pass legislation for the funding of the Contras. Legislation in 1985 retained the prohibition on military aid to rebel groups in Nicaragua but authorized $27 million in humanitarian aid for the "Nicaraguan democratic resistance."[184] The assistance "shall be provided to such department or agency of the United States as the President shall designate, except the Central Intelligence Agency or the Department of Defense."[185] The Nicaraguan Humanitarian Assistance Office (NHAO) was created in the State Department to administer this financial aid.[186]

Legislation in 1986 provided $100 million for the Nicaraguan opposition, of which $70 million could be used for non-humanitarian assistance.[187] The Secretary of State (or his designee) was made responsible for policy guidance, coordination, and supervision of U.S. government activities under this title of the statute. Nothing in the title was to be construed as permitting the President to furnish additional assistance to the Nicaraguan democratic resistance from funds other than the funds specified in this statute or otherwise specifically authorized by Congress.[188]

## *B. The story breaks*

On October 5, 1986, one of the aircraft used by the administration to provide covert assistance to the Contras was shot down in Nicaragua. On board was Eugene Hasenfus, who survived the crash. The Sandinista government found in the wreckage an identification card issued to Hasenfus by the Air Force and an identification card issued to the pilot, William Cooper, by a CIA front company. Those documents were shared with reporters. Although senior officials in the administration, including President Reagan, denied any connection with the flight, it had been assisted by National Security Adviser Robert McFarlane, Col. Oliver North in the White House, the U.S. ambassador in Costa Rica, and the CIA station chief for Central America.[189] Elliott Abrams, Assistant Secretary of State for Inter-American Affairs, assured congressional committees there was no connection between the administration and the plane carrying Hasenfus.[190] Clair George, CIA Deputy Director for Operations, also testified at congressional

---

183. *Department of Defense Appropriations for 1986* (Part 2), hearings before the House Committee on Appropriations, 99th Cong., 1st Sess. 1092 (1985).

184. 99 Stat. 190, 249, sec. 722 (1985).

185. Id. at 254.

186. *Iran-Contra Affair*, *supra* note 180, at 402.

187. 100 Stat. 1783, 1783–300 (1986)

188. Id. at 1783–301.

189. *Iran-Contra Affair*, *supra* note 180, at 144–45.

190. Id. at 145–46.

hearings that his agency was not involved, directly or indirectly, in assisting resupply missions conducted by private individuals in support of the Contras.[191]

On November 3, 1986, a Lebanese weekly (*Al-Shiraa*) reported that the Reagan administration had sold arms to Iran. Initial reports claimed that the purpose was to win the release of American hostages held in Lebanon.[192] Such a policy would have violated U.S. policy and public announcements by President Reagan. The Secretary of State had designated Iran as a country supporting terrorism. On July 1, 1985, Reagan declared his opposition to any type of bargaining with terrorists: "We make no concessions. We make no deals."[193] It was later learned that some of the funds from those transactions were diverted to support the Contra rebels in Nicaragua. Selling arms to Iran violated the administration's policy called "Operation Staunch," which advocated no arms sales to either side in the war between Iran and Iraq.[194] In its report released in November 1987, the Iran-Contra Committee concluded that the sale of weapons to Iran violated the Arm Export Control Act on several grounds: arms could not be transferred to a terrorist nation, no presidential finding authorized the sale, and no notice had been given to Congress.[195]

Three weeks after the *Al-Shiraa* report, President Reagan created a Special Review Board (called the Tower Commission) to investigate the administration's involvement in Iran-Contra. Serving on the board were former Senator John Tower, former Senator Edmund Muskie, and former National Security Adviser Brent Scowcroft. With regard to arms sales to Iran, the board concluded: "The President appeared to be unaware of key elements of the operation."[196] However, Reagan admitted to the board that he had approved "a convoluted plan whereby Israel would free 20 Hezballah prisoners, Israel would sell TOW [tube-launched, optically tracked, wire-guided] missiles to Iran, the five U.S. citizens in Beirut would be freed, and the kidnappings would stop."[197] A draft finding for the covert operation had been signed by Reagan, although he told the board he did not recall signing it.[198] He advised the board on January 26, 1987 that "he did not know that the NSC staff was engaged in helping the Contras."[199]

In a book published in 1991, Senator Tower said he doubted Reagan's statements when he met with the board. Tower sat opposite Reagan, listening to his "rather convoluted statement," and was "shocked" at what he heard.[200] At one point Reagan recanted a previous statement, although that testimony was "fully consistent" with documentary evidence the board possessed.[201] Responding to a question from Tower, Reagan stood up and walked to his desk, picked up a sheet of paper and, as Tower recalled, said to the board: "This is what I am supposed to

---

191. Id. at 147.

192. Id. at xv.

193. Id. at 157.

194. George P. Shultz, Turmoil and Triumph 237, 239–41, 785, n.1 (1993); *Iran-Contra Affair, supra* note 180, at 157, 159.

195. *Iran-Contra Affair, supra* note 180, at 418–19.

196. Tower Commission Report 2 (N.Y. Times ed., 1987).

197. Id. at 37.

198. Id.

199. Id. at 61.

200. John G. Tower, Consequences: A Personal and Political Memoir 283 (1991).

201. Id.

say."[202] He read an answer prepared for him by White House Counsel Peter Wallison. To Tower, it "was obvious that the president had been prepped by Wallison and words were being put into his mouth."[203]

To Attorney General Edwin Meese, the combination of funding the Contras and sending arms to Iran could cause the "possible toppling" of Reagan through impeachment proceedings. He believed it was essential for the administration to release information and get it "out the door first."[204] The administration called NATO Ambassador David Abshire back to Washington, D.C., to ensure that executive documents—many of them highly classified—were made available to Congress in an expeditious manner. He described the problems he faced: "there had been so much lying within the White House that no one could know the real truth. There had been too much shredding of documents and too much falsification of records."[205] Presidential aides worried about Reagan's vulnerability to impeachment.[206]

Recalling Nixon's experience with Watergate, the Reagan administration decided to get facts out quickly to prevent opponents from charging a cover-up and obstruction of justice.[207] Reagan permitted two former National Security Advisers, Robert McFarlane and John Poindexter, to testify before Congress.[208] Other administration officials who testified included Secretary of State George Shultz and Secretary of Defense Caspar Weinberger. They were at liberty to publicly discuss their conversations with the President.[209] Because Reagan authorized the release of documents, ordered executive officials to testify before Congress, and waived executive privilege, members of Congress never seriously considered a move to impeach him.[210]

Reagan directed Attorney General Meese to go to a special judicial panel and request an independent counsel. The judges appointed Lawrence Walsh. His efforts to uncover the full scope of illegalities, however, were limited by the decision of the Reagan and Bush I administrations to withhold key documents.[211] In the course of Walsh's investigation, McFarlane pled guilty to withholding information from Congress, Abrams pled guilty to giving false statements to Congress, George was charged with making false statements to Congress, and other administration officials were either charged or found guilty.[212]

---

202. Id.

203. Id.

204. Theodore Draper, A Very Thin Line: The Iran-Contra Affairs 521 (1991).

205. David M. Abshire, Saving the Reagan Presidency 27 (2005).

206. Lawrence B. Walsh, Firewall: The Iran-Contra Conspiracy and Cover-up 9, 189, 355, 358–59, 360, 397 (1997).

207. Id. at 189, 379.

208. Draper, *supra* note 204, at 498.

209. *Iran-Contra Investigation*, joint hearings before the Senate Select Committee on Secret Military Assistance to Iran and the Nicaraguan Opposition and the House Select Committee to Investigate Covert Arms Transactions with Iran (Part 100-9), 100th Cong., 1st sess. 1–2 (1987); id. (Part 100-10), at 132.

210. William S. Cohen & George J. Mitchell, Men of Zeal: A Candid Inside Story of the Iran-Contra Hearings 45–50 (1988).

211. Walsh, *supra* note 206, at 210–11, 218–19.

212. Paul Gumina, *Title VI of the Intelligence Authorization Act, Fiscal Year 1991: Effective Covert Action Reform or "Business as Usual?,"* 20 Hastings Const. L.Q. 149, 175–76 (1992). See also David Fagelson, *The Constitution and National Security: Covert Action in the Age of Intelligence Oversight*, 5 J. Law & Politics 275 (1989).

On December 24, 1992, President Bush pardoned six executive officials involved in Iran-Contra: Weinberger, McFarlane, Abrams, and three CIA officials (Duane Clarridge, Alan Fiers, and Clair George).[213] The pardons eliminated the opportunity to learn the full extent of CIA involvement. Had Weinberger gone to trial, he would have likely sought Bush's testimony. Bush therefore had personal reasons to pardon Weinberger.[214] On October 30, 1992, four days before the presidential election between Bush and Bill Clinton, Walsh indicted Weinberger a second time. Walsh released information that indicated Bush had not been truthful when he claimed to be "out of the loop" and unaware of key decisions to send arms to Iran. In the closing days of the campaign, Clinton publicly challenged Bush's credibility in Iran-Contra, one of several factors that led to Bush's defeat.[215]

## C. Using outside funds

Denied appropriated funds to assist the Contras, the Reagan administration solicited money from foreign governments and private citizens. The countries were variously referred to as Countries 1 through 6 in the congressional investigation.[216] The one country actually identified in the congressional report is Brunei, which agreed to provide $10 million to the Contras but a typographical error in the bank account number by either Colonel North or his secretary blocked this form of assistance.[217] The administration also sought funds from a number of private individuals. When prosecuted by Walsh, some pled guilty to various counts of conspiracy to defraud the United States.[218]

In congressional testimony, Colonel North claimed that the President could authorize and conduct covert operations by using nonappropriated funds.[219] He was asked: "And it is also clear, isn't it, that if Congress told the President he could not ask foreign countries or private individuals for financial or other official assistance for the Contras, there would be serious doubt about whether Congress had exceeded its constitutional power, correct?" North replied: "If the Congress had passed such a measure, it would clearly, in my opinion, be unconstitutional."[220] The purpose of those questions was to challenge the constitutionality of Boland II. If Congress closed the door to the Treasury, could a President go elsewhere for funds to implement White House objectives?

Former National Security Adviser John Poindexter testified that the administration was justified in withholding information from Congress because the Contras were being assisted with nonappropriated funds: "we weren't using appropriated funds. They were private, third-country funds."[221] He argued that the President possesses plenary power over foreign policy and Congress

---

213. 57 Fed. Reg. 62145–57 (1992).

214. Jeffrey Crouch, The Presidential Pardon Power 95, 106–07 (2009).

215. Id. at 102–03.

216. *Iran-Contra Affair, supra* note 180, at 38–40, 44–45, 63, 69.

217. Id. at 71, 352–53.

218. Id. at 85–103; Walsh, *supra* note 206, at 95.

219. *Iran-Contra Investigation, supra* note 180, Vol. 100-7 (Part 2), at 37.

220. Id., Vol. 100-7 (Part 2), at 37.

221. Id., Vol. 100-8, at 158.

may not interfere with his decisions: "The point was, and still is, that the President has the constitutional right and, in fact, the constitutional mandate to conduct foreign policy. His policy was to support the Contras. Congress had put some restrictions on the use of appropriated funds. Those restrictions didn't apply to private funds. They didn't apply to third-country funds. And the restrictions in the Boland Amendment, as I have said, did not apply to the NSC staff."[222]

At these hearings, Secretary of State Shultz rejected the theory that an administration, denied funds by Congress, could seek financial support from private parties and foreign governments: "it is totally outside of the system of government that we live by and must live by. You cannot spend funds that the Congress doesn't either authorize you to obtain or appropriate. That is what the Constitution says, and we have to stick by it."[223] He said that when he was asked in 1984 about third-country solicitations for the Contras, he advised: "in the end if this is going to work, we have to persuade the Congress to support it."[224] The idea of circumventing Congress and relying on funds from private parties and foreign governments "is a piece of junk and it ought to be treated that way."[225]

Some members of the Iran-Contra Committee agreed with Poindexter. Senator Orrin Hatch asked him: "But regarding Boland, would you say that you were trying to comply with the law while still attempting to pursue the President's policies; is that right?" Poindexter agreed. Hatch continued: "OK. Boland didn't really apply to the President, did it?" Poindexter concurred. Hatch: "I don't know of one person who has any semblance of constitutional authority or law or background who will say that it did.... There was nothing in Boland, though, or in any of these Boland Amendments that prohibited private donations to the Contras.... Private donations could be made to the Contras.... There was nothing in Boland that prohibited foreign governments from donating to the Contras...."[226]

Hatch's position raises several political and constitutional issues. If Congress were to authorize military operations against another country, the President would be permitted to seek financial assistance from other countries and have those funds deposited in the Treasury to be appropriated by Congress. That process was followed in deciding to go to war against Iraq in 1990–1991.[227] But if Congress denies funds for a program, could the President go, hat in hand, to private groups and foreign governments for financial assistance to carry out White House policy? Such conduct would invite a major confrontation with Congress by acting in defiance of statutory policy. The President would fail in his constitutional duty to see that the laws are faithfully executed and would likely face impeachment proceedings. Also, soliciting funds from foreign governments to promote U.S. foreign policy would open the door to widespread compromise

---

222. Id. at 159.

223. Id., Vol. 100-9, at 74–75.

224. Id. at 75.

225. Id.

226. Id., Vol. 110-8, at 290. For a position that the President has broad authority in foreign affairs to solicit funds from foreign governments, but could not use those funds in such an operation as Iran-Contra, see George W. Van Cleve, *The Constitutionality of the Solicitation or Control of Third-Country Funds for Foreign Policy Purposes by United States Officials Without Congressional Approval*, 11 HOUSTON J. INT'L L. 69 (1988). The author limits this argument to foreign policy, not to domestic programs or military actions over which the power of Congress is "complete." Id. at 77–78, 82.

227. LOUIS FISHER, PRESIDENTIAL WAR POWER 169 (3d ed., 2013).

and corruption through various quid pro quos. Having received funds from another country, an administration would likely reciprocate by giving donor countries special consideration in terms of foreign assistance, military assistance, arms sales, and trade concessions.[228]

At the time of Iran-Contra, constitutional and statutory restrictions already existed on receiving gifts or funds from foreign governments. Article I, section 9 requires an appropriation to draw money from the Treasury and contains the Statement and Account Clause. Immediately following is this language: "No title of Nobility shall be granted by the United States: And no Person holding any Office of Profit or Trust under them, shall, without the Consent of the Congress, accept of any present, Emolument, Office, or Title, of any kind whatever, from any King, Prince, or foreign state." At the Virginia ratifying convention, Edmund Randolph defended this limitation as a means of excluding "corruption and foreign influence."[229] Justice Story in his *Commentaries* explained that this provision originated "in a just jealousy of foreign influence."[230]

It is possible to conduct federal operations with private and foreign funds, but only when specifically authorized by Congress. Statutes create trust funds to receive gifts from the private sector and from foreign government.[231] Gift funds must be placed in the Treasury and spent only for objects defined by Congress.[232] The purpose is to "ensure that the executive branch remains dependent upon the congressional appropriations process."[233] Failure to comply with statutory policy on contributions from private parties and foreign nationals is subject to criminal laws that provide for fines and prison sentences.[234]

Quid pro quos were covered by the Pell Amendment of 1985, which placed prohibitions on military and paramilitary operations in Nicaragua. No funds could be used to provide "assistance of any kind, directly or indirectly, to any person or group engaging in an insurgency or other act of rebellion against the Government of Nicaragua."[235] The intent: prevent the United States from entering into any arrangement that conditioned, "expressly or impliedly," the provision of defense articles and services to recipients of U.S. funds with the understanding that they will assist others engaged "in an insurgency or other act of rebellion against the Government of Nicaragua."[236]

Congress drafted legislation to place new limits on quid pro quos. In November 1989, President Bush vetoed two bills that attempted to do that. The first prohibited the solicitation of funds from any foreign government or U.S. person for the purpose of furthering a military or foreign policy objective that is contrary to statutory law. Bush believed the bill was designed to prohibit consultation between the United States and another country, even though the bill

228. Alex Whiting, *Controlling Tin Cup Diplomacy*, 99 YALE L.J. 2043 (1990).

229. 3 Farrand 327.

230. 3 JOSEPH STORY, COMMENTARIES ON THE CONSTITUTION OF THE UNITED STATES 215–16 (1833).

231. 31 U.S.C. § 1321 (1982); 5 U.S.C. § 7342 (1982).

232. 31 U.S.C. § 3302 (1982).

233. GENERAL ACCOUNTING OFFICE, PRINCIPLES OF FEDERAL APPROPRIATIONS LAWS 5–65 (1982); see also 5–82 to 5–89.

234. *The Foreign Agents Registration Act*, prepared for the Senate Committee on Foreign Relations by the American Law Division of the Congressional Research Service, 95th Cong., 1st Sess. 186-96 (committee print, August 1977).

235. 99 Stat. 254, sec. 722(d) (1985).

236. Id.

stated there was no such intent.[237] Two days later he vetoed another bill that contained criminal penalties for the use of third-party funds by executive branch officials. His objections to both bills centered not on concerns that he recognized as legitimate, but on language he found to be too "vague and sweeping."[238]

He did sign a bill, on November 21, 1989, that covered quid pro quos. The legislation prohibited the use of appropriated funds to provide assistance to a foreign government in exchange for that government undertaking "any action which is, if carried out by the United States Government, a United States official or employee, expressly prohibited by a provision of United States law."[239] In his signing statement, Bush accepted the legislative purpose of prohibiting "quid pro quo" transactions. As he put it: "transactions in which U.S. funds are provided to a foreign nation on the express condition that the foreign nation provide specific assistance to a third country, which assistance U.S. officials are expressly prohibited from providing by U.S. law."[240]

Congress enacted a more comprehensive statute in 1991. The 1980 Intelligence Oversight Act required Presidents to make a confidential "finding" that a covert operation was necessary. With regard to Iran-Contra, President Reagan issued an "oral" finding and attempted to retroactively authorize what the CIA had done. Congress rewrote the Intelligence Oversight Act in 1991 to specify that presidential findings "shall be in writing," may not have retroactive effect, and "may not authorize any action that would violate the Constitution or any statute of the United States." If the President determines that "it is essential to limit access to the finding to meet extraordinary circumstances affecting vital interests of the United States," the finding may be reported to what is called the "Gang of Eight": the chairmen and ranking minority members of the intelligence committees, the House Speaker and minority leader, and the Senate majority and minority leaders.[241]

In signing the bill, President Bush raised this objection: "I remain concerned about legislatively directed policy determinations in the Act and provisions that are without effect because they are unconstitutional under the Supreme Court decision in *INS v. Chadha*, 462 U.S. 919 (1983). I reiterate that the inclusion of such provisions is inappropriate."[242] He did not identify the particular provisions or explain why they were invalid under *Chadha*. He might have had in mind the requirement that the CIA Director and the heads of all departments, agencies and entities involved in a covert action furnish to the intelligence committees any information or material concerning covert actions "which is requested by either of the intelligence committees in order to carry out its authorized activities."[243] This type of reporting requirement is not barred by *Chadha*. The Court noted that the Constitution provides Congress "with abundant means to oversee and control its administrative creatures. Beyond the obvious fact that Congress ultimately controls administrative agencies in the legislation that creates them, other means of

---

237. PUBLIC PAPERS OF THE PRESIDENTS, 1989, II, at 1545–46.

238. Id. at 1567–68.

239. 103 Stat. 1251, sec. 582 (1989).

240. PUBLIC PAPERS OF THE PRESIDENTS, 1989, II, at 1573.

241. 105 Stat. 442–43, sec. 503 (1991). See Gumina, *supra* note 212.

242. PUBLIC PAPERS OF THE PRESIDENTS, 1991, II, at 1043–44.

243. 105 Stat. 443, sec. 503(b)(2).

control, such as durational limits on authorizations and formal reporting requirements, lie well within Congress' constitutional power."[244]

# 10. CONTROLLING THE NATIONAL DEBT

A House committee in 1919 concluded that economy and efficiency at the federal level could be secured only by making an officer responsible for receiving and scrutinizing agency budget requests: "In the National Government there can be no question but that the officer upon whom should be placed this responsibility is the President of the United States."[245] That political and constitutional principle led to the Budget and Accounting Act of 1921 and the expectation that the President would be personally responsible for submitting a national budget, especially with regard to aggregates and the projection of budget surpluses and deficits. If the President presents a budget with realistic aggregates, Congress is able to operate within those numbers and change the priorities. Each branch has the institutional capacity to perform those tasks.

As explained earlier in this chapter, presidential and congressional duties changed radically with the Budget Act of 1974. The nation no longer had a single budget: the President's. It had several, including the President's, the House budget resolution, the Senate budget resolution, and the budget resolution agreed to by the two chambers. The single measuring rod disappeared. Lawmakers could claim they were "under" the budget without the public knowing which budget they meant. The Appropriations Committees lost their traditional purpose of producing bills under the President's budget. They were now pressured to come "up to" the numbers in the budget resolution. Presidents were more than happy to let Congress make the budget and step away from their statutory duty to submit a responsible budget, especially with regard to aggregates and deficits.

When President Reagan entered office, the national debt—accumulated from 1789 to 1981—had reached one trillion dollars. Instead of the budget resolution serving as a mechanism to strengthen congressional authority, Reagan managed to gain control of the now centralized legislative process to cut taxes and increase military spending. The deficit tripled during his eight years. Both branches avoided accountability by creating the "automatic" control of the Gramm-Rudman Act, which failed egregiously to control deficits. The national debt rose to $4 trillion under President George H. W. Bush, but seemed to be brought under control by the two branches during the Clinton years. A combination of spending constraints and tax increases projected sizable budget surpluses.

Under the presidencies of George W. Bush and Barack Obama, the national debt climbed beyond $16 trillion. Part of that increase came from Bush's decision to cut taxes and fight wars in Iraq and Afghanistan without paying for them. If conditions after the terrorist attacks of 9/11 were indeed a national crisis, it was appropriate to ask the public to pay for military expenditures

---

244. INS v. Chadha, 462 U.S. 919, 955 n.19 (1983). Budgetary and constitutional issues of Iran-Contra are carefully examined by WILLIAM C. BANKS & PETER RAVEN-HANSEN, NATIONAL SECURITY LAW AND THE POWER OF THE PURSE (1994). For an analysis of Iran-Contra and statutory remedies: HAROLD HONGJU KOH, THE NATIONAL SECURITY CONSTITUTION: SHARING POWER AFTER THE IRAN-CONTRA AFFAIR (1990).

245. H. Rep. No. 362, 66th Cong., 1st Sess. 5 (1919).

or cut other programs. That was not done. The economic collapse in 2008 reduced revenues and increased the debt still further. No one expected President Obama to immediately produce a balanced budget, given joblessness and economic conditions, but it was within his capacity to present a budget that brought deficits under control ten years out. That was not done either.

The failure of the elected branches to address the problem of budget deficits raises several issues. One is the growing expense to pay interest on the debt, consuming each year a greater portion of the national budget. Second, the United States is increasingly dependent on foreign countries (China, Japan, and others) to purchase U.S. bonds. Concerns about budget irresponsibility in the United States creates the likelihood that they may refrain from buying the bonds, or would agree to do so only if the rates are substantially increased. That would add still further to the cost of paying for the annual debt. Third, what accounts for the unwillingness of contemporary Presidents and members of Congress to provide leadership for controlling deficit spending? The magnitude of the national debt and its increase over the coming decade makes it a legitimate topic of national security. Other nations, allies and adversaries, judge the United States in part on its capacity to manage indebtedness in a responsible manner. Instead of addressing the problem head-on, both branches searched for new mechanisms, including a fiscal commission and a "supercommittee" in Congress that would supposedly do what Presidents and lawmakers refused to do.

## A. Fiscal commission

In 2009, members of Congress debated the idea of creating a fiscal commission to confront massive federal deficits. Bills were introduced to empower a commission to develop legislation to "reform tax policy and entitlement benefit programs and ensure a sound fiscal future for the United States"—code words for raising revenue, cutting entitlements, and bringing budget deficits under control.[246] Sponsors of this legislation regarded it as crucial to create a process that would ensure bipartisan support. Senator Kent Conrad, chairman of the Senate Budget Committee, concluded that "the regular legislative process is simply not going to get it done."[247] Democrats and Republicans, acting alone, would not agree to cut popular entitlement programs (Medicare, social security, etc.) or raise taxes. To guarantee that a proposal would have bipartisan support, the fiscal commission would need a supermajority (for example, 12 of 16 members) before making its recommendations.

Hearings on these proposals generally ignored a role for the President. Lawmakers and budget experts in 2009 blamed Congress for the fiscal crisis: a national debt of $12 billion at that time and an annual deficit that exceeded $1.4 trillion. The next decade was projected to add another $9 trillion of debt. At a hearing on November 10, 2009, Senator George Voinovich offered this view: "Congress is simply not willing or not capable of enduring short term pain for long term gain."[248] Certainly that is a fair point, but the same could be said of Presidents George

---

246. H.R. 1557, 111th Cong., 1st Sess. (2009); S. 1056, 111th Cong., 1st Sess. (2009); S. 2853, 111th Cong., 1st Sess. (2009).

247. Transcript of remarks by Senate Budget Committee Chairman Kent Conrad at hearing on Bipartisan Process Proposals for Long-Term Fiscal Stability, Nov. 10, 2009, at 1.

248. Id., statement by Senator Voinovich, at 1–2.

Bush and Barack Obama. During the hearing, Senator Lamar Alexander asked: "What about the President? The President has to be involved.... He is the agenda setter.... No one else can come close to that."[249]

In December 2009, the cover of *Newsweek* captured the budget crisis dramatically with this headline: "How Great Powers Fall: Steep Debt, Slow Growth, and High Spending Kills Empires—And America Could Be Next." In the background was the Capitol, upside down.[250] Where was the White House? It should have been upside down also. At a hearing in December 2009, Senator Joe Lieberman remarked that confronting the deficit problem required "facing the hard choices Congress has shown in the past it hasn't got the stomach for."[251] The record supports his judgment about the legislative branch, but recent Presidents demonstrated no stomach for the fight either. At that same hearing, Senator Voinovich said that President Obama and his OMB Director "realize we have a crisis that needs to addressed."[252] If that was the case, why not address it? Why leave it to Congress and a fiscal commission?

The basic idea of a Senate bill (S. 2853) was to create a fiscal commission, consisting of 18 task force members to study methods of reducing the federal deficit. Sixteen would be members of Congress; two would come from the executive branch. The bill empowered the commission to draft a bill to include changes in entitlement programs, taxes, and appropriations. A majority of 14 would be needed to report the bill for floor action. No floor amendments were allowed. The choice for lawmakers: vote it up or down, without any changes. A majority of 60 percent in each house was required to pass the bill. If it cleared both chambers, the bill would go to the President for his signature or veto. Needing a supermajority of 60 percent, the bill fell short on a vote of 53 to 46.[253]

At that point, President Obama issued an executive order on February 18, 2010, establishing an 18-member National Commission on Fiscal Responsibility and Reform.[254] He had been in office for one year without addressing the deficit issue. Another year would be lost waiting for the commission to complete its work and present a plan no later than December 1, 2010, after the November elections. Issuing the report required the approval of not less than 14 of the 18 members of the Commission.[255]

Obama's first budget message in February 2009 spoke frankly about the seriousness of the debt: "[W]e cannot lose sight of the long-run challenges that our country faces and that threaten our economic health—specifically, the trillions of dollars of debt that we inherited."[256] He noted that his initial budgets carried high deficits because of the deep recession and the need

249. Id.

250. NEWSWEEK, Dec. 7, 2009.

251. *Safeguarding the American Dream: Prospects for Our Economic Future and Proposals to Secure It*, opening statement of Chairman Joseph Lieberman, Homeland Security and Governmental Affairs Committee, Dec. 17, 2009, at 3.

252. Id., statement by Senator Voinovich, at 2.

253. Lori Montgomery, *Senate Rejects Plan to Create Commission on the Deficit*, WASH. POST, Jan. 27, 2010, at A8.

254. *Remarks on Signing an Executive Order Establishing the National Commission on Fiscal Responsibility and Reform and an Exchange With Reporters*, DAILY COMP. PRES. DOC., Feb. 18, 2010; http://www.whitehouse.gov/the-press-office/executive-order-national-commission-fiscal-responsibility-and-reform.

255. Id.

256. President Obama, budget message of Feb. 26, 2009.

to stimulate economic recovery but pledged: "we must begin the process of making the tough choices necessary to restore fiscal discipline, cut the deficit in half by the end of my first term in office, and put our Nation on sound fiscal footing."[257] Those words were never followed by actions needed to achieve that goal.

A year later, in his budget message of February 2010, Obama told the nation: "we cannot continue to borrow against our children's future," spoke of the urgency of "getting our fiscal house in order," and admitted that "our fiscal situation remains unacceptable."[258] Instead of making concrete proposals to cut the deficit, he issued his executive order to create a fiscal commission. On July 13, 2010, when he announced the appointment of his new OMB Director, Jacob Lew, it was reported that Lew would be responsible for reducing the deficit "to 3 percent of the size of the economy by 2015."[259] Based on the gross domestic product (GDP) of $19.190 trillion projected for fiscal 2015,[260] the annual deficit at that time would be $575.7 billion. Projections of that order did not reflect a policy of fiscal discipline to control deficits.

In December 2010, the fiscal commission failed to attract the necessary 14 votes to produce a deficit control plan. Another year had slipped by without moving toward a balanced budget or to surpluses. Obama could have adopted some of the proposals of his fiscal commission, which urged reductions in social security, cuts in defense spending, and increased taxes.[261] But nothing in his third budget, released in February 2011, dealt substantively with long-term deficits.[262] OMB Director Lew spoke the language of budget restraint, claiming that Obama's budget is one "that lives within our means."[263] However, this budget projected deficits of $8 trillion over the next decade.

## B. Statutory action in 2011

With President Obama unwilling to bring deficits—near-term and long-term—under control, Congress passed the Budget Control Act of 2011, signed into law on August 2. The legislation created a new process to reduce the deficit by up to $2.4 trillion over ten years. Part of that reduction came from statutory caps for fiscal years 2012 through 2021, amounting to an estimated $917 billion in savings. To enforce the caps, the legislation borrowed from the "sequesters" of Gramm-Rudman. If Congress were to exceed the caps, automatic across-the-board spending cuts would occur within discretionary accounts.

The second step in potential savings depended on the work of a new 12-member "supercommittee." The statute directed the Joint Select Committee on Deficit Reduction to recommend an additional $1.5 trillion in deficit reduction over ten years. Once again Congress decided it could not rely on its regular legislative process or the procedures of the Budget Act of 1974. Recommendations from this new committee would be voted on by the end of the year. If a

---

257. Id.

258. President Obama, budget message of Feb. 1, 2010.

259. Anne E. Kornblut & Ed O'Keefe, *Obama Taps New Budget Chief*, WASH. POST, July 14, 2010, at A3.

260. Historical Tables: Budget of the U.S. Government, Fiscal Year 2011, at 211.

261. Jackie Calmes, *Panel Seeks Cuts in Social Security and Higher Taxes*, N.Y. TIMES, Nov. 11, 2010, at A1.

262. President Obama, budget message of Feb. 14, 2011.

263. Dana Milbank, *Keep Passing the Budget on Budget Reform? Yes, We Can*, WASH. POST, Feb. 15, 2011, at A2.

majority of the committee agreed on proposed legislative language, lawmakers had to vote by December 23, with no amendments allowed. Enactment had to occur by January 15, 2012, to avoid automatic spending cuts. If the committee failed to achieve at least $1.2 trillion in deficit reduction, automatic sequesters would be triggered to achieve the savings. As with Gramm-Rudman, a number of programs were exempted from these cuts.[264] The supercommittee failed to reach agreement.

In February 2012 Obama submitted his fourth budget.[265] Including the $1 trillion in discretionary spending required by the Budget Control Act, his budget proposed an estimated $4 trillion in additional cuts by 2018. Even with those projections, the estimated annual deficit for 2022 was $704 billion.[266] If some of his proposals for spending cuts and tax increases are not accepted by Congress, the deficits will be higher.[267] In mid-2013, higher tax revenues and spending cuts through the sequestration process reduced the annual deficit by about $200 billion (from $973 billion to $759 billion), but OMB projected deficits in 2023 at a half-trillion dollars.[268] CBO estimates for 2023 anticipated a deficit of $895 billion.[269] Deficits in the short term remain a problem for the long term.

THE GROWTH OF the national debt over the last three decades has been too extraordinary to ignore. Nevertheless, elected officials from both branches have allowed an urgent matter to persist with little remedy. They have resorted to new mechanisms—budget resolutions, the Gramm-Rudman Act, item vetoes, fiscal commissions, and supercommittees—to replace the regular, political legislative process. Repeatedly those substitutes failed. Presidents and members of Congress are public servants, elected to resolve problems that threaten the nation's fiscal health and stability. The picture that emerges after 1981 is a lack of leadership skills in both elected branches needed to protect republican and constitutional government.

The political process requires the President to play a central role in submitting a responsible budget on aggregates, especially the deficit. There is no substitute for that personal involvement, but the Budget Act of 1974 helped erode presidential accountability. Other factors contribute to the crisis, such as a public that wants more services than it is willing to pay for, and increased polarization that drives moderates out of both parties. The budget system can work when the President provides leadership, including frank talks with the nation to help voters understand what steps are needed. That has not been done for many decades.

264. 125 Stat. 240 (2011); *Highlights of Budget Control Act*, CONG. Q. WEEKLY REPT., Aug. 8, 2011, at 1761–62.

265. President Obama, budget message of Feb. 13, 2012.

266. These estimates come from "Key Budget Facts" in President Obama's budget of Feb. 13, 2012.

267. Jackie Calmes, *Military Cuts and Tax Plan Are Central To a Budget*, N.Y. TIMES, Feb. 14, 2012, at A12.

268. Zachary A. Goldfarb, *OMB Shrinks Its Deficit Forecast*, WASH. POST, July 9, 2013, at A4.

269. Erik Wasson, *CBO Says Deficit Shrinking at Faster Rate*, THE HILL, May 15, 2013, at 13.

# SEVEN

# Foreign Affairs

IT BECAME COMMONPLACE AFTER WORLD WAR II FOR PRESIDENTS, FEDERAL judges, scholars, and even members of Congress to associate all of "foreign policy" with the President.[1] Those assertions do not merely disregard the intent of the Framers. They ignore the text of the Constitution. The Framers gave explicit reasons for rejecting political systems that vested plenary control over external affairs in the executive. That understanding is basic to America's system of checks and balances. When Congress and the judiciary equate foreign policy with the President, decisions are transferred from republican government to a branch with two elected officials. The Framers repeatedly warned about the dangers of placing unchecked power in the executive.

## 1. THE BRITISH MODEL

The American Framers studied the prevailing models of government in ancient times and in contemporary Europe. They knew that foreign policy in England was largely placed with the executive. It was their decision, after personal experience and careful debate, to vest a substantial part of that power in the legislative branch. Their judgment drew heavily from a political commitment to self-government. In a republic, the sovereign power rests with citizens and the individuals they select to represent them in Congress. The U.S. Constitution depends on the principle of collective judgment, shared power in foreign affairs, and "the cardinal tenet of republican ideology that the conjoined wisdom of many is superior to that of one."[2] Some powers of foreign affairs belong solely to the President, such as receiving ambassadors, but they are few.

A number of federal courts and scholars have drawn presidential power from English sources. In a state secrets privilege case in 1953, the Supreme Court noted in *United States v. Reynolds*

---

1. In 1972, the Supreme Court recognized that foreign affairs is entrusted to the President and the Congress. Having said that on pages 765 and 767 of its decision, the Court proceeded in between those pages to claim that several of its cases "emphasized the exclusive competence of the Executive Branch in the field of foreign affairs." First Nat. City Bk. v. Banco Nacional de Cuba, 406 U.S. 759, 766 (1972).

2. David Gray Adler, *Foreign Policy and the Separation of Powers: The Influence of the Judiciary*, in JUDGING THE CONSTITUTION: CRITICAL ESSAYS ON JUDICIAL LAWMAKING 158 (Michael W. McCann & Gerald L. Houseman eds., 1989).

that the experience of English courts with the privilege "has been more extensive" than in the United States "but still relatively slight compared with other evidentiary privileges."[3] The Court cited language from a British case of 1942 for guidance.[4] When the Third Circuit decided this case two years earlier, it rejected the government's reliance on the British case, explaining that the plans of the submarine *Thetis* in that case "were obviously military secrets," the suit was between private parties (whereas *Reynolds* involved a private suit against the government), and the British case should not be "controlling in any event."[5] The basic reason: "For whatever may be true in Great Britain the Government of the United States is one of checks and balances."[6]

In 2001, an article by Saikrishna Prakash and Michael Ramsey advocated a "residual" presidential power that incorporates broad executive prerogatives developed by Locke and Blackstone from British practice.[7] Although they acknowledged that the President "had a greatly diminished foreign affairs power as compared to the English monarchy,"[8] they looked to Locke, Blackstone, and other British writers of the eighteenth century to treat "foreign affairs as an aspect of executive power."[9] Claims of "residual" authority open the door to relying on British precedents when defining the authority of the U.S. President. In a separate study published in 2001, Ramsey rejected the notion that the President possesses "inherent powers in foreign affairs."[10]

A study by Prakash in 2003 developed the theory of executive branch "essentialism" (whatever powers are essential in carrying out the duties of a President). According to this theory, "even if the Constitution did not vest the American executive with all of the English crown's executive powers, it still might have codified the executive's essential power."[11] John Yoo, in a lengthy article in 1996, argued that the U.S. Constitution "did not break with the tradition of their English, state, and revolutionary predecessors, but instead followed in their footsteps."[12] He concluded that "the war powers provisions of the Constitution are best understood as an adoption, rather than a rejection, of the traditional British approach to war powers."[13] That theme reappears in his subsequent writings.[14]

A number of scholars reject this dependence on British precedents. Writing in 1989, Louis Henkin observed that the Framers "turned their backs on Locke and Montesquieu, on British and European practice."[15] More recent evaluations conclude that the Framers "self-conscious[ly]"

---

3. United States v. Reynolds, 345 U.S. 1, 7 (1953).

4. Id. at 8, n.20; Duncan v. Cammell, Laird & Co., A. C. 624, 638 (1942).

5. Reynolds v. United States, 192 F.2d 987, 997 (3d Cir. 1951).

6. Id.

7. Saikrishna B. Prakash & Michael D. Ramsey, *The Executive Power over Foreign Affairs*, 111 YALE L.J. 231, 234–36 (2001).

8. Id. at 254.

9. Id. at 272.

10. Michael D. Ramsey, *The Myth of Extraconstitutional Foreign Affairs Power*, 42 W&M L. REV. 379, 442 (2001).

11. Saikrishna Prakash, *The Essential Meaning of Executive Power*, 2003 U. ILL. L. REV. 701, 810 (2003).

12. John C. Yoo, *The Continuation of Politics by Other Means: The Original Understanding of War Powers*, 84 CAL. L. REV. 167, 197 (1996).

13. Id. at 242.

14. E.g., JOHN YOO, THE POWERS OF WAR AND PEACE: THE CONSTITUTION AND FOREIGN AFFAIRS AFTER 9/11, at 30–54, 88–89, 91–92 (2005).

15. Louis Henkin, *Treaties in a Constitutional Democracy*, 10 MICH. J. INT'L L. 406, 409 (1989).

discarded the British model of government.[16] They "consciously rejected" the British monarch as their model "when thinking about executive power."[17] Other scholars agree that Yoo "relies too much on the English experience, without recognizing ways the Framers sought to depart from that experience."[18] Writing in 2007, David Gray Adler concluded that the Framers "rejected the British model—the monarchical model, a design that emphasized executive unilateralism."[19]

A study in 2009 reviewed British history to demonstrate that the Framers dismissed royal prerogatives and limited the President to a combination of enumerated and implied powers.[20] In 2011, I offered this assessment: "The American framers could not have been more explicit in rejecting the British model of an executive who possesses exclusive control over external affairs."[21] An article in 2012 noted that the Framers "made it clear that they consciously and deliberately rejected the British constitutional model, particularly with respect to the powers of war and foreign affairs."[22]

The English Parliament gained the power of the purse in the 1660s to restrain the king, but the power over foreign policy and war remained a monarchical prerogative.[23] In his *Second Treatise of Civil Government* (1690), John Locke identified three functions of government: legislative, executive, and "federative."[24] The last embraced "the power of war and peace, leagues and alliances, and all the transactions with all persons and communities without the commonwealth."[25] To Locke, the federative power (or what today we call foreign policy) was "always almost united" with the executive.[26] Any effort to separate the executive and federative powers, he wrote, would invite "disorder and ruin."[27]

William Blackstone, the eighteenth-century jurist, described exclusive executive powers in the field of foreign affairs. He defined the king's prerogative as "those rights and capacities which the king enjoys alone."[28] Some of those powers were *direct*, i.e., powers that are "rooted in and

---

16. Curtis A. Bradley & Martin S. Flaherty, *Executive Branch Essentialism and Foreign Affairs*, 102 MICH. L. REV. 545, 552 (2004).

17. Id. at 560.

18. Michael D. Ramsey, *Toward a Rule of Law in Foreign Affairs*, 106 COLUM. L. REV. 1450, 1458 (2006). In an earlier coauthored article, Ramsey maintained that the "executive power" of the President drew from the writings of Locke, Montesquieu, and Blackstone to include all of foreign affairs. Saikrishna B. Prakash & Michael D. Ramsey, The Executive Power over Foreign Affairs, 111 YALE L. REV. 231, 253–61, 266–72 (2001). For additional views by Ramsey and Yoo on the Framers' dependence on the British model: Ramsey, *Textualism and War Powers*, 69 U. CHI. L. REV. 1543 (2002); Yoo, *War and the Constitutional Text*, 69 U. CHI. L. REV. 1639 (2002); and Ramsey, *Text and History in the War Powers Debate*, 69 U. CHI. L. REV. 1685 (2002).

19. David Gray Adler, *George W. Bush and the Abuse of History: The Constitution and Presidential Power in Foreign Affairs*, 12 UCLA J. INT'L L. & FOR. AFFAIRS 75, 76 (2007).

20. Robert J. Reinstein, *The Limits of Executive Power*, 59 AM. U. L. REV. 259 (2009).

21. Louis Fisher, *John Yoo and the Republic*, 41 PRES. STUD. Q. 177, 183 (2011).

22. Janet Cooper Alexander, *John Yoo's War Powers: The Law Review and the World*, 100 CAL. L. REV. 101, 120 (2012).

23. PAUL EINZIG, THE CONTROL OF THE PURSE: PROGRESS AND DECLINE OF PARLIAMENT'S FINANCIAL CONTROL (1959).

24. JOHN LOCKE, SECOND TREATISE OF CIVIL GOVERNMENT, § 146 (1690).

25. Id.

26. Id., § 147.

27. Id., § 148.

28. 1 WILLIAM BLACKSTONE, COMMENTARIES ON THE LAWS OF ENGLAND 232 (1765).

spring from the king's political person," including the right to send and receive ambassadors and the power "of making war or peace."[29] By placing in the king the sole power to make war, individuals who entered society and accepted the laws of government necessarily surrendered any private right to make war: "It would indeed be extremely improper, that any number of subjects should have the power of binding the supreme magistrate, and putting him against his will in a state of war."[30]

In 1794, Congress rejected Blackstone's definition of foreign affairs and war as an exclusive executive power. The Neutrality Act passed by Congress that year imposed criminal penalties on citizens who attempt to make war on another country.[31] The statute did not in any way accept Blackstone's model. It expressed congressional policy about the power of the national government. As explained in this chapter and the next, early decisions by federal courts understood it in that manner. In time of war, if a collision occurred between presidential actions and statutory policy, the will of Congress prevailed (Chapter 8, section 2B).

Blackstone recognized other exclusive foreign policy powers for the Executive. The king could make "a treaty with a foreign state, which shall irrevocably bind the nation."[32] He could issue letters of marque and reprisal (authorizing private citizens to use their ships and other possessions to undertake military actions). As he explained, that power was "nearly related to, and plainly derived from, that other of making war."[33] Blackstone regarded the king as "the generalissimo, or the first in military command," who had "the sole power of raising and regulating fleets and armies."[34] When the king exercised those powers he "is and ought to be absolute; that is, so far absolute, that there is no legal authority that can either delay or resist him."[35] Article I, section 8 vests exclusively in Congress the authority to raise and regulate the military.

The implication of Blackstone's last position—that the king possesses certain powers that may not be limited by any legal authority, including the legislative branch—has become known as "inherent powers." Several administrations, starting with Harry Truman, advanced that view of presidential power. This type of inherent power, rooted in the British prerogative model, was rejected by the Framers and has been consistently repudiated by Congress and the federal courts (Chapter 3, section 4).

## A. Creating a republic

Unlike England, with its history of monarchy over which Parliament gradually gained some control, America as a national government started with a legislative branch and no other. After America declared its independence from England, all national powers (including executive) were vested in a Continental Congress. The ninth article of the first national constitution, the Articles of Confederation, provided: "The United States in Congress assembled, shall have the

---

29. Id. at 232–33.
30. Id. at 249.
31. 1 Stat. 381–84 (1794).
32. BLACKSTONE, *supra* note 28, at 244.
33. Id. at 250.
34. Id. at 254.
35. Id. at 243.

sole and exclusive right and power of determining on peace and war."[36] The single exception to that principle lay in the sixth article, which allowed states to engage in war if invaded by enemies or when threatened by Indian tribes.[37] The powers of the national government were limited by the need to receive approval from nine of the thirteen states if it wanted to engage in war, enter into treaties, borrow money, appropriate money, and take other actions.[38]

The Framers rejected both the British monarchical model and the Articles of Confederation, especially with regard to foreign policy and the war power. At the Philadelphia convention, Charles Pinckney said he was for "a vigorous Executive but was afraid the Executive powers of <the existing> Congress might extend to peace & war which would render the Executive a Monarchy, of the worst kind, towit an elective one."[39] John Rutledge wanted the executive power placed in a single person, "tho' he was not for giving him the power of war and peace."[40] James Wilson supported a single executive but "did not consider the Prerogatives of the British Monarch as a proper guide in defining the Executive powers. Some of these prerogatives were of a Legislative nature. Among others that of war & peace &c."[41] Edmund Randolph worried about executive power, calling it "the fœtus of monarchy." The delegates at the convention, he said, had "no motive to be governed by the British Governmt. as our prototype." If the United States had no other choice it might adopt the British model, but "the fixt genius of the people of America required a different form of Government."[42] Wilson agreed that the British model "was inapplicable to the situation of this Country; the extent of which was so great, and the manners so republican, that nothing but a great confederated Republic would do for it."[43]

In a lengthy speech at the Philadelphia Convention, Alexander Hamilton shared with his colleagues that in his "private opinion he had no scruple in declaring...that the British Govt. was the best in the world."[44] Having expressed a personal preference, he admitted that the models of Locke and Blackstone had no application to America and its commitment to republican government. Hamilton's draft constitution required the Executive to seek the Senate's approval for treaties and ambassadors. The Senate had "the sole power of declaring war."[45] In Federalist No. 69, Hamilton detailed the vast difference between the war powers vested in the British king and the "inferior" powers granted to the President.[46]

## B. Sole-organ doctrine

This framework of republican government and congressional powers in foreign affairs is wholly at odds with what is known as the "sole organ" doctrine, which asserts independent and

---

36. 1 U.S.C. L (2006 ed.).
37. Id.
38. Id. at L–LII.
39. 1 Farrand 64–65.
40. Id. at 65.
41. Id. at 65–66.
42. Id. at 66.
43. Id.
44. Id. at 288.
45. Id. at 292.
46. The Federalist 446.

unchecked presidential authority in foreign affairs. Such a doctrine largely mirrors Blackstone's theory of exclusive monarchical control over external affairs. The belief that the President is "sole organ" appears to come with impressive credentials. It relies on a speech in 1800 by John Marshall, when he served in the House of Representatives. A year later he would be Chief Justice of the Supreme Court. Yet Marshall never took the position that is frequently attributed to him.

During the Iran-Contra controversy of 1987 (Chapter 6, section 9), several members of the Reagan administration cited the sole-organ doctrine to defend two actions: giving assistance to Iran (in violation of the administration's public pledge of neutrality in the Iran-Iraq war) and providing funds to the Contras in Nicaragua (in violation of statutory policy). They claimed that the Supreme Court in the 1936 *Curtiss-Wright* case recognized that the President possessed "plenary and exclusive power as sole organ" of the national government in the field of international relations, "a power which does not require as a basis for its exercise an act of Congress."[47] The language from *Curtiss-Wright* was not merely extraneous to the issue before the Court. It falsely portrayed Marshall's reference to the President as "sole organ."[48]

In defending the secret warrantless surveillance program that President Bush authorized after the terrorist attacks of 9/11, the Justice Department in 2006 relied on the sole-organ doctrine. The Department claimed that the activities of the National Security Agency "are supported by the President's well-recognized inherent constitutional authority as Commander in Chief and sole organ for the Nation in foreign affairs."[49] Well-recognized within the Department, perhaps, and even by many courts, but not by anyone who reads Marshall's speech with care. In an OLC memo written on September 25, 2001, Deputy Assistant Attorney General John Yoo reached out to the sole-organ doctrine: "As future Chief Justice John Marshall famously declared [in 1800]: 'The President is the sole organ of the nation in its external relations, and its sole representative with foreign nations.... The [executive] department... is entrusted with the whole foreign intercourse of the nation.' 10 Annals of Cong. 613–14 (1800)."[50] On that ground, Yoo argued, "it has not been difficult for the executive branch consistently to assert the President's plenary authority in foreign affairs ever since."[51] Marshall's speech had nothing to do with plenary presidential power.

Justice Sutherland's decision in *Curtiss-Wright* helped spread misconceptions about the sole-organ doctrine. The issue before the Court involved only *legislative* power, not presidential power. How much may Congress delegate *its* power to the President in the field of international affairs? In upholding the delegation, Sutherland added pages of dicta that were wholly irrelevant

---

47. *Iran-Contra Investigation*, joint hearings before the Senate Select Committee on Secret Military Assistance to Iran and the Nicaraguan Opposition and the House Select Committee on Investigate Covert Arms Transactions with Iran, 100th Cong., 1st Sess., Vol. 100-2, at 558; Vol. 100-5, at 419–21, 426; Vol. 100-7 (Part II), at 38–39, 133–34.

48. *Iran-Contra Affair*, H. Rep. No. 100-433, S. Rep. No. 100-216, 100th Cong., 1st Sess. 472–74 (Nov. 1987).

49. Memo from Attorney General Alberto R. Gonzales to the Majority Leader of the U.S. Senate, *Legal Authorities Supporting the Activities of the National Security Agency Described by the President*, Jan. 19, 2006, at 1, http://www. justice.gov/olc/2006/nsa-white-paper.pdf.

50. Memo opinion for Timothy Flanigan, the Deputy Counsel to the President, from John C. Yoo, Deputy Assistant Attorney General, *The President's Constitutional Authority to Conduct Military Operations Against Terrorists and Nations Supporting Them*, Sept. 25, 2001, at 4–5 (hereafter "Yoo Memo"), http://www.usdoj.gov/ olc/warpowers925.htm.

51. Id. at 5.

to the constitutional question before the Court. He claimed that the principle that the federal government is limited to enumerated and implied powers "is categorically true only in respect to our internal affairs."[52] In arguing for independent and exclusive presidential powers in the field of foreign affairs, he distorted Marshall's speech.

What Sutherland, the Justice Department, and John Yoo failed to understand is Marshall's purpose in giving his speech. When read in whole, it is evident that Marshall never advocated inherent, plenary, or independent powers for the President in foreign affairs.[53] Some members of the House of Representatives wanted to censure or impeach President John Adams for turning over to Great Britain a British subject charged with murder.[54] Marshall took the floor to explain why there were no grounds to criticize or punish Adams. The Jay Treaty provided for extradition in cases involving the charge of murder. Adams acted not on the basis of any plenary or inherent power but on the express language in a treaty, with treaties under Article VI of the Constitution included as part of the "supreme Law of the Land."[55] Marshall spoke about *express* presidential authority, not inherent or plenary powers. In his later service as Secretary of State and Chief Justice of the Supreme Court, Marshall never advanced any notion of inherent, plenary, exclusive, or independent powers of the President in external affairs. As Chief Justice he looked solely to Congress in matters of war.[56] He understood that when a conflict arose between what Congress provided by statute and what a President announced by proclamation, in time of war, the statute represents the law of the nation.[57]

Scholarly studies of *Curtiss-Wright* have thoroughly repudiated Sutherland for his careless and false mischaracterization of Marshall's speech. Writing in 1944, C. Perry Patterson described Sutherland's position on the existence of inherent presidential powers as "(1) contrary to American history, (2) violative of our political theory, (3) unconstitutional, and (4) unnecessary, undemocratic, and dangerous."[58] Two years later, David M. Levitan described Sutherland's theory as "the furthest departure from the theory that [the] United States is a constitutionally limited democracy. It introduces the notion that national government possesses a secret reservoir of unaccountable power."[59] Law professor Michael Glennon characterized Sutherland's opinion as "a muddled law review article wedged with considerable difficulty between the pages of the United States Reports."[60] Other scholarly evaluations of Sutherland's decision are similarly

---

52. United States v. Curtiss-Wright Corp., 299 U.S. 304, 315 (1936).

53. 10 ANNALS OF CONG. 596, 613 (1800); the full speech appears at http://loufisher.org/docs/pip/444.pdf.

54. There was some controversy whether he was British (Thomas Nast) or American (Jonathan Robbins), but the evidence demonstrates he was British but adopted an American name. Ruth Wedgwood, *The Revolutionary Martyrdom of Jonathan Robbins*, 100 YALE L.J. 229, 310–11 (1990).

55. For greater detail on Marshall's speech: Louis Fisher, *Presidential Inherent Power: The "Sole-Organ" Doctrine*, 37 PRES. STUD. Q. 139 (2007), http://loufisher.org/docs/pip/439.pdf, and Louis Fisher, *The "Sole Organ" Doctrine*, Law Library of Congress, Aug. 2006, http://loufisher.org/docs/pip/441.pdf.

56. Talbot v. Seeman, 5 U.S. (1 Cr.) 1, 28 (1801) ("The whole powers of war being, by the Constitution of the United States, vested in congress, the acts of that body can alone be resorted to as our guides in this enquiry.").

57. Little v. Barreme, 6 U.S. (2 Cr.) 170, 179 (1804) (holding that a proclamation issued by President Adams during the Quasi-War was invalid because it conflicted with a congressional statute).

58. C. Perry Patterson, *In Re The United States v. The Curtiss-Wright Corporation*, 22 TEX. L. REV. 286, 297 (1944).

59. David M. Levitan, *The Foreign Relations Power: An Analysis of Mr. Justice Sutherland's Theory*, 55 YALE L.J. 467, 493 (1946).

60. Michael J. Glennon, *Two Views of Presidential Foreign Affairs Power: Little v. Barreme or Curtiss-Wright?*, 13 YALE J. INT'L L. 5, 13 (1988).

harsh.[61] Some studies provide excellent background on *Curtiss-Wright* but do not explain how and why Justice Sutherland seriously misinterpreted Marshall's speech.[62]

Federal courts continue to cite the sole-organ doctrine to uphold broad definitions of presidential power in foreign relations and provide support for extensive delegations of legislative power to the President.[63] Those decisions have a routine, mechanical quality, citing precedents without any understanding of the erroneous view of presidential power advanced by Justice Sutherland.[64] Most judges and Justices (and their law clerks) appear never to have read Marshall's speech to form an independent and informed judgment. The Supreme Court in 1972 described the President as authorized "to speak as the sole organ" of the national government.[65] Authority to *speak* is not equivalent to exclusive authority to *make* or *formulate* foreign policy. Although some Justices in concurrences have described the President's foreign relations powers as "exclusive,"[66] the Court itself has never denied to Congress its constitutional authority to enter the field of foreign affairs and limit, reverse, or modify presidential decisions.

## 2. FOREIGN RELATIONS

Those who believe that foreign policy is assigned exclusively to the President must contend with a host of powers that Article I expressly vests in Congress. The next chapter focuses on the war powers assigned to Congress. This chapter concentrates on the foreign policy powers of Congress enumerated in Article I, section 8: the power to "lay and collect Taxes, Duties, Imposts and Excises"; to "regulate Commerce with foreign Nations"; to establish a "uniform Rule of Naturalization"; to coin money, "regulate the Value thereof, and of foreign Coin"; to "define and punish Piracies and Felonies committed on the high Seas, and Offenses against the Law of Nations"; and to "make all Laws which shall be necessary and proper for carrying into Execution the foregoing Powers, and all other Powers vested by this Constitution in the Government of the United States or in any Department or Officer thereof." It is often forgotten that the Necessary and Proper Clause supplements not merely the legislative powers identified in Article I but those vested in executive departments and officers.[67]

---

61. For a review of those articles, see Fisher, *The "Sole-Organ" Doctrine*, Aug. 2006, *supra* note 55.

62. H. Jefferson Powell, *The Story of* Curtiss-Wright Export Corporation, in PRESIDENTIAL POWER STORIES 222 (Christopher H. Schroeder & Curtiss A. Bradley eds., 2009). In his book, THE PRESIDENT'S AUTHORITY OVER FOREIGN AFFAIRS (2002), Powell states clearly that *Curtiss-Wright* "misread one of its sources, an 1800 speech of John Marshall" (id. at 23); Robert A. Devine, *The Case of the Smuggled Bombers*, in QUARRELS THAT HAVE SHAPED THE CONSTITUTION (John A. Garrity ed., 1966 ed).

63. Fisher, *The "Sole-Organ" Doctrine*, Aug. 2006, *supra* note 55, at 23-27.

64. For perceptive and critical evaluations of Sutherland's opinion: Justice Jackson's concurrence in the Steel Seizure Case, Youngstown Co. v. Sawyer, 343 U.S. 579, 635–36 n.2 (1952), and American Intern. Group v. Islamic Republic of Iran, 657 F.2d 430, 438 n.6 (D.C. Cir. 1981).

65. First Nat. City Bk. v. Banco Nacional de Cuba, 406 U.S. 759, 766 n.2 (1972), citing United States v. Belmont, 301 U.S. 324, 330 (1937).

66. E.g., Webster v. Doe, 486 U.S. 592, 605–06 (1988) (O'Connor, J., concurring).

67. "To make all Laws which shall be necessary and proper for carrying into Execution the foregoing Powers, and all other Powers vested by this Constitution in the Government of the United States or in any Department or Officer thereof" (Article I, section 8, clause 18).

The delegates at Philadelphia faced two issues of foreign policy: how to divide that power between the two elected branches, and how to protect national authority against competing state actions. After the American colonies broke with England, many of the states entered into treaties and functioned like sovereign governments.[68] The Framers faced the question of how the Constitution should be drafted to vest foreign relations in the national government. Madison pointed to the need to protect against "the influence of foreign powers."[69]

As drafted and ratified, the Constitution excludes states from several areas of foreign relations. Under Article I, section 10, no state "shall enter into any Treaty, Alliance, of Confederation; grant Letters of Marque and Reprisal; coin Money; emit Bills of Credit; make any Thing but gold and silver coin a Tender in Payment of Debts; pass any Bill of Attainder; ex post facto Law, or Law impairing the Obligation of Contracts; or grant any Title of Nobility." Further, no state shall, "without the Consent of Congress, lay any Imposts or Duties on Imports or Exports, except what may be absolutely necessary for executing it's [sic] inspection Laws; and the net Produce of all Duties and Imposts, laid by any State on Imports or Exports, shall be for the Use of the Treasury of the United States; and all such Laws shall be subject to the Revision and Controul of the Congress." Finally, no state shall, "without the Consent of Congress, lay any Duty of Tonnage, keep Troops, or Ships of War in time of Peace, enter into any Agreement or Compact with another State, or with a foreign Power, or engage in War, unless actually invaded, or in such imminent Danger as will not admit of delay."[70]

Several essays in the *Federalist Papers* warned about the dangers of foreign influence. In Federalist No. 4, Jay said that if foreign nations saw the national government as efficient and well administered, its trade "prudently regulated," and the militia and finances properly managed, they would be "much more disposed to cultivate our friendship than provoke our resentment." If they found the nation ineffectual and fragmented, with different states showing partiality to different foreign countries, "what a poor, pitiful figure will America makes in their eyes!"[71] Weak republics, Hamilton warned in Federalist No. 22, "afford too easy an inlet to foreign corruption."[72]

In Federalist No. 6, Hamilton spoke of commerce as having "a tendency to soften the manners of men, and to extinguish those inflammable humors which have so often kindled into wars."[73] Commercial republics, he said, "will never be disposed to waste themselves in ruinous contentions with each other." They will be governed by "mutual interest, and will cultivate a

---

68. 1 Farrand 316; Claude H. Van Tyne, *Sovereignty in the American Revolution: An Historical Study*, 12 Am. Hist. Rev. 529 (1907).

69. 1 Farrand 319.

70. State actions in such fields as commerce inevitably have an impact on foreign relations. Harold G. Maier, *Cooperative Federalism in International Trade: Its Constitutional Parameters*, 27 Mercer L. Rev. 391 (1976). The Supreme Court in 1968 struck down an Oregon statute as an impermissible involvement in foreign affairs and international relations, treating those areas as entrusted solely to the federal government. Zschernig v. Miller, 389 U.S. 429 (1968). Other decisions have limited state actions that interfere with national powers over foreign affairs. American Ins. Assn. v. Garamendi, 539 U.S. 396 (2003); Crosby v. National Foreign Trade Council, 530 U.S. 363 (2000); and Hines v. Davidowitz, 312 U.S. 52 (1941). See Michael D. Ramsey, The Constitution's Text in Foreign Affairs 258–82 (2007), and Louis Henkin, Foreign Affairs and the United States Constitution 163–65 (2d ed. 1996).

71. The Federalist 104.

72. Id. at 196.

73. Id. at 110.

spirit of mutual amity and concord."[74] Yet he recognized that many wars had been "founded upon commercial motives."[75] In vesting in Congress the power to regulate foreign commerce, the Framers understood it was an activity closely related to the war power. Commercial conflicts between nations had sparked wars. In *Gibbons v. Ogden* (1824), Chief Justice Marshall said the commerce power "may be, and often is, used as an instrument of war."[76]

In allocating authority over foreign policy, the Framers gave substantial powers to both Congress and the President. How the two branches exercise their powers and fulfill constitutional principles depends on the individuals who serve in public office. Powers expressly conferred but not exercised will atrophy. If exercised too vigorously the other branches might stage a counterattack. Edward Corwin framed the issue well: "What the Constitution does, *and all that it does*, is to confer on the President certain powers capable of affecting our foreign relations, and certain other powers of the same general kind on the Senate, and still other such powers on Congress; but which of these organs still have the decisive and final voice in determining the course of the American nation is left for events to resolve."[77]

Jefferson Powell, in a book generally supportive of presidential authority, cautioned those who insist on placing plenary and unchecked power over foreign policy in the President: "The conclusion that the Constitution lodges in the president the authority to determine United States foreign policy—in the sense of taking the initiative in formulating that policy—does not, and indeed cannot, ground any claim that Congress has no role to play in foreign affairs. No such assertion is tenable."[78]

In recent decades, sweeping claims of presidential power over foreign policy have been advanced without recognizing congressional powers in Article I. In 1981, Interior Secretary James Watt refused to give a House subcommittee 31 documents related to a reciprocity provision with Canada. He based his refusal on the judgment of Attorney General William French Smith that the documents were "either necessary and fundamental to the deliberative process presently ongoing in the Executive Branch or relate to sensitive foreign policy considerations."[79] Smith's decision marked the first claim of executive privilege by President Reagan.[80] In seeking the documents, the subcommittee based its request on the express constitutional authority of Congress to "regulate Commerce with foreign Nations." After the subcommittee and full committee voted to hold Watt in contempt, the documents were submitted to the subcommittee for its review.[81]

---

74. Id. at 110–11.

75. Id. at 111.

76. 22 U.S. (9 Wheat.) 1, 192 (1824).

77. EDWARD S. CORWIN, THE PRESIDENT: OFFICE AND POWERS, 1787–1957, at 171 (4th ed. 1957) (emphasis in original).

78. H. JEFFERSON POWELL, THE PRESIDENT'S AUTHORITY OVER FOREIGN AFFAIRS: AN ESSAY IN CONSTITUTIONAL INTERPRETATION 107–08 (2002).

79. 43 OP. ATT'Y GEN. 327, 328 (1981).

80. Martha M. Hamilton, *Executive Privilege Invoked to Back Watt*, WASH. POST, Oct. 15, 1981, at D12.

81. LOUIS FISHER, THE POLITICS OF EXECUTIVE PRIVILEGE 124–26 (2004).

# 3. TREATY POWER

The Framers' uncertainty about the President's role in foreign policy is reflected in the debates over the treaty power. As late as August 7, 1787, the draft constitution entirely excluded the President from both treaties and the appointment of ambassadors. Those duties were vested in the Senate.[82] By early September, the delegates decided to include the President in this process. Different proposals were advanced. On September 7, James Wilson recommended that the House be included in the treaty power: "As treaties...are to have the operation of laws, they ought to have the sanction of laws also." His motion fell, ten states to one.[83] As agreed to, Article II, section 2 empowers the President to make treaties "by and with the Advice and Consent of the Senate" and to nominate "and by and with the Advice and Consent of the Senate" appoint ambassadors. Article VI states that the Constitution, congressional statutes, and "all Treaties made, or which shall be made, under the Authority of the United States, shall be the supreme Law of the Land; and the Judges in every State shall be bound thereby, any Thing in the Constitution or Laws of any State to the Contrary notwithstanding."

In Federalist No. 69, Hamilton compared the joint action of the President and the Senate in treaty-making with the British king, who "is the sole and absolute representative of the nation in all foreign transactions" and may on "his own accord make treaties of peace, commerce, alliance, and of every other description."[84] In Federalist No. 75, Hamilton rejected the view that treaty-making was by nature an executive authority: "if we attend carefully to its operation, it will be found to partake more of the legislative than of the executive character, though it does not seem strictly to fall within the definition of either of them."[85]

Article II, section 2 stipulates that treaties need the concurrence of "two thirds of the Senators present." The Constitution does not require a roll-call vote (as it does for veto overrides). No constitutional language demands that a quorum be present. In 1952, the Senate gave its advice and consent to three treaties with only two Senators on the floor. One of those Senators did not even vote. The presiding officer cast an "aye" vote and stated that "two-thirds of the Senators present concurring therein, the resolution of ratification is agreed to, and the convention is ratified."[86] The following year, Senate Majority Leader William Knowland announced that future treaties would be preceded by a quorum call and subjected to "a yea-and-nay vote, at least on the first of a series of treaties."[87] The purpose was to attract Senators to the floor to deliberate and vote on a series of treaties. That has remained the practice.

The word "treaty" in a statute does not necessarily mean an international agreement requiring the advice and consent of the Senate. Unless Congress in legislation specifically defines the word in that sense, courts may interpret treaties to mean an international agreement concluded between sovereigns without Senate participation.[88] Extensive scholarship explores whether

---

82. 1 Farrand 292; 2 Farrand 145, 155, 169, 183, 197.

83. 2 Farrand 538.

84. The Federalist 447–48.

85. Id. at 476.

86. 98 Cong. Rec. 7222, 7223, 7228 (1952).

87. 99 Cong. Rec. 9231 (1953). See Carl Marcy, *A Note on Treaty Ratification*, 47 Am. Pol. Sci. Rev. 1130 (1953).

88. Weinberger v. Rossi, 456 U.S. 25 (1982).

treaties and bills enacted by both houses of Congress are "interchangeable."[89] Legislation often authorizes the President to enter into executive agreements to carry out the statutory purpose, producing what are called congressional-executive agreements.[90] This subject is covered later in this chapter in section 6.

## A. Treaty negotiation

In *Curtiss-Wright*, Justice Sutherland claimed that when the President makes treaties with the advice and consent of the Senate "he alone negotiates. Into the field of negotiation the Senate cannot intrude; and Congress itself is powerless to invade it."[91] His statement was false when written, false when serving earlier as U.S. Senator from Utah, and false ever since. In making that assertion, Sutherland ignored his own experiences in the Senate and demonstrated little understanding of how often Presidents in the past had invited members of Congress (both Senators and Representatives) to share in treaty negotiation. Presidents have no constitutional obligation to include lawmakers in treaty negotiation. They do so to promote executive interests.

Justice Sutherland knew from his service on the Senate Foreign Relations Committee that treaty negotiation had never been a presidential monopoly. In a book published in 1919, he recognized that Senators participated in the negotiation phase and that Presidents had often acceded to this "practical construction."[92] Presidents frequently consulted the Senate "before initiating negotiations, or completing negotiations already undertaken, with a view to obtaining advice in advance. Thus the right and authority of the Senate to participate in the making of treaties at any stage of the process has been again and again recognized and acted upon by the Executive."[93] It is extraordinary that someone with Sutherland's personal experience in the Senate could write such plainly erroneous passages about treaty negotiation.

Edward Corwin, a leading constitutional and presidential scholar, assigned treaty negotiation exclusively to the President. He called the process of drafting and negotiating a treaty a "presidential monopoly," a phrase that appeared in his 1952 annotated Constitution and reappears in subsequent editions as updated by the Congressional Research Service.[94] In his classic work on the presidency, Corwin claimed: "it is today established that the President alone has

---

89. Edwin Borchard, *Shall the Executive Agreement Replace the Treaty?*, 54 YALE L.J. 664 (1944); Myres S. McDougal & Asher Lans, *Treaties and Congressional-Executive or Presidential Agreements: Interchangeable Instruments of National Policy*, 54 YALE L.J. 181, 534 (1945); Bruce Ackerman & David Golove, *Is NAFTA Constitutional?*, 108 HARV. L. REV. 799 (1995); Laurence H. Tribe, *Taking Text and Structure Seriously: Reflections on Free-Form Method in Constitutional Interpretation*, 108 HARV. L. REV. 1221 (1995); John C. Yoo, *Laws as Treaties?: The Constitutionality of Congressional-Executive Agreements*, 99 MICH. L. REV. 757 (2001).

90. WALLACE MCCLURE, INTERNATIONAL EXECUTIVE AGREEMENTS (1941); Oona A. Hathaway, *Treaties' End: The Past, Present, and Future of International Lawmaking in the United States*, 117 YALE L.J. 1236 (2008); Oona A. Hathaway, *Presidential Power over International Law: Restoring the Balance*, 119 YALE L.J. 140 (2009).

91. United States v. Curtiss-Wright Corp., 299 U.S. 304, 319 (1936).

92. GEORGE SUTHERLAND, CONSTITUTIONAL POWERS AND WORLD AFFAIRS 123 (1919).

93. Id.

94. THE CONSTITUTION OF THE UNITED STATES: ANALYSIS AND INTERPRETATION, S. Doc. No. 108-17, at 492 (2004).

the power to negotiate treaties with foreign governments."[95] He quoted favorably from Justice Sutherland's language in *Curtiss-Wright* that the President "alone negotiates."[96]

The title page of Corwin's *The President's Control of Foreign Relations* (1917) features this sentence from Thomas Jefferson: "The transaction of business with foreign nations is executive altogether."[97] When read in context, that statement is not as sweeping as it might first appear. First, Jefferson understood that the President's power in foreign affairs is not plenary. Second, his statement applies to an extremely narrow area of the appointment process. Here is the full passage, written while Jefferson served as Secretary of State in 1790:

> The transaction of business with foreign nations is Executive altogether. It belongs then to the head of that department, *except* as to such portions of it as are specially submitted to the Senate. *Exceptions* are to be construed strictly. The Constitution itself indeed has taken care to circumscribe this one within very strict limits: for it gives the *nomination* of the foreign Agent to the President, the *appointment* to him and the Senate jointly, the *commissioning* to the President.[98]

The issue arose when President Washington asked Jefferson whether the Senate could not only reject a nominee but also the *grade* (level) the President might want for the foreign mission. Jefferson replied that if the Constitution intended to give the Senate a negative over the grade, "it would have said so in direct terms, and not left it to be effected by a sidewind."[99] As explained later in this chapter, with regard to the Algerine Treaty, Jefferson fully appreciated that the two elected branches must work together to form and implement foreign policy.

Do Senators offer "advice" on a treaty only at the final stage, after the President has fashioned it, or at early stages as well? The Constitution does not divide treaty-making into two distinct and sequential stages: negotiation by the President followed by Senate advice and approval. The President "makes" treaties, by and with the advice and consent of the Senate. The constitutional text for treaties differs significantly from that of appointments. The President "shall nominate, and by and with the Advice and Consent of the Senate, shall appoint Ambassadors." Here the President's authority to nominate appears to be set apart as an executive action, even if in practice members of Congress and other parties exert a substantial influence on who is nominated (Chapter 4, section 5B). Treaty-making more clearly seems to invite joint action by the two branches. The President "shall have Power, by and with the Advice and Consent of the Senate, to make Treaties."

When President Washington first communicated with the Senate regarding the appropriate procedure for treaties, he did not treat negotiation as an exclusively executive preserve. He explained that oral communications with the Senate "seem indispensably necessary; because in these a variety of matters are contained, all of which not only require consideration, but some of them may undergo much discussion; to do which by written communications would be tedious without being satisfactory."[100]

A letter from Washington two days later underscored the partnership status of the Senate in treaty-making: "In the appointment to offices, the agency of the Senate is purely executive,

---

95. EDWARD S. CORWIN, THE PRESIDENT: OFFICE AND POWERS, 1787–1957, at 211–12 (4th ed., 1957).

96. Id. at 442 n.122.

97. EDWARD S. CORWIN, THE PRESIDENT'S CONTROL OF FOREIGN RELATIONS (1917).

98. 16 THE PAPERS OF THOMAS JEFFERSON 379 (Boyd ed., 1961) (emphasis in original).

99. Id. at 380.

100. 20 THE WRITINGS OF GEORGE WASHINGTON 373 (Fitzpatrick ed.)

and they may be summoned to the President. In treaties, the agency is perhaps as much of a legislative nature and the business may possibly be referred to their deliberations in their legislative chamber."[101] Repeatedly he spoke of sending "propositions" to the Senate, implying that he would forward a working draft, not the final product. Senators would have an opportunity to make changes and offer recommendations to his draft.[102]

What happened next has been widely misinterpreted as such a sour experience for Washington that he closed the door to any future Senate participation in treaty negotiations. On August 21, 1789, he sent a message to the Senate, stating his intention to meet with Senators in the Senate Chamber "to advise with them on the terms of the treaty *to be negotiated* with the Southern Indians."[103] He met with Senators the following day and put to them a series of seven questions, requesting advice on the instructions to be given to the commissioners chosen to negotiate the treaty.[104] The Senators did not want to act solely on the information supplied by the Secretary of War, who accompanied Washington. The sound of carriages passing by made it difficult to hear what was being said. When each question was read, Washington expected to receive a yes or no. Senators eventually told him they were unable to commit themselves to any positions that day. According to Senator William Maclay, Washington "started up in a violent fret. *This defeats every purpose of my coming here*, were the first words that he said."[105] The diary of John Quincy Adams reports (perhaps apocryphally) that when Washington left the Senate chamber "he said he would be damned if he ever went there again."[106]

Washington returned two days later and obtained the Senate's answers to his questions and its consent to the treaty. He never again met personally with Senators to seek their advice on a treaty draft. It was an error for John Quincy Adams (and many others) to conclude: "And ever since that time treaties have been negotiated by the Executive *before* submitting them to the consideration of the Senate."[107] Washington continued to ask for the Senate's advice, but did so through written communications rather than personal appearances.[108] Senators were asked to approve the appointment of treaty negotiators and even advise on their negotiating instructions.[109] Far from being a "presidential monopoly," treaty negotiation is often shared with both houses of Congress to build legislative understanding and support.[110]

President Andrew Jackson encouraged Senators to assist in the negotiation of Indian treaties. Obtaining the Senate's views in advance "on this important and delicate branch of our future negotiations would enable the President to act much more effectively in the exercise of his particular functions. There is also the best reason to believe that measures in this respect emanating from the united counsel of the treaty-making power would be more satisfactory to the American

---

101. Id. at 378.

102. Id.

103. 1 ANNALS OF CONG. 67 (1789) (emphasis added).

104. Id. at 69–71.

105. WILLIAM MACLAY, SKETCHES OF DEBATE IN THE FIRST SENATE OF THE UNITED STATES 124 (1880) (emphasis in original). Also on Washington's visit to the Senate chamber: RALSTON HAYDEN, THE SENATE AND TREATIES, 1789–1817, at 16–26 (1920).

106. 6 MEMOIRS OF JOHN QUINCY ADAMS 427 (Charles Francis Adams ed., 1875).

107. Id. (emphasis in original).

108. 1 Richardson 64–65, 68–69, 71–72, 81–84, 110–13, 115.

109. THOMAS M. FRANCK & EDWARD WEISBAND, FOREIGN POLICY BY CONGRESS 136 (1979).

110. Examples are provided in 2 GEORGE H. HAYNES, THE SENATE OF THE UNITED STATES 576–602 (1938).

people and to the Indians."[111] President James K. Polk followed the same course, deciding it was prudent for a President to consult Senators in advance of "important measures of foreign policy which may ultimately come before them for their consideration."[112] Through such initiatives the President "secures harmony of action between that body and himself."[113] Presidents William McKinley, Warren Harding, and Herbert Hoover included Senators as members of U.S. delegations to negotiate treaties.[114]

President Woodrow Wilson decided to pursue treaty negotiations independently, at great cost to himself and the country. He believed that presidential leadership would compel legislative compliance by getting the country "into such scrapes, pledged in the view of the world to certain courses of action, that the Senate hesitates to bring about the appearance of dishonor which would follow its refusal to ratify the rash promises or to support the discreet threats of the Department of State."[115] Excluding prominent Senators from the negotiation of the Versailles Treaty marked a grave miscalculation, both constitutionally and politically.[116]

A more effective and constructive model of presidential-Senate cooperation appears in the legislative history of the United Nations Charter. Half of the eight members of the U.S. delegation that met in San Francisco in 1945 came from Congress: Senators Tom Connally (D-Tex.) and Arthur H. Vandenberg (R-Mich.), and Representatives Sol Bloom (D-N.Y.) and Charles A. Eaton (R-N.J.).[117] Ranking members of the Senate Foreign Relations Committee worked closely with the Truman administration on the North Atlantic Treaty. They actively engaged in negotiations and wrote some of the provisions.[118] As explained in Chapter 8, section 6, Truman would later renege on his promise not to use the Charter as a unilateral presidential means for ordering military operations against another country.

Although members of Congress often participate in treaty negotiation and this practice is generally in the interest of the executive branch, scholars continue to treat the negotiation stage as a presidential monopoly. Writing in 1996, Louis Henkin remarked: "In a word, 'advice and consent' has effectively been reduced to 'consent.'"[119] In an article in 2009, Oona Hathaway cited this position by Henkin: "as early as the presidency of George Washington, the 'advice and consent'

---

111.  4 J. Sen. Exec. Proc. 99 (1887).

112.  5 Richardson 2299.

113.  Id.

114.  Treaties and Other International Agreements: The Role of the United States Senate, S.Prt. 106–71, 106th Cong., 2d Sess. 109 (2001).

115.  Woodrow Wilson, Congressional Government 233–34 (1885). Similar views appear in his Constitutional Government in the United States 77–78 (1908). His belief in presidential monopoly of treaty negotiation has been thoroughly refuted: William Whitwell Dewhurst, *Does the Constitution Make the President Sole Negotiator of Treaties?*, 30 Yale L.J. 478 (1921); Forrest R. Black, *The United States Senate and the Treaty Power*, 4 Rocky Mt. L. Rev. 1 (1931); Richard E. Webb, *Treaty-Making and the President's Obligation to Seek the Advice and Consent of the Senate with Special Reference to the Vietnam Peace Negotiations*, 31 Ohio State L.J. 490 (1970); and Louis Fisher, *Congressional Participation in the Treaty Process*, 137 U. Pa. L. Rev. 1511 (1989).

116.  Townsend Hoopes & Douglas Brinkley, FDR and the Creation of the U.N. 1–9 (1997). See also Deena Frank Fleming, The Treaty Veto of the American Senate 124–57 (1930).

117.  *The Charter of the United Nations*, hearings before the Senate Committee on Foreign Relations, 79th Cong., 1st Sess. 644 (1945).

118.  Testimony by Dean Acheson, *Executive Privilege: The Withholding of Information by the Executive*, hearing before the Senate Committee on the Judiciary, 92d Cong., 1st Sess. 262–64 (1971). See also Richard H. Heindel et al., *The North Atlantic Treaty in the United States Senate*, 43 Am. J. Int'l L. 633 (1949).

119.  Louis Henkin, Foreign Affairs and the United States Constitution 177 (2d ed. 1996).

of the Senate was effectively reduced to consent.'"[120] The Office of Legal Counsel continues to cite Justice Sutherland's "clear dicta" that "Into the field of negotiation the Senate cannot intrude; and Congress itself is powerless to invade it"[121] These statements, no matter how frequently and confidently expressed, have no relationship to the regular practice of treaty negotiation by both branches.

## B. The Jay Treaty

Several constitutional misconceptions are commonly held about the Jay Treaty of 1796. President Washington rebuffed the House request for documents on two grounds: (1) treaties require secrecy in foreign negotiations, and (2) the Senate is the exclusive legislative participant in treaty-making. His explanation does not bear up under scrutiny and marks possibly the only time that he made a public statement that was trite and disingenuous.

The treaty was highly controversial. Chief Justice John Jay negotiated the agreement with England. Had it been litigated, it might come before him in his judicial capacity.[122] Moreover, it was widely known that Jay had departed from his negotiation instructions and acquiesced in substantial restrictions on American commerce.[123] What Washington identified as a matter of secrecy was in large part a decision to avoid public embarrassment about a treaty with many flaws. He decided to withhold from the House treaty documents, but the House had every constitutional reason to receive documents to permit it to make an informed judgment when voting on legislation and appropriations needed to *implement* the treaty. The treaty cleared the Senate by the bare minimum two-thirds majority, 20 to 10.[124] Lawmakers voted along party lines. Alexander Hamilton advised President Washington not to release the treaty instructions to the House, warning that they were "in general a crude mass" and would do "no credit to the administration."[125]

The House requested the treaty instructions, including correspondence and other related documents. It provided some discretion: "Excepting such of said papers as any negotiation may render improper to be disclosed."[126] That language applied to pending negotiations, not previous negotiations. Representative Edward Livingston highlighted the key constitutional authority of

---

120. Oona Hathaway, *Presidential Power Over International Law: Restoring the Balance*, 119 YALE L.J. 140, 207 (2009).

121. Office of Legal Counsel, *Memorandum Opinion for the Acting Legal Adviser, Department of State*, June 1, 2009, at 9, http://www.justice.gov/olc/2009/section7054.pdf.

122. HAYDEN, *supra* note 105, at 69–70. For documents on the Jay Treaty: 1 Goldsmith 414–21.

123. ABRAHAM D. SOFAER, WAR, FOREIGN AFFAIRS, AND CONSTITUTIONAL POWER: THE ORIGINS 85 (1976). For further analysis of the Jay Treaty: WILLIAM R. CASTO, THE SUPREME COURT IN THE EARLY REPUBLIC: THE CHIEF JUSTICES OF JOHN JAY AND OLIVER ELLSWORTH 87-98 (1995); STANLEY ELKINS & ERIC MCKITRICK, THE AGE OF FEDERALISM: THE EARLY AMERICAN REPUBLIC, 1788–1800, at 375–449 (1993); DANIEL N. HOFFMAN, GOVERNMENTAL SECRECY AND THE FOUNDING FATHERS: A STUDY IN CONSTITUTIONAL CONTROLS 131–77 (1981); SAMUEL FLAGG BEMIS, JAY'S TREATY: A STUDY IN COMMERCE AND DIPLOMACY (1975, originally published in 1923); and RALSTON HAYDEN, THE SENATE AND TREATIES, 1789–1817; THE DEVELOPMENT OF THE TREATY-MAKING FUNCTIONS OF THE UNITED STATES SENATE DURING THEIR FORMATIVE PERIOD 58–94 (1920).

124. ELKINS & MCKITRICK, *supra* note 123, at 419.

125. 20 THE PAPERS OF ALEXANDER HAMILTON 83 (Syrett ed. 1974).

126. ANNALS OF CONG., 4th Cong., 1st Sess. 400–01, 426 (March 2 & 7, 1796).

the House, which possessed "a discretionary power of carrying the Treaty into effect, or refusing it their sanction."[127] The President and the Senate could agree on a treaty, but the House was at liberty to decide whether to vote for necessary legislation and funding. Few treaties are self-executing.[128] Generally they depend on legislative action by both houses.

The Livingston resolution passed on a vote of 62 to 37.[129] Even before the confrontation with President Washington, members of the House had gained access to most of the treaty documents. Livingston, as chairman of the House Committee on American Seamen, "together with the whole committee, had been allowed access to these papers, and had inspected them." The same privilege, said one lawmaker, "he doubted not, would be given to any member of the House who would request it."[130] A House member, commenting on the Jay Treaty papers, observed: "he did not think there were any secrets in them. He believed he had seen them all."[131] Another lawmaker explained that his colleagues could have walked over to the office of the Secretary of the Senate to see the treaty papers, but why, he asked, "depend upon the courtesy of the Clerk for information which might as well be obtained in a more direct channel?"[132] Madison tried to weaken Livingston's resolution by authorizing the President to withhold papers that, "in his judgment, it may not be consistent with the interest of the United States, at this time, to disclose." His amendment failed, 37 to 47.[133]

President Washington did not invoke executive privilege to block congressional access. He acknowledged that "all the papers affecting the negotiation with Great Britain were laid before the Senate, when the Treaty itself was communicated for their consideration and advice."[134] His justification for withholding documents from the House is unpersuasive. He referred to the exclusive role of the Senate to participate as a member of the legislative branch in treaty matters.[135] Members of the House did not need a reminder that the Constitution excludes them from treaty-making. They knew that. The issue was whether to pass legislation to *implement* the Jay Treaty, and in that task the House was equal to the Senate.

Initially, Washington seemed to understand that point. A letter from Hamilton suggests that Washington agreed to give the House access to the treaty papers. Instead of delivering the documents to the House, Washington considered an alternative: having House members travel to the office of the Secretary of State to read the papers.[136] The editor of Hamilton's papers indicated that Washington planned to comply with Livingston's resolution.[137] Hamilton later advised Washington to deny House access to the treaty papers, fearing the documents "cannot fail to start [a] new and unpleasant Game—it will be fatal to the Negotiating Power of the Government

---

127. Id. at 427–28.

128. Jordan J. Paust, *Self-Executing Treaties*, 82 Am. J. Int'l L. 760 (1988).

129. Annals of Cong., 4th Cong., 1st Sess. 759 (March 14, 1796).

130. Id. at 461 (Rep. Harper). Legislation drafted by Livingston's committee concerned the relief and protection of American seamen who had been forced into naval service by Great Britain. Id. at 802–20.

131. Id. at 642 (Rep. Williams).

132. Id. at 588 (Rep. Freeman).

133. Id. at 438.

134. Id. at 761.

135. Id. at 759.

136. Letter from Hamilton to Washington, March 24, 1795, in 20 The Papers of Alexander Hamilton 81–82 (Syrett ed., 1974).

137. Id. at 66 (editor's introductory note to letter from Hamilton to Washington, March 7, 1796).

if it is to be a matter of course for a call of either House of Congress to bring forth all the communication however confidential."[138]

After Washington declined to give the House access to the treaty papers, Representative Thomas Blount introduced two resolutions to restate the principles of the Livingston resolution. The House adopted each resolution, 57 to 35. The language stated that when a treaty stipulates regulations on any of the subjects submitted to the constitutional power of Congress, "it must depend, for its execution, as to such stipulations, on a law or laws to be passed by Congress." It then becomes the constitutional right and duty of the House "to deliberate on the expediency or inexpediency of carrying such Treaty into effect, and to determine and act thereon, as, in their judgment, may be most conducive to the public good."[139]

Washington needed $90,000 from Congress to implement the Jay Treaty.[140] The House could have decided to deny funding until it gained full access to the treaty documents. Yet the appropriation passed the House by the narrow margin of 51 to 48.[141] An earlier test vote was even closer, 49 to 49, with the Speaker breaking the tie to support funding.[142] The appropriation became law.[143] Had a few House members shifted their votes, Washington would have faced this choice: release the treaty documents to the House or permit the treaty to fail of implementation.

Washington's constitutional arguments regarding the Jay Treaty are particularly artificial and misleading when we review his actions with the Algerine treaty of 1793. The Continental Congress paid bribes ("tributes") to four countries in North Africa—Morocco, Algiers, Tunis, and Tripoli—to permit American merchant vessels to operate safely in those waters.[144] In 1792, Washington had to decide whether to continue this practice. Could he rely only on the treaty process and Senate support, or did he need approval from both houses of Congress? He thought of taking out a loan, but repayment would have required him to seek an appropriation from both houses.

Secretary of State Jefferson did not think abstractly about treaty-making resting solely with the President and the Senate. On any question of funding, he knew the House was an equal partner. Jefferson looked at the matter practically. Just as Senators "expect to be consulted beforehand" about a pending treaty, if Representatives were being called on to fund a treaty, "why should not they expect to be consulted in like manner, when the case admits?"[145] Washington followed Jefferson's advice and agreed to seek support from both houses for the Algerine treaty.

Some Senators objected to the House participating in a treaty matter. If the House were allowed to vote, they reasoned, "it would not be a secret."[146] The Senate had little trust in the House. Washington's attitude toward the Senate was not any better. Lacking any confidence "in the secrecy of the Senate," he decided against borrowing money.[147] On December 16, 1793, he forwarded to both houses of Congress a message regarding a treaty with Morocco to pay ransom and establish

---

138. Id. at 68 (letter from Hamilton to Washington, March 7, 1796).

139. ANNALS OF CONG., 4th Cong., 1st Sess. 771 (1796). For the votes, see id. at 782–83.

140. Id. at 991.

141. Id. at 1291.

142. Id. at 1280.

143. 1 Stat. 459 (1796).

144. GERARD CASPER, SEPARATING POWER: ESSAYS ON THE FOUNDING PERIOD 45–50 (1997).

145. "The Anas," 1 WRITINGS OF THOMAS JEFFERSON 294 (Bergh ed. 1903).

146. Id. at 306.

147. Id.

peace with Algiers. He asked lawmakers to protect the confidentiality of certain letters.[148] Meeting in secret session, the House debated the treaty and supported funding.[149] Whatever treaty documents Washington gave the Senate he shared with the House. The treaty included an annual amount to be paid to the ruler of Algiers.[150] Having recognized the vital role of the House in implementing treaties, it was simplistic and inconsistent for Washington a few years later to tell the House it could not have Jay Treaty documents because it lacked a constitutional role in treaty-making and its access would undermine the need for secrecy.

## C. The Logan Act

Presidential responsibility to negotiate with foreign nations was tested in 1798 when George Logan, a Philadelphia physician, traveled to Europe to try his hand at diplomacy. American negotiations with France had foundered and he thought he could be of assistance.[151] His trip provoked a resolution in Congress directed against private citizens who "usurp the Executive authority of this government, by commencing or carrying on any correspondence with the Government of any foreign Prince or State."[152] The Logan Act provided fines and imprisonment for American citizens who conduct unauthorized correspondence or intercourse with foreign governments for the purpose of influencing American policy.[153] The word "unauthorized" is significant. Presidents and administration officials have often asked members of Congress and private parties to meet with foreign governments to resolve disputes.

Lacking an official invitation, thousands of individuals have defied the Logan Act. Only one was indicted and he was found not guilty.[154] During the Vietnam War, pacifist leaders and other Americans met frequently with North Vietnam officials and the peace delegations in Paris. The State Department took the position that members of Congress may engage in discussions with foreign officials pursuant to their legislative duties under the Constitution, provided they advise the officials they have no authority to negotiate on behalf of the United States.[155]

In 1976, former President Nixon traveled to China at the time of the New Hampshire presidential primary. Senator Barry Goldwater announced that Nixon violated the Logan Act and would do the United States a favor by remaining in China.[156] The State Department interpreted

---

148. 4 ANNALS OF CONG. 20–21 (Dec. 16, 1793).

149. Id. at 149–55 (Dec. 27, 1793–Jan. 2, 1794); 8 Stat. 133 (1795). See CASPER, *supra* note 144, at 51–65.

150. 8 Stat. 136 (art. XXII). See FISHER, *supra* note 81, at 30–33.

151. Frederick B. Tolles, *Unofficial Ambassador: George Logan's Mission to France, 1798*, 7 WM. & MARY Q. 3 (1950).

152. 1 Stat. 613 (1799); 18 U.S.C. § 953; ANNALS OF CONG. 5th Cong., 3d Sess. 2489 (1798).

153. See Charles Warren, *History of Laws Prohibiting Correspondence with a Foreign Government and Acceptance of a Commission*, S. Doc. No. 696, 64th Cong., 2d Sess. (1917).

154. Detlev F. Vagts, *The Logan Act: Paper Tiger or Sleeping Giant?*, 60 AM. J. INT'L L. 268 (1966). His analysis concluded that the statute is probably unconstitutional. For similar judgments: Kevin M. Kearny, *Private Citizens in Foreign Affairs: A Constitutional Analysis*, 36 EMORY L.J. 285 (1987), and Curtis C. Simpson, III, *The Logan Act: May It Rest in Peace*, 10 CAL. WEST. INT'L L.J. 365 (1980). Constitutional doubts were raised in Waldron v. British Petroleum Co., 231 F. Supp. 72, 88–89 (S.D.N.Y. 1964).

155. DIGEST OF UNITED STATES PRACTICE IN INTERNATIONAL LAW, 1975, at 749–50.

156. 122 CONG. REC. 4216, 4919 (1976); WASH. POST, Feb. 26, 1976, at A7.

Nixon's trip as one undertaken entirely as a private citizen and was "unaware of any basis for believing that Mr. Nixon acted with the intent prohibited by the Logan Act."[157] In 1979, after more than 50 Americans were held hostage in Iran, American legislators, professors, clergymen, and parents of the hostages traveled to that country in an effort to negotiate their release. When American citizens traveled to the Middle East to talk to Arab and Israeli leaders, President Carter said: "I don't have any authority, nor do I want to have any authority, to interrupt or to interfere with the right of American citizens to travel where they choose and to meet with whom they choose. I would not want that authority; I think it would be a violation of the basic constitutional rights that are precious to our Nation."[158]

A year later, Carter's position shifted when former Attorney General Ramsey Clark attended a conference in Iran despite a presidential ban. Some members of Congress charged that Clark violated the Logan Act.[159] Carter said he was inclined to prosecute Clark and several other Americans who ignored his travel restrictions.[160] Attorney General Benjamin Civiletti subsequently announced it would be "inappropriate" to prosecute Clark in a criminal suit. Nor were steps taken in a civil action.[161]

Jesse Jackson traveled frequently to foreign countries during the Reagan years, visiting with foreign leaders in Syria, Cuba, Central America, and other regions. Often he negotiated for the release of U.S. citizens. After visiting Cuba in 1984 and meeting with Fidel Castro, President Reagan told reporters "there is a law, the Logan Act, with regard to unauthorized personnel, civilians, simply going to…other countries and, in effect, negotiating with foreign governments. Now, that is the law of the land." But he said he had no plans to take legal action.[162] Louis Farrakhan in 1996 traveled to African and Middle Eastern countries, including Libya, Nigeria, Iraq, and Iran. Some members of Congress claimed a Logan Act violation but there was no prosecution.[163]

In 2007, Speaker Nancy Pelosi traveled to Syria and met with leaders of the government. Representative Dan Burton criticized her trip to a "terrorist state" after the State Department and the White House "disapproved" her visit. In a floor statement, Burton said: "We must not send a signal of weakness. I think the Speaker did the wrong thing. I believe she violated the Logan Act because she didn't have the approval of both the White House and the Defense Department."[164] No legal action resulted. The President's claim to a monopoly over diplomatic negotiation does not criminalize interaction by private citizens and members of Congress with foreign governments. Any agreements they reach are private and not binding on the nation.

157. DIGEST OF UNITED STATES PRACTICE IN INTERNATIONAL LAW, 1976, at 75–76.

158. PUBLIC PAPERS OF THE PRESIDENTS, 1979, at 1861.

159. 126 CONG. REC. 13005–08, 13581–82, 13727–31, 13842–43 (1980).

160. PUBLIC PAPERS OF THE PRESIDENTS, 1980–81, II, at 1087.

161. *Prosecution of Clark Rejected by Civiletti*, WASH. POST, Jan. 8, 1981, at A6.

162. PUBLIC PAPERS OF THE PRESIDENTS, 1984, II, at 990.

163. 142 CONG. REC. 3667 (1996).

164. 153 CONG. REC. H3444 (daily ed. April 17, 2007).

# D. Supremacy of treaties

Article VI provides that all treaties shall be "the supreme Law of the Land; and the Judges in every State shall be bound thereby; any Thing in the Constitution or Laws of any State to the contrary notwithstanding." Under Article III, section 2, the power of the Supreme Court applies to "Treaties made, or which shall be made." Those provisions clearly establish national superiority over the states with regard to treaties. Article I, section 10 adds: "No State shall enter into any Treaty, Alliance, or Confederation." The Supreme Court has held that in cases of conflict between state law and a treaty, the latter prevails.[165] In 1920, the Supreme Court seemed to suggest that what Congress could not do by statute might be done by treaty.[166] However, there is no question, under the "last in time" doctrine, that a statute may override a treaty just as a treaty may override a statute.[167]

Many questions remain. Are all treaties "self-executing" or do some require implementing legislation by Congress? When the President and the Senate agree to a treaty, does that compel the House to pass authorizing and appropriating bills? There is no reason to believe that. Does the judiciary have the superior voice in interpreting treaties? In 1829, the Supreme Court for the first time held that portions of a treaty may require legislation by Congress. Although a treaty is the law of the land and may be regarded by courts "as equivalent to an act of the legislature," that principle applies only when "it operates of itself without the aid of any legislative provision."[168] Such treaties are called self-executing. However, "when the terms of the stipulation import a contract, when either of the parties engages to perform a particular act, the treaty addresses itself to the political, not the judicial department; and the legislature must execute the contract before it can become a rule for the Court."[169]

A study by Jordan Paust in 1988 referred to the distinction between "self-executing" and "non-self executing" treaties as a "judicially invented notion that is patently inconsistent with express language in the Constitution affirming that '*all* Treaties . . . shall be the supreme Law of the Land.' "[170] Although the decision in 1829 was the first to judicially make that distinction, the elected branches understood the difference from the beginning. Certainly President Washington realized that the Algerine and Jay Treaties could not take effect unless both houses of Congress passed implementing legislation. The burden was on him to do what was necessary, politically, to gain that support. The two houses were not constitutionally compelled to pass the legislation.

The study by Paust in 1988 appeared to reject "the current insistence that certain treaties are inherently non-self-executing because legislative power exists, for example, to regulate commerce, to define and punish crimes, and to appropriate money."[171] His study assigned control not to Congress but to the judiciary. To claim that certain treaties "should be inherently

---

165. Ware v. Hylton, 3 U.S. (3 Dall.) 199 (1796).

166. Missouri v. Holland, 252 U.S. 416, 432 (1920) ("If the treaty is valid there can be no dispute about the validity of the statute under Article I, § 8, as a necessary and proper means to execute the powers of Government.")

167. Whitney v. Robertson, 124 U.S. 190, 193–94 (1888); see also The Chinese Exclusion Case, 130 U.S. 581, 600–02 (1889); Head Money Cases, 112 U.S. 580, 597–99 (1894); and MICHAEL J. GLENNON, CONSTITUTIONAL DIPLOMACY 233 (1990).

168. Foster v. Neilson, 27 U.S. (2 Pet.) 253, 314 (1829).

169. Id.

170. Jordan J. Paust, *Self-Executing Treaties*, 82 AM. J. INT'L L. 760, 760 (1988) (emphasis in original).

171. Id. at 775.

non-self-executing merely because Congress has a relevant concurrent power is to ignore or subvert the separation of powers between the legislative and judicial branches, to rewrite the Constitution at the expense of the treaty power. It is the judiciary, not Congress, that has been granted the power (indeed the textual commitment) under Article III of the Constitution to apply treaty law in cases or controversies otherwise properly before the courts."[172]

Under that interpretation, the President and the Senate could reach agreement on a treaty that commits specific dollar amounts of economic and military assistance to another country and the two houses would be compelled to pass implementing legislation. That position dismisses the independent constitutional role of the House, discussed in the next section. Moreover, there is nothing to prevent Congress from passing a statute to override a treaty. Under the Constitution, a treaty and a statute are equally the law of the land. One instrument is not superior to the other. If the two are inconsistent, the most recent prevails. The Court has frequently acknowledged this last-in-time rule.[173]

According to a study by John Yoo, if the elected branches "wished to render a treaty self-executing they would have to make that clear in the text."[174] However, if the Jay Treaty had somehow said it was "self-executing," President Washington still needed to convince both houses of Congress to pass authorizations and appropriations. He and the Senate could not, through the treaty process, compel House action and approval. Yoo's study also maintained that whether a treaty is self-executing depends on "the intent of the treatymakers."[175] Intent is not sufficient or even relevant. President Washington and the Senate could have been crystal clear about their intent of self-execution with the Jay Treaty but the House always retained the right to say, "No." A treaty may not provide: "This agreement is self-executing and hereby appropriates funds." In 1978 the D.C. Circuit noted: "[t]he expenditure of funds by the United States cannot be accomplished by self-executing treaties; implementing legislation appropriating such funds is indispensable."[176]

What is the role of courts in enforcing treaties? Article VI regards treaties as "laws" ("the supreme Law of the Land") and Article III, section 2 grants the Supreme Court jurisdiction over treaties. Does that imply that the Supreme Court has final reviewing authority over the meaning and application of a treaty? Some studies would make federal courts "the primary enforcers" of all three elements of the Supremacy Clause: the Constitution, statutes, and treaties.[177] If a treaty promised specific amounts of financial assistance to another country, could the judiciary order the houses of Congress to pass the necessary implementing legislation, requiring action from authorizing and appropriating committees? Such a doctrine would create a serious

172. Id. at 777.

173. The Cherokee Tobacco, 78 U.S. (11 Wall.) 616, 620–21 (1870); Head Money Cases, 112 U.S. 580, 597–99 (1884); Whitney v. Robertson, 124 U.S. 190, 194 (1888).

174. John C. Yoo, *Globalism and the Constitution: Treaties, Non-Self Execution, and the Original Understanding*, 99 COLUM. L. REV. 1955, 1971 (1999).

175. Id.

176. Edwards v. Carter, 580 F.2d 1055, 1058 (D.C. Cir. 1978).

177. Carlos Manuel Vázquez, *Treaty-Based Rights and Remedies of Individuals*, 92 COLUM. L. REV. 1092, 1108 (1992).

confrontation between the judicial and legislative branches, with Congress having full legitimacy to prevail in such a contest. It is in the interest of courts to avoid that collision.[178]

In 2008, the Supreme Court decided that neither a decision by the International Court of Justice nor a memorandum issued by President George W. Bush were enforceable as domestic law in a state court. A treaty may constitute an international commitment, but it is not binding as domestic law unless Congress enacts legislation implementing it or the treaty conveys an intention that it be "self-executing." No such intention applied in this case.[179]

# 4. ROLE OF THE HOUSE

In addition to passing legislation and appropriations to implement treaties, the House has a broad role in international agreements. Several delegates at the Philadelphia convention favored a check on treaties by both houses rather than by the Senate alone. Because treaties have the status of law under the Constitution, they reasoned that the entire Congress should register its approval. At one point it was suggested that "no Treaty shall be binding on the U.S. which is not ratified by a law."[180] Madison wondered whether a distinction might be made between two types of treaties: those allowing the President and the Senate to make "Treaties eventual and of Alliance for limited terms—and requiring the concurrence of the whole Legislature in other Treaties."[181] A later proposal, joining the House with the Senate in advising and consenting to treaties, was decisively rejected, with one state in favor and ten opposed."[182]

## A. Funding disputes

On the basis of a provisional appropriation of $2 million to be applied toward the purchase of New Orleans and the Floridas, the Jefferson administration entered into an agreement with France to buy the whole of Louisiana. Jefferson understood that successful implementation of the treaty with France required close cooperation and support from both houses of Congress. He sent copies of the ratified treaty to the House and the Senate, explaining: "You will observe that some important conditions can not be carried into execution but with the aid of the Legislature, and that time presses a decision on them without delay."[183] The House joined the Senate in passing legislation to enable Jefferson to take possession of the Louisiana Territory.[184] On the Louisiana Purchase, see also Chapter 3, section 5.

---

178. Vázquez in a subsequent article discusses the need to seek House action to implement treaties, if not before then later. Carlos Manuel Vázquez, *Laughing at Treaties*, 99 COLUM. L. REV. 2154, 2161 (1999).

179. Medellin v. Texas, 552 U.S. 491 (2008). For the analysis of Vázquez of this decision, see *Treaties as Law of the Land: The Supremacy Clause and the Judicial Enforcement of Treaties*, 122 HARV. L. REV. 599 (2008). Also on this issue: Edward T. Swaine, *Taking Care of Treaties*, 108 COLUM. L. REV. 331 (2008).

180. 2 Farrand 392.

181. Id. at 394.

182. Id. at 538.

183. 1 Richardson 350–51 (Oct. 21, 1803).

184. 2 Stat. 245, 247 (1803); ANNALS OF CONG., 8th Cong., 1st Sess. 385–419.

On some occasions the House has opposed treaties that required appropriations, such as the Gadsden purchase treaty with Mexico in 1853 and the Alaskan purchase treaty with Russia in 1867. The need to have the support of both houses for certain treaties was recognized in a reciprocity treaty with the Hawaiian Islands in 1876. A proviso made the treaty dependent on legislative consent by both houses.[185]

A dispute over the Spanish Bases Treaty of 1976 began as a conflict between the Senate and the President. It ended up as a struggle between the two houses and the need to protect the jurisdiction of committees. Senators insisted that the agreement with Spain over military bases be accomplished not by an executive agreement, as in the past, but by treaty. Members of both houses objected to language in the treaty that appeared to make mandatory the appropriation of funds over a five-year period. The administration also argued that the treaty constituted an *authorization* to have funds appropriated, thus threatening to circumvent the jurisdictions of the Senate Committee on Foreign Relations and the House Committee on Foreign Affairs.[186]

Responding to these issues, the Senate Resolution of Advice and Consent contained a declaration that the sums referred to in the treaty "shall be made available for obligation through the normal procedures of the Congress, including the process of prior authorization and annual appropriations."[187] The language guaranteed congressional control by the authorizing and appropriation committees of both houses. Congress enacted legislation in 1976 to authorize the appropriation of funds needed to implement the treaty.[188] This treaty was replaced by an executive agreement in 1982. It stipulated that the supply of defense articles and services is subject to "the annual authorizations and appropriations contained in United States security assistance legislation." Although the agreement promised support "in the highest amounts, the most favorable terms, and the widest variety of forms," it conditioned support on what "may be lawful and feasible."[189] In short, the two countries could negotiate as they like; what Spain received depended on legislative action by both houses.

A dispute over the Panama Canal in the 1970s raised questions about the United States having to surrender control over the canal. Members of the House looked to language in the Constitution about ceding U.S. property. Article IV, section 3, clause 2 states: "The Congress shall have Power to dispose of and make all needful Rules and Regulations respecting the Territory or other Property belonging to the United States." Several dozen members of the House asked the courts to declare illegal President Carter's submission of the Panama Canal treaties to the Senate. They argued that the treaty process violated their right to vote on the disposition of U.S. property. A district court held that the lawmakers lacked standing. The D.C. Circuit affirmed that ruling but also held that the Property Clause in Article IV is not the exclusive method of disposing of federal property. The use of treaties for that purpose is constitutionally authorized.[190]

---

185. Chalfant Robinson, *The Treaty-Making Power of the House of Representatives*, 12 YALE REV. 191 (1903). See also Ivan M. Stone, *The House of Representatives and the Treaty-Making Power*, 17 KY. L.J. 216 (1929).

186. *Treaty With Spain: Congress' Powers An Issue*, CONG. Q. WEEKLY REPT., April 10, 1976, at 852–56.

187. See 122 CONG. REC. 19074–75, 30219–20, 30225–31 (1976); S. Rep. No. 94-941, 94th Cong., 2d Sess. (1976).

188. 90 Stat. 765, sec. 507 (1976); 90 Stat. 2498 (1976).

189. *Agreement on Friendship, Defense, and Cooperation Between the United States of America and the Kingdom of Spain*, Complimentary Agreement Three, Article 2, signed July 2, 1982.

190. Edwards v. Carter, 445 F. Supp. 1279 (D.D.C. 1978); Edwards v. Carter, 580 F.2d 1055 (D.C. Cir. 1978), cert. denied, 436 U.S. 907 (1978).

## *B. Statutes vs. treaties*

Legislation can serve as a substitute for treaties. When the Senate failed to ratify a treaty for the annexation of Texas, President John Tyler advised the House of Representatives: "The power of Congress is, however, fully competent in some other form of proceeding to accomplish everything that a formal ratification of the treaty could have accomplished."[191] He laid before the House the rejected treaty, together with all the correspondence and documents that had previously been made available to the Senate. Instead of needing a two-thirds majority from the Senate, the annexation of Texas was consummated by simple majority vote from both houses.[192] Hawaii was annexed in 1898 by the same procedure.[193] The Senate had earlier blocked action on a treaty. The St. Lawrence Seaway Plan, rejected by the Senate in 1934 as a treaty, passed Congress in 1954 as a regular bill.[194] There has been extensive debate about whether SALT (Strategic Arms Limitation) agreements required approval by treaty or by statute.[195]

The role of the House in international agreements was at issue in 1994 when President Clinton submitted the Uruguay Round Agreements to Congress as a bill rather than a treaty. The purpose of the bill was to implement the worldwide General Agreements on Tariffs and Trade (GATT). Laurence Tribe testified that certain features of the bill would so alter the dynamics of state-federal relations that ratification of a treaty by two-thirds of the Senate was constitutionally required, given the Senate's special role in representing the states as political units.[196] There are few clear guidelines on what must be done by treaty rather than by statute. The subject matter of GATT—international trade—was certainly within the jurisdiction of Congress as a whole to "regulate Commerce with foreign nations" and therefore merited action by both houses through the regular legislative process. The same constitutional issue arose with action on the North American Free Trade Agreement (NAFTA), which passed not as a treaty but a statute.[197]

In 2001, the Eleventh Circuit was asked to decide whether NAFTA was a "treaty" requiring Senate ratification pursuant to the Treaty Clause. It had been passed as a regular bill and submitted to the President for his signature. The court held that there were no standards available to the

---

191. 5 Richardson 2176 (June 10, 1844).

192. 5 Stat. 797 (1845).

193. Hawaii v. Mankichi, 190 U.S. 197 (1903). Myres S. McDougal & Asher Lans, *Treaties and Congressional-Executive or Presidential Agreements: Interchangeable Instruments of National Policy* (Parts I & II), 54 Yale L.J. 181, 534 (1945).

194. 68 Stat. 92 (1954). For an opinion by Acting Attorney General James McGranery in 1946, upholding the legality of an executive agreement made pursuant to a joint resolution (instead of a treaty), see 40 Op. Att'y Gen. 569 (1946).

195. *Treaty Ratification Process and Separation of Powers*, hearing before the Subcommittee on Separation of Powers of the Senate Committee on the Judiciary, 97th Cong., 2d Sess. (1982); Armen R. Vartian, *Approval of SALT Agreements by Joint Resolution of Congress*, 21 Harv. Int'l L.J. 421 (1980).

196. *S. 2467, GATT Implementing Legislation*, hearings before the Senate Committee on Commerce, Science, and Transportation, 103d Cong., 2d Sess. 302–12 (1994).

197. Bruce Ackerman & David Golove, *Is NAFTA Constitutional?*, 108 Harv. L. Rev. 799 (1995). See also Laurence H. Tribe, *Taking Text and Structure Seriously: Reflections on Free-Form Method in Constitutional Interpretation*, 108 Harv. L. Rev. 1223 (1995), and Peter J. Spiro, *Treaties, Executive Agreements, and Constitutional Method*, 79 Tex. L. Rev. 961 (2011).

judiciary to determine whether one procedure was constitutionally superior to the other. The issue represented a nonjusticiable political question.[198]

## C. Fast-track procedures

The Trade Act of 1974 included both houses of Congress in trade policy by authorizing a "fast track" procedure. The statute created the following procedure: the executive branch negotiates a trade policy, invites members of Congress to participate, and the President's proposal is then submitted in the form of a bill. It may not be amended by Congress or buried in committee. Congress must vote within a specified time period, either to pass or defeat the bill. That procedure was used in 1993 to pass NAFTA. The prohibition on amendments is somewhat misleading. Although the implementing bill may not be amended in committee or on the floor, a draft bill is circulated and subject to congressional hearings, committee markups, and pressures for changes.[199] The executive branch ignores these congressional demands at its peril. Failure to address legislative concerns can result in the implementing bill being voted down.

The notion that the President is the exclusive negotiator of treaties and international agreements is belied by this process. Administrations greatly value the procedural benefits of fast-track, particularly the ban on amendments and the deadline for Congress voting on the bill, up or down. In return, the executive branch agrees that lawmakers will be closely involved in the negotiation. In 1991, after President Bush asked Congress to extend fast-track to cover a trade pact with Mexico, U.S. Trade Representative Carla Hills told the Senate Finance Committee that the procedure demands "a genuine partnership between the two branches." Because Congress retains the power to defeat implementing bills, she emphasized that Congress "has a full role in close consultation as the negotiations proceed."[200]

# 5. TREATY TERMINATION AND REINTERPRETATION

The Constitution does not explain how treaties are terminated. The delegates did not discuss that issue at the Philadelphia convention. Article VI vests treaties with the same domestic status as federal statutes. The Constitution, statutes, and treaties "shall be the supreme Law of the Land." Some of the early treaties were terminated or abrogated by statute. To the extent that a statute conflicts with an existing treaty, it operates to abrogate those portions of the treaty.[201] Other treaties have been terminated by presidential action, Senate resolutions, and new treaties.[202]

---

198. Made in the USA Foundation v. United States, 242 F.3d 1300 (11th Cir. 2001), cert. denied, sub nom. United Steelworkers of America, AFL-CIO, CLC, et al., 534 U.S. 1039 (2001).

199. Harold Hongju Koh, *The Fast Track and United States Trade Policy*, 18 BROOK. J. INT'L L. 143 (1992).

200. *Extension of Fast Track Legislative Procedures*, hearings before the Senate Committee on Finance, 102d Cong., 1st Sess. 9 (1991).

201. The Chinese Exclusion Case, 130 U.S. 581, 600–02 (1889). See also Whitney v. Robertson, 124 U.S. 190, 193–94 (1888), and the Head Money Cases, 112 U.S. 580, 597–99 (1884).

202. DIGEST OF UNITED STATES PRACTICE IN INTERNATIONAL LAW, 1978, at 734–65.

## A. *The Goldwater case*

After President Nixon made overtures to the People's Republic of China (PRC), some members of Congress were concerned that steps might be taken to terminate U.S. treaties with the Republic of China (Taiwan). The Mutual Defense Treaty of 1954 permitted "either party" to end the pact after giving the other country one year's notice. The treaty did not explain the particular process to be used. In legislation enacted in 1978, Congress adopted this nonbinding language: "It is the sense of the Congress that there should be prior consultation between the Congress and the executive branch" on any changes affecting the U.S.-Taiwan treaty.[203] Two months later, when Congress was out of session, President Carter announced his decision to recognize the PRC and terminate the defense treaty with Taiwan.

A resolution by Senator Harry Byrd provided it was the sense of the Senate that "approval of the United States Senate is required to terminate any Mutual Defense Treaty between the United States and another nation."[204] The Senate Foreign Relations Committee retained the nonbinding language but recommended the concurrence of both houses of Congress.[205] On a vote of 59 to 34, Byrd successfully restored his position on Senate approval. Other issues of treaty termination were debated.[206] Senator Barry Goldwater brought the issue to the courts. A decision by District Judge Oliver Gasch, placed in the *Congressional Record,* concluded that the power to terminate treaties is shared by the two elected branches and the President could not act alone. But he noted that Congress had yet to assert its position.[207] The Senate debate continued without final legislative action.[208]

The D.C. Circuit rejected the district court decision. The appellate court ruled that the President, in the particular circumstances before the court, was empowered to terminate the Taiwan treaty. The judiciary, it said, was incapable of distinguishing between treaties that could be terminated by the President alone and those that required joint executive-legislative action.[209] It noted that Congress was aware that it possessed strong powers to express its disapproval of Carter's action but "simply did not take those measures."[210] Even if the Senate had acted on the Byrd resolution, it was merely a sense-of-the-Senate measure and would not have been legally binding. The court underscored a crucial fact: "Congress as a body has chosen not to confront the President directly on the treaty termination."[211]

Without oral argument and acting within days of the scheduled treaty termination, the Supreme Court was poorly positioned to issue a thoughtful and reasoned decision. In dismissing Goldwater's complaint, the Justices scattered in so many directions that no position emerged to provide clear guidance for future disputes over treaty termination.[212] Powell counseled that

---

203. 92 Stat. 746, sec. 26 (1978).

204. 125 CONG. REC. 475 (1979).

205. Id. at 13672.

206. Id. at 13705, 13712–13.

207. Id. at 13707–09; Goldwater v. Carter, 481 F. Supp. 949 (D.D.C. 1979).

208. 125 CONG. REC. 13711–21, 14840, 15209–11 (1979).

209. Goldwater v. Carter, 617 F.2d 697, 707 (D.C. Cir. 1979).

210. Id. at 712.

211. Id. at 714.

212. Goldwater v. Carter, 444 U.S. 996 (1979).

the case should be dismissed as not ripe for judicial review.[213] In his judgment, the judiciary should not decide executive-legislative conflicts until the two branches reach an impasse, which had not yet occurred. Had Congress challenged Carter's action with legislation, it would have been appropriate for the Court to resolve the dispute. Rehnquist, joined by Burger, Stewart, and Stevens, regarded the matter as a nonjusticiable political question that had no place in the courts.[214] Blackmun, joined by White, believed the Court should have heard oral argument and given the case plenary consideration.[215] Brennan did not agree the case represented a political question. He would have granted the President authority to terminate treaties as an incident of his power to recognize foreign governments.[216]

Senator Goldwater introduced legislation in 1981 to require a two-thirds affirmative vote in the Senate to terminate defense treaties.[217] Two years later he introduced a concurrent resolution (which is not legally binding) to require congressional action by either a two-thirds vote of the Senate or a majority vote of both houses.[218] In 1985, he proposed that the Senate act by simple resolution to establish the procedures for terminating defense and security treaties.[219] Two members of the House introduced legislation in 1987 to establish treaty termination procedures. None of those measures received action by Congress.[220]

On December 13, 2001, President George W. Bush announced the withdrawal of the United States from the Antiballistic Missile (ABM) Treaty that had been signed with the Soviet Union in 1972. He concluded that the treaty hindered the ability of the United States "to develop ways to protect our people from future terrorist or rogue state missile attacks."[221] Thirty-two members of the House of Representatives filed suit, contending that because the Supremacy Clause classifies treaties, like statutes, as the "supreme Law of the Land," the President may not terminate a treaty without congressional consent. A district court held that the lawmakers lacked standing to bring the case, which also raised a nonjusticiable political question.[222] The House plaintiffs did not appeal the decision.[223] The treaty was terminated.

213. Id.

214. Id. at 1002–06.

215. Id. at 1006.

216. Id. at 1006–07. For analysis of treaty termination and the cases that followed *Goldwater v. Carter*: Roy E. Brownell II, *Foreign Affairs and Separation of Powers in the Twenty-first Century*, 2 J. NAT'L SECURITY L. & POL'Y 367, 391–96 (2008) (reviewing JOHN YOO, THE POWERS OF WAR AND PEACE (2005)). See also Raoul Berger, *The President's Unilateral Termination of the Taiwan Treaty*, 75 Nw. U. L. REV. 577 (1980); Karin Lee Lawson, *The Constitutional Twilight Zone of Treaty Termination:* Goldwater v. Carter, 20 VA. J. INT'L L. 147 (1979).

217. S.J. Res. 31 (1981); 127 CONG. REC. 2286–87 (1981).

218. 129 CONG. REC. 3414–15 (1983).

219. 131 CONG. REC. 678–80 (1985).

220. 133 CONG. REC. 36646, 36666–67 (1987).

221. PUBLIC PAPERS OF THE PRESIDENTS, 2001, II, at 1510.

222. Kucinich v. Bush, 236 F. Supp. 2d 1 (D.D.C. 2002). See David Gray Adler, *Termination of the ABM Treaty and the Political Question Doctrine: Judicial Succor for Presidential Power*, 34 PRES. STUD. Q. 156 (2004).

223. For additional analysis of treaty termination: MICHAEL D. RAMSEY, THE CONSTITUTION'S TEXT IN FOREIGN AFFAIRS 155–73, 321–41 (2007); Adler, *Termination of the ABM Treaty, supra* note 222; MICHAEL J. GLENNON, CONSTITUTIONAL DIPLOMACY 145–61, 318–23 (1990); and DAVID GRAY ADLER, THE CONSTITUTION AND THE TERMINATION OF TREATIES (1986).

## B. Treaty reinterpretation

Once a treaty takes effect, the President and executive officials are largely responsible for implementing and interpreting the treaty. Federal courts may also interpret a treaty, at times in ways contrary to executive interpretations.[224] An executive-legislative clash may occur when the President "reinterprets" a treaty to reach a meaning different from what Senators understood at the time they ratified the treaty.[225]

Treaty reinterpretation became a prominent issue in 1983 when President Reagan pressed for a sophisticated antimissile defense shield consisting of satellites armed with laser weapons. The administration referred to it as the Strategic Defense Initiative (SDI); the press called it "Star Wars." Some lawmakers argued that deployment or even testing of the SDI would violate the ABM treaty. According to others, appropriated funds could be spent only for research and development. Administration officials wanted to use funds for development, testing, and deployment of space-based ABMs contingent on future technologies. The conflict intensified when proponents of the broader interpretation relied on the treaty negotiation record, which was classified and had not been shared with the Senate.[226]

What disturbed many lawmakers was the administration's position that Senators give advice and consent to a treaty, not to the explanations of the treaty offered by executive officials.[227] Under that theory, executive officials could explain to Senators the meaning of a treaty without being bound by those explanations. During hearings in 1987, Senator Arlen Specter asked: "Can we function in a system where the Senate cannot rely on explanations made by executive officers?"[228] These complex issues, both legal and political, were resolved by the power of the purse. In 1987, Congress passed legislation stating that the Secretary of Defense "may not deploy any anti-ballistic missile system unless such deployment is specifically authorized by law after the date of the enactment of this Act."[229]

Presidents continue to exercise broad authority in interpreting treaties, but their decisions are not absolute. President George W. Bush offered his interpretation of Common Article 3 of the Third Geneva Convention in deciding to try Salim Ahmed Hamdan by military commission. In rejecting his interpretation, the Supreme Court noted the requirement in Common Article 3 that Hamdan be tried by a regularly constituted court that affords all the judicial guarantees recognized as indispensable by civilized peoples. It acknowledged that Common Article 3 "tolerates a great degree of flexibility in trying individuals captured during armed conflict."

224. Rainbow Nav., Inc. v. Department of Navy, 699 F. Supp. 339 (D.D.C. 1988); Rainbow Nav., Inc. v. Department of Navy, 686 F. Supp. 354 (D.D.C. 1988).

225. Michael J. Glennon, *Interpreting "Interpretation": The President, the Senate, and When Treaty Interpretation Becomes Treaty Making*, 20 U.C. Davis L. Rev. 913 (1987).

226. Abram Chayes & Antonia Handler Chayes, *Testing and Development of "Exotic" Systems Under the ABM Treaty: The Great Reinterpretation Caper*, 99 Harv. L. Rev. 1956 (1986); Abraham D. Sofaer, *The ABM Treaty and the Strategic Defense Initiative*, 99 Harv. L. Rev. 1972 (1986).

227. *The ABM Treaty and the Constitution*, joint hearings before the Senate Committees on Foreign Relations and the Judiciary, 100th Cong., 1st Sess. 130 (1987).

228. Id. at 143.

229. 101 Stat. 1057, sec. 226 (1987). The treaty reinterpretation issue is debated in detail at 137 U. Pa. L. Rev. 1351–1557 (1989). See also Gary Michael Buechler, *Constitutional Limits on the President's Power to Interpret Treaties: The Sofaer Doctrine, the Biden Condition, and the Doctrine of Binding Authoritative Representations*, 78 Geo. L.J. 1983 (1990).

Its requirements are general ones, "crafted to accommodate a wide variety of legal systems. But *requirements* they are nonetheless." The commission that Bush convened did not meet those requirements.[230]

# 6. EXECUTIVE AGREEMENTS

Some differences between treaties and executive agreements are clear. Treaties require the advice and consent of the Senate; executive agreements do not. Treaties, unlike executive agreements, may supersede prior conflicting statutes.[231] The executive branch may at times insist that a statutory provision interferes with executive presidential authority. Otherwise, there is substantial discretion on the part of the executive branch to choose between treaties and executive agreements. A major constraint is when Senators are willing to assert their institutional interests to ensure that their role in the treaty process is not circumvented.

Although the term executive agreement may suggest unilateral and perhaps even inherent authority, most executive agreements are entered into to implement treaties and statutes. They are done to carry out the law. Legislation in 1792 authorized the Postmaster General to make arrangements with foreign postmasters for the receipt and delivery of letters and packets.[232] To fulfill the statute, many executive agreements with other countries were necessary. Executive officials often enter into reciprocal trade agreements on the basis of statutory authority. The Supreme Court in 1912 said these agreements lacked the "dignity" of a treaty because they do not require Senate approval, but they are nevertheless valid international compacts.[233]

The executive branch cites four sources of constitutional authority under which the President may enter into executive agreements: (1) the President's authority as chief executive to represent the nation in foreign affairs, (2) the President's authority to receive ambassadors and other public ministers, and to recognize foreign governments, (3) the President's authority as Commander in Chief, and (4) the President's authority to "take care that the laws be faithfully executed."[234]

In the period after World War II, Congress grew increasingly concerned about presidential dominance in foreign policy, exercised in part through treaties and executive agreements. In 1952, Senator John Bricker expressed his belief that U.S. sovereignty and its constitutional system were put at risk by treaties pursued by the United Nations and its specialized agencies to move toward "world government."[235] His proposed constitutional amendment stated that no treaty or executive

---

230. Hamdan v. Rumsfeld, 548 U.S. 557, 635 (2006) (emphasis in original). See also Brownell, *supra* note 216, at 396–401.

231. United States v. Schooner Peggy, 5 U.S. (1 Cr.) 103 (1801); memorandum by Monroe Leigh, Legal Adviser to the State Department, Oct. 8, 1975, reprinted at 121 Cong. Rec. 36718–21 (1975).

232. 1 Stat. 239 (1792).

233. Altman & Co. v. United States, 224 U.S. 583, 600–01 (1912). In United States v. Pink, 315 U.S. 203, 230 (1942), Justice Douglas regarded executive agreements as having a "similar dignity" to treaties. Acting Attorney General McGranery in 1946 upheld the legality of an executive agreement made pursuant to a joint resolution; 40 Op. Att'y Gen. 469.

234. 11 FAM [Foreign Affairs Manual] 723.2-2(C), Sept. 25, 2006, http://www.state.gov/documents/organization/88317.pdf.

235. 98 Cong. Rec. 909 (1952).

agreement "shall be made respecting the rights of citizens of the United States protected by this Constitution, or abridging or prohibiting the free exercise thereof." Nor could any treaty or executive agreement "vest in any international organization or in any foreign power any of the legislative, executive, or judicial powers vested by this Constitution in the Congress, the President, and in the courts of the United States." Executive agreements "shall not be made in lieu of treaties." Executive agreements "shall, if not sooner terminated, expire automatically 1 year after the end of the term of office for which the President making the agreement shall have been elected." Congress and the new President would have the option of extending the executive agreement.[236] The language of the amendment changed over time. In 1954, the final version failed to receive the required two-thirds majority. The vote in the Senate was 60 to 31, or one vote short.[237]

## A. Litigation

Recognition of foreign governments may involve the settlement of claims and legal disputes. President Roosevelt's recognition of Soviet Russia led to the "Litvinov Assignment" in 1933 and subsequent property claims in the courts. In 1937, the Supreme Court unanimously upheld the assignment as a valid international compact.[238] Five years later, in a second case involving the recognition of the Soviet Union, Justice Douglas declared that the powers of the President in the conduct of foreign affairs "included the power, without consent of the Senate, to determine the public policy of the United States with respect to the Russian nationalization decrees." To Douglas, the President possessed authority to do more than simply determine which government to recognize. Presidential authority included the power to decide the policy to accompany recognition. Objections to the policy or the recognition "are to be addressed to the political department and not to the courts."[239]

His decision swept too broadly. Executive agreements may affect private claims and the constitutional privileges of the Due Process and Just Compensation Clauses of the Fifth Amendment. Presidents are not at liberty to enter into executive agreements that violate constitutional provisions. As the State Department acknowledges, the President "may conclude an international agreement on any subject within his constitutional authority so long as the agreement is not inconsistent with legislation enacted by the Congress in the exercise of its constitutional authority."[240] That principle surfaced in a Fourth Circuit decision in 1953. The court struck down an executive agreement that contravened an existing commercial statute with Canada. Imports from a foreign country represented foreign commerce "subject to regulation, so far as this country is concerned, by Congress alone."[241]

---

236. Id. at 908.

237. 100 CONG. REC. 2349–2375 (1954). See GLEN S. KRUTZ & JEFFREY S. PEAKE, TREATY POLITICS AND THE RISE OF EXECUTIVE AGREEMENTS: INTERNATIONAL COMMITMENTS IN A SYSTEM OF SHARED POWERS (2009); DUANE TANANBAUM, THE BRICKER AMENDMENT CONTROVERSY (1988); LOCH K. JOHNSON, THE MAKING OF INTERNATIONAL AGREEMENTS: CONGRESS CONFRONTS THE EXECUTIVE (1984).

238. United States v. Belmont, 301 U.S. 324 (1937).

239. United States v. Pink, 315 U.S. 203, 229 (1942). See Note, *United States v. Pink—A Reappraisal*, 48 COLUM. L. REV. 890 (1948).

240. 11 FAM 723.2-2(C).

241. United States v. Guy W. Capps, Inc., 204 F.2d 655, 660 (4th Cir. 1953), aff'd on other grounds, 348 U.S. 296 (1955).

Other cases limited the reach of executive agreements. A decision by the Court of Claims in 1955 examined an executive agreement under which the United States agreed to pay Austria a flat sum to settle all obligations incurred by U.S. armed forces. A naturalized U.S. citizen sued to recover damages to her home in Austria, which U.S. troops used as an officers' club. The Court of Claims held that the woman was entitled to compensation under the Fifth Amendment: "we think that there can be no doubt that an executive agreement, not being a transaction which is even mentioned in the Constitution, cannot impair Constitutional rights."[242]

In 1956, the Court upheld an executive agreement that permitted American military courts in Great Britain to use trial by court martial for offenses committed by American military personnel and their dependents. The plaintiff, a dependent wife of an Air Force sergeant, was sentenced to life imprisonment by the military.[243] She insisted on the constitutional right to trial by jury in a civilian court. Four Justices objected to the hasty handling of this case and one other in the closing days of the Term. They urged the Court to rehear the two cases and give them more thorough consideration.[244]

The Court did so. The next year it withdrew both decisions. Writing for the Court, Justice Black observed: "These cases are particularly significant because for the first time since the adoption of the Constitution wives of soldiers have been denied trial by jury in a court of law and forced to trial before courts-martial."[245] After a rehearing and further argument, he said the two decisions "cannot be permitted to stand."[246] He rejected "the idea that when the United States acts against citizens abroad it can do so free of the Bill of Rights." He referred to the Fifth and Sixth Amendment rights to trial by jury, action by grand jury, and right to a speedy and public trial in civilian court.[247] Black held that no executive agreement with another nation could confer power "on the Congress, or on any other branch of Government, which is free from the restraints of the Constitution."[248]

The Iranian hostage crisis of 1979 led to several actions by President Carter to freeze Iran's assets in the United States and suspend claims pending in American courts. The Supreme Court found statutory support only for the first action. Legal justification for the second was located in a combination of past presidential practices to settle claims by executive agreement, the history of "implicit" congressional approval, and the decision of Congress not to contest the Iranian agreement. The Court limited the reach of its opinion by confining it to the particular circumstances of the case.[249] Congress can restrict presidential power, but it must do so explicitly and not by silence or implication.

---

242. Seery v. United States, 127 F. Supp. 601, 606 (Ct. Cl. 1955). See Arthur E. Sutherland, Jr., *The Flag, the Constitution, and International Agreements*, 68 HARV. L. REV. 1374 (1955).

243. Reid v. Covert, 351 U.S. 487 (1956). The Court relied on Kinsella v. Krueger, 351 U.S. 470 (1956), on the constitutional issue.

244. The reasons of these four Justices (Frankfurter, Warren, Black, and Douglas) are set forth in Kinsella v. Krueger, 351 U.S. at 481–86.

245. Reid v. Covert, 354 U.S. 1, 3 (1957).

246. Id. at 5.

247. Id. at 5–7.

248. Id. at 16.

249. Dames & Moore v. Regan, 453 U.S. 654 (1981). For congressional "support" through acquiescence, the Court relied on Haig v. Agee, 453 U.S. 280, 290 (1981).

## B. The Case Act

Prior to 1950, executive agreements were published in the *U.S. Statutes at Large*. They then appeared in *Treaties and Other International Agreements*.[250] A number of sensitive agreements were never disclosed to Congress or to the public. During a Senate hearing in 1972, a State Department official was asked: "Now, you do have some executive agreements in force that are not listed in this publication, do you not?" He replied: "A very small percentage, classified."[251]

The extent of secret executive agreements had been discovered earlier by the Symington Subcommittee during hearings in 1969 and 1970. Travels by committee staff uncovered significant agreements that U.S. administrations had made covertly with South Korea, Thailand, Laos, Ethiopia, and Spain, among others. The hearings revealed that the United States offered substantial secret subsidies to foreign nations. In return, they provided modest amounts of assistance to the war in Southeast Asia. These secret agreements allowed the administration to boast about the existence of Free World Forces dedicated to fighting communism.[252]

Congress passed legislation in 1972, called the Case Act. It required the Secretary of State to transmit to Congress within 60 days the text of "any international agreement, other than a treaty," to which the United States is a party. If the President decided that publication of the agreement would be prejudicial to national security, he could transmit it to the Senate Committee on Foreign Relations and the House Committee on Foreign Affairs under an injunction of secrecy removable only by the President.[253]

Over the next few years, several Senators objected that the Nixon and Ford administrations were not complying with the Case Act. In 1975, Senator James Abourezk testified that administration officials had "admitted to both Senator Case and myself that there are some agreements they do not submit at all under the Case Act."[254] A report by the General Accounting Office in 1976 disclosed that a number of agreements (called "arrangements" by the executive branch) had not been submitted to Congress or even to the Office of Treaty Affairs in the State Department.[255] A Senate study in 1977 concluded that 39 percent of the executive agreements entered into the previous year had been submitted to Congress after the 60-day period (171 out of 440). Of those, 35 were submitted a *year* late.[256]

Responding to those problems, Congress passed legislation in 1977 to require any department or agency of the U.S. government that enters into an international agreement to transmit to the State Department the text of the agreement no later than 20 days after its signing.[257] A year later, Congress further refined the meaning of executive agreement to include the text of any "oral international agreement, which agreement shall be reduced to writing."[258]

---

250. 64 Stat. 979 (1950).

251. *Congressional Oversight of Executive Agreements*, hearing before the Senate Committee on the Judiciary, 92d Cong., 2d Sess. 284 (1972).

252. Louis Fisher, Presidential War Power 135–37 (3d ed. 2013).

253. 86 Stat. 619 (1972), 1 U.S.C. § 112b.

254. *Early Warning System in Sinai*, hearing before the Senate Committee on Foreign Relations, 94th Cong., 1st Sess. 6 (1975).

255. General Accounting Office, *U.S. Agreements with the Republic of Korea*, ID-76-20, Feb. 20, 1976.

256. 123 Cong. Rec. 16127 (1977).

257. 91 Stat. 224, sec. 5 (1977).

258. 92 Stat. 993, sec. 708 (1978).

Confusion over terms increased when the Carter administration decided to act not by treaty or executive agreement but by a third option: "parallel policy statements." On September 23, 1977, ten days prior to the expiration date of SALT I, the United States and the Soviet Union issued statements promising to adhere to the arms ceilings. Because the statements were issued separately and unilaterally, the State Department said they did not constitute an "agreement" and therefore did not have to be reported to Congress.[259]

As in the past, Congress invoked its power of the purse to gain control. In 1987, it passed legislation to tighten the reporting requirements for executive agreements. If any international agreement required to be transmitted to Congress under the Case Act was not submitted within the 60-day period, "then no funds authorized to be appropriated by this or any other act shall be available after the end of that 60-day period to implement that agreement until the text of that agreement has been so transmitted."[260] Still, problems persisted. In 1994, President Clinton entered into an "agreed framework" with North Korea to assist in the replacement of its graphite-moderated reactors with light-water reactor power plants. The objective was to prevent North Korea from developing nuclear weapons. The administration regarded the framework as a "political agreement" that was nonbinding and therefore not required to be submitted to Congress under the Case Act. President Clinton wrote to North Korea, stating that he would use the powers of his office to implement the framework, with much of that effort "subject to the approval of the U.S. Congress." According to the administration, the effect of the framework was to make political and moral, not legal, commitments.[261]

# 7. AMBASSADORS AND RECOGNITION POLICY

Article II, section 2 specifies that the Senate's advice and consent is required for two classes of public office: Justices of the Supreme Court and "Ambassadors, other public Ministers and Consuls." Senate advice and consent is also needed for other federal offices "whose Appointments are not herein otherwise provided for, and which shall be established by Law." The Constitution permits Congress, by statute, to vest the appointment of "such inferior Officers, as they think proper, in the President alone, in the Courts of Law, or in the Heads of Departments." The decision to specify diplomatic officers in the Constitution reflects the Senate's responsibilities with treaties. The advice and consent process provides a legislative opportunity to control the substance of treaties. Senators may discuss with a nominee the type of instructions to be used in negotiating with a foreign country.

## A. *Special envoys*

In addition to relying on ambassadors and submitting their names for confirmation, Presidents have frequently circumvented the Senate by directly appointing agents and special envoys. They justify this shortcut by claiming the appointments are temporary and not technically, under the

---

259. Thomas M. Franck & Edward Weisband, Foreign Policy by Congress 152–54 (1979).

260. 101 Stat. 1347, sec. 139 (1987).

261. 141 Cong. Rec. 8206 (1995).

Constitution, "officers." Henry Wriston observed that the insistence that someone "performing official duties, with officials to help him, is not an officer skirts the borders of legal fiction."[262] Some of these "temporary" officers exercised their duties for up to seven years.[263] These appointees discharged significant diplomatic duties. Presidents acted unilaterally, making no reference to statutory authority other than "a few appropriation acts, where men who have served in this capacity have been granted extra compensation by congress."[264]

Attorney General Cushing prepared a lengthy opinion in 1855, explaining the difference between ambassadors who are confirmed by the Senate and those who are not. Of the various questions put to him the first was: "Can the President, without the advice and consent of the Senate, appoint envoys extraordinary and ministers plenipotentiary in the place of the ministers resident, and a secretary of legation to each of them?"[265] Before answering that question he provided examples of Presidents doing precisely that. On October 13, 1789, President Washington instructed Gouverneur Morris to travel to London to represent the United States. There was no Senate action.[266] Cushing cites similar examples before stating: "the President may negotiate a treaty through the intervention of a person not commissioned, or intended to be commissioned, on a nomination to the Senate."[267]

A Senate report in 1888 provides details on special envoys. The majority of the Senate Committee on Foreign Relations objected to the President appointing unconfirmed "plenipotentiaries" to negotiate treaties. They said it was "not difficult to see that, in evil times, when the President of the United States may be under influence of foreign and adverse interests, such a course of procedure might result in great disaster to the interests and even the safety of our Government and people."[268] A minority on the committee disagreed with the report and its recommendation to reject the treaty. They found "no fault in the manner of negotiating this treaty, and the President has not in any way exceeded his constitutional powers."[269] The minority report included a table listing the names of 438 persons who acted as agents in conducting negotiations and concluding treaties. Three had been appointed by the Secretary of State. Thirty-two were appointed by the President with the advice and consent of the Senate. The rest were unconfirmed special envoys.[270]

---

262. Henry M. Wriston, *The Special Envoy*, 38 FOREIGN AFFAIRS 219, 221 (1960). See also ELMER PLISCHKE, DIPLOMAT IN CHIEF: THE PRESIDENT AT THE SUMMIT 63–118 (1986).

263. Wriston, *supra* note 262, at 221.

264. Henry Merritt Wriston, *Presidential Special Agents in Diplomacy*, 10 AM. POL. SCI. REV. 481, 482 (1916). Wriston explains that Presidents had access to the small amounts set aside by Congress for "contingent expenses."

265. 7 OP. ATT'Y GEN. 186, 189 (1855).

266. Id. at 194.

267. Id. at 197.

268. S. Mis. Doc. No. 109, 50th Cong., 1st Sess. 17 (1888).

269. Id. at 103.

270. Id. at 103–05, 110–34. The major work is by HENRY MERRITT WRISTON, EXECUTIVE AGENTS IN AMERICAN FOREIGN RELATIONS (1929).

## B. Recognition policy

Article II, section 3 provides that the President "shall receive Ambassadors and other public Ministers." From that language Presidents have claimed the exclusive right to recognize other governments, a power that has been widely exercised. Does the express authority to receive ambassadors carry with it the right to recognize foreign governments? In Federalist No. 69, Hamilton said this about the President's authority to receive ambassadors and other public ministers: "This, though it has been a rich theme of declamation, is more a matter of dignity than of authority."[271] Was Hamilton deliberately downplaying presidential power to build support for the Constitution?

Even if that is a possibility, the Constitution does not expressly grant the President the power to recognize foreign governments. Nor is there any "recorded evidence that any of the participants in the drafting and ratifying of the Constitution—Federalists and Anti-Federalists alike— understood that any provision in the Constitution *vested* such a power in the presidency, and certainly not a power that is plenary in nature."[272]

Presidents have acknowledged limits to their power to recognize. President Andrew Jackson, certainly a jealous defender of executive authority, refused to recognize the independence of Texas after it broke from Mexico in 1836. Both houses of Congress passed resolutions urging that the independence of Texas ought to be recognized by the United States, but Jackson decided not to take that step. He believed that recognizing the independence of Texas could provoke war with Mexico and therefore invade the prerogatives of Congress. He advised: "Prudence, therefore, seems to dictate that we should still stand aloof and maintain our present attitude, if not until Mexico itself or one of the great foreign powers shall recognize the independence of the new Government, at least until the lapse of time or the course of events shall have proved beyond cavil or dispute the ability of the people of that country to maintain their separate sovereignty and to uphold the Government constituted by them."[273]

Federal courts have done little to clarify the President's recognition power. At least in part, this lack of clarity flows from the general pattern of the courts deciding to leave recognition to the elected branches.[274] Judicial involvement in the recognition power might be changed significantly with the Supreme Court's involvement in the case of *Zivotofsky v. Secretary of State*. At issue is a collision between a congressional statute and the claim by the executive branch that the recognition power belongs exclusively to the President. Legislation by Congress in 2002 stated that for purposes of the registration of birth, certification of nationality, or issuance of a passport of a U.S. citizen born in the city of Jerusalem, the Secretary of State "shall, upon the request of the citizen or the citizen's legal guardian, record the place of birth as Israel."[275] In signing

---

271. The Federalist 448.

272. Robert J. Reinstein, *Recognition: A Case Study on the Original Understanding of Executive Power*, 45 U. Rich. L. Rev. 801, 862 (2011) (emphasis in original).

273. 4 Richardson 1487–88 (Dec. 21, 1836).

274. Williams v. Suffolk Insurance Co., 38 U.S. (13 Pet.) 414, 419–20 (1839). See also Kennett et al. v. Chambers, 55 U.S. 38, 50–51 (1852); Oetjen v. Central Leather Co., 246 U.S. 297, 302 (1918); Ricaud v. American Metal Co., 246 U.S. 304, 309 (1918); Guaranty Trust Co. v. U.S., 304 U.S. 126, 137–38 (1938); United States v. Pink, 315 U.S. 203, 228–30 (1942); National Bank v. Republic of China, 348 U.S. 356, 358 (1955); Baker v. Carr, 369 U.S. 186, 212 (1962); Banco Nacional de Cuba v. Sabbatino, 376 U.S. 398, 410 (1964); and David Gray Adler, *The President's Recognition Power: Ministerial or Discretionary?*, 25 Pres. Stud. Q. 267 (1995).

275. 116 Stat. 1366, sec. 214 (d) (2002).

the bill, President Bush objected that several provisions "impermissibly interfere with the constitutional functions of the presidency in foreign affairs, including provisions that purport to establish foreign policy that are of significant concern." Three times he referred to "the unitary executive branch." He expressed constitutional concerns about seven provisions, including one on Jerusalem.[276]

A federal district court in 2004 granted the administration's motion to dismiss, finding that the plaintiffs lacked standing and the issue was a nonjusticiable political question.[277] The D.C. Circuit held that one of the plaintiffs, a three-year child, suffered injury and remanded the case to the district court. The constitutional issue posed a number of questions, including which should prevail: a statute passed by Congress pursuant to its legislative authority over passport policy, or the administration's policy included in the State Department's Foreign Affairs Manual? Which had greater weight: a statute or an agency manual?[278]

On remand, the district court held that the case presented a nonjusticiable political question.[279] The D.C. Circuit affirmed.[280] On a request to rehear the case en banc, the D.C. Circuit denied the petition. Only three of the nine judges wanted to rehear the case.[281] During oral argument before the Supreme Court on November 7, 2011, Justice Elena Kagan wondered on what basis the administration insisted the President possesses exclusive power over recognition policy. She asked Solicitor General Donald Verrilli: "Is it the receipt of ambassadors clause alone, or is it something else? Because I was frankly a little bit surprised that your brief put so much weight on that receipt of ambassadors clause, which arguably meant to give the President a purely ministerial function."[282] When Verrilli seemed to concede that no textual commitment exists for the President to recognize foreign governments, he added: "Well, I think it's the historical gloss on the vesting power is—functions as has [sic] the equivalent of the specific textual commitment."[283]

On March 26, 2012, the Court vacated the D.C. Circuit ruling and remanded the case for further proceedings. It specifically rejected the position of the D.C. Circuit that the political question doctrine prohibits judicial review of Zivotofsky's claim. It concluded that federal courts "are fully capable of determining whether this statute may be given effect, or instead must be struck down in light of authority conferred on the Executive by the Constitution."[284] On July 23, 2013, the D.C. Circuit supported the President's implied authority to recognize foreign governments over the implied authority of Congress to decide passport policy, relying in substantial part on the judicial error by the Supreme Court in *Curtiss-Wright* on the President's "sole organ" authority.

---

276. Public Papers of the Presidents, 2002, II, at 1697–99.

277. Zivotofsky v. Secretary of State, 2004 WL 5835212 (D.D.C. 2004).

278. Zivotofsky v. Secretary of State, 444 F.3d 614 (D.C. Cir. 2006).

279. Zivotofsky v. Secretary of State, 511 F. Supp. 2d 97 (D.D.C. 2007).

280. Zivotofsky v. Secretary of State, 571 F.3d 1227 (D.C. Cir. 2009).

281. Zivotofsky v. Secretary of State, 610 F.3d 84 (D.C. Cir. 2010). Judges Ginsburg, Rogers, and Kavanaugh supported a rehearing. A separate statement by Judge Edwards indicated he wanted to rehear it.

282. Oral argument, Zivotofsky v. Secretary of State, U.S. Supreme Court, Nov. 7, 2011, at 39–40.

283. Id. at 47.

284. Zivotofsky v. Clinton, 566 U.S. ___, ___ (2012).

# 8. RIGHT TO TRAVEL

There is broad agreement that the federal government may ban travel to regions affected by pestilence and war. Presidents and their administrations have also limited travel for other reasons. Claiming both constitutional and statutory authority, the executive branch has used control over passports and visas to restrict travel by foreigners to this country and by Americans to other countries, generally citing concerns about their connections to "communist" or "subversive" organizations. In one case a member of Congress was denied a passport to attend a conference to aid Greek rebels, a purpose contrary to U.S. policy.[285] Opponents of these travel restrictions raised First Amendment issues of access to information and right of association.

In 1958, the Supreme Court split 5 to 4 in holding that statutory policy did not delegate to the Secretary of State authority to withhold passports to U.S. citizens because of their beliefs or associations. Any statute purporting to do so would raise grave constitutional questions.[286] The Court held that the right to travel is part of the "liberty" of which a citizen may not be deprived without due process of law under the Fifth Amendment.[287] Instead of reaching the question of constitutionality, the Court held that congressional policy expressed in statutes did not delegate to the Secretary of State the kind of authority exercised.[288] The Court dealt with "a constitutional right of the citizen, a right we must assume Congress will be faithful to respect."[289] On that same day the Court, split again 5 to 4, held that the Secretary of State lacked statutory authority to deny a passport to Weldon Bruce Dayton. The State Department had used a mix of "suspicions," allegations, and confidential files to deny his travel to India. The Court found the reasons for the denial to be "impermissible."[290]

In 1964, the Court struck down a congressional provision that prevented individuals from applying for a passport if they belonged to a "Communist-active" or "Communist-front" organization. If they already held a passport, it could be revoked. The Court concluded that the statutory provision was too broad and indiscriminate in restricting the right to travel and abridged "the liberty guaranteed by the Fifth Amendment."[291] Under that amendment, an individual may not be deprived of life, liberty, or property without due process of law. The Court referred to freedom of travel as a "constitutional liberty closely related to rights of free speech and association."[292]

A year later, the Court upheld the authority of the State Department to impose *area* restrictions (in this case, travel to Cuba). It concluded that it was permissible to deny all citizens the right to travel to a certain country, in contrast to *Kent v. Dulles* which singled out a particular individual's belief or association.[293] The Court decided that the Passport Act of 1926 was

---

285. Louis L. Jaffe, *The Right to Travel: The Passport Problem*, 35 FOREIGN AFFAIRS 17, 24 (1956).

286. Kent v. Dulles, 357 U.S. 116 (1958).

287. Id. at 125.

288. Id. at 129.

289. Id. at 130. See *Passports: At the Brink of the Constitution*, 47 GEO. L.J. 142 (1958).

290. Dayton v. Dulles, 357 U.S. 144, 150 (1958).

291. Aptheker v. Secretary of State, 378 U.S. 500, 505 (1964).

292. Id. at 517.

293. Zemel v. Rusk, 381 U.S. 1 (1965).

sufficiently broad to justify the department's action.[294] The plaintiff had requested permission to travel to Cuba as a tourist "to satisfy my curiosity about the state of affairs in Cuba and to make me a better informed citizen."[295] In dissents, Justices Black, Douglas, and Goldberg denied that the Passport Act authorized area restrictions.[296]

Subsequent cases circumscribed the State Department's authority to impose area restrictions. Limits were necessary in cases where the department attempted to prosecute individuals for criminal conduct when a statutory provision made no reference to criminal sanctions.[297] Judicial rulings relied entirely on interpretations of relevant statutes and regulations.[298] The judiciary made no effort to discover some type of implied or inherent power of the President to restrict travel.

Later cases offered broad support for executive restrictions on foreign travel. In 1981, the Supreme Court upheld the authority of the Secretary of State to revoke the passport of Philip Agee, a former CIA employee who had announced his intention to identify undercover CIA agents and reveal intelligence sources in foreign countries. To the Court, the revocation inhibited his actions, not his speech. The Secretary's decision was based on a departmental regulation, a broad interpretation of statutory authority, and the "silence" of Congress in acquiescing to the department's action. Specific congressional authorization, said the Court, was not required.[299] A dissent by Justice Brennan expressed this concern: "The Constitution allocates the lawmaking function to Congress, and I fear that today's decision has handed over too much of that function to the Executive."[300]

In 1984, the Court divided 5 to 4 in upholding a Treasury Department regulation that prohibited general tourist and business travel to Cuba. The Reagan administration decided to retaliate against Cuba for its political and military interventions in Latin America and Africa. Congress passed the International Emergency Economic Powers Act (IEEPA) in 1977 to place limits on presidential power, but the Court read the statute broadly to permit the sanctions against Cuba.[301] The dissenters disagreed with the Court's statutory interpretation.

Many cases focus on the right of aliens to visit the United States to speak on public issues. At issue are two rights: the right of aliens to speak and the right of Americans to hear their views and thoughts.[302] A right to travel case arose in 2003 when Ryan Clancy, a U.S. citizen, traveled to Iraq on January 28, 2003, with the intent to serve as a "human shield" to protect Iraqi facilities from U.S. military action, which began in March 2003. The Treasury Department's Office of Foreign Asset Control (OFAC) fined him $8,000 for violating OFAC's regulations. A district

---

294. Id. at 8.

295. Id. at 4.

296. Id. at 20–40. See Thomas Ehrlich, *Passports*, 19 Stan. L. Rev. 129 (1966) and *Constitutional Law: Resolving Conflict between the Right to Travel and Implementation of Foreign Policy*, 1966 Duke L.J. 233.

297. United States v. Laub, 385 U.S. 475 (1967).

298. Id. at 477. See also Travis v. United States, 385 U.S. 491 (1967).

299. Haig v. Agee, 453 U.S. 280 (1981).

300. Id. at 319 (Brennan, J. dissenting, joined by Marshall, J.). See Case Comment, *Authority of the Secretary of State to Revoke Passports for National Security Reasons:* Haig v. Agee, 66 Minn. L. Rev. 667 (1982).

301. Regan v. Wald, 468 U.S 222 (1984).

302. Abourezk v. Reagan, 592 F. Supp. 880, 882 (D.D.C. 1984), denying visas to aliens seeking to speak in the United States. This decision was reversed and remanded on appeal; Abourezk v. Reagan, 785 F.2d 1043 (D.C. Cir.

court upheld the fine, as did the Seventh Circuit.[303] The right to travel demands the interest and involvement not only of all three branches but the public at large.

# 9. EXCLUDING ALIENS

The power to exclude aliens is a necessary incident of national sovereignty. At times the United States has excluded aliens on racial lines. Congressional legislation in 1875 required U.S. consular officers to determine whether an immigrant from China, Japan, "or any Oriental country" had entered into an agreement for a term of service within the United States "for lewd and immoral purposes." If such an agreement existed, the individual would be denied a certificate to enter the country.[304] Whoever attempted to bring these individuals into the country for illegal purposes faced fines and imprisonment. During this period, California passed legislation to block access to "lewd and debauched women" arriving from other countries. In 1876, the Supreme Court struck down this statute, in part because of the power it placed "in the hands of a single man."[305] The opportunity for ignorant, biased, and corrupt actions was too great.

Legislation drafted by Congress to restrict the immigration of Chinese encountered vetoes from Presidents Rutherford B. Hayes and Chester A. Arthur. Their vetoes were sustained. Both Presidents urged Congress not to repudiate treaty obligations with China governing trade and immigration.[306] In these years, mobs forced Chinese from their homes, often with only four hours' notice, and torched their communities.[307] Federal courts occasionally intervened to place some constraints on arbitrary executive enforcement of exclusion statutes. In 1908, the Supreme Court ruled that Chin Yow, claiming to be a U.S. citizen, must have an opportunity to show his citizenship in a deportation proceeding. His attorney stated that he was not allowed to see and read evidence presented to an immigration officer.[308]

Detailed studies on the enforcement of deportation laws revealed marked abuses by executive officials. In deciding whether an alien should be deported, it was the practice to make a preliminary examination of the suspect under oath, in a private hearing, without the alien having assistance of counsel or other representation.[309] Often the alien did not understand the

---

1986). The D.C. Circuit was affirmed per curiam by an equally divided Supreme Court, 484 U.S. 1 (1987). Justices Blackmun and Scalia took no part in this case. See Kenneth Dana Greenwald, Abourezk v. Reagan: *The Need for Further Clarification and Reform of Alien Excludability Law*, 77 GEO. L.J. 217 (1988).

303. Clancy v. Office of Foreign Asset Control, 2007 WL 1051767 (E.D. Wis. 2007), aff'd, Clancy v. Geithner, 559 F.3d 595 (7th Circuit. 2009). See Christiaan Highsmith, *The Liberty-Speech Framework: Resolving the Tension Between Foreign Affairs Powers and First Amendment Freedoms*, 88 BOSTON U. L. REV. 745 (2008).

304. 18 Stat. 477 (Part 3) (1875).

305. Chy Lung v. Freeman, 92 U.S. 275, 278 (1876).

306. 9 Richardson 4466 (March 1, 1879); 10 Richardson 4699 (April 4, 1882).

307. JEAN PFAELZER, DRIVEN OUT: THE FORGOTTEN WAR AGAINST CHINESE AMERICANS (2007).

308. Chin Yow v. United States, 208 U.S. 8, 9 (1908).

309. NATIONAL COMMISSION ON LAW OBSERVANCE AND ENFORCEMENT, REPORT ON THE ENFORCEMENT OF THE DEPORTATION LAWS OF THE UNITED STATES 59 (1931).

significance of questions asked.[310] After the preliminary examination, aliens were entitled to have counsel but few could afford one. Other objectionable features of the process included illegal searches and seizures to obtain evidence against an alien and the use of hearsay testimony and rumors to support a final decision.[311]

In addition to excluding aliens on racist grounds, Congress prepared legislation to block anarchists and other unwanted ideologies. Opponents of labor rights viewed the violence of the Haymarket Affair in 1886, in Chicago, as the work of foreign anarchists. The bomb explosions spread fear throughout the country, with newspapers lashing out at "long-haired, wild-eyed, bad-smelling, atheistic, reckless foreign wretches."[312] The 1901 assassination of President William McKinley by Leon Czolgosz, an anarchist born in Detroit of Polish immigrants, added one more justification to pass restrictive legislation on immigrants.

In his first annual message on December 3, 1901, President Theodore Roosevelt recommended prompt passage of legislation to bar anarchists from the United States. He urged Congress to prohibit such people from entering the United States and to deport those already here. In addition, he advised Congress to exclude "all persons who are of a low moral tendency or unsavory reputation."[313] Legislation passed two years later identified broad categories of aliens who would not be admitted into the United States under any circumstances: "All idiots, insane persons, epileptics, and persons who have been insane within five years previous; ... persons who have been convicted of a felony or other crime or misdemeanor involving moral turpitude; polygamists, anarchists, or persons who believe in or advocate the overthrow by force or violence of the Government of the United States or of all government or of all forms of law, or the assassination of public officials ..."[314]

From 1903 to 1921, the United States excluded 38 persons charged with anarchistic beliefs.[315] John Turner, one of the individuals excluded, was represented by Clarence Darrow and Edgar L. Masters. They argued that the statute abridged Turner's freedom of speech.[316] Finding no constitutional violation, the Supreme Court said that Turner did not "become one of the people to whom these things are secured by our Constitution by an attempt to enter forbidden by law."[317] Darrow and Masters also objected that Congress had provided for the trial of an alien "by a Board of Special Inquiry, secret and apart from the public; without indictment; without confrontation of witnesses; without the right of counsel."[318] The Court answered that constitutional rights available to an accused in a criminal proceeding do not apply to the exclusion or deportation of an alien.[319]

---

310. Id. at 64.

311. Id. at 133–37, 144. See WILLIAM C. VAN VLECK, THE ADMINISTRATIVE CONTROL OF ALIENS: A STUDY IN ADMINISTRATIVE LAW AND PROCEDURE 111–12, 170–74 (1932), and JANE PERRY CLARK, DEPORTATION OF ALIENS FROM THE UNITED STATES TO EUROPE (1931).

312. JOHN HIGHAM, STRANGERS IN THE LAND: PATTERNS OF AMERICAN NATIVISM, 1860–1925, at 55 (2004 ed.).

313. 13 Richardson 6641, 6651 (Dec. 3, 1901).

314. 32 Stat. 1214, sec. 2 (1903).

315. WILLIAM PRESTON, JR., ALIENS AND DISSENTERS: FEDERAL SUPPRESSION OF RADICALS, 1903–1933, at 33 (2d ed. 1994).

316. Turner v. Williams, 194 U.S. 279, 286 (1904).

317. Id. at 292.

318. Id. at 286.

319. Id. at 289–90.

The lack of basic procedural safeguards is evident in the case of Ellen Knauff, who was held on Ellis Island from 1948 to 1951 and threatened with exclusion. The Truman administration justified its action on the basis of "confidential information" that it need not show to Knauff, her attorney, or even to federal courts. She was born in Germany and lived in Prague. Her mother, father, and other Jewish relatives perished in the Nazi camps. She managed to escape to England, where she worked during World War II. After the war, she returned to Germany to assist the American military government. On February 28, 1948, she married Kurt Knauff, a U.S. citizen and veteran who had been honorably discharged. Intent on becoming a U.S. citizen, she booked a ship to America and arrived in New York Harbor on August 14, 1948.[320]

Instead of being permitted to land and meet her husband's family, she was taken to Ellis Island. Over a period of weeks she was questioned without being able to receive visitors or obtain any legal assistance. Within two months, on October 6, an immigration official recommended that she be permanently excluded from America. There was no hearing. The official justified exclusion because her admission would be "prejudicial" to the United States. No other reasons were given. On that same day, Attorney General Tom Clark entered a final order of exclusion.[321]

With legal assistance, Knauff filed a habeas petition with a district court. It dismissed the petition, as did the Second Circuit.[322] Neither court objected to excluding her on the basis of confidential information that she, her attorney, and federal judges could not see. The Second Circuit was willing to defer wholly to unsupported and uncorroborated executive claims. Lacking information on why she was being excluded, the courts had no basis to judge whether the administration's action was reasonable. On January 16, 1950, the Supreme Court decided 4 to 3 in favor of the Truman administration.[323] In one of the dissents, Justice Jackson found no evidence that Congress had authorized "an abrupt and brutal exclusion of the wife of an American citizen without a hearing."[324] He said the administration told the judiciary "that not even a court can find out why the girl is excluded."[325] To Jackson, the claim that evidence of guilt "must be secret is abhorrent to free men, because it provides a cloak for the malevolent, the misinformed, the meddlesome, and the corrupt to play the role of informer undetected and uncorrected."[326] He added: "Security is like liberty in that many are the crimes committed in its name."[327] He would have directed the Attorney General "either to produce his evidence justifying exclusion or to admit Mrs. Knauff to the country."[328]

Several times she faced deportation. On one occasion, immigration officials in the Truman administration suggested to her attorney that he travel to Washington, D.C., to block deportation, even though the agency had already decided to immediately deport her on the morning

---

320. For details on her arrival in New York City and subsequent detention on Ellis Island, see ELLEN RAPHAEL KNAUFF, THE ELLEN KNAUFF STORY (1952).

321. Id. at 78.

322. United States ex rel. Knauff v. Watkins, 173 F.2d 599 (2d Cir. 1949).

323. Knauff v. Shaughnessy, 338 U.S. 537 (1950).

324. Id. at 550 (Jackson, J., dissenting).

325. Id. at 551.

326. Id.

327. Id.

328. Id. at 552.

of May 17, 1950. Agency officials drove her to Idlewild Airport and had a plane ready. In his capacity as circuit justice, Jackson learned of the ploy and issued an emergency stay. His order reached the airport about 20 minutes before her scheduled departure.[329]

President Truman, Attorney General Clark, and the Supreme Court did not protect Knauff's rights. A number of newspapers came to her defense, as did Representative Francis Walter.[330] The House Judiciary Committee unanimously supported a private bill to permit Knauff to enter the country. The committee report included a letter from the Justice Department that the President and the Attorney General had sole authority to deny entry for "security reasons." Knauff had "to stand the test of security" and "she failed to meet that test."[331] Confidentiality prevented lawmakers and judges from knowing on what ground she was being excluded. They did not know what the test was or how she failed to meet it. The private bill reached the House floor on May 2, 1950, and passed unanimously.[332] Legislation was introduced in the Senate but no further action was taken.

On March 26, 1951, after the Supreme Court had ruled in the case, the Immigration Service finally held a hearing. Three witnesses selected by the administration testified that Ellen Knauff was a security risk. Although their statements relied entirely on hearsay, the immigration board found the information sufficient.[333] Two questions were taken to an immigration appeals board: (1) did evidence before the Immigration Service justify its findings?, and (2) was Knauff accorded a fair and impartial hearing?[334] On August 29, 1951, the appeals board held there was not adequate evidence to justify her exclusion. Having answered the first question, it found it unnecessary to answer the second. The appeals board ordered Knauff admitted for permanent residence.[335]

The careful reasoning of the appeals board merits close attention. It referred to "several kinds of hearsay." One consists of statements "purporting to be based on the declarant's own knowledge, but is unsworn." The second is a sworn statement regarding matters known to the declarant through hearsay. To the appeals board, the statements of the three witnesses fell in the second category. As to anything dealing with espionage or subversive activities by Knauff, they had no personal knowledge. "The sum total then of all the testimony is hearsay."[336] Hearsay in an administrative hearing might be admissible if corroborated by direct evidence, but "all we have in this case is hearsay."[337] On November 2, 1951, Attorney General J. Howard McGrath

329. Jackson's order is reprinted at 96 Cong. Rec. A3750–51 (1950).

330. Louis Fisher, *Truman's National Security Policy: Constitutional Issues*, Congress and Harry S. Truman: A Conflicted Legacy 166 (Donald A. Ritchie ed., 2011). The *New York Times* protested the "remarkably un-American aspect of our immigration procedures." The *St. Louis Post-Dispatch* condemned the administration for acting contemptuously toward Congress and the courts. Regarding the scheduled flight from Idlewild, the *Post-Dispatch* said the Justice Department had tried to get away with a "Fascistlike scheme."

331. *Mrs. Ellen Knauff*, H. Rep. No. 1940, 81st Cong., 2d Sess. 4 (1950).

332. 96 Cong. Rec. 6174 (1950).

333. Knauff, *supra* note 320, at 194–201.

334. Id., Appendix 2.

335. Id., 217–30, Appendix 18.

336. Id., Appendix 16.

337. Id.

approved the decision of the appeals board and Ellen Knauff left Ellis Island to begin her life in America.[338]

She survived because her case did not depend on the world of shadows, secrets, and confidentiality embraced by the executive branch. Her rights moved into the public arena, to be helped by the press and members of Congress. Statements by the three witnesses could be analyzed by those who knew them, including individuals following the case from Europe. Citizens and aliens should not be condemned by informers who rely on speculation, secondhand conjectures, and perhaps malice. That was the climate encouraged by President Truman's loyalty review board, discussed in the next section.

# 10. LOYALTY DISMISSALS

Efforts to suppress communism and subversion have been a prominent theme for more than a century, beginning with legislation in 1903 to block "anarchists" from entering the country (discussed in previous section), the "Red Scare" after World War I, and initiatives by FBI Director J. Edgar Hoover in 1939 and 1940 to have his agency develop a secret list of organizations considered to be Communist or Communist-front. The organizations were not given notice of why they were put on the list or an opportunity to offer objections at a hearing.[339] Fears of communism and fascism during World War II created pressures within the United States for some type of loyalty pledge that citizens and aliens would have to sign.[340]

In 1943, President Roosevelt issued Executive Order 9300 to create an interdepartmental committee to review allegations that federal employees were engaged in "subversive activity."[341] He acted shortly after Representative Martin Dies, chairman of the Special Committee to Investigate Un-American Activities, claimed that hundreds of federal employees were affiliated with Communist groups or causes. The executive order directed departments and agencies to refer suspect employees to the FBI for investigation. The previous year, Attorney General Francis Biddle had released a report stating that 36 federal employees had been discharged for activities associated with alleged subversive organizations. Of those discharged, only two were on the list of 1,100 names assembled by the Dies Committee.[342]

Looking back on his lengthy career of public service, Clark Clifford said his "greatest regret" was that he did not "make more of an effort to try to kill the loyalty program at its inception in 1947–48."[343] On March 25, 1947, President Truman issued Executive Order 9835, prescribing

---

338. Id., final page (unnumbered). See Charles D. Weisselberg, *The Exclusion and Detention of Aliens: Lessons from the Lives of Ellen Knauff and Ignatz Mezei*, 143 U. PA. L. REV. 933 (1995).

339. ROBERT JUSTIN GOLDSTEIN, AMERICAN BLACKLIST: THE ATTORNEY GENERAL'S LIST OF SUBVERSIVE ORGANIZATIONS 18–20 (2008). See also M. J. HEALE, AMERICAN ANTICOMMUNISM: COMBATING THE ENEMY WITHIN, 1830–1970 (1990).

340. In 1942, a group called Bundles for America drafted the text of "A Pledge for Americans." *Loyalty Pledge to Be Circulated*, N.Y. TIMES, May 28, 1942, at 12.

341. Executive Order 9300, *Subversive Activities by Federal Employees*, Feb. 5, 1943, reprinted in ELEANOR BONTECOU, THE FEDERAL LOYALTY-SECURITY PROGRAM 272–73 (1953).

342. *Names Committee on Subversion*, N.Y. TIMES, Feb. 7, 1943, at 20.

343. CLARK CLIFFORD, COUNSEL TO THE PRESIDENT: A MEMOIR 175 (1991).

procedures for determining the loyalty of federal employees.[344] His order claimed that the presence within the government "of any disloyal or subversive person" constituted a threat to democratic processes, but the order did not include a clear and understandable definition of either loyalty or subversion.[345] In an effort to guard against abusive and irresponsible assertions, Truman insisted on safeguards to protect employees "from unfounded accusations of disloyalty."[346] The safeguards were minimal. His order permitted federal agencies to rely on secret informants whose identities and credibility could be withheld from the accused.

Truman's order covered two categories: individuals seeking jobs with the federal government and those already employed. Applicants needed to undergo a loyalty investigation conducted by the Civil Service Commission (CSC). Employees would be investigated by their department or agency. The executive branch relied on FBI files, CSC files, military and naval intelligence files, the files of any other appropriate government investigative or intelligence agency, and other sources, without the capacity of the accused to determine or verify the credibility of information presented against them. If "derogatory information" appeared to exist regarding the "loyalty" of an applicant or employee, a full field investigation would be conducted.[347]

Damaging information could come from unreliable or malicious sources: former spouses, employers, associates, and neighbors. The individual being investigated had no right to know who said they were subversive, disloyal, or a security risk. Nor could the individual explore the basis for the accusations. In a loyalty case decided several years later, in 1955, Justice Douglas noted that informers "may bear old grudges. Under cross-examination their stories might disappear like bubbles. Their whispered confidences might turn out to be yarns conceived by twisted minds or by people who, though sincere, have poor faculties of observation and memory."[348] Truman's executive order offered no protection from those risks.

Agency loyalty boards, usually consisting of three employees, heard complaints and wrote regulations. Employees charged with disloyalty had a right to a hearing and could appear before the board personally. They had access to counsel and could present evidence, call witnesses, submit affidavits, and challenge efforts to remove them. During this period, agency heads were authorized to suspend the employee. To defend themselves, employees were supposed to be informed of the nature of the charges in sufficient detail to permit a reasoned defense. However, charges were stated

---

344. 12 FED. REG. 1935 (1947). For political context of Truman's order, see RICHARD M. FREELAND, THE TRUMAN DOCTRINE AND THE ORIGINS OF MCCARTHYISM: FOREIGN POLICY, DOMESTIC POLITICS, AND INTERNAL SECURITY, 1946–1948 (1985 ed.); PETER L. STEINBERG, THE GREAT "RED MENACE": UNITED STATES PROSECUTION OF AMERICAN COMMUNISTS, 1947–1952 (1984); ATHAN THEOHARIS, SEEDS OF REPRESSION: HARRY S. TRUMAN AND THE ORIGINS OF MCCARTHYISM (1977 ed.); ROBERT GRIFFITH & ATHAN THEOHARIS, eds., THE SPECTER: ORIGINAL ESSAYS ON THE COLD WAR AND THE ORIGINS OF MCCARTHYISM (1974); and ALAN D. HARPER, THE POLITICS OF LOYALTY: THE WHITE HOUSE AND THE COMMUNIST ISSUE, 1945–1952 (1969).

345. Representative John Kerr was chairman of a House subcommittee to determine whether federal employees were unfit to remain in office because of their present or past associations with organizations "whose aims or purposes are or have been subversive to the Government of the United States." He later acknowledged: "We discovered after organization the fact that there had never been declared judicially or by any legislative body what constituted subversive activities in respect to this Government." 89 CONG. REC. 4582 (1943).

346. 12 FED. REG. 1935 (fourth "Whereas").

347. Id., Part IV.1.

348. Peters v. Hobby, 349 U.S. 331, 351 (1955) (Douglas, J., concurring).

"as specifically and completely as, in the discretion of the employing department or agency, security considerations permit."[349]

Executive agencies were authorized to withhold the names of confidential informants, "provided it furnishes sufficient information about such informants on the basis of which the requesting department or agency can make an adequate evaluation of the information furnished by them."[350] There was no assurance that the loyalty boards had either the time or competence to determine the reliability or motivation of informers or judge with confidence the quality of information they received from investigative agencies. A few agencies, through their regulations, allowed employees access to the name of confidential informants.[351]

Loyalty boards within the executive branch received from the Justice Department the names of each foreign or domestic organization that the Attorney General designated as "totalitarian, fascist, communist or subversive, or as having adopted a policy of advocating or approving the commission of acts of force or violence to deny others their rights under the Constitution of the United States, or as seeking to alter the form of government of the United States by unconstitutional means."[352] Private organizations and federal courts did not know how the Attorney General or the Justice Department prepared the list. The terms "totalitarian," "fascist," "communist," and "subversive" were never defined. Organizations placed on the list were not notified and had no opportunity to challenge and contest their designation. The loyalty security program depended on secret investigations, confidential information, and secret deliberations.[353]

In 1951 the Supreme Court, after reviewing three "communist" organizations that had been placed on the Attorney General's list, found the designations "patently arbitrary." The Justice Department had not relied on "either disclosed or undisclosed facts supplying a reasonable basis for the determination."[354] Adding names to the list without any substantial or reasonable basis would "cripple the functioning and damage the reputation of those organizations in their respective communities and in the nation."[355] The Court required the Justice Department to either substantiate its judgments and conclusions or delete organizations from the list. In a concurrence, Justice Frankfurter said that due process was violated whenever the executive branch felt at liberty to "maim or decapitate" an organization "on the mere say-so of the Attorney General."[356] Critics of the list objected that it discouraged individuals from joining organizations, promoted "conformity and standardization," and unconstitutionally limited the freedoms of thought and association.[357]

The breadth of Truman's executive order reached to sabotage, espionage, treason, and sedition.[358] Those categories were already covered by existing criminal law. Individuals subject to

---

349. 12 FED. REG. 1937, Part II.2b.

350. Id. at 1938, Part IV.2.

351. BONTECOU, *supra* note 341, at 60–64.

352. 12 FED. REG. 1938, Part III.3.

353. For details on the Attorney General's list, see BONTECOU, *supra* note 341, at 157–204.

354. Anti-Fascist Committee v. McGrath, 341 U.S. 123, 126 (1951).

355. Id. at 139.

356. Id. at 161 (Frankfurter, J., concurring).

357. JOHN LORD O'BRIAN, NATIONAL SECURITY AND INDIVIDUAL FREEDOM 25–25 (1955). See also Clifford J. Durr, *The Loyalty Order's Challenge to the Constitution*, 16 U. CHI. L. REV. 298 (1949), and John Lord O'Brian, *Loyalty Tests and Guilt by Association*, 61 HARV. L. REV. 592 (1948).

358. 12 FED. REG. 1938, Part V.2.

prosecution under those statutes had full access to procedural safeguards, unlike those swept up in the loyalty security program. The order affected people with prominent names and inconspicuous agency employees. In the first category is O. Edmund Clubb, director of the State Department's Office of Chinese Affairs in 1950. Mao's Communist Party had won the civil war in China the previous year, leading some in the United States to look for scapegoats responsible for "losing" China. Charges against Clubb were vague: he had engaged in "political unorthodoxy," kept "dangerous associations," and had "distinct pink tendencies."[359] Through the appeals process he was eventually cleared and restored to active duty, but he understood that no one who undergoes that type of investigation is ever "cleared." Inevitably, a shadow of disloyalty remains over the individual. On February 12, 1952, Clubb retired from federal service.[360]

After leaving the presidency, Truman noted in his memoirs that "if a man cannot be prosecuted in the courts, then he should not be persecuted by a Senate or House committee."[361] A sound principle, but such individuals should not be persecuted by the executive branch either. Truman spoke out against "taking hearsay charges against any person, especially against anyone who has the background to qualify as a government servant."[362] He seemed unaware that his executive order had allowed precisely that. As President, he understood that the files of the CSC, the FBI, and other agencies "contain many unsupported, uninvestigated, and unevaluated charges... [and may] contain items based on suspicion, rumor, prejudice, and malice, and therefore, if released, may do great harm to the reputation and careers of many innocent people."[363] Yet he allowed loyalty security boards to rely on that kind of material without providing procedural safeguards for government employees.

IT IS MISLEADING to assume that a bright line exists between "domestic policy" and "foreign policy." There has always been substantial overlap between the two, as U.S. merchants understood when President Jefferson adopted an embargo policy against Great Britain. Whatever penalty he thought he was imposing on England did severe damage to American businesses.[364] Subsequent Presidents have appreciated the degree to which domestic and foreign policy intermix. In 1991, the first President Bush was criticized for spending too much time traveling abroad while neglecting problems at home. He explained that his efforts to promote trade agreements with other nations would benefit U.S. exports: "I guess my bottom line... is you can't separate foreign policy from domestic."[365] President Clinton reached a similar conclusion in 1993: "There is no longer a clear division between what is foreign and what is domestic."[366] There never was.

359. Fisher, *supra* note 330, at 161. See O. Edmund Clubb, The Witness and I (1974).

360. Fisher, *supra* note 330, at 161. For other casualties of Truman's executive order, see id. at 161–63.

361. 2 Harry S. Truman, Memoirs: Years of Trial and Hope 270 (1956).

362. Id.

363. Id. at 281.

364. Forrest McDonald, The Presidency of Thomas Jefferson 142–52, 155–58 (1976).

365. Public Papers of the Presidents, 1991, II, at 1629.

366. Id., 1993, II, at 2.

# EIGHT

# War Powers

UNDERSTANDING THE ALLOCATION OF THE WAR POWER BEGINS BY studying the text of the Constitution. Article II, section 2 provides that the President "shall be Commander in Chief of the Army and Navy of the United States, and of the Militia of the several States, when called into the actual Service of the United States." As explained by Attorney General Bates in this chapter, in section 3, a major purpose of the Commander in Chief Clause is to maintain civilian supremacy and prevent war from falling in the hands of military leaders. The President's control over the militia is governed by Article I, section 8, which empowers Congress to "provide for calling forth the Militia to execute the Laws of the Union, suppress Insurrections and repel invasions." The President commands the militia after Congress does the calling.

Article I, section 8 grants Congress a number of war powers that William Blackstone vested solely in the Executive: "To define and punish Piracies and Felonies committed on the high Seas, and Offense against the Law of Nations" and "declare War, grant Letters of Marque and Reprisal, and make Rules concerning Captures on Land and Water." Moreover, to "raise and support Armies," "provide and maintain a Navy," "make Rules for the Government and Regulation of the land and naval Forces," and "provide for organizing, arming, and disciplining, the Militia, and for governing such Part of them as may be employed in the Service of the United States, reserving to the States respectively, the Appointment of the Officers, and the Authority of training the Militia according to the discipline prescribed by Congress."[1] Finally, section 8 empowers Congress to exercise authority over territories "purchased by the Consent of the Legislature of the State in which the Same shall be, for the Erection of Forts, Magazines, Arsenals, dock-Yards and other needful Buildings." That language is significant because Blackstone placed those powers with the king (section 1A of this chapter).

Additional guidance on the allocation of the war power comes from the Philadelphia debates, statements at the ratifying conventions, the Federalist Papers, and precedents set over the next 160 years. All three branches—from 1789 to 1950—understood that Congress alone possessed the constitutional authority to take the country from a state of peace to a state of war. Matters changed abruptly in 1950 when President Truman went to war against North Korea without seeking approval from Congress. For all previous wars, Presidents asked Congress either for a declaration or authorization. Part of the shift away from constitutional and republican

---

1. With regard to raising and supporting armies, section 8 stipulates that "no Appropriation of Money to that Use shall be for a longer Term than two Years."

government resulted from the creation of the UN Security Council in 1945, which Truman and his successors illegitimately used as an alternative way to authorize war (this chapter, sections 4 and 5). Contributing to the imbalance between executive and legislative powers has been the failure of Congress to exercise and defend its institutional powers and the general pattern of federal courts to accept broad interpretations of independent presidential power (this chapter and Chapter 9).

# 1. INITIATING WAR

The Framers gave to Congress alone the authority to take the nation to war. One need not accept that principle merely by analyzing the constitutional record from 1787 to 1789. That principle was continually reinforced for 160 years. Presidents could exercise defensive powers in case of sudden attack, but mobilizing the nation for an offensive war rested solely with Congress. From 1789 to 1950, Presidents publicly stated their understanding and respect for the essential difference between defensive and offensive wars.

## A. *Dispensing with the prerogative*

Under the British model described by William Blackstone, the king possessed a number of prerogatives in external affairs. The word prerogative, he said, "can only be applied to those rights and capabilities which the king enjoys alone."[2] He divided prerogatives between "direct" and "incidental." The first included powers "rooted in and spring from the king's political person," including the right "of making war or peace."[3] To Blackstone, the law "ascribes to the king, in his political capacity, absolute *perfection*. The king can do no wrong."[4] He is "not only incapable of *doing* wrong, but even of *thinking* wrong; he can never mean to do an improper thing: in him is no folly or weakness."[5] In exercising the prerogative, "the king is, and ought to be absolute; that is, so far absolute, that there is no legal authority that can either delay or resist him."[6] The king has "the sole prerogative of making war and peace."[7] He is empowered "to issue letters of marque and reprisal" and has "sole power of raising and regulating fleets and armies."[8] The "erection of beacons, light-houses, and sea-marks, is also a branch of the royal prerogative."[9]

The powers that Blackstone ascribed to the British king are assigned almost exclusively to Congress in Article I, section 8. Because the authority to "grant Letters of Marque and Reprisal"

---

2. 1 WILLIAM BLACKSTONE, COMMENTARIES ON THE LAWS OF ENGLAND 238 (1775) (citing pages at the top, not in the margin).

3. Id. at 239.

4. Id. at 245 (emphasis in original).

5. Id. (emphases in original).

6. Id. at 250.

7. Id. at 257.

8. Id. at 258, 262.

9. Id. at 264.

is not as familiar as other powers cited in section 8, some discussion is merited. Reprisal consists of the use of military force short of war. Letters of marque authorize private citizens to equip their vessels for attack and to plunder enemy ships. Blackstone described the prerogative to issue letters of marque and reprisal as "nearly related to, and plainly derived from, that other of making war."[10] Although the Framers' rejection of his prerogative was sweeping and complete, arguments continue to be advanced that the President possesses certain "inherent" and "prerogative" powers that may not be limited by the legislative and judicial branches. Those assertions lack any substantive grounds (Chapter 3, sections 4 and 5).

## B. Declare War Clause

The Framers chose to take one of the royal prerogatives—to declare war—and place it solely with Congress. The reason for that choice has been vigorously debated. Does it mean that Congress is empowered to "declare" war but the President may "make" war? Is the President at liberty to take the country to war, after which Congress merely acknowledges the President's action by officially "declaring" it? Which branch is empowered by the Constitution to take the country to war?

Part of the Framers' concern about the war power focused on the weakness of the national government under the Articles of Confederation. As Edmund Randolph explained at the Philadelphia convention on May 29, 1787, "particular states might by their conduct provoke war without controul."[11] The Framers settled that issue with language in Article I, section 10: "No State shall, without the Consent of Congress, lay any Duty of Tonnage, keep Troops, or Ships of War in time of Peace, enter into Agreement or Compact with another state, or with a foreign Power, or engage in War, unless actually invaded, or in such imminent Danger as will not admit of delay."

Having placed the war power with the national government, not the states, the delegates debated how to allocate that power between Congress and the President. On June 1, 1787, Charles Pinckney offered support for "a vigorous Executive but was afraid the Executive powers of <the existing> Congress might extend to peace & war &c which would render the Executive a Monarchy, of the worst kind, towit an elective one."[12] John Rutledge expressed a similar concern. He was "for vesting the Executive power in a single person, tho' he was not for giving him the power of war and peace."[13] James Wilson "preferred a single magistrate, as giving most energy dispatch and responsibility to the office," but "did not consider the Prerogatives of the British Monarch as a proper guide in defining the Executive powers. Some of these prerogatives were of a Legislative nature. Among others that of war & peace &c."[14]

Five days later, George Mason objected to placing the "purse and sword" in the same hands.[15] By June 18, delegates considered language giving the Senate "the sole power of declaring war."[16] Alexander Hamilton believed the President should have power "to make war or peace, with

---

10. Id. at 258.

11. 1 Farrand 19.

12. Id. at 65.

13. Id.

14. Id. at 65–66.

15. Id. at 144.

16. Id. at 292.

the advice of the senate."[17] A draft constitution by the Committee of Detail in July placed the power to "make war" in the legislative branch.[18] By August 6, the language under consideration empowered Congress to "make war."[19]

Extensive debate occurred on August 17. Regarding language to give Congress the power to "make war," Charles Pinckney objected that legislative proceedings "were too slow" for the safety of the country in an emergency.[20] He anticipated that Congress would meet "but once a year."[21] Also, the House of Representatives "would be too numerous for such deliberations."[22] The Senate "would be the best depositary, being more acquainted with foreign affairs, and most capable of proper resolutions."[23] Pierce Butler announced he was "for vesting the power in the President, who will have all the requisite qualities, and will not make war but when the Nation will support it."[24] No delegate offered any support for Butler's position. As explained in subsequent paragraphs in this section, Butler at the South Carolina ratification debates distanced himself from this trust in presidential wars.

James Madison and Elbridge Gerry moved to insert "declare" for "make," thereby "leaving to the Executive the power to repel sudden attacks."[25] Roger Sherman expressed his approval: the President "shd. be able to repel and not to commence war."[26] Gerry expressed astonishment at Butler's proposal. He "never expected to hear in a republic a motion to empower the Executive alone to declare war."[27] Mason was "agst giving the power of war to the Executive, because not <safely> to be trusted with it; or to the Senate, because not so constructed as to be entitled to it."[28] He was "for clogging rather than facilitating war; but for facilitating peace."[29] The motion to strike "make" and insert "declare" carried, 7 states to 2. Pennsylvania, Delaware, Maryland, Virginia, North Carolina, South Carolina, and Georgia voted aye. New Hampshire and Connecticut voted no.[30]

The Framers recognized that the President may act unilaterally in taking certain *defensive* actions in a time of emergency, but Congress possessed constitutional authority to take offensive actions against another country. At the South Carolina ratifying convention on January 16, 1788, Butler summarized the main points of debate at the constitutional convention on the war power. The proposal to place that authority in the Senate, he said, was "objected to as inimical

17. Id. at 300.

18. 2 Farrand 143, 168.

19. Id. at 182.

20. Id. at 318.

21. Id.

22. Id.

23. Id.

24. Id.

25. Id.

26. Id.

27. Id.

28. Id. at 319.

29. Id.

30. Id.

to the genius of a republic, by destroying the necessary balance they were anxious to preserve."[31] He next remarked: "Some gentlemen were inclined to give this power to the President; but it was objected to, as throwing into his hands the influence of a monarch, having an opportunity of involving his country in a war whenever he wished to promote her destruction."[32] Obviously unwilling to identify himself as the only person who promoted independent presidential war power, apparently he realized how far out of step he was and accepted Congress as the branch of government authorized to involve the nation in war.

At the Pennsylvania ratifying convention, James Wilson explained that the system of government contained in the Constitution "will not hurry us into war; it is calculated to guard against it. It will not be in the power of a single man, or a single body of men, to involve us in such distress; for the important power of declaring war is vested in the legislature at large."[33] Clearly he understood that the authority to *go to war*, and not simply to "declare" it, was reserved to Congress. At the North Carolina ratifying convention, James Iredell underscored the difference between the President and the British king. Both were designated Commander in Chief, but the king "has power, in time of war, to raise fleets and armies. He has also authority to declare war."[34] The President, Iredell said, "has not the power of declaring war by his own authority, nor that of raising fleets and armies. Those powers are vested in other hands. The power of declaring war is expressly given to Congress."[35] The war power was lodged not in the Executive but in the two chambers of Congress "deputed by the people at large."[36]

## C. Contemporary analysis

Some studies have urged Congress to approve wars not by authorizing bills (as with the Quasi-War in 1798) but solely by declarations of war. Writing in 1991, J. Gregory Sidak argued that an authorizing bill of January 12, 1991, supporting military action against Iraq, "was a legal nullity, a merely precatory or hortatory gesture."[37] However, the authorizing bill passed each house, was submitted to the President, and signed into law. It was a public law, not a legal nullity. To Sidak, political accountability is achieved only with a declaration, not an authorization. A declaration of war "fulfills Congress's representative function because it is more immediately visible to the electorate, less susceptible to ambiguity and disagreement once it is made, and thus more conducive to effective monitoring of the performance of political actors."[38] A declaration signals "whether America's political representatives favor or oppose the use of warfare in a particular instance."[39] For Sidak, a "formal declaration of war is a more politically accountable means to record these representatives' approval or rejection of war."[40]

31. 4 Elliot 263.
32. Id.
33. 2 Elliot 528.
34. 4 Elliot 107.
35. Id. at 107–08.
36. Id. at 108.
37. J. Gregory Sidak, *To Declare War*, 41 Duke L.J. 27, 33 (1991).
38. Id.
39. Id. at 121.
40. Id.

However, the authorization of January 1991 enabled the public to determine if a lawmaker favored or opposed the use of military force. In response to Sidak, Harold Koh noted that the votes of Representatives and Senators were "intensely scrutinized."[41] Speeches before the votes "were nationally televised, and the roll-call votes were published in every newspaper—both the next day and during the war."[42] Because of this publicity, Koh found it "difficult to see what additional accountability would have been gained had the resolution been styled as a declaration of war."[43]

Even a declaration of war may not satisfy those who promote more formal actions. Similar to Sidak, Brien Hallett concludes that Congress in January 1991 should have voted not on an authorization bill but a declaration of war. He looked to the Declaration of Independence as a model of a fully "reasoned" declaration, setting forth in detail why Americans found it necessary to break with England. However, when he examined the declarations of war in 1812, 1846, 1898, 1917, and 1941, Hallett found them "unreasoned" declarations.[44] Under some circumstances, authorizations of war have several advantages over declarations. Koh explained that formal declarations "are blunt instruments that do not lend themselves as easily as joint resolutions [authorizations] to modulated use of force. They tend to be tersely worded documents, enacted hastily in crisis situations, and with only minimal deliberation. They announce that a state of war exists with an enemy, but they neither name our allies nor detail our objectives; nor do they generally set either substantive or procedural limitations upon the authorities granted to the President."[45]

In an article published in 1996, John Yoo maintained that the Framers "established a system which was designed to encourage presidential initiative in war."[46] The only delegate at the Philadelphia convention who supported that presidential power was Pierce Butler. By the time of the South Carolina ratifying convention, he dissociated himself from that position. With regard to the Declare War Clause, Yoo concluded that a declaration by Congress "did not create or authorize; it recognized."[47] A declaration "announced Congress' judgment that a *legal* state of war existed between the United States and another country," even if the President was the branch that initiated war.[48] In that sense, according to Yoo, the Declare War Clause vested Congress "with a *judicial* function, which involves a capacity for judgment in the manner of a court, rather than the enactment of positive law in the style of a legislature."[49] Nothing in the debates at Philadelphia, the ratifying conventions, the Federalist Papers, or public statements by

41.  Harold Hongju Koh, *The Coase Theorem and the War Power: A Response*, 41 Duke L.J. 122, 127 (1991).

42.  Id.

43.  Id.

44.  Brien Hallett, The Lost Art of Declaring War 9 (1998). See also Brien Hallett, Declaring War: Congress, the President, and What the Constitution Does Not Say (2012); Kenneth B. Moss, Undeclared War and the Future of U.S. Foreign Policy (2008); Edward Keynes, Undeclared War: Twilight Zone of Constitutional Power (1991 ed.); and Lawrence R. Velvel, Undeclared War and Civil Disobedience: The American System in Crisis (1970).

45.  Koh, *supra* note 41, at 128.

46.  John C. Yoo, *The Continuation of Politics by Other Means: The Original Understanding of War Powers*, 84 Cal. L. Rev. 167, 174 (1996).

47.  Id. at 246.

48.  Id. (emphasis in original).

49.  Id. at 248–49 (emphasis in original).

any of the three branches from 1789 to 1950 supports that interpretation. No one offered that argument until Yoo's article in 1996. As he acknowledged, his interpretation of the Declare War Clause "provides a new understanding of Congress' role in war."[50]

In an article in 2007, Saikrishna Prakash concluded that only Congress can decide whether the United States will start a war against another nation.[51] He drew attention to the position of some scholars who argue that although the President may not declare war on another nation, if a nation declared war against the United States the President could order the military to wage war against that country without securing a prior congressional declaration of war.[52] Yet there is no automatic requirement that the United States must respond militarily simply because a nation declares war on it. As Prakash notes, the Creek Nation declared war against the United States in the spring of 1793 but Congress felt no obligation to declare war on the Creeks.[53] On December 8, 1801, President Jefferson advised Congress that the Pasha of Tripoli had declared war on the United States.[54] Congress did not declare war on Tripoli, but it did pass a number of statutes authorizing Jefferson (and later Madison) to take military action against the Barbary powers.[55]

Writing in 2008, Prakash states that if Congress "requires the President to wage war, the President must both wage the war that Congress declared and adhere to the restrictions on the use of military force in the declaration."[56] "As a matter of constitutional law, there is no good reason to think that the Commander in Chief can choose to ignore a congressional declaration of war that orders hostilities."[57] Yet he also acknowledges that the President "might be able to exploit changes in circumstances or public sentiment to take a different course."[58] An example might be that the President discovers on the basis of new information that a pending dispute can be settled short of war. Under those conditions, the President in good faith could advise Congress of his decision to delay military action in pursuit of a negotiated settlement.

## D. Commander in Chief Clause

Article II, section 2 provides that the President "shall be Commander in Chief of the Army and Navy of the United States, and of the Militia of the several States, when called into the actual Service of the United States." There is little discussion of this clause at the Philadelphia convention. The New Jersey plan, offered on June 15, did not decide whether the Executive should be a single person or several. It resolved that Congress "be authorized to elect a federal Executive to

50. Id. at 248. Yoo's interpretation of the Declare War Clause also appears in subsequent writings; e.g., JOHN YOO, THE POWERS OF WAR AND PEACE: THE CONSTITUTION AND FOREIGN AFFAIRS AFTER 9/11, at 145–47 (2005). For a recent evaluation of Yoo's 1996 article in the *California Law Review*: Janet Cooper Alexander, *John Yoo's War Powers: The Law Review and the World*, 100 CAL. L. REV. 331 (2012).

51. Saikrishna Prakash, *Unleashing the Dog of War: What the Constitution Means by "Declare War,"* 93 CORNELL L. REV. 45 (2007).

52. Id. at 47.

53. Id. at 97–98.

54. 11 ANNALS OF CONG. 12 (1801).

55. LOUIS FISHER, PRESIDENTIAL WAR POWER 35 (3d ed. 2013).

56. Saikrishna Prakash, *Exhuming the Seemingly Moribund Declaration of War*, 77 G.W. L. REV. 89 (2008).

57. Id.

58. Id. at 131–32.

consist of persons, to continue in office for the term of years....”[59] None of the persons composing the federal Executive “shall on any occasion take command of any troops, so as personally to conduct any enterprise as General, or in other capacity.”[60] Command of the military remained unclear during debate on July 20.[61]

The draft constitution prepared by the Committee of Detail provided that the Executive “shall consist of a single person” elected by Congress.[62] The Executive would serve six or seven years “and shall be ineligible thereafter.”[63] The powers of the Executive included: “to (command and superintend the militia,) <to be Commander in Chief of the Land & Naval Forces of the Union & of the Militia of the sevl. States.>”[64] On August 27, the delegates agreed to add language giving the President command “of the militia of the several States when called into the actual service of the United States.” It passed, 6 states to 2.[65] No other significant changes were made to the Commander in Chief Clause.[66]

The Federalist Papers offer some insights into presidential power over war. Hamilton in Federalist No. 69 claimed that the President’s role as Commander in Chief “would amount to nothing more than the supreme command and direction of the military and naval forces, as first General and admiral of the Confederacy; while that of the British king extends to the *declaring* of war and to the *raising* and *regulating* of fleets and armies,—all which, by the Constitution under consideration, would appertain to the legislature.”[67] Even if Hamilton’s political intention was to support ratification of the Constitution, nothing in his remarks here or in subsequent years endorsed presidential authority to unilaterally take the country to war. In Federalist No. 70, Hamilton spoke about the benefits that in “the conduct of war...the energy of the Executive is the bulwark of the national security,” but that authority existed only after Congress had decided to initiate war.[68]

In Federalist No. 4, John Jay explained why the power to initiate war could not be placed in the President. From his study he concluded that nations made war “whenever they have a prospect of getting any thing by it; nay, absolute monarchs will often make war when their nations are to get nothing by it, but for purposes and objects merely personal, such as a thirst for military glory, revenge for personal affronts, ambition, or private compacts to aggrandize or support their particular families or partisans.”[69] These and other motives often lead an Executive “to engage in wars not sanctified by justice or the voice and interests in his people.”[70] Those

---

59. 1 Farrand 244.

60. Id.

61. 2 Farrand 69–70.

62. Id. at 145.

63. Id.

64. Id. Similar language appears in subsequent drafts by the Committee of Detail. Id. at 157–58, 171–72, 185.

65. Id. at 422, 426–27.

66. Id. at 575, 599, 621.

67. The Federalist 446 (emphases in original).

68. Id. at 454.

69. The Federalist 101.

70. Id.

sentiments are from a Framer with extensive experience and expertise in foreign policy as well as an appreciation of historical and constitutional values.[71]

# 2. MILITARY ACTION IN PRACTICE

When the First Congress assembled in 1789, lawmakers, executive officials, and federal judges understood that the Declare War Clause did not mean a perfunctory legislative act to acknowledge that a President had initiated war. Contrary to the change from "make" war to "declare" war, the clause continued to mean *making war* and *going to war*. The legislative authority to declare war covered offensive, not defensive, operations. Presidents understood the difference.

## A. Offensive and defensive operations

The Framers realized that the country might be subject to sudden attack, requiring the President to act without coming to Congress for authority. Especially was that so when Congress was not in session and could not speedily return to the nation's capital. The opportunity for executive discretion, however, did not open the door to unchecked presidential use of force. President Washington explained in 1793: "The Constitution vests the power of declaring war with Congress; therefore no offensive expedition of importance can be undertaken until after they shall have deliberated upon the subject, and authorized such a measure."[72]

Also in 1793, during his service as Secretary of State, Jefferson gave reasons why U.S. citizens had no authority to initiate military actions against another nation: "If every citizen has that right, then the nation (which is composed of all it's [sic] citizens) has a right to go to war, by the authority of it's [sic] individual citizens. But this is not true either on the general principles of society, or by our Constitution, which gives that power to Congress alone...."[73] In that same year, Jefferson emphasized that "the making of reprisal on a nation is a very serious thing.... When reprisal follows it is considered as an act of war.—Besides, if the case were important enough to require reprisal, & ripe for that step, Congress must be called on to take it; the right of reprisal being expressly lodged with them by the constitution, & not with the executive."[74]

In 1794, President Washington decided to use military force in western Pennsylvania to suppress the Whiskey Rebellion. He followed the procedures established in the Militia Act of 1792, which included several checks on presidential power. Whenever the United States was invaded

---

71. Major studies on the principles of the war power include Abraham D. Sofaer, War, Foreign Affairs and Constitution Power: The Origins (1976); W. Taylor Reveley III, War Powers of the President and Congress: Who Holds the Arrows and Olive Branch? (1981); Francis D. Wormuth & Edwin B. Firmage, To Chain the Dog of War: The War Power of Congress in History and Law (2d ed. 1989); John Hart Ely, War and Responsibility: Constitutional Lessons of Vietnam and Its Aftermath (1993); Louis Fisher, Presidential War Power (3d ed. 2013); The Constitution Project, Deciding to Use Force Abroad: War Powers in a System of Checks and Balances (2005).

72. 33 The Writings of George Washington 73 (Fitzpatrick ed. 1940).

73. 6 The Writings of Thomas Jefferson 381 (Ford ed. 1895).

74. Id. at 259.

or "in imminent danger of invasion from any foreign nation or Indian tribe," the President was authorized to call forth such number of the state militia as he may judge necessary to repel the invasion.[75] In case of an insurrection in any state against public authority, the President was authorized—on application of the state legislature or of the governor when the legislature was unable to sit—to call forth the militia to suppress the insurrection.[76] If federal laws were opposed or the execution of the laws obstructed, "by combinations too powerful to be suppressed by the ordinary course of judicial proceedings," a Supreme Court Justice or district judge would have to notify the President. Only after this independent judicial determination could the President call up the militia. The statute further specified that these emergency powers were available to the President only "if the legislature of the United States be not in session."[77]

President Washington gave Justice James Wilson the evidence needed to verify the rebellion in western Pennsylvania. He received from Wilson a certification that ordinary legal means were insufficient to carry out national law.[78] Washington called upon the military in four states to put down the rebellion. District Judge Richard Peters joined Treasury Secretary Hamilton and District Attorney William Rawle in accompanying the troops. Hamilton and Rawle conducted hearings before Judge Peters to identify the instigators, who were later tried in Philadelphia.[79]

Alexander Hamilton, generally a strong proponent of independent (though limited) presidential power, understood that the decision to take the country from a state of peace to a state of war was vested solely with Congress. Writing as "Pacificus" in 1793 to defend the Neutrality Proclamation (Chapter 3, section 3A), he wrote: "[T]he Legislature can alone declare war, can alone actually transfer the nation from a state of peace to a state of hostility.... It is the province and duty of the executive to preserve the nation and blessings of peace. The Legislature alone can interrupt them by placing the nation in a state of war."[80] In 1798, after Congress had authorized President Adams to seize French armed vessels, Hamilton was asked what American ship commanders could do prior to that statute. He was "not ready to say that [the President] has any other power than merely to employ" ships as convoy with authority "to *repel* force by *force*, (but not to capture), and to repress hostilities within our waters including a marine league from our coasts."[81] However, any actions beyond those measures "must fall under the idea of *reprisals* & requires the sanction of that Department which is to declare or make war."[82]

Similarly, Jefferson interpreted the Declare War Clause broadly to include steps to *make* or *go to* war. On March 3, 1801, one day before Jefferson took office as President, Congress passed legislation to provide for a "naval peace establishment."[83] Acting under that statute, Jefferson

---

75. 1 Stat. 264, sec. 1 (1792).

76. Id.

77. Id., sec. 2. For further legislation on the militia: 1 Stat. 271 (1792). The judicial check was removed three years later: 1 Stat. 424 (1795). For these early militia statutes: Louis Fisher, *Domestic Commander in Chief: Early Checks by Other Branches*, 29 Cardozo L. Rev. 961 (2008) and Stephen I. Vladeck, *Emergency Power and the Militia Acts*, 114 Yale L.J. 149 (2004).

78. 1 Richardson 152 (Aug. 7, 1794).

79. Homer Cummings & Carl McFarland, Federal Justice 43–45 (1937). See Thomas P. Slaughter, The Whiskey Rebellion (1986).

80. 4 The Works of Alexander Hamilton 443 (Lodge ed.).

81. 21 The Papers of Alexander Hamilton 461–62 (Syrett ed. 1974) (emphases in original).

82. Id. at 462 (emphasis in original).

83. 2 Stat. 110 (1801).

sent a squadron to the Mediterranean. In the event the Barbary powers declared war on the United States, the American vessels were directed to "protect our commerce & chastise their insolence—by sinking, burning or destroying their ships & Vessels wherever you shall find them."[84] On December 8, Jefferson informed Congress about the actions of U.S. ships in the Mediterranean, stating he was "[u]nauthorized by the Constitution, without the sanction of Congress, to go beyond the line of defence."[85] Congress might want to consider, he suggested, "measures of offence also."[86] He communicated all information to Congress to permit it to decide what to do about "this important function confided by the constitution to the Legislature exclusively."[87]

Hamilton studied Jefferson's message with care. With regard to the Declare War Clause, Hamilton said "the plain meaning" is that "it is the peculiar and exclusive province of Congress, *when the nation is at peace*, to change that state into a state of war; whether from calculations of policy or from provocations or injuries received; in other words, it belongs to Congress only, *to go to War*." But when a foreign nation "declares, or openly and avowedly makes war upon the United States, they are then by the very fact, already at *war*, and any declaration on the part of Congress is nugatory: it is at least unnecessary."[88] As explained earlier in this chapter when discussing the Creek Indians and the Pasha of Tripoli, Hamilton's reasoning is too broad. There is no requirement for the United States to declare war simply because a nation declares war on it.

An OLC opinion in 1980 incorrectly states that Jefferson's use of the navy against the Barbary pirates represented one of many examples of Presidents using military force abroad "without congressional authorization."[89] Jefferson did not claim an independent or inherent power to take the country to war. He came to Congress to seek statutory authority. Beginning in 1802, Congress passed ten statutes expressly authorizing military action by Presidents Jefferson and Madison against the Barbary powers.[90] By the end of 1815, President Madison could report to Congress on the successful termination of the war with Algiers.[91]

President Jefferson often distinguished between defensive and offensive military operations, recognizing presidential initiatives for the former but not the latter. In 1805, he notified Congress about a conflict with the Spanish along the eastern boundary of the Louisiana Territory (West Florida). After describing the problem, he publicly articulated his legal principles: "Congress alone is constitutionally invested with the power of changing our condition from peace to war."[92]

84. 1 Naval Documents Relating to the United States Wars Within the Barbary Powers 467 (1939).

85. 11 Annals of Cong. 12 (Dec. 8, 1801).

86. Id.

87. Id. For details on Jefferson's military actions in the Mediterranean: Abraham D. Sofaer, War, Foreign Affairs and Constitutional Power: The Origins 209–14 (1976).

88. 25 The Papers of Alexander Hamilton 455–56 (Syrett ed. 1977) (emphases in original).

89. 4A Op. O.L.C. 185, 187 (1980).

90. 2 Stat. 129 (1802), 2 Stat. 206 (1803), 2 Stat. 291 (1804), 2 Stat. 391 (1806), 2 Stat. 436 (1807), 2 Stat. 456 (1808), 2 Stat. 511 (1809), 2 Stat. 614 (1811), 2 Stat. 675 (1812), 2 Stat. 809 (1813).

91. 2 Richardson 547 (Dec. 5, 1815). See R. Ernest Dupuy & William H. Baumer, The Little Wars of the United States 26–64 (1968). For documents on Commander in Chief power during the early decades: 1 Goldsmith 367–86.

92. 1 Richardson 377 (Dec. 6, 1805).

He thought it his "duty to await their authority for using force in any degree which could be avoided."[93]

In 1812, President Madison detailed for Congress "a series of acts, hostile to the United States," taken by Great Britain.[94] Although he referred to those actions as constituting "a state of war against the United States," he understood that the decision to go to war was left solely to Congress.[95] Conflicts with Great Britain posed a "solemn question, which the Constitution wisely confides to the Legislative Department of the Government."[96] Congress responded by issuing a declaration of war.[97]

## *B. Early legal judgments*

Federal courts understood that the branch of government authorized to "make" war and "go to war" is Congress. The Quasi-War against France prompted the Supreme Court in 1800 and 1801 to recognize that Congress has a choice in going to war and defining the scope of military operations. It may issue a formal declaration or pass statutes providing authority. In 1800 the Court explained: "Congress is empowered to declare a general war, or congress may wage a limited war; limited in place, in objects, and in time [as with the Quasi-War].... Congress has authorized hostilities on the high seas by certain persons in certain cases. There is no authority given to commit hostilities on land."[98] In the second decision, a year later, Chief Justice Marshall wrote for the Court: "The whole powers of war being, by the constitution of the United States, vested in congress, the acts of that body can alone be resorted to as our guides in this inquiry."[99]

In 1804, the Court decided a conflict between a congressional statute passed during the Quasi-War and a proclamation issued by President Adams that exceeded the statute. Writing for a unanimous Court, Chief Justice Marshall ruled that the statute necessarily prevailed. Presidential orders, even those issued as Commander in Chief, must comply with restrictions imposed by Congress.[100] Two years later, a circuit court reviewed the indictment of Colonel William S. Smith for engaging in military actions against Spain. He claimed that his military enterprise "was begun, prepared, and set on foot with the knowledge and approbation of the executive department of our government."[101] The court denied that a President or his aides may unilaterally authorize military actions against another country. The court asked: "Does [the President] possess the power of making war? That power is exclusively vested in congress."[102]

---

93. Id. Also reprinted at Annals of Cong., 9th Cong., 1st Sess. 18–19 (1805).

94. Annals of Cong., 12th Cong., 1st Sess. 1624 (1812).

95. Id. at 1629.

96. Id.

97. 2 Stat. 755 (1812).

98. Bas v. Tingy, 4 U.S. 37, 43 (1800). In Federalist No. 25, Hamilton noted: "As the ceremony of a formal denunciation of war has of later fallen into disuse," nations had authorized but not declared the initiation of hostilities. The Federalist 211. Under the Constitution, the decision either to authorize or declare war belongs to Congress.

99. Talbot v. Seeman, 5 U.S. (1 Cr.) 1, 28 (1801).

100. Little v. Barreme, 6 U.S. (2 Cr.) 170 (1804).

101. United States v. Smith, 27 Fed. Cas. 1192, 1229 (C.C.N.Y. 1806) (No. 16,342).

102. Id. at 1230.

The President could resist an invasion as a defensive action, but "it is the exclusive province of congress to change a state of peace into a state of war."[103]

A report by the Senate Committee on Foreign Relations in 1835 discussed the use of reprisals against another nation: "The framers of our constitution have manifested their sense of the nature of this power, by associating it in the same clause with grants to Congress of the power to declare war, and to make rules concerning captures on land and water."[104] Given the assignment of the authority to grant letters of marque and reprisal specifically to Congress, the committee recommended that the legislative branch "ought to retain to itself the right of judging of the expediency of granting them" and lacked constitutional grounds for delegating that authority to the President.[105]

# 3. AVAILABILITY OF A STANDING ARMY

The Framers understood the risk of executive wars whenever Presidents had ready access to armed forces. At the Philadelphia convention, Elbridge Gerry "took notice that there was <no> check here agst. standing armies in time of peace."[106] He thought "an army dangerous in time of peace & could never consent to a power to keep up an indefinite number."[107] The Framers sought to limit that risk by including in Article I, section 8 this language: "To raise and support Armies, but no Appropriation of Money to that Use shall be for a longer Term than two Years." An Attorney General opinion in 1904 concluded that to "raise and support an army is one thing. To render it effective, by equipping it with guns, ammunition, and other means for attack and defense, is another."[108] According to his analysis, the two-year constitutional limit applied only to the former. Entering into military contracts that might extend beyond a period of two years did not, in his opinion, violate the two-year limit.

This analysis may appear to be playing with words, but the constitutional debates at Philadelphia offer some support for his interpretation. Initially, the word "equip" was used in reference to the Navy, as in "raise armies. <& equip. Fleets.>", "raising a military Land Force—and of equiping a Navy," and "raise Armies; to build and equip Fleets."[109] The delegates agreed later to insert the words "and support" after "raise" and to adopt "provide and maintain" in place of "build and equip."[110] The two-year limit applied to armies, not to navies. Whereas Article I, section 8 empowers Congress to "raise and support armies" and no appropriation for that use shall be for a longer term than two years, it next states: "To provide and maintain a Navy." The Framers appeared to be mainly concerned about the potential for misuse or abuse by a

---

103. Id.

104. S. Rep. No. 40, 23d Cong., 2d Sess. 21 (1835).

105. Id. at 22. For analysis of contemporary military actions by Presidents, without any delegated authority, that amount to reprisals: Jules Lobel, *"Little Wars" and the Constitution*, 50 U. MIAMI L. REV. 61 (1995).

106. 2 Farrand 329.

107. Id.

108. 25 OP. ATT'Y GEN. 105, 106 (1904). See also 40 OP. ATT'Y GEN. 555 (1948).

109. 2 Farrand 143, 158, 168, 182.

110. Id. at 323, 329–30.

standing army while recognizing the need to make funds available over a period of many years for the construction of vessels. Carried a step further, the same reasoning could apply to any long lead-time construction items for the Army, Air Force, and Marine Corps. It is not unusual in contemporary appropriations bills for the military services to receive money for five years and even "no-year" money, where funds are available until obligated and spent.[111]

When President John Adams decided there were sufficient grounds to use military force against France in 1798, he lacked capacity to move on his own. He had to come to Congress to ask for legislation to prepare the country for war. Congress passed several dozen bills to provide supplemental funds for a naval armament, a regiment of artillertists and engineers, reinforcement of ports and harbors, and money for additional cannons, arms, and ammunition.[112] Although there was no formal declaration of war, no one doubted that Congress had acted to authorize war. Representative Edward Livingston considered the country "now in a state of war, and let no man flatter himself that the vote which has been given is not a declaration of war."[113] In fact, it was not a declaration of war. It marked legislative authorization for the undeclared Quasi-War.[114]

Matters changed dramatically in 1846 when President Polk decided it was in his political interest to provoke war with Mexico. Those intentions are clear from his diary.[115] The previous year he informed Congress about diplomatic efforts to resolve several disputes with Mexico, including the location of the boundary between it and the state of Texas.[116] Yet in the following spring he sent U.S. troops to the border and reported on May 11, 1846, about military hostilities. He claimed that Mexican forces "have at last invaded our territory and shed the blood of our fellow-citizens on our own soil."[117] There was no evidence that the territory on which Mexican and American forces clashed belonged to the United States. Nevertheless, Congress promptly passed legislation that "a state of war exists" between the two countries.[118] Even after the war, no one knew the location of the boundary line. On July 6, 1848, Polk admitted to Congress that the border remained uncertain and efforts would again be made to define national territory.[119]

In 1850, the Supreme Court observed that the President as Commander in Chief "is authorized to direct the movements of the naval and military forces placed by law at his command, and to employ them in the manner he may deem most effectual to harass and conquer and subdue the enemy."[120] There is no implication of an independent presidential authority to take the country to war. Military forces are *placed by law* at his command. The President is constrained by appropriations, authorizations, and statutory limitations. Once war begins the President "may invade the hostile country, and subject it to the sovereignty and authority of the United

---

111. Louis Fisher, Presidential Spending Power 127–30 (1975).

112. 1 Stat. 547–611 (1798).

113. 8 Annals of Cong. 1519 (1798).

114. Fisher, *supra* note 55, at 23-26. See Alexander DeConde, The Quasi-War: The Politics and Diplomacy of the Undeclared War with France, 1797–1801 (1966).

115. 1 The Diary of James K. Polk 71, 228–29, 235–39, 287, 319, 325–26, 337, 343, 354 (M. Quaife, ed., 1910).

116. 5 Richardson 2241 (Dec. 1, 1845).

117. Id. at 2288 (May 11, 1846).

118. 9 Stat. 9 (1846).

119. 5 Richardson 2246 (July 24, 1848). For a recent analysis of the Mexican War: Amy S. Greenberg, A Wicked War: Polk, Clay, Lincoln, and the 1946 U.S. Invasion of Mexico (2012).

120. Fleming v. Page, 50 U.S. (9 How.) 603, 615 (1850).

States," but presidential conquests "do not enlarge the boundaries of this Union, nor extend the operation of our institutions and laws beyond the limits before assigned to them by the legislative power."[121]

On July 5, 1861, after the Civil War began, Attorney General Edward Bates explored the meaning of the Commander in Chief Clause. He asked why the Constitution puts the President in charge of the army, the navy, and the militia when called into actual service. His answer: "Surely not because the President is supposed to be, or commonly is, in fact, a military man, a man skilled in the art of war and qualified to marshal a host in the field of battle."[122] He is assigned that position for a different reason: "it is that whatever skilful soldier may lead our armies to victory against a foreign foe, or may quell a domestic insurrection; however high he may raise his professional renown, and whatever martial glory he may win, still he is subject to the orders of the *civil magistrate*, and he and his army are always 'subordinate to the civil power.' "[123] The civil power is not merely the President. It includes Congress and the judiciary. When President Truman invoked his Commander in Chief power in 1952 to seize steel mills in order to prosecute the war in Korea, a district judge and later the Supreme Court ruled that he lacked that constitutional power.[124] See section 6 of this chapter.

In his message to Congress on July 4, 1861, President Lincoln reviewed his actions in authorizing "the Commander General in proper cases, according to his discretion, to suspend the privilege of the writ of *habeas corpus*."[125] Initially the writ was suspended between Washington and Philadelphia to protect the northern flank of the capital and ensure that Union troops could reach it.[126] Suspending this constitutional privilege made it easier for the North to apprehend and detain those who sympathized with the South and were willing to sabotage Union efforts. Later, the suspension applied more broadly.[127] Lincoln acknowledged that the "legality and propriety" of his actions "are questioned, and the attention of the country has been called to the proposition that one who is sworn to 'take care that the laws be faithfully executed' should not himself violate them.' "[128] He never claimed exclusive authority to justify what he had done. Instead, he "believed that nothing has been done beyond the constitutional competency of Congress."[129] In short, he had exercised not only his Article II powers but the Article I powers of Congress and for that reason needed Congress to authorize what he had done, which Congress provided by statute.[130]

Lincoln's Attorney General, Edward Bates, never argued that the President had independent and unchecked authority to suspend the writ. Bates reasoned that in times of "a great and dangerous insurrection, the President has the lawful discretionary power to arrest and hold in custody persons known to have criminal intercourse with the insurgents, or persons against

121. Id.

122. 10 Op. Att'y Gen. 74, 79 (1861).

123. Id. (emphasis in original).

124. Youngstown Co. v. Sawyer, 343 U.S. 579 (1952); Youngstown Sheet & Tube Co. v. Sawyer, 103 F. Supp. 569 (D.D.C. 1952).

125. 7 Richardson 3225 (July 4, 1861).

126. James M. McPherson, Tried by War: Abraham Lincoln as Commander in Chief 27 (2008).

127. Id.

128. 7 Richardson 3226.

129. Id. at 3225.

130. 12 Stat. 326 (1861).

whom there is probable cause for suspicion of such criminal complicity."[131] He qualified his opinion by saying that if the constitutional language meant "a repeal of all power to issue the writ, then I freely admit that none but Congress can do it."[132] In the event of "a great and dangerous rebellion, like the present," the President's power to suspend the privilege was "temporary and exceptional."[133]

Both Lincoln and Bates acknowledged congressional power to pass legislation that limits how a President may suspend the writ of habeas corpus during a rebellion. On March 3, 1863, Congress enacted a bill that directed the Secretary of State and the Secretary of War to furnish federal judges with a list of the names of all persons held as prisoners by order of the President or executive officers.[134] Submitting this list was mandatory.[135] Failure to furnish someone's name to the judiciary could result in the discharge of a prisoner.[136]

Military authorities arrested John Merryman and held him at Fort McHenry in Baltimore. Chief Justice Roger Taney, sitting as circuit judge, issued a writ of habeas corpus to the commandant of the fort, directing him to bring Merryman to the circuit courtroom in Baltimore on May 27, 1861.[137] The commandant, acting under Lincoln's orders, refused to produce Merryman. Taney issued an opinion stating that Merryman was entitled to be set at liberty, but Taney, in May 1861, was not the federal officer responsible for preserving the Union. He had neither the authority nor the capacity. His decision in *Dred Scott* in 1857 had helped propel the country toward civil war. In May 1861, Lincoln faced a difficult choice. Having lost Virginia to the South, he could not afford to lose Maryland to the North and have the nation's capital encircled. At that moment in time, it was Lincoln's constitutional call, not Taney's.[138]

Lincoln's blockade of the South during the Civil War reached the Supreme Court in 1863. An OLC opinion in 1980 described the decision in this manner: "In the only major case dealing with the role of the courts with regard to this general subject [presidential power to use armed force without statutory authorization], the Supreme Court upheld presidential power to act in an emergency without prior congressional authority."[139] The dispute before the Court in 1863 was, in fact, much narrower. Justice Robert Grier said that while the President had no authority to initiate war, in the event of a foreign invasion he was not only authorized "but bound to resist force by force. He does not initiate the war, but is bound to accept the challenge without waiting for the special legislative authority."[140] Grier limited the President to *defensive* actions, noting that he "has no power to initiate or declare a war against either a foreign nation or a domestic

---

131. 10 Op. ATT'Y GEN. 74, 81 (1861).

132. Id. at 90.

133. Id.

134. 12 Stat. 755, sec. 2 (1863).

135. Id.

136. Id., § 3, 12 Stat. at 756.

137. Ex parte Merryman, 17 F. Cas. 144, 147 (C.C.D. Md. 1861) (No. 9,487).

138. See Michael Stokes Paulsen, *The Merryman Power and the Dilemma of Autonomous Executive Branch Interpretation*, 15 CARDOZO L. REV. 81 (1993), and Martin S. Sheffer, *Presidential Power to Suspend Habeas Corpus: The Taney-Bates Dialogue and* Ex parte Merryman, 11 OKLA. CITY U. L. REV. 1 (1986).

139. 4A Op. O.L.C. 185, 188 (1980).

140. The Prize Cases, 67 U.S. 635, 668 (1863).

State."[141] The executive branch took exactly the same position. Richard Henry Dana, Jr., who represented the President, acknowledged that Lincoln's actions had nothing to do with "the right *to initiate a war, as a voluntary act of sovereignty. That is vested only in Congress.*"[142] At issue in *The Prize Cases* was a domestic civil war, not a military action against another nation.

Unlike President Truman and many of his successors, Lincoln never claimed he possessed unilateral legal and constitutional authority to act as he did in the months following the outbreak of the Civil War. When he issued proclamations calling out the state militia and suspending the writ of habeas corpus, he did not claim or invoke "inherent" presidential authority. He forthrightly admitted that he exceeded his constitutional boundaries and needed the sanction of Congress. When lawmakers returned he explained that his actions, "whether strictly legal or not, were ventured upon under what appeared to be a popular demand and a public necessity, trusting then, as now, that Congress would readily ratify them."[143] In language that is extraordinarily frank, he described his initiatives as not "beyond the constitutional competency of Congress."[144] Congress debated his request at length, with members supporting him on the explicit understanding that his acts were illegal unless they receive retroactive congressional approval.[145] Congress eventually passed legislation "approving, legalizing, and making valid all the acts, proclamations, and orders of the President, etc., as if they had been issued and done under the previous express authority and direction of the Congress of the United States."[146]

# 4. INTERNATIONAL AND REGIONAL BODIES

Following the Civil War, Presidents came to Congress to receive a declaration of war against Spain in 1898 and two declarations when entering World War I in 1917.[147] Six declarations were enacted for World War II in 1941 and 1942.[148] Truman was the first President to initiate a war without seeking congressional authorization or declaration. He did so in June 1950, citing "authorization" not from Congress but from the United Nations Security Council. By acting in that manner, he violated a public pledge he made to Congress in 1945 and violated the UN Participation Act of 1945. The precedent he set has been followed by other Presidents, including

---

141. Id.

142. Id. at 660 (emphasis in original).

143. 7 Richardson 3225 (July 4, 1861).

144. Id.

145. Cong. Globe, 37th Cong., 1st Sess. 393 (1861) (Senator Howe).

146. 12 Stat. 326 (1861).

147. Declarations of war against Spain, 30 Stat. 364 (1898), the Imperial German Government, 40 Stat. 1 (1917), and the Imperial and Royal Austro-Hungarian Government, 40 Stat. 429 (1917).

148. Declarations of war against Japan, 55 Stat. 795 (1941), Germany, 55 Stat. 795 (1941), Italy, 55 Stat. 797 (1941), Bulgaria, 56 Stat. 307 (1942), Hungary, 56 Stat. 307 (1942), and Rumania, 56 Stat. 307 (1942). For President Roosevelt's proclamation announcing arrest and detention policy for U.S. non-citizens of the later three countries: 56 Stat. 1970–72 (1942).

George H. W. Bush, Bill Clinton, and Barack Obama. Presidents also circumvent Congress by seeking "authorization" from NATO allies.

A fundamental question of constitutional government has been inadequately explored by the elected branches, the judiciary, and scholars. Here is the basic issue: May a President and the Senate through the treaty process (as with the UN Charter and NATO) create an international or regional body that functions as a constitutional substitute for the Senate and the House of Representatives? Put differently: May a treaty transfer Article I authority to an organization outside of the United States?

## A. Creating the UN

In June 1950, when President Truman ordered U.S. troops to Korea, for legal footing he cited resolutions passed by the UN Security Council. How can UN machinery be a legal substitute for congressional approval? Is it possible for the President and the Senate through the treaty process to strip from the House of Representatives (and future Senates) their constitutional role to decide questions of war? Did the UN Charter transfer part of the U.S. Constitution to the Security Council?

Part of the answer comes from reviewing the experience with the Treaty of Versailles and the Covenant of the League of Nations. The Senate defeated the treaty in 1919 and again in 1920, after a number of Senators insisted that any commitment of U.S. troops to a world body (the League of Nations) first had to be approved by Congress. Senator Henry Cabot Lodge favored U.S. participation in the League but proposed certain "reservations" to be attached to the treaty. The second of 14 reservations concerned the congressional prerogative to decide questions of war:

> The United States assumes no obligation to preserve the territorial integrity or political indepen-
> dence of any other country or to interfere in controversies between nations—whether members
> of the league or not—under the provisions of article 10, or to employ the military or naval forces
> of the United States under any article of the treaty for any purpose, unless in any particular case
> the Congress, which, under the Constitution, has the sole power to declare war or authorize the
> employment of the military or naval forces of the United States, shall by act or joint resolution so
> provide.[149]

Wilson vigorously opposed the Lodge reservations, advising the public they "cut out the heart of this Covenant."[150] His principal advisers, including Secretary of State Robert Lansing, Bernard Baruch, Herbert Hoover, and Colonel Edward Mandell House, saw nothing objectionable to the reservations and urged Wilson to accept them.[151] Personal spite caused Wilson to dig in his heels. Newspapers reported he had "strangled his own child."[152] Wilson had no principled reason to oppose the reservations. On March 8, 1920, he wrote to Senator Gilbert Monell Hitchcock to

---

149.  58 CONG. REC. 8777 (1919).

150.  63 THE PAPERS OF WOODROW WILSON 451 (Link ed. 1990).

151.  TOWNSEND HOOPES & DOUGLAS BRINKLEY, FDR AND THE CREATION OF THE U.N. 6 (1977).

152.  65 THE PAPERS OF WOODROW WILSON 71, n.3 (Link ed. 1991).

explain why Congress need not be concerned about any military action the League of Nations might consider. Whatever obligations the U.S. government undertook "would of course have to be fulfilled by its usual and established constitutional methods of action," and there "can be no objection to explaining again what our constitutional method is and that our Congress alone can declare war or determine the causes or occasions for war, and that it alone can authorize the use of the armed forces of the United States on land or on the sea."[153] He regarded acceptance of the Lodge reservation as "a work of supererogation," by which he meant it was superfluous and unnecessary.[154]

It was important for Wilson to accept the Senate reservations and move forward with the treaty, but he was personally incapable of doing that. Having excluded the Senate from the nego-tiating sessions, he tried to present the final product to Senators as a fait accompli. The result: a resounding political defeat for Wilson. He chose to mount an exhausting campaign across the country to build public support, resulting in his physical and emotional collapse. His dismal experience of "going it alone" remained fixed in the nation's memory and cast a long shadow over efforts during World War II to create a United Nations.

On March 16, 1943, Senator Joseph Hurst Ball introduced a resolution calling for the for-mation of a United Nations.[155] During Senate debate on his resolution, nothing was said about which branch of government could commit U.S. troops to the organization and the military actions it engaged in. The House debated a resolution introduced by J. William Fulbright to support the concept of a United Nations. Unlike the Senate measure, which was only a Senate resolution, Fulbright's bill was a concurrent resolution requiring action by both houses. The House passed the Fulbright resolution 252 to 23.[156] An amendment was adopted to require that the United States act "through its constitutional processes."[157] The next day, by roll call vote, the amended resolution passed 360 to 29.[158] The Senate ignored Fulbright's resolution and concen-trated on its own resolution, which passed 85 to 5.[159] It included the phrase "through its consti-tutional processes" with respect to committing troops to UN military operations. Little was said during this lengthy debate about specific congressional controls over the use of American troops in a UN military action.

The United States, the United Kingdom, the Soviet Union, and China met at Dumbarton Oaks, in Washington, D.C., to further develop this international organization. Yale law professor Edwin Borchard observed: "Constitutionally, the plan seems to assume that the President, or his delegate, without consulting Congress, the war-making and declaring authority, can vote for the use of the American quota of armed forces, if that can be limited when the 'aggressor' resists."[160] Two weeks later, after the close of the conference at Dumbarton Oaks, President Roosevelt indi-cated the need for advance congressional approval of military actions. In order for the UN "to act quickly and decisively to keep the peace by force, if necessary,... [it] must be endowed in

153. Id. at 68.

154. Id.

155. 89 Cong. Rec. 2030–31 (1943).

156. Id. at 7655.

157. Id.

158. Id. at 7728–29.

159. Id. at 9221–22.

160. Edwin Borchard, *The Dumbarton Oaks Conference*, 39 Am. J. Int'l L. 97, 101 (1945).

advance by the people themselves, by constitutional means through their representatives in the Congress, with authority to act."[161] He appeared to anticipate congressional support for a UN military force able to act at a moment's notice.

In following the debate over the UN Charter, Borchard in 1945 focused on a "serious question of constitutional law."[162] The draft charter provided in Article 43 that all member states make available to the Security Council, "on its call and in accordance with a special agreement or agreements, armed forces,... necessary for the purpose of maintaining international peace and security." Borchard asked: How was that to be done? By the President and the Senate through the treaty process? By both houses of Congress acting by statute? By the President alone, issuing an executive agreement?[163] He learned that President Truman sent a cable from Potsdam announcing his intent to submit any and all agreements "of this nature to a majority vote of both Houses."[164] To Borchard, it was uncertain whether Truman's commitment applied only to the original agreement or to subsequent agreements.[165]

Here is the language that Truman used in a cable of July 2, 1945, sent to Senator Kenneth McKellar: "When any such agreement or agreements are negotiated it will be my purpose to ask the Congress for appropriate legislation to approve them."[166] In that manner, Truman made it clear that U.S. action on special agreements would not be done by the President alone, or by the President and the Senate through the treaty process, but by both houses of Congress passing a bill or joint resolution to be submitted to the President.

Borchard explored two other issues. If the United Nations engaged in "any belligerent action against a proclaimed 'aggressor'" and "bombs or shoots up that nation's inhabitants, it is hard to see how the conclusion can be avoided that this is an act of war and the United States is at war, even if the 'aggressor' fails to resist."[167] To avoid calling it war by speaking of "'peace enforcement' or any other pleasant name does not alter the fact that it is an act of war."[168] Employing military force against another nation "is admittedly an 'act of war' requiring the consent of Congress."[169] Borchard's reference to euphemisms proved prescient. In addition to "peace enforcement," UN military operations against North Korea in 1950 would be referred to as a "police action" (discussed later in this chapter).

As a second point, Borchard commented on those who argued that if the President may use armed forces to protect U.S. citizens abroad, "it follows that he can make these agreements or give his consent without the consent of Congress or the Senate."[170] He cited a study by James G. Rogers, *World Policing and the Constitution* (1945), that described about 150 American

---

161. *American Foreign Policy: Address by the President*, 11 Dep't of State Bull. 447, 448 (1944) (excerpts from an address delivered before the Foreign Policy Association in New York, N.Y., Oct. 21, 1944).

162. Edwin Borchard, *The Charter and the Constitution*, 39 Am. J. Int'l L. 767, 767 (1945).

163. Id.

164. Id. at 767–68.

165. Id. at 768, n.3.

166. 91 Cong. Rec. 8185 (1945).

167. Borchard, *supra* note 162, at 768.

168. Id.

169. Id.

170. Id.

military interventions without a declaration or authorization from Congress.[171] Those interventions, however, were "occasioned mostly by local disorders, revolutions, supervising elections, offenses against American citizens (and therefore punitive in nature), the pursuit of pirates and slavers, at the request of the local government, under extraterritoriality or other treaty, a mere demonstration of force and a variety of other occasions."[172] The number of troops "was usually very few, under 100, although about 5,000 were involved in the Boxer troubles in China."[173] None of the presidential interventions "were expected to lead to war."[174] For those who argued that military initiatives under the UN could be handled by treaty, Borchard responded: "The trouble with this construction is a Constitutional one. The Constitution provides that Congress alone, not the treaty-making power, has the power to declare war and make regulations governing the use of the armed forces of the United States."[175] He concluded that "an Act of Congress is necessary to reconcile the Charter with the Constitution of the United States."[176]

## B. Statutory action on the Charter

Chapter VII of the UN Charter covers UN responses to threats of peace, breaches of peace, and acts of aggression. All UN members would make available to the Security Council, "on its call and in accordance with a special agreement or agreements," armed forces and other assistance for the purpose of maintaining international peace and security.[177] Agreements concluded between the Security Council and member states "shall be subject to ratification by the signatory states in accordance with their respective constitutional processes."[178] Each nation therefore had to determine its "constitutional processes." For the United States, would that be solely by the President, the President and the Senate through the treaty process, or the two houses and the President acting by statute?

From July 9 through July 13, 1945, the Senate Foreign Relations Committee held hearings on the Charter. Leo Pasvolsky, a special assistant to the Secretary of State, was asked whether Congress would have ultimate control over the special agreements to use armed forces. He replied: "That is a domestic question which I am afraid I cannot answer."[179] Senator Arthur Vandenberg offered his view that if the consent of Congress were required for every use of our armed forces "it would not only violate the spirit of the Charter, but it would violate the spirit of the Constitution of the United States, because under the Constitution the President has certain

---

171. Id., n.4.

172. Id. at 769, n.5.

173. Id.

174. Id.

175. Id. at 770.

176. Id. at 771. On military actions short of war, an earlier reference was to *The Little War of the United States* by R. Ernest Dupuy & William H. Baumer, *supra* note 91. See also MAX BOOT, THE SAVAGE WARS OF PEACE: SMALL WARS AND THE RISE OF AMERICAN POWER (2002), and PETER HUCHTHAUSEN, AMERICA'S SPLENDID LITTLE WARS: A SHORT HISTORY OF U.S. MILITARY ENGAGEMENTS: 1975–2000 (2003).

177. UN CHARTER, Ch. VII, Art. 43, para. 1.

178. Id., para. 3.

179. *The Charter of the United Nations*, hearings before the Senate Committee on Foreign Relations, 79th Cong., 1st Sess. 298 (1945).

rights to use our armed forces in the national defense without consulting Congress. It has been done 72 times within the last 150 years. It is just as much a part of the Constitution as is the congressional right to declare war."[180] The precedents Vandenberg referred to were small scale, limited military actions. They had nothing to do with the scope of UN actions against North Korea in 1950.

John Foster Dulles, an adviser to the U.S. delegation at San Francisco, testified that special agreements would need the approval of the Senate and could not be done unilaterally by the President. Twice he said he had "no doubt" that Senate advice and consent by a two-thirds vote would satisfy the meaning of "constitutional processes" in the United States.[181] As discussion of Senate ratification continued, Dulles used the phrases "no doubt" and "no doubt in my mind" to describe his position.[182] During floor debate, some Senators took sharp exception to Dulles' position and insisted that approval of special agreements would need the support of not merely the Senate but of both houses. They pointed to language in Article I, section 8 of the U.S. Constitution that places the war power in Congress, not the Senate.[183]

As the debate continued, Senator Vandenberg decided to telephone Dulles and get a better understanding. On this occasion Dulles was less cocksure. He explained that at the hearing it was his intention to reject the notion that the President could act alone in approving a special agreement. For that reason he insisted that Senate approval would be needed. The central point he tried to make was that the use of force could not be made by exclusive presidential authority through an executive agreement. On the issue whether Congress should act by treaty or by both houses, he had not thought it through.[184] It was evident that Dulles was an international lawyer, not a constitutional lawyer. On July 28, 1945, the Senate received Truman's cable from Potsdam, pledging that he would ask the full Congress for legislation to approve special agreements. Several minutes later the Senate supported the UN Charter by a vote of 89 to 2.[185]

Congress now had to decide the meaning, for the United States, of "constitutional processes" as called for by the Charter. It did so through the UN Participation Act, enacted on December 20, 1945.[186] Section 6 authorizes the President to negotiate a special agreement or agreements with the Security Council, "which shall be subject to the approval of the Congress by appropriate Act of joint resolution," providing for the numbers and types of armed forces, their degree of readiness and general location, and other requirements.[187] The language is consistent with Truman's pledge. Presidents could commit armed forces to the United Nations only after Congress had given its explicit approval by statute. The President could not act unilaterally by executive agreement or simply seek the support of two-thirds of the Senate by treaty. That point is crucial. The League of Nations Covenant foundered precisely on the issue of needing congressional approval

---

180. Id. at 299.

181. Id. at 645–45.

182. Id. at 651.

183. 91 Cong. Rec. 8021–27 (1945).

184. Id. at 8027–28.

185. Id. at 8190.

186. 59 Stat. 619 (1945).

187. Id. at 621, sec. 6; 22 U.S.C. § 287d.

before using armed force in an international body. The framers of the UN Charter understood that history and very consciously included safeguards for congressional authority.[188]

The legislative history of the UN Participation Act reinforces the need for advance congressional approval. Under Secretary of State Dean Acheson explained in congressional testimony that only after the President receives the consent of Congress is he "bound to furnish that contingent of troops to the Security Council; and the President is not authorized to furnish any more than you [Congress] have approved of in that agreement."[189] In reporting the UN Participation Act, the Senate Foreign Relations Committee anticipated a shared, coequal relationship between the President and Congress in committing U.S. troops to a UN military action: "The Congress will be asked annually to appropriate funds to support the United Nations budget and for the expenses of our representation. It will be called up to approve arrangements for the supply of armed forces to the Security Council and thereafter to make appropriations for the maintenance of such forces."[190] The report by the House Foreign Affairs Committee underscored that "it is eminently appropriate that the Congress as a whole pass upon these agreements under the constitutional powers of the Congress."[191]

Statutory restrictions on presidential war power were reinforced by amendments in 1949 to the UN Participation Act. They permitted the President on his own initiative to provide military forces to the United Nations "for cooperative action."[192] Presidential authority in this limited area was subject to stringent limitations. The forces could serve only "for peaceful settlement of disputes and not involving the employment of armed forces contemplated by chapter VII of the United Nations Charter."[193] U.S. armed forces could serve only "as observers, guards, or in any noncombatant capacity, but in no event shall more than a total of one thousand of such personnel be so detailed at any one time."[194] Nothing in the text or legislative history of the UN Charter, the UN Participation Act, or the amendments in 1949 anticipated or authorized unilateral presidential decisions to commit U.S. troops to an offensive action without prior congressional approval.

## C. NATO and other mutual security treaties

In addition to seeking support from the Security Council for military operations, Presidents have turned to NATO allies as an "authorizing" body. However, the issue of defining "constitutional processes" under Article 43 of the UN Charter applies as well to language in mutual defense treaties. The NATO (North Atlantic Treaty Organization) treaty was signed in 1949 by the United States, Canada, and ten European countries. Article 5 provides that "an armed attack against one or more of them in Europe or North America shall be considered an attack against

---

188. Michael J. Glennon, *The Constitution and Chapter VII of the United Nations Charter*, 85 Am. J. Int'l L. 74, 75–77 (1991).

189. *Participation by the United States in the United Nations Organization*, hearings before the House Committee on Foreign Affairs, 79th Cong., 1st Sess. 23 (1945).

190. S. Rep. No. 717, 79th Cong., 1st Sess. 5 (1945).

191. H. Rep. No. 1383, 79th Cong., 1st Sess. 7 (1945).

192. 63 Stat. 735, sec. 5 (1949).

193. Id.

194. Id. at 736.

them all."[195] It further states that, in the event of an attack, NATO countries may exercise the right of individual or collective self-defense recognized by Article 51 of the UN Charter and assist the country or countries attacked by taking "such action as it deems necessary, including the use of armed force."[196] Article 11 of the North Atlantic Treaty provides that it shall be ratified "and its provisions carried out by the Parties in accordance with their respective constitutional processes."[197] Like the UN Charter, the NATO treaty does not provide Presidents with any unilateral authority to commit military forces to war.

Similar procedures appear in the Rio Treaty, signed in 1947 by the United States and 18 countries in Central America, South America, and the Caribbean. Nicaragua joined the pact a year later. Those nations agreed to assist one another in the event of an attack, with an armed attack against one state considered "as an attack against all the American states."[198] A mutual defense treaty between the United States and the Republic of Korea in 1953 declared the "common determination" of both countries to "defend themselves against external armed attack."[199] Each party recognized that "an armed attack in the Pacific area on either of the Parties in territories now under their respective administrative control…would be dangerous to its own peace and safety and declares that it would act to meet the common danger in accordance with its constitutional processes."[200]

A treaty in 1954 created the Southeast Asia Treaty Organization (SEATO), consisting of the United States, Australia, France, New Zealand, Pakistan, the Philippines, Thailand, and the United Kingdom. Each party recognized that armed aggression against one of the parties "would endanger its own peace and safety, and agreed that it will in that event act to meet the common danger in accordance with its constitutional processes."[201] As with NATO, the SEATO treaty "shall be ratified and its provisions carried out by the Parties in accordance with their respective constitutional processes."[202]

These mutual security treaties did not—and could not—transfer the war power to the President. Action by the President and the Senate through the treaty process may not transfer the Article I powers of Congress to an international or regional body. The treaties were clearly designed for defensive operations. As explained in section 9 of this chapter, Presidents Clinton and Obama used NATO military forces against countries that did not attack or threaten the United States. The operations were offensive, not defensive. Finally, these mutual security treaties require action through "constitutional processes." Unilateral offensive wars by the President are not constitutional.

During Senate hearings in 1949, Secretary of State Dean Acheson testified that the NATO treaty "does not enlarge, nor does it decrease, nor does it change in any way, the relative constitutional position of the President and the Congress."[203] Nevertheless, Presidents Clinton and Obama would later rely on NATO to use military force against Bosnia, Yugoslavia, and Libya

195. 63 Stat. 2244, art. 5 (1949).

196. Id.

197. Id. at 2246, art. 11.

198. 62 Stat. 1700, art. 3 (1947).

199. 5 UST 2371.

200. Id. at 2372–73.

201. 6 UST 83, art. IV (1954).

202. Id. at 84, art. IX.2.

203. *North Atlantic Treaty* (Part 1), hearings before the Senate Committee on Foreign Relations, 81st Cong., 1st Sess. 80 (1949).

without coming to Congress for authority. By providing that the NATO treaty be carried out in accordance with constitutional processes, the Senate Foreign Relations Committee "intended to ensure that the Executive Branch of the Government should come back to the Congress when decisions were required in which the Congress has a constitutional responsibility."[204] The treaty "does not transfer to the President the Congressional power to make war."[205] Congress reinforced that constitutional principle when it enacted the War Powers Resolution of 1973. Section 8(a) provides that authority to introduce U.S. forces into hostilities shall not be inferred "from any treaty heretofore or hereafter ratified unless such treaty is implemented by legislation specifically authorizing" the introduction of American troops.[206] Section 8 of this chapter provides further analysis on this issue.

In considering the North Atlantic Treaty, the Senate rejected an amendment that would have required explicit, advance congressional approval before the President could use armed force. The amendment lost on a vote of 84 to 11.[207] An interesting amendment, but a Senate vote to defeat an amendment does not change the Constitution or nullify the Article I authority of the House of Representatives and future Senates. In legislative history, a negative vote does not augment presidential authority.

# 5. THE KOREAN WAR

With statutory safeguards supposedly in place to protect congressional powers and constitutional government, President Truman on June 26, 1950, announced to the American public that he had conferred with his Secretaries of State and Defense, their senior advisers, and the Joint Chiefs of Staff "about the situation in the Far East created by unprovoked aggression [by North Korea] against the Republic of Korea."[208] He said the Security Council had ordered a withdrawal of the invading forces to positions north of the 38th parallel and that in "accordance with the resolution of the Security Council, the United States will vigorously support the effort of the Council to terminate this serious breach of the peace."[209] At that point, Truman had made no commitment of U.S. forces to the conflict.

One day later, Truman announced that North Korea had failed to cease hostilities and withdraw to the 38th parallel. He described the UN process in this manner: "The Security Council called upon all members of the United Nations to render every assistance to the United Nations in the execution of this resolution. In these circumstances I have ordered United States air and sea forces to give the [South] Korean Government cover and support."[210] He made no mention of

---

204. Richard H. Heindel, Thorsten V. Kalijarvi & Francis O. Wilcox., *The North Atlantic Treaty in the United States Senate*, 43 Am. J. Int'l L. 633, 649 (1949).

205. Id. at 650. See also Michael J. Glennon, *United States Mutual Security Treaties: The Commitment Myth*, 24 Colum. J. Transnat'l L. 509 (1986).

206. 87 Stat. 555, 558, sec. 8(a)(2) (1973).

207. 95 Cong. Rec. 9806, 9898, 9916 (1949).

208. Public Papers of the Presidents, 1950, at 491.

209. Id.

210. Id. at 492. See Glenn D. Paige, The Korean Decision: June 24–30, 1950 (1968).

his public pledge from Potsdam five years earlier about obtaining prior congressional approval and did not refer to the UN Participation Act of 1945 and its specific requirement to do precisely that. How was that possible?

Part of the answer is that the Soviet Union chose to be absent from the Security Council and did not exercise its veto power. Without the Russians, the Council voted 9 to zero to call upon North Korea to cease hostilities and withdraw their forces. Two days later the Council requested military assistance from member states to repel the attack. By that time, Truman had already ordered U.S. air and sea forces to assist South Korea. Can it be reasonably argued that the President's constitutional authority fluctuates with the presence or absence of Soviet delegates at the Security Council? Robert Bork noted in 1971: "the approval of the United Nations was obtained only because the Soviet Union happened to be boycotting the Security Council at the time, and the President's Constitutional powers can hardly be said to ebb and flow with the veto of the Soviet Union in the Security Council."[211]

Why was there no compliance with Section 6 of the UN Participation Act? Some supporters of Truman's sending of troops to Korea offered this explanation: "As no Article 43 agreements had been concluded by the United States—or any other nation—section 6 of the UNPA did not apply."[212] According to this analysis, the statutory requirement for prior congressional approval (to ensure that the UN Charter conformed to U.S. "constitutional processes") was without meaning or effect. In 1945, executive officials and members of Congress agreed that the President could not act unilaterally by executive agreement in making troops available for a UN military action, or even through the treaty process with the Senate, but must obtain approval from both houses of Congress. A Security Council resolution "authorizing" the use of military force does not change the allocation of the war-making power in the United States.[213] And yet Truman in 1950 acted alone without congressional authority.

Other arguments were presented to defend Truman's action. At a June 29, 1950, news conference, he was asked whether the country was at war. He replied: "We are not at war."[214] A reporter asked whether it might be more correct to call the military conflict "a police action under the United Nations." Truman readily agreed: "That is exactly what it amounts to."[215] Robert Turner has pointed out that Truman "met personally with the top congressional leaders" and they "*unanimously* supported the President's actions."[216] He did indeed meet with lawmakers. On July 3, Senate Majority Leader Scott Lucas told Truman that he questioned the need for a congressional resolution of approval: "He said that the President had very properly done what he had to

211. Robert H. Bork, *Comments on the Articles on the Legality of the United States Action in Cambodia*, 65 Am. J. Int'l L. 79, 81 (1971).

212. Thomas M. Franck & Faiza Patel, *UN Police Action in Lieu of War: "The Old Order Changeth,"* 85 Am. J. Int'l L. 63, 70 (1991).

213. The requirement for congressional approval comes not from Section 6 alone but from the U.S. Constitution: Michael J. Glennon, *The Constitution and Chapter VII of the United Nations Charter*, 85 Am. J. Int'l L. 74, 80–81, 85–88 (1991).

214. Public Papers of the Presidents, 1950, at 504.

215. Id. On July 13, at another news conference, Truman again called military actions in Korea a "police action." Id. at 522.

216. Robert F. Turner, *Truman, Korea, and the Constitution: Debunking the "Imperial President" Myth*, 19 Harv. J. L. & Pub. Pol'y 533, 568 (1996) (emphasis in original).

without consulting the Congress."[217] These comments are interesting, but remarks by individual members of Congress—even party leaders—do not amend the Constitution or nullify the UN Participation Act.[218]

On July 3, the State Department released a memo offering legal arguments for independent presidential authority over unilateral wars, including: "The President, as Commander in Chief of the Armed Forces of the United States, has full control over the use thereof."[219] No President from 1789 to 1950 took the country to war singlehandedly. The memo pointed to "many instances" in the past where armed forces had been used by Presidents unilaterally to protect American lives and property.[220] None of those examples took the country to war. Did military activities in Korea actually constitute "war" or a "police action"? Federal and state courts had to interpret legal documents, such as life insurance policies, to determine whether the insured died while "in the military, naval or air forces of any country at war." Judges had no difficulty in reaching this conclusion: "We doubt very much if there is any question in the minds of the majority of the people in this country that the conflict now raging in Korea can be anything but war."[221]

# 6. TRUMAN'S SEIZURE OF STEEL MILLS

On April 8, 1952, President Truman issued Executive Order 10340, authorizing and directing the Secretary of Commerce to take possession "of all or such of the [steel] plants, facilities, and other property of the companies named in the list attached hereto, or any part thereof, as he may deem necessary in the interests of national defense."[222] The companies included on the list numbered 87. Truman acted to avert a nationwide strike of steel companies. His executive order referred to "American fighting men and fighting men of other nations of the United Nations…now engaged in deadly combat with the forces of aggression in Korea."[223] Weapons and other materials needed by the armed forces "are produced to a great extent in this country, and steel is an indispensable component of substantially all of such weapons and materials."[224] He identified his legal and constitutional authority: "NOW, THEREFORE, by virtue of the authority vested in me by the Constitution and laws of the United States, and as President of the United States and Commander in Chief of the armed forces of the United States."[225]

---

217. 7 Foreign Relations of the United States, 1950, Korea, 82d Cong., 1st Sess., H. Doc. No. 82-264, at 287 (1976).

218. Louis Fisher, *The Korean War: On What Legal Basis Did Truman Act?*, 89 Am. J. Int'l L. 21, 32–39 (1995).

219. *Authority of the President to Repel the Attack in Korea*, 23 Dep't of State Bull. 173, 173 (1950).

220. Id. at 174–78.

221. Weissman v. Metropolitan Life Ins. Co, 112 F. Supp. 420, 425 (S.D. Cal. 1953). See also Western Reserve Life Ins. Co. v. Meadows, 261 S.W.2d 554, 558–59 (Tex. 1953); Gagliormella v. Metropolitan Life Ins. Co., 122 F. Supp. 246, 249–50 (D. Mass. 1954); Carius v. New York Life Insurance Co., 124 F. Supp. 388, 391 (S.D. Ill. 1954); and A. Kenneth Pye, *The Legal Status of the Korean Hostilities*, 45 Geo. L.J. 45 (1956).

222. 17 Fed. Reg. 3139, 3142 (1952).

223. Id. at 3139.

224. Id.

225. Id. at 3142.

Justifications for the executive order depended heavily on the claim of "inherent" presidential power. To Representative John McCormack, the "action of the President, as we all know, was based on the inherent executive powers vested in the President under the Constitution, acting during an emergency, and for the public welfare and the common good of our people."[226]

Senator Wayne Morse said the Supreme Court "has yet to render its first decision denying that the President of the United States, whoever he may be, has the inherent power to protect the interests of the American people in time of emergency and crisis."[227] Twice more on that page and four times on the next page, Morse referred to inherent presidential powers. It was equally true when Morse spoke that the Court had yet to render a decision that the President *did have* inherent power. Implied power? Yes. Inherent power (incapable of being checked by other branches)? No. In the Steel Seizure Case, the Supreme Court squarely rejected the claim that inherent and emergency powers justified Truman's action.

In response to Truman's definition of presidential authority, newspapers across the country warned that "dictatorial powers" were "dangerous," "ugly," "fear-inspiring," and "a constitutional and political crisis."[228] The seizure of steel mills, said one newspaper, "will probably go down in history as one of the most high-handed acts committed by an American President."[229] On April 17, a reporter at a news conference asked: "Mr. President, if you can seize the steel mills under your inherent powers, can you, in your opinion, also seize the newspapers and/or the radio stations?"[230] Truman replied: "Under similar circumstances the President of the United States has to act for whatever is for the best of the country. That's the answer to your question."[231] Several days later Senator Richard Russell said he had "always mistrusted and feared the doctrine of what is called inherent power. I fear the invocation of inherent power even in the greatest emergency.... Any statute, even a poor one, even a bad one, is highly preferable in any case to the assertion of the naked power of an individual."[232]

## A. In district court

A number of steel companies took the dispute to federal district court. Holmes Baldridge of the Justice Department defended the steel seizure as "a legal taking under the inherent executive powers of the President."[233] For constitutional authority he relied on the "executive power" that Article II vests in the President, the President's oath, the Take Care Clause, the Commander in Chief Clause, and "that he shall be the sole organ of the nation in its external relations."[234] To District Judge Alexander Holtzoff, "executive power" meant "the power to execute statutes."[235]

---

226. 98 CONG. REC. 3916 (1952).

227. Id. at 3964.

228. Id. at 4033–34.

229. Id. at 4034.

230. PUBLIC PAPERS OF THE PRESIDENTS, 1952, at 272–73.

231. Id. at 273.

232. 98 CONG. REC. 4154 (1952).

233. *The Steel Seizure Case*, H. Doc. No. 534 (Part I), 82d Cong., 2d Sess. 253 (1952). This document contains proceedings in district court and the D.C. Circuit.

234. Id. at 255.

235. Id.

Baldridge defined it more broadly: "among other things it is the power to protect the country in times of national emergency by whatever means seems appropriate to achieve the end."[236] Judge Holtzoff dismissed the request for a temporary restraining order against the government, with the understanding that the companies could bring actions either for just compensation in the Court of Claims or a tort claims case in district court.[237]

The following day the companies brought the case to district court for a full hearing on the merits, with Judge David A. Pine presiding. Baldridge confronted the court with this challenge: "Our position is that there is no power in the Courts to restrain the President and, as I say, Secretary Sawyer is the alter ego of the President and not subject to injunctive order of the Court."[238] Judge Pine asked this question: "If the President directs Mr. Sawyer to take you into custody, right now, and have you executed in the morning you say there is no power by which the court may intervene even by habeas corpus?" Baldridge said statutory remedies might be available but he could not recall any "at the moment."[239] Pine suggested the Fifth Amendment should offer protection: "No person shall...be deprived of life, liberty, or property, without due process of law." Interestingly, Baldridge made no mention of a UN "police action" in Korea. He said U.N. armed forces, "largely American, are today fighting a war with Communist armies and Air forces in Korea."[240]

Baldridge agreed with Judge Pine that the government was not asserting any statutory power. Instead, the President's power was based on Sections 1, 2, and 3 of Article II "and whatever inherent, implied or residual powers may flow therefrom."[241] He argued that the President "has the power to take such action as is necessary to meet the emergency," subject to two limitations: "One is the ballot box and the other is impeachment."[242] Judge Pine inquired about the role of the judiciary. When the Executive determines the emergency, was it the case that "the Courts cannot even review whether it is an emergency"? Baldridge: "That is correct."[243] He continued to insist that the President "is accountable only to the country" and "the decisions of the President are conclusive."[244] Where an executive officer, such as Commerce Secretary Sawyer, acts at the direction of the President and is the "alter ego of the President, the courts will not interfere."[245] Yet Baldridge also told the court the steel companies had an "available remedy": filing suit for "just compensation under the Fifth Amendment."[246] Throughout his appearance in district court, he emphasized how earlier Presidents had successfully invoked "inherent" power,[247] and he concluded his presentation with two more references to presidential inherent power.[248]

236. Id.
237. Id. at 266.
238. Id. at 362.
239. Id.
240. Id. at 367.
241. Id. at 371.
242. Id.
243. Id. at 372.
244. Id. at 380.
245. Id.
246. Id.
247. Id. at 386.
248. Id. at 426–27.

On April 29, nineteen days after he first heard the case, Judge Pine ruled that Truman's action in seizing the plants was illegal. He found no express or implied constitutional authority for the seizure. No "residuum of power" or "inherent" power existed to justify this exercise of emergency power for the good of the public.[249] The Constitution lodges the power to provide "for the common defense and general welfare" not in the President but in Congress.[250] Although Baldridge had argued for a presidential inherent power in the nature of eminent domain, Pine said the power of eminent domain "is a Congressional power."[251] To Pine, the scope of presidential power described by Baldridge "spells a form of government alien to our Constitutional government of limited powers."[252]

Pine also rejected Baldridge's claim that judicial action against the seizure posed unacceptable costs because of the emergency, and that Congress had been unable to reach an acceptable and constructive remedy. Pine said he was "unwilling to indulge in that assumption, because I believe that our procedures under the Constitution can stand the stress and strains of an emergency today as they have in the past, and are adequate to meet the test of emergency and crisis."[253] He acknowledged that his ruling might precipitate the heavy costs that Baldridge warned of, such as "the contemplated strike, if it came, with all its awful results." Yet such a consequence "would be less injurious to the public than the injury which would flow from a timorous judicial recognition that there is some basis for this claim to unlimited and unrestrained Executive power, which would be implicit in a failure to grant the injunction. Such recognition would undermine public confidence in the very edifice of government as it is known under the Constitution."[254]

## B. The Supreme Court decides

The Supreme Court on May 3 granted certiorari and heard oral argument on May 12. Solicitor General Philip Perlman presented the case for the executive branch. Although he emphasized the grave nature of the national emergency, not once did he rely on the constitutional doctrine regularly promoted by Baldridge: "inherent presidential power."[255] Also, Perlman did not refer to a "police action" in Korea. He explained that an "uninterrupted production of steel" was required for "the war effort."[256] Justice Frankfurter agreed "we are at war" and "this is wartime."[257] At one point, Justice Jackson suggested that Congress had "categorically disclaimed this as war, but denominates it rather as a police action." He added: "It looks like war; people know it."[258]

---

249. Youngstown Sheet & Tube Co. v. Sawyer, 103 F. Supp. 569, 573 (D.D.C. 1952).

250. Id. at 573–74.

251. Id. at 575.

252. Id. at 576.

253. Id. at 577.

254. Id.

255. 48 LANDMARK BRIEFS 877–995. With other parties, the Justices debated the existence of inherent presidential powers; e.g., id. at 986–94.

256. Id. at 922–23.

257. Id. at 959.

258. Id.

Perlman responded: "You can say without contradiction to anyone that we are under war conditions, and whether it may be a police action, nevertheless we are engaged with every other nation in an effort to repeal aggression overseas."[259] Justice Frankfurter advised Perlman: "You cannot say that you are not in a war on one hand and on the other say that the President is exercising war powers when he is not."[260]

After the Court concluded oral argument, President Truman at a news conference on May 22 remarked on his power to seize steel mills: "nobody can take it away from the President, because he is the Chief Executive of the Nation, and he has to be in a position to see that the welfare of the people is met."[261] Reporters asked if "nobody" meant the judiciary.[262] Truman said he was "not going to comment on what the Court is going to do," but added: "Nobody can take it away from the President, because it is inherent in the Constitution of the United States."[263] Inconsistently, when another reporter asked whether he would abide with whatever decision the Supreme Court handed down, Truman answered: "That is exactly what I expect to do."[264]

On June 2, by a 6 to 3 vote, the Supreme Court invalidated Truman's executive order.[265] The decision is difficult to summarize because the majority consists of the opinion by Justice Black followed by concurrences from Frankfurter, Douglas, Jackson, Burton, and Clark. The dissent came from Chief Justice Vinson, joined by Reed and Minton. All six Justices in the majority rejected the claim of inherent presidential power.[266]

## C. Jackson's tripartite analysis

Federal courts and scholars have long debated whether language in Article II merely confers a title (Commander in Chief) or includes additional powers for the President variously described as inherent, emergency, and residual. In a concurring opinion in *Youngstown*, Justice Jackson remarked that the Commander in Chief Clause implies "something more than an empty title.

---

259. Id.

260. Id.

261. Public Papers of the Presidents, 1952–53, at 362.

262. Id.

263. Id. at 363.

264. Id. At the end of the news conference, the White House incoherently added a note: "Neither the Congress nor the courts could deny the inherent powers of the Presidency without tearing up the Constitution. The President said that the Supreme Court, in the pending steel case, might properly decide that the conditions existing did not justify the use by the President of his inherent powers, but that such a decision would not deny the existence of inherent powers."

265. Youngstown Co. v. Sawyer, 343 U.S. 579 (1952).

266. For analyses of this case, a series of articles are devoted to the Steel Seizure Case: at Youngstown *at Fifty: A Symposium*, 19 Const. Comm. 1 (Spring 2002). See also Maeva Marcus, Truman and the Steel Seizure Case (1994 ed.); Alan F. Westin, The Anatomy of a Constitutional Law Case: Youngstown Sheet and Tube Co. v. Sawyer (1958), Glendon A. Schubert, Jr., *The Steel Case: Presidential Responsibility and Judicial Irresponsibility*, 6 West. Pol. Q. 61 (1953); Edward S. Corwin, *The Steel Seizure Case: A Judicial Brick Without Straw*, 53 Colum. L. Rev. 53 (1953); Robert F. Banks, *Steel, Sawyer, and the Executive Power*, 14 U. Pitt. L. Rev. 467 (1953); Lucius Wilmerding, Jr., *The President and the Law*, 67 Pol. Sci. Q. 321 (1952); Donald R. Richberg, *The Steel Seizure Cases*, 38 Va. L. Rev. 713 (1952); and Paul G. Kauper, *The Steel Seizure Case: Congress, the President and the Supreme Court*, 51 Mich. L. Rev. 141 (1952).

But just what authority goes with the name has plagued presidential advisers who would not waive or narrow it by nonassertion yet cannot say where it begins or ends."[267]

Justice Jackson lamented the meager guidance left by the Framers: "Just what our forefathers did envision, or would have envisioned had they foreseen modern conditions, must be divined from materials almost as enigmatic as the dreams Joseph was called upon to interpret for Pharaoh."[268] Here he let his gifts as a writer momentarily outrun his excellent skills as an analyst, amply displayed elsewhere in his opinion. In fact, he did not throw his hands in the air and say: "The constitutional text and intent are too vague for us to possibly interpret." Instead, he identified basic principles: "While the Constitution diffuses power the better to secure liberty, it also contemplates that practice will integrate the dispersed powers into a workable government. It enjoins upon its branches separateness but interdependence, autonomy but reciprocity."[269] He objected to the Solicitor General's dependence on "nebulous powers never expressly granted" and to "[l]oose and irresponsible use of adjectives" used to augment presidential power, including "inherent," "implied," "incidental," "plenary," "war," and "emergency," all of which he said were invoked "often interchangeably and without fixed or ascertainable meanings."[270]

The Justice Department urged the Court to "declare the existence of inherent powers *ex necessitate* to meet an emergency," asking the Justices "to do what many think would be wise, although it is something the forefathers omitted."[271] Here Justice Jackson found the Framers' intent sufficiently clear. The Framers "knew what emergencies were, knew the pressures they engender for authoritative action, knew, too, how they afford a ready pretext for usurpation. We may also suspect that they suspected that emergency powers would tend to kindle emergencies."[272] He concluded that "emergency powers are consistent with free government only when their control is lodged elsewhere than in the Executive who exercises them."[273] Toward the end of his opinion, Jackson rested on these fundamental principles: "With all its defects, delays and inconveniences, men have discovered no technique for long preserving free government except that the Executive be under the law, and that the law be made by parliamentary deliberations."[274]

Jackson's concurrence in the Steel Seizure Case is generally praised and cited for his tripartite analysis of presidential power. Yet he warned the reader that he was beginning with "a somewhat over-simplified grouping of practical situations in which a President may doubt, or others may challenge, his powers, and by distinguishing roughly the legal consequences of this factor of relativity."[275] He was offering a starting-point, not a formula to settle every particular dispute. He knew as well as anyone that general frameworks and models may be manipulated to justify illegal ends.

In Jackson's first category, where the President acts pursuant to an express or implied authorization of Congress, "his authority is at its maximum, for it includes all that he possesses in his

267. Youngstown Co. v. Sawyer, 343 U.S. 579, 641 (1952) (Jackson, J., concurring).

268. Id. at 634.

269. Id. at 635.

270. Id. at 646–47.

271. Id. at 649–50 (emphasis in original).

272. Id. at 650.

273. Id. at 652.

274. Id. at 655.

275. Id. at 635.

own right plus all that Congress can delegate."[276] In the second category, the President acts without a congressional grant or denial of authority and relies only on his independent powers. In this "zone of twilight" the President and Congress may have "concurrent authority, or in which its distribution is uncertain." In such cases, "congressional inertia, indifference or quiescence may sometimes, at least as a practical matter, enable, if not invite, measures on independent presidential responsibility. In this area, any actual test of power is likely to depend on the imperatives of events and contemporary imponderables rather than on abstract theories of law."[277] Among abstract theories, surely Jackson would have included his three categories.

The third category covered instances in which the President "takes measures incompatible with the expressed or implied will of Congress." Here executive power "is at its lowest ebb, for then he can rely only upon his own constitutional powers minus any constitutional powers of Congress over the matter."[278] Note that presidential power survives in this category, even at a low ebb. Note also that the judiciary is asked to perform some type of mathematical exercise, determining the constitutional power of the President and subtracting from it certain congressional powers. Not much guidance. Jackson adds: "Courts can sustain exclusive presidential control in such a case only by disabling the Congress from acting upon the subject. Presidential claim to a power at once so conclusive and preclusive must be scrutinized with caution, for what is at stake is the equilibrium established by our constitutional system."[279]

In 1981, Justice Rehnquist found Jackson's three categories "analytically useful," but underscored that Jackson himself recognized that the categories represented "a somewhat over-simplified grouping." Rehnquist added: "it is doubtless the case that executive action in any particular instance falls, not neatly in one of three pigeonholes, but rather at some point along a spectrum running from explicit congressional authorization to explicit congressional prohibition."[280] This observation is helpful because it discourages efforts to locate a presidential action in one of three categories.

The capacity for producing wholly conflicting legal analyses by relying on Jackson's three categories is illustrated by two studies on warrantless surveillance after 9/11. The program by the Bush administration did not become public until it was leaked to *The New York Times* and published on December 16, 2005.[281] On January 5, 2006, two attorneys in the Congressional Research Service reviewed the Foreign Intelligence Surveillance Act (FISA) and its express language that it provided the "exclusive means" for domestic surveillance.[282] They concluded that the warrantless surveillance by the administration was incompatible with FISA and therefore placed presidential power "at its lowest ebb" in Jackson's third category.[283] On January 19, 2006, the Justice Department released its analysis, concluding that President Bush operated under the Authorization for Use of Military Force (AUMF) enacted after 9/11 and was therefore within

---

276. Id. at 635.

277. Id. 637.

278. Id.

279. Id. at 637–38.

280. Dames & Moore v. Regan, 453 U.S. 654, 669 (1981).

281. James Risen & Eric Lichtblau, *Bush Lets U.S. Spy on Callers Without Courts*, N.Y. Times, Dec. 16, 2005, at A1.

282. Elizabeth B. Bazan & Jennifer K. Elsea, Congressional Research Service, *Presidential Authority to Conduct Warrantless Electronic Surveillance to Gather Foreign Intelligence Information*, Jan. 5, 2006, at 27.

283. Id. at 44.

Jackson's first category, placing presidential power "at the zenith" because the President acted "pursuant to an express or implied authorization of Congress" plus the powers "he possesses in his own right."[284] These two studies illustrate that Jackson's tripartite model can produce mutually conflicting results.

# 7. THE VIETNAM WAR

In August 1964, after President Lyndon Johnson reported two attacks on U.S. vessels in the Gulf of Tonkin, Congress hurriedly passed legislation to authorize the use of armed force in Southeast Asia. There were doubts at the time about the second attack, but Congress did not take the time to verify Johnson's claims. As explained later in this section, the National Security Agency in 2005 publicly acknowledged that the second attack never occurred. The poor performance of Congress in 1964, the escalation of the war, heavy casualties, and massive expenses prompted Congress in 1973 to pass the War Powers Resolution and cut off funding for military actions in Southeast Asia.

## A. Tonkin Gulf claims

On August 3, 1964, President Johnson announced he had ordered the Navy to take retaliatory actions against the North Vietnamese for their operations in the Gulf of Tonkin.[285] He spoke following an attack on the U.S. destroyer *Maddox* by Communist PT boats. On the following day he reported a second attack, this one against two American destroyers.[286] A special message to Congress on August 5 requested a joint resolution to affirm the U.S. determination to respond to North Vietnam's attacks. He explained: "As I have repeatedly made clear, the United States intends no rashness, and seeks no wider war."[287]

Congress spent little time debating the resolution. Senate discussion began August 6 and concluded the next day, with the resolution passing 88 to 2.[288] Senator Daniel Brewster said he would "look with dismay" at landing large land armies in Southeast Asia and asked if anything in the resolution would permit that. Senator J. William Fulbright, the floor manager, agreed "that that is the last thing we would want to do," but the language of the resolution did not prevent it.[289] Senator Wayne Morse predicted that "if we follow a course of action that bogs down

---

284. U.S. Justice Department, *Legal Authorities Supporting the Activities of the National Security Agency Described by the President*, Jan. 19, 2006, at 2, http://www.justice.gov/olc/2006/nsa-white-paper.pdf. For recent evaluations of Jackson's tripartite framework: Joseph M. Bessette, *Confronting War: Rethinking Justice Jackson's Concurrence in* Youngstown v. Sawyer, THE LIMITS OF CONSTITUTIONAL DEMOCRACY 194 (Jeffrey K. Tulis & Stephen Macedo eds., 2010); Mark D. Rosen, *Revisiting Youngstown: Against the View That Jackson's Concurrence Resolves the Relation Between Congress and the Commander-in-Chief*, 54 UCLA L. REV. 1703 (2007); and Adam J. White, *Justice Jackson's Draft Opinions in The Steel Seizure Case*, 69 ALB. L. REV. 1107 (2006).

285. PUBLIC PAPERS OF THE PRESIDENTS, 1963–64, II, at 926–27.

286. Id. at 927.

287. Id. at 931.

288. 110 CONG. REC. 18442 (1964).

289. Id. at 18403.

thousands of American boys in Asia, the administration responsible for it will be rejected and repudiated by the American people. It should be."[290] An uncanny gift for prophecy.

Having listened to the debate, Senator Gaylord Nelson objected that "there is no agreement in the Senate on what the joint resolution means."[291] He offered an amendment that President Johnson would seek "no extension of the present military conflict" and that "we should continue to attempt to avoid a direct military involvement in the southeast Asian conflict."[292] Fulbright refused to accept the amendment, explaining that any amendment would delay enactment because it would have to be settled in conference with the House. But he remarked that Nelson's amendment stated "fairly accurately what the President has said would be our policy, and what I stated my understanding was as to our policy."[293] Fulbright stated his belief that the resolution "is calculated to prevent the spread of war, rather than to spread it."[294] The House passed the measure on August 7 without a single dissenting vote, 416 to zero.[295] Fulbright would later regret his failure to protect legislative prerogatives instead of acting on behalf of presidential interests.

The Tonkin Gulf Resolution approved and supported the determination of the President as Commander in Chief to take "all necessary measures to repel any armed attack against the forces of the United States and to prevent further aggression."[296] It declared that the United States was prepared, "as the President determines, to take all necessary steps, including the use of armed force," to assist any member or protocol state (South Vietnam, Cambodia, and Laos) of SEATO requesting assistance in defense of its freedom. The resolution could expire by two procedures: by presidential decision or if terminated earlier by concurrent resolution.[297]

Beginning early in 1965, the war in Southeast Asia began to escalate, eventually involving 500,000 U.S. troops and the deaths of 58,000 American soldiers, with no expectation that the war could be contained or successfully concluded. The cost of the war, in lives lost and financial burdens, resulted in Johnson deciding not to seek reelection in 1968. The war continued under President Richard Nixon, spreading from Vietnam to Cambodia and Laos.

## B. Was there a second attack?

The first attack on August 2, 1964, was too minor to justify asking Congress for a resolution. There were strong doubts that the second attack, reported on August 4, ever occurred. Conflicting accounts had been given. The ship's radar showed blips that might have indicated gunfire from North Vietnamese boats, but the evidence was inconclusive. The commander of the *Maddox* sent this cable on August 4: "Review of action makes many recorded contacts and torpedoes fired appear doubtful. Freak weather effects and over-eager sonarman may have accounted for many reports. No actual visual sightings by *Maddox*. Suggest complete evaluation before any

290. Id. at 18427.
291. Id. at 18458.
292. Id. at 18459.
293. Id.
294. Id. at 18462.
295. Id. at 18555.
296. 78 Stat. 384 (1964).
297. Id., 50 U.S.C. §§ 1541–48.

further action."[298] Some studies suggested that most, if not all, of the sonar reports identifying torpedoes were probably reflections from the *Maddox* as it made its evasive weaving turns.[299]

Edwin E. Moïse concluded in 1996, after studying documents and taking interviews, that the second attack never took place. He attributed the mistaken report to error rather than an intentional lie by the Johnson administration.[300] In 1964, Defense Secretary Robert McNamara was convinced the second attack occurred. After a trip to Vietnam in 1995, he announced that he was "absolutely positive" the second attack never took place. He was prepared to say, "without a doubt, there was no second attack."[301] In 2005, the National Security Agency released a study that affirmed what had long been suspected: there was no second attack. The agency explained that what had been reported as a second attack consisted of late signals coming from the first.[302]

## C. Rethinking national commitments

The escalation of the war in Vietnam caused Senator Fulbright to abandon his position of innate trust in presidential power. In 1961 he wrote that "for the existing requirements of American foreign policy we have hobbled the President by too niggardly a grant of power."[303] The break began in 1965 when President Johnson sent troops into the Dominican Republic. Fulbright repudiated the military action, accusing the Johnson administration of relying on an exaggerated fear of communism.[304] By 1967, Fulbright could "now see how great the Executive's foreign policies powers are and how limited the Congress' restraining powers are and I see great merit in the checks and balances of our 18th century Constitution."[305] Fulbright entered the House of Representatives in 1943. It is remarkable that not until 1965 did he reach an understanding that Congress needed to exercise checks and balances to protect its institution and prevent a concentration of power in the presidency.

Under Fulbright's direction, the Senate Foreign Relations Committee drafted a national commitments resolution. The committee report attributed "a fair share" of the expansion of presidential power to congressional acquiescence and passivity.[306] That conduct "is probably the most important single fact accounting for the speed and virtual completeness of the transfer" of

298. *The Gulf of Tonkin, The 1964 Incidents*, hearing before the Senate Foreign Relations Committee, 90th Cong., 2d Sess. 54 (1968).

299. Joseph C. Goulden, Truth is the First Casualty: The Gulf of Tonkin Affair—Illusion and Reality (1969); William Conrad Gibbons, The U.S. Government and the Vietnam War: Executive and Legislative Roles and Relationships, Part I: 1961–1964, at 291–92 (1986).

300. Edwin E. Moïse, Tonkin Gulf and the Escalation of the Vietnam War (1996).

301. Keith B. Richburg, *Mission to Hanoi*, Wash. Post, Nov. 11, 1995, at A21, A25.

302. Robert J. Hanyok, *Skunks, Bogies, Silent Hounds, and the Flying Fish: The Gulf of Tonkin Mystery*, Aug. 2–4, 1964, Cryptologic Quarterly, declassified by the National Security Agency on Nov. 3, 2005, http://www.nsa. gov/public_info/_files/gulf_of_tonkin/articles/rel1_skunks_bogies.pdf.

303. J. William Fulbright, *American Foreign Policy in the 20th Century under an 18th-Century Constitution*, 47 Corn. L.Q. 1, 2 (1961).

304. 111 Cong. Rec. 23858–59 (1965).

305. *U.S. Commitments to Foreign Powers*, hearings before the Senate Foreign Relations Committee, 90th Cong., 1st Sess. 3 (1967).

306. S. Rep. No. 129, 91st Cong., 1st Sess. 8 (1969).

the war power to the President.[307] Turning to the Tonkin Gulf Resolution, the report admitted that the language was broad enough to support a full-scale war in Vietnam and regarded the scope of that delegation as careless and irresponsible. By adopting a resolution with such sweeping terms, Congress "committed the error of making a *personal* judgment as to how President Johnson would implement the resolution when it had a responsibility to make an *institutional* judgment, first, as to what *any* President would do with so great an acknowledgment of power, and, second, as to whether under the Constitution, Congress had a right to grant or concede the authority in question."[308]

The National Commitments Resolution passed the Senate by a vote of 70 to 16.[309] It defined a national commitment as the use of U.S. armed forces on foreign territory or a promise to assist a foreign country by using U.S. armed forces or financial resources "either immediately or upon the happening of certain events." The resolution further provided that "it is the sense of the Senate that a national commitment by the United States results only from affirmative action taken by the executive and legislative branches of the United States government by means of a treaty, statute, or concurrent resolution of both Houses of Congress specifically providing for such commitment."[310] In 1971, Congress repealed the Tonkin Gulf Resolution.[311]

## D. Involvement of the courts

After intervening in Cambodia in 1970, President Nixon told the nation that the "only remaining American activity in Cambodia after July 1 [1970] will be air missions to interdict the movement of enemy troops and material where I find that is necessary to protect the lives and security of our men in South Vietnam."[312] Congress enacted other restrictions. Section 601 of the military authorization bill in 1971 declared it the policy of the United States to terminate "at the earliest practicable date" all military operations in Southeast Asia and to provide for the "prompt and orderly withdrawal of all United States military forces at a date certain," subject to the release of all American prisoners of war. The statutory language required the President to establish a final date for the withdrawal of all U.S. military forces.[313]

In signing the bill, Nixon announced that Section 601 "does not represent the policies of this Administration" and was "without binding force or effect."[314] A federal district judge chided Nixon for his language, noting that when the bill embodying Section 601 was signed into law "it established 'the policy of the United States' to the exclusion of any different executive or administrative policy, and had binding force and effect on every officer of the Government. No

---

307. Id. at 15.

308. Id. at 23 (emphases in original).

309. 115 Cong. Rec. 17245 (1969).

310. Id.

311. 84 Stat. 2055, sec. 12 (1971).

312. Public Papers of the Presidents, 1970, at 478.

313. 85 Stat. 430, sec. 601 (1971).

314. Public Papers of the Presidents, 1971, at 1114.

executive statement denying efficacy to the legislation could have either validity or effect." The judge described Nixon's signing statement as "very unfortunate."[315]

Federal courts differed on whether appropriations by Congress authorized military actions. Officials in the Johnson administration argued that Congress had authorized the Vietnam War by funding it. Initially, federal judges accepted appropriations as sufficient authority and rejected claims to the contrary. Said one judge: "That some members of Congress talked like doves before voting with the hawks is an inadequate basis for a charge that the President was violating the Constitution in doing what Congress by its words had told him he might do."[316]

Experts advised the courts that appropriations bills do not encompass major declarations of policy. They explained that House and Senate rules are designed to prevent substantive legislation from being included in appropriations bills.[317] Some court decisions continued to accept the theory that Congress may indirectly assent to war by funding it.[318] When private parties argued that the repeal of the Tonkin Gulf Resolution removed congressional authorization for the war in Vietnam, courts disagreed, pointing to the continued appropriation of funds.[319]

After learning more about the procedural distinction in Congress between the authorization and appropriation processes, some judges no longer believed that funding was the legal equivalent of endorsing a policy. Federal appellate judge Charles E. Wyzanski remarked in a 1973 decision that courts "cannot be unmindful of what every schoolboy knows: that in voting to appropriate money or to draft men a Congressman is not necessarily approving of the continuation of a war no matter how specifically the appropriation or draft act refers to that war." A lawmaker wholly opposed to a war's commencement and continuation might support funds and the draft "because he was unwilling to abandon without support men already fighting." To Wyzanski, an "honorable, decent, compassionate act of aiding those already in peril is no proof of consent to the actions that placed and continued them in that dangerous posture." Courts should "not construe votes cast in pity and piety as though they were votes freely give to express consent."[320]

Similarly, federal appellate judge Arlan Adams concluded that it would be impossible to decide whether lawmakers, by voting on appropriations, meant to authorize the military activities in Vietnam: "to explore these issues would require the interrogation of members of Congress regarding what they intended by their votes, and then synthesization of the various answers. To do otherwise would call for a gross speculation in a delicate matter pertaining to foreign relations."[321] As explained in the next section, the War Powers Resolution of 1973 clarified that appropriations alone do not constitute an authorization for war.

---

315. DaCosta v. Nixon, 55 F.R.D. 145, 146 (E.D. N.Y. 1972). See also DaCosta v. Laird, 471 F.2d 1146, 1156–57 (2d Cir. 1973).

316. Berk v. Laird, 317 F. Supp. 715, 724 (E.D. N.Y. 1970), aff'd sub nom. Orlando v. Laird, 443 F.2d 1039 (2d Cir. 1971), cert. denied, 404 U.S. 869 (1971).

317. Berk v. Laird, 317 F. Supp. at 718, 721 (testimony of Professors Richard F. Fenno, Jr. & Don Wallace, Jr.).

318. Orlando v. Laird, 317 F. Supp. 1013, 1018–19 (E.D.N.Y. 1970); Orlando v. Laird, 443 F.2d 1039, 1042 (2d Cir. 1971), cert. denied, 404 U.S. 869 (1971), and Berk v. Laird, 429 F.2d 302, 305 (2d Cir. 1970).

319. DaCosta v. Laird, 448 F.2d 1368, 1369 (2d Cir. 1971), cert. denied, 405 U.S. 979 (1972), and DaCosta v. Laird, 471 F.2d 1146, 1154 (2d Cir. 1973).

320. Mitchell v. Laird, 476 F.2d 533, 538 (D.C. Cir. 1973). This decision was later withdrawn by court order.

321. Atlee v. Laird, 347 F. Supp. 689, 706 (E.D. Pa. 1972) (three-judge court), aff'd, Atlee v. Richardson, 411 U.S. 911 (1973).

In 1973, Congress passed language to forbid the use of any funds to support U.S. combat activities in Cambodia or Laos—a restriction that covered funds contained in a supplemental appropriations bill as well as all funds made available by previous appropriations. President Nixon vetoed the bill on June 27, claiming that the Cambodia rider would "cripple or destroy the chances for an effective negotiated settlement in Cambodia and the withdrawal of all North Vietnamese troops." He also warned that the bill contained a number of appropriations that were essential for the continuation of government operations.[322]

An effort by the House to override the veto failed by a vote of 241 to 173, short of the necessary two-thirds majority.[323] Congress drafted a revised supplemental bill to delay the effect of the funding cutoff until August 15, allowing the administration to bomb Cambodia for another 45 days. Nixon signed that bill. The compromise affected litigation that had been progressing in the federal courts. Representative Robert Drinan and three other members of the House asked that the 1973 bombing of Cambodia be declared a violation of domestic and international law. District judge Joseph Tauro ruled that only in situations when a conflict between the executive and legislative branches appeared to be incapable of resolution should the courts intervene. The August 15 compromise, he said, "demonstrates clearly and objectively that the branches were not in resolute conflict." Had Congress been unwilling to compromise, "we would have a clear issue of conflict before us that would have required judicial determination."[324]

The August 15 compromise also affected a suit by Representative Elizabeth Holtzman, who had asked the courts to rule that Nixon could not engage in combat operations in Cambodia and elsewhere in Southeast Asia unless he received explicit congressional authorization. A federal district court held that Congress had not authorized the bombing in Cambodia. The inability of Congress to override Nixon's veto could not be interpreted as an affirmative grant of authority: "It cannot be the rule that the President needs a vote of only one-third plus one of either House in order to conduct a war, but this would be the consequence of holding that Congress must override a Presidential veto in order to terminate hostilities which it has not authorized."[325] The court enjoined Nixon from engaging in combat operations in Cambodia but postponed the injunction for 48 hours to permit the administration to apply for a stay.

The Second Circuit ordered a stay of the injunction until August 13. Holtzman took her case to the Supreme Court. Justice Marshall, assigned to the Second Circuit, denied her motion to vacate the stay. He noted that once the August 15 deadline was reached, "the contours of this dispute will then be irrevocably altered. Hence, it is difficult to justify a stay for the purpose of preserving the status quo, since no action by this Court can freeze the issues in their present form."[326] The district court order was reversed by the Second Circuit on August 8, treating the dispute as essentially a political question to be settled by the elected branches. However, the Second Circuit did note that the August 15 compromise constituted congressional approval of the bombing in Cambodia.[327]

322. PUBLIC PAPERS OF THE PRESIDENTS, 1973, at 621–22.

323. 119 CONG. REC. 21778 (1973).

324. Drinan v. Nixon, 364 F. Supp. 854, 860, 861 (D. Mass. 1973).

325. Holtzman v. Schlesinger, 361 F. Supp. 553, 565 (E.D.N.Y. 1973).

326. Holtzman v. Schlesinger, 414 U.S. 1304, 1310 (1973). On August 4, Justice Douglas vacated the stay, 414 U.S. 1316, but later that same day Justice Marshall reinstated the stay and announced that other members of the Court were unanimous in overruling the Douglas order. 414 U.S. 1321.

327. Holtzman v. Schlesinger, 484 F.2d 1307, 1313–14 (2d Cir. 1973).

# 8. WAR POWERS RESOLUTION

The Vietnam War underscored what should have been obvious to Congress by the Korean War: its constitutional powers over military commitments had been sharply undermined by unilateral presidential actions and legislative acquiescence. Efforts to restore congressional powers produced sharply divergent positions in the House and the Senate. The House passed legislation in 1970 that conceded a large measure of the war power to the President. Its bill, passed by a vote of 289 to 39, recognized that the President "in certain extraordinary and emergency circumstances has the authority to defend the United States and its citizens without specific prior authorization by the Congress."[328] Instead of trying to identify the precise circumstances under which a President may act, the House preferred procedural safeguards. The President would be required, "whenever feasible," to consult with Congress before sending American troops into combat and would be required to report the circumstances necessitating the action; the constitutional, legislative, and treaty provisions that authorized the action, together with his reasons for not seeking specific prior congressional authorization; and the estimated scope of activities.[329] The House passed the same legislation a year later, with one change: elimination of the words "whenever feasible."[330]

In 1973, the House supported a similar procedure of requiring the President to consult with Congress, report within 72 hours, and explain why it was necessary to use military force against another nation. Unless Congress declared war within 120 days or specifically authorized the use of force, the President would be required to terminate hostilities and withdraw the troops. Congress could also, during the 120-day period, pass a concurrent resolution to direct disengagement of military force.[331]

The Senate rejected this degree of deference to presidential military commitments. In the absence of congressional declaration, it believed that unilateral presidential action could be justified only in three situations: (1) to repel an armed attack upon the United States and its territories and possessions, retaliate in the event of such an attack, and forestall the direct and imminent threat of such an attack; (2) repel an armed attack against U.S. armed forces located outside the United States and its territories and possessions, and forestall the direct and imminent threat of such an attack; and (3) rescue endangered American citizens and nationals in foreign countries or at sea.[332] The first situation (except for the final clause) conforms to the understanding reached at the Philadelphia convention. The other situations reflect defensive actions and steps taken to protect American lives and property.

The Senate bill required the President to cease military action unless Congress, within 30 days, specifically authorized him to continue. A separate provision allowed the President to sustain military operations beyond the 30-day period if he determined that "unavoidable military necessity respecting the safety" of the armed forces required their continued use for

---

328. 116 Cong. Rec. 37398 (1970).

329. Id. The roll-call vote appears at 37407–08.

330. 117 Cong. Rec. 28870–78 (1971). The bill passed under suspension of the rules without a roll-call vote. For explanation of the deletion of "whenever feasible," see H. Rep. No. 92-383 (1971), at 1–2.

331. 119 Cong. Rec. 24653–708 (1973).

332. Id. at 25119, sec. 3.

purposes of "bringing about a prompt disengagement."[333] After meeting in conference, the two houses produced what became the War Powers Resolution. President Nixon vetoed the bill because he believed it encroached upon the presidential responsibilities as Commander in Chief. He also thought it was impractical and dangerous to try to fix in a statute specific procedures to govern the war power.[334] Both houses overrode the veto, the House narrowly (284 to 135), the Senate more easily (75 to 18).[335]

Some Democrats in the House recognized that the conference report tilted the war power too much toward the President.[336] Senator Tom Eagleton, a major sponsor of the bill in the Senate, denounced the version that emerged from conference as a "total, complete distortion of the war powers concept."[337] Instead of the three exceptions in the Senate bill, the conference bill gave the President full authority to use military force for up to 90 days. To Eagleton, the bill marked a sellout, a surrender. With memories so fresh about presidential expansion of the war in Southeast Asia, he asked "how can we give unbridled, unlimited total authority to the President to commit us to war?"[338]

## A. Statutory provisions

Section 2(a) of the War Powers Resolution (WPR) states that its purpose is "to fulfill the intent of the framers of the Constitution of the United States and insure the collective judgment" of both branches when U.S. forces are introduced into hostilities.[339] It does neither. The Framers would not have permitted the President to use force anywhere in the world, for whatever reason, and to do so for up to 90 days. Nor is there is any "collective judgment" to this unilateral decision by the President. Under Section 3, the President is to consult with Congress "in every possible instance," leaving full discretion to the President. The legislative history makes it clear that consultation should go beyond simply being informed that the President has made a decision. Consultation means that "a decision is pending on a problem and that Members of Congress are being asked by the President for their advice and opinions and, in appropriate circumstances, their approval of action contemplated."[340] That legislative intent is not binding on the President, who may consult with no lawmakers or with a handful who support his initiative. Section 4 directs the President, after introducing forces into hostilities, to report to Congress within 48 hours.

---

333. Id. at 25120, sec. 6.

334. PUBLIC PAPERS OF THE PRESIDENTS, 1973, at 893.

335. House vote: 119 CONG. REC. 36221–22 (1973); Senate vote: id. at 36198.

336. E.g., Id. at 36204 (Rep. Green), 36207 (Rep. Thomson), 36208 (Rep. Eckhardt), 36212 (Rep. Brown), 36220 (Rep. Dellums), 36220–21 (Rep. Culver) (1973).

337. Id. at 36177.

338. Id. See THOMAS F. EAGLETON, WAR AND PRESIDENTIAL POWER: A CHRONICLE OF CONGRESSIONAL SURRENDER (1974), and Louis Fisher. *Thomas F. Eagleton: A Model of Integrity*, 52 ST. LOUIS U. L.J. 97 (2007), http://loufisher.org/docs/wpr/429.pdf.

339. 87 Stat. 555 (1973).

340. H. Rep. No. 287, 93d Cong., 1st Sess. 6–7 (1973).

The WPR contemplated two means of legislative control: the 60-to-90-day limit on presidential initiatives to use force, and reliance on a concurrent resolution to require him to remove troops engaged in hostilities. Neither mechanism ensures congressional control. The clock does not start ticking unless the President reports under a very specific section: Section 4(a)(1). Presidents do not submit reports with that specificity. They report generally under Section 4 or "consistent with the War Powers Resolution."[341] Therefore the clock never starts. Concurrent resolutions are not legally binding, especially after the Supreme Court in *INS v. Chadha* (1983) struck down the legislative veto.

Even if the clock does not formally tick on the 60-to-90-day deadline, executive officials often behave as though it does, attempting to complete military action before 60 and certainly before 90 days have passed. The examples of Kosovo and Libya, to be discussed, are instances of presidential military commitments exceeding 60 days. For military operations that are expected to last for lengthy periods, Presidents come to Congress for statutory authorization, as with Afghanistan in 2001 and Iraq in 2002.

The principal problem with the WPR is its statutory incoherence. Section 2 promises collective judgment and keeping faith with the Framers. But Section 4 allows Presidents to use military force unilaterally for up to 90 days. Section 2(c) limits the President to the use of armed force under three conditions: "(1) a declaration of war, (2) specific statutory authorization, or (3) a national emergency created by attack upon the United States, its territories or possessions, or its armed forces." Those conditions are consistent with the Constitution and Framers' intent. Section 4, however, contemplates much broader military action, introducing U.S. troops "(1) into hostilities or into situations where imminent involvement in hostilities is clearly indicated by the circumstances; (2) into the territory, airspace or waters of a foreign nation, while equipped for combat, except for deployments which related solely to supply, replacement, repair, or training of such forces; or (3) in numbers which substantially enlarge United States Armed Forces equipped for combat already located in a foreign nation." Those situations are unrelated to attacks against U.S. territory and troops. They go beyond defensive actions to endorse offensive operations.[342]

Section 8 contains some valuable provisions. President Truman claimed he could seek authority from the UN Security Council. President Johnson referred to SEATO in justifying military action in Vietnam. Administrations regularly insist that statutes providing funds constituted legislative authorization. Section 8 eliminated this reliance on treaties and appropriations,

---

341. E.g., when President Reagan reported to Congress on his air strikes against Libya in 1986, he reported "consistent with the War Powers Resolution." Public Papers of the Presidents, 1986, I, at 478.

342. For evaluation of the War Powers Resolution: Robert F. Turner, The War Powers Resolution: Its Implementation in Theory and Practice (1983); Robert F. Turner, *The War Powers Resolution: Unconstitutional, Unnecessary, and Unhelpful*, 17 Loy. L.A. L. Rev. 683 (1984); Michael J. Glennon, *The War Powers Resolution: Sad Record, Dismal Promise*, 17 Loy. L.A. L. Rev. 657 (1984); Michael Ratner & David Cole, *The Force of Law: Judicial Enforcement of the War Powers Resolution*, 17 Loy. L.A. L. Rev. 715 (1984); Michael J. Glennon, *The War Powers Resolution Ten Years Later: More Politics than Law*, 78 Am. J. Int'l L. 571 (1984); Patrick D. Robbins, *The War Powers Resolution After Fifteen Years: A Reassessment*, 38 Am. U. L. Rev. 141 (1988); John Hart Ely, *Suppose Congress Wanted a War Powers Act That Worked*, 88 Colum. L. Rev. 1336 (1988), Robert F. Turner, Repealing the War Powers Resolution: Restoring the Rule of Law in U.S. Foreign Policy (1991); Edward Keynes, *The War Powers Resolution: A Bad Idea Whose Time Has Come and Gone*, 23 U. Toledo L. Rev. 343 (1992); James

requiring Presidents to obtain specific authorization from Congress. Section 8(a) provides that authority to introduce U.S. troops into hostilities or imminent hostilities

> shall not be inferred (1) from any provision of law (whether or not in effect before the date of the enactment of this joint resolution), including any provision contained in any appropriation Act, unless such provision specifically authorizes the introduction of United States Armed Forces into hostilities or into such situations and states that it is intended to constitute specific statutory authorization within the meaning of this joint resolution; or (2) from any treaty heretofore or hereafter ratified unless such treaty is implemented by legislation specifically authorizing the introduction of United States Armed Forces into hostilities or into such situations and stating that it is intended to constitute specific statutory authorization within the meaning of this joint resolution.[343]

It has been argued that Section 8 proceeds to contradict itself on the treaty power and is therefore a nullity. Section 8(d) states that nothing in the joint resolution "is intended to alter the...provisions of existing treaties." According to one analysis: "This internal contradiction in its terms makes the treaty-breaking provisions of the Resolution meaningless."[344] Section 8(d) can be read not as a contradiction but as a truism: A statute by itself does not alter the terms of a treaty. The parties to a treaty must consent to changes. The legislative history of Section 8 provides further evidence that the language in Section 8(a) does what it was intended to do: treaties (such as the UN Charter, NATO, and SEATO) do not provide "authorization" for presidential wars.[345]

## B. Reform proposals

After the Supreme Court's decision in *Chadha*, efforts were made in 1983 to change the concurrent resolution in the War Powers Resolution to a joint resolution, to comply with both bicameralism and presentment. Instead of amending the WPR, the joint resolution was placed in a freestanding statute as an alternative procedure.[346] In 1995, House Republicans proposed an amendment to repeal all of the WPR except the sections on consultation and reporting. Representative David Skaggs objected that the amendment carried an "unfortunate implication" that presidential war power "is restrained only by a consultative and reporting requirement."[347] Toward the end of the debate, Speaker Newt Gingrich appealed to the House "to, at least on paper, increase the power of President Clinton" because the President "on a bipartisan

Nathan, *Salvaging the War Powers Resolution*, 23 Pres. Stud. Q. 235 (1993); Louis Fisher & David Gray Adler, *The War Powers Resolution: Time to Say Goodbye*, 113 Pol. Sci. Q. 1 (1998).

343. 87 Stat. 558, sec. 8(a).

344. Thomas M. Franck & Faiza Patel, *UN Police Action in Lieu of War: "The Old Order Changeth*," 85 Am. J. Int'l L. 63, 72 (1991).

345. Michael J. Glennon, *The Constitution and Chapter VII of the United Nations Charter*, 85 Am. J. Int'l L. 74, 83–84 (1991).

346. 97 Stat. 1062–63, sec. 1013 (1983); 50 U.S.C. § 1546a. See 129 Cong. Rec. 28406–08, 28673–74, 28683–84, 28686–89, 33385, 33395–96 (1983).

347. 141 Cong. Rec. 15203 (1995).

basis deserves to be strengthened in foreign affairs and strengthened in national security."[348] Forty-four Republicans, repelled by that objective, abandoned Gingrich. The amendment failed on a vote of 201 to 217.[349]

In 2008, former Secretaries of State James Baker and Warren Christopher headed a war powers commission. It recommended the repeal of the War Powers Resolution and offered a substitute that promised "equal respect" to the legislative and executive branches. In fact, the commission's proposal greatly strengthened the President's capacity to initiate war and weakened both congressional and public control. Under the commission's proposal, the President need only consult with a newly formed "consultation committee" of 20 senior lawmakers before sending U.S. troops into armed conflict. The President would have no obligation to heed the advice of the committee. Little, if any, role is assigned to the other 515 members of Congress. Congressional action would take the form of a concurrent resolution of approval, without any legal or constitutional force. During the consideration of this concurrent resolution, for close to two months, the President could initiate and continue an unauthorized war. If the concurrent resolution of approval failed to pass, any lawmaker could file a joint resolution of disapproval. Of course the President could veto it, requiring Congress to muster a two-thirds majority in each house to regain control. Bottom line: the President could initiate war and continue it as long as he had one-third plus one votes in a single chamber.[350]

# 9. BYPASSING CONGRESS

Beginning with the Korean War in 1950, Presidents developed the practice of going to war without coming to Congress for a declaration or authorization. Instead, they sought "authorization" from the UN Security Council or from NATO. Presidents who took that path include Truman, Bush I, Clinton, and Obama. Institutionally, Congress has expressed little interest in Presidents circumventing the legislative branch and treating the Security Council and NATO as constitutional substitutes.

After Saddam Hussein invaded Kuwait on August 2, 1990, President Bush sent several hundred thousand troops to Saudi Arabia and the Middle East. At that point the commitment could be interpreted as defensive: to deter further Iraqi aggression. Bush's decision in November to double the size of U.S. forces gave him the capacity to wage offensive war. He made no effort to seek authority from Congress. Rather, the strategy was to build a strong coalition with other nations. His Secretary of State, James Baker, later explained: "from the very beginning, the President recognized the importance of having the express approval of the international community if at all possible."[351] Approval of Congress was not important.

International support was sought because Saudi Arabia, Kuwait, the United Arab Emirates, Japan, Germany, France, Great Britain, and other nations were willing to shoulder the financial

---

348. Id. at 15209.

349. Id. at 15209–10.

350. NATIONAL WAR POWERS COMMISSION REPORT (Miller Center of Public Affairs, University of Virginia, Charlottesville. Va., 2008), http://millercenter.org/policy/commissions/warpowers. For a critique of this report, see Louis Fisher, *The Baker-Christopher War Powers Commission*, 39 PRES. STUD. Q. 128 (2009).

351. JAMES A. BAKER III, THE POLITICS OF DIPLOMACY 304 (1995).

costs. The administration wanted those contributions to go directly to the Defense Department as "gifts," with the money later allocated to such needs as the administration decided.[352] The purpose was to circumvent the appropriations power of Congress. Senator Robert C. Byrd intervened to insist that contributions from foreign government be deposited in the Treasury, subject to appropriation decisions by Congress.[353]

The next step in building support for offensive action against Iraq was the United Nations. On November 29, 1990, at the urging of the Bush administration, the Security Council passed Resolution 678, authorizing member states to use "all necessary means" to force Iraqi troops out of Kuwait. The phrase "all necessary means" anticipated military force. Thomas M. Franck, a specialist in international law, wrote an article for *The New York Times* titled "Declare War? Congress Can't."[354] In his view, once the Security Council acts, member states have no grounds to wait and seek authority from their legislatures. Franck's position is not supported by the language "constitutional processes" in the UN Charter, the legislative history of the Charter, or the text of the UN Participation Act.

Secretary of Defense Dick Cheney, appearing before the Senate Armed Services Committee on December 3, 1990, testified that President Bush did not require "any additional authorization from Congress" before attacking Iraq.[355] The phrase "additional authorization" implied that a Security Council resolution provided constitutionally sufficient grounds. On the day following Cheney's claim, the House Democratic Caucus adopted a resolution stating that the President must first seek authorization from Congress unless American lives were in danger. The resolution passed, 177 to 37.[356]

Fifty-four members of Congress filed a suit in district court, challenging the authority of President Bush to initiate war in the Persian Gulf. The Justice Department argued that Bush could order offensive actions without seeking advance authority from Congress. Although the court held that the case was not ripe for judicial determination, it rejected many of the sweeping assertions of independent presidential war powers. The Justice Department insisted that definitions of the war power were in the hands of the elected branches, not the judiciary. The court disagreed. If the President "had the sole power to determine that any particular offensive military operation, no matter how vast, does not constitute war-making but only an offensive military attack, the congressional power to declare war will be at the mercy of a semantic decision by the Executive. Such an 'interpretation' would evade the plain language of the Constitution, and it cannot stand."[357]

The Justice Department argued that the judiciary had no role in deciding such questions because it would have to "inject itself into foreign affairs, a subject which the Constitution commits to the political branches." That position, said the court, "must fail."[358] Either because of the court's decision or other factors, President Bush on January 8, 1991, asked Congress to

352. H. Doc. No. 101-237, 101st Cong., 2d Sess. (1990).

353. 136 Cong. Rec. 25067–68 (1990).

354. Thomas M. Franck, *Declare War? Congress Can't*, N.Y. Times, Dec. 11, 1990, at A27.

355. *Crisis in the Persian Gulf Region: U.S. Policy Options and Implications*, hearings before the Senate Committee on Armed Services, 101st Cong., 2d Sess. 701 (1990).

356. 1990 C.Q. Almanac 742.

357. Dellums v. Bush, 752 F. Supp. 1141, 1145 (D.D.C. 1990).

358. Id. at 1146.

pass legislation supporting his use of the military. When questioned by reporters the next day whether he needed a statute from Congress, he replied: "I don't think I need it....I feel that I have the authority to fully implement the United Nations resolutions."[359] Given the experience of the "police action" in Korea and the clear plan for offensive operations in 1991, Congress "insisted that *it* was the body with the constitutional authority to decide whether U.S. forces should be sent to combat against Iraq."[360]

Congress passed legislation authorizing offensive action against Iraq. In signing the bill, Bush indicated he could have acted without congressional authority: "As I made clear to congressional leaders at the outset, my request for congressional support did not, and my signing this resolution does not, constitute any change in the long-standing positions of the executive branch on either the President's constitutional authority to use the Armed Forces to defend vital U.S. interests or the constitutionality of the War Powers Resolution."[361] His signing statement did not alter the fact that the resolution passed by Congress specifically authorized him to act. What counted legally was what the law provided, not what Bush said about it.

Early in 1999, Bush gave a talk to the Senate and discussed the war-declaring power. He said: "there was a fundamental difference of opinion between the Senate and the White House over the Senate's role in declaring war—one that dated back to the War Powers Act."[362] Of course the issue did not date back to passage of the WPR in 1973. It originated in 1788 with ratification of the Constitution. Moreover, the power to declare war is not vested in the Senate; it is granted to both houses.

President Clinton circumvented Congress several times by citing "authority" from the United Nations and NATO. On July 31, 1994, the Security Council adopted a resolution authorizing all member states, particularly those in the region of Haiti, to use "all necessary means" to remove the military leadership on that island.[363] On this occasion, the Senate spoke promptly and clearly by passing a "sense of the Senate" amendment, stating that the Security Council resolution "does not constitute authorization for the deployment of United States Armed Forces in Haiti under the Constitution of the United States or pursuant to the War Powers Resolution (Public Law 93-148)." The Senate vote: 100 to zero.[364]

On September 15, in a nationwide televised address, President Clinton announced he was prepared to use military force against Haiti "to carry out the will of the United Nations."[365] He made no reference to carrying out the will of Congress or adhering to the requirements of the U.S. Constitution. An invasion became unnecessary when former President Jimmy Carter helped negotiate an agreement to have the military leaders in Haiti step down.[366] House and

---

359. Public Papers of the Presidents, 1991, I, at 20.

360. Jane E. Stromseth, *Treaty Constraints: The United Nations Charter and War Powers*, in The Constitution and the Power to Go to War 88 (Gary M. Stern & Morton H. Halperin eds., 1994) (emphasis in original).

361. Public Papers of the Presidents, 1991, I, at 40. The authorizing statute: 105 Stat. 3 (1991). See Marcia Lynn Whicker, James P. Pfiffner & Raymond A. Moore, eds., The Presidency and the Persian Gulf War (1993).

362. 145 Cong. Rec. 1333 (1999).

363. Julia Preston, *U.N. Authorizes Invasion of Haiti*, Wash. Post, Aug. 1, 1994, at A1.

364. 140 Cong. Rec. 19306-24 (1994).

365. Public Papers of the Presidents, 1994, II, at 1559.

366. John F. Harris & Douglas Farah, *Clinton Halts Invasion as Haiti Leaders Agree to Quit; U.S. Forces Land Today*, Wash. Post, Sept. 19, 1994, at A1.

Senate debates were strongly critical of Clinton's insistence that he could act militarily against Haiti without authority from Congress. Both houses passed legislation stating the "the President should have sought and welcomed Congressional approval before deploying United States Forces to Haiti."[367] Even lawmakers who voted against this legislation agreed that Clinton should have received approval from Congress.[368]

On September 27, OLC released an analysis on the deployment of U.S. armed forces to Haiti. It concluded that President Clinton possessed legal authority to deploy the troops, his decision satisfied the requirements of the War Powers Resolution, and the military operation was not a "war" within the meaning of the Constitution. On the latter point, OLC said the planned deployment "was to take place with the full consent of the legitimate government, and did not involve the risk of major or prolonged hostilities or serious casualties to either the United States or Haiti."[369] According to OLC, it was sufficient to have the consent of another government, not of Congress. To demonstrate a measure of congressional support, OLC cited "sense of Congress" language in an appropriations bill enacted on November 11, 1993.[370] OLC ignored language in Section 8(a) the War Powers Resolution that specifically states that no previous statutes, including appropriations bills, shall be used to "infer" congressional authority for military action. Furthermore, the language in the 1993 statute was clearly non-binding and did not constitute congressional authorization for military action against Haiti.[371]

Although Presidents and their administrations have generally criticized the WPR for improperly and unwisely constraining presidential power, in this case OLC looked to the statute as support for military operations in Haiti. The structure of the WPR "recognizes and presupposes the existence of unilateral presidential authority to deploy armed forces 'into hostilities or into situations where imminent involvement in hostilities is clearly indicated by the circumstances.' "[372] Moreover, the "overriding interest" of the statute "was to prevent the United States from being engaged, without express congressional authorization, in major, prolonged conflicts such as the wars in Vietnam and Korea, rather than to prohibit the President from using or

367. 140 CONG. REC. 28239 (1994), passing S. J. Res. 229; id. at 28565–78, passing H. J. Res. 416. A day later the House, by voice vote, agreed to S. J. Res. 229; 140 CONG. REC. 29223–24 (1994).

368. E.g., of the eight Senators who voted against S. J. Res. 229, at least four agreed that Clinton should have first obtained approval from Congress: Baucus (140 Cong. Rec. 28236–37), Bradley (id. at 28233), Byrd (id. at 28212–16), and Feingold (id. at 28205–06). For further analysis of Clinton's military actions in Haiti: Michael J. Glennon, *Too Far Apart: Repeal the War Powers Resolution*, 50 U. MIAMI L. REV. 17 (1995); Morris Morley & Chris McGillion, *"Disobedient" Generals and the Politics of Redemocratization: The Clinton Administration and Haiti*, 112 POL. SCI. Q. 363 (1997); RYAN C. HENDRICKSON, THE CLINTON WARS: THE CONSTITUTION, CONGRESS, AND WAR POWERS 43–67 (2002); and FISHER, *supra* note 55, at 178–81.

369. 18 OP. O.L.C. 173, 173 (1994).

370. Id. at 174–75; 107 Stat. 1418, 1474–75, sec. 8147 (1993).

371. Ten professors of constitutional law and foreign relations law disagreed with much of OLC's memo on Haiti: 89 AM. J. INT'L L. 96, 127–30 (1995). Additional legal analysis appears at *Agora: The 1994 U.S. Action in Haiti*, 89 AM. J. INT'L L. 58–87 (1995), with evaluations by Lori Fisler Damrosch, Michael J. Glennon, Monroe Leigh, Theodor Meron, W. Michael Reisman, and Phillip R. Trimble. Walter Dellinger, author of the OLC memo, offered some reflections on academic lawyers versus executive branch attorneys and responded to some of the critiques directed at his memo; Walter Dellinger, *After the Cold War: Presidential Power and the Use of Military Force*, 50 U. MIAMI L. REV. 107 (1995).

372. 18 OP. O.L.C. at 175.

threatening to use troops to achieve important diplomatic objectives where the risk of sustained military conflict was negligible."[373]

In 1993, President Clinton cited support from both the Security Council and NATO in ordering air strikes in Bosnia. The next year he explained: "The authority under which air strikes can proceed, NATO acting out of area pursuant to UN authority, requires the common agreement of our NATO allies."[374] In other words, he had to seek approval from France, Italy, and other NATO allies, but not from Congress. NATO carried out the war's biggest air raid at the end of August 1995.[375] On September 12, 1995, Clinton stated that he regarded the bombing attacks as "authorized by the United Nations."[376] Toward the end of 1995, Clinton sent 20,000 American ground troops to Bosnia. At no time did he seek or receive congressional authority for these military actions.[377]

By October 1998, Clinton was again threatening the Serbs with air strikes, operating through NATO.[378] Although Congress was not asked to grant its approval, some legislatures in NATO countries had to take explicit votes to authorize military action. The Italian Parliament voted to approve the NATO strikes.[379] The Bundestag had to be brought back in special session to approve deployment of German aircraft and troops to Kosovo.[380] The House and Senate took several votes on concurrent resolutions, but they have no legal value and cannot be used for authorization. Other votes were taken but the provisions did not become law.[381] The war against Yugoslavia began on March 24, 1999, without any statutory or constitutional support. Representative Tom Campbell and 25 colleagues went to court to seek a declaration that Clinton had violated the Constitution and the WPR. A district court held they lacked standing, in large part because Congress had never passed restrictive legislation to create a constitutional impasse for the court to resolve.[382]

In 2001 and 2002, President George W. Bush received advance authority from Congress for the wars against Afghanistan and Iraq.[383] In 2011, President Barack Obama continued the pattern of initiating military action against another country without congressional authorization. Although Libya had not threatened or attacked the United States, he cited "authorization" from the Security Council to bomb air defense systems and Libyan forces as part of a no-fly

---

373. Id. at 176.

374. PUBLIC PAPERS OF THE PRESIDENT, 1994, I, at 186.

375. Rick Atkinson & John Pomfret, *NATO Bombs Serbs in War's Biggest Air Raid*, WASH. POST, Aug. 30, 1995, at A1.

376. PUBLIC PAPERS OF THE PRESIDENTS, 1995, II, at 1353.

377. HENDRICKSON, *supra* note 368, at 68–98, and FISHER, *supra* note 55, at 181-91.

378. PUBLIC PAPERS OF THE PRESIDENTS, 1998, II, at 1765.

379. Alessandra Stanley, *Italy's Center-Left Government Is Toppled by One Vote*, N.Y. TIMES, Oct. 10, 1998, at A3.

380. William Drozdiak, *Allies Grim, Milosevic Defiant Amid Kosovo Uncertainty*, WASH. POST, Oct. 8, 1998, at A32.

381. HENDRICKSON, *supra* note 368, at 117–37, and FISHER, *supra* note 55, at 197-200.

382. Campbell v. Clinton, 52 F. Supp. 2d 34, 43 (D.D.C. 1999). That decision was affirmed by the D.C. Circuit; Campbell v. Clinton, 203 F.2d 19 (D.C. Cir. 2000). See Louis Fisher, *Litigating the War Power with* Campbell v. Clinton, 30 PRES. STUD. Q. 564 (2000).

383. 115 Stat. 224 (2001); 116 Stat. 1498 (2002).

zone policy.[384] Later, Obama and administration officials spoke of receiving "authorization" from NATO allies.[385] He was the first President to conduct offensive military operations beyond the 90-day limit of the WPR, stretching them out to seven months. The administration concluded that the military operations did not constitute "war" or "hostilities."[386] An OLC memo in April 2011 argued that in order to meet the constitutional meaning of war there had to be "prolonged and substantial military engagements, typically involving exposure of U.S. military personnel to significant risk over a significant period."[387] Under that interpretation, a nation with superior military force could pulverize another country—including use of nuclear weapons—and there would be neither war nor hostilities if the aggressor state sustained no or minimal hostilities.

Ten members of Congress filed suit, claiming that Obama's military actions in Libya violated the Constitution and the War Powers Resolution. As with many similar lawsuits in the past, a district court on October 11, 2011, held that they lacked standing to bring the case.[388] On war power cases, Representative Holtzman was the last member of Congress to obtain standing in 1973 and actually prevail in district court. As explained earlier, in section 7D, her case was mooted by an accommodation reached between Congress and the Nixon administration. Other war power cases are typically dismissed on grounds of the political question doctrine, ripeness, mootness, standing, and the equitable/remedial doctrine. If Congress were to direct the President to take a particular action, or prohibit him from doing so, presidential noncompliance could result in a court granting standing to lawmakers and reaching the merits of a dispute.[389]

There has been little legislative, judicial, or scholarly focus on Presidents who use offensive military force against another nation on the basis of "authorization" from international and regional bodies. Presidents typically rely on such treaties as the UN Charter, NATO, and SEATO. Michael Glennon and Allison Hayward wrote in 1994: "Just as Congress cannot amend the Constitution via statute, the Senate cannot alter the balance of constitutional powers via treaty. Thus, the Senate cannot take from the full Congress its power to declare war by guaranteeing in a treaty that the United States will go to war in the event an ally is threatened."[390] In an article published that year, Charles Ernest Edgar concluded: "Authorization is given by majority votes from both houses of Congress; under no circumstance is the judgment of another body, including the Security Council, a valid substitute for the judgment of Congress."[391] That point has been reinforced by Jane Stromseth: "To claim that the President as Commander in Chief has

---

384. March 21, 2011, letter from President Obama to the Speaker of the House of Representatives and the President Pro Tempore of the Senate, http://www/whitehouse.gov/the-press-office/2011/03/21/letter-president-regarding-commencement-operations-libya.

385. Harold Koh, Legal Adviser to the State Department, *Statement Regarding Use of Force in Libya*, March 26, 2011, appearing before the American Society of International Law Annual Meeting, Washington, D.C., http://www.state.gov/s/l/releases/remarks/159201.htm.

386. Louis Fisher, *Military Operations in Libya: No War? No Hostilities?*, 42 Pres. Stud. Q. 176 (2012).

387. Office of Legal Counsel, *Authority to Use Military Force in Libya*, April 1, 2011, at 8.

388. Kucinich v. Obama, 821 F. Supp. 2d 110 (D.D.C. 2011).

389. Michael John Garcia, *War Powers Litigation Initiated by Members of Congress Since the Enactment of the War Powers Resolution*, Feb. 17, 2012, CRS Report RL30352.

390. Michael J. Glennon & Allison R. Hayward, *Collective Security and the Constitution: Can the Commander in Chief Power Be Delegated to the United Nations?*, 82 Geo. L.J. 1573, 1597 (1994).

391. Charles Ernest Edgar, *United States Use of Armed Force Under the United Nations… Who's in Charge?*, 10 J.L. & Pol. 299, 337 (1994).

unilateral authority to send U.S. forces to combat whenever he thinks it is in the interest of the United States or the United Nations to do so, regardless of the size or riskiness of the operation, is essentially to read Congress's power to declare war out of the Constitution."[392]

MANY STUDIES IN recent decades explore the scope of the President's power as Commander in Chief. Some scholars conclude that although Presidents increasingly act independently to engage the country in war, Congress retains a capacity to control and limit executive policy.[393] Jack Goldsmith analyzed the overreach of the Bush II administration in promoting unilateral presidential power after 9/11 and the resulting corrections taken during the second term.[394] In a subsequent book, he argued that those legal adjustments in the Bush II administration largely carried over into the Obama administration.[395]

In 2008, David Barron and Martin Lederman published a lengthy two-part series in the *Harvard Law Review*, analyzing the President's unilateral authority to use military force even if Congress adopts statutory constraints. They conclude that the Founding era provides little support for the claim that the President as Commander in Chief possesses a general power to initiate military operations, free from statutory and judicial control.[396] Barron and Lederman distinguish between "inherent" presidential power (claimed by Presidents beginning in 1950) and "preclusive" powers, asserted from that time forward. The two terms seem to overlap to some degree, but "inherent" denies the availability of congressional and judicial checks, while "preclusive" recognizes that the legislative and judicial branches may curb presidential power. Many of the issues that Barron and Lederman discuss, including treatment of detainees, torture, military commissions, and warrantless surveillance, are covered in Chapter 9.

On June 25, 2013, Representative Walter Jones introduced H.R. 2496 to prohibit the deployment of U.S. armed forces in support of a UN or mutual security treaty military operation absent express prior statutory authorization from Congress for such deployment. His bill underscores the principle that the Constitution does not permit the President and the Senate through the treaty process to transfer Article I congressional authority to international and regional organizations.

---

392. Jane E. Stromseth, *Rethinking War Powers: Congress, the President, and the United Nations*, 81 GEO. L.J. 597, 661 (1993). See also David Golove, *From Versailles to San Francisco: The Revolutionary Transformation of the War Powers*, 70 U. COLO. L. REV. 1491 (1999); Louis Fisher, *Sidestepping Congress: Presidents Acting Under the UN and NATO*, 47 CASE WEST. RES. L. REV. 1237 (1997); Matthew D. Berger, *Implementing a United Nations Security Council Resolution: The President's Power to Use Force Without the Authorization of Congress*, 15 HASTINGS INT'L & COMP. L. REV. 83 (1991).

393. DOUGLAS L. KRINER, AFTER THE RUBICON: CONGRESS, PRESIDENTS, AND THE POLITICS OF WAGING WAR (2010); WILLIAM G. HOWELL & JON C. PEVEHOUSE, WHILE DANGERS GATHER: CONGRESSIONAL CHECKS ON PRESIDENTIAL WAR POWERS (2007).

394. JACK GOLDSMITH, THE TERROR PRESIDENCY: LAW AND JUDGMENT INSIDE THE BUSH ADMINISTRATION (2007).

395. JACK GOLDSMITH, POWER AND CONSTRAINT: THE ACCOUNTABLE PRESIDENCY AFTER 9/11 (2012).

396. David J. Barron & Martin S. Lederman, *The Commander in Chief at the Lowest Ebb—Framing the Problem, Doctrine, and Original Understanding (Part 1)*, 121 HARV. L. REV. 689 (2008), and *The Commander in Chief at the Lowest Ebb—A Constitutional History (Part 2)*, 121 HARV. L. REV. 941 (2008).

# NINE

# The President and the Judiciary

PRESIDENTS HAVE A SIGNIFICANT OPPORTUNITY TO INFLUENCE JUDICIAL rulings by nominating individuals to district courts, circuit courts, and the Supreme Court. Through those choices, Presidents can attempt to place an ideological stamp on the federal judiciary. Senators have a similar opportunity when they recommend nominees and reject or block presidential selections. Both elected branches recognize that courts play an ongoing policymaking role that competes with, and sometimes prevails over, executive and legislative efforts. Notwithstanding their influence, Presidents successful in having their nominees confirmed are often disappointed by the results, especially at the level of the Supreme Court. Once elevated to a position with a lifetime appointment, Justices may move in directions wholly unanticipated by Presidents who nominated them. At times, the Court conflates the power of judicial review with judicial supremacy and misrepresents the holding in *Marbury v. Madison* (1803).

## 1. UNDERSTANDING *MARBURY*

Federal courts and constitutional scholars often cite a sentence from *Marbury* as evidence that the Supreme Court possesses authority not merely to strike down the acts of Presidents, Congress, and the states but to do so permanently. Here is the sentence: "It is emphatically the province and duty of the judicial department to say what the law is."[1] Judicial finality is not present in that sentence. First, remove some of the frills about "emphatically the province and duty" and restate the sentence in this manner: "It is the duty of the judicial department to say what the law is." Simplify the sentence still further by replacing "the judicial department" with "courts" to yield: "It is the duty of courts to say what the law is." Basically: Courts decide the law. Yes, quite

---

1. Marbury v. Madison, 5 U.S. (1 Cr.) 137, 177 (1803). Examples of the Court claiming judicial supremacy by relying on this sentence in *Marbury*: Citizens United v. FEC, 558 U.S. 310, 365 (2010); Boumediene v. Bush, 553 U.S. 723, 765 (2008); United States v. Morrison, 529 U.S. 598, 617 n.7 (2000); Boerne v. Flores, 521 U.S. 507, 536 (1997); United States v. Nixon, 418 U.S. 683, 703, 705 (1974); Powell v. McCormack, 395 U.S. 486, 549 (1969); and Cooper v. Aaron, 358 U.S. 1, 18 (1958). In Baker v. Carr, 369 U.S. 186, 211 (1962), the Court described itself "as ultimate interpreter of the Constitution."

true. That is why courts exist, but the sentence says nothing about judicial finality. A reworked sentence is equally true: "It is emphatically the province and duty of the legislative department to say what the law is." No one could dispute that sentence, but it does not make Congress superior or final. Here is a third rewrite: "It is emphatically the province and duty of the executive department to say what the law is." Presidents and executive agencies say what the law is through executive orders, proclamations, and agency rules that implement statutes. All three branches are involved in saying what the law is. The historical record does not elevate a particular branch to a position of supremacy in constitutional interpretation. They all jockey for influence and control. That is the nature of a republican form of government.

*Marbury* is justly remembered as a case of extraordinary importance, but not for the principle of judicial supremacy. Rather, it is for the principle of judicial survival. Chief Justice Marshall fully understood that the federal judiciary in 1803 occupied a highly vulnerable position. The Federalist Party, in control of the presidency for the first 12 years of the republic's existence, had succeeded in placing its supporters on the federal bench. In the last weeks of the John Adams administration, the Federalists added still more of their followers to the courts. The election of 1800 swept the Federalists out of power, replaced by the Republicans under the leadership of Thomas Jefferson. Over a period of years, these Republicans formed the base for what would later be called the Democratic Party.

In February 1801, with a few weeks remaining in the lame-duck Congress, the Federalists passed two bills to create a number of new federal judges.[2] One statute created 16 lifetime judges to serve in newly created circuits, relieving Justices of the Supreme Court of the need to travel outside Washington, D.C., to perform the onerous duty of "circuit riding."[3] Upon entering office, the Jeffersonians passed legislation to abolish those positions, an issue discussed in the next section. The second statute created new justices of the peace for the District of Columbia, each with a five-year term.[4] President Adams nominated Federalists to those positions and the Federalist Senate quickly confirmed them. The day before Jefferson took office, the Senate confirmed 42 justices of the peace.[5]

Marshall was serving as Secretary of State under Adams, even though he had already been confirmed as Chief Justice of the Supreme Court for the next term. After the Senate confirmed the new judgeships, it was Marshall's duty as Secretary of State to have the commissions delivered to the new officeholders. Because of last-minute pressures and distractions, some of the commissions never reached the confirmed individuals, including one for William Marbury to be justice of the peace in the District of Columbia. Upon entering the White House, Jefferson ordered that the judicial nominations confirmed by the Federalist Senate and signed and sealed by President Adams, but not yet delivered, be withheld.

Marbury and other plaintiffs brought their case directly to the Supreme Court instead of starting in district court. In that manner they asked the Court to exercise original jurisdiction. The Constitution, in Article III, section 2, distinguishes between original and appellate jurisdiction. In all cases "affecting Ambassadors, other public Ministers and Consuls, and those in which a State shall be Party, the supreme Court shall have original jurisdiction." In all other cases, the

2. Kathryn Turner, *The Midnight Judges*, 109 U. Pa. L. Rev. 494 (1961).

3. 1 Stat. 89 (1801).

4. Id. at 103, 107, sec. 11 (1801).

5. William W. Van Alstyne, *A Critical Guide to Marbury v. Madison*, 1969 Duke L.J. 1, 4 (1969).

Court "shall have appellate Jurisdiction, both as to Law and Fact, with such Exceptions and under such Regulations as the Congress shall make." The language about exceptions and regulations appears to grant Congress some discretion in legislating on the two types of jurisdiction.

To Marshall, the Court lacked jurisdiction to do what Congress authorized in section 13 of the Judiciary Act of 1789: to issue a writ of mandamus to compel Jefferson or Secretary of State Madison to deliver the commissions.[6] Marshall concluded that section 13 was unconstitutional because it expanded the original jurisdiction of the Court. Congress, he said, could alter the boundaries only of appellate jurisdiction. The word "original" might appear to imply exclusivity, suggesting that what is granted by the Constitution may not be abridged or altered by Congress. But Congress divided original jurisdiction into two categories: (1) original and exclusive and (2) original but not exclusive.[7] The Judiciary Act of 1789 spoke of "original but not exclusive jurisdiction."[8] The two categories were not as distinct as Marshall argued.

Many scholars have found Marshall's reasoning unpersuasive. To one critic: "The learned Justice really manufactured an opportunity to declare an act void."[9] William Van Alstyne discovered no convincing reasoning by Marshall on the issue of jurisdiction. To Van Alstyne, one might argue that Congress has no authority to reduce the Court's original jurisdiction, but what prohibited Congress from increasing original jurisdiction?[10] An article by law professor Michael McConnell referred to Marshall's analysis of original and appellate jurisdiction as "strained reading."[11]

Upon his retirement from the Supreme Court in 2010, John Paul Stevens offered a number of thoughts about the Court in his book *Five Chiefs*. Marshall decided that Marbury had a "right" to receive his commission, and one method of securing that right was to ask the Court to issue a writ of mandamus "commanding Madison to deliver it."[12] Yet Marshall concluded that the provision for a writ of mandamus in the 1789 law was unconstitutional. Stevens wrote: "For me, the case has always been puzzling because I have never found satisfying Marshall's explication of why the statute was unconstitutional."[13] He added: "Why would not the statute not have been perfectly valid in cases in which the Court properly had original jurisdiction, such as a suit by a foreign ambassador seeking relief against the secretary of state?"[14]

If the constitutional meaning of original jurisdiction were as clear as Marshall maintained, the Court should have disposed of the case by informing Marbury and the other plaintiffs: "Gentlemen, the Constitution plainly prohibits you from bringing this dispute directly to the Supreme Court. You must initiate your action in district court. Case dismissed." Moreover, there are good reasons why Marshall should not have participated in the case. His previous

---

6. 1 Stat. 81, sec. 13 (1789).

7. 28 U.S.C. § 1251.

8. 1 Stat. 80, sec. 13 (1789).

9. Andrew C. McLaughlin, *Marbury v. Madison Again*, 14 Am. Bar Ass'n J. 155, 157 (1928).

10. Van Alstyne, *supra* note 5, at 15–16, 30–33.

11. Michael W. McConnell, *The Story of* Marbury v. Madison, in Constitutional Law Stories 29 (Michael C. Dorf, ed., 2004).

12. John Paul Stevens, Five Chiefs 17 (2011).

13. Id.

14. Id. at 17–18.

position as Secretary of State and failure to deliver the commission to Marbury disqualified him. He should have recused himself. The conflict of interest was so overwhelming he could not possibly claim impartiality, a quality essential for those who judge.[15]

But Marshall had things he wanted to say, particularly about the new administration. He proceeded to deliver an ad hominem about what he described as Jefferson's illegal conduct: "To withhold his commission, therefore, is an act deemed by the court not warranted by law, but violative of a vested right."[16] Law professor Barry Friedman remarked: this "gratuitous tongue-lashing of Jefferson and Madison for failing to deliver Marbury's commission was entirely unwarranted."[17] Political scientist Edward Corwin made a similar observation in 1914: "The court was bent on reading the President a lecture on his legal and moral duty to recent Federalist appointees to judicial offices."[18] Corwin later praised Marshall for sidestepping a collision with the executive branch he could not have won. Yet Marshall, he said, "stigmatized his enemy Jefferson as a violator of the laws which as President he was sworn to support."[19]

Marshall spoke disingenuously about Marbury's "right" to have his job. Marshall claimed that because Jefferson and Madison refused to take required steps, Marbury "has a consequent right to the commission."[20] Given the manner in which Marshall decided to void the writ of mandamus, combined with his own earlier failure as Secretary of State to see that Marbury received his commission, Marshall guaranteed that Marbury and his fellow plaintiffs would walk away empty-handed. They could have refiled their case in district court but chose not to. What was Marshall's purpose, other than some political and partisan objectives, of speaking loftily about rights and entitlements that did not exist?

In *Cohens v. Virginia* (1821), Marshall returned to the distinction between original and appellate jurisdiction, treating it this time with greater thought, less rigidity, and less partisanship. He objected to litigants who read *Marbury* carelessly, failing to separate what was at its core from "some *dicta* of the Court."[21] When it appeared that litigants were rummaging around *Marbury* to find nuggets favorable to their position, Marshall insisted that general expressions in a case "are to be taken in connection with the case in which those expressions are used." If those expressions "go beyond the case, they may be respected, but ought not to control the judgment in a subsequent suit when the very point is presented for decision."[22] A question before a court must be "investigated with care, and considered to the full extent."[23] In *Marbury*, the "single

---

15. For studies concluding that Marshall should have withdrawn from the case: J. A. C. Grant, *Marbury v. Madison Today*, 23 AM. POL. SCI. REV. 673, 678 (1929), and JEFFREY ROSEN, THE MOST DEMOCRATIC BRANCH: HOW THE COURTS SERVE AMERICA 22 (2006). Writing in 1950, Justice Harold Burton noted that had Marshall disqualified himself "there would not have been the required quorum of four present." Harold H. Burton, *The Cornerstone of Constitutional Law: The Extraordinary Case of Marbury v. Madison*, 36 AM. BAR ASS'N J. 805, 807 (1950).

16. Marbury v. Madison, 5 U.S. (1 Cr.) 137, 162 (1803).

17. BARRY FRIEDMAN, THE WILL OF THE PEOPLE: HOW PUBLIC OPINION HAS INFLUENCED THE SUPREME COURT AND SHAPED THE MEANING OF THE CONSTITUTION 63 (2009).

18. Edward S. Corwin, *Marbury v. Madison and the Doctrine of Judicial Review*, 12 MICH. L. REV. 538, 543 (1914).

19. EDWARD S. CORWIN, JOHN MARSHALL AND THE CONSTITUTION 66 (1919).

20. Marbury v. Madison, 5 U.S. (1 Cr.) at 168.

21. Cohens v. Virginia, 19 U.S. (6 Wheat.) 264, 397 (1821).

22. Id.

23. Id.

question" before the Court was "whether the legislature could give this Court original jurisdiction in a case in which the constitution had clearly not given it."[24] That was the core holding. Everything else, including what might be read as claims of judiciary supremacy, amounted to dicta. Some of the language in *Marbury* was not only too broad, he said, "but in some instances contradictory to its principle."[25]

Marshall knew that the Supreme Court in 1803 could not confront the President and Congress and have any chance of prevailing. Claims of "judicial supremacy" would merely whet the appetite of lawmakers who wanted to impeach and remove Federalist judges. Congress removed District Judge John Pickering through the impeachment process and the House impeached Justice Samuel Chase. Marshall had every reason to believe he could be next. It would have been an institutional error of the highest order for the Court to order Jefferson or Madison to deliver the commission to Marbury and allow him to take his seat as a justice of the peace in the District of Columbia. Marshall's sound political judgment ruled out such error.

Marshall's reaction to the impeachment actions against Pickering and Chase underscores that he was quite willing to share constitutional interpretations with the elected branches. He issued *Marbury* on February 24, 1803. The House impeached Pickering a week later, on March 2. The Senate convicted him on March 12, 1804. Congress then turned its guns on Chase, making it clear that Justices were proper targets. Under these precarious conditions, Marshall wrote to Chase on January 23, 1805, suggesting that if members of Congress did not like a particular judicial opinion, there was no need to impeach a judge. Instead, just pass a statute to reverse objectionable decisions. Here is Marshall's language to Chase: "I think the modern doctrine of impeachment shoud [sic] yield to an appellate jurisdiction in the legislature. A reversal of those legal opinions deemd [sic] unsound by the legislature would certainly better comport with the mildness of our character than [would] a removal of the Judge who has renderd [sic] them unknowing of his fault."[26] Nothing in those words imply judicial supremacy or arrogance. Marshall did not speak as someone empowered and determined to impose his will on the elected branches. In both tone and content, he recommended judicial modesty and an understanding that the Court must operate in a government of three branches, fully respectful of institutional limits imposed on the judiciary.

Toward the end of *Marbury*, Marshall argued that he was required to strike down the statutory provision in Section 13 of the Judiciary Act of 1789 because of his oath of office: "Why otherwise does [the Constitution] direct the judges to take an oath to support it? This oath certainly applies in an especial manner, to their conduct in their official character." It would be "immoral," he continued, to impose the oath on judges "if they were to be used as the instruments, and the knowing instruments, for violating what they swear to support!"[27] He asked: "Why does a judge swear to discharge his duties agreeably to the constitution of the United States, if that constitution forms no rule for his government? [I]f it is closed upon him, and cannot be inspected by

---

24. Id. at 400.

25. Id. at 401.

26. 3 Albert J. Beveridge, The Life of John Marshall 177 (1919). Marshall dated the letter January 23, 1804, but modern scholarship fixes the date a year later, January 23, 1805. 6 The Papers of John Marshall 348 n.1 (Charles F. Hobson ed., 1990). Like the rest of us often do, Marshall forgot to switch to the new year.

27. Marbury v. Madison 5 U.S. (1 Cr.) at 180.

him?" If such were the real state of things, "this is worse than solemn mockery. To prescribe, or to take the oath, becomes equally a crime."[28]

Quite a flight of rhetoric! Supreme Court Justices are not unique in taking an oath of office. So do Presidents, members of Congress, federal executive officers, and state officials (Chapter 2, section 5). No doubt Marshall took the oath when he served as Secretary of State and failed to get the commission to Marbury. The important ceremony of oath taking does not give the Court the final word on the meaning of the Constitution or some exalted status over the other branches.

Marshall's writing skills enabled him to present a conclusion as though no other alternative could possible exist. In *Marbury* he wrote: "It is a proposition too plain to be contested, that the constitution controls any legislative act repugnant to it; or, that the legislature may alter the constitution by an ordinary act." Continuing: "The constitution is either a superior paramount law, unchangeable by ordinary means, or it is on a level with ordinary legislative acts, and, like other acts, is alterable when the legislature shall please to alter it."[29] Here he leans in the direction of judicial supremacy. If lawmakers treat the Constitution as an ordinary statute and seek to amend it with another statute, the Court must intervene to protect the Constitution. But if a statute contrary to the constitution text may not stand, why allow a Supreme Court decision that is contrary to the Constitution? Legal scholar Nelson Lund has asked: "[I]f statutes enacted by the people's representatives are always trumped by the Constitution, it would seem to follow by inexorable logic that mere judicial opinions must also be trumped by the Constitution."[30]

## 2. ABOLISHING ARTICLE III JUDGES

The Court decided *Marbury* on February 24, 1803. One week later it decided an important case that unfortunately receives far less attention than Marshall's famous decision. The second case highlights the fact that constitutional interpretation is determined by the President and Congress, not just the judiciary, and that the Court in 1803 understood that often the "final word" is decided, and appropriately so, by the elected branches.

One of the first actions by President Jefferson and Congress was to repeal a statute, passed by the Federalists toward the end of the Adams administration, that created 16 new federal judgeships with lifetime appointments. Did Congress have authority to abolish Article III judges? Many Federalists found it constitutionally repugnant to argue that Congress could not take a judge out of an office (save for impeachment) but could take the office out of the judge. After vigorous debate, the repeal bill became law on March 8, 1802. All actions, suits, process, pleadings, and other actions in the abolished courts were transferred to circuit courts and district courts.[31]

---

28. Id.

29. Id. at 177.

30. Nelson Lund, *Resolved, Presidential Signing Statements Threaten to Undermine the Rule of Law and the Separation of Power* (con), in RICHARD J. ELLIS & MICHAEL NELSON, eds., DEBATING THE PRESIDENCY: CONFLICTING PERSPECTIVES ON THE AMERICAN EXECUTIVE 150 (2010).

31. 2 Stat. 132, sec. 4 (1802). For details on the congressional debate: MITCHEL A. SOLLENBERGER, JUDICIAL APPOINTMENTS AND DEMOCRATIC CONTROLS 17–19 (2011).

The constitutionality of the repeal statute reached the Court in *Stuart v. Laird*. Opponents of the repeal argued: "The words *during good behavior* can not mean *during the will of Congress*. The people have a right to the services of those judges who have been constitutionally appointed; and who have been unconstitutionally removed from office."[32] If Marshall and the other Justices exercised judicial review by striking down the repeal law, it would likely have intensified congressional efforts to impeach and remove Federalist judges, including those on the Supreme Court. The Justices were thus confronted not merely with a constitutional issue but an institutional question about the continued survival of the courts.

Although Marshall did not disqualify himself from the *Marbury* case, as he should have, he stepped aside in *Stuart* because he had tried the case in the court below.[33] Would his colleagues on the Supreme Court invoke its newfound strength of judicial review by invalidating what the Jeffersonians had done by passing the repeal statute? There was barely any chance of that. The constitutional judgment of Congress and the President would stand.

To the Court, the issue of circuit judges had been settled by congressional action in 1789 when it created circuit courts that combined district judges and Supreme Court Justices. From 1789 to the end of the John Adams administration, Justices had ridden circuit and no one raised a constitutional objection. Said the Court in *Stuart*: "it is sufficient to observe, that practice and acquiescence under it for a period of several years, commencing with the organization of the judicial system, affords an irresistable [sic] answer, and has indeed fixed the construction."[34] The congressional judgment represented "a contemporary interpretation of the most forcible nature. This practical exposition is too strong and obstinate to be shaken or controlled."[35] The Court deferred to the constitutional judgment of Congress in 1789 and to the constitutional judgment of Congress and President Jefferson in 1801. The final voice on constitutionality in this dispute went to the elected branches.

It has been argued that Chief Justice Marshall and Justice Chase resented the Jeffersonian repeal of the Circuit Court Act and gave some consideration to refusing to abide by it, including the requirement of circuit riding. That course of action needed a united Court, but Justices Bushrod Washington and William Paterson declined to join that outcome. Justices had ridden circuit for the previous decade without constitutional complaint. A judicial objection in 1803 would have lacked credibility.[36] Given Marshall's sensitivity to the fragile nature of judicial power following the Jeffersonian victory, combined with the ever-present specter of impeachment, it is highly doubtful that he would have supported a judicial ruling striking down the repeal statute. He understood the need to protect the institutional interests of the Court by avoiding a costly confrontation with Jefferson.[37]

---

32. Stuart v. Laird, 5 U.S. (1 Cr.) 299, 304 (1803) (emphasis in original).

33. Id. at 308.

34. Id. at 309.

35. Id.

36. Bruce Ackerman, The Failure of the Founding Fathers: Jefferson, Marshall, and the Rise of Presidential Democracy 163–76 (2007 ed).

37. James F. Simon, What Kind of Nation: Thomas Jefferson, John Marshall, and the Epic Struggle to Create a United States (2002). Marshall's political skills in avoiding collisions with Jefferson are evident in his handling of United States v. Schooner Peggy (id. at 160–61), Marbury v. Madison (id. at 180, 183, 185, 187, 238), and Stuart v. Laird (id. at 168–71).

Marshall had just joined the Court and intended to make it a career. He remained as Chief Justice until 1835. *Marbury* marked the only time that the Marshall Court invalidated a congressional statute. Marshall's genius lay in a political sophistication of what a Court may and may not do. Constitutional scholar Michael McConnell makes that point: "*Marbury* was brilliant, then, not for its effective assertion of judicial power, but for its effective avoidance of judicial humiliation."[38] Marshall did not use *Marbury* to elevate himself and the Court above the President and Congress. Quite the contrary. Judicial review became a mechanism to regularly affirm, not invalidate, the constitutional judgments of elected officials. He found ways to bestow a judicial blessing on what Presidents and lawmakers wanted to do with the commerce power and in creating a national bank. In a series of cases, he exercised judicial review by strengthening national power over the states.[39]

The congressional decision in 1802 to abolish Article III courts was highly unusual. Federal judges with supposedly lifetime terms lost their jobs. The next attempt did not occur until the Civil War, when Congress became concerned about the D.C. circuit court. Because of questions about the loyalty of some of the judges, bills were introduced to abolish the court. After lengthy debate, both houses passed the legislation and President Lincoln signed it into law. The statute abolished the circuit court, district court, and criminal court of the District of Columbia.[40] Congress in 1911 also abolished some federal courts when it restructured circuit courts. No federal judges were removed because Congress in 1891 had created new circuit courts of appeal, establishing nine new appellate level courts.[41]

# 3. INDEPENDENT PRESIDENTIAL JUDGMENT

A year after *Marbury*, President Jefferson wrote to Mrs. John Adams: "You seem to think it devolved on the judges to decide on the validity of the sedition law. But nothing in the Constitution has given them a right to decide for the Executive, more than to the Executive to decide for them."[42] In articulating the doctrine of "coordinate construction," Jefferson said each branch was "equally independent in the sphere of action assigned to them."[43] Judges could fine and imprison someone, but the President under his independent power of pardon could then "remit the execution of it."[44] Giving judges the right to decide exclusively a constitutional question "would make the judiciary a despotic branch."[45]

---

38. McConnell, *supra* note 11, at 31.

39. E.g., McCulloch v. Maryland, 17 U.S. (4 Wheat.) 316 (1819), and Gibbons v. Ogden, 22 U.S. (9 Wheat.) 1 (1824).

40. 12 Stat. 762, 764, sec. 16 (1863). For analysis of this statute: Sollenberger, *supra* note 31, at 21–26.

41. 36 Stat. 1087 (1911) and 26 Stat. 826 (1891). See Sollenberger, *supra* note 31, at 26.

42. 11 The Writings of Thomas Jefferson 50 (Bergh ed., 1904).

43. Id.

44. Id. at 51.

45. Id.

Jefferson and his followers regarded the Alien and Sedition Acts of 1798 as patently uncon-stitutional and hoped the federal courts would strike them down.[46] Federalist judges declined to invalidate those statutes passed by a Federalist administration. Once in office as President, Jefferson "discharged every person under punishment or prosecution under the sedition law, because I considered, and now consider, that law to be a nullity, as absolute and as palpable as if Congress had ordered us to fall down and worship a golden image."[47] Congress later determined that the Sedition Act was "unconstitutional, null, and void" and appropriated funds to reimburse those who had been fined under the statute.[48] In 1964, the Supreme Court acknowledged that the Sedition Act was rejected not by a court of law but by the "court of history."[49]

Toward the end of his life, Jefferson continued to advocate coordinate construction. Writing to a correspondent in 1820: "You seem...to consider the judges as the ultimate arbiters of all constitutional questions; a very dangerous doctrine indeed, and one which would place us under the despotism of an oligarchy."[50] Jefferson said he regarded judges "as honest as other men, but not more so," and have "the same passions for party, for power, and the privilege of their corps."[51] They represented a danger because they were not responsible to the people in the same manner as the elected branches. The Constitution "has more wisely made all the departments coequal and co-sovereign within themselves."[52] He knew of no "safe depository" for the power of society other than "the people."[53] To those who insisted "there must be an ultimate arbiter somewhere," Jefferson agreed, but selected as the ultimate arbiter "the people of the Union, assembled by their deputies in convention, at the call of Congress, or of two-thirds of the States."[54]

President Andrew Jackson inherited Jefferson's distrust of the judiciary, but at times looked to federal courts as a potential ally to combat the nullification doctrine promoted by some southern states. To keep the nation intact, it might be necessary for the presidency and the judiciary to join forces.[55] He announced his own theory of coordinate construction in 1832 when he vetoed a bill to recharter the Bank of the United States. He was urged to sign the bill because the Bank had been upheld by the Supreme Court in *McCulloch v. Maryland* (1819) and previous Presidents and Congresses had given it their blessing. In vetoing the bill on both policy and constitutional grounds, Jackson announced that each public officer who takes an oath to support the Constitution "swears that he will support it as he understands it, and not as it is understood by others."[56] The opinion of judges had "no more authority over Congress than the opinion of Congress has over the judges, and on that point the President is independent of

---

46. Id., 10: 61 ("the laws of the land, administered by upright judges, would protect you from any exercise of power unauthorized by the Constitution of the United States," letter to R. H. Rowan, Sept. 2, 1798).

47. Id., 11: 43–44 (letter to Mrs. John Adams, July 22, 1804).

48. H. Rep. No. 86, 26th Cong., 1st Sess. 2 (1840); 6 Stat. 802, ch. 45 (1840).

49. New York Times Co. v. Sullivan, 376 U.S. 254, 276 (1964).

50. 15 The Writing of Thomas Jefferson 277 (Bergh ed., 1904), letter to William Charles Jarvis, Sept. 28, 1820.

51. Id.

52. Id.

53. Id. at 278.

54. Id. at 451, letter to Judge William Johnson, June 12, 1823.

55. Richard P. Longaker, *Andrew Jackson and the Judiciary*, 71 Pol. Sci. Q. 341 (1956).

56. 3 Richardson 1145.

both."[57] Constitutional struggles over the U.S. Bank were covered in Chapter 3, section 1, and Chapter 5, section 1D.

Abraham Lincoln and Stephen Douglas debated judicial finality during their campaign for the U.S. Senate in 1858. Douglas supported the Supreme Court's decision in *Dred Scott v. Sandford* issued the previous year. Lincoln said he supported the decision only with regard to its impact on the particular litigants but refused to accept the decision as a policy for the nation. Lincoln opposed the spread of slavery to the new territories and rejected the Court's ruling as a basis for nationalizing slavery.[58] He regarded the Supreme Court as a coequal, not superior, branch of government. In his inaugural address in 1861, Lincoln denied that constitutional questions could be settled solely by the Supreme Court. If government policy on "vital questions affecting the whole people is to be irrevocably fixed" by the Supreme Court, "the people will have ceased to be their own rulers."[59] Presidents and lawmakers were at liberty to exercise their own independent constitutional judgments, even if at odds with past Court rulings.

At times the Supreme Court will decide a constitutional case in a manner that invites the elected branches to revisit the issue and adopt a different policy. In 1890, the Court ruled that a state's prohibition of intoxicating liquors could not be applied to original packages or kegs. Only after the original package was broken into smaller units could the state exercise control. The Court qualified its ruling by saying that states could not exclude incoming articles "without congressional permission."[60] Within a matter of months Congress passed legislation that gave states regulatory powers over intoxicating liquors that entered their territory and the Court upheld the statute.[61]

Another type of judicial invitation appears in 1943, after the Court and the elected branches had traded interpretations of the taxing power. The Court encouraged lawmakers to pass new legislation to challenge previous rulings: "There is no reason to doubt that this Court may fall into error as may other branches of the Government. Nothing in the history or attitude of this Court should give rise to legislative embarrassment if in the performance of its duty a legislative body feels impelled to enact laws which may require the Court to reexamine its previous judgment or doctrine."[62] The Court explained that it is less able than other branches "to extricate itself from error" because it can reconsider a matter "only when it is again properly brought before it as a case or controversy."[63]

An example of this constitutional dialogue appears in the history of child labor legislation. In 1918, the Court struck down a federal statute regulating child labor as an impermissible use of the commerce power.[64] Congress promptly passed new legislation, this time based on the taxing power, but in 1922 the Court invalidated that statute.[65] Congress passed a constitutional amendment in 1924 to give itself authority to regulate child labor but could not attract sufficient

57. Id.

58. 2 Collected Works of Abraham Lincoln 516 (Basler ed., 1953).

59. 7 Richardson 3210.

60. Leisy v. Hardin, 135 U.S. 100, 125 (1890).

61. 26 Stat. 313 (1890); In re Rahrer, 140 U.S. 545 (1891).

62. Helvering v. Griffiths, 318 U.S. 371, 400–01 (1943).

63. Id. at 401.

64. Hammer v. Dagenhart, 247 U.S. 251 (1918).

65. Bailey v. Drexel Furniture Co., 259 U.S. 20 (1922).

states to ratify it. In 1938, Congress returned to the commerce power as a basis for passing child labor legislation, precisely what the Court had earlier disallowed. Not only did the Court uphold the law this time but did so unanimously, admitting that its earlier rulings contained indefensible reasoning and doctrines.[66]

This type of constitutional dialogue is reflected in contemporary disputes over presidential power, such as the independent counsel created in 1978 as part of post-Watergate reforms. As discussed in Chapter 4, section 8, substantial questions were raised as to whether this office encroached upon the President's powers over appointments, removals, and law enforcement. The Supreme Court upheld the constitutionality of the independent counsel in *Morrison v. Olson* (1988),[67] but the elected branches retained the right to terminate the office at any time for any reason. *Morrison* did not command that the office exist. It merely announced that if the elected branches wanted to create such an office, it saw no constitutional objections. From 1978 to 1994, Presidents signed periodic reauthorizations while voicing constitutional concerns. They could have vetoed those bills—on both policy and constitutional grounds—but for political reasons signed them. Eventually, both elected branches in 1999 decided not to reauthorize the office.

Although classes in constitutional law at universities and law schools focus heavily on case law, some professors and practitioners recognize the important role played by the elected branches in shaping constitutional law. What emerges from studies over the years is the realization that no single institution, including the Supreme Court, has the final word on constitutional questions. Instead, courts engage in a continuing colloquy with the elected branches and society at large. The Court has a pattern of rethinking constitutional issues and reversing earlier holdings. At times that reflects a change in the Court's composition, but even without the addition of new Justices the Court may decide to break with its own rulings. There are also situations where the Court will decline to decide a constitutional issue, pushing it back to Presidents and lawmakers for resolution.[68]

66. United States v. Darby, 312 U.S. 100 (1941).

67. 478 U.S. 654 (1988).

68. WILLIAM G. ANDREWS, COORDINATE MAGISTRATES: CONSTITUTIONAL LAW BY CONGRESS AND THE PRESIDENT (1969); JOHN AGRESTO, THE SUPREME COURT AND CONSTITUTIONAL DEMOCRACY (1984); LOUIS FISHER, CONSTITUTIONAL DIALOGUES: INTERPRETATION AS POLITICAL PROCESS (1988); NEAL DEVINS, SHAPING CONSTITUTIONAL VALUES: ELECTED GOVERNMENT, THE SUPREME COURT, AND THE ABORTION DEBATE (1996); ROBERT A. KATZMANN, COURTS & CONGRESS (1997); COLTON C. CAMPBELL & JOHN F. STACK, JR., eds.,CONGRESS CONFRONTS THE COURT: THE STRUGGLE FOR LEGITIMACY AND AUTHORITY IN LAWMAKING (2001); MARK C. MILLER & JEB BARNES, eds., MAKING POLICY, MAKING LAW: AN INTERBRANCH PERSPECTIVE (2004); NEAL DEVINS & LOUIS FISHER, THE DEMOCRATIC CONSTITUTION (2004); J. MITCHELL PICKERILL, CONSTITUTIONAL DELIBERATION IN CONGRESS: THE IMPACT OF JUDICIAL REVIEW IN A SEPARATED SYSTEM (2004); NEAL DEVINS & KEITH E. WHITTINGTON, eds., CONGRESS AND THE CONSTITUTION (2005); CHARLES GARDNER GEYH, WHEN COURTS & CONGRESS COLLIDE: THE STRUGGLE FOR CONTROL OF AMERICA'S JUDICIAL SYSTEM (2006); LOUIS FISHER, THE SUPREME COURT AND CONGRESS: RIVAL INTERPRETATIONS (2009); BARRY FRIEDMAN, THE WILL OF THE PEOPLE: HOW PUBLIC OPINION HAS INFLUENCED THE SUPREME COURT AND SHAPED THE MEANING OF THE CONSTITUTION (2009); LOUIS FISHER & NEAL DEVINS, POLITICAL DYNAMICS OF CONSTITUTIONAL LAW (5th ed., 2011); and LOUIS FISHER, ON THE SUPREME COURT: WITHOUT ILLUSION AND IDOLATRY (2013).

# 4. ADVISORY OPINIONS

The federal judiciary decides cases through the adversary process, listening to litigants on each side of a dispute to reach an informed judgment. At times federal judges have been asked to provide advice in an extrajudicial setting. An advisory opinion is a legal interpretation that lacks binding effect. Some state courts render advisory opinions.[69] Federal courts, restricted to cases or controversies under Article III, should not, but the record has been quite mixed. Presidents, executive officials, and other parties attempt to seek the advice of Supreme Court Justices and federal judges about legal and political matters. Supposedly advisory opinions are barred at the federal level, but they survive in various forms.

At the Philadelphia convention, Charles Pinckney submitted a number of proposals to the Committee of Detail. In one, each house of Congress and the President "shall have authority to require the opinions of the supreme Judicial Court upon important questions of law, and upon solemn occasions."[70] No action was taken on his proposal. Delegates next considered creating a Council of State to assist the President "in conducting the Public affairs."[71] The Council included the heads of executive departments. The Chief Justice of the Supreme Court, as part of that council, "shall from time to time recommend such alterations of and additions to the laws of the U.S. as may in his opinion be necessary to the due administration of Justice, and such as may promote useful learning and inculcate sound morality throughout the Union."[72] In the absence of the President, the Chief Justice would preside over the Council.[73] The idea of a Council of State, or Privy Council, was debated but not adopted.[74] The draft constitution included language permitting the President to seek the written opinions of his department heads (Chapter 3, section 9).

In debating the authority of the Supreme Court to decide "cases or controversies" under Article III, Madison "doubted whether it was not going too far to extend the jurisdiction of the Court generally to cases arising under the Constitution, & whether it ought not to be limited to cases of a Judiciary Nature. The right of expounding the Constitution in cases not of this nature ought not to be given to that Department."[75] Efforts to distinguish between judicial and nonjudicial duties produced many controversies, not only in the early years of the republic but throughout its history, including presidential decisions to appoint Supreme Court Justices to participate in commissions regarding Pearl Harbor and the Kennedy assassination (Chapter 3, section 12C).

The administration of George Washington tested the boundaries of advisory opinions. In November 1790, Secretary of the Treasury Alexander Hamilton contacted Chief Justice John Jay about a pending legal dispute. Resolutions adopted by the Virginia House of Representatives challenged the constitutional authority of the national government to assume state debts.

---

69. Note, *Advisory Opinions on the Constitutionality of Statutes*, 69 HARV. L. REV. 1302 (1956).

70. 2 Farrand 341.

71. Id. at 342.

72. Id.

73. Id.

74. Id. at 367.

75. Id. at 430.

The resolutions objected that nothing in the U.S. Constitution expressly granted such action. Hamilton viewed this development as "the first symptom of a spirit which must either be killed or it will kill the Constitution of the United States."[76] He recommended that the "collective weight" of all three branches be marshaled to repudiate the resolutions.[77] In Jay's judgment, it was inadvisable to take the course Hamilton proposed. To treat the resolutions "as very important might render them more so than I think they are."[78] Every "indecent interference of State Assemblies will diminish their influence; the National Government has only to do what is right, and, if possible, be silent. If compelled to speak, it should be in few words, strongly evinced of temper, dignity and self-respect."[79]

In 1793, Secretary of State Thomas Jefferson sought legal advice from the Supreme Court regarding certain questions of international law and U.S. treaty obligations.[80] On this occasion, Chief Justice Jay wrote to President Washington on August 8, 1793, explaining why it was inappropriate for the Court to render advice to the executive branch. Jay referred to the constitutional system of the three branches checking each other and "our being judges of a court in the last resort."[81] Those considerations, he said, "afford strong arguments against the propriety of our extra-judicially deciding the questions alluded to...."[82] Additionally, Jay pointed to language in Article II that enabled the President to call on the heads of departments for opinions, which "seems to have been *purposely* as well as expressly united to the *executive* departments."[83] In closing, Jay said he was confident that Washington's "judgment will discern what is right, and that your usual prudence, decision, and firmness will surmount every obstacle to the preservation of the rights, peace, and dignity of the United States."[84]

During that same period, however, federal judges did not hesitate to advise the administration about matters they regarded as unconstitutional. One example is the Judiciary Act of 1789, which required Justices to perform not only as a high court but to "ride circuit" and participate as judges in the lower courts. The statute created circuit courts to meet twice a year in each district. Circuit courts consisted of any two Justices of the Supreme Court and one district judge.[85] On April 3, 1790, President Washington wrote to the Justices, inviting their thoughts about the judiciary.[86] They raised several objections about the statute. Riding circuit was an arduous and hazardous enterprise, requiring Justices to travel great distances over primitive roads. Moreover, participation in circuit courts might require a Justice to later review his own decision. Were the

---

76. 1 CHARLES WARREN, SUPREME COURT IN UNITED STATES HISTORY 52 (1937).

77. Id.

78. Id. at 53.

79. Id.

80. 3 THE CORRESPONDENCE AND PUBLIC PAPERS OF JOHN JAY 486–87 (Johnston ed., 1890).

81. Id. at 488.

82. Id.

83. Id. at 488–89 (emphases in original).

84. Id. at 489. See also Robert P. Dahlquist, *Advisory Opinions, Extrajudicial Activity and Judicial Advocacy: A Historical Perspective*, 14 SW. U. L. REV. 46, 58–62 (1983). For multiple occasions on which Chief Justice Jay was willing to advise on legal matters facing the Washington administration, including the Neutrality Proclamation of 1793, see WILLIAM R. CASTO, THE SUPREME COURT IN THE EARLY REPUBLIC 71-75 (1995).

85. 1 Stat. 73, 74, sec. 4 (1789).

86. Dahlquist, *supra* note 84, at 50–51.

Court to take and decide such cases, the Justices predicted that "the public confidence would diminish almost in proportion to the number of cases in which the Supreme Court might affirm acts of any of its members."[87]

All six Justices appealed to President Washington and Congress to reduce their labors. Congress offered modest relief in 1793 by requiring the attendance of only one Justice for the holding of circuit court.[88] One of the last acts of the Adams administration was to abolish these circuit courts, with its mixed membership, and create new circuit courts of appeal. As explained earlier, in section 2, the Jeffersonians repealed that statute and revived the practice of "riding circuit."

Another dispute over advisory opinions involved legislation in 1792 that authorized the payment of pensions to disabled war veterans. A circuit court would have to examine the nature of the wound, determine the cause of disability, and certify that an applicant be placed on the pension list.[89] The statute authorized the Secretary of War to reject certified applications if he "shall have cause to suspect imposition or mistake."[90] Judgments by federal judges were thus made subordinate to decisions by a department head. Circuit judges from New York, Pennsylvania, and North Carolina wrote to President Washington, setting forth reasons why this statutory procedure was unconstitutional. These letters were advisory opinions. The views expressed were not based on a specific litigated case covered by "cases or controversies" under Article III. Among the federal judges sitting on those circuit courts were five Justices of the Supreme Court: Jay, Cushing, Wilson, Blair, and Iredell.[91]

The letters to President Washington made two basic points. The duties assigned to circuit judges in certifying pensions were not "of a judicial nature."[92] Second, the statutory policy was unconstitutional because certifications agreed to by circuit courts were subject to review and reversal by the Secretary of War. Judges were reduced to making non-binding and non-final judgments, subject to the appellate review of an executive officer. Judicial certifications were treated as mere advisory opinions.[93] The issue reached the Court in the *Hayburn's Case* in 1792, but there was no need to decide the constitutional issue. The dispute became moot when Congress passed legislation to repeal the offending statutory provision.[94] The following year, the Court noted that the 1792 statute would have been unconstitutional if it sought to impose nonjudicial duties on the circuit courts.[95]

After settling this controversy, Congress continued to vest in federal judges a number of non-judicial and fact-finding duties far short of a case or controversy.[96] The Chief Justice was named a member of two administrative bodies, one to superintend the reduction of the Revolutionary War debt, the other to evaluate the quality of sample coins produced by the United States Mint.

---

87. Id. at 52.

88. 1 AMERICAN STATE PAPERS: MISCELLANEOUS 24, 52 (1834); 1 Stat.333, sec.1 (1793).

89. 1 Stat. 243, 244, sec. 2 (1792).

90. Id. at 244, sec. 4.

91. Dahlquist, *supra* note 84, at 55.

92. Id. at 56.

93. Id.

94. 1 Stat. 324 (1793); Hayburn's Case, 2 Dall. 409 (1792).

95. United States v. Yale Todd, 13 How. 52 (1794). This decision was not published until 1851.

96. Russell Wheeler, *Extrajudicial Activities of the Early Supreme Court*, 1973 SUP. CT. REV. 123, 131–35.

The Chief Justice served with other executive officials, including the Attorney General and the Secretaries of State and Treasury.[97] On numerous occasions, President Washington reached out to Chief Justice Jay for advice.[98] Of course, Jay accepted Washington's request that he travel to London to negotiate a treaty (Chapter 7, section 3B). Many Chief Justices and Justices maintained close associations with Presidents and cabinet heads, quite comfortable in visiting the White House and offering suggestions. Those who fostered this advisory relationship include Roger Taney, Robert Grier, Louis Brandeis, William Howard Taft, Harlan Fiske Stone, Fred Vinson, and Felix Frankfurter.[99] Other Justices, including James Byrnes and Abe Fortas, were heavily involved in congressional politics and provided advice to Presidents on appointments and other matters.[100]

The Supreme Court's formal position on advisory opinions appeared in 1911. Congress had authorized certain Indians to bring suit to determine the constitutionality of a statute. Justice Day reviewed earlier instances in which federal judges concluded that Congress could not impose nonjudicial duties on the courts. The suit, as authorized by Congress, did not create a case or controversy between adverse parties. The Court held it was inappropriate for the judiciary "to give opinions in the nature of advice concerning legislative action, a function never conferred upon it by the Constitution and against the exercise of which this court has steadily set its face from the beginning."[101]

Nevertheless, in the course of writing an opinion, judges often include dicta to advise executive and legislative officers. In 1978, Justice Stevens warned against the practice of offering advisory opinions: "We are not statesmen; we are judges. When it is necessary to resolve a constitutional issue in the adjudication of an actual case or controversy, it is our duty to do so. But whenever we are persuaded by reasons of expediency to engage in the business of giving legal advice, we chip away a part of the foundation of our independence and our strength."[102] A year later, Justice Stevens and three colleagues accused the members of the Court of rendering an advisory opinion for the state of Massachusetts. In defense, Justice Powell explained that his decision merely provided "some guidance" for state lawmakers. This exchange took place in two intriguing footnotes.[103] In 1994, a concurrence by Justice O'Connor offered suggestions to New York State on how to create a school district for a religious minority without running into constitutional problems.[104] Justices may decide to express concerns about broad legislative language in a manner that encourages Congress to revisit a statute and clarify it.[105]

---

97. Id. at 140–44.

98. Id. at 144–55.

99. WALTER MURPHY, ELEMENTS OF JUDICIAL STRATEGY 147–55 (1964).

100. Robert B. McKay, *The Judiciary and Nonjudicial Activities*, 35 LAW & CONTEMP. PROB. 9, 27–36 (1970).

101. Muskrat v. United States, 219 U.S. 346, 362 (1911).

102. Duke Power Co. v. Carolina Environmental Study Group, 438 U.S. 59, 103 (1978) (Stevens, J., concurring).

103. Bellotti v. Baird, 443 U.S. 622, 651–52 n.32 (1979) (Powell, J., opinion), 656 n.4 (Stevens, J., concurring, joined by Brennan, J., Marshall, J., and Blackmun, J.).

104. Board of Ed. of Kiryas Joel v. Grumet, 512 U.S. 687, 717 (1994) (O'Connor, J., concurring).

105. Brogan v. United States, 522 U.S. 398, 408–18 (1998) (Ginsburg, J., concurring, joined by Souter, J.). For contemporary examples of judicial advisory opinions: LOUIS FISHER & KATY J. HARRIGER, AMERICAN CONSTITUTIONAL LAW 77-78, 80 (10th ed., 2013).

# 5. NOMINATING JUDGES

Subjecting federal judges to presidential nomination and Senate advice and consent creates an intensely political process, opening the door to influence by public officials, private parties, and the press.[106] What qualifications do Presidents take into account when nominating Justices and lower court judges? In 1970, President Nixon insisted that constitutional philosophy was an appropriate factor for him to consider but not for the Senate. He advised Senator William Saxbe about the "constitutional responsibility of the President to appoint members of the Court and whether this responsibility can be frustrated by those who wish to substitute their own philosophy or their own subjective judgment for that of the one person entrusted by the Constitution with the power of appointment."[107]

His statement raises two issues. First, why should Presidents have the right to reflect on philosophy and make subjective judgments but not Senators? Second, the power of appointment is not granted to the President. It is shared with the Senate. At times Senators will agree with Nixon that "the ideology of the nominee is the responsibility of the President," whereas the Senate should focus "solely upon grounds of qualifications."[108] However, both branches have legitimate reasons to evaluate a nominee's "ideology," which is a broad word encompassing beliefs, theories, assertions, and ideas. Political and legal orientations may be grounds for a President—and the Senate—to find someone unacceptable for a judicial post, including a Supreme Court Justice.

When the Senate rejected Clement Haynsworth for Associate Justice in 1969, the *Washington Post* criticized opponents whose votes seemed "ideological."[109] If ideology is a permissible consideration for a President, it is permissible for the Senate. Not only Haynsworth but other nominees have failed to gain confirmation as Justices because of their ideology, constitutional philosophy, and socioeconomic views. Over the last century, the names include John J. Parker in 1930 (rejected), Abe Fortas in 1968 (filibustered on an attempted elevation to Chief Justice), G. Harrold Carswell in 1970 (rejected), and Robert Bork in 1987 (rejected).[110] Other potential nominees to the Court were withdrawn by the White House because of likely defeat in the Senate: Homer Thornberry in 1968, Douglas Ginsburg in 1987, and Harriet Miers in 2005.[111]

---

106. Lee Epstein & Jeffrey A. Segal, Advice and Consent: The Politics of Judicial Appointments (2005).

107. Sollenberger, *supra* note 31, at 97.

108. Letter from Senator Marlow W. Cook, Oct. 21, 1969, cited by A. Mitchell McConnell, Jr., *Haynesworth and Carswell: A New Senate Standard of Excellence*, 59 Ky. L.J. 7, 15 (1970).

109. Id. at 20.

110. See Paul A. Freund, *Appointment of Justices: Some Historical Perspectives*, 10 Harv. L. Rev. 1146 (1988), and William F. Swindler, *The Politics of "Advice and Consent,"* 56 Am. Bar Ass'n J. 533 (1970).

111. For general studies on presidential nominations to the Supreme Court: Henry J. Abraham, Justices, Presidents, and Senators: A History of the U.S. Supreme Court Appointments from Washington to Bush II (2007); Epstein & Segal, *supra* note 106; Jeffrey K. Tulis, *Constitutional Abdication: The Senate, the President, and Appointments to the Supreme Court*, 47 Case W. Res. L. Rev. 1331(1997); Mark Silverstein, Judicious Choices: The New Politics of Supreme Court Appointments (1994); and John Massaro, Supremely Political: The Role of Ideology and Presidential Management in Unsuccessful Supreme Court Nominations (1990).

The American Bar Association (ABA) performs a role in evaluating potential judicial nominees. Its influence increased during the Truman administration when it established a special committee to judge the professional qualifications of candidates submitted to it by the Justice Department.[112] ABA screening reached a point in the Eisenhower administration where opposition by the bar functioned as a near veto power over judicial candidates. Subsequent Presidents refused to give ABA the power to block candidates. Presidents insisted that their constitutional authority to nominate could not be diminished simply because the ABA decided a candidate was "not qualified."[113] In 2001, the Bush White House advised the ABA that it would no longer receive advance notice of judicial nominees.[114] The Senate Judiciary Committee continued to rely on ABA evaluations. In 2009, President Obama agreed to submit names to the ABA before issuing a judicial nominee to the Senate.[115]

The ABA has recognized that its capacity to evaluate nominees for the Supreme Court is much less than for lower courts. Lawrence Walsh, who served as chairman of the ABA Standing Committee on Federal Judiciary, explained that with the lower courts the Committee had time to investigate and interview judges and lawyers and to report to the Attorney General whether a prospective nominee was "not qualified," "qualified," "well qualified," or "exceptionally well qualified." With Supreme Court nominations, the Committee had at most 24 hours notice and often no notice at all.[116] The Committee said it did not attempt to express a view on political and ideological factors that might "dominate the question of confirmation."[117]

In 1989, the Supreme Court received a challenge to ABA's participation in the nomination process. The ABA had refused a request from a foundation for the names and potential nominees it was considering and for its reports and meetings of its meetings. The request was brought under the Federal Advisory Committee Act (FACA). After a district court decided that applying FACA to the ABA would unconstitutionally infringe on the President's Article II authority to nominate federal judges and would violate the principle of separation of powers, the Supreme Court held that FACA did not apply to ABA's advisory relationship.[118]

President Carter altered the selection process for appellate judges by establishing nominating panels. They were directed to recommend five candidates for each vacancy, with the President selecting one from the list. The announced purpose was to ensure that judges were selected on the basis of merit, not politics, but political considerations can never be eliminated. Part of Carter's reason for creating the panels was to increase the number of women and minorities, which was itself a political objective.[119] Politics entered in other ways, such as the practice of panels devising litmus tests for potential nominees. They would be asked questions about

112. JOEL B. GROSSMAN, LAWYERS AND JUDGES: THE ABA AND THE POLITICS OF JUDICIAL SELECTION (1965). See also HAROLD W. CHASE, FEDERAL JUDGES: THE APPOINTING PROCESS (1972).

113. SOLLENBERGER, *supra* note 31, at 81.

114. Neil A. Lewis & David Johnston, *Bush Would Sever Law Group's Role in Screening Judges*, N.Y. TIMES, March 17, 2001, at A1; Neil A. Lewis, *White House Ends Bar Association's Role in Screening Federal Judges*, N.Y. TIMES, March 23, 2001, at A13.

115. SOLLENBERGER, *supra* note 31, at 82.

116. Lawrence E. Walsh, *Selection of Supreme Court Justices*, 56 AM. BAR ASS'N J. 555, 556 (1970).

117. Id. at 558.

118. Public Citizen v. Department of Justice, 491 U.S. 440 (1989).

119. CORNELL W. CLAYTON, THE POLITICS OF JUSTICE: THE ATTORNEY GENERAL AND THE MAKING OF LEGAL POLICY 63 (1992).

specific policy issues.[120] Administrations developed their own inventory of preferred ideologies. If a panel declined to include a particular name, a Senator could intervene to request the administration to ignore the panel's list and nominate the Senator's choice.[121] As part of an accommodation, Senators retained their power to recommend district judges. Some Senators decided to set up their own panels. When President Reagan took office, he abolished the judicial nominating commissions for appellate judges.[122] Subsequent administrations followed a variety of practices, relying on screening committees or panels, recommendations from the state bar or lawyers associations, and procedures developed by Senators.

To ensure that names finally selected as judicial nominees can be confirmed, the Justice Department and the White House regularly consult with Congress, especially the Senate Judiciary Committee. Failure to consult may be costly: "resourceful senators may exercise a near absolute control over the fate of judicial positions in their states."[123] The same methods used for the general appointment process—including filibusters, blue slips, and holds—apply to judicial nominees (Chapter 4, section 5C).[124] The Senate Judiciary Committee conducts an extensive investigation into each nominee to the courts. The committee provides nominees with a questionnaire that probes the candidate's qualifications, including a financial disclosure report to provide information on income, assets, and liabilities.[125] The committee relies on documents it receives from the White House, Justice Department, and FBI. Until the committee receives those documents, including materials that are highly confidential, it will not act.[126] Often the press uncovers important information about the qualifications (or not) about a judicial nominee.[127]

During his time as Associate Justice, William Rehnquist wrote about presidential appointments to the Supreme Court. He spoke about the need for judicial independence and the President's constitutional authority, but added this qualification: "When a vacancy occurs on the Court, it is entirely appropriate that that vacancy be filled by the President, responsible to a national constituency, as advised by the Senate, whose members are responsible to regional constituencies. Thus, public opinion has some say in who shall become Justices of the Supreme Court."[128] In that article, he said that Justices should be "independent of popular opinion when deciding the particular cases or controversies that come before them."[129] Independence need not mean being unaware. Elsewhere, when writing about the Steel Seizure Case of 1952, Rehnquist said, "the tide of public opinion suddenly began to run against" the Truman administration, and "for a number of reasons...[that] tide of public opinion had a considerable influence on the Court."[130] As law clerk to Justice Jackson that year, he was well placed to make that judgment.

---

120. Id. at 64.

121. Id.

122. Id.

123. Sollenberger, *supra* note 31, at 83.

124. Id. at 99–104, 129–53.

125. Id. at 106–09.

126. Id. at 109–11.

127. Nina Totenberg, *The Confirmation Process and the Public: To Know or Not to Know*, 101 Harv. L. Rev. 1213 (1988).

128. William H. Rehnquist, *Presidential Appointments to the Supreme Court*, 2 Const. Comment. 319, 320 (1985).

129. Id.

130. William H. Rehnquist, The Supreme Court: How It Was, How It Is 95 (1987).

Rehnquist analyzed the capacity of Presidents (long before Franklin D. Roosevelt) "to pack the Supreme Court." He said, "like murder suspects in a detective novel, [they] must have both motive and opportunity."[131] Rehnquist reviewed the success of President Lincoln in appointing Justices who would support his political objectives. In *The Prize Cases* (1863), which upheld Lincoln's blockade of the South, all three of his nominees to the Court (Noah Swayne, David Davis, and Samuel F. Miller) supported this wartime initiative. Along with Justices Wayne and Grier, they made up a majority. Rehnquist concluded it "seems obvious that this case would have been decided the other way had the same Justices been on the Court who had decided the *Dred Scott* case six years earlier."[132] Lincoln's appointments thus worked in his favor. In *Ex parte Milligan* (1866),[133] decided after his assassination, his nominees split on the question of a President's authority to use military commissions instead of civil trial.[134]

Highly instructive are the Court's decisions on the constitutionality of "greenback legislation" to finance the Civil War. Lincoln had named Salmon P. Chase, his Secretary of the Treasury, as Chief Justice in part to uphold this statute.[135] Yet in *Hepburn v. Griswold* (1870),[136] Chase wrote for the Court that the legislation was unconstitutional. Field, a Lincoln appointee, joined Chase. The other three Lincoln choices—Miller, Swayne, and Davis—dissented. Rehnquist described this decision as "a textbook example of the proposition that one may look at a legal question differently as a judge than one did as a member of the executive branch."[137]

Rehnquist did not complete the greenback story, which later embarrassed the Court. In 1870, a 4-3 Court declared that it was unconstitutional for Congress to treat paper money as legal tender to discharge prior debts. Justice Grier's retirement and the authorization by Congress the previous year of a new Justice allowed President Grant to appoint two new members. The Senate confirmed his second nominee, Edwin Stanton, but he died four days later. Grant had reason to believe his next two appointments would support the statute. William Strong, a member of the Supreme Court of Pennsylvania, had already sustained the Legal Tender Act.[138] Joseph P. Bradley appeared to be no less sympathetic.[139] Fifteen months after the statute had been declared unconstitutional, a reconstituted Court upheld the statute by a 5-4 margin. Strong and Bradley joined the three original dissenters to form a majority. The four Justices who had decided the case in 1870 were now in the minority.[140]

The public received another reminder that the Constitution means not what it says but what those on the Court say it means. In a book published in 1936, Chief Justice Charles Evans Hughes spoke of "three notable instances the Court has suffered severely from self-inflicted

131. Rehnquist, *supra* note 128, at 322.

132. Id. at 323.

133. 71 U.S. (4 Wall.) 2 (1866).

134. Rehnquist, *supra* note 128, at 323.

135. Brian McGinty, Lincoln and the Court 233–34 (2008).

136. 75 U.S. (8 Wall.) 603 (1870).

137. Rehnquist, *supra* note 128, at 324.

138. McGinty, *supra* note 135, at 283.

139. Charles Fairman, *Mr. Justice Bradley's Appointment to the Supreme Court and the Legal Tender Cases*, 54 Harv. L. Rev. 1128, 1131 (1941). See also Sidney Ratner, *Was the Supreme Court Packed by President Grant?*, 50 Pol. Sci. Q. 343 (1935).

140. Legal Tender Cases, 12 Wall. (79 U.S.) 457 (1871).

wounds."[141] The first, he said, was *Dred Scott* in 1857, a decision he called "a public calamity" that "undermined confidence in the Court." It was "many years before the Court, even under new judges, was able to retrieve its reputation."[142] The second example that "brought the Court into disesteem" were the legal tender cases.[143] Invalidation in the first case, followed by validation in the second, "caused widespread criticism." The "overruling in such a short time, and by one vote, of the previous decision shook popular respect for the court."[144]

Hughes described a third self-inflicted wound: the two income tax cases in 1895. In the first, the Court held that the tax on rents or income of real estate was a direct tax and violated the Constitution by not following the apportionment rule.[145] In that case, the Court split 4 to 4 on the constitutionality of the income tax. Justice Howell E. Jackson, who was ill and did not participate in the first case, voted to sustain the income tax. That should have created a 5 to 4 decision upholding the income tax, but the Court voted 5 to 4 to strike it down.[146] Obviously one Justice switched his vote. Who he was and why he switched was not disclosed. Hughes wrote: "There can be no objection to a conscientious judge changing his vote, but the decision of such an important question by a majority of one after one judge had changed his vote aroused a criticism of the Court which has never been entirely stilled."[147] Public support for a federal income tax resulted in the Sixteenth Amendment.

# 6. RECESS APPOINTMENTS

The Framers understood that when the Senate is not in session to give advice and consent, the President may need to make recess appointments. There have been ongoing struggles by all three branches to define the scope of that power in Article II, section 2 (Chapter 4, section 6). The use of recess appointments for federal judges, however, has significant implications for judicial independence. Beginning with George Washington, Presidents have invoked their recess appointment power many times to place individuals on the courts. The practice attracted special attention when President Eisenhower unilaterally placed three individuals on the Supreme Court: Earl Warren, William Brennan, and Potter Stewart. Warren's appointment as Chief Justice occurred on October 2, 1953. He took his seat three days later and received Senate confirmation for a lifetime term on March 1, 1954. The recess appointments of Justices Brennan and Stewart in 1956 and 1958 followed a similar path. Brennan took his seat one day after the recess appointment and was confirmed by the Senate on March 19, 1957. Stewart took his seat on the same day as the recess appointment, on October 14, 1958, and was confirmed on

---

141. Charles Evans Hughes, The Supreme Court of the United States: Its Foundation, Methods, and Achievements: An Interpretation 50 (1936).

142. Id. at 50–51.

143. Id. at 51.

144. Id. at 52.

145. Pollock v. Farmers' Loan & Trust Co., 157 U.S. 429 (1895).

146. Pollock v. Farmers' Loan and Trust Co., 158 U.S. 601, 637 (1895).

147. Hughes, *supra* note 141, at 54.

May 5, 1959. All three joined the Court and participated in decisions before the Senate had an opportunity to review their credentials.

These presidential initiatives raised serious issues. During the time the three nominees served in a recess capacity, they lacked the lifetime term that ensures judicial independence. Their decisions and opinions during that period would be reviewed by the President and White House aides in deciding to nominate them for a full term. The Senate would scrutinize those rulings during the confirmation process. In anticipation of presidential and Senate actions, would a recess nominee calculate that certain decisions and opinions might raise concerns in the White House and the Senate? Would they revise initial drafts to maximize the prospect of a lifetime term?[148] Litigants are entitled to have their case heard and decided by federal judges with full independence. They lack that confidence with recess appointees.

The House of Representatives, without a formal role in the confirmation process, released a study in 1959 raising objections to appointing federal judges on a recess basis.[149] In 1960, Senator Philip Hart introduced a resolution to discourage reliance on recess appointments for judicial positions. As a Senate resolution, it would have no legally binding effect but was meant to send a strong signal to Presidents and the Senate. Some Senators objected to Hart's resolution, insisting that Presidents need to exercise the constitutional power of recess appointments to relieve the heavy workload of federal courts. They also objected to the lack of Senate hearings. The Senate passed the resolution 48 to 37, essentially along party lines, with Democrats favoring it more than Republicans.[150] The resolution, after a preamble that details the disadvantages of making recess appointments to the Supreme Court, reads as follows:

> *Resolved*, That it is the sense of the Senate that the making of recess appointments to the Supreme Court of the United States may not be wholly consistent with the best interests of the Supreme Court, the nominee who may be involved, the litigants before the Court, nor indeed the people of the United States, and that such appointments, therefore, should not be made except under unusual circumstances and for the purpose of preventing or ending a demonstrable breakdown in the administration of the Court's business.

Although legally nonbinding, the resolution has had its intended effect. No President since Eisenhower has made a recess appointment to the Supreme Court. They have, however, used that authority for the lower courts. In 1962, the Second Circuit upheld Eisenhower's recess appointment of a district court judge.[151] In 1983, however, a panel of the Ninth Circuit ruled that presidential authority to make recess appointments could not supplant the lifetime tenure guaranteed to judges by Article III. Federal judges serving under a recess appointment lacked the independence required by the Constitution. A judge receiving a commission under the Recess

---

148. Scott E. Graves & Robert M. Howard, Justice Takes a Recess: Judicial Recess Appointments from George Washington to George W. Bush (2009).

149. House Committee on the Judiciary, *Recess Appointments of Federal Judges*, 86th Cong., 1st Sess. (Comm. Print, January 1959). See Note, *Recess Appointments to the Supreme Court—Constitutional But Unwise?*, 10 Stan. L. Rev. 124 (1957).

150. 106 Cong. Rec. 18145 (1960). See S. Rep. No. 1893, 86th Cong., 2d Sess. (1960).

151. United States v. Allocco, 305 F.2d 704 (2d Cir. 1962), cert. denied, 371 U.S. 964 (1963). Comments, *A New Look at Recess Appointments to the Federal Judiciary—United States v. Allocco*, 12 Cath. U. L. Rev. 29 (1963).

Appointment Clause "may be called upon to make politically charged decisions while his nomination awaits approval by popularly elected officials. Such a judge will scarcely be oblivious to
the effect his decision may have on the vote of these officials."[152]

The Ninth Circuit, sitting en banc, reversed the three-judge panel. Divided 7 to 4, the court
held there was no reason to favor the constitutional provision for lifetime tenure for federal
judges over the constitutional provision for recess appointments. It pointed out that Presidents
had been making judicial recess appointments ever since 1789, totaling approximately 300
appointments. Acknowledging that historical acceptance alone cannot conclusively establish
constitutionality, the court decided that the recess provision to appoint federal judges "has been
inextricably woven into the fabric of our nation."[153] The dissenters denied the permanence of this
pattern, noting that with one exception (the appointment prompting this case), federal courts
had functioned since 1964 without the assistance of recess appointees.[154]

The exception involved District Judge Walter M. Heen of Hawaii. He was recess appointed
by President Carter on December 31, 1980, almost two months after Carter lost to Ronald
Reagan. As a U.S. Attorney, Heen knew he would be out of a job in the next administration and
thought it was a good idea to help out on the district court. Later he regarded his decision as
"an exercise in futility" when "you know you're not going to be around."[155] After serving about
11 months as a federal judge, he was appointed to the state's appeals court and sat on the state's
Supreme Court.[156]

President Clinton made several recess appointments to federal courts. Initial selections were
not to Article III courts with lifetime terms. In December 1997, he made a recess appointment of
Christine Odell Cook Miller to the U.S. Court of Federal Claims. Her previous term by President
Reagan had expired and Clinton appointed her to a second term.[157] In January 2001, he recess
appointed Sarah L. Wilson to be a judge of the U.S. Court of Federal Claims, which has a term
of 15 years. Questions were raised whether she could be paid under the provisions of 5 U.S.C.
§ 5503, but the Administrative Office of the United States Courts determined she could be paid
under one of the exceptions identified in that statute.[158]

On December 27, 2000, President Clinton made a recess appointment of Roger L. Gregory
to the Fourth Circuit, the first time since 1980 that a President had named an Article III judge

---

152. United States v. Woodley, 726 F.2d 1328, 1330 (9th Cir. 1983).

153. United States v. Woodley, 751 F.2d 1008, 1012 (9th Cir. 1985), cert. denied, 475 U.S. 1048 (1986).

154. Id. at 1024. See Steven M. Pyser, *Recess Appointments to the Federal Judiciary: An Unconstitutional
Transformation of Senate Advice and Consent*, 8 U. Pa. J. Const. L. 61 (2006); Edward A. Hartnett, *Recess
Appointments of Article III Judges: Three Constitutional Questions*, 26 Cardozo L. Rev. 377 (2005); Michael
Herz, *Abandoning Recess Appointments?: A Comment on Hartnett (and Others)*, 26 Cardozo L. Rev. 443
(2005); William Ty Mayton, *Recess Appointments and an Independent Judiciary*, 20 Const. Comment. 515
(2003–2004); Paul Ferris Solomon, *Answering the Unasked Question: Can Recess Appointees Constitutionally
Exercise the Judicial Power of the United States?*, 54 U. Cinn. L. Rev. 631 (1985); Virginia L. Richards, *Temporary
Appointments to the Federal Judiciary: Article II Judges?*, 60 N.Y.U. L. Rev. 702 (1985); and Thomas A. Curtis,
*Recess Appointments to Article III Courts: The Use of Historical Practice in Constitutional Interpretation*, 84
Colum. L. Rev. 1758 (1984).

155. Al Kamen, *Recess Appointee Says It's Not a Great Idea*, Wash. Post, Nov. 8, 1999, at A19.

156. Id.

157. White House Press Release, *President Clinton Appoints Christine O. C. Miller to the Court of Federal Claims*,
Dec. 10, 1997.

158. Letter from William R. Burchill, Jr., Associate Director and General Counsel, Administrative Office of the
United States Courts, to Senator Strom Thurmond, May 24, 2001.

as a recess appointee.[159] President Bush submitted Gregory's name on May 9, 2001, for a lifetime appointment and the Senate approved, 93 to 1.[160] Bush made two other recess appointments to the federal courts early in 2004: Charles W. Pickering for the Fifth Circuit and William H. Pryor for the Eleventh Circuit. When Pickering's recess appointment expired he announced he would not seek a lifetime position.[161] His appointment came between the first and second sessions of the 108th Congress and was thus an intersession action.

Pryor's appointment was intrasession during a short Senate recess (February 12 to February 23, 2004). Of the more than 300 recess appointments to Article III courts, only 14 have been intrasession.[162] The Senate recessed 145 days for one appointee, 112 days for two, 79 days for two, 73 days for one, 64 days for three, 35 days for four, and only ten days for Pryor.[163] The distinction between intersession and intrasession session has a practical effect. Someone who receives an intersession appointment serves until the end of the next session, about a year or slightly more. An individual with an intrasession appointment made early during a session serves close to two years. Litigation to disqualify Pryor because he sat as a recess appointee was unsuccessful.[164]

The Senate could protect itself from judicial recess appointments by establishing a clear policy that individuals placed on the bench by that process will serve out their interim term and be ineligible for confirmation. Under that policy, if the President submitted their names for a lifetime appointment, the Senate Judiciary Committee would take no action. At the end of a Congress, the names would be returned to the White House. This publicly announced legislative policy would send a clear message to Presidents that circumvention of the Senate would have limited effect. Presidents and their aides could then decide whether it is worth the laborious process of completing background checks on nominees and interviewing them, merely to have judges serve for brief periods. The disruption to federal courts of short-term judges is substantial, in part because they might be involved in cases they cannot complete before their recess appointment ends. Their departure leaves a vacancy that takes time to fill. Nominees asked to accept a recess appointment should understand that lifetime tenure will be denied them, perhaps casting an unfavorable light on their professional careers. Under these conditions, individuals asked if they would like to leave their current position to serve a year or so as a federal judge may decide to decline the offer.

The validity of most recess appointments has been questioned by *Noel Canning v. NLRB*, an exceptionally broad opinion issued by the D.C. Circuit on January 25, 2013. It held that recess appointments may be made only between one session and another (not within a session) and only if a vacancy arises during that period (Chapter 4, section 6A).

---

159. Henry B. Hogue, *Recess Appointments to Article III Courts*, 34 Pres. Stud. Q. 656, 659 (2004).

160. Sollenberger, *supra* note 31, at 40.

161. Id.

162. Id. at 670.

163. Id.

164. Evans v. Stephens, 387 F.3d 1220 (11th Cir. 2004), cert. denied, 544 U.S. 942 (2005), but see separate statement by Justice Stevens at 544 U.S. 942–43 (2005). See also Sollenberger, *supra* note 31, at 38–43.

# 7. FDR'S COURT-PACKING

Congress has altered the number of Justices on the Supreme Court several times throughout its history. It authorized six Justices in 1789, lowered it to five in 1801, returned to six a year later, and increased the size of the Court in subsequent years to keep pace with the creation of new circuits. From 1869 to the present the number of Justices has remained fixed at nine. An effort by President Franklin D. Roosevelt in 1937 to add up to six Justices to the Supreme Court provoked intense debate in all three branches and the public about the independence of the judiciary.

In his inaugural address on March 4, 1933, President Roosevelt spoke confidently about presidential-judicial relations. He said the Constitution "is so simple and practical that it is possible always to meet extraordinary needs by changes in emphasis and arrangements without loss of essential form."[165] Privately, he tempered public optimism with the knowledge that most members of the Supreme Court were conservative, business-oriented, and unsympathetic to his political orientation. Given the composition of the Court, it was unlikely to be receptive to many of the reform measures designed to cope with the Great Depression.

On May 27, 1935, known as "Black Monday," the Supreme Court unanimously struck down the National Industrial Recovery Act (NIRA), Roosevelt's program for bringing about economic recovery (Chapter 4, section 11C).[166] On the same day, it ruled that Presidents could remove members of independent regulatory commissions only by following the statutory grounds for removal (Chapter 3, section 7C).[167] The Court also invalidated a statute for the relief of farm mortgagors.[168] Roosevelt wondered why liberal members of the Court had abandoned him: "Well, where was Ben Cardozo? And what about old Isaiah [Louis Brandeis]?"[169] The public reacted unfavorably to Roosevelt's sneering accusation at a press conference that the Justices had adopted a "horse-and-buggy definition of interstate commerce."[170]

## A. *The proposal*

At a cabinet meeting in December 1935, Roosevelt reviewed his options. The notion of packing the Court, Interior Secretary Harold Ickes recorded in his diary, "was a distasteful idea."[171] A month later, the Court struck down the processing tax in the Agricultural Adjustment Act. The decision divided the Court, 6 to 3. In a stinging dissent, Justice Stone deplored the Court's "tortured construction of the Constitution" and reminded the other Justices that they were not "the only agency of government that must be assumed to have capacity to govern."[172]

---

165. Arthur M. Schlesinger, Jr. & Fred L. Israel, eds., My Fellow Citizens: The Inaugural Addresses of the Presidents of the United States, 1789–2009, at 286 (2010).

166. Schechter Corp. v. United States, 295 U.S. 495 (1935).

167. Humphrey's Executor v. United States, 295 U.S. 602 (1935).

168. Louisville Bank v. Radford, 295 U.S. 555 (1935).

169. William E. Leuchtenburg, *The Origins of Franklin D. Roosevelt's "Court-Packing" Plan*, 1966 Sup. Ct. Rev. 347, 357.

170. Id. at 357–58.

171. 1 The Secret Diary of Harold L. Ickes 495 (1953).

172. United States v. Butler, 297 U.S. 1, 87 (1936).

Other decisions in 1936, striking down federal and state laws, supplied extra incentives for Roosevelt to curb the Court. Some of the rulings attracted three or four dissents.[173] Roosevelt's landslide victory in 1936, capturing all but two states, prepared what seemed to him the political foundation to challenge the Court. He regarded constitutional amendments as wholly impracticable. They were difficult to frame and extremely difficult to pass. Statutory remedies, such as requiring more than a majority of the Court to invalidate legislation, were of doubtful constitutionality. After eliminating a number of alternatives, Roosevelt selected court packing as the only feasible remedy.

Working closely with Attorney General Homer Cummings and Solicitor General Stanley Reed, but without the advice of congressional leaders, Roosevelt ordered preparation of a draft bill. The President would be authorized to nominate Justices to the Supreme Court whenever an incumbent over the age of 70 declined to retire or resign. The same procedure would apply to the lower federal courts, with additional appointments limited to 50. The maximum size of the Supreme Court would be 15. Under this proposal, Roosevelt could name as many as six new Justices to the Court.[174]

When Roosevelt submitted his proposal to Congress on February 5, 1937, he attempted to disguise it primarily as an economy and efficiency measure. Additional Justices and judges would help relieve the delay and congestion he claimed resulted from aged or infirm judges.[175] What some called his "indirection" (a euphemism for deception and deviousness) offended some potential supporters.[176] A month later, Roosevelt revealed his real intent: to pack the Court with liberal Justices who would support his public policies. In a "fireside chat" on March 9, 1937, he told the country he wanted a Court that "will enforce the Constitution as written."[177] But a mechanical application of that document by six additional Justices would not automatically alleviate the problems Roosevelt faced.

Later in that address he spoke of the need "to infuse new blood into all our Courts." He called for judges "who will bring to the Courts a present-day sense of the Constitution."[178] Was he recommending the Constitution as written in 1787 or as applied in 1937? He wanted "new and younger blood...younger men who have had personal experience and contact with modern facts and circumstances under which average men have to live and work." His plan, he said, would "save our national Constitution from hardening of the judicial arteries."[179] Roosevelt

---

173. Jones v. SEC, 298 U.S. 1 (1936) (Cardozo, J., Brandeis, J., and Stone, J. dissenting); St. Joseph Stock Yards Co. v. United States, 298 U.S. 38 (1936) (Cardozo, J., Brandeis, J., Stone, J. dissenting); Carter v. Carter Coal Co., 298 U.S 238 (1936) (Hughes, C.J., Cardozo, J., Brandeis, J., Stone, J. disagreeing in part with the Court); Morehead v. New York ex rel. Tipaldo, 298 U.S. 587 (1936) (Hughes, C.J., Brandeis, J., Stone, J., Cardozo, J. dissenting).

174. WILLIAM E. LEUCHTENBURG, THE SUPREME COURT REBORN: THE CONSTITUTIONAL REVOLUTION IN THE AGE OF ROOSEVELT 108–31 (1995). For documents on FDR's court-packing plan: 3 Goldsmith 1953-2004.

175. 6 PUBLIC PAPERS AND ADDRESSES OF FRANKLIN D. ROOSEVELT, 1937 Volume, at 35–50 (1941).

176. FDR's proposal "lacked the simplicity and clarity which was the President's genius and, to men not learned in the procedures of the Court, much of it seemed technical and confusing....the plan never lived down its initial indirection." ROBERT H. JACKSON, THE STRUGGLE FOR JUDICIAL SUPREMACY 189, 191 (1941).

177. 6 PUBLIC PAPERS AND ADDRESSES OF FRANKLIN D. ROOSEVELT, 1937 volume, 126 (1941).

178. Id. at 127.

179. Id. at 127-28.

pledged to appoint Justices "who will not undertake to override the judgment of the Congress on legislative policy."[180] His reform promised "a reinvigorated, liberal-minded Judiciary."[181]

Roosevelt denied he was "seeking to 'pack' the Supreme Court."[182] If by that phrase was meant placing "on the bench spineless puppets who would disregard the law and would decide specific cases as I wished them to be decided, I make this answer: that no President fit for his office would appoint, and no Senate of honorable men fit for their office would confirm, that kind of appointees to the Supreme Court." But the phrase appeared to mean he would ask the Senate to confirm Justices who "understand modern conditions" and would not reverse the judgment of Congress on legislative policy, a result he said he and "the vast majority of the American people favor doing just that thing—now."[183]

## B. Senate repudiation

The Senate Judiciary Committee held hearings on Roosevelt's bill from March 10 to April 23, 1937. Attorney General Cummings testified first, defending the proposal. He was followed by Robert H. Jackson, Assistant Attorney General, public and private attorneys, academic experts, and Senator Burton K. Wheeler, who testified that the administration "did not take into its confidence any of the members of the Committee on the Judiciary or the leaders among either the Democrats or Progressives."[184]

During the course of the hearings, the committee received from Chief Justice Hughes a letter of March 21 that discredited Roosevelt's claim that the judiciary was behind in its work and needed additional judges. Hughes reported that the Court "is fully abreast of its work" and provided statistics to document his statement. He also said that increasing the number of Justices on the Court, "apart from any question of policy, which I do not discuss, would not promote the efficiency of the Court." He believed it would "impair that efficiency so long as the Court acts as a unit." There would be more judges to hear, more judges to confer and discuss, and more judges to be convinced and decide.[185]

The Senate Judiciary Committee, heavily controlled by Democrats, issued a report that denounced Roosevelt's proposal. The report methodically shredded the bill's premises, structures, content, and motivation. The purpose behind this legislative indictment appeared to be a desire to so pulverize Roosevelt's recommendation that no President in the future would attempt to revive it. In the first of six reasons to reject the plan, the committee bluntly noted: "the bill does not accomplish any of the objectives for which it was originally offered."[186] The committee observed that the courts "with the oldest judges have the best records in the disposition of business."[187] The bill called for retirement only of judges who had served for ten years (penalizing

---

180. Id. at 129.

181. Id. at 133.

182. Id. at 128.

183. Id. at 129.

184. *Reorganization of the Federal Judiciary* (Part 3), hearings before the Senate Committee on the Judiciary, 75th Cong., 1st Sess. 486 (1937).

185. Id. at 488, 491.

186. S. Rep. No. 711, 75th Cong., 1st Sess. 3 (1937).

187. Id. at 4.

not age itself but age combined with experience). Nothing in the bill prevented Roosevelt from nominating someone 69 years and eleven months of age without prior judicial service. A possible result: a Court of 15, all of them older than 70 and with no means of altering its composition. To the committee, the bill had one purpose and one purpose only: to apply "force to the judiciary" and undermine its independence.[188]

The committee described Roosevelt's proposal as a "needless, futile, and utterly dangerous abandonment of constitutional principle."[189] The bill was presented to Congress "in a most intricate form and for reasons that obscured its real purpose."[190] The proposal violated "every sacred tradition of American democracy."[191] Through this meticulous and blunt analysis, the committee hoped the bill would "be so emphatically rejected that its parallel will never again be presented to the free representatives of the free people of America."[192]

Several developments undermined prospects for the bill. Roosevelt hoped that Senate Majority Leader Joe Robinson would steer the bill through the Senate, but he died on July 14, 1937, after a week of debate. By that time the Court, on March 29, had upheld a state law establishing a minimum wage law for women, basically reversing a decision handed down ten months earlier.[193] This reversal occurred because of a change in positions by Justice Roberts, leading some to refer to the "switch in time that saved nine." However, several years before Roosevelt submitted his court-packing plan, Roberts had already broken with his laissez-faire colleagues. He wrote the opinion for a 5-4 Court in a 1934 case that upheld a New York price-setting statute.[194] With his support, the Court was prepared to sustain minimum-wage legislation in the fall of 1936 but delayed its ruling because of Justice Stone's illness. Late in 1936, Roberts voted with the liberal Justices to affirm a state unemployment insurance law.[195]

Other rulings in 1937 confirmed that the Court had become more accepting of New Deal programs. After Congress passed legislation early in 1937 to provide full judicial pay during retirement, Justice Van Devanter stepped down on June 2, 1937, giving Roosevelt his first chance in more than four years to nominate a Justice. He chose Hugo Black to replace Van Devanter. In 1938 and 1939, Justices Sutherland and Butler retired, replaced by Stanley Reed and Frank Murphy. Roosevelt was able to "reorganize" the Court through the regular constitutional process.

Interest remained in some type of court-packing bill. The original proposal was unlikely to pass Congress, but modified versions were drafted, such as changing the triggering age from 70 to 75 and limiting Roosevelt to three or four additional Justices instead of six. This substitute bill appeared to have the votes to pass the Senate, but the death of Senator Robinson, the acrimonious debate that gripped the Senate, and the decision of eight Freshmen Senators to withdraw

---

188. Id. at 3.

189. Id. at 23.

190. Id.

191. Id.

192. Id.

193. West Coast Hotel Co. v. Parrish, 300 U.S. 379 (1937), overturning Adkins v. Children's Hospital, 261 U.S. 525 (1923) and "distinguishing" (in fact reversing) Morehead v. New York ex rel. Tipaldo, 298 U.S. 587 (1936).

194. Nebbia v. New York, 291 U.S. 502 (1934).

195. W. H. H. Chamberlin, Inc. v. Andrews, 299 U.S. 515, decided November 23, 1936. The Court was equally divided. For Roberts' vote, see John W. Chambers, *The Big Switch: Justice Roberts and the Minimum-Wage Cases*, 10 LABOR HIST. 44, 57 (1969). See also Felix Frankfurter, *Mr. Justice Roberts*, 104 U. PA. L. REV. 311 (1955); 2 MERLO J. PUSEY, CHARLES EVANS HUGHES 757 (1963). For a challenge to Roberts' recollection of key events in

their support, sent the bill back to committee from which it never emerged.[196] Congress did enact legislation on August 24, 1937, affecting the judiciary, but it merely expedited constitutional challenges to federal laws. It did not change the Court's composition.[197]

By 1941, the composition of the Supreme Court had shifted dramatically. Retirements of three conservative Justices (Van Devanter, Sutherland, and Butler) led to the appointments of more moderate replacements: Hugo Black, Stanley Reed, and Frank Murphy. In a statement on June 3, 1941, President Roosevelt expressed satisfaction with the court-packing fight, concluding that although his reform bill was not enacted, the Court had altered its position to begin providing judicial support for legislation passed by the elected branches.[198]

# 8. NATIONAL SECURITY AND JUDICIAL DEFERENCE

In his concurrence in the Steel Seizure Case of 1952, Justice Jackson asked fundamental questions about the U.S. Constitution. Does it apply fully only in time of peace? Do individual liberties decline in periods of emergencies? How many "emergencies" are real and how many contrived? What is the role of the judiciary? Should federal judges stay their hand when the President acts alone, or with the support of Congress, and announces that conditions in the country are so perilous that the balance must shift from customary individual freedoms to the "national interest"? At such times is it necessary, or advisable, for the federal judiciary to defer to arguments by elected leaders about national security, especially arguments later shown to be deceptive and without substance? What damage flows from judicial deference to presidential claims: for individual rights, the constitutional system of checks and balances, and the reputation of the judiciary as an independent branch? This section focuses on those general issues. The next section concentrates on the "state secrets privilege" that developed in 1953 and has grown over the years to largely insulate presidential initiatives from judicial scrutiny.

## A. *Reflections by Justice Jackson*

When Truman ordered the seizure of steel mills, Justice Jackson said the Court "should not use this occasion to circumscribe, much less to contract, the lawful role of the President as Commander in Chief." He would "indulge the widest latitude of interpretation to sustain his exclusive function to command the instruments of national force, at least when turned against

---

1936, see Clement E. Vose, Constitutional Change: Amendment Politics and Supreme Court litigation Since 1900, at 228–34 (1972).

196. Leuchtenburg, *supra* note 174, at 148–54.

197. 50 Stat. 751 (1937).

198. 6 Public Papers and Addresses of Franklin D. Roosevelt, 1937 Volume, at xlvii-lxxii (1941). For other studies on the court-packing plan: William Lasser, *Justice Roberts and the Constitutional Revolution of 1937: Was there a "Switch in Time"?*, 78 Tex. L. Rev. 1347 (2000), Michael Nelson, *The President and the Court: Reinterpreting the Court-packing Episode of 1937*, 103 Pol. Sci. Q. 267 (1988), Gregory A. Caldeira, *Public*

the outside world for the security of our society."[199] Jackson added an appropriate qualification: the President's *lawful* role as Commander in Chief. Who decides if the President acts lawfully? Examples are provided in this section of Presidents acting without law and courts failing to supply a countercheck.

Jackson spoke too broadly about the President's "exclusive" function in commanding U.S. forces. He gave no recognition to the constitutional role of Congress in authorizing offensive operations and in placing limits on what a President may and may not do, such as authorizing only naval actions in the Quasi-War against France in 1798. Congress placed restrictions on the capture of ships, a statutory limitation upheld unanimously by the Supreme Court in *Little v. Barreme* (1804). Those constitutional and statutory limitations on the President's Commander in Chief powers are reviewed in Chapter 8.

Having described presidential power overseas too broadly, Jackson then added: "But, when it is turned inward, not because of rebellion but because of a lawful economic struggle between industry and labor, it should have no such indulgence."[200] The President's command power over troops "is not such an absolute as might be implied from that office in a militaristic system but is subject to limitations consistent with a constitutional Republic whose law and policy-making branch is a representative Congress."[201] His distinction between foreign and domestic affairs is artificial and seems to invoke Justice Sutherland's misconceived sole-organ doctrine in *Curtiss-Wright* and his separation between external and internal affairs (Chapter 7, section 1B). Presidents have never had a free hand when operating abroad. At various times they are restricted by Congress and the courts. The Court's decision in *Little v. Barreme* (1804) is an early precedent. Other examples include judicial restrictions on executive agreements that affect private claims and the constitutional privileges of the Due Process and Just Compensation Clauses (Chapter 7, section 6A) and litigation after the terrorist attacks of September 11, 2001, to be discussed in this section.

Justice Jackson was on stronger ground when he warned about "loose and irresponsible" adjectives that attempt to expand presidential power beyond constitutional limits: " 'Inherent' powers, 'implied' powers, 'incidental' power, 'plenary' powers, 'war' powers and 'emergency' powers," used "often interchangeably and without fixed or ascertainable meanings."[202] Other adjectives have been added after 1952, including the President's "residual" powers,[203] "preclusive" powers,[204] the "unitary executive,"[205] and the President's "completion power."[206]

*Opinion and the U.S. Supreme Court: FDR's Court-Packing Plan*, 81 AM. POL. SCI. REV. 1139 (1987), and Theresa A. Niedziela, *Franklin D. Roosevelt and the Supreme Court*, 6 PRES. STUD. Q. 51 (1976).

199. Youngstown Co. v. Sawyer, 343 U.S. 579, 645 (1952) (Jackson, J., concurring).

200. Id.

201. Id. at 645–46.

202. Id. at 646–47.

203. Saikrishna B. Prakash & Michael D. Ramsey, *The Executive Power over Foreign Affairs*, 111 YALE L.J. 231 (2001).

204. David J. Barron & Martin S. Lederman, *The Commander in Chief at the Lowest Ebb—Framing the Problem, Doctrine, and Original Understanding* (Part 1), 121 HARV. L. REV. 689 (2008), and *The Commander in Chief at the Lowest Ebb—A Constitutional History* (Part 2), 121 HARV. L. REV. 941 (2008).

205. STEVEN G. CALABRESI & CHRISTOPHER S. YOO, THE UNITARY EXECUTIVE: PRESIDENTIAL POWER FROM WASHINGTON TO BUSH (2008).

206. Jack Goldsmith & John F. Manning, *The President's Completion Power*, 115 YALE L.J. 2280 (2006).

Later in his concurrence, Jackson abandoned his model of Presidents exercising unfettered power abroad but subject to limits when he acts in the domestic arena. The Constitution, he said, was created for good times and bad times. Asserted emergencies do not suspend the Constitution. The appeal that "we declare the existence of inherent powers *ex necessitate* to meet an emergency asks us to do what many think would be wise, although it is something the forefathers omitted."[207] Jackson said the Framers "knew what emergencies were, knew the pressures they engender for authoritative action, knew, too, how they afford a ready pretext for usurpation. We may also suspect that they suspected that emergency powers would tend to kindle emergencies."[208] In reviewing the history of the Weimar Constitution in Germany and Hitler's reign of emergency government, Jackson concluded that "emergency powers are consistent with free government only when their control is lodged elsewhere than in the Executive who exercises them."[209] That position parts company with his earlier support for the President's "exclusive function" of commanding military force against outside threats.

## B. The judicial record: 1936 to 2001

Part of judicial deference to presidential power in external affairs is the result of courts repeatedly citing Justice Sutherland's erroneous dicta in *Curtiss-Wright* without ever reading John Marshall's speech. Describing the President as "sole organ" carries with it a range of associations about inherent, independent, and plenary executive power that Marshall never embraced (Chapter 7, section 1B). Mechanical citations to *Curtiss-Wright* suggest that federal courts lack the capacity, or interest, to do their homework and avoid false and misleading platitudes. That type of judicial conduct weakens the constitutional system of checks and balances.

A second judicial ruling routinely cited to uphold broad presidential power in external affairs is from 1948. The Supreme Court reviewed a statutory provision that authorized judicial review of orders issued by the Civil Aeronautics Board, including those that grant or deny applications by citizen carriers to engage in overseas and foreign air transportation. Those orders were subject to the President's approval.

Justice Jackson, writing for the Court, acknowledged that Congress has constitutional authority over foreign commerce and may delegate "large grants" to the President. But he also said that the President "also possesses in his own right certain powers conferred by the Constitution on him as Commander-in-Chief and as the Nation's organ in foreign affairs."[210] Two pages later he cited *Curtiss-Wright* and explained why courts could not review orders that result from presidential direction: "The President, both as Commander-in-Chief and as the Nation's organ for foreign affairs, has available intelligence services whose reports are not and ought not to be published to the world."[211] Independent judicial review obviously does not mean publication in the world. Yet he said it would be "intolerable" that courts, "without the relevant

---

207. Youngstown Co. v. Sawyer, 343 U.S. at 649–50.

208. Id. at 650.

209. Id. at 652.

210. C.& S. Air Lines v. Waterman Corp., 333 U.S. 103, 109 (1948).

211. Id. at 111.

information, should review and perhaps nullify actions of the Executive taken on information properly held secret."[212]

Although the President was acting under a provision of the Civil Aeronautics Act, Jackson chose to interpret this authority not as a statutory grant but as a power that the President possesses "in his own right"—i.e., *inherent* powers, precisely what Jackson would reject four years later in the Steel Seizure Case. He denied that courts may "sit *in camera* in order to be taken into executive confidences."[213] But courts frequently sit in camera to receive confidential information that cannot be aired in public. Jackson further argued that "even if courts could require full disclosure, the very nature of executive decisions as to foreign policy is political, not judicial. Such decisions are wholly confided by our Constitution to the political departments of the government, Executive and Legislative."[214]

Nothing in the Constitution confides all of foreign affairs to the elected branches. Jackson could cite nothing in the Constitution to defend his claim. He described foreign policy as "delicate, complex, and involv[ing] large elements of prophecy."[215] Much the same could be said about issues involving agriculture, the economy, housing, and taxation. Jackson urged that such questions "should be undertaken only by those directly responsible to the people whose welfare they advance or imperil." What happens if the elected branches imperil legal and individual rights? No recourse to the judiciary?

Precisely that issue arose with the Japanese-American cases of 1943 and 1944, two decisions that severely undermined the Supreme Court's claim to be the "guardian" of individual liberties. On February 19, 1942, President Roosevelt issued Executive Order 9066, leading to the transfer of more than 110,000 Americans of Japanese descent (about two-thirds of them natural-born U.S. citizens) to what were euphemistically called "relocation centers." Roosevelt said he acted under his authority as President and Commander in Chief.[216] With no evidence of disloyalty or subversive activity, and without benefit of any procedural safeguards, these individuals were imprisoned solely on grounds of race. A month later, Congress enacted legislation to ratify the executive order.[217]

A unanimous Court upheld a curfew order directed against Japanese Americans. In a concurrence, Justice Murphy said the curfew policy "bears a melancholy resemblance to the treatment accorded to members of the Jewish race in Germany and in other parts of Europe."[218] The following year, with the Justices divided 6 to 3, the Court supported the exclusion of Japanese Americans and their relocation to detention camps. In one of the dissents, Justice Murphy protested that the exclusion order resulted from an "erroneous assumption of racial guilt" found in the commanding general's report, which referred to all individuals of Japanese descent as "subversives" belonging to "an enemy race" whose "racial strains are undiluted."[219] He dissented

---

212. Id.

213. Id.

214. Id.

215. Id.

216. 7 Fed. Reg. 1407 (1942).

217. 56 Stat. 173 (1942).

218. Hirabayashi v. United States, 320 U.S. 81, 111 (1943).

219. Korematsu v. United States, 323 U.S. 214, 235–36 (1944) (Murphy, J., dissenting).

from "this legalization of racism."[220] In another dissent, Justice Jackson remarked that "here is an attempt to make an otherwise innocent act a crime merely because this prisoner is the son of parents to which he had no choice, and belongs to a race from which there is no way to resign."[221]

Why did the Court extend its blessing to this military operation? It did so for the same reason Justice Jackson offered in his 1948 decision: deference to independent presidential power in the field of external affairs. The majority (and some of the dissenters) claimed they lacked a capacity to determine whether President Roosevelt and his military advisers possessed sufficient grounds to act as they did. Writing for the Court, Justice Black acquiesced to military experts: "we are unable to conclude that it was beyond the war power of Congress and the Executive to exclude those of Japanese ancestry from the West Coast war area at the time they did."[222] The words "we are unable to conclude" are frequently used when courts acquiesce to actions in the field of national security without any grounds for doing so. Although Jackson dissented, he also wrote: "the Court, having no real evidence before it, has no choice but to accept General DeWitt's own unsworn, self-serving statement, untested by any cross-examination, that what he did was reasonable. And thus it will always be when courts try to look into the reasonableness of a military order."[223]

Thus it will always be? It was not always that way before 1944 and certainly not always that way after 1944. Jackson had an opportunity, as a member of an independent branch, to probe the basis for the exclusion order. He claimed the Court had "no choice." Justices always have a choice. Certainly they had a choice when Jackson described DeWitt's statement as unsworn, self-serving, and untested by any cross-examination. The Justices had a duty under their oath of office to insist: "We decide cases based on evidence. You have provided none, other than crude assertions of racism. Both for the rights of Japanese Americans and our own institutional self-respect, we must hold against the exclusion order." In his dissent, Justice Murphy identified an effective and principled way to challenge executive assertions: "Justification for the exclusion is sought, instead, mainly upon questionable racial and sociological grounds not ordinarily within the realm of expert military judgment."[224] The Court was not faced with what might be called a "military judgment." There was no reason to defer to DeWitt's purely prejudiced and ignorant beliefs about race and sociology.[225]

In a law review article in 1962, Chief Justice Warren reflected on the Court's performance in the Japanese-American cases. In times of emergency, he suggested that the judiciary could not function as an independent and coequal branch: "The consequence of the limitations under which the Court must sometimes operate in this area is that other agencies of government must bear the primary responsibility for determining whether specific actions they are taking are consonant with our Constitution."[226] Next comes a remarkable sentence: "To put it another way, the fact that the Court rules in a case like *Hirabayashi* that a given program is constitutional,

220. Id. at 242.

221. Id. at 243 (Jackson, J., dissenting).

222. Id. at 217–18.

223. Id. at 245 (Jackson, J., dissenting).

224. Id. at 236–37 (Murphy, J., dissenting).

225. Eugene V. Rostow, *The Japanese American Cases—A Disaster*, 54 YALE L.J. 489 (1945); Nanette Dembitz, *Racial Discrimination and the Military Judgment: The Supreme Court's Korematsu and Endo Decisions*, 45 COLUM. L. REV. 175 (1945).

226. Earl Warren, *The Bill of Rights and the Military*, 37 N.Y.U. L. REV. 181, 192 (1962).

does not necessarily answer the question whether, in a broader sense, it actually is."[227] In so many words: the Court held the government's action constitutional when it was not.

On February 20, 1976, President Gerald Ford issued a proclamation publicly apologizing for the treatment of Japanese Americans, calling it the "uprooting of loyal Americans."[228] The proclamation called upon Americans "to affirm with me this American Promise—that we have learned from the tragedy of that long-ago experience forever to treasure liberty and justice for each individual American, and resolve that this kind of action shall never again be repeated."[229] In 1980, Congress established a commission to gather facts to determine the wrong done by Roosevelt's order. Released in December 1982, the report stated that the order "was not justified by military necessity" and the policies that followed from it—curfew and detention—"were not driven by analysis of military conditions." The factors that shaped those decisions were "race prejudice, war hysteria and a failure of political leadership."[230]

Congress passed legislation in 1988 to establish a trust fund of $1.25 billion to pay up to $20,000 to eligible individuals.[231] No financial payment could compensate for the lost years, humiliation, and economic sacrifices of having to sell property at reduced values when forced to relocate to detention camps. In signing the bill, President Reagan said the larger purpose had less to do with economic benefits that with honor: "For here we admit a wrong; here we reaffirm our commitment as a nation to equal justice under the law."[232]

The price of judicial deference to executive assertions surfaced when Gordon Hirabayashi and Fred Korematsu returned to court after newly discovered documents revealed that executive officials had deceived federal courts. The two men learned that the executive branch had withheld vital evidence from the judiciary. At the time of Korematsu's case in 1944, Justice Department attorneys were aware that a 618-page document called *Final Report*, prepared by the War Department for General DeWitt, contained erroneous claims about alleged espionage efforts by Japanese Americans. The FBI and the Federal Communications Commission rejected War Department assertions that some Japanese Americans had sent signals from shore to assist Japanese submarine attacks along the Pacific coast.

Justice Department officials had a professional obligation to inform the judiciary about these false allegations. A footnote, to be included in the Justice Department brief for *Korematsu*, should have clearly identified the errors that appeared in the *Final Report*. Yet the footnote was so reworked and watered down that the courts could not possibly have understood the extent to which the administration had misled them.[233] A district court in 1984 concluded that the executive branch had "knowingly withheld information from the courts when they were considering the critical question of military necessity in this case."[234] To the court, there was "substantial support in the record that the government deliberately omitted relevant information and provided

227. Id. at 192–93.

228. Proclamation 4417, 42 Fed. Reg. 7741 (1976).

229. Id.

230. Commission on Wartime Relocation and Internment of Civilians. Personal Justice Denied 18 (1982).

231. 102 Stat. 903, 905–06, sec. 104-05 (1988).

232. Public Papers of the Presidents, 1988, II, at 1054.

233. Peter Irons, Justice at War: The Story of the Japanese American Internment Cases 278 (1983).

234. Korematsu v. United States, 584 F. Supp. 1406, 1417 (D. Cal. 1984).

misleading information in papers before the court."[235] On that basis, the district court vacated Korematsu's conviction. The Justice Department did not appeal this decision.

Hirabayashi also challenged his conviction for violating a curfew order. The Justice Department had argued that the government lacked time to separate loyal Japanese from those who might be subversive. It did not claim it was impossible to distinguish between loyal and disloyal Japanese. However, General DeWitt believed that because of racial ties, filial piety, and strong bonds of common tradition, culture, and customs, it was "impossible to establish the identity of the loyal and the disloyal with any degree of safety."[236] For DeWitt, there was no "such a thing as a loyal Japanese."[237] The initial draft report contained his remarks. The final report, after War Department editing, did not. The Justice Department received the final report but not the draft version.

In 1986, a district court ruled that although the Justice Department "did not knowingly conceal" from Hirabayashi's counsel and the Supreme Court the reasons DeWitt offered, it was necessary to charge the executive branch with concealment because the information was known to the War Department, an arm of government. The failure of the executive branch to disclose DeWitt's position "was an error of the most fundamental character." Hirabayashi "was in fact seriously prejudiced by that non-disclosure in his appeal from his conviction for failing to report."[238] The district court vacated that conviction but declined to vacate his conviction for violating the curfew order.[239] On appeal, the Ninth Circuit vacated both convictions.[240] The Supreme Court has never overruled its decisions in *Hirabayashi* and *Korematsu*. On May 20, 2011, Acting Solicitor General Neal Katyal pointed out that the Solicitor General in *Korematsu* failed to inform the Supreme Court of evidence that undermined the rationale for internment.[241]

Other judicial decisions, by adding careless and extraneous dicta, have artificially inflated presidential authority in the field of national security. In the Pentagon Papers Case of 1971, the Supreme Court held that two newspapers were constitutionally entitled to publish a secret Defense Department study of the Vietnam War. Writing for the Court, Justice Black denied that the President possessed "inherent power" to halt publication to make the country "secure."[242] He said the guarding of military and diplomatic secrets "at the expense of informed representative government provides no real security for our Republic."[243]

Justice Stewart, agreeing that the Pentagon documents should be published in the newspapers, wrote a confused concurrence that promoted independent presidential power. Citing Justice Sutherland's dicta in *Curtiss-Wright*, Stewart wrote: "The responsibility must be where the power is."[244] By that he meant the President. He continued: "If the Constitution gives the Executive a large degree of unshared power in the conduct of foreign affairs and the maintenance of our

235. Id. at 1420.

236. Hirabayashi v. United States, 627 F. Supp. 1445, 1449 (W.D. Wash. 1986).

237. Id. at 1452.

238. Id. at 1457.

239. Id. at 1457–58.

240. Hirabayashi v. United States, 828 F.2d 591 (9th Cir. 1987).

241. Neal Katyal, *Confession of Error: The Solicitor General's Mistakes During the Japanese-American Internment Cases*, May 20, 2011, http://blogs.justice.gov/main/archives/1346.

242. New York Times Co. v. United States, 403 U.S. 713, 719 (1971).

243. Id.

244. Id. at 728 (Stewart, J., concurring).

national defense, then under the Constitution the Executive must have the largely unshared duty to determine and preserve the degree of internal security necessary to exercise that power successfully."[245]

Why begin a broad assertion with an "if"? Does the Constitution grant that authority to the President or not? Second, the President's largely unshared power to *conduct* foreign affairs does not imply a largely unshared power to *make* foreign policy. The conduct of foreign affairs generally follows implementation of national security policy arrived at jointly by Congress and the President. John Marshall made that precise point in 1800 with his sole-organ speech. Collective judgment is especially required for "maintenance of our national defense," the phrase Stewart used.

Stewart referred to the "constitutional duty of the Executive—as a matter of sovereign prerogative."[246] By referring to "sovereign prerogative" and citing *Curtiss-Wright*, Stewart embraced inherent presidential power. Yet he immediately states: "This is not to say that Congress and the courts have no role to play."[247] If guarding the nation's secrets is an inherent power to be exercised by the President, what possible authority remains for the other two branches? After suggesting that Congress and the courts might have a role, Stewart proceeds to write: "We are asked ... to perform a function that the Constitution gave to the Executive, not the Judiciary."[248] At no point does Stewart identify the constitutional powers that justify unchecked presidential power in national security.

In 1974, the Supreme Court concluded that in matters of criminal prosecution the decision to release the Watergate tapes is reserved to the courts, not the President.[249] An important ruling, but the Court suggested the outcome of the case might have been different had President Nixon claimed the need "to protect military, diplomatic, or sensitive national security secrets."[250] That issue was not before the Court and had not been argued or briefed. It was error to imply that the corruption and illegality within the Nixon administration could have been forever sealed, with defendants denied evidence to clear their names, if the administration had invoked "national security." Still, the dictum is available to justify unchecked presidential power.

Careless writing by the Supreme Court in a 1988 case converted what was a purely statutory issue into constitutional dimensions. The dispute involved the Navy's denial of a security clearance to Thomas Egan, who worked on the Trident submarine. He was subsequently removed. Egan sought review by the Merit Systems Protection Board (MSPB), but the Supreme Court upheld the Navy's action by ruling that the denial of a security clearance is a sensitive discretionary judgment call *committed by law* to the executive agency with the necessary expertise to protect classified information.[251] The conflict was within the executive branch (Navy versus the MSPB), not between Congress and the executive branch.

The focus on statutory questions was evident throughout the litigation. The Justice Department noted in its brief submitted to the Supreme Court: "The issue in this case is one

---

245. Id. at 728–29.
246. Id. at 729–30.
247. Id. at 730.
248. Id.
249. United States v. Nixon, 418 U.S. 683 (1974).
250. Id. at 706.
251. Department of the Navy v. Egan, 484 U.S. 518, 529–30 (1988).

of statutory construction and 'at bottom...turns on congressional intent.' "[252] The parties were directed to address this question: "Whether, in the course of reviewing the removal of an employee for failure to maintain a required security clearance, the Merit Systems Protection Board is *authorized by statute* to review the substance of the underlying decision to deny or revoke the security clearance."[253] The statutory questions centered on 5 U.S.C. §§ 7512, 7532, and 7701.

The entire oral argument before the Supreme Court on December 2, 1987, was devoted to the meaning of statutes and what Congress intended by them. The Court merely decided the "narrow question" whether MSPB had statutory authority to review the substance of a decision to deny a security clearance.[254] Although the Court referred to independent constitutional powers of the President, including those as Commander in Chief and head of the executive branch,[255] and noted the President's responsibilities with regard to foreign policy,[256] the case was decided on statutory grounds. In stating that courts "traditionally have been reluctant to intrude upon the authority of the Executive in military and national security affairs," the Court added this basic point: "*unless Congress specifically has provided otherwise.*"[257] The Court appears to have borrowed that condition, and language, from the Justice Department's brief: "Absent an unambiguous grant of jurisdiction by Congress, courts have traditionally been reluctant to intrude upon the authority of the executive in military and national security affairs."[258]

In his opinion for the Court, Justice Blackmun began by referring to the "narrow" statutory question of MSPB review of security clearances.[259] He analyzed the various statutes. He then moved to the President's authority as Commander in Chief, concluding that his authority to classify and control access to national security information "flows primarily from this constitutional investment of power in the President and exists quite apart from the explicit congressional grant."[260] Because of Blackmun's discursive opinion, straying from the statutory issue, readers can pick through different passages to build a distorted and erroneous view of independent presidential authority. A review of over 180 judicial decisions that cite *Egan* illustrates how Blackmun's opinion produced a variety of judicial interpretations: analyzing statutory grounds, the level of judicial deference, lack of jurisdiction, interpreting Article II powers, disclosing classified information, and other strands of his opinion. Nothing in *Egan*, however, recognized a plenary or exclusive power on the part of the President over classified information.[261]

In 1988, District Judge Oliver Gasch ruled that Congress lacked constitutional authority to interfere, by statute, with nondisclosure agreements drafted by the executive branch to protect

252. U.S. Department of Justice, *Brief for the Petitioner*, Department of the Navy v. Egan, October Term, 1987, at 22 (citing Clarke v. Securities Industry Ass'n, No. 85-971, January 14, 1987).

253. Id. at (I) (emphasis added).

254. 484 U.S. at 520.

255. Id. at 527.

256. Id. at 529.

257. Id. at 530 (emphasis added).

258. U.S. Department of Justice, *Brief for the Petitioner*, Department of the Navy v. Egan, October Term, 1987, at 21.

259. 484 U.S. at 520.

260. Id. at 527.

261. Louis Fisher, *Judicial Interpretations of* Egan, Law Library of Congress, Nov. 13, 2009, http://www.loufisher.org/docs/ep/466.pdf.

classified information.[262] Among other authorities, Gasch relied on *Curtiss-Wright* and *Egan*.[263] From the latter, he extracted a sentence ("The authority to protect such [national security] information falls on the President as head of the Executive Branch and as Commander in Chief") without acknowledging that *Egan* was decided on statutory, not constitutional, grounds, and that the Supreme Court recognized that Congress in appropriate circumstances may by statute narrow presidential action. Having mischaracterized *Egan*, Gasch concluded that Congress had passed legislation regarding nondisclosure agreements that "impermissibly restricts the President's power to fulfill obligations imposed upon him by his express constitutional powers and the role of the Executive in foreign relations."[264]

On October 31, 1988, the Supreme Court noted probable jurisdiction over this case.[265] Both the House and the Senate submitted briefs objecting to Judge Gasch's interpretation of presidential power over foreign affairs. On April 18, 1989, the Court issued a per curiam order that vacated Gasch's order and remanded the case for further consideration.[266] In doing so, the Court advised him to tread with greater caution in expounding on constitutional matters.[267] On remand, Judge Gasch resolved the dispute without addressing any constitutional issues.[268]

## C. After 9/11

Following the terrorist attacks of September 11, 2001, federal courts were once again asked to define the limits of presidential power in foreign affairs and national security. Many courts followed the customary ritual of expressing deference to the executive branch in a time of emergency, but on this occasion the judiciary demonstrated greater independence and confidence on a number of fronts. Much of this judicial assertiveness resulted from poor judgments committed by executive officials: mechanically invoking "inherent" presidential power and making legal and constitutional arguments that were too shallow and strained to survive scrutiny.

On November 13, 2001, President George W. Bush issued a military order to create military tribunals to try individuals who gave assistance to the terrorist attacks of 9/11.[269] Military tribunals had not been used since World War II, but the administration looked to a Supreme Court decision of 1942, *Ex parte Quirin*, as an "apt precedent" to support Bush's order.[270] The administration justified the order by referring to the availability of presidential inherent powers. As with similar assertions by Presidents Truman and Nixon to justify their actions in seizing steel mills, impounding funds, and ordering warrantless domestic surveillance (Chapter 3, section 4; Chapter 6, section 6; Chapter 8, section 6), Bush's claim of inherent power would similarly misfire.

---

262. National Federation of Federal Employees v. United States, 688 F. Supp. 671 (D.D.C. 1988).

263. Id. at 676, 684–85.

264. Id. at 685.

265. American Foreign Service Ass'n., et al. v. Garfinkel,  488 U.S. 923 (1988).

266. American Foreign Service Ass'n v. Garfinkel, 490 U.S. 153 (1989).

267. Id. at 158, 161.

268. American Foreign Service Ass'n v. Garfinkel, 732 F. Supp. 13 (D.D.C. 1990).

269. 66 Fed. Reg. 57833 (2001).

270. William P. Barr & Andrew G. McBride, *Military Justice for al Qaeda*, Wash. Post, Nov. 18, 2001, at B7.

The Bush order borrowed heavily from language in a proclamation and military order issued by President Roosevelt in 1942 to try eight German saboteurs.[271] Instead of pressing the limits of presidential power, the administration would have been better served, politically and legally, by going to Congress and receiving statutory authority, as it was eventually forced to do. By attempting a shortcut by military order, the executive branch placed a shadow of illegitimacy over the tribunals that remained there for the next decade, never to be fully removed despite many revisions of Pentagon regulations and statutory rewrites.

It has been pointed out that Roosevelt's use of a military commission "received widespread praise" while the Bush military order issued after 9/11 "was greeted with impassioned criticism in the press, the legal academy, and Congress."[272] As for the supposed appeal of Roosevelt's tribunal in 1942 and the Supreme Court's decision in *Ex parte Quirin*, a number of procedural and constitutional deficiencies were present. Roosevelt issued the proclamation and military order, appointed the generals to serve on the tribunal, selected the prosecutors and defense counsel, and then, after the tribunal completed its work and reached a verdict, the trial record went to Roosevelt as the "final reviewing authority." The generals, prosecutors, and defense counsel (two colonels) were all subordinate to Roosevelt.[273] It would be difficult to conceive of a trial system more procedurally flawed. It was a complete closed circle without any independent checks.

What about the quality of the Court's decision in *Quirin*? The Justices agreed to take the case before there had been any lower court rulings. On the evening of July 28, 1942, a district court turned down a petition for a writ of habeas corpus brought by the defense counsel for the German saboteurs. Oral argument before the Supreme Court began the next day at noon and continued on July 30. The Court did not receive briefs by the two sides until July 29. Justices were therefore unprepared to debate highly technical issues involving the Articles of War and whether Roosevelt violated them. At oral argument, objections were raised because the D.C. Circuit had not acted. The Court allowed the case to continue while defense counsel filed papers with the appellate court. On July 31, at 11:59 a.m., the Court received papers from the D.C. Circuit, granted certiorari, and released a short per curiam that contained no legal reasoning but upheld the jurisdiction of the military tribunal.[274]

In the per curiam, Chief Justice Stone explained that a "full opinion" would be released as soon as possible. It took the Court three months to do that, with a clear understanding that Justices would not be permitted to write dissents or even concurrences. Chief Justice Stone did not want any show of disunity. The generals completed their work, recommended the execution of all eight men, and Roosevelt ordered that punishment for six. On August 6, they were electrocuted. The Court continued to work on its opinion, aware now that Roosevelt had violated a number of Articles of War. On September 10, Chief Justice Stone wrote to Justice Frankfurter,

---

271. Louis Fisher, Military Tribunals and Presidential Power: American Revolution to the War on Terrorism 168–70 (2005).

272. Jack Goldsmith & Cass R. Sunstein, *Military Tribunals and Legal Culture: What a Difference Sixty Years Makes*, 19 Const. Comment. 261, 261 (2002).

273. Louis Fisher, Nazi Saboteurs on Trial: A Military Tribunal and American Law 50–53 (2003). Perceptive analyses of the Nazi saboteur case include David J. Danelski, *The Saboteurs' Case*, 1 J. Sup. Ct. Hist. 61–82 (1996); Michal Belknap, *Frankfurter and the Nazi Saboteurs*, Yearbook 1982: Sup. Ct. Hist. Soc. 66–71; and Michal R. Belknap, *The Supreme Court Goes to War: The Meaning and Implications of the Nazi Saboteur Case*, 89 Mil. L. Rev. 59 (1980).

274. Fisher, *supra* note 273, at 87–108.

saying it "seems almost brutal to announce this ground of decision for the first time after six of the petitioners have been executed and it is too late for them to raise the question if in fact the articles as they construe them have been violated."[275]

The Court released the full opinion on October 29, 1942. Frankfurter was sufficiently troubled by the decision that he asked Frederick Bernays Wiener, an expert on military justice, to evaluate *Quirin*. Wiener said the weaknesses in the decision flowed "in large measure" from the administration's disregard for "almost every precedent in the books" when it established the military tribunal.[276] Three lengthy letters from Wiener to Frankfurter amounted to a sweeping condemnation of the Court's October 29 decision. In 1953, when the Court considered sitting in summer session to hear the espionage case of Ethel and Julius Rosenberg, a Justice recalled that the Court sat in summer session in 1942 to hear the saboteur case. Frankfurter regarded the Court's process as "not a happy precedent."[277] In *Hamdi v. Rumsfeld* (2004), Justice Scalia, joined by Justice Stevens, properly referred to *Quirin* as "not this Court's finest hour."[278]

The plurality ruling in *Hamdi* contains several limitations on presidential power. The administration argued that no "explicit congressional authorization" is required because the President "possesses plenary power to detain [enemy combatants] pursuant to Article II of the Constitution."[279] The plurality did not reach that question, agreeing that Congress in the Authorization for Use of Military Force (AUMF), enacted on September 18, 2001, had provided adequate authority. The claim of inherent presidential power was expressly rejected in *Hamdan*, discussed next. The plurality in *Hamdi* felt comfortable in relying on *Quirin*. It offered a number of procedural considerations that had not been briefed or argued.[280] The plurality identified a basic constitutional principle: "Whatever power the United States Constitution envisions for the Executive in its exchanges with other nations or with enemy organizations in times of conflict, it most assuredly envisions a role for all three branches when individual liberties are at stake."[281]

The constitutionality of President Bush's military tribunal reached the Court in *Hamdan v. Rumsfeld* (2006). The Court held that Bush's military order to create tribunals violated both the Uniform Code of Military Justice (UCMJ) and the Geneva Conventions. Congress had enacted the UCMJ, and it was the President's duty to comply with it. No inherent presidential authority existed to circumvent the statutory policy established by Congress under its Article I authority.[282] In this litigation, I filed three amicus briefs in opposition to the Bush administration: when the case was in D.C. Circuit, when a motion had been filed for certiorari, and after the Court had granted cert.[283] The Bush administration claimed that the Founding-era history supported presidential establishment of military tribunals: "It was well established when the Constitution was written and ratified that one of the powers inherent in military command was

275.  Id. at 110. See also id. at 111–13.

276.  Id. at 129.

277.  Id. at 134.

278.  Hamdi v. Rumsfeld, 542 U.S. 507, 569 (2004).

279.  Id. at 516–17.

280.  Id. at 533–35, 537–39. For critique of this approach, see the dissent by Justices Scalia and Stevens, id. at 576–77.

281.  Id. at 536.

282.  Hamdan v. Rumsfeld, 548 U.S. 557 (2006).

283.  *Brief* Amicus Curiae *of Louis Fisher in Support of Petitioner-Appellee Urging Affirmance*, Hamdan v. Rumsfeld, No. 04-5393, D.C. Circuit, Dec. 29, 2004; *Brief* Amicus Curiae *of Louis Fisher in Support of Petitioner*,

the authority to institute tribunals for punishing enemy violations of the laws of war," and that General Washington had appointed a "Board of General Officers" in 1780 to try British Major John André as a spy.[284] The Justice Department argued: "there was no provision in the American Articles of War providing for the jurisdiction in a court-martial to try an enemy for the offense of spying."[285]

Those arguments were false. As my brief explained, the Continental Congress adopted a resolution in 1776 expressly providing that enemy spies "shall suffer death ... by sentence of a court martial, or such other punishment as such court martial shall direct," and ordered the resolution "be printed at the end of the rules and articles of war."[286] The previous year, Congress had made it punishable by court-martial for members of the Continental Congress to "hold correspondence with" or "give intelligence to" the enemy.[287] It was a conceptual and historical mistake for the Bush administration to rely on the John André trial of 1780. There was no President at that time. There was no separate executive branch. There was only one branch of government: the Continental Congress. In convening Major André's trial, Washington did not act unilaterally as an Executive possessing inherent power but as a military general carrying out procedures established by Congress. Other military tribunals were created after 1789, raising important questions about presidential power and judgment.[288]

Several legal and political embarrassments confronted the Bush administration. In April 2004, during oral argument on the Yaser Esam Hamdi and Jose Padilla cases (both of them U.S. citizens), Justice Stevens asked Deputy Solicitor General Paul Clement whether he thought there was "anything in the law that curtails the method of interrogation that may be employed." Clement assured the Court that safeguards existed. The United States was "signatory to conventions that prohibit torture and that sort of thing. And the United States is going to honor its treaty obligations."[289] To Clement, drawing on the experience of those who actually conduct interrogations, "the last thing you want to do is torture somebody or try to do something along those lines."[290] Using coercion to get information leaves one wondering "about the reliability of the information you were getting." The lessons drawn from interrogations is that the way to "get the best information from individuals is that you interrogate them, you try to develop a relationship of trust."[291]

During the Padilla oral argument on the same day, Justices continued to ask how the executive branch treated detainees. To Clement, the President should be free to use "traditional authority to make discretionary judgments" in deciding what is the necessary appropriate force for military actions, as in Afghanistan. He counseled against "judicial management of

Hamdan v. Rumsfeld, No. 05-184, on petition for writ of certiorari, Sept. 7, 2005; *Brief* Amicus Curiae *of Louis Fisher in Support of Petitioner [Commissions—History]*, Hamdan v. Rumsfeld, No. 05-184, on writ of certiorari, Jan. 6, 2006.

284. Brief for Appellants, Hamdan v. Rumsfeld, No. 04-5393 (D.C. Cir. Dec. 8, 2004), at 58.

285. Id.

286. 5 JOURNALS OF THE CONTINENTAL CONGRESS, 1774–1789, at 693.

287. American Articles of War of 1775, art. 28, reprinted in WILLIAM WINTHROP, MILITARY LAW AND PRECEDENTS 955 (2d ed. 1920).

288. FISHER, *supra* note 271.

289. U.S. Supreme Court, Hamdi v. Rumsfeld, oral argument, April 28, 2004, at 48–49.

290. Id. at 50.

291. Id.

the executive's war-making power."[292] One of the Justices observed that "if the law is what the executive says it is, whatever is necessary and appropriate in the executive's judgment," the result would be an "executive, unchecked by the judiciary." Under those circumstances, "what is it that would be a check against torture?" Clement reassured the Justices: "Well, first of all, there are treaty obligations." Moreover, if a U.S. military person committed a war crime "on a harmless, you know, detained enemy combatant or a prisoner of war," the government would put the soldier or officer on trial in a court-martial.[293]

The Court wanted to know from Clement what would happen if the President or executive officials said that mild torture would be helpful in extracting information. What would constrain such conduct? "Is it just up to the good will of the executive? Is there a judicial check?" Having earlier referred to treaty constraints and the understanding of interrogators that torture is ineffective in getting reliable information, Clement now discouraged any judicial interference with presidential decisions. The fact that executive discretion during war "can be abused is not a good and sufficient reason for judicial micromanagement and overseeing of that authority." In time of war "you have to trust the executive to make the kind of quintessential military judgments that are involved in things like that."[294] After Clement concluded his oral argument, that evening photos of U.S. abuse of detainees held at the Abu Ghraib prison in Iraq began to be broadcast around the world on the CBS News program "60 Minutes."[295]

The U.S. military had already begun an inquiry into these abuses. An investigation initiated on January 19, 2004, led to the appointment of Maj. Gen. Antonio Taguba, who described "numerous incidents of sadistic, blatant, and wanton criminal abuses" inflicted on detainees, referring to the actions as "systemic and illegal."[296] His report detailed such actions as keeping detainees naked for several days at a time, a male military police guard having sex with a female detainee, using unmuzzled dogs to intimidate and terrify detainees, and sodomizing a detainee with a chemical light and perhaps a broomstick.[297] Taguba limited his report to the 800th Military Police Brigade and the Abu Ghraib prison. He did not investigate abuses in other prisons in Iraq and Afghanistan. He said that abusive interrogation methods used in Guantánamo had been transferred to Iraq by Maj. Gen. Geoffrey Miller, the previous commander at the naval base.[298] Documentary records reveal deliberate planning of abusive and illegal interrogations by Bush administration officials.[299]

On June 22, 2004, the Bush administration released a number of documents about interrogation policies. In one, dated August 1, 2002, OLC head Jay Bybee concluded that for an act of interrogation to constitute torture "it must inflict pain that is difficult to endure. Physical pain

---

292. U.S. Supreme Court, Rumsfeld v. Padilla, oral argument, April 28, 2004, at 17.

293. Id. at 22.

294. Id. at 23.

295. *Photos Show U.S. Troops Abusing Iraqi Prisoners*, L.A. TIMES, April 29, 2004, at A4; James Risen, *G.I.'s Are Accused of Abusing Iraqi Captives*, N.Y. TIMES, April 29, 2004, at A13; *Photographs Reveal Atrocities by U.S. Soldiers*, WASH. TIMES, April 29, 2004, at A5.

296. Article 15-6 Investigation of the 800th Military Police Brigade, at 16.

297. Id. at 16–17. The Taguba Report is reprinted in MARK DANNER, TORTURE AND TRUTH: AMERICA, ABU GHRAIB, AND THE WAR ON TERROR 279–328 (2004).

298. Seymour M. Hersh, *The General's Report*, NEW YORKER, June 24, 2007, at 63–65.

299. JAMEEL JAFFER & AMRIT SINGH, ADMINISTRATION OF TORTURE: A DOCUMENTARY RECORD FROM WASHINGTON TO ABU GHRAIB AND BEYOND (2007).

amounting to torture must be equivalent in intensity to the pain accompanying serious physical injury, such as organ failure, impairment of bodily function, or even death."[300] The legal deficiencies of this memo were considered so flagrant that it was withdrawn and replaced by an OLC memo dated December 30, 2004.[301]

In OLC memos, the administration argued that the U.S. naval base in Guantánamo was outside the United States and therefore beyond the jurisdiction of federal judges to hear cases brought by detainees.[302] That analysis prevailed on July 30, 2002, when District Judge Colleen Kollar-Kotelly ruled that the detainees held at the naval base were beyond the sovereign territory of the United States and could not use federal courts to hear petitions for habeas relief.[303] She relied heavily on the Supreme Court's decision in *Johnson v. Eisentrager* (1950), but that case did not resemble the conditions at Guantánamo. Unlike the detainees at the naval base, the individuals in *Eisentrager* had been charged, tried, and found guilty.[304]

*Eisentrager* applied to German citizens captured in China and tried in Germany, where no possible claim of U.S. sovereignty could be made. In contrast, the United States occupies the naval base at Guantánamo under a lease entered into with the Cuban government in 1903. The lease provides: "While on the one hand the United States recognizes the continuance of the ultimate sovereignty of the Republic of Cuba over [the military base at Guantánamo Bay], on the other hand the Republic of Cuba consents that during the period of occupancy by the United States of said areas under the terms of this agreement the United States shall exercise complete jurisdiction and control over and within said areas...."[305] The United States possessed full jurisdiction but not sovereignty.

In handling this case, the Supreme Court heard oral argument on April 20, 2004. John J. Gibbons for the detainees pointed out that the habeas statute is not limited to U.S. citizens. With certain exceptions, the writ of habeas corpus extends to a "prisoner."[306] Several Justices expressed discomfort about the scope of power sought by the administration. Justice Breyer remarked: "It seems rather contrary to an idea of a Constitution with three branches that the executive would be free do to whatever they want, whatever they want without a check." He said "several hundred years of British history" on habeas corpus ran against the administration's position.[307] Gibbons distinguished *Eisentrager* from the naval base. The 1950 case covered admitted enemy aliens who received a hearing before a military tribunal. The detainees at Guantánamo denied being enemy aliens and had never received a hearing.[308]

---

300. Memorandum from Jay S. Bybee, Assistant Attorney General, Office of Legal Counsel, to Alberto R. Gonzales, Counsel to the President, Aug. 1, 2002, *Re: Standards of Conduct for Interrogation under 18 U.S.C. §§ 2340-2340A*, at 1, http://www.justice.gov/olc/docs/memo-gonzales-aug2002.pdf.

301. Daniel Levin, Office of Legal Counsel, Legal Standards Applicable Under 18 U.S.C. §§ 2340-2340A, Dec. 30, 2004, http://www.justice.gov/olc/18usc23402340a2.htm. For background on the rewriting of the Bybee memo: JACK GOLDSMITH, THE TERROR PRESIDENCY: LAW AND JUDGMENT INSIDE THE BUSH ADMINISTRATION (2007).

302. Patrick F. Philbin & John C. Yoo, Office of Legal Counsel, to William J. Haynes, II, General Counsel, Department of Defense, *Possible Habeas Jurisdiction over Aliens Held in Guantanamo Bay, Cuba*, Dec. 28, 2001.

303. Rasul v. Bush, 235 F. Supp. 2d 55 (D.D.C. 2002).

304. Johnson v. Eisentrager, 339 U.S. 763 (1950).

305. Rasul v. Bush, 235 F. Supp. 2d at 69 n.14.

306. 28 U.S.C. § 2241(c).

307. U.S. Supreme Court, Rasul v. Bush, oral argument, April 20, 2004, at 42.

308. Id. at 9.

Solicitor General Ted Olson told the Court the question of sovereignty at the naval base was "a political question." It would be "remarkable," he said, "for the judiciary to start deciding where the United States is sovereign and where the United States has control."[309] He compared the situation at the naval base to detainees "in a field of combat where there are prisons in Afghanistan where we have complete control with respect to the circumstances." Several Justices found his analogy strained and unconvincing, noting that Afghanistan "is not a place where American law is, and for a century, has customarily been applied to all aspects of life," as with the naval base.[310]

On June 28, 2004, in a 6 to 3 decision, the Court rejected *Eisentrager* as an automatic bar on detainee access to habeas relief.[311] It ruled that federal courts have jurisdiction to consider challenges to the legality of detaining foreign nationals captured abroad, in connection with hostilities, and held at Guantánamo. Writing for the majority, Justice Stevens identified six key elements of the 1950 *Eisentrager* case. The prisoners (1) were enemy aliens, (2) had never been or resided in the United States, (3) were captured outside U.S. territory and held there in military custody as POWs, (4) were tried and convicted by a military tribunal sitting outside the United States, (5) were tried and convicted for offenses against laws of war committed outside the United States, and (6) were at all times imprisoned outside the United States. The detainees at the naval base were not nationals of countries at war with the United States, denied being engaged in or plotting acts of aggression against the United States, were not afforded access to any tribunal or even charged with or convicted of wrongdoing, and for two years had been detained in a territory over which the United States exercised exclusive jurisdiction and control.[312] The dissenters claimed the Court had overruled *Eisentrager*, but Justice Stevens clearly explained how several facts about the 1950 case differed from conditions at the naval base.[313]

Following the decisions in *Hamdi*, *Hamdan*, and *Rasul*, the Supreme Court delivered another significant ruling on the 9/11 cases. *Hamdan* forced the administration to seek statutory authority from Congress to create military tribunals. At a congressional hearing on July 11, 2006, Acting OLC head Steven Bradbury testified that the Court "did not address the President's constitutional authority and did not reach any constitutional question."[314] In fact, the Court in *Hamdan* reached (and decided) two constitutional issues: (1) the President lacked inherent authority to create tribunals and needed statutory authority; and (2) Congress possessed constitutional authority under Article I to impose on the President the procedural requirements of the Uniform Code of Military Justice.

During debate on the legislation, prominent issues included the use of evidence derived from hearsay or coercion, exclusion of defendants from their trials, allowing classified information to be shared with a defense lawyer but not the defendant, and access by the defendant to informers. As enacted, the Military Commissions Act (MCA) of 2006 placed restrictions on habeas petitions. The D.C. Circuit held that the MCA denied jurisdiction to federal courts to consider

---

309. Id. at 51.

310. Id. at 52.

311. Rasul v. Bush, 542 U.S. 466 (2004).

312. Id. at 475–76.

313. See JONATHAN HAFETZ, HABEAS CORPUS AFTER 9/11: CONFRONTING AMERICA'S NEW GLOBAL DETENTION SYSTEM (2011), and DARREN A. WHEELER, PRESIDENTIAL POWER IN ACTION: IMPLEMENTING SUPREME COURT DETAINEE DECISIONS (2008).

314. *The Supreme Court's Decision in Hamdan v. Rumsfeld*, hearing before the Senate Committee on the Judiciary, 109th Cong., 2d Sess. (2006), http://judiciary.senate.gov/print_testimony.cfm?id=1986&wit_id=5505.

habeas petitions filed by detainees at Guantánamo previous to the date of the statute."[315] The court revived the issue in *Rasul*. Was Guantánamo "sovereign" U.S. territory or merely under the "jurisdiction" of the United States? The D.C. Circuit denied that a "*de facto* sovereignty" existed at the naval base.[316]

On June 12, 2008, the Supreme Court in *Boumediene v. Bush* held that both the Military Commissions Act of 2006 and the Detainee Treatment Act of 2005 operated as an unconstitutional suspension of the writ of habeas corpus.[317] The Court ruled that the Suspension Clause was designed to protect against abuses of the writ by the elected branches, and the Clause had full effect at the naval base. Detainees at Guantánamo were thus entitled to petition a federal district court for habeas review. After *Boumediene*, approximately 250 habeas petitions were filed on behalf of Guantánamo detainees.[318]

Although federal district courts began granting habeas relief to a number of Guantánamo detainees, in some cases ordering their release, in each instance the D.C. Circuit reversed and the Supreme Court denied review. Instead of acting as an independent branch, the D.C. Circuit regularly favored the position advanced by the executive branch. Rather than assert the constitutional principles it announced in *Boumediene*, the Supreme Court chose to reject all appeals to it in these cases, including the denial of seven certiorari on June 11, 2012.[319]

In periods of national emergencies, both Congress and the judiciary have at times failed to exercise their independent checks against presidential initiatives, resulting in great harm to the nation, its citizens, and aliens. Lawmakers and judges take a constitutional oath to safeguard individual rights and structural checks. Those values are more important than a mechanical show of national unity behind a particular President. When legislators and judges uphold those values—as they sometimes have—by setting limits on presidential power, they faithfully perform their constitutional duties.

# 9. STATE SECRETS PRIVILEGE

The *New York Times* in December 2005 revealed warrantless eavesdropping by the Bush administration. When lawsuits challenged the legality of the program, the administration invoked the "state secrets privilege" to block disclosure of agency documents. In cases involving the government's "extraordinary rendition" program, used to transfer individuals to other countries for interrogation and torture, the administration also asserted the state secrets privilege. The Justice Department relies primarily on *United States v. Reynolds* (1953), the first time the Supreme

---

315. Boumediene v. Bush, 476 F.3d 981, 991 (D.C. Cir. 2007), citing Zadvydas v. Davis, 533 U.S. 678, 693 (2001).

316. Id. at 992.

317. 553 U.S. 723 (2008).

318. Michael John Garcia, Boumediene v. Bush: *Guantanamo Detainees' Right to* Habeas Corpus, Congressional Research Service, RL34536, Sept. 8, 2008, at 9. See also Jennifer K. Elsea and Michael John Garcia, *Enemy Combatant Detainees*: Habeas Corpus *Challenges in Federal Court*, Congressional Research Service, RL33180, Feb. 3, 2010.

319. Erwin Chemerinsky, *Losing Interest: Since the Supreme Court's Latest Ruling Guaranteeing Habeas Corpus Rights to Guantánamo Detainees, in 2008, It has Refused to Hear a Single Detainee Case*, Nat'l L.J., June 25, 2012, at 34.

Court recognized the privilege in its full scope. The case involved the crash of a B-29 that killed five crewmen and four civilian engineers. The widows of three engineers sought damages under the Federal Tort Claims Act, requesting access to the official accident report to determine government negligence.

The trial judge in *Reynolds* insisted that the government give him the report, to be read in his chambers, and the Third Circuit affirmed. The Supreme Court ruled for the executive branch without ever looking at the report. In the 1990s, the government declassified the report. It contains no confidential or state secrets but does reveal government negligence. The plane should not have been allowed to fly. The Court allowed itself to be misled by not independently examining the report.

## A. The Burr trial

In its brief in *Reynolds*, the Justice Department attempted to add legitimacy to the state secrets privilege by citing two early precedents: the Aaron Burr trial of 1807 and a Civil War case that involved a spy for President Lincoln.[320] The Burr trial adds no support for the state secrets privilege. The Civil War case applies only to a very specific set of circumstances unrelated to the facts of *Reynolds*.

In citing the Burr trial, the Department compiled a list of what it called successful assertions of the evidentiary privilege, with the second example dating from 1807: "Confidential information and letters relating to Burr's conspiracy."[321] According to a district court in 1977, the state secrets privilege "can be traced as far back as Aaron Burr's trial in 1807."[322] In 1989, the D.C. Circuit conceded that the "exact origins" of the privilege "are not certain," yet found its "initial roots" in Burr's trial.[323] In the judgment of a district court in 2004, the origins of the state secrets privilege "can be traced back to the treason trial of Aaron Burr."[324] In fact, there is no connection between Burr's trial and the state secrets privilege. It is regularly cited because courts routinely repeat a cite without ever double-checking its validity.

On December 6, 1806, President Jefferson alerted Congress to the plans of several private individuals who had armed themselves to carry out a military expedition against the territories of Spain.[325] In a message of January 16, 1807, he said that much of the information was in the form of letters "containing such a mixture of rumors, conjectures, and suspicions" that it would be inappropriate and unjust to name particular individuals involved in the conspiracy "except that of the principal actor, whose guilt is placed beyond question."[326] He identified Burr as "the prime mover" and referred to three letters received from General James Wilkinson.

320. *Brief for the United States*, United States v. Reynolds, No. 21, Supreme Court of the United States, at 10–11, 24, 32–33 (Sept. 1952).

321. Id. at 24.

322. Jabara v. Kelley, 75 F.R.D. 475, 483 (D. Mich. 1977).

323. In re U.S., 872 F.2d 472, 474–75 (D.C. Cir. 1989).

324. Edmonds v. U.S. Dept. of Justice, 323 F. Supp. 2d 65, 70 (D.D.C. 2004).

325. 1 Richardson 394.

326. Id. at 400.

In its brief in *Reynolds*, the Justice Department stated that during Burr's trial Chief Justice Marshall issued a subpoena to Jefferson to produce the letter from Wilkinson, "which Burr alleged contained information vital to his defense."[327] The brief made three claims: Jefferson "ignored the subpoena," the court "avoided the ultimate test of power with the executive," and whenever the question arises whether disclosure of information would be detrimental to the public interest, "the determination of the executive is conclusive."[328] All three statements by the Justice Department are false.

Burr, charged with treason and facing the death penalty, had every right to see the letters and determine their credibility and worth. Jefferson did not ignore the subpoena. Understanding that the government may not charge and convict someone on the basis of secret evidence, he directed George Hay, a government attorney handling the prosecution, and Attorney General Caesar Rodney to ensure that Burr receive the letters needed to prepare his defense.[329] Chief Justice Marshall, presiding over the trial as part of his circuit duties, said he would deplore any action on his part to deny an accused the information needed to rebut the government's charges.[330] The trial was run by Chief Justice Marshall, not by the executive branch. It was Marshall who made the conclusive determination about Burr's access to information.

On September 1, 1807, the jury found Burr not guilty on the charge of treason.[331] The court then considered seven counts of a misdemeanor charge. Again Burr sought documents, only to be told in one case the administration could not locate the original but would furnish a copy. Marshall ruled that a copy could not be admitted unless the administration proved the loss of the original.[332] Hay said he would produce a letter but indicated that some matters in the Wilkinson letters "ought not to be made public." He was willing, however, to put them "in the hands of the clerk confidentially" and allow Burr's attorneys to examine them. Hay indicated that some parts of the letters should not be made public, but he never argued that Burr and his attorneys could not see the materials.[333]

As negotiations continued over giving documents to Burr and what portions should be withheld from the public, a series of rulings by Marshall greatly undermined the government's case. At one point he inquired of the government: "gentlemen will consider whether they are not wasting the time and money of the United States, and of all those persons who are forced to attend here, whilst they are producing such a mass of testimony which does not bear upon the cause."[334] When the government moved to discharge the jury, Burr objected and insisted on a verdict. The jury retired and returned with a judgment: "Not guilty."[335]

Nothing in the Burr trial provides any precedent or support for the state secrets privilege. The government may not prosecute and convict someone on the basis of evidence withheld from

327. *Brief for the United States, supra* note 320, 32.

328. Id. at 32–33.

329. United States v. Burr, 25 Fed. Cas. 30, 65, 69, 253–54 (C.C.D. Va. 1807) (No. 24,692d); 9 THE WRITINGS OF THOMAS JEFFERSON 61n (Ford ed., 1898).

330. United States v. Burr, 25 Cas. 37.

331. United States v. Burr, 25 Fed. Cas. 180-81 (C.C.D. Va. 1807) (No. 14,693).

332. Id. at 189.

333. Id. at 190–92.

334. United States v. Burr, 25 Fed. Cas. 201 (C.C.D. Va. 1807) (No. 14,694). See also 193–98.

335. Id. at 201.

the accused. If the government decides it cannot surrender sensitive or confidential documents to the accused, it must drop the charges. President Jefferson knew that, as did Chief Justice Marshall. The state secrets privilege is entirely unrelated to cases of prosecution brought by the government. It applies solely to civil cases brought by private parties against the government.[336]

In *United States v. Nixon* (1974), the Supreme Court replayed the issue posed by the Burr trial. Defendants in criminal court required evidence held by the government. President Nixon claimed he had exclusive authority to decide what documents to share with Special Prosecutor Archibald Cox and federal judges, but the Court rejected his argument. In a criminal case, where an accused needs information to protect rights in court, the President's general authority over executive privilege may not override a defendant's specific need for evidence.[337]

## B. Lincoln's spy and its progeny

In *Reynolds*, the Supreme Court described the government's attempt to invoke the state secrets privilege as "well established in the law of evidence."[338] Among the cases the Court cited for that proposition, and standing first in line, is a Civil War government spy case, *Totten v. United States* (1875).[339] President Lincoln entered into a contract with William A. Lloyd, directing him to travel behind Confederate lines to collect information about its military strength. Lloyd was to receive $200 a month, but he received funds only to cover his expenses.[340] After he died his family sued to recover compensation for his services.

The Supreme Court rejected the lawsuit because "public policy forbids the maintenance of any suit in a court of justice, the trial of which would inevitably lead to the disclosure of matters which the law itself regards as confidential, and respecting which it will not allow the confidence to be violated."[341] Following that principle, suits "cannot be maintained which would require a disclosure of the confidences of the confessional, or those between husband and wife, or of communications by a client to his counsel for professional advice, or of a patient to his physician for a similar purpose."[342] "Much greater reason exists," said the Court, "for the application of the principle to cases of contract for secret services with the government, as the existence of a contract of that kind is itself a fact not to be disclosed."[343]

The lawsuit could not proceed for several reasons. First, President Lincoln paid Lloyd from a contingency fund that Congress, by statute, placed exclusively under presidential control.[344] Second, by its very nature, a secret contract between the government and a private citizen may not be taken to court at some later date to be enforced. When Lloyd entered into the contract

336. For details on the Burr trial: Louis Fisher, In the Name of National Security: Unchecked Presidential Power and the *Reynolds* Case 212–21 (2006).

337. United States v. Nixon, 418 U.S. 683 (1974).

338. United States v. Reynolds, 345 U.S. 1, 6–7 (1953).

339. 92 U.S. 105 (1875).

340. Id. at 106.

341. Id. at 107.

342. Id.

343. Id.

344. Id. at 106.

with President Lincoln, he understood it was a secret agreement and needed to remain so. The Court distinguished between ordinary contracts (enforceable in court) and secret contracts (which are not). *Totten* has no relevance to the case brought by the three widows in *Reynolds*.

The *Totten* principle applies to lawsuits involving spies for the government.[345] In 1954, the Court of Claims dismissed a petition seeking expenses and compensation for secret services allegedly performed for the federal government.[346] In two rulings in 1980 and 1981, the Court of Claims rejected efforts by individuals to be compensated for work they said they did for the CIA.[347] Another unsuccessful case involved a Vietnamese man who claimed he did covert work for the CIA from 1962 to 1964 and deserved back pay for his services.[348] In 2001, a district court applied *Totten* against an individual who tried to recover damages for breach of an alleged contract with the CIA.[349] Also rejected on *Totten* grounds was a case brought by someone who presented himself as a CIA agent.[350] The principle of *Totten* reached the Supreme Court in 2005. A husband and wife team ("John and Jane Doe") alleged that the CIA failed to provide them with financial assistance it had promised for their espionage services during the Cold War. Unanimously, the Court held the suit barred by *Totten*.[351]

A basic difference between these cases and the broad privilege of state secrets is this: the lawsuit in *Totten* was not justiciable. A state secrets case *is* justiciable. The question is how a court decides to balance the interests of private plaintiffs and counterclaims made by the executive branch. In the *Reynolds* case, both in district court and in the Third Circuit, federal judges told the government: You are entitled to protect the confidentiality of certain documents and withhold them from the plaintiffs and from us, but in doing so you will lose the tort claims action brought against you.

## C. A B-29 explodes in midair

On October 6, 1948, over Waycross, Georgia, a B-29 lost control at 20,000 feet and exploded. Killed in the blast were five of eight crew members and four of five civilian engineers who served as technical advisers of secret equipment. Military personnel may not sue the government, but three widows of the civilian engineers brought an action under the Federal Tort Claims Act of 1946. The statute authorizes federal agencies to settle claims against the United States caused by negligent or wrongful acts of federal employees acting within the scope of their official duties.[352] Congress directed federal courts to treat the government like a private individual, deciding a dispute on the basis of facts and with no partiality in favor of the government. The United States "shall be liable in respect of such claims…in the same manner, and to the same extent as a

---

345.  De Arnaud v. United States, 151 U.S. 483 (1894); Allen v. United States, 27 Ct. Cl. 9 (1892).

346.  Tucker v. United States, 118 F. Supp. 371 (Ct. Cl. 1954).

347.  Simrick v. United States, 224 Ct. Cl. 724 (1980); Mackowski v. United States, 228 Ct. Cl. 717 (1981), cert. denied, 454 U.S. 1123 (1981).

348.  Guong v. United States, 860 F.2d 1063 (Fed. Cir. 1988).

349.  Kielczynski v. U.S. C.I.A., 128 F. Supp. 2d 151 (E.D.N.Y. 2001).

350.  Monarch Assur. P.L.C. v. United States, 42 Fed. Cl. 258, 264 (1998); Monarch Assur. P.L.C. v. United States, 36 Fed. Cl. 324 (1996); Monarch Assur. P.L.C. v. United States, 244 F.3d 1356 (Fed. Cir. 2001).

351.  Tenet v. Doe, 544 U.S. 1 (2005). For details on these cases: FISHER, *supra* note 336, at 223–27.

352.  60 Stat. 843, sec. 403(1) (1946).

private individual under like circumstances, except that the United States shall not be liable for interest prior to judgment, or for punitive damages."[353]

There was no reason for judges in a tort claims case to accept at face value a government's claim or assertion. Courts have a duty to examine evidence from both sides. To uncritically accept the government's word in these cases would be to abdicate the court's duty to protect the rights of private parties to present their case in the most effective manner. Permitting executive officials to withhold documents that revealed government negligence would make a nullity of the tort claims statute and abandon the adversary process needed to inform a court.

In a district court in Pennsylvania, attorneys for the three widows submitted a number of interrogatories to the government. One question asked whether the government had prescribed modifications for the B-29 engines to prevent overheating and reduce fire hazards. If so, when were the modifications prescribed? If any modifications had been carried out, the interrogatory asked for details. The government answered: "No."[354] When the declassified accident report was discovered on the Internet in 2000 by the three families, they realized the government's answer was false.

The district court looked for guidance from earlier cases where the government considered certain documents too sensitive, privileged, or secret to be shared with a private plaintiff. Federal judges consistently ruled that they needed access to documents to independently verify that the government accurately characterized their contents.[355] Guided by those precedents, District Judge William Kirkpatrick decided on June 30, 1950, that the accident report on the B-29 crash was not "privileged."[356] He issued an order permitting the plaintiffs to inspect the requested documents, including the official accident report. The government presented an undated claim of privilege by the Secretary of the Air Force, Thomas K. Finletter, which turned out to be the key document. He spoke about state secrets and the official accident report, but never said explicitly that the accident report contained state secrets. We know now, after the report was declassified and made public, it contained no state secrets.

Judge Kirkpatrick directed the government to produce several documents, including the accident report and statements of the three surviving crew members, to be examined in his chambers. When the government failed to produce the documents he ruled in favor of the three widows.[357] On December 11, 1951, a unanimous Third Circuit upheld the district court's decision. In tort claims cases, where the government has consented to be sued as a private person, whatever claims of public interest might exist in withholding accident reports "must yield to what Congress evidently regarded as the greater public interest involved in seeing that justice is done to persons injured by governmental operations whom it has authorized to enforce their claims by suit against the United States."[358]

Beyond questions of statutory policy, the Third Circuit concluded that granting the government a "sweeping privilege" of state secrets would be "contrary to a sound public policy."[359] It would be

---

353. Id. at 843–44, sec. 410(a).

354. Transcript of Record, Supreme Court of the United States, October Term, 1952, No. 21, United States v. Reynolds, at 14.

355. FISHER, *supra* note 336, at 36–42.

356. Brauner v. United States, 10 F.R.D. 468, 472 (D. Pa. 1950).

357. FISHER, *supra* note 336, at 56–58.

358. Reynolds v. United States, 192 F.2d 987, 994 (3d Cir. 1951).

359. Id. at 995.

a small step, said the court, "to assert a privilege against the disclosure of records merely because they might prove embarrassing to government officers."[360] The court rejected the government's position that it was within "the sole province of the Secretary of the Air Force [Finletter] to determine whether any privileged material is contained in the documents."[361] To allow the government as a party to "conclusively determine the Government's claim of privilege is to abdicate the judicial function and permit the executive branch of the Government to infringe the independent province of the judiciary as laid down by the Constitution."[362]

This thoughtful and principled analysis by the lower courts was not followed by the Supreme Court. The fundamental issue, which the executive branch repeatedly muddled, was whether the accident report contained secret information. At various places the government's brief to the Supreme Court was misleading about the contents of the accident report. It asserted: "to the extent that the report reveals military secrets concerning the structure or performance of the plane that crashed or deals with these factors in relation to projected or suggested secret improvements it falls within the judicially recognized 'state secrets' privilege."[363] *To the extent*? In the case of the official accident report, the extent was zero.[364]

On March 9, 1953, the Supreme Court decided that the executive branch had presented a valid claim of privilege. It acted without ever looking at the accident report. Speaking for a 6 to 3 Court, Chief Justice Fred Vinson announced incoherent principles of judicial responsibility: "The court itself must determine whether the circumstances are appropriate for the claim of privilege, and yet do so without forcing a disclosure of the very thing the privilege is designed to protect."[365] Disclosure to the public is a reasonable concern, but has no application to disclosure to a court for in camera inspection. If a court does not examine a disputed document, it is incapable of determining "whether the circumstances are appropriate for the claim of privilege." In this case, the Supreme Court accepted at face value an assertion by the executive branch, an assertion that proved to be false. As to the privilege against disclosing documents, the Court said it "must be satisfied from all the evidence and circumstances" before it decides to accept the privilege.[366] Without inspecting actual documents, a court has no "evidence" other than self-serving assertions by one party to the case: the executive branch.

Chief Justice Vinson cautioned that judicial control "over the evidence of a case cannot be abdicated to the caprice of executive officers."[367] If, as in this case, an executive officer acted capriciously and arbitrarily, a court would have no capacity to make that discovery without reading the contested document. Deciding the case as it did, the Court clearly "abdicated to the caprice of executive officers." It surrendered to the executive branch the fundamental judicial duty to decide questions of privileges and evidence. The majority served not justice but the

---

360. Id.

361. Id. at 996–97

362. Id. at 997.

363. *Brief for the United States*, United States v. Reynolds, No. 21, U.S. Supreme Court, October Term, 1952, at 45.

364. For access to the accident report: http://www.fas.org/sgp/othergov/reynoldspetapp.pdf, at 10a-68a.

365. United States v. Reynolds, 345 U.S. at 8.

366. Id. at 9.

367. Id. at 9–10.

executive branch. It signaled that in this type of national security case, the courtroom tilted away from the private litigant and became a safe haven for executive power.

The Court could have followed the responsible path taken by the district court and the Third Circuit: decide for the three widows because the government refused to release the accident report to the trial judge. Vinson adopted an option that was the least justified. He assumed on the basis of highly ambiguous claims by the executive branch that the assertion of state secrets had merit. By so doing, the Court resorted to a jumbled reasoning process that led future lower courts to damage the rights of private litigants, fair procedures, the rule of law, and the system of checks and balances. Unwilling to examine the accident report to ensure it was properly informed, the majority in *Reynolds* took the chance of being fooled by the executive branch. As it turned out, it was.

## D. Fraud against the court

In 1996, the Air Force decided to declassify and release some accident reports, including one that contained the investigation of the B-29 crash. The daughter of one of the civilian engineers who died on the plane learned of the report and obtained a copy. She discovered that the report contained no secrets but did describe negligence on the part of the government. The three families discussed the matter and decided to sue the government for deceiving the judiciary.[368] Their attorneys filed a motion for a writ of *coram nobis*, charging that the government had misled the Supreme Court and committed fraud against it.

As explained by the Supreme Court in an earlier ruling, a court needs to revisit a judgment after learning that fraud cast a shadow over an original ruling. Tolerating fraud in a particular case lowers respect for judges and reduces confidence in the courts. Injury is done not merely to the litigant but against "the institutions set up to protect and safeguard the public.... The public welfare demands that the agencies of public justice be not so impotent that they must always be mute and helpless victims of deception and fraud."[369]

On March 4, 2003, the three families petitioned the Supreme Court for a writ of error *coram nobis*. They asked the Court to vacate its 1953 decision and reinstate the district court's judgment: awarding the widows and their families damages, attorney fees, and single or double costs as a sanction against the government's misconduct.[370] The petition included specific negligence detailed in the accident report. The Air Force failed to install required heat shields for the engines and did not instruct the civilian engineers on the use of parachutes and emergency aircraft evacuation. Several answers by the government to interrogatories were either inaccurate or patently false. Without explanation, the Supreme Court on June 23, 2003, denied the petition.[371]

---

368. For the discovery of the declassified accident report and the decision to sue the government: Fisher, *supra* note 336, at 165–71.

369. Hazel-Atlas Co. v. Hartford Co., 322 U.S. 238, 246 (1944). For recent experiences with *coram nobis* cases: Fisher, *supra* note 336, at 171–76.

370. *Petition for a Writ of Error* Coram Nobis *to Remedy Fraud upon This Court*, In re Patricia J. Herring, No. 02M76, at i.

371. In re Herring, 539 U.S. 940 (2003).

On October 1, 2003, the families filed an action in district court in Pennsylvania to remedy fraud on the court. The following September, the court granted the government's motion to dismiss.[372] The Third Circuit affirmed, and the Supreme Court on May 1, 2006, denied certiorari.[373] Unprotected in this litigation was the fundamental need to protect the integrity, independence, and reputation of the federal judiciary. By accepting the government's assertion that the accident report contained state secrets and failing to examine the document, the Supreme Court in 1953 appeared to function as an agency of the executive branch. Even when the executive branch's dissembling was exposed decades later, courts failed to hold it accountable. When courts operate in that manner, litigants and citizens lose faith in the judiciary, the rule of law, and the system of checks and balances.

## E. State secrets after 9/11

The scope of the state secrets privilege expanded after the terrorist attacks of 9/11. On a range of issues, the privilege defeated challenges of illegal and unconstitutional conduct by the executive branch.[374] The Bush administration secretly authorized the National Security Agency (NSA) to eavesdrop on telephone conversations and e-mails without first seeking warrants from the Foreign Intelligence Surveillance Court. Congress created this court in 1978 in response to illegal warrantless surveillance by the Nixon administration, an action struck down by a district court, the Sixth Circuit, and the Supreme Court. The judiciary dismissed the claim that the President possesses a broad "inherent" power to conduct such operations.[375] The Foreign Intelligence Surveillance Act (FISA) of 1978 provided that court-approved procedures for electronic surveillance within the United States for foreign intelligence purposes "shall be the exclusive means" of conducting such surveillance.

On December 16, 2005, *The New York Times* broke the story on the secret NSA program.[376] OLC produced a 42-page "white paper" defending NSA's activities.[377] The analysis offered two arguments: one statutory, the other constitutional. OLC claimed that Congress, in passing the Authorization for Use of Military Force (AUMF) after 9/11, had "confirmed and supplemented the President's recognized authority under Article II of the Constitution to conduct such warrantless surveillance to prevent further catastrophic attacks on the homeland."[378] If Congress after 9/11 wanted to change FISA procedures to grant the President greater authority to act

---

372. Memorandum and Order, Herring v. United States, Civil Action No. 03-CV-5500-LDD (E.D. Pa. 2004).

373. Herring v. United States, 424 F.3d 384 (3d Cir. 2005), cert. denied, 547 U.S. 1123 (2006). For details on the briefs and oral argument: Fisher, *supra* note 336, at 176–211.

374. Robert M. Chesney, *State Secrets and the Limits of National Security Litigation*, 75 G.W. L. Rev. 1249 (2007); Robert M. Pallitto & William G. Weaver, Presidential Secrecy and the Law (2007); and William G. Weaver & Robert M. Pallitto, *State Secrets and Executive Power*, 120 Pol. Sci. Q. 120 (2005).

375. United States v. United States District Court, 407 U.S. 297 (1972). For details on this decision and rulings by the lower courts: Louis Fisher, The Constitution and 9/11: Recurring Threats to America's Freedoms 287–90 (2008).

376. James Risen & Eric Lichtblau, *Bush Lets U.S. Spy on Callers Without Courts*, N.Y. Times, Dec. 16, 2005, at A1.

377. Office of Legal Counsel, *Legal Authorities Supporting the Activities of the National Security Agency Described by the President*, Jan. 19, 2006.

378. Id. at 2.

without a judicial check, it could have amended FISA but did not do that. Amendments to statutes are made expressly, not by implication, especially to a statute that unambiguously provided the "exclusive means" for conducting foreign intelligence surveillance.

OLC's constitutional argument referred to the President's "well-recognized inherent constitutional authority as Commander in Chief and sole organ for the Nation in foreign affairs to conduct warrantless surveillance of enemy forces for intelligence purposes to detect and disrupt armed attacks on the United States."[379] The sole-organ doctrine, of course, is a misconception of John Marshall's speech in 1800 (Chapter 7, section 1B). In FISA, Congress left no room for inherent presidential authority to conduct warrantless surveillance. Court-approved procedures supplied the only means. OLC essentially argued that Congress may not, by statute, limit powers the executive branch considers to be "inherent" in the President.

On July 20, 2006, a federal district court held that the state secrets privilege did not block action on a lawsuit challenging the constitutionality of the surveillance program.[380] A month later, a federal district court in Detroit ruled that the program violated the Constitution and several statutes, but the Sixth Circuit reversed the district court on the ground that the plaintiffs lacked standing to sue.[381] On February 19, 2008, the Supreme Court declined to take the case.[382] Major litigation involved the Al-Haramain Islamic Foundation, a case that moved back and forth between trial and appellate courts. On July 2, 2008, District Judge Vaughn Walker asked what should happen in a conflict between FISA and the state secrets privilege. He stated flatly that "FISA preempted the state secrets privilege."[383] Litigation continued until December 21, 2010, when Judge Walker ordered the government to pay nearly $2.6 million in lawyers' fees and damages to attorneys who represented Al-Haramain. He refused to grant punitive damages against the government because he found insufficient evidence that the NSA had shown "reckless or callous indifference" to the plaintiffs rights.[384]

The state secrets privilege was regularly invoked by the government in cases of "extraordinary rendition": seizing individuals and transferring them to other countries for interrogation and torture. Rendition, sometimes used as a substitute for an extradition treaty, means surrendering someone to another jurisdiction *for trial*. Over time, rendition became associated with kidnappings and forcible abductions, but the purpose continued to be bringing someone to trial.[385] With extraordinary rendition, there is no trial or procedural safeguards. Only interrogation and physical abuse.

Khaled El-Masri, born in Kuwait of Lebanese parents, moved to Germany in 1985 and became a German citizen. At the end of 2003 he traveled to Macedonia for vacation. Border

---

379. Id.

380. Hepting v. AT&T Corp., 439 F. Supp. 2d 974 (N.D. Cal. 2006).

381. American Civil Liberties Union v. National Sec. Agency, 438 F. Supp. 2d 754 (E.D. Mich. 2006); ACLU v. National Sec. Agency, 493 F.3d 644 (6th Cir. 2007).

382. American Civil Liberties Union v. National Security Agency, 552 U.S. 1179 (2008).

383. In re National Sec. Agency Telecommunications Rec., 564 F. Supp. 2d 1109, 1111 (D. Cal. 2008).

384. Eric Lichtblau, *U.S. Ordered to Pay Group of Muslims*, N.Y. TIMES, Dec. 22, 2010, at A23. Further details on this litigation: Louis Fisher, *National Security Surveillance*, in CONGRESS AND THE POLITICS OF NATIONAL SECURITY 213–29 (David P. Auerswald & Colton C. Campbell eds., 2012).

385. For analysis of extraordinary rendition and litigation during the administration of George W. Bush: FISHER, *supra* note 375, at 321–60, and Louis Fisher, *Extraordinary Rendition: The Price of Secrecy*, 57 AM. U. L. REV. 1405 (2008).

guards detained him because of confusion about his name. They thought he was Khalid al-Masri, a suspect from the al Qaeda Hamburg cell. There was also suspicion (later shown to be false) that El-Masri's passport was a forgery. In early January 2004, he was transferred to CIA agents and flown to a secret prison called the "Salt Pit" in Afghanistan. Held for five months, he was repeatedly refused counsel or access to a representative of the German government.

The CIA concluded that his passport was genuine and they had imprisoned the wrong person. On May 28, 2004, he was flown to Albania and left alone, at night, on a hill. Later he was taken to the airport and flown to Frankfurt. On December 6, 2005, he sued CIA Director George Tenet, the airlines used by the CIA, and current and former employees of the agency. The Bush administration asserted the state secrets privilege to block his case from moving toward discovery and access to government documents. On May 21, 2006, a federal district court held that the privilege has been validly asserted and dismissed El-Masri's case.[386]

As with many state secrets cases, the court spoke inconsistently about a plaintiff's rights and executive branch authority. The judge said that courts "must not blindly accept the Executive Branch's assertion" about state secrets but "must instead independently and carefully determine whether, in the circumstances, the claimed secrets deserve the protection of the privilege."[387] Courts "must carefully scrutinize the assertion of the privilege lest it be used by the government to shield 'material not strictly necessary to prevent injury to national security.' "[388] Yet "courts must also bear in mind the Executive Branch's preeminent authority over military and diplomatic matters" and must accept the executive branch's assertion of the privilege "whenever its independent inquiry discloses a '*reasonable danger* that compulsion of the evidence will expose military matters which, in the interest of national security, should not be divulged.' "[389] Once a court is satisfied that the claim is validly asserted, "the privilege is not subject to a judicial balancing of the various interests at stake."[390]

For some reason, the court decided to offer a balancing test: El-Masri's "private interests must give way to the national interest in preserving state secrets."[391] The private interest of one individual is unlikely to outweigh the claimed interest of the entire government or the nation, unless one analyzes more closely "national interest." What national interest is served by picking up the wrong person, keeping him in prison for five months, and with no capacity to seek damages and have the government concede error? Actually, on El-Masri's side are all individuals, U.S. citizen or alien, who do not want to experience his fate. It is in the national interest to have an independent court pass judgment on abusive executive actions. Checks and balances are in the national interest. Government apologies and restitution for wrongs done are in the national interest.

El-Masri appealed his case to the Fourth Circuit, which noted that a draft report by the Council of Europe substantially affirmed El-Masri's account of his rendition. Yet the Fourth Circuit affirmed the district court decision, in part because the case "pits the judiciary's search

386. El-Masri v. Tenet, 437 F. Supp. 2d 530, 539 (E.D. Va. 2006).

387. Id. at 536.

388. Id., citing Ellsberg v. Mitchell, 709 F.2d 51, 58 (D.C. Cir. 1983).

389. Id. at 536–37, citing United States v. Reynolds, 345 U.S. 1, 10 (1953) (emphasis added by district court).

390. Id. at 536, 537.

391. Id. at 539.

for truth against the Executive's duty to maintain the nation's security."[392] The judiciary certainly cannot search for truth if it uncritically accepts executive assertions about state secrets, blocks access to documents, and eliminates the adversary process that serves to inform a court. The Fourth Circuit repeated the warning in *Reynolds* that courts should not force the disclosure "of the very thing the privilege is designed to protect."[393] Evidence is not "disclosed" when a judge reads disputed documents in a private chamber.

On December 13, 2012, a unanimous opinion from the European Court of Human Rights ruled that El-Masri was an innocent victim of torture and abuse. It held Macedonia responsible for his ill-treatment and transfer to U.S. authorities. The Court ordered Macedonia to pay about $78,000 in damages. Macedonia's Ministry of Justice said it would comply.[394]

The executive branch inflicted much greater abuse on Maher Arar, a Canadian citizen. Upon returning home to Ottawa in September 2002, he was questioned at the JFK airport by New York police and FBI agents. The next day he was transferred to the Metropolitan Detention Center. Several weeks later the administration sent him to Syria, which the State Department lists as a country with a known record of torture.[395] For nearly a year he was subjected to beatings and threatened with electric shocks and other abuse. He was never formally charged with anything. Syria found no evidence linking him to terrorism.[396]

Arar filed a civil suit seeking money damages and declaratory relief from a number of U.S. officials in their individual and official capacities. The Justice Department invoked the state secrets privilege, claiming that the documents sought by Arar were "properly classified" and that disclosure "would interfere with foreign relations, reveal intelligence-gathering sources or methods, and be detrimental to national security."[397] A federal district court held that Arar lacked standing to bring a claim against U.S. officials responsible for holding him incommunicado in New York and removing him to Syria for detention and torture.[398] The court explained the importance of secrecy in foreign affairs: "One need not have much imagination to contemplate the negative effect on our relations with Canada if discovery were to proceed in this case and were it to turn out that certain high Canadian officials had, despite public denials, acquiesced in Arar's removal to Syria."[399]

Canada had been conducting its own investigation. Seven months after the district court's ruling, a three-volume, 822-page judicial report concluded that Canadian intelligence officials had passed false warnings and unreliable information about Arar to the United States. On January 26, 2007, Prime Minister Stephen Harper released a public apology to Arar and his

392. El-Masri v. United States, 479 F.3d 296, 304 (4th Cir. 2007).

393. Id.

394. Nicholas Kulish, *Court Finds Rights Violation in C.I.A. Rendition Case*, N.Y. TIMES, Dec. 14, 2012, at A13.

395. U.S. Department of State, Country Reports on Human Rights Practices, Syria, 2002, at 1; http://www.state.gov/g/drl/rls/hrrpt/2002/18289.htm.

396. For details on his prison conditions: FISHER, *supra* note 375, at 346–49.

397. U.S. Department of Justice, *Memorandum in Support of the United States' Assertion of State Secrets Privilege*, Arar v. Ashcroft, C.A. No. 04-CV-249-DG-VVP (E.D.N.Y. 2005), at 2–3.

398. Arar v. Ashcroft, 414 F. Supp. 2d 250 (E.D.N.Y. 2006).

399. Id. at 281.

family and provided $9.75 million in compensation.[400] Arar's appeal to the Second Circuit was unsuccessful. On June 14, 2010, the Supreme Court denied his petition for certiorari. No apology or statement of regret came from the United States.

LOYALTY DOES NOT mean automatic support for what the three branches do, either separately or in combination. Self-government requires federal officials and the public to think independently in an informed manner. After World War II, Presidents asserted greater power under the theory that their energy, activism, and initiative would promote the public good. That period includes costly wars in Korea, Vietnam, and Iraq II, the scandals of Watergate and Iran-Contra, and impeachment actions against Nixon and Clinton. Instead of demonstrating reliable judgment and a commitment to the national interest, the presidential record has often been one of miscalculation, deceit, and incompetence. Toward the end of his concurrence in the Steel Seizure Case, Justice Jackson put his trust in structural checks that are basic to the U.S. Constitution: "With all its defects, delays and inconveniences, men have discovered no technique for long preserving free government except that the Executive be under the law, and that the law be made by parliamentary deliberations." He acknowledged that these institutional strengths "may be destined to pass away. But it is the duty of the Court to be last, not first, to give them up."[401]

---

400. Prime Minister releases letter of apology to Maher Arar and his family and announces completion of mediation process, http://www.pm.gc.ca/eng/media.asp?id=1510.

401. Youngstown Co. v. Sawyer, 343 U.S. 579, 655 (Jackson, J., concurring).

# Conclusions

PRESIDENTIAL POWER HAS PROGRESSED THROUGH TWO MAIN PERIODS. From 1789 to World War II, the pattern consisted of strong Presidents followed by weak Presidents, with Congress playing the alternate roles of descendant and ascendant. Assertions of independent executive power triggered a response by the legislative branch, determined to regain control. No President over those years claimed the right to take the country from a state of peace to a state of war without first coming to Congress to obtain either a declaration or authorization for military action.

From 1950 to the present, political power has moved steadily toward the White House. This shift gained support from the constant international shadow of communism, the Cold War, and the War on Terrorism. Military threats, whether real or contrived, expanded presidential power not only over external affairs but domestic policy as well. On a regular basis, the executive branch appealed to federal courts to promote assertions of presidential authority. Over those seven decades, Congress recognized it was losing power to the executive branch and made efforts to strengthen the legislative branch. Reforms included increases in professional committee staff and seeking assistance from such legislative agencies as the General Accounting Office (now the Government Accountability Office), the Congressional Research Service, the Congressional Budget Office, and the short-lived Office of Technology Assessment.

Prominent scholars promoted the growth of presidential power. Beginning in the 1940s, they described the President in idealized and reverential tones: a national officer dedicated to keeping the nation safe, committed to the "national interest," and surrounded by experts available to provide informed and reliable advice. The public law model that had previously restrained the President was largely discarded in favor of a more independent officer, less subject to the constitutional system of checks and balances.[1]

The contrast between this highly theoretical construct of the President and the actual occupants of the White House has been striking. The record over those seven decades includes presidential wars that did substantial harm to the nation, particularly the Korean War, the Vietnam War, and military actions against Iraq in 2003. Presidents Richard Nixon and Bill Clinton faced impeachment proceedings. President Ronald Reagan became embroiled in the Iran-Contra

---

1. Louis Fisher, *Teaching the President: Idealizing a Constitutional Office*, 45 PS: POLITICAL SCIENCE & POLITICS 17 (2012). For a symposium on political scientists who conduct research on constitutional law and public policy and challenge broad claims of presidential power, see *Law and (Disciplinary) Order: A Dialogue about Louis Fisher, Constitutionalism, and Political Science*, 46 PS: POLITICAL SCIENCE & POLITICS 483-523 (2013).

affair, involving a decision by executive officials to seek funds from foreign nations and private citizens to carry out a program that violated statutory policy. Other Presidents displayed limited skills in using political power. They learned that the oratorical abilities that enabled them to win elections did not ensure accomplishments once in office. Thomas Cronin criticized scholarly efforts to promote romantic and unrealistic models of the presidency. After reviewing the period from 1920 to 2009, he offered this judgment about presidential performance:

> Maybe about three were successful. At least half a dozen failed in one way or another. Nixon was ingloriously forced from the office. Bill Clinton was impeached. The American voters vetoed four others when they sought reelection (Hoover, Ford, Carter, and Bush I). Two others (Truman and LBJ) wisely stepped aside rather than almost surely face voter rebuke in 1952 and 1968.[2] [The three Presidents who gained a "successful" score from Cronin were Franklin D. Roosevelt, Dwight D. Eisenhower, and Ronald Reagan.]

Federal judges have contributed to the expansion of presidential power. Courts regularly depend on precedents that were false when first issued and remain so over time. A prominent example is language that appears in the *Curtiss-Wright* case of 1936. Justice Sutherland's description of the President as "sole organ" in external affairs served to place unchecked power in the executive branch. It is irresponsible for courts to continue to rely on his misconception. Anyone reading the sole-organ speech by John Marshall delivered in 1800 can understand that he never promoted plenary, independent, or exclusive power for the President in foreign affairs (Chapter 7, section 1B). Lawmakers, courts, and scholars need to study original documents, not repeat secondhand errors. Similarly careless is the judicial acceptance of the executive branch assertion that the state secrets privilege may be traced back to the Aaron Burr trial in 1807. That is plain error (Chapter 9, section 9A). Congress and the judiciary have a constitutional duty to independently scrutinize executive assertions to ensure they are not used to implement misguided and illegal programs.

Shifting power to the President and the judiciary moves the nation toward a dramatically less democratic political system: an executive branch with only two elected officials and a judiciary with none. At risk, then, is the Framers' commitment to self-government. Under their framework, people were not "subjects" under an all-powerful Executive. They were capable of governing themselves through elected representatives. In Federalist No. 49, Madison referred to the people as "the only legitimate fountain of power."[3] In Federalist No. 51, he said that in "republican government, the legislative authority necessarily predominates."[4]

The Constitution is not self-executing. The three branches are expected to fulfill the duties assigned them: protecting their powers and fighting off encroachments. In Federalist No. 48, Madison explained why the U.S. Constitution could not maintain its meaning and survival simply by putting words to paper: "a mere demarcation on parchment of the constitutional limits of the several departments, is not a sufficient guard against those encroachments which lead to a tyrannical concentration of all the powers of government in the same hands."[5] Unless those

---

2. Thomas E. Cronin, On the Presidency: Teacher, Soldier, Shaman, Pol 2 (2009).

3. The Federalist 348.

4. Id. at 356.

5. Id. at 347.

departments "be so far connected and blended as to give to each a constitutional control over the others, the degree of separation which the maxim requires, as essential to a free government, can never in practice be duly maintained."[6]

Madison's system of checks and balances has not been easy to grasp or apply. To exercise their checking function, branches must overlap to some degree. He cautioned: "the powers properly belonging to one of the departments ought not to be directly and completely administered by either of the other departments."[7] What powers "properly" belong to a branch? Congress may not actually exercise the presidential powers of pardon or veto, although lawmakers and private citizens often apply pressure to influence those decisions.

Other powers, seemingly assigned to a particular branch, invite competition. Each house of Congress is specifically empowered to "determine the Rules of its Proceedings." Presidents and their advisers on occasion will attempt to interpret those rules. In January 2012, the Obama administration decided that pro forma sessions of the Senate did not prevent the President from making recess appointments (Chapter 4, section 6A). Litigants asked the judiciary to offer its own interpretation of legislative rules, as it did in 1932 in deciding that a Senate rule did not permit it to "reconsider" a nominee who had been confirmed, taken the oath, and entered into the duties of office.[8]

Similar complexities apply to the President's power to nominate. Article II, section 2, specifies that the President "shall nominate" individuals to begin the confirmation process. The language may appear to vest that decision exclusively in the President, but the executive branch has long understood the practical need to permit Senators (and others) a role in deciding who is actually nominated. The two elected branches have agreed that the political system works best by allowing part of the nominating process to originate outside the executive branch. If Presidents and their advisers regard a name as not suitable, they can advise a Senator or other party to recommend someone else (Chapter 4, sections 5A and 5B). This type of accommodation helps government function effectively. The Framers wanted a workable political system capable of meeting public needs.

Federal judges recognize that a compromise entered into by the elected branches "is most likely to meet their essential needs and the country's constitutional balance."[9] In adopting a Constitution with general and overlapping provisions, the Framers anticipated that "a spirit of dynamic compromise would promote resolution of the dispute in the manner most likely to result in efficient and effective functioning of our governmental system."[10] The executive and legislative branches "should take cognizance of an implicit constitutional mandate to seek optimal accommodation through a realistic evaluation of the needs of the conflicting branches in the particular fact situation."[11]

Article II, section 2 specifies that the President "shall have Power, by and with the Advice and Consent of the Senate, to make Treaties, provided two thirds of the Senators present concur." Nothing is said about the process of negotiating treaties. Contrary to Justice Sutherland's

---

6. Id. at 343.

7. Id.

8. United States v. Smith, 286 U.S. 6 (1932); 74 Cong. Rec. 3939–40 (1931).

9. United States v. American Tel. & Tel. Co., 551 F.2d 384, 394 (D.C. Cir. 1976).

10. United States v. AT&T, 567 F.2d 121, 127 (D.C. Cir. 1977).

11. Id.

statement in *Curtiss-Wright* that Congress may not "intrude" on treaty negotiation, Presidents have long understood the benefit of inviting Senators and Representatives to be part of the negotiating team as a mean of building support for a treaty and its funding (Chapter 7, section 3A). The Senate discovered that the constitutional requirement of two-thirds of its members "present" could result in a treaty being agreed to by three members on the floor. It therefore changed its procedures to require a quorum call and a yea-and-nay vote to ensure that Senators assemble in greater numbers (Chapter 7, section 3).

In the *Chadha* legislative veto case of 1983, the Supreme Court appeared to speak against the value of governmental efficiency. The mere fact that a law or procedure is "efficient, convenient, and useful in facilitating functions of government, standing alone, will not save it if it is contrary to the Constitution. Convenience and efficiency are not the primary objectives—or the hallmarks—of democratic government."[12] To the Court, it was "crystal clear from the records of the Convention, contemporary writings and debates, that the Framers ranked other values higher than efficiency."[13] The Court spoke too broadly in trying to settle the dispute over legislative vetoes. It failed to understand that some Presidents encouraged legislative vetoes as a means of receiving greater delegated authority. The elected branches had earlier agreed to subject certain agency decisions to the review and approval of designated congressional committees. Those accommodations continue unabated despite *Chadha* (Chapter 5, section 6).

The pursuit of efficiency has its limits. One cannot reasonably argue it would be more efficient for Congress to enact bills without submitting them to the President for possible veto, or more efficient for the President to make national law unilaterally. Efficiency is not an overriding value, but the decade prior to the Philadelphia convention reveals a persistent search for a form of government that would perform more efficiently and effectively than the discredited Articles of Confederation. In his *Commentaries*, Justice Story remarked that the Framers adopted a separation of powers but "endeavored to prove that a rigid adherence to it in all cases would be subversive of the efficiency of the government, and result in the destruction of the public liberties."[14] To avoid disorder and rebellion, government must function and retain the confidence of the people.

A dissent in 1926 by Justice Brandeis claimed that the doctrine of separation of powers "was adopted by the Convention of 1787, not to promote efficiency but to preclude the exercise of arbitrary power."[15] His dictum is, at best, a half-truth. The separation doctrine was intended to provide checks on arbitrary actions, but it can also contribute to efficiency. The ineffectiveness of the Continental Congress—with delegates having to perform legislative, executive, and judicial functions—convinced the Framers at Philadelphia to create three distinct branches. Unfortunately, the language in a Brandeis dissent later found its way into majority rulings. In 1965, for example, the Court insisted: "This 'separation of powers' was obviously not instituted with the idea that it would promote governmental efficiency."[16] Nothing in that sentence is obvious or well-founded.[17]

12. INS v. Chadha, 462 U.S. 919, 944 (1983).

13. Id. at 958–59.

14. 1 Joseph Story, Commentaries on the Constitution of the United States 396 (5th ed., 1891, reprinted in 1994).

15. Myers v. United States, 272 U.S. 52, 293 (1926) (Brandeis, J., dissenting).

16. United States v. Brown, 381 U.S. 437, 443 (1965).

17. Louis Fisher, *The Efficiency Side of Separated Powers*, 5 J. Am. Stud. 113 (1971).

As supplements to the checks and balances exercised by the three branches, private groups actively monitor federal activities to ferret out abuse and misconduct. They go to court to challenge executive actions, testify before Congress, and seek information from the executive branch. This is a healthy development and part of self-government. Important checks come from the press. Agency whistleblowers disclose mismanagement and corruption, often at fearful cost to their careers. However, democratic checks from outside the tripartite system are no substitutes for having three independent branches willing to push back against encroachments.

Of great concern is the unwillingness of Congress and the judiciary to independently check executive actions that violate statutes, treaties, and the Constitution. In the Watergate scandal, top officials in the Nixon administration were prosecuted, convicted, and sent to prison. There has been little executive accountability since then. Presidential pardons (Iran-Contra), court rulings on executive immunity, and judicial acquiescence to executive claims of state secrets have provided regular shelter for abusive and criminal actions. In this protective environment, Presidents and executive officials weaken constitutional government with little risk of being called to account.

Much of the national government operates not on formal statutes, written presidential messages, and court rulings but on informal understandings entered into by the elected branches. This treatise highlights a number of these agreements: lawmakers involved in the nomination process, in negotiating treaties, and participating in agency funding decisions through committee and subcommittees vetoes. Political settlements usually resolve most disputes over executive privilege. Informal accommodations keep executive-legislative conflicts to a manageable level. Alexander Bickel recognized that large societies will explode if they cannot devise accommodations and middle positions to overcome disagreements. His advice in 1961 remains sound today: "No good society can be unprincipled; and no viable society can be principle-ridden."[18]

---

18.  Alexander M. Bickel, *Foreword: The Passive Virtues*, 75 HARV. L. REV. 40, 49 (1961).

# About the Author

LOUIS FISHER IS SCHOLAR IN RESIDENCE AT THE CONSTITUTION PROJECT. Previously he worked for four decades at the Library of Congress as Senior Specialist in Separation of Powers (Congressional Research Service, 1970–2006) and Specialist in Constitutional Law (the Law Library, 2006–2010). Fisher's specialities include constitutional law, war powers, budget policy, executive-legislative relations, and judicial-congressional relations. After completing his doctoral work in political science at the New School for Social Research in 1967, Fisher taught at Queens College, the William and Mary law school, the Catholic University law school, Georgetown University, American University, Catholic University, Indiana University, and Johns Hopkins University. Currently he is Visiting Professor at the William and Mary law school.

Many of Fisher's articles and congressional testimony are available at http://loufisher.org. His books, listed in the front of this treatise, cover various aspects of presidential power. More than 500 of his articles have appeared in law reviews, political science journals, encyclopedias, books, magazines, and newspapers.

He has twice won the Louis Brownlow Book Award (for *Presidential Spending Power* and *Constitutional Dialogues*). The encyclopedia on the presidency he co-edited with Leonard W. Levy was awarded the Dartmouth Medal in 1995. In that same year, Fisher received the Aaron B. Wildavsky Award "For Lifetime Scholarly Achievement in Public Budgeting" from the Association for Budgeting and Financial Management. In 2006, the Neustadt Book Award went to his book *Military Tribunals and Presidential Power*. Three of his books were selected by Choice as "Outstanding Academic Titles": *On Appreciating Congress: The People's Branch* (2010), *Nazi Saboteurs on Trial* (2004), and *Congressional Abdication on War and Spending* (2000).

In 2011, Fisher was presented with the Walter Beach Pi Sigma Alpha Award. It is given by the National Capital Area Political Science Association for a political scientist who makes a substantial contribution to strengthen the relationship between political science and public service. In 2012, he received the Hubert H. Humphrey Award, given annually by the American Political Science Association in recognition of notable public service by a political scientist.

Fisher has been invited to testify before Congress over 50 times on such issues as war powers, state secrets privilege, NSA surveillance, executive spending discretion, presidential reorganization authority, Congress and the Constitution, the legislative veto, the item veto, the

Gramm-Rudman deficit control act, executive privilege, committee subpoenas, executive lobbying, CIA whistleblowing, covert spending, the pocket veto, recess appointments, the budget
process, the balanced budget amendment, biennial budgeting, and presidential impoundment
powers.

He has been active with CEELI (Central and East European Law Initiative) of the American Bar
Association, traveling to Bulgaria, Albania, and Hungary to assist constitution-writers. He par-
ticipated in CEELI conferences in Washington, DC with delegations from Bosnia-Herzegovina,
Lithuania, Romania, and Russia; served on CEELI "working groups" on Armenia and Belarus;
and assisted in drafting constitutional amendments for the Kyrgyz Republic. As part of CRS
delegations he traveled to Russia and Ukraine to assist on constitutional questions. For the
International Bar Association he helped analyze the draft constitutions of Swaziland and
Zimbabwe.

In response to invitations, Fisher has spoken in Albania, Australia, Belgium, Bulgaria,
Canada, China, the Czech Republic, Denmark, France, Germany, Great Britain, Greece, Israel,
Japan, Macedonia, Malaysia, Mexico, the Netherlands, Oman, the Philippines, Poland, Romania,
Russia, Slovenia, South Korea, Sweden, Taiwan, Ukraine, and the United Arab Emirates. The
topics include a range of constitutional, political, and institutional issues.

# Index of Cases

# Index of Subjects